I0822963

ANDRE DE DIENES

MARILYN

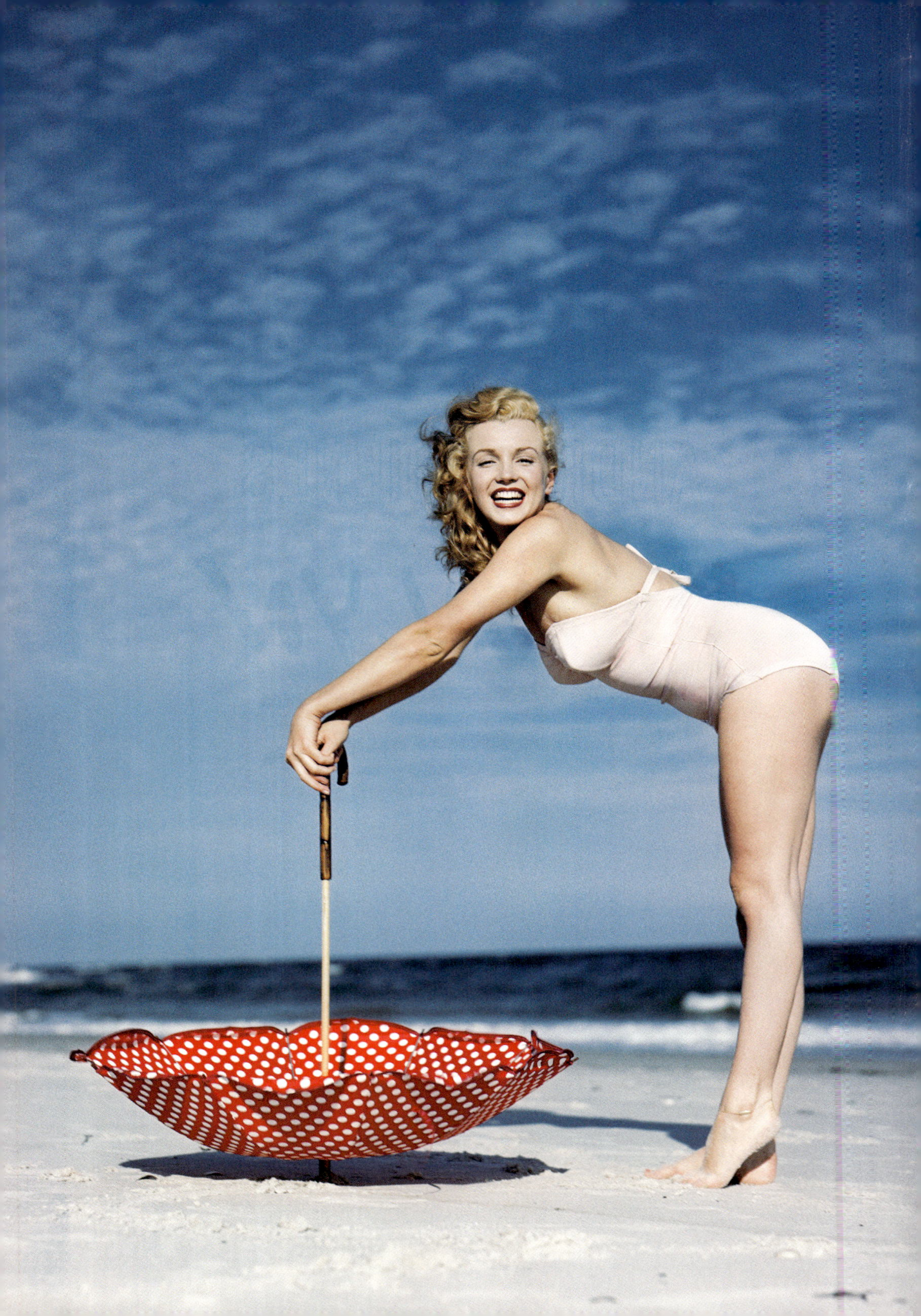

ANDRE DE DIENES

MARILYN

Edited by Steve Crist and Shirley T. Ellis de Dienes

TASCHEN

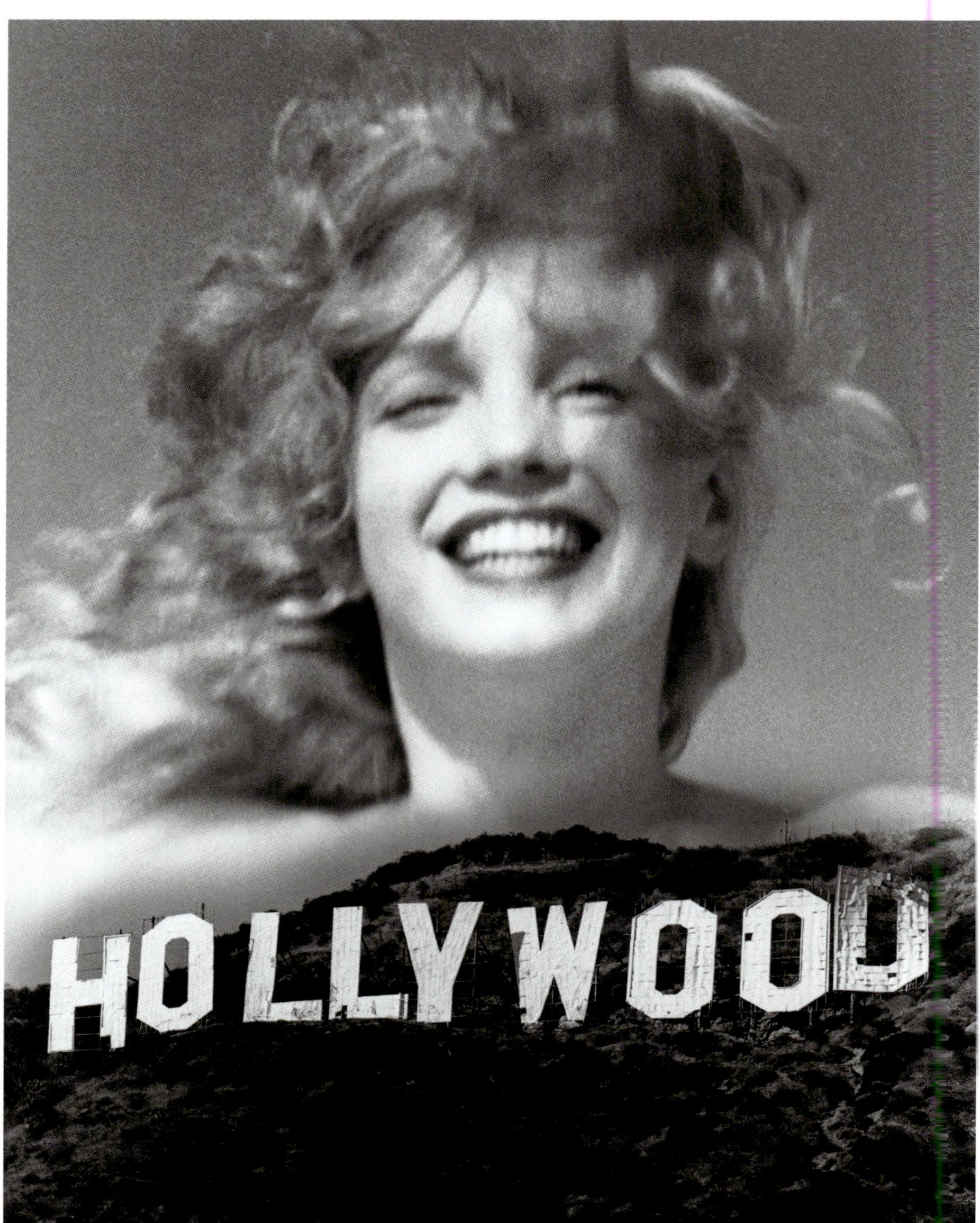
HOLLYWOOD

Contents

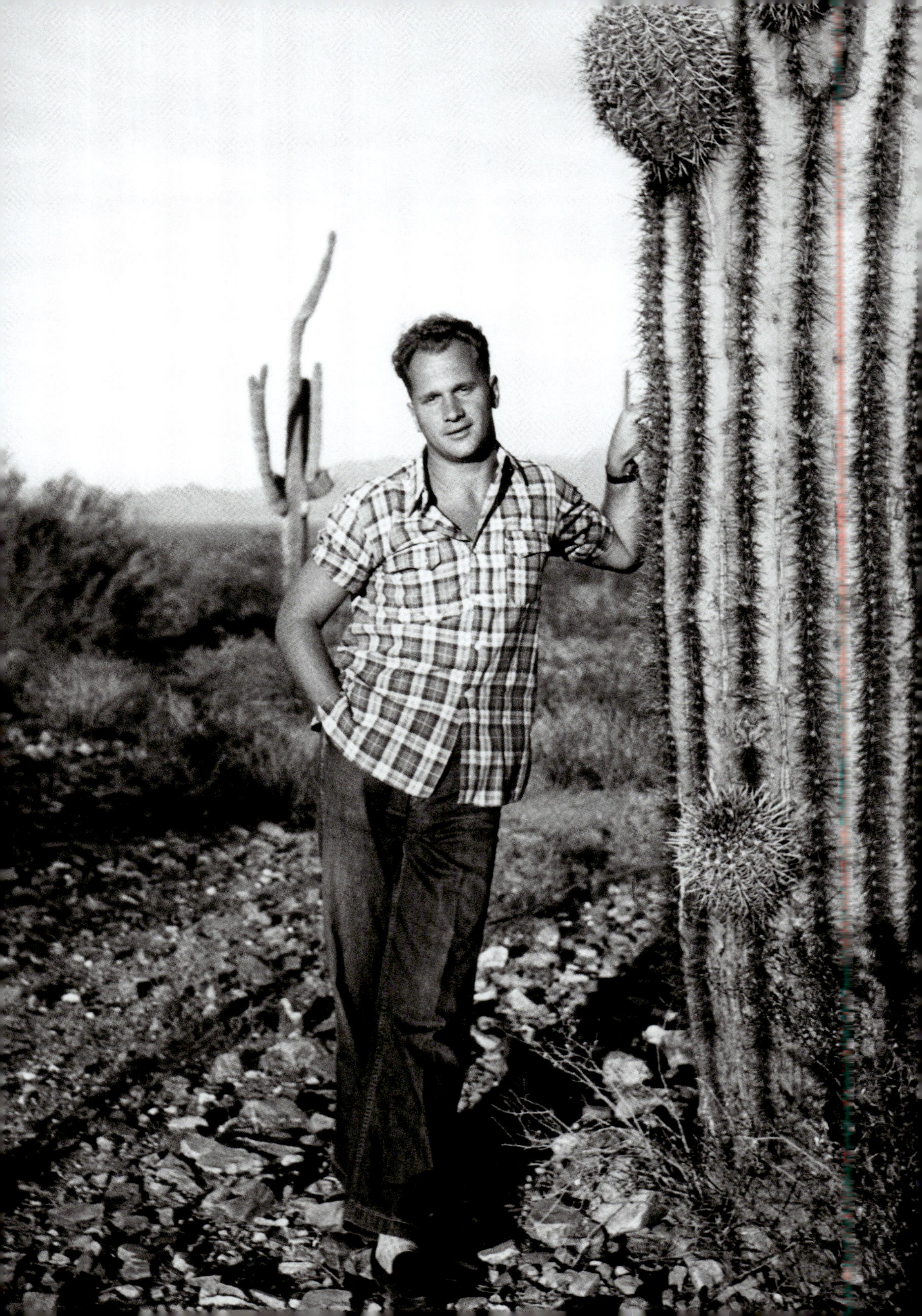

(Re)Discovering André   When a young photographer on assignment for *Vogue* left New York for Los Angeles in the early 1940s, he could have hardly imagined the future that awaited him. Ultimately, he would end up relocating to California and spending the next four decades of his life photographing beautiful women – famous and those aspiring to fame alike – while living an impassioned and sometimes tormented existence in the hills above Hollywood. Of the many beautiful women who would ultimately cross his path, one woman would come to have special significance in his life: Marilyn Monroe.

This book is the first substantial view of André de Dienes's work since his death in 1985, as well as the definitive collection of his images and writings pertaining to the young Norma Jeane – the future Marilyn Monroe. André became Marilyn's confidant and lover, but she would also become a source of frustration – driving him to near obsession at various times throughout his life. From a simple chance meeting in November of 1945, André de Dienes would forever be changed by his personal and private moments with a Hollywood star who perhaps has no comparison in today's celebrity-filled society.

Images of Marilyn Monroe as a Hollywood icon are so prolific that they almost blend together in our collective memory of her. The entire world seems to know Marilyn, and the many photographs of her are hard to distinguish from one another, revealing little of the artistry or identity of the individual photographers who created them. Despite this, André's vision of Marilyn is unique. He captured a young

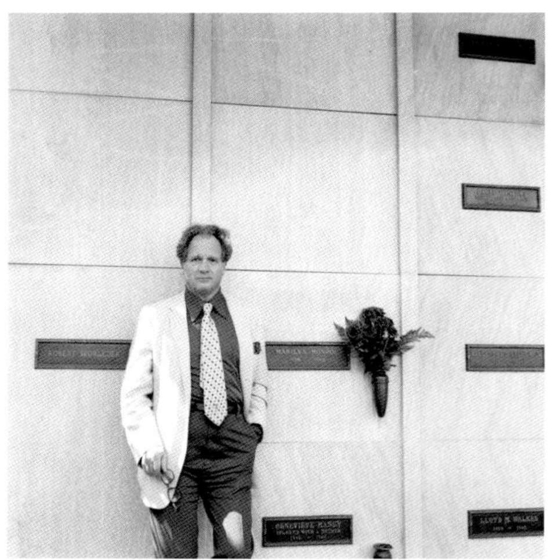

Norma Jeane and a newly-named Marilyn's innocence, naïveté and natural beauty long before her transformation into the epitome of Hollywood glamour. Photographs of Marilyn later in life show an experienced model and actress who knew how to work the camera and her adoring audience. It was before André's camera that Marilyn first attempted her craft. Decades later, André's images of her are significant and refreshing, in that they suggest a naturalness and sincerity, and even in some instances reveal a darker, more hidden side of who Marilyn truly was.

Interestingly, André often refrained from photographing Marilyn during their relationship. He felt that many exploited her to their own advantage, and his diaries unveil his desire to maintain a special friendship with her that was based on more than simple image making to further enhance either of their careers. He never solicited her for work and he protectively kept their affairs private. His feelings for her were genuine and his photographs of her lovingly reflect that. Despite all of this, André did become consumed with Marilyn. In the final analysis, it can be said that André seemed to both love her personally, and adore her with a passion similar to that of any fervent fan.

In the last few years before his death from cancer, André began typing his memoirs, a good portion of which comprise this volume. Knowing full well that he was dying, André wrote in a loose, passionate style that was true to his real life personality. Most of

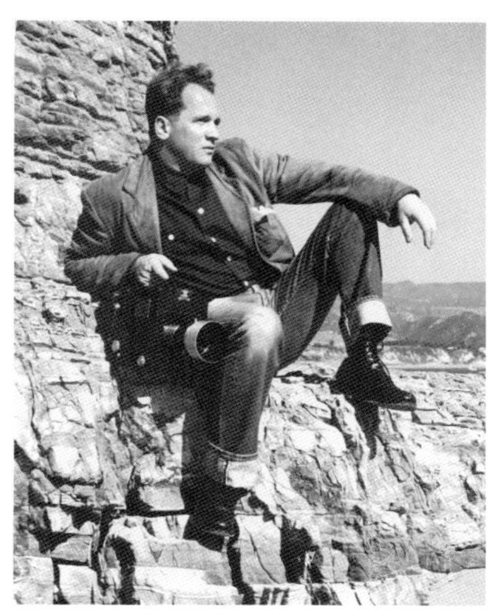

his life, André was considered a colorful character. He had a temper and hated injustice. His life and writing contained many exclamation points. It should be mentioned that it's unlikely that André, unlike numerous others who have written about their relationships with Marilyn, embellished much on what really occurred. He loved his privacy, but realized the importance of the special experiences he had with her. Knowing André, it's also probable that he purposely left some stories out. To the end, he remained a gentleman. Perhaps to some, events in his memoirs may seem at times almost unbelievable – but the reality of André's life was almost as remarkable as Marilyn's.

Andor Ikafalvi de Dienes was born in 1913 in the Transylvanian village of Turia, a former possession of Hungary. When André was eleven, with the Hungarian currency devalued and his family in crisis, André's mother committed suicide by throwing herself down a well on the family property. Devastated by the loss and the breakup of his family, André struck out on his own at age fourteen. He found his way to Budapest and tried to rejoin his estranged father. Unable to make a lasting connection, he was alone at a very young age. He took a job in a fabric store and spent the formative years of his youth surrounded by wealthy women and expensive fabrics. At night, he would work as a stagehand in order to see the operas and musicals he loved in the Budapest theater. These years in Budapest nurtured his interest in the arts, culture, and women.

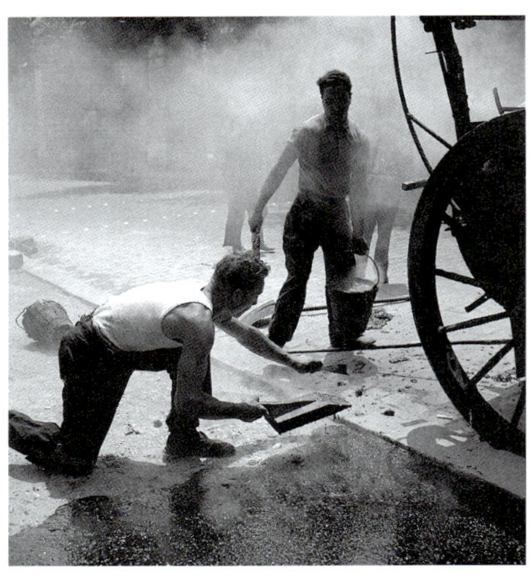

Eager to see the world and bored with the routine of fabric sales – he left Budapest to travel through Europe and Africa at age eighteen. Joining a group of traveling artists, he learned to paint and took his first photographs on that journey. While photographing statues in a park in Paris in 1934, he was stopped by a British clothing designer, Captain Edward Molyneux, and was asked to become his exclusive fashion photographer. Opting for a more French-sounding name, he remade himself as André de Dienes. His photographs from that time period were primarily fashion assignments for Molyneux, but from 1935 to 1938 he created thousands of portraits and street images in Paris and all over France. It was André's first venture into photographing people from all walks of life, something he continued to do throughout his photographic career. Very few of André's fashion images have survived from his days in France (he destroyed many and later wrote that he regretted it) – but happily almost two thousand images of France remain in his archive.

After meeting Arnold Gingrich, the editor of *Esquire* magazine on holiday in Paris, André accepted his offer to relocate to New York and pursue assignments with *Esquire's* sponsorship. His decision to move to New York ushered in a new chapter of his life and put him on a course that would ultimately define his career. Arriving in New York in 1938, André began shooting for *Vogue*, *Bazaar*, and *Town and Country*. He was quite comfortable with the powerful editors who ran and influenced the magazines in New York and quickly established himself in the city.

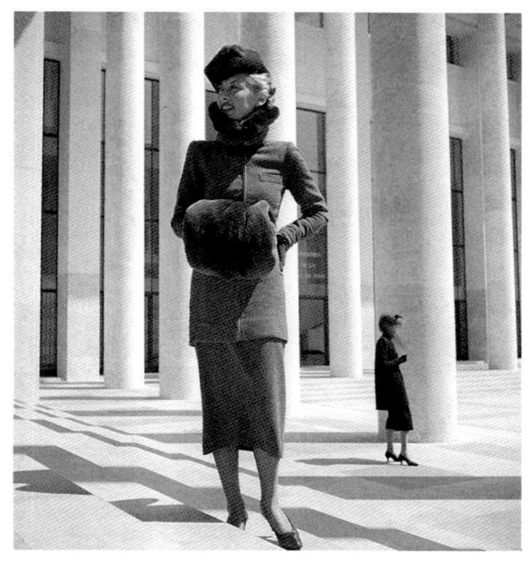

As time progressed however, André felt increasingly stifled by the confinements of fashion photography. Although he had become quite successful as a fashion photographer, he always made time for personal image making. He began to use every opportunity to photograph subjects that he felt drawn to in his newly adopted country. His adventurous spirit led him to explore many diverse subjects, including female nudes. As a European in America, he did not subscribe to the common prejudices of the day. He took many opportunities to photograph African Americans in Harlem, as well as the Southern states, and Native American tribes across the entire United States. Back in New York, André was dumbfounded by the lack of interest photo editors had for these images. He was shocked at the injustice of it all, yet continued to photograph all people he felt a connection to. It was a theme that would continue, and his lack of interest in assignment photography led him to seek out a direction that was more soulful and artistic.

In Harlem, André found a prosperous and successful community of African Americans that captured his attention. He walked the streets and made hundreds of unposed and spontaneous portraits, giving much attention to the children playing on the streets. On the reverse side of some Harlem prints, he would sometimes write about the people he met and photographed. He was moved by the dignity, poise and beauty of this rarely photographed American community. When he proudly showed these images to a major publication

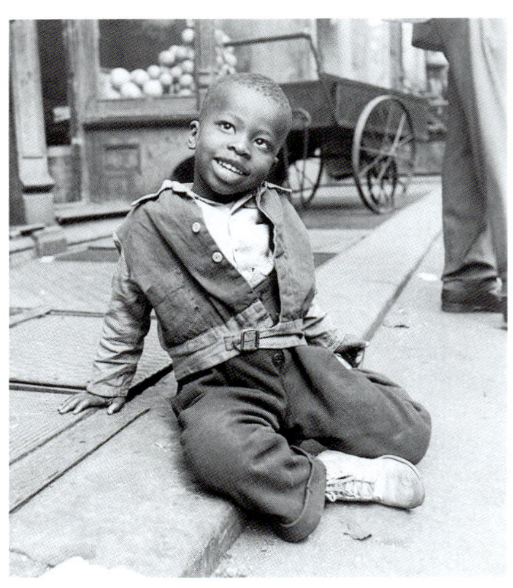

of the day, he was devastated that they were totally uninterested in publishing them.

When his travels took him to the southern states of Louisiana, Mississippi and Georgia, he encountered African American workers in the fields. He relished the opportunity to photograph the workers and made many return trips to the area to continue the effort. His images of the workers showed a proud and dignified people rarely recorded on film during that time period.

Native American tribes became another great source of inspiration in his life. The majority of tribes were certainly not the subject of much serious photography. André fell in love with many different tribes, and proceeded to document thousands of images over many decades. Frequently, he would find himself at the end of a road, walking with his cameras and introducing himself to a secluded group of Native Americans unused to visitors or interest from mainstream America. Presenting himself to tribal leaders, he was often invited to stay as a guest, allowed to embrace tribal life and photograph rituals like few outsiders had.

André was an excited, wide-eyed student of life who loved the promise of the vast, open countryside. The West beckoned to him, and he dove into all it had to offer. Like his earlier travels throughout the eastern parts of America, André loved the western states and especially their indigenous peoples. He also loved the open skies and the outdoor lifestyle agreed with his free spirit. He envisioned

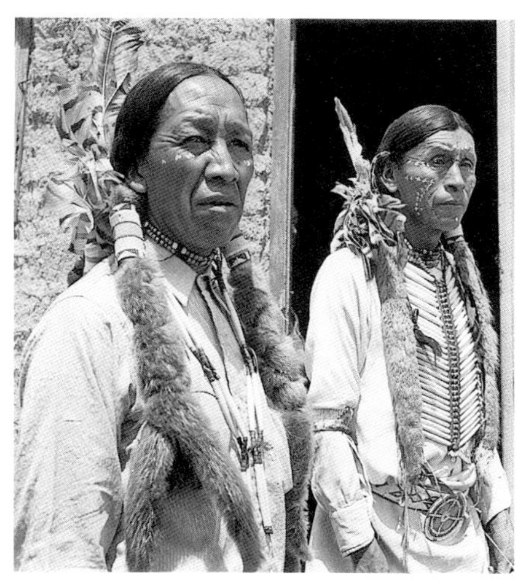

a career for himself photographing women with the western landscape as the backdrop. This desire led him to move to the famed Garden of Allah Hotel in Hollywood in 1945. Many well-known artists, writers and actors had called the hotel home at one time or another. It was on that fateful first day that he met the future Marilyn Monroe. His life would never be the same.

The Norma Jeane of 1945 was married and all of nineteen years old. In a strained relationship while her husband was shipped out to the events of World War II, she was a story waiting to happen. Norma Jeane stepped through André's hotel door, and in typical André style, he fell head over heels for the young brunette. She was a simple girl from a troubled background and was just gaining confidence in her aspiration to become a model. Even by today's standards, it's hard to imagine how quickly events unfolded in her life. Less than six months after he first photographed her, André's status as a photographer landed Norma Jeane her first magazine cover. André's photograph of her debuted on the cover of *Family Circle*, April 26, 1946 – despite the fact she was an unknown model at the time. In short time, many more André covers followed.

Traveling extensively during this time period, André happened to be in New York when news broke out of the end of World War II. He rushed to Times Square and made an indelible set of images from the street celebrations of the day. In typical André style, he would file these photographs away and they would stay there for the rest of his life, with no explanation as to why they were overlooked.

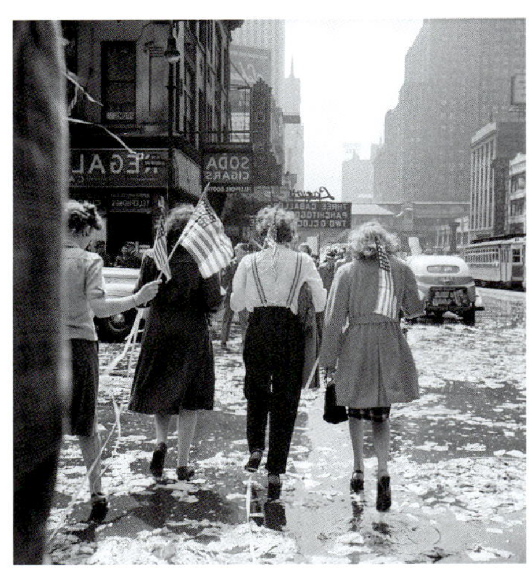

Wine, good food, and opera were all part of André's daily requirements for life. His love of books, physical exercise, and time in the outdoors became his mantra. Women would come and go, and Marilyn left for the stardom and marriages she was destined for. There were frequent relationships in his life – usually short-term lovers who seemed not to satisfy him for long. A fellow well-known photographer of the time period, Peter Gowland, recalled, "Many times André and I were shooting different girls at opposite ends of the same beach. The only difference between us was that André always left with the girl, a loaf of bread, and a bottle of wine – while I went home to my wife and family."

Seeking artistic autonomy and independence from assigned image making, André built a career of photographing women. It would give him great excitement and cause him great torment for many years. Los Angeles allowed him to live out his fantasy like no other city would. The constant flow of aspiring actresses and models seemed to be endless, and all wanted to be recognized and put on film. André carved out a life for himself, and built a home by hand on a lot he purchased high in the Hollywood hills above Sunset Boulevard. During these years his life moved quickly – aided by his Hollywood locale and the famous people he photographed.

The André de Dienes of the 1950s was a bit older and wiser – and suddenly a well-known photographic commodity. As a European, he pushed himself into a medium that was still considered taboo in many parts

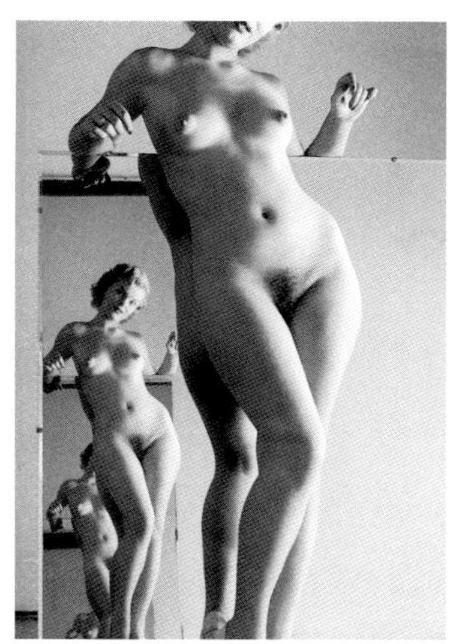

of postwar America. He clearly stood out as a major photographer of the female form in that time period. In 1953, the front cover of a brand new magazine called *Playboy* led with the headline "At home with André de Dienes". André had made it – and would ride the new trend of "girlie" magazines that would start to proliferate on American newsstands. Publishers from Europe and America sought his material, and he had a wealth of monographs published that are highly sought after and collectible to this day.

In his latter years, André became a recluse in his hillside home. The last decade of his life included little picture taking. Instead, he sequestered himself in his darkroom and printed and reprinted his life of negatives in all subject matter. After his death, André's estate and photograph collection were upset by legal battles for many years. Despite his long absence from publication, the recent resurgence of his work is refreshing and his images are vital once again.

In the coming years, André de Dienes will undoubtedly be rediscovered as a significant contributor to the medium of photography. As an individual, he will always be remembered as an independent, passionate and emotionally charged man, inseparable from his association with Marilyn Monroe.

The Hollywood version of the photographer and model romance story has been told many times over. Indeed, André was the first of many photographers with whom Marilyn would become romantically involved. Despite this, the story of André and Marilyn is most poignant as it

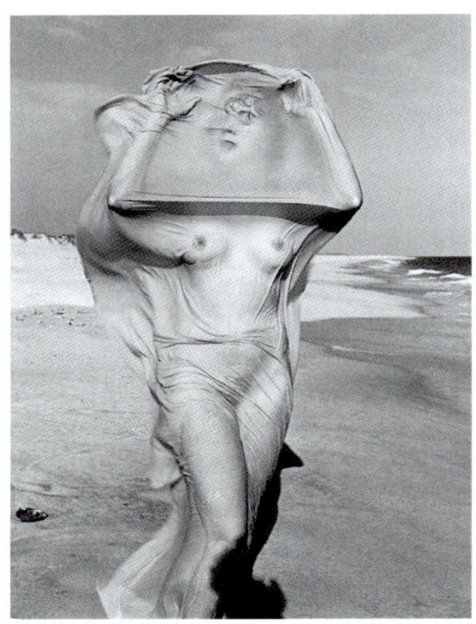

took place during a time of rare innocence in the life of Marilyn. As André commented many times, Norma Jeane was not Marilyn Monroe back in 1945! She was simply a girl who possessed an unexplainable, almost mystical ingredient that propelled her to a level of fame almost incomparable to that of any other celebrity. To a great extent, many will always consider André and Marilyn inseparable. Appropriately, André's and Marilyn's graves lie very near each other in Westwood Memorial Cemetery in Los Angeles.

Steve Crist
Los Angeles, April 2002

A Note about the Text André de Dienes wrote his memoirs in the last days of his life, typing them and making additions and corrections by hand. The section of these memoirs that deals with Marilyn Monroe has been reproduced here in facsimile form, with reworked excerpts that make it easier to follow the chronology of the photographs.

N.B. That Marilyn Monroe's name was originally spelled "Norma Jean" is a common misconception. The correct spelling, and the one she herself used, was "Norma Jeane."

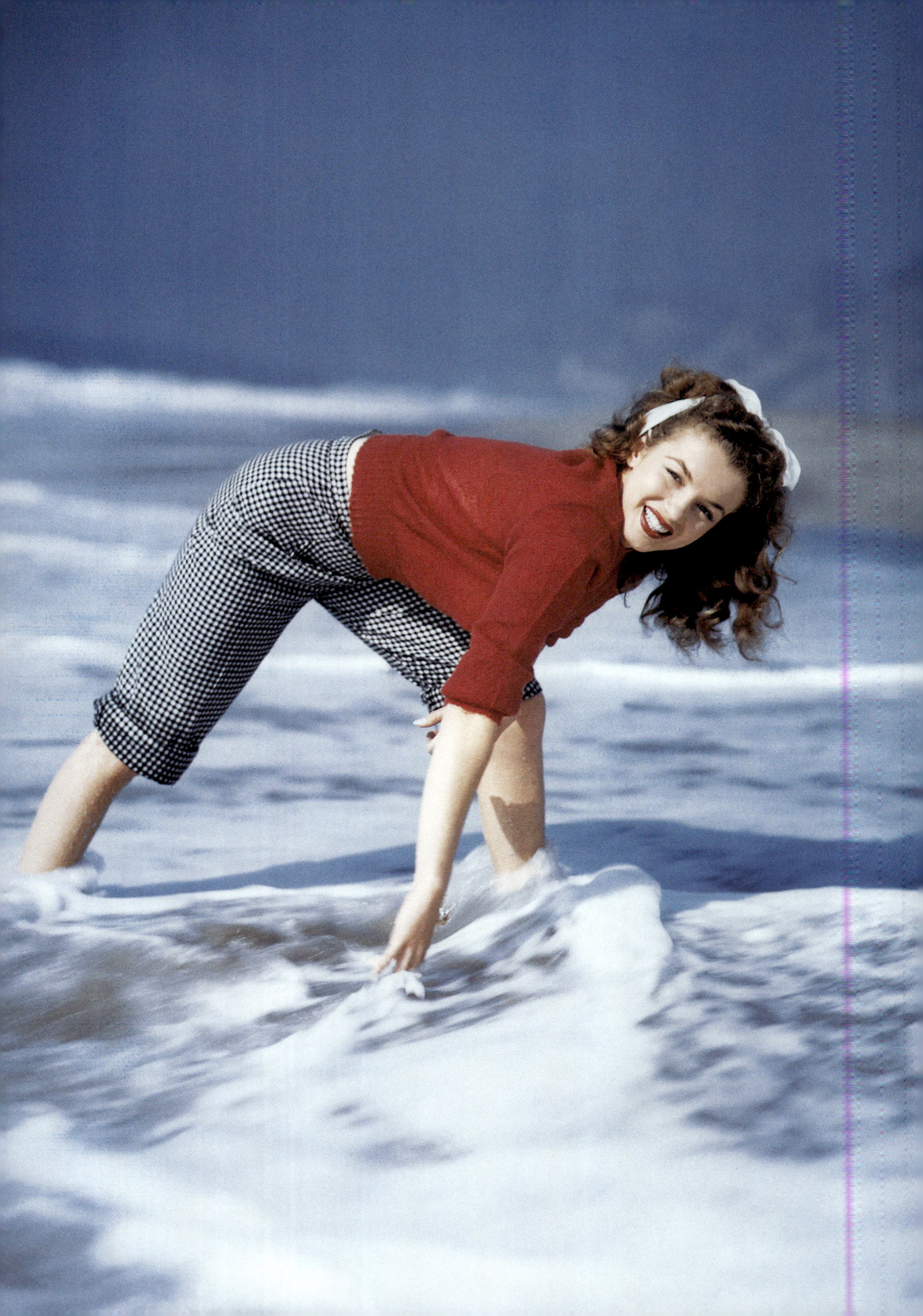

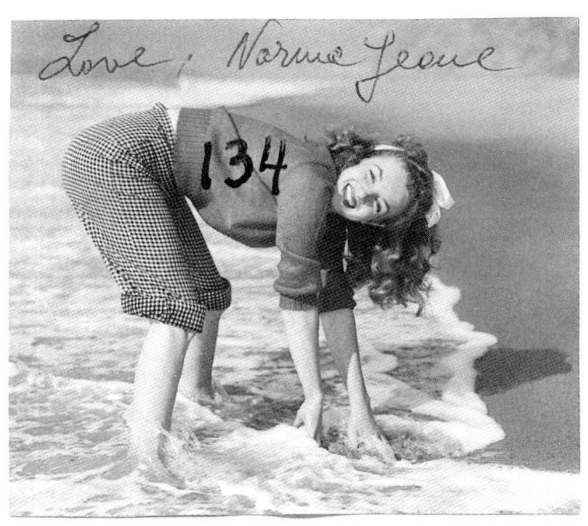

Norma Jeane   Reality can be stranger than fiction. Soon after I got myself installed in a bungalow at the Garden of Allah in Hollywood, I phoned Emmeline Snively, who had the Blue Book Model Agency at the Ambassador Hotel, and I explained to her that I was back in Hollywood again and that I needed models for photos of nudes, artistic nudes, for a new project I had in mind. Miss Snively said there was a very pretty girl in her office, waiting for her first modeling assignment, a model who just started in the profession, and perhaps she would pose for nudes. Miss Snively said she would send the young lady to see me right away and that her name was Norma Jeane Baker.

When Norma Jeane arrived at my bungalow later in the afternoon, it was as if a miracle had happened to me. Norma Jeane seemed to be like an angel. I could hardly believe it for a few moments. An earthly, sexy-looking angel! Sent expressly for me! The impact Norma Jeane had on me was tremendous. As minutes passed, I fell more and more in love with Norma Jeane; there was an immediate rapport between us. She responded to everything I said. She started to look around in my room, examining all the pictures I put on the walls, and began asking questions. I had the immediate feeling that she was something special, something different from most girls and models I had met before her, mainly because she was so eager to ask questions about me and the pictures I put on the walls. She wanted to know many things right away, she was interested in me! She was utterly sincere; she did not wish to speak about herself, except when I asked her my own questions. She was

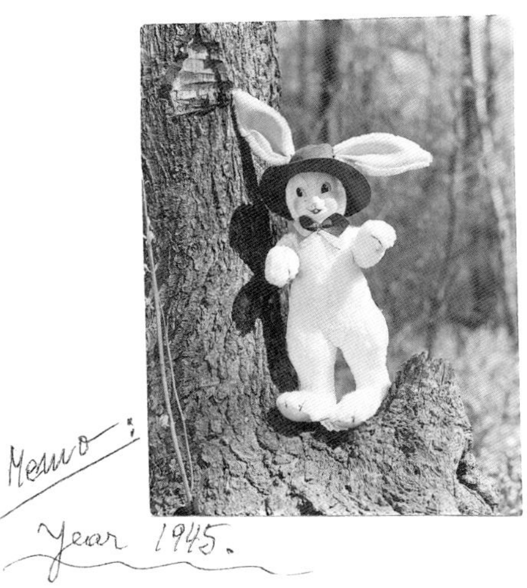

Memo: Year 1945.

sincere in wanting to know who I was and what I was doing with my life and I began to amuse her exceedingly with all sorts of stories that ran through my mind and I just kept dishing them out to her. I still remember it as clearly as if it happened just recently.

Norma Jeane wore a pale pink sweater, tight to her body, and her curly ash-blonde hair was tied around her head with pink ribbon; her rosy pinkish face and her blue eyes reminded me of a pretty Easter bunny. I told her I had bought two large rabbit dolls in a toy shop in New York, which I intended to photograph for a new magazine I was planning to start (to be financed by a wealthy literary agent), and how sorry I was not to have brought them with me to Hollywood, because I would have loved to photograph her with the rabbits for my new magazine. Norma Jeane loved the idea, and laughed heartily.

(Thinking back to all that, I find it a bizarre coincidence, or a premonition, that I told Norma Jeane in 1945 about wanting to start a new kind of magazine, the picture of the rabbit as the emblem of the magazine and pictures of her nude inside the magazine. Eight years later, Hugh Hefner, a genius businessman, made it a reality! Norma Jeane was going to be the cover star of the first issue of my magazine; correspondingly, the first issue of *Playboy* featured my darling Norma Jeane, but as Marilyn Monroe, on the cover, and nude on the inside.)

I noticed Norma Jeane had a wedding ring on her finger. She informed me she was married, but separated from her husband and no longer in

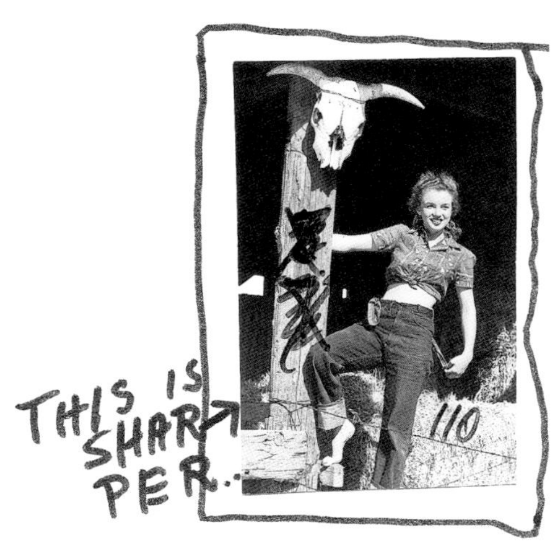

love with him. He was a merchant marine away at sea, and she was free and modeling was her new goal. She mentioned nothing about wanting to become an actress. The few words of explanation she gave me freed my mind from inhibition. The truth was that I wanted to photograph her very much, but I wanted her more than anything else in the world! I was completely love struck from the moment she appeared at the door.

While we were talking, Norma Jeane took a good look at one of several old engravings I had on the wall — a nude Indian girl sitting on a rock, surrounded by mountainous scenery and animals, sort of an allegorical representation of the vision of America, the way Europeans figured life was like in America a few centuries ago. Norma Jeane was very interested in the picture and I told her I brought the pictures with me all the way from Transylvania. I went into a long story, telling her that in Spain in the 16th century, it was believed that California was an island inhabited by beautiful and strong native women — who lived in the nude. And that the entire continent of the West was rumored to be rich with gold, so Cortes, the famous Spanish explorer, outfitted ships and came to explore and conquer California, driven by the lust for gold and women. She laughed like crazy when I told her that I had the same thing in mind coming here to Hollywood, and my intentions were to photograph beautiful girls in the nude all throughout the West, but at the same time to explore old forgotten gold mines and look for gold in the mountains too. I came straight to the point in our conversation, asking her whether

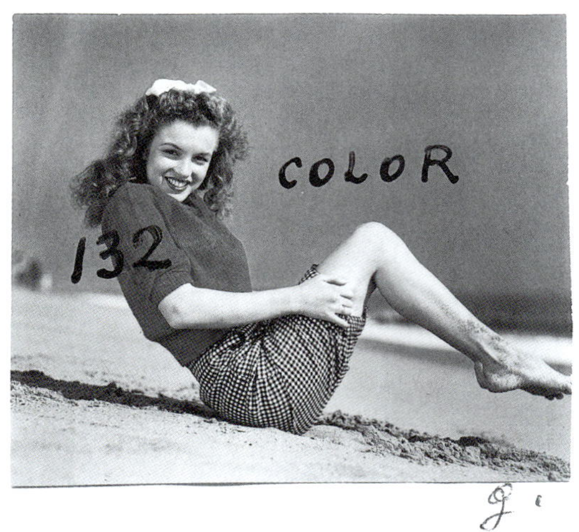

she would like to come travel with me. We would go by car to explore the vast West and take pictures everywhere – glamour photos for magazine covers, and nudes too!

I had a stack of large enlargements of photos I took of movie stars the year before, and some nudes, and Norma Jeane looked through them with great approval. She was excited and wanted to pose for me. She asked, "Would you like to see my figure?" In a jiffy, she grabbed her hatbox, went to the adjoining room (the bedroom), put on a bathing suit, and, smiling, beaming with happiness, she swirled around the center of the living room, happy to be able to show me her beautiful figure.

A day later, I took her to the beach to take pictures of her. Again and again, I photographed her each day. My mind was made up for sure – I wanted to take her away from Hollywood right away on a long trip. Just go with her, everywhere! I felt completely enamored by her!

I offered to pay her 100 dollars per week for posing plus all expenses, and that I would buy all sorts of things for her to wear for pictures (jeans, blouses, sweaters, bathing suits) and promised she could eat as much and as well as she pleased, because I noticed she loved food. She was young and she had a good appetite!

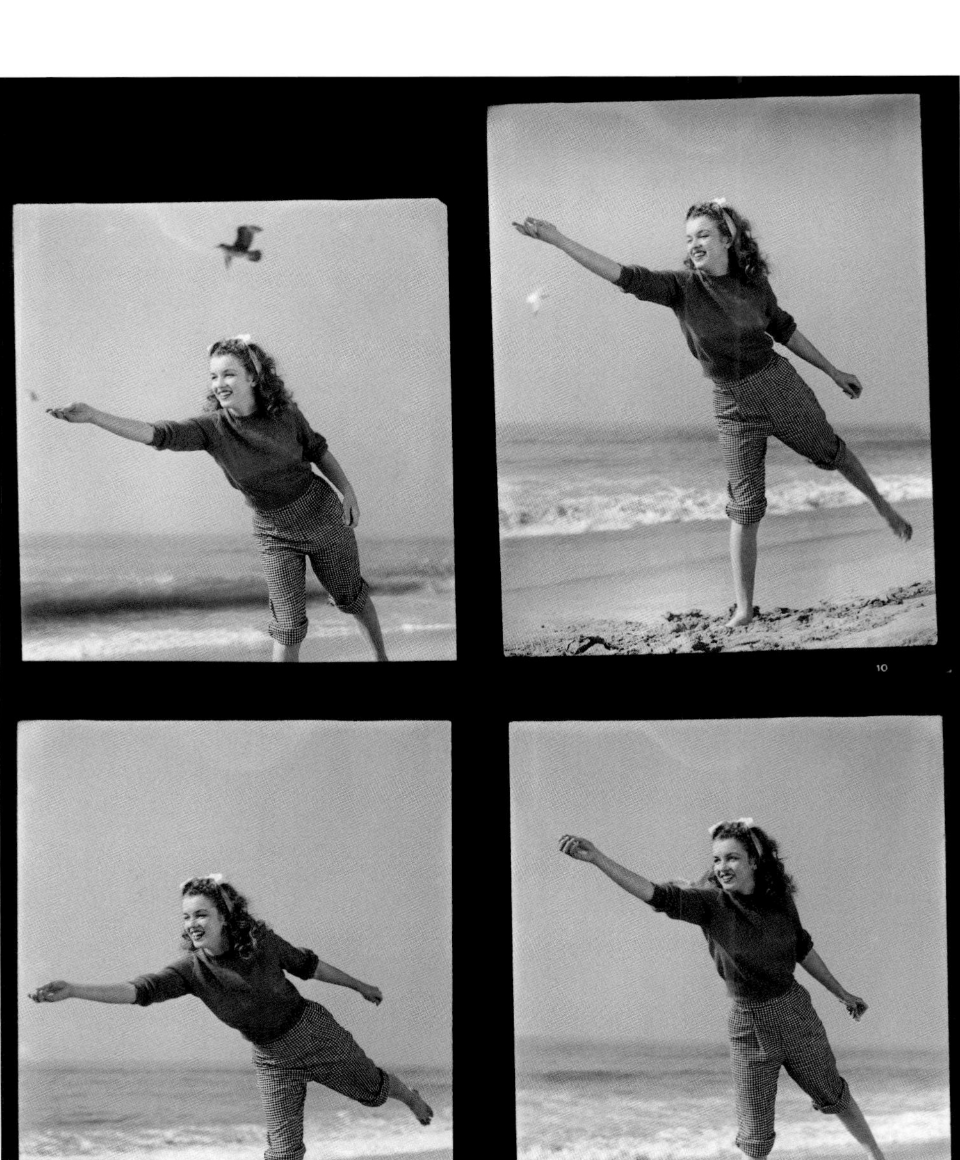

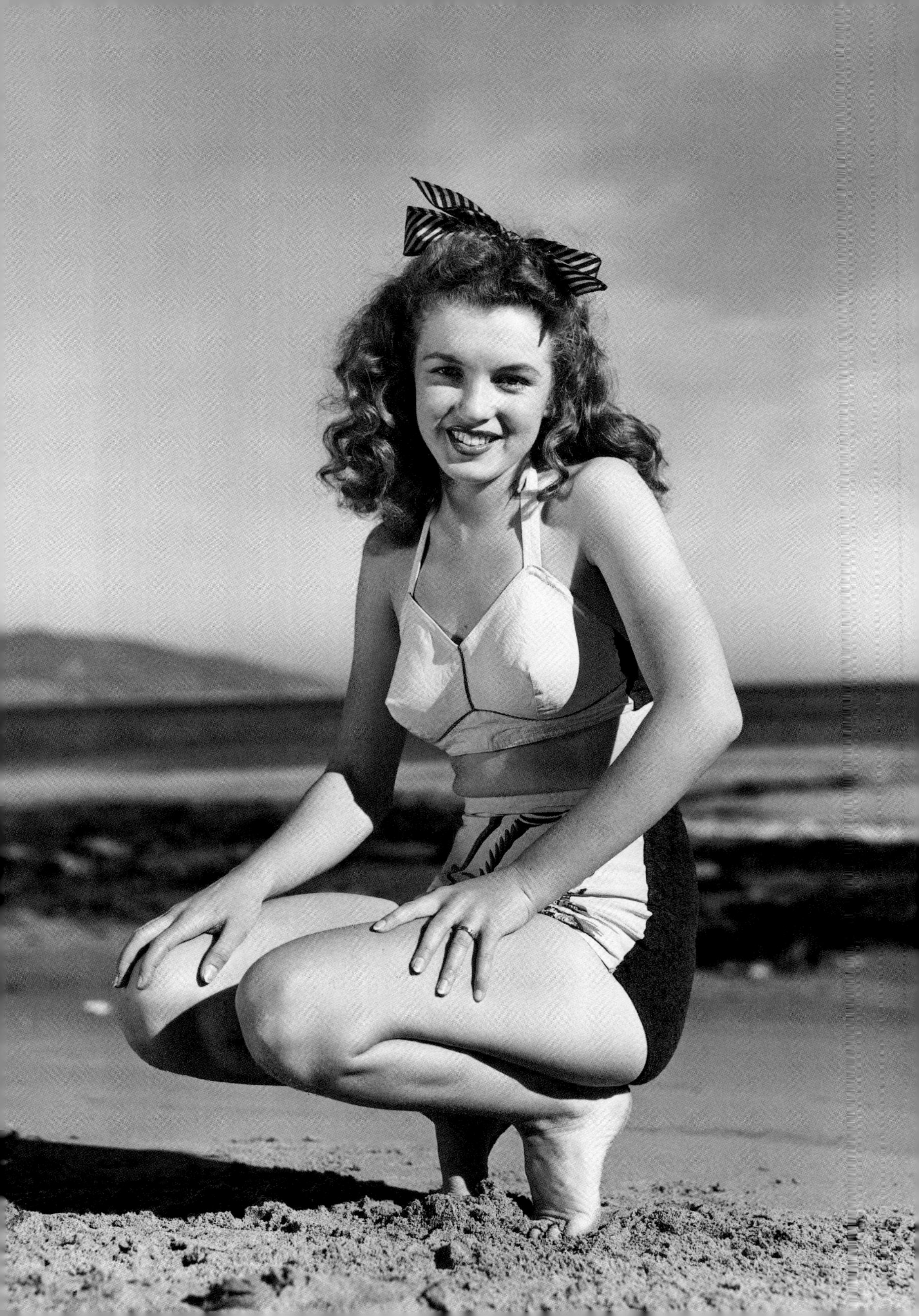

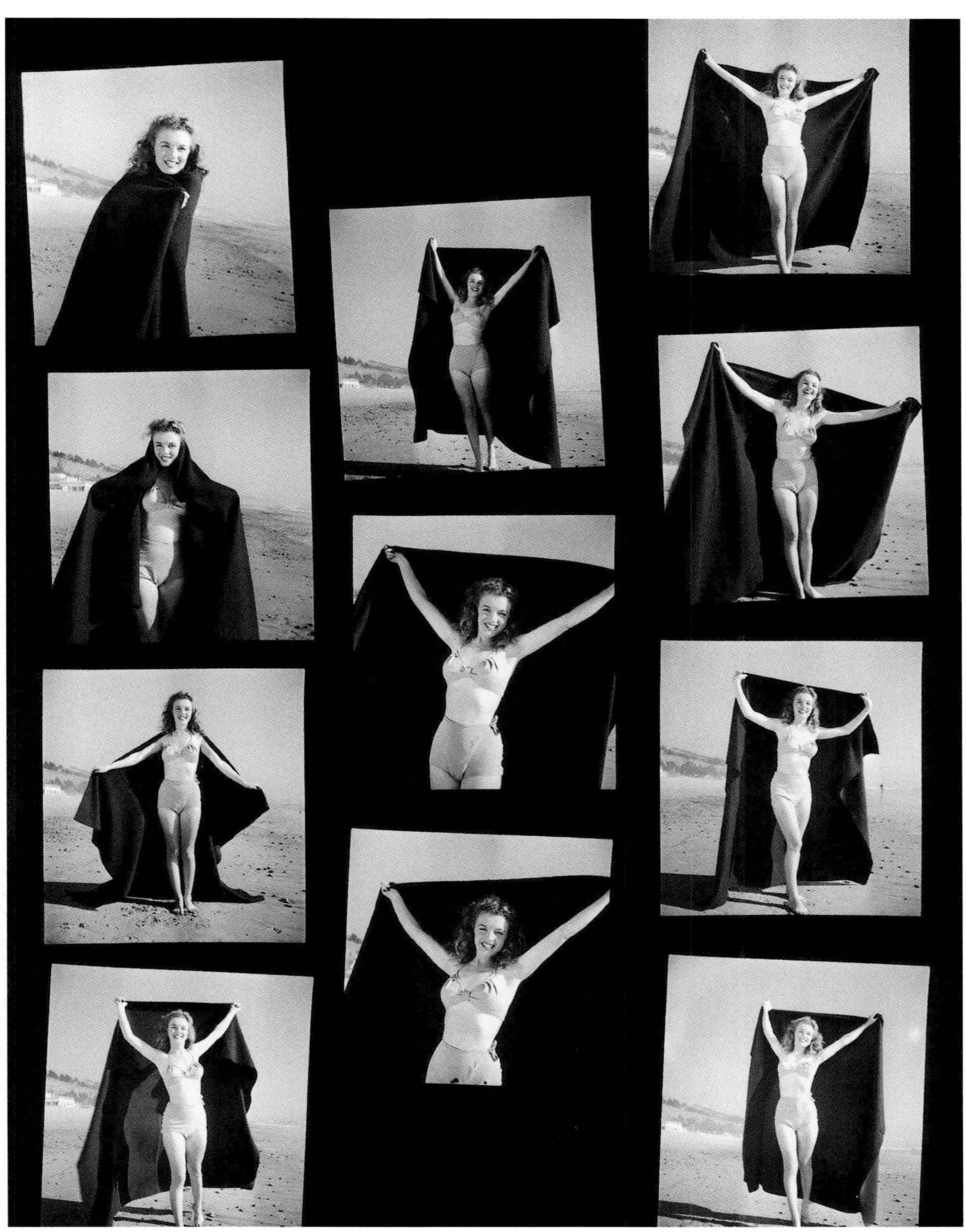

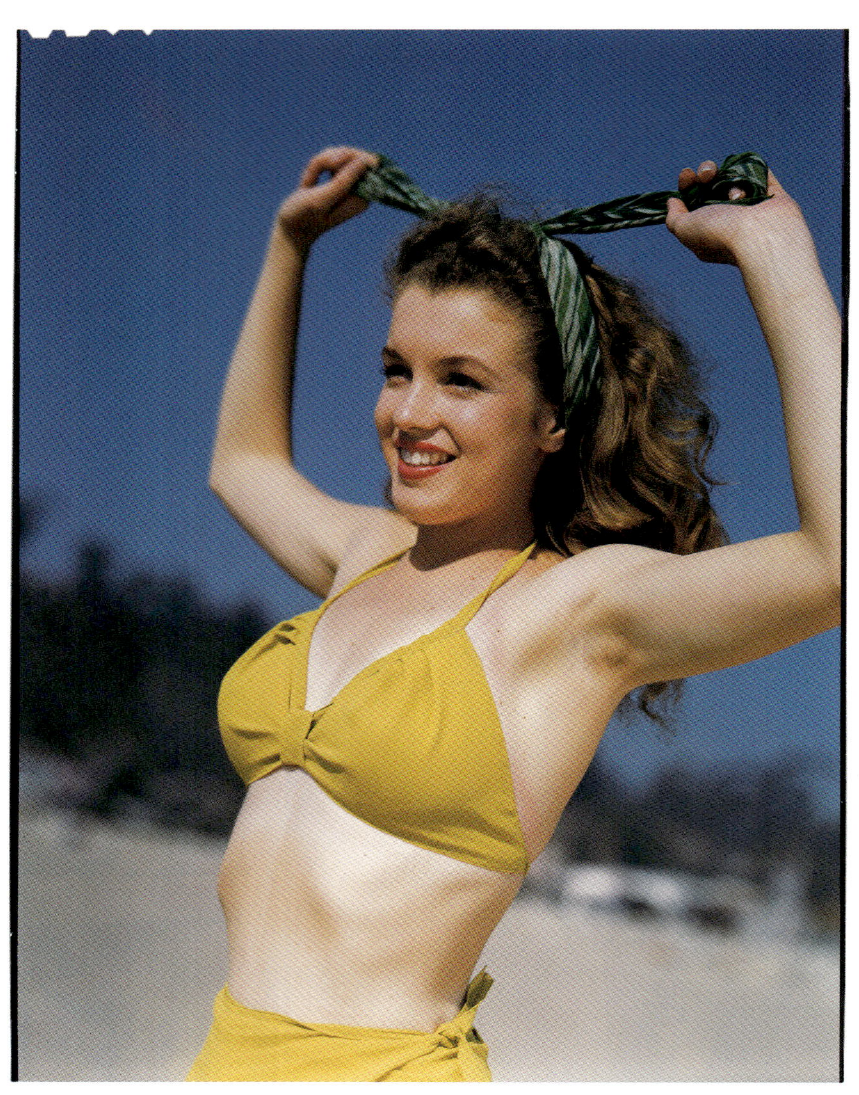

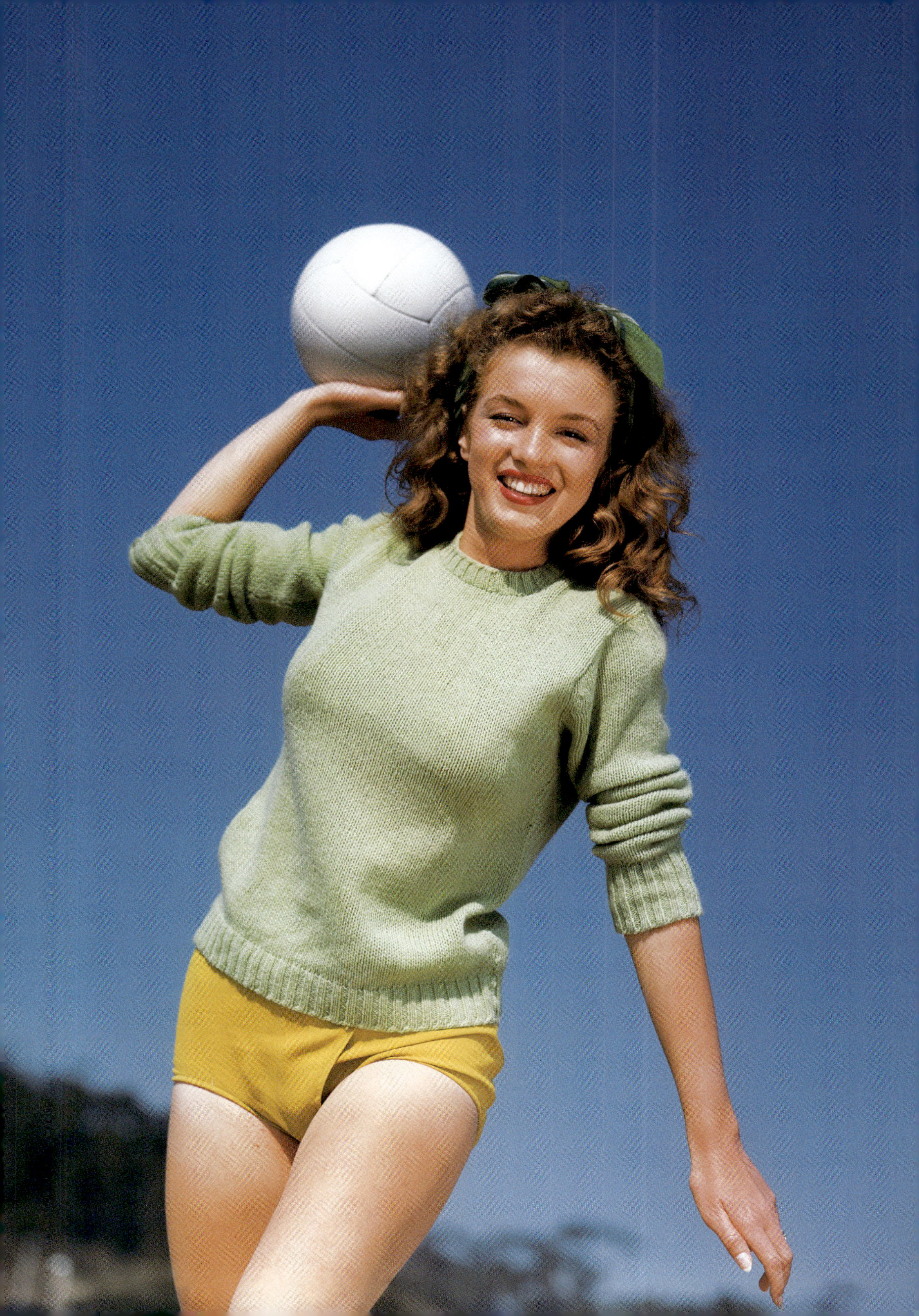

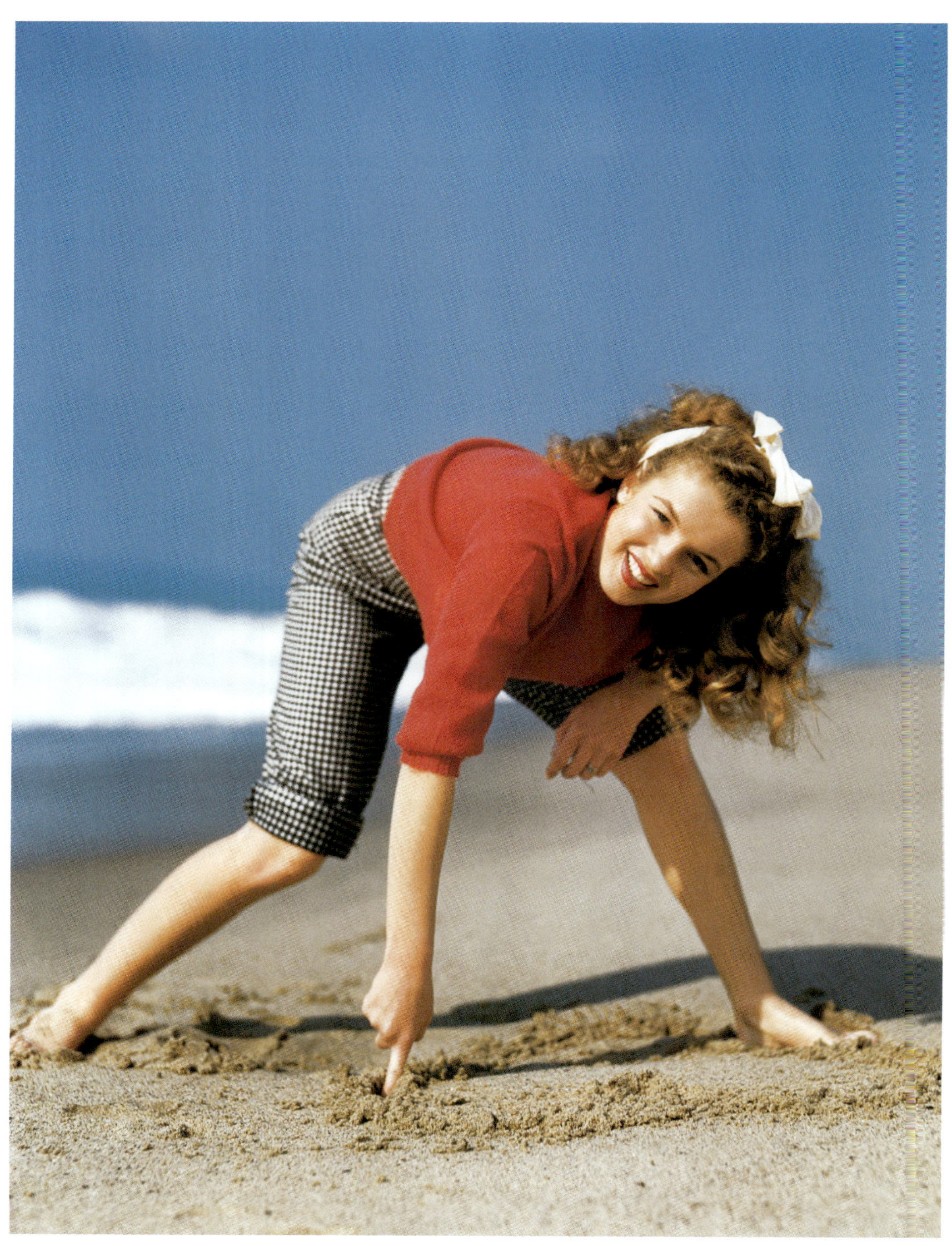

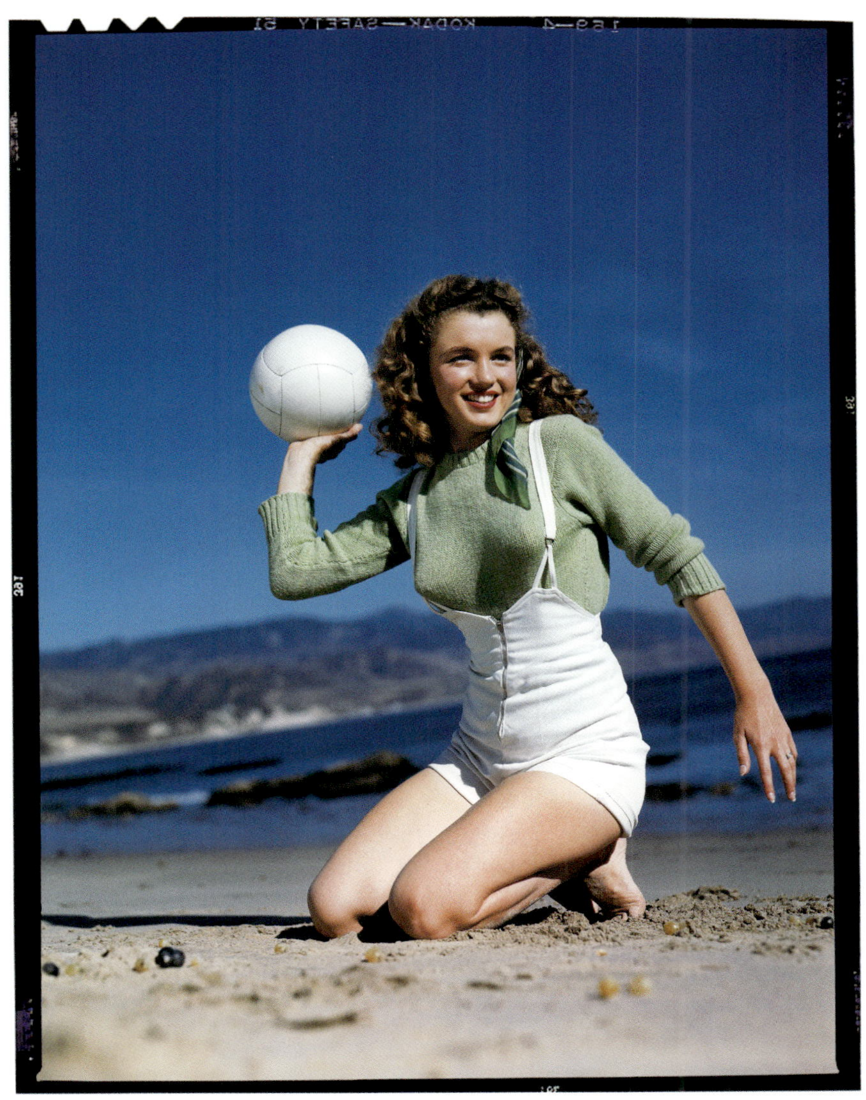

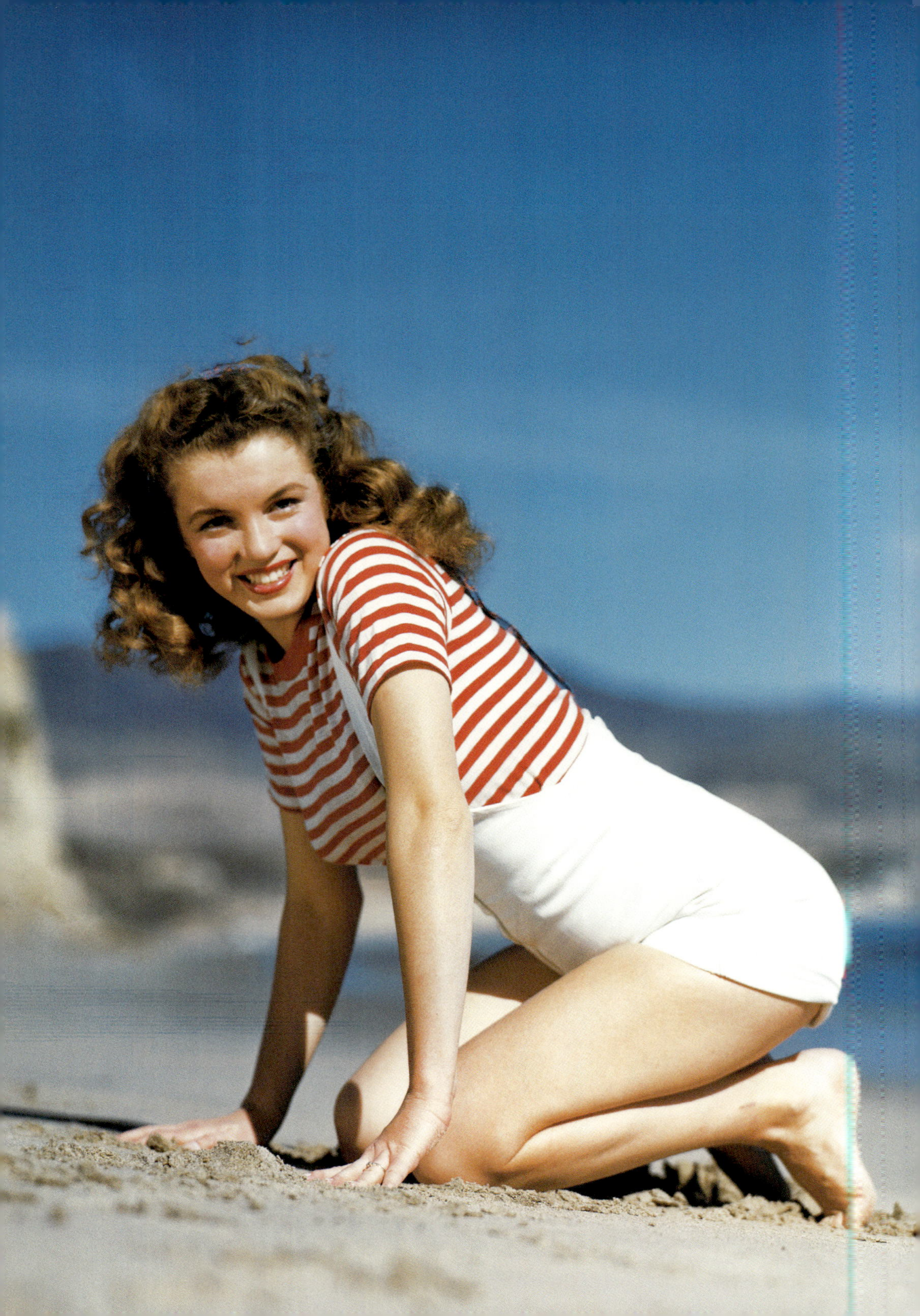

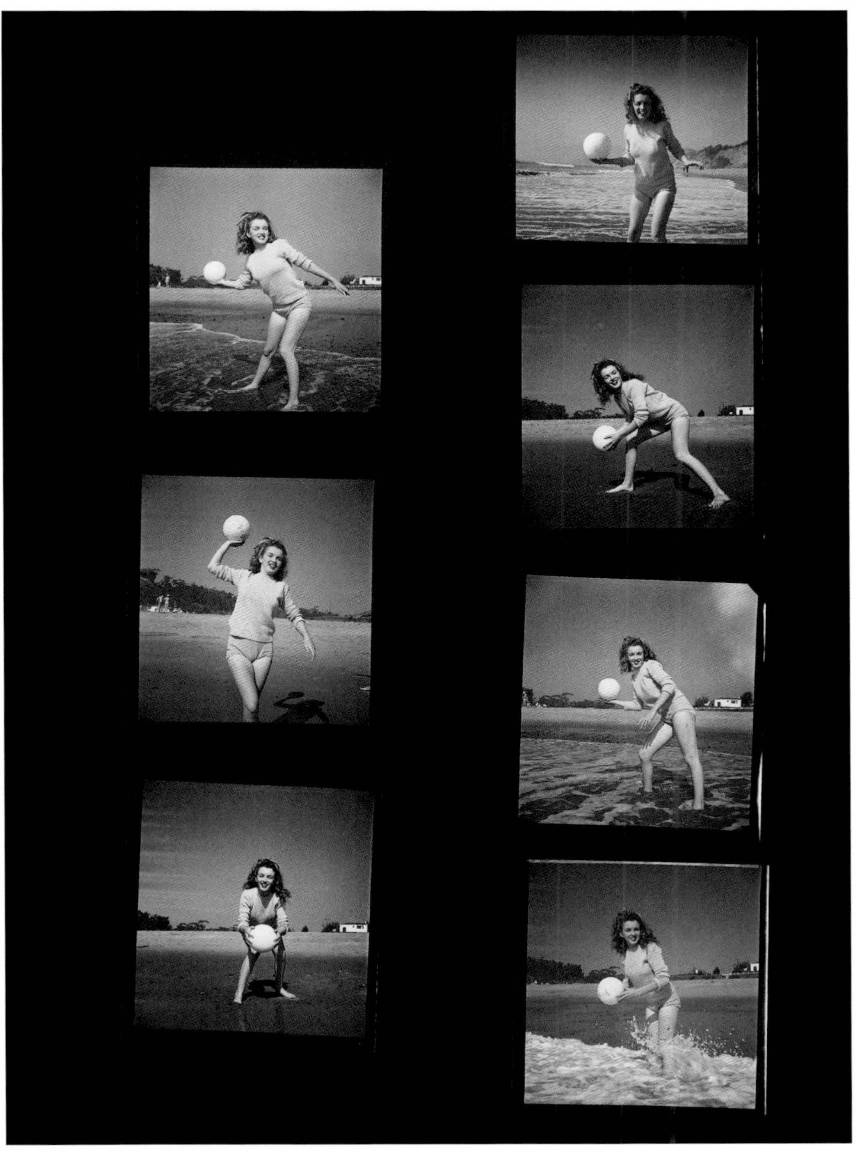

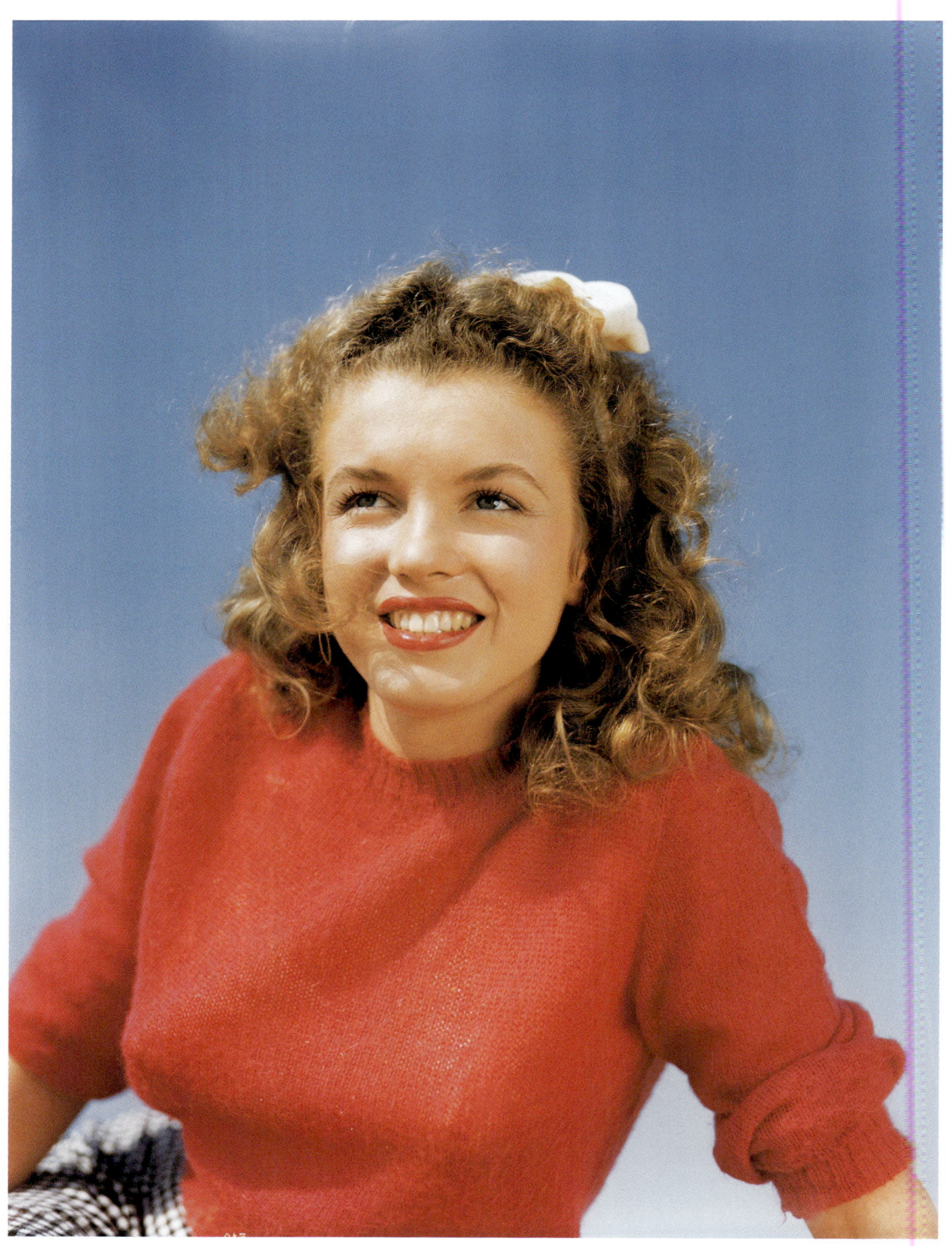

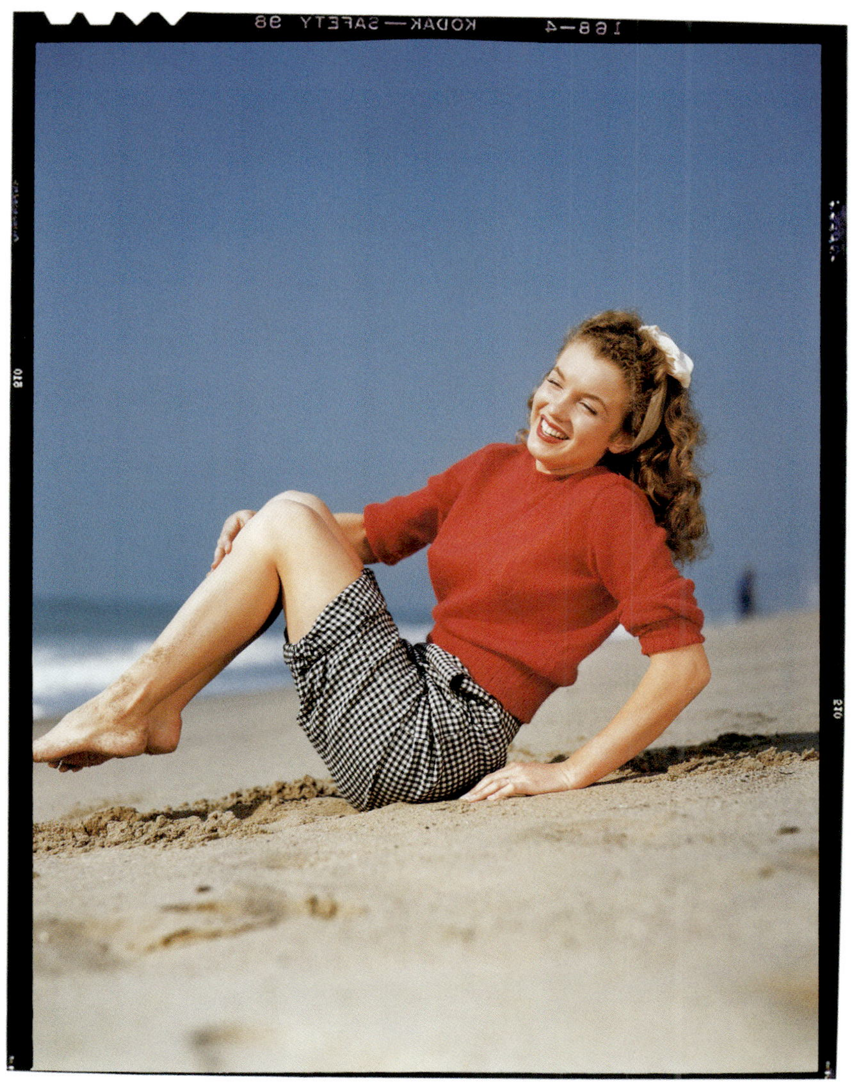

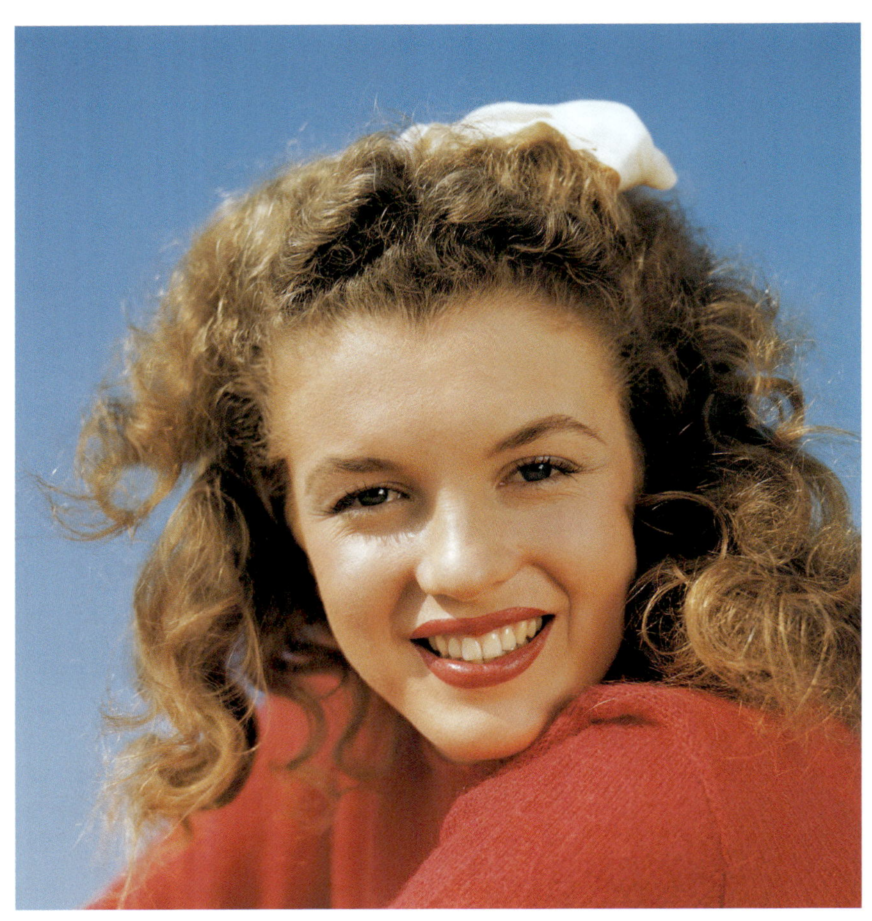

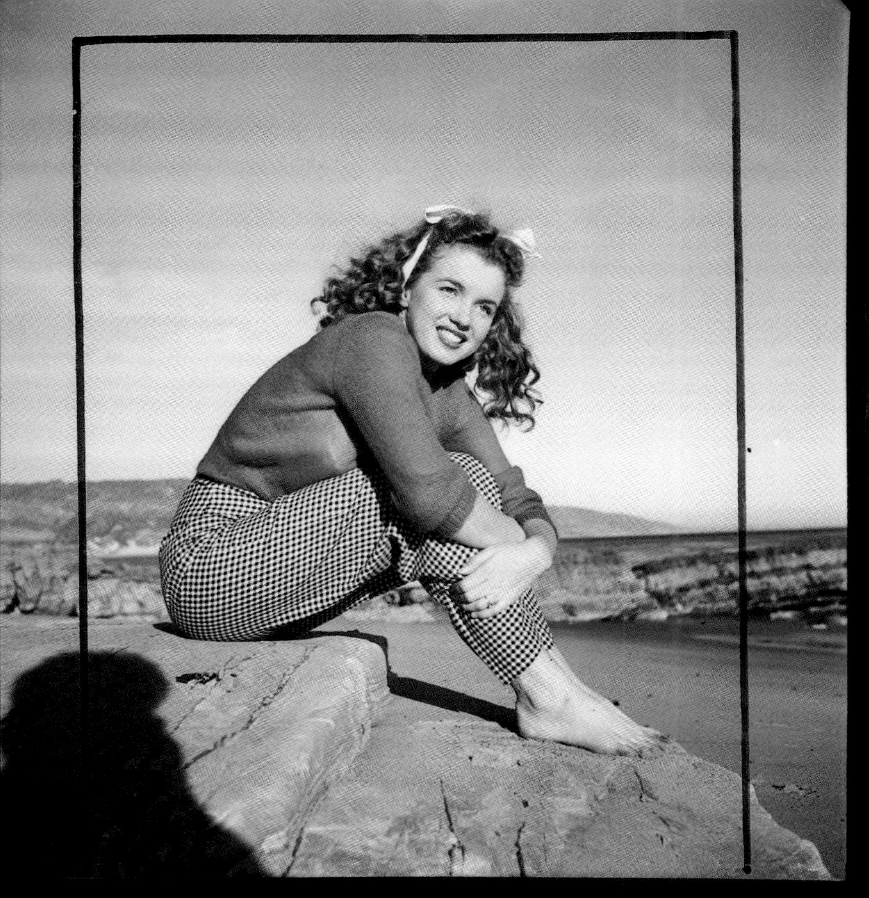

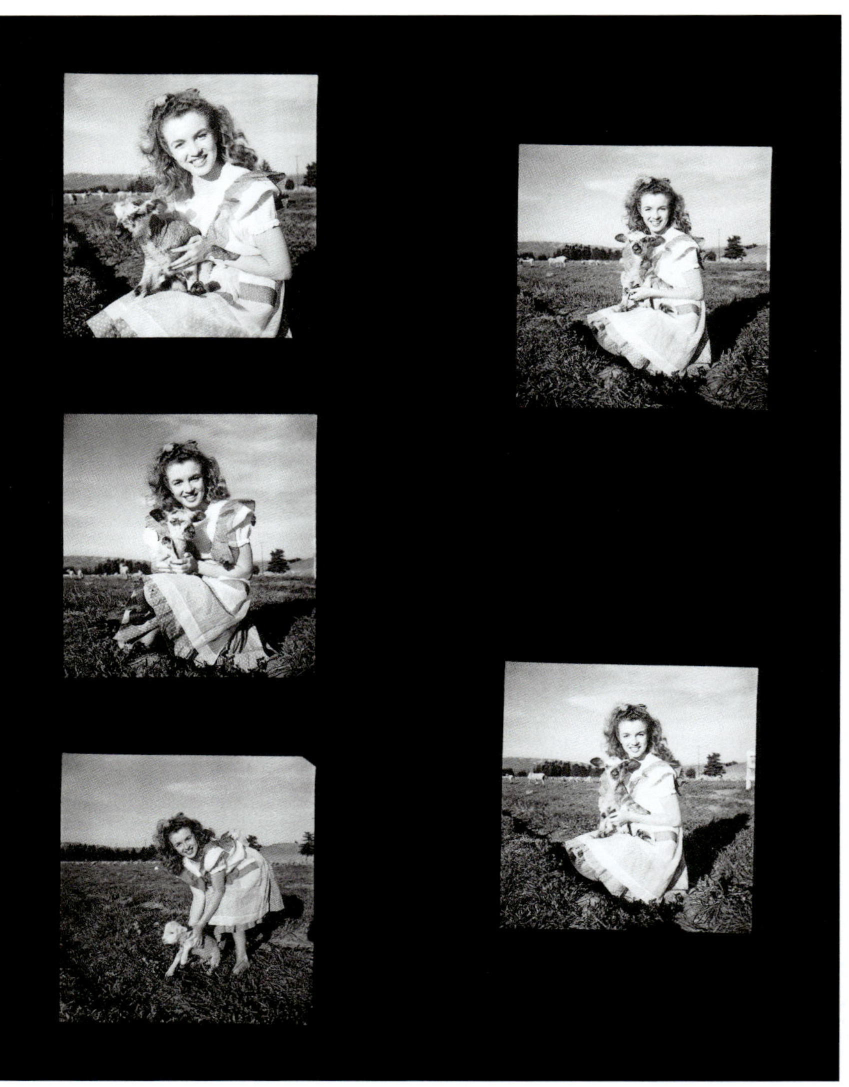

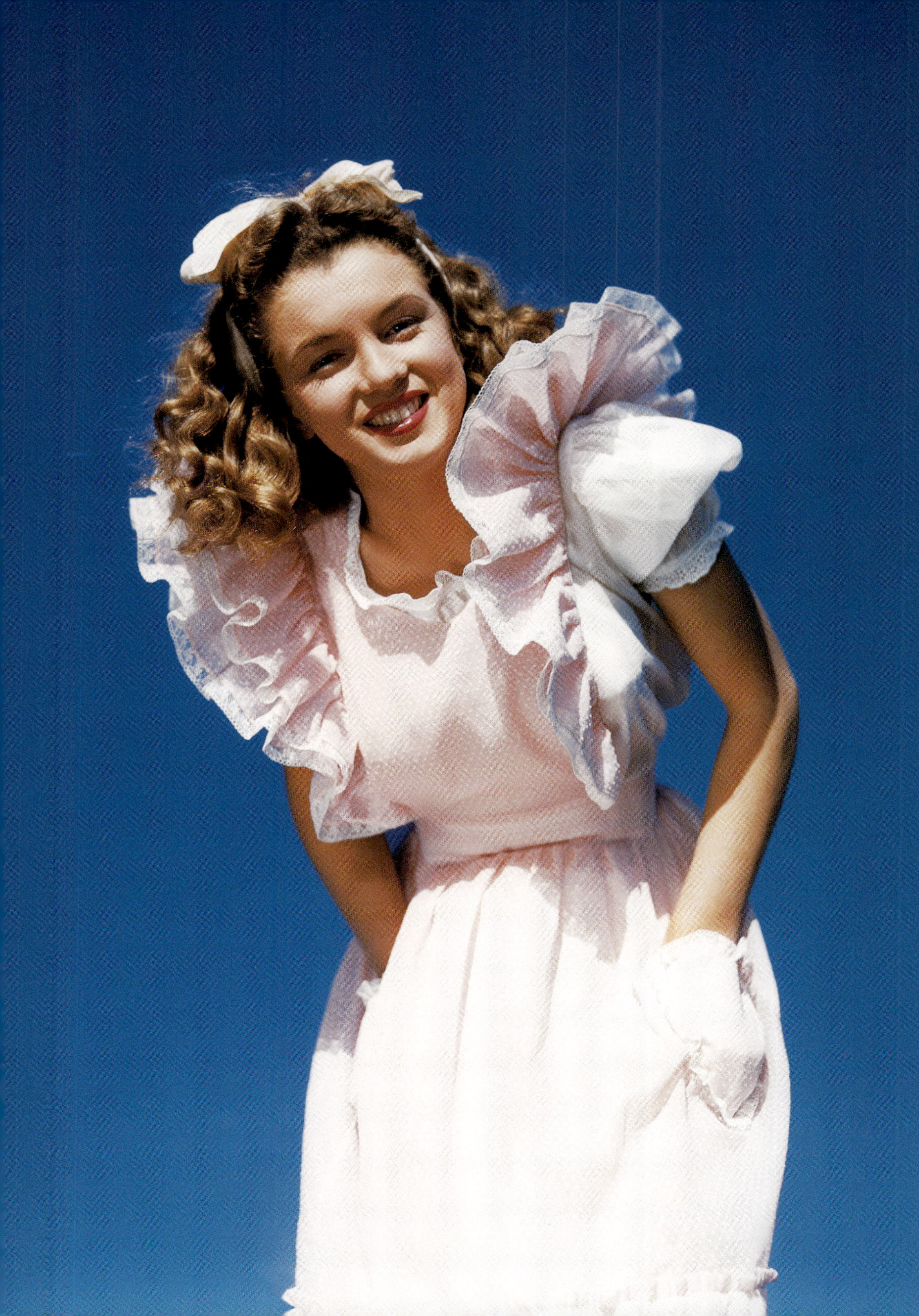

VIII. "NORMA JEAN"

Reality can be stranger than fiction. Soon after I got installed myself in a bungalow at the Garden of Allah, in Hollywood, what the man have predicted came through with amazing accuracy. This is how it went:

I phoned Dorothy Preble, a than lady model-agent who had her office on the Sunset Strip, just 2 blocks away from the Garden of Allah. She sent me many beautiful models the year before. (in 1944) I told Dorothy I need models for nudes, and she promised she shall try to find some for me. But I said, Dorothy, I was in a hurry, something very Urgent, a fortune-teller predicted there was a girl in Hollwyood "waiting for me" to photograph her! Waiting as soon as I got to Hollwyood! Dorothy said no; she does not see any girl waiting for a job in the office. I hanged up the phone, I called another lady model agent I knew, Emiline Snively, who had the "Blue Book model Agency" at the Amassador Hotel, I explained to Emiline that I was back in Hollwyood, again, and I needed models for photos of nudes, artistic nudes, for a new project I had in mind. And Miss Snively said, there was a very pretty girl in her office, waiting for her first modellling assignment, a model who just started in the profession, and perhaps she would pose for nudes. Miss Snively said she will send the young lady to see me right away, and that her name was Norma Jeane Baker.

When Norma Jeane arrived to my bungalow, later in the afternoon, it was, as if a miracle had happened to me. From the instant I looked at her, and we began to talk, her voice, her smile, her beautiful blue eyes revived in my mind Krisztina, the maid in Transylvania whom I loved so much. Norma Jeane was like the spitting image of Krisztina, (except that N.J. was only 19) Her movements, her vitality, her enthusiasm, her entire countenance, reflecting purity of soul, and honesty, was exacly like Krisztina's. Even her outbursting loughter seemed the same! Norma Jeane seemed to be like an Angel into my memory ! I could hardly believe it for a few moments. An earthly, sexy-looking angel ! Sent expressly for me !

And reminded Dorothy how my photos brought success to many models the year before.

P.S. This became the first-- Urgent. Everything about Marilyn Monroe was forever after "Urgent". Always important. Something extraordinary ! (Fate!)

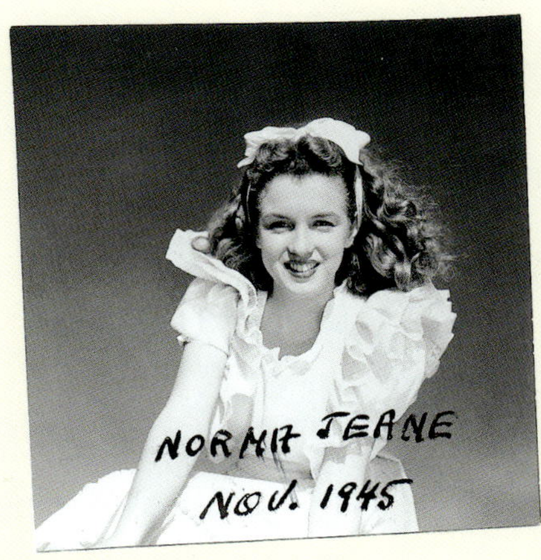

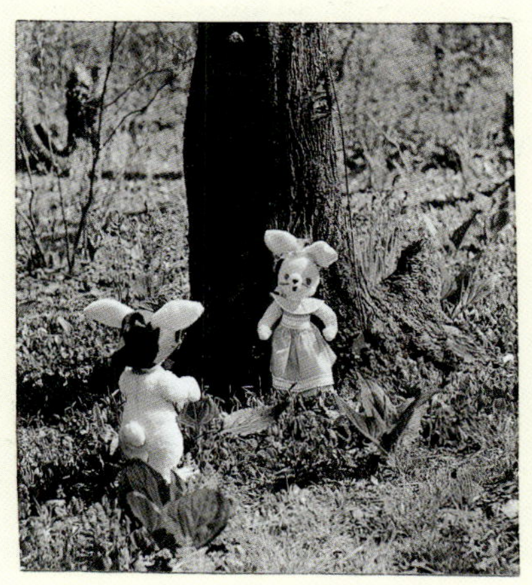

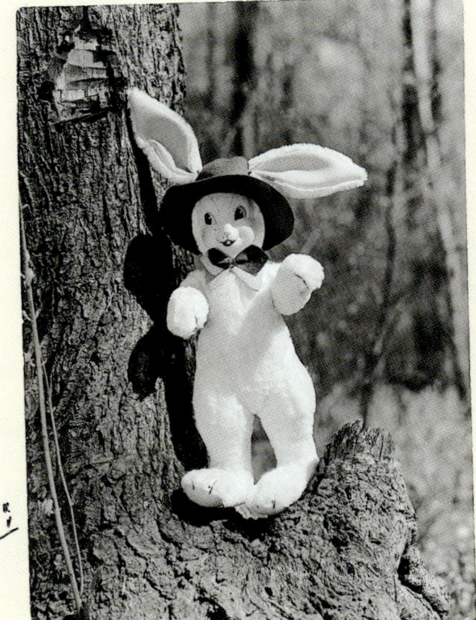

NOV. 1945

Year 1945.
My idea to use a bunny for the emblem of a new magazine I was planning to publish – was 8 years prior to Hugh Hefner's "PLAYBOY"!

R. D.

The impact Norma Jeane had on me was tremendous. A new "Krisztina" entered into my life! But this time I was a grown up man, and as minutes passed, I fell more and more in love with Norma Jeane. There was an immediate rapport between us; She reacted, responded to everything I said. She started to look around in my room examining all the pictures I put on the walls, and began asking questions. I had the immediate feeling that she was something special, something different from most girls and models I met before her, not only because she reminded me Krisztina, but mainly because she was so eager to ask questions about the pictures I put on the walls, and asked many questions about me; She wanted to know many things, right away. She was interested in me ! Mind you, reader, she was just an unknown 19 years old girl, not Marilyn Monroe ! She was utterly sincere; she did not wish to speak about herself, except when I asked her my own questions. She was sincere in wanting to know who I was, what was I doing with my life..... and I began to amuse her exceedingly with all sorts of stories what ren through my mind, and I kept dishing them out to her. I still remember it so clearly as if it happened just recently:

Norma Jeane wore a **pale** pink sweather, tight to her body, and her curly ash-blonde hair was tied around her head with pink ribbon; her rosy, pinkish face, her blue eyes, reminded me of a pretty Easter bunny! And I told her I bought two large rabbit dolls in a toy shop in New York, which I intened to photograph for a new magazine I was planning to start, to be financed by a very wealthy literary agent, and how sorry I was not having brought them with me to Hollywood, because I would have loved to photograph her with the rabbits for my new magazine, and to put her picture on the cover of the magazine, and inside the magazine, also, intermingling with the pictures of the rabbits. Norma Jeane loved the idea, and loughed heartily.

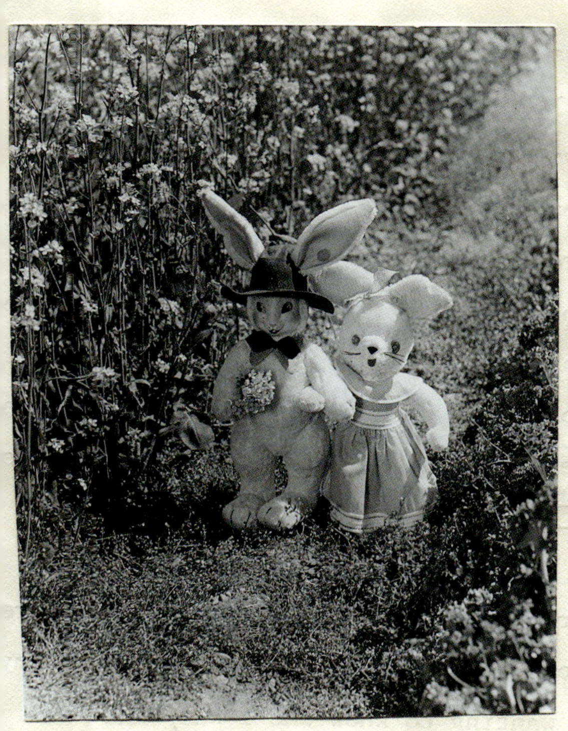

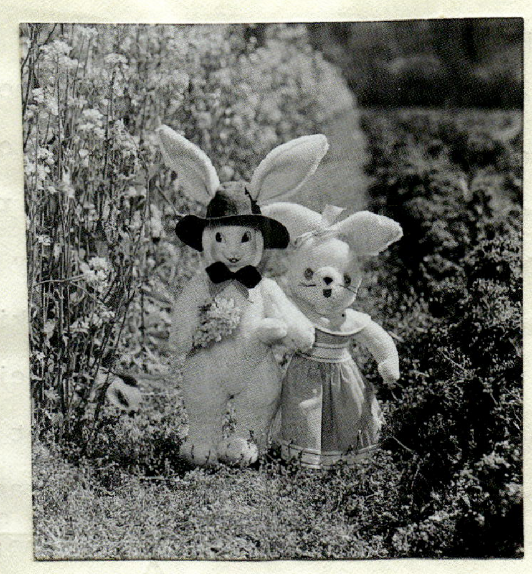

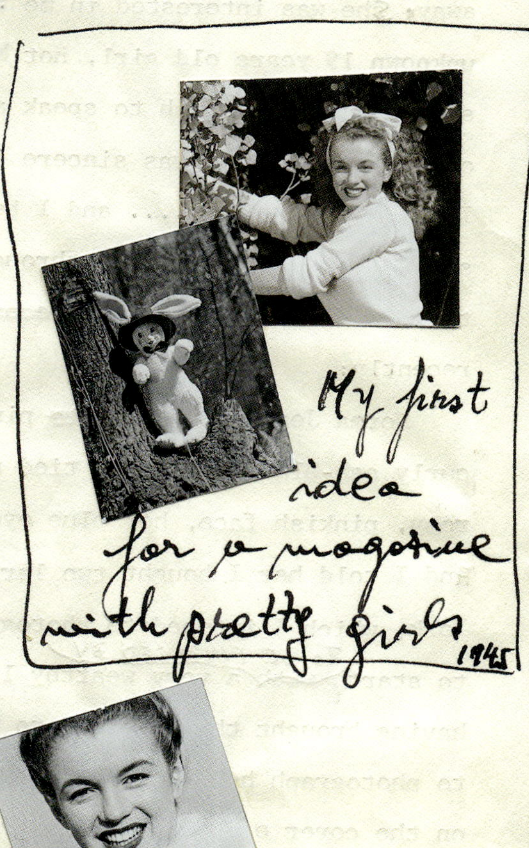
My first
idea
for a magazine
with pretty girls
1945

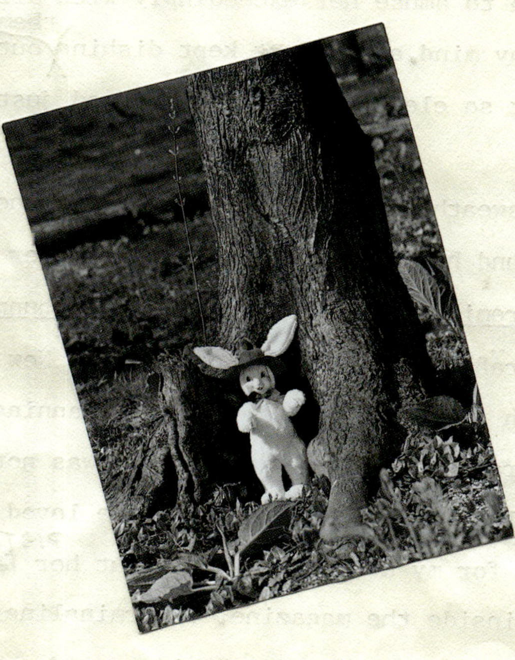

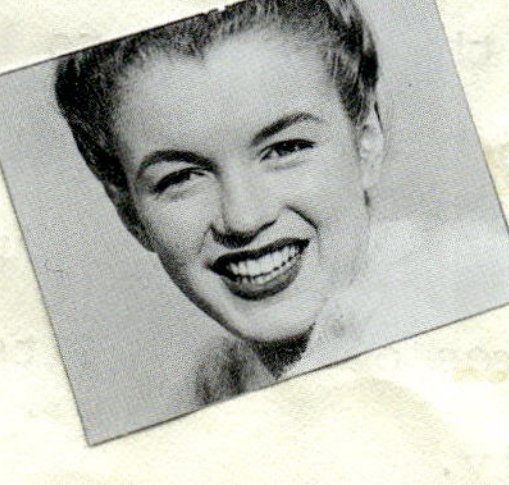

Thinking back to all that, I find it a bizarre coincidence, or a premonition, that, what I told to Norma Jean in 1945, about wanting to start a new kind of magazine, with the picture of the rabbit as the emblem of the magazine, and pictures of nudes inside the magazine, eight years later, Hugh Hefner, a genius of a businessman, made it a rality! Norma Jeane was going to be the star of the first issue of my magazine, on the cover, and inside the magazine. ~~and~~ Correspondingly, the first issue of PLAYBOY featured my darling Norma Jeane, but as Marilyn Monroe, on the cover of the magazine, and A NUDE OF her ~~nude~~ inside. ~~Hugh Hefner could not have known about my idea,~~ And this is not an implication that he stole the idea from me ! It is just an amazing coincidence !

But my idea was good, ~~and~~ BUT my misfortune was that I wasn't born to be business man! And that the literary agent (~~Jacques Chambrun~~) did not take my visions REALLY seriously !

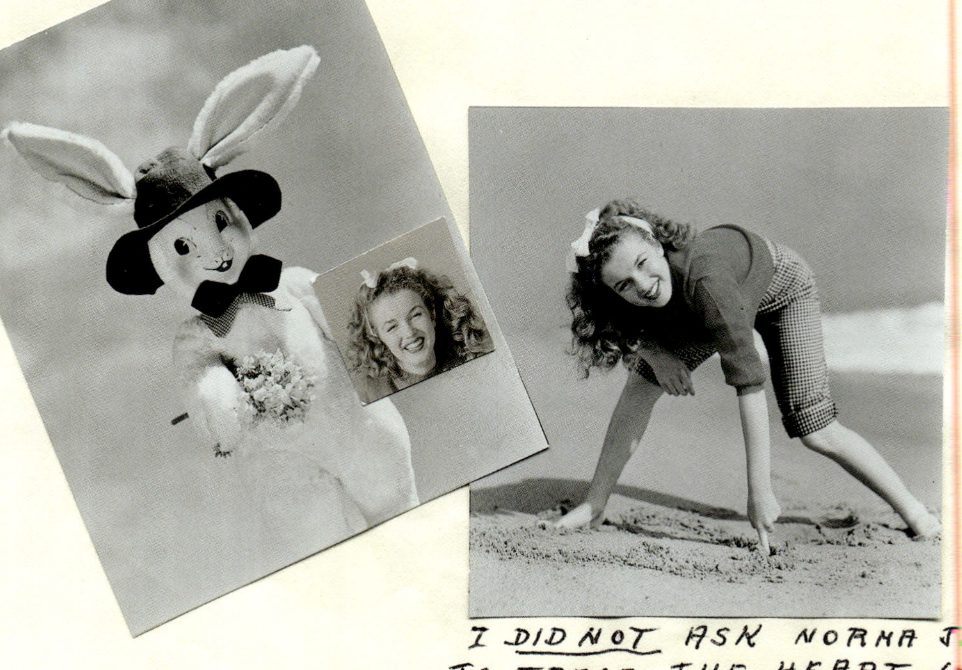

I DID NOT ASK NORMA JEAN TO TRACE THE HEART INTO THE SAND. SHE DID IT ON HER OWN!

MEMO:

(Most of the small contact print proofs I made 35 years ago have began turning yellow, dark brown, etc, or are fading away, and some of the negatives have started having spots in the emulsion. It's a matter of a few more years, and they will gradually start deteriorating completely. No wonder that, intuitively, I want some of my photos to be published now. At least, the printed page will last much much longer. Even a few centuries! And who wouldn't like to have his work preserved for posterity ! ~~Partly,~~ Its Vanity, but also common sense !)

I SHOUTED TO "NORMA JEAN" "PULL UP YOUR PANTS TIGHT! I LOVE YOU!"

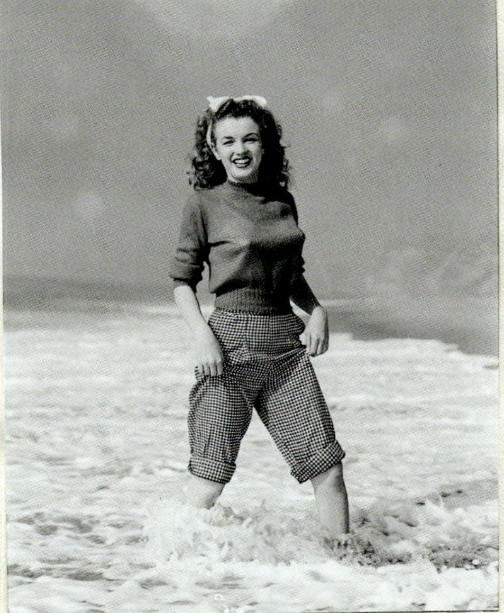

This was Marilyn Monroe's first magazine cover, in 1946 (a completely unknown young model)

NOTICE SPOTS ALL OVER IN THE NEGATIVE

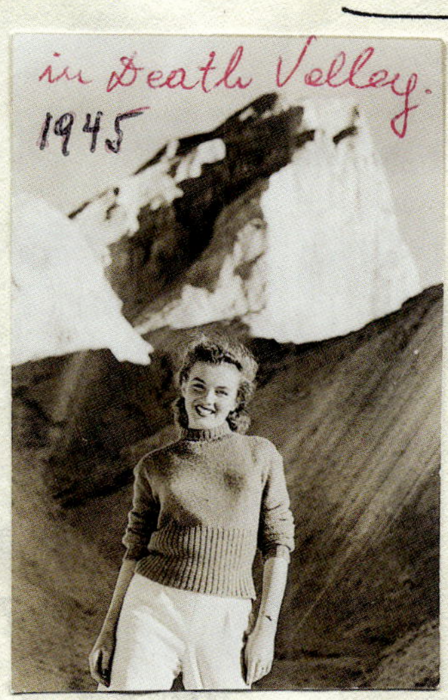

1945, AT "PARADISE COVE" NORTH OF MALIBU.

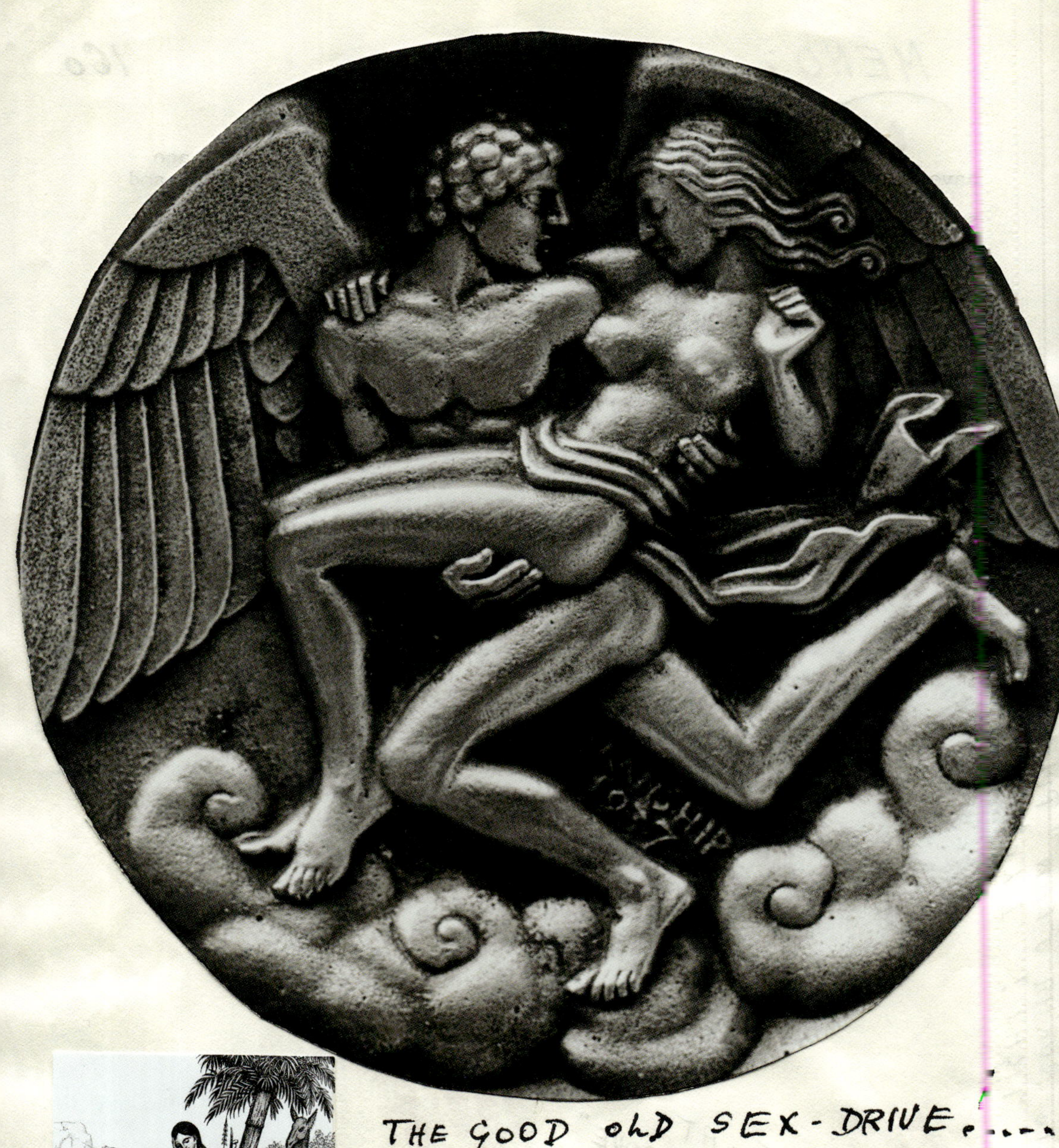

THE GOOD OLD SEX-DRIVE!.....
MOTIVATED ME!.....
NORMA JEANE HAVE SENSED IT
RIGHT AWAY!

I noticed Norma Jean had a wedding ring on her finger. She informed me she was married, but separated from her husband, and no longer in love with him. He was a merchant marine sea-man, away, on the sea, and she was free, and modelling was her new goal. She mentioned nothing about wanting to become an actress!

The few words of explanations she gave me freed my mind from inhibition; the truth was that I wanted to photograph her very much, but I wanted her more than anything else in the world! I was completely love-struck from the moment she appeared at the entrance door!

While we were talking, Norma Jean took a good look at one of the several engravings I put on the wall; a nude indian girl sitting on a rock, surrounded by mountaineous scenery, and anilmals, sort of an allegorical representation of the vision of America. The way Europeans figured life was like in America, a few centuries ago. Norma Jeane was very interested in the picture, I told her I brought the pictures with me all the way from Transylvania, Hungary, and I went into a long story, telling her that in Spain, in the 16th Century, it was believed that California was an island, inhabited by beautiful and strong native women only-- who lived nude --in. And, that the entire continent of the West was rumored to be rich with gold; So, Cortes, the famous Spanish explorer outfitted ships and came to explore and conquer California -- driven by the lust for gold, and lust for women. The good old sex-drive was the reason Califroania became invaded by the Spaniards -- I said to Norma Jean. And she loughed like crazy when I told her that I had the same thing in mind coming here to Hollywood, and my intentions were to photograraph beautiful girls in the nude all throughout the west, but at the same time, to explore old forgotten gold mines, and look for gold, too, in the mountains, because I believed there was still plenty there, if only one takes the trouble to look for it. I came straight to the point in our conversation, asking

"NORMA JEAN", 1945

Dec'

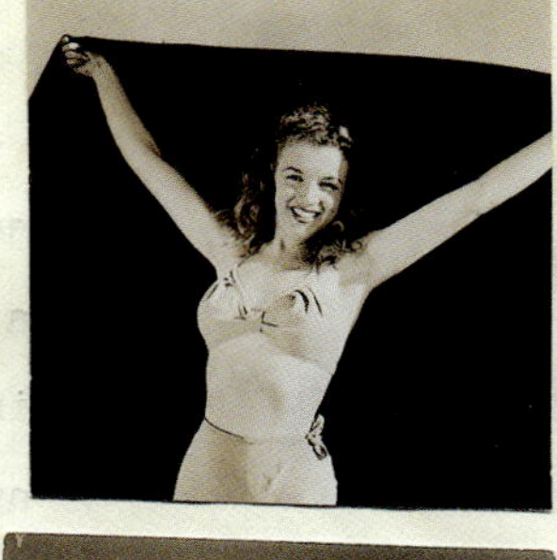

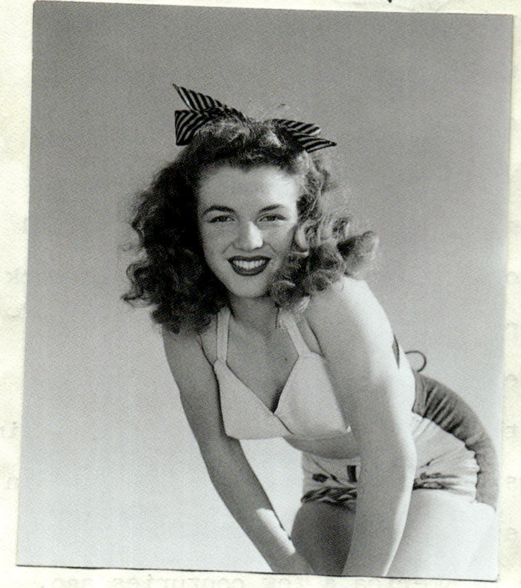

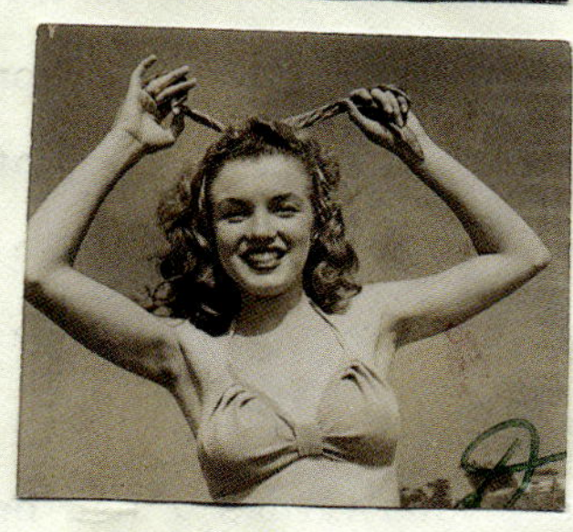

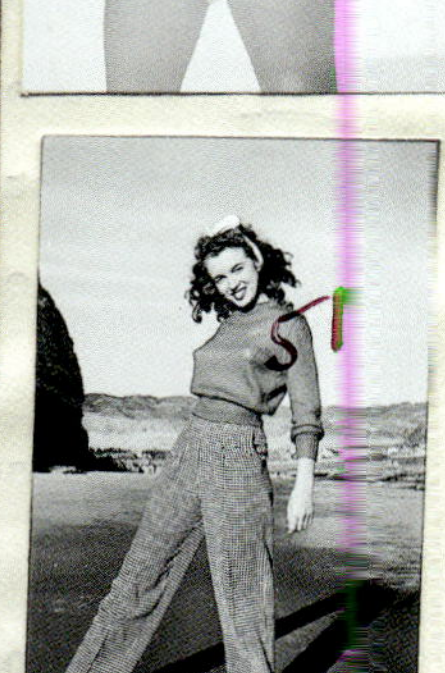

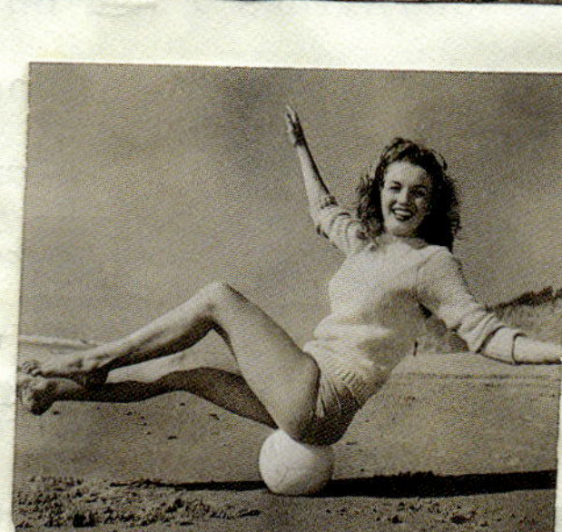

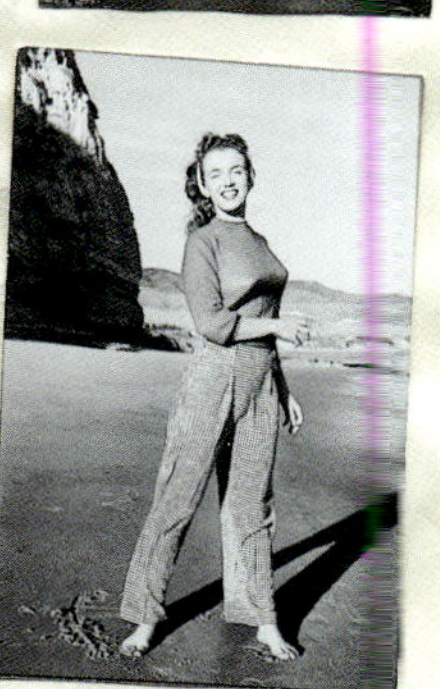

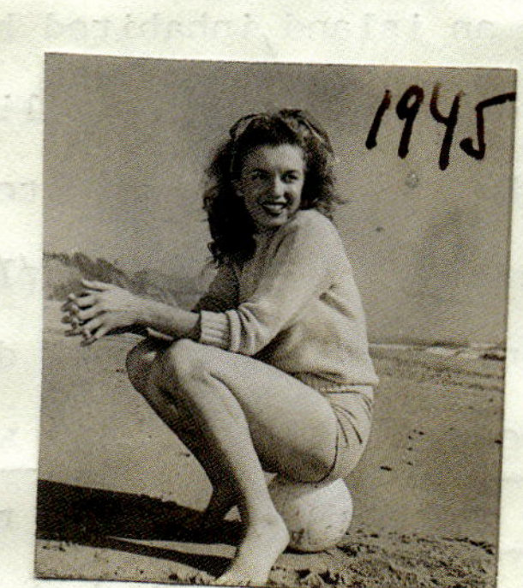

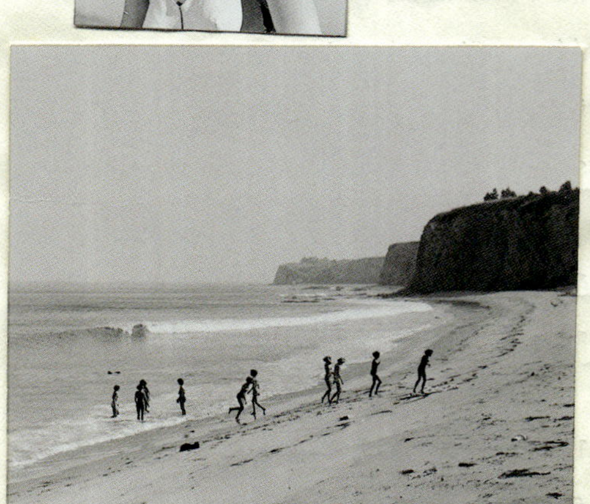

"PARADISE COVE", NORTH OF MALIBU. SECLUDED BEACH. THIS IS WHERE I TOOK NORMA JEANE THE FIRST TIME OUT. 1/1945

her whether she would like to come to travel with me. We would go by car to explore the vast West, and take pictures everywhere -- glamour photos for magazine covers, and nudes, too!
I had a stack of large enlargments of photos I took of movie stars the year before, and some nudes, and Norma Jeane looked through them with great approval. She was excited, and wanted to pose for me. And she asked " Would you like to see my figure ? ". In a jiffy, she grabbed her hatbox, went to the adjoining room (the bedroom) to put on a bathing suit, and smiling, beaming with happiness, she swirled around the center of the living room, happy to be able to show me her beautiful figure.

A day later, I took her to the beach to take pictures of her. And again, and again, I photographed her each day. My mind was made up for sure; I wanted to take her away from Hollywood right away, on a long trip. Just go with her anywhere, everywhere! I felt completely enamored by her!

I offered to pay her one hundred dollars per week for posing, plus all expenses, and that I would buy all sorts of things for her to wear for pictures: jeans, blouses, sweathers, bathings suits; and promised she can eat as much, and as well as she pleased, because, I noticed she loved food. She was young, she had a good appetite !

Norma Jeane wanted to come with me on the trip, but since she lived with her aunt, she had to have her aunt's permission to go with me. As for posing for nudes, she said she might, maybe, but neither of us attached much importance to the issue. I was trembling, I was so much in love with her! And the thought of her with me on a trip was my main issue. I felt she liked me, and she was very enthusastic about going away with me. I reassured her she will be safe and sound in my company. And we hugged and kissed, sincerely, and innocently. I took more pictures of her on the deserted beach at Paradise Cove, near Mailbu,

checks for first photos

90-1388 LAUREL-SUNSET BRANCH 90-1388

Bank of America
NATIONAL TRUST AND SAVINGS ASSOCIATION

No. ______

HOLLYWOOD, CALIF. 11. 20 1945

PAY TO THE ORDER OF Norma Jeane Dougherty $ 30 00/100

thirty 00/100 DOLLARS

MEMBER FEDERAL RESERVE SYSTEM

André de Dienes

SAMPLE

90-1388 LAUREL-SUNSET BRANCH 90-1388

Bank of America
NATIONAL TRUST AND SAVINGS ASSOCIATION

No. ______

HOLLYWOOD, CALIF. 11. 26 1945

PAY TO THE ORDER OF Norma Jeane Dougherty $ 20 00/100

twenty 00/100 DOLLARS

MEMBER FEDERAL RESERVE SYSTEM

André de Dienes

SAMPLE

Norma Jeane Dougherty
11348 Nebraska Ave
W. LA.

ANY BANK, BANKER OR TRUST CO. OR THRU LOS ANGELES CLEARING HOUSE ALL PRIOR ENDORSEMENTS GUARANTEED

NOV 29 '45 0099

16-66 LOS ANGELES HEADQUARTERS 16-66
BANK OF AMERICA N.T.&S.A.
LOS ANGELES CALIFORNIA
11

SAMPLE

Norma Jeane's lovely handwriting on the reverse side of the check.

NORMA JEAN 1945

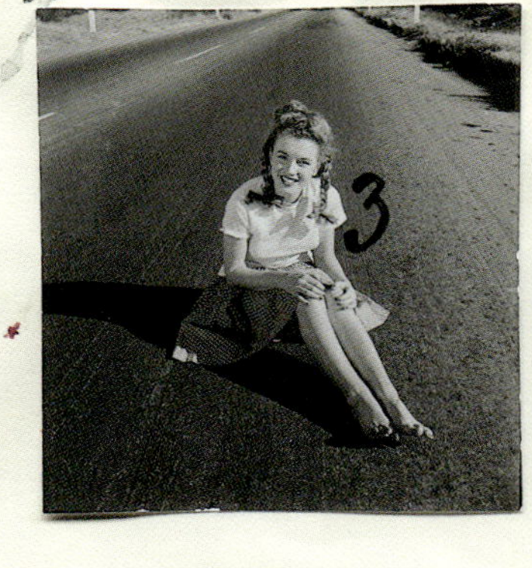

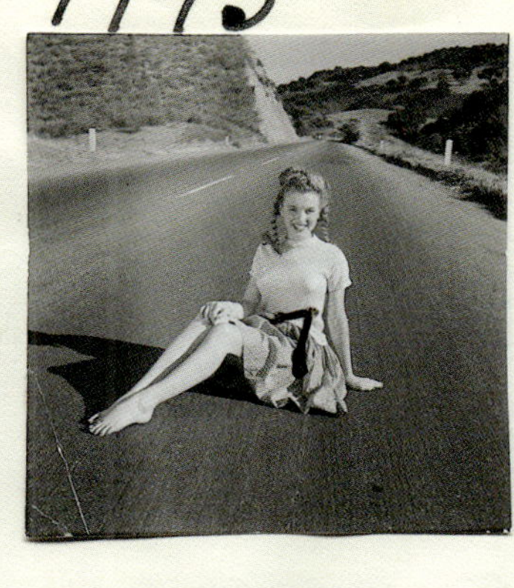

G.I.P. had
...is set 1981-1982.
Xeroted

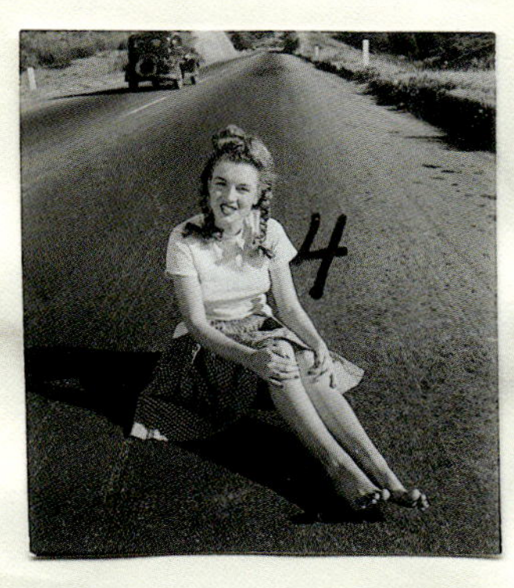

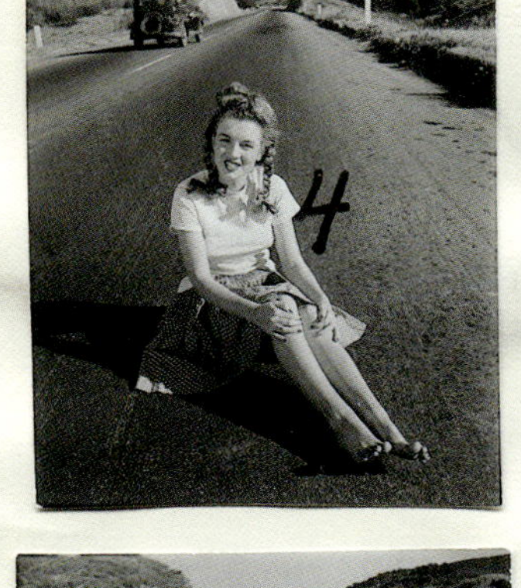

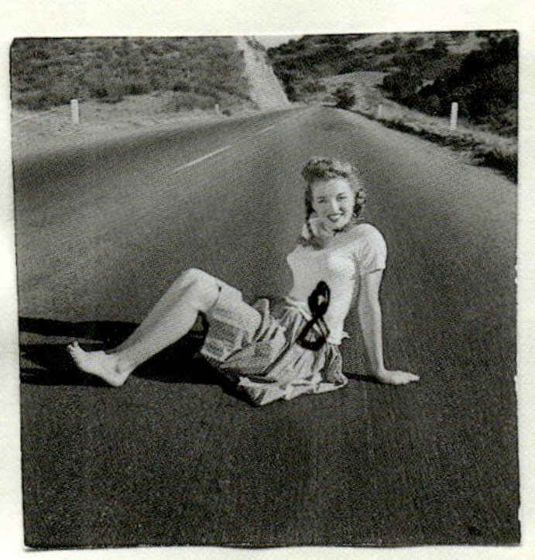

SHE STARTED
HERE

1945

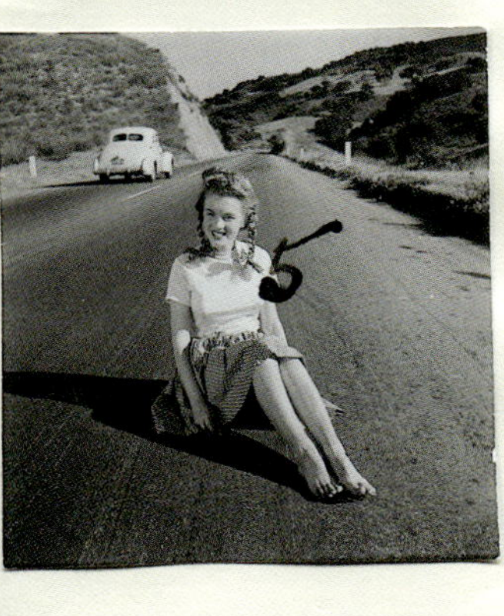

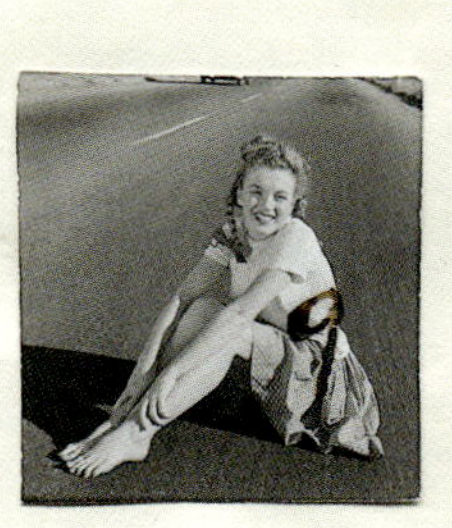

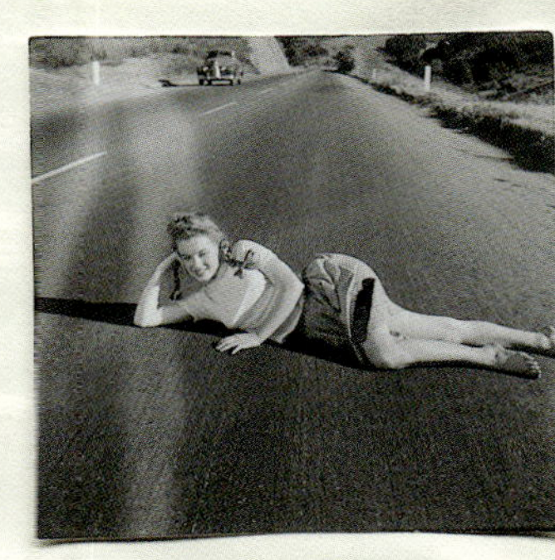

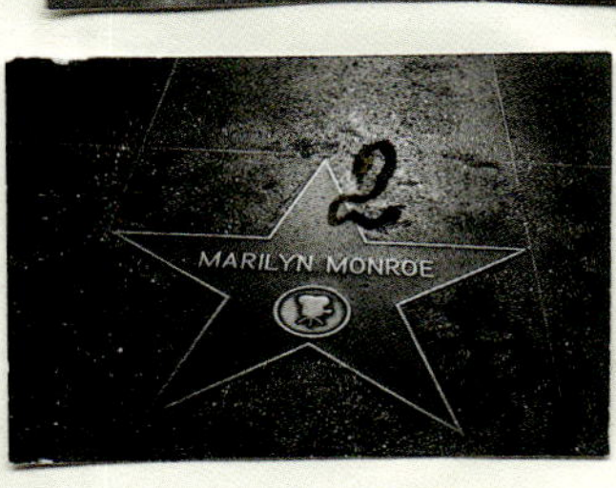

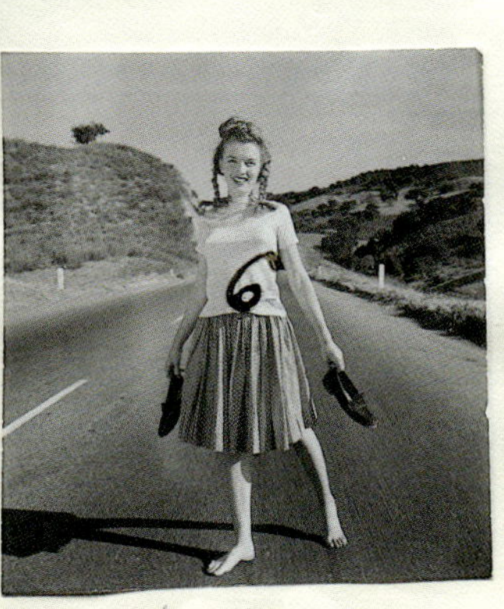

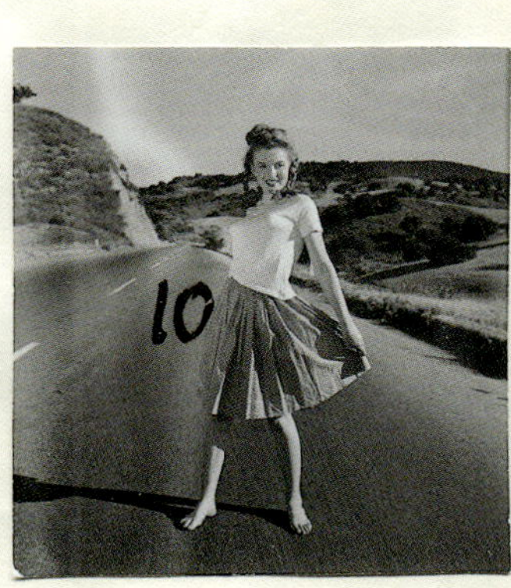

AND HER NAME
BECAME A LEGEND...

1.

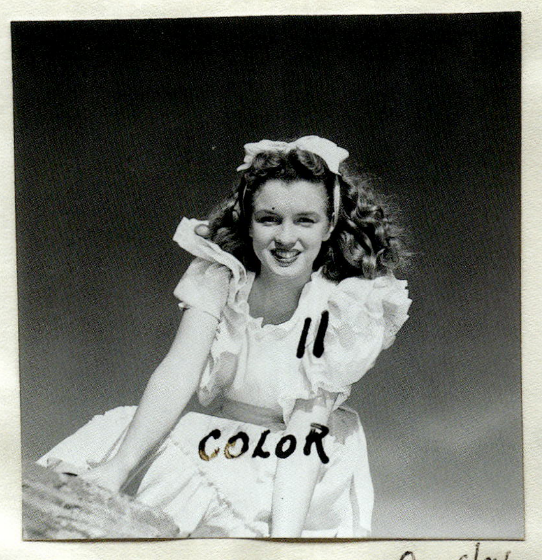

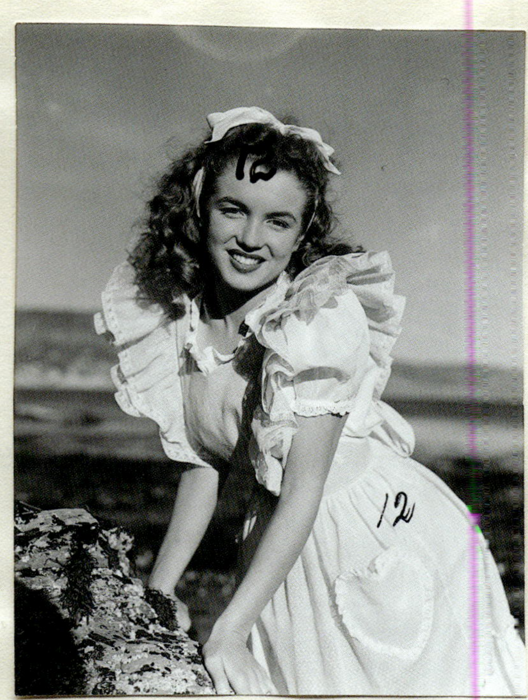

g - 6/24/82

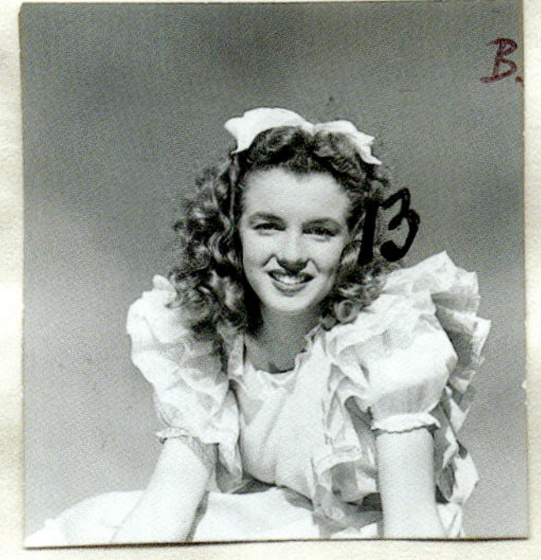

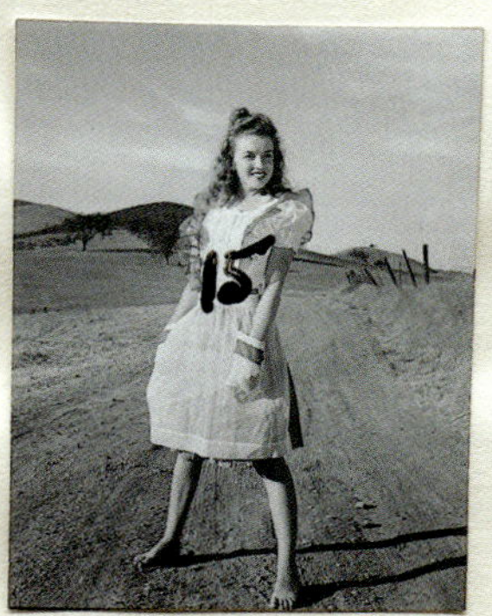

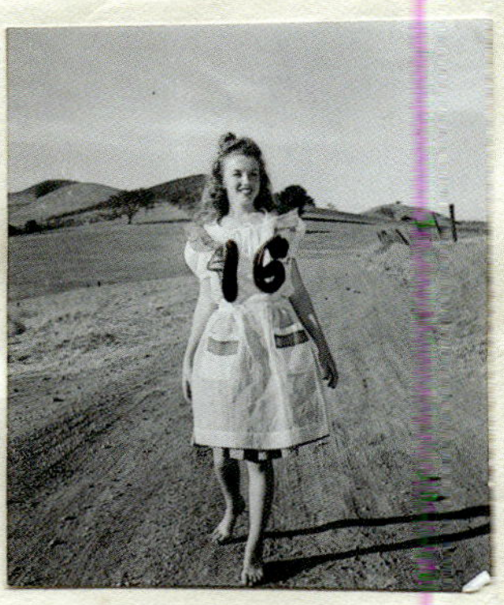

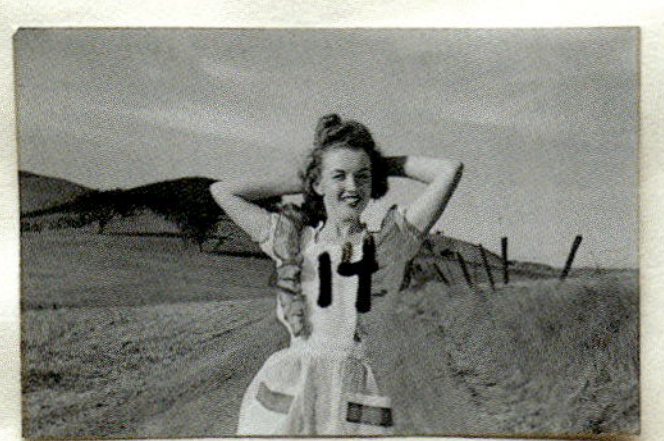

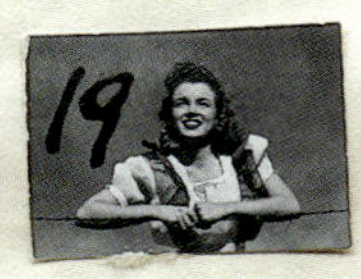

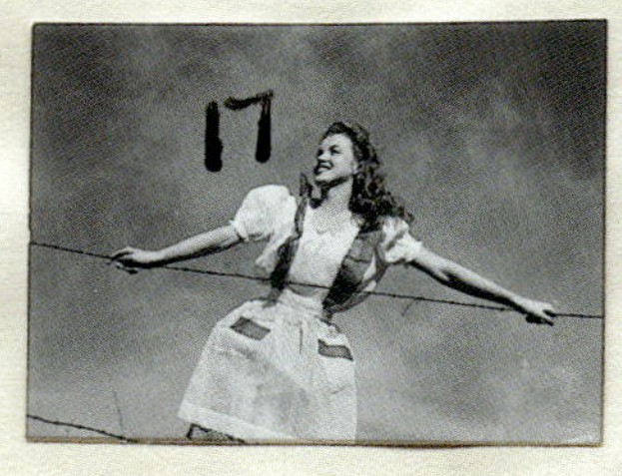

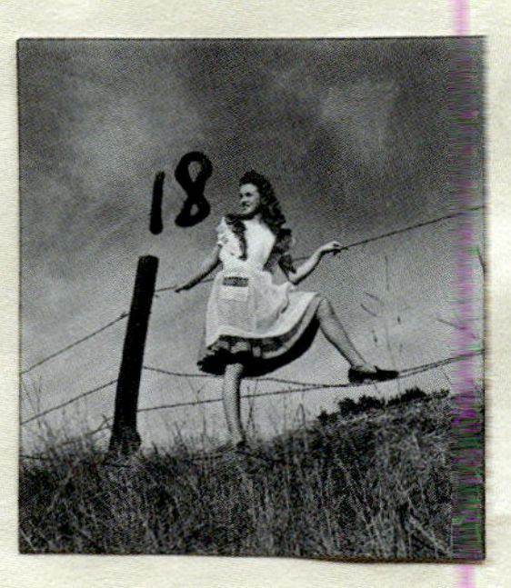

ANDRE DE DIENES
1401 SUNSET PLAZA DRIVE
HOLLYWOOD, CALIF. 90069

2

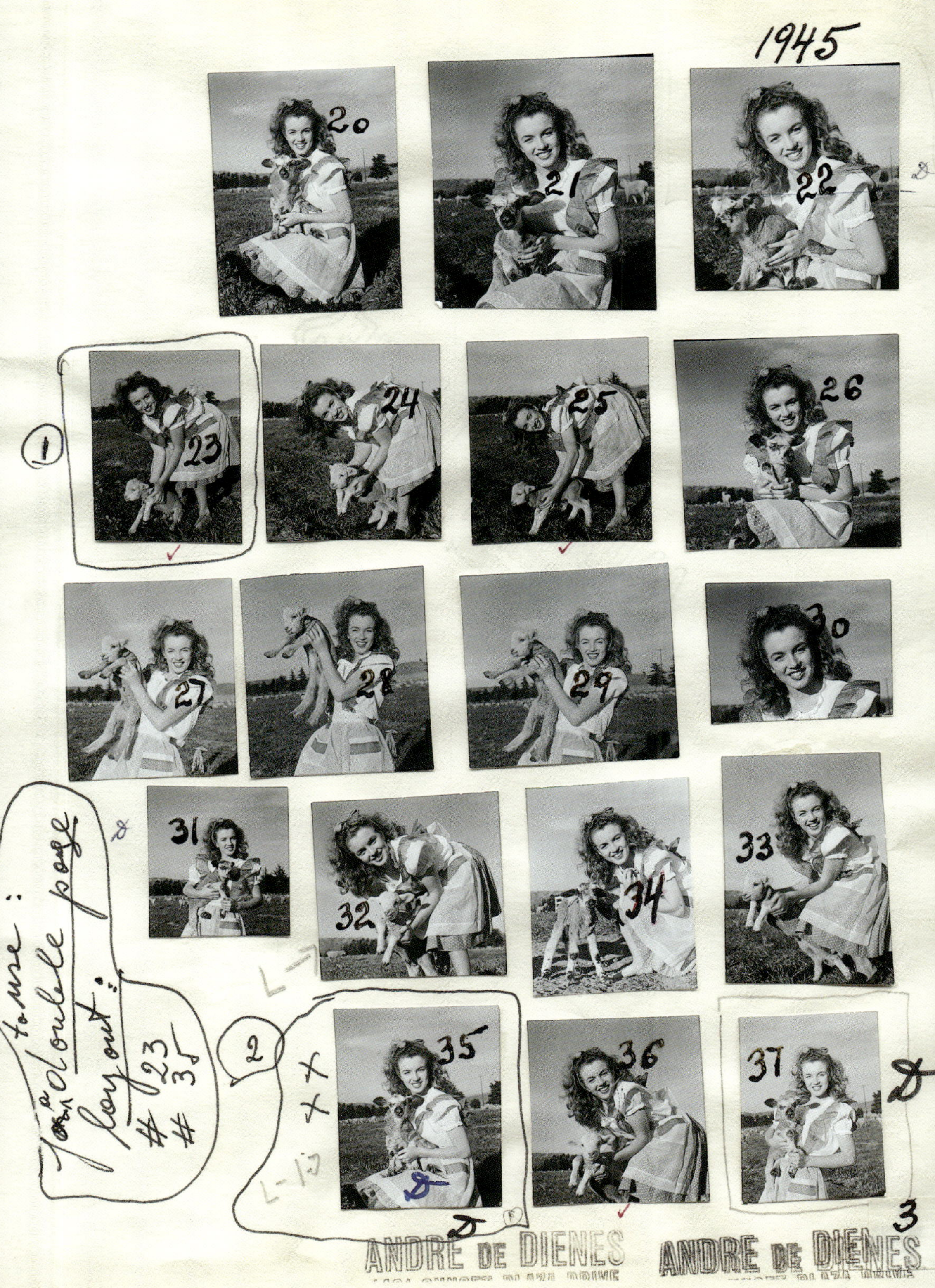

1945
20
21
22
23
24
25
26
27
28
29
30
31
32
33
34
35
36
37
1
2
to use: for double page layout: # 23 # 35
3
ANDRE DE DIENES
ANDRE DE DIENES

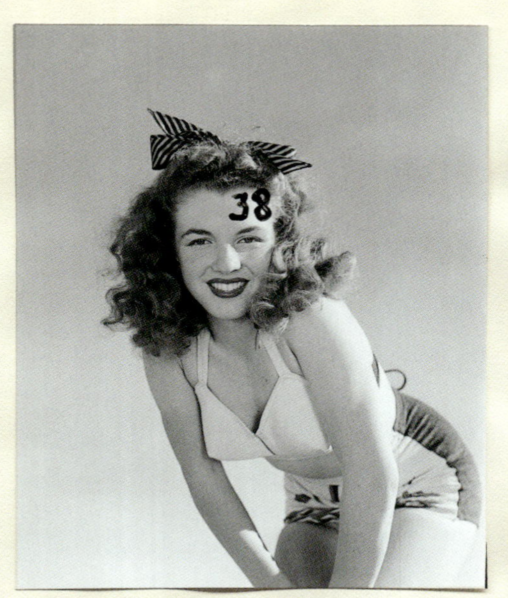

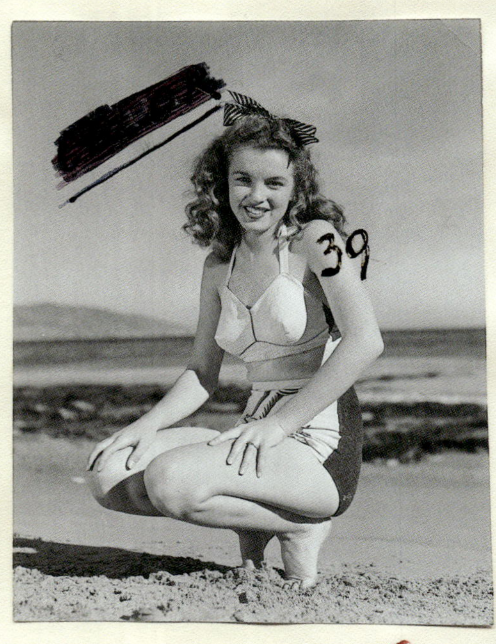

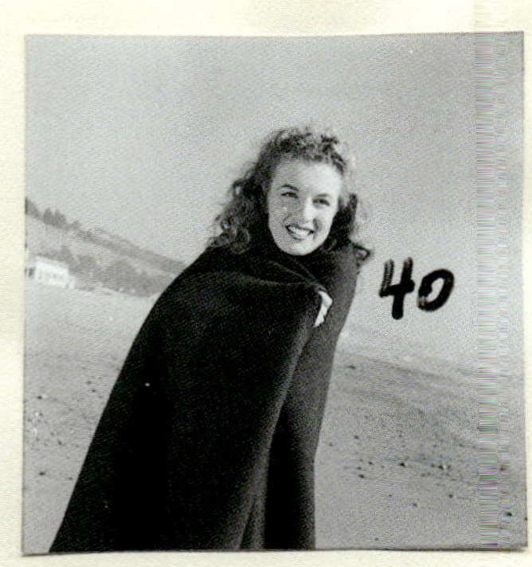

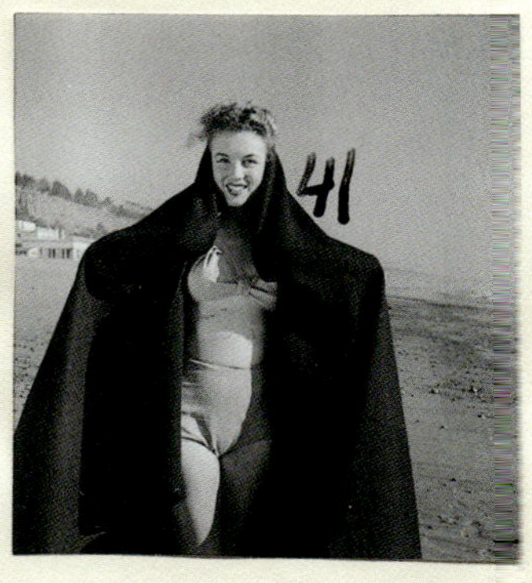

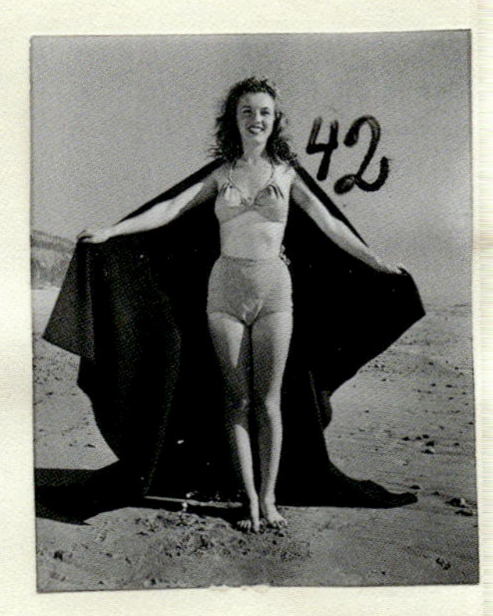

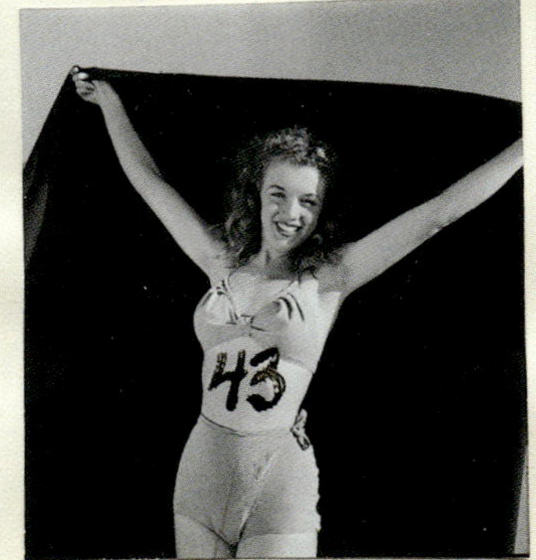

g.

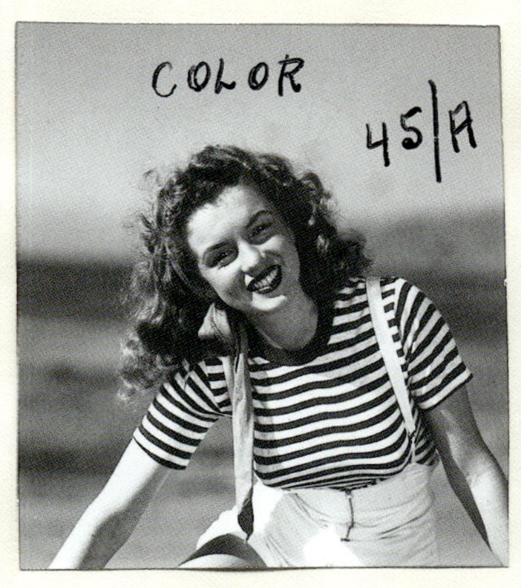

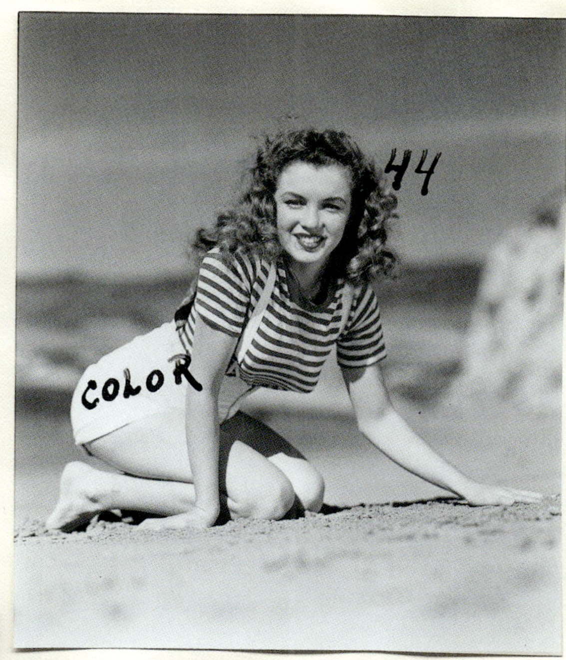

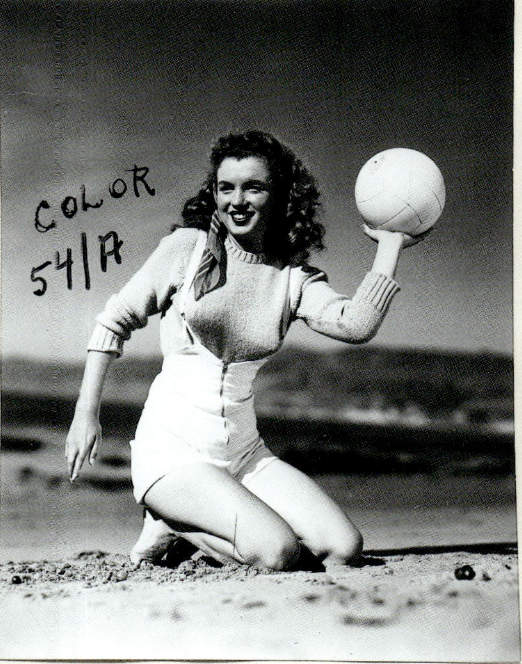

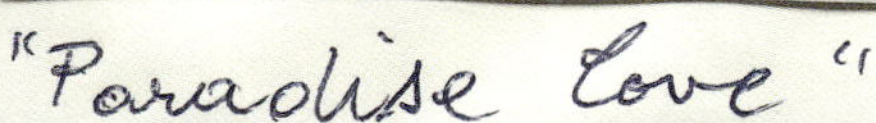

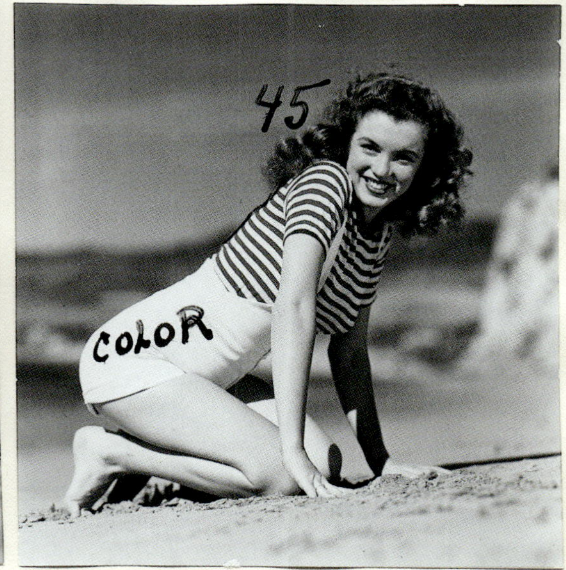

north of Malibu

ANDRE DE DIENES
1401 SUNSET PLAZA DRIVE
HOLLYWOOD, CALIF. 90069

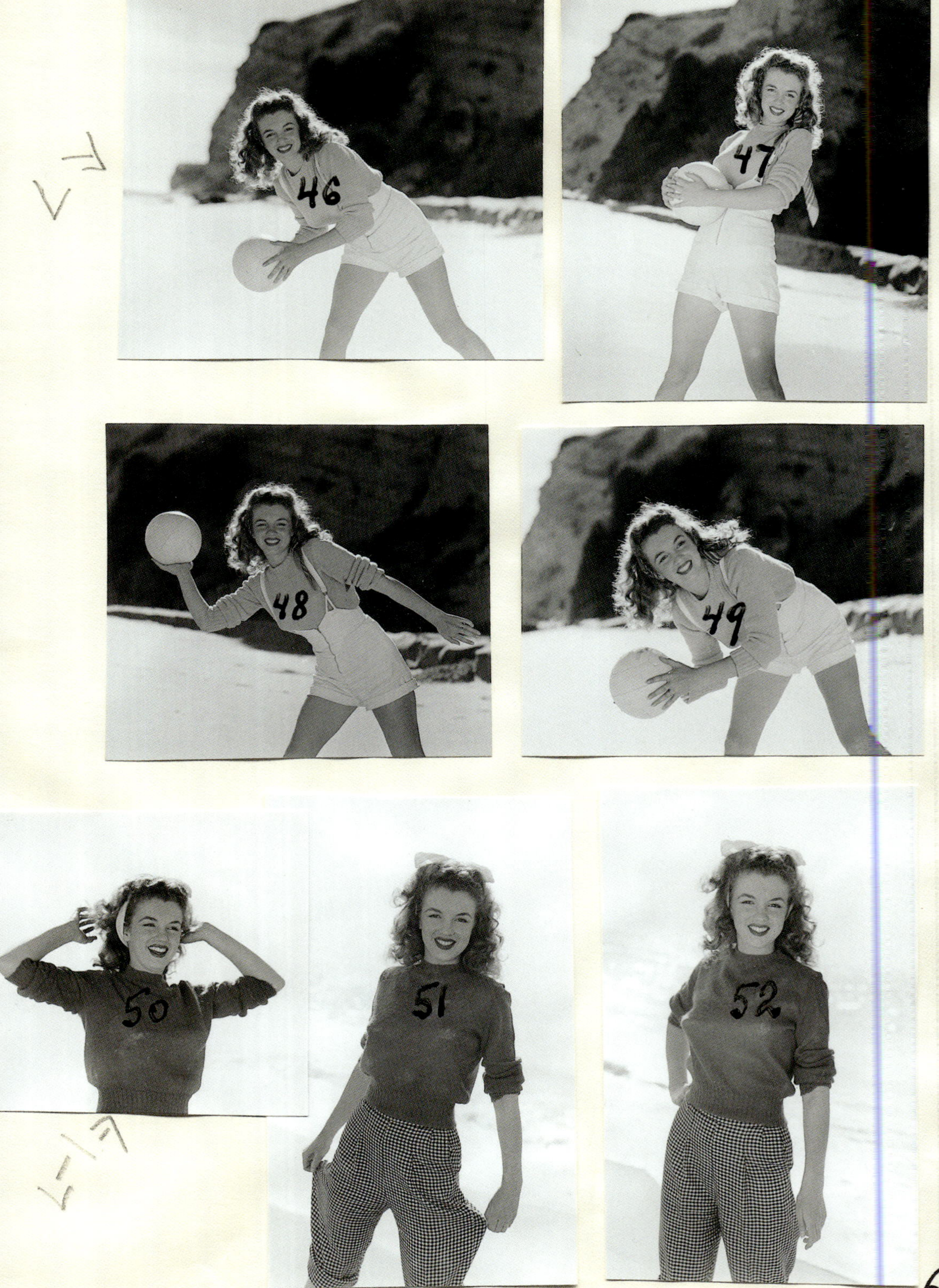
46
47
48
49
50
51
52
ANDRE DE DIENES

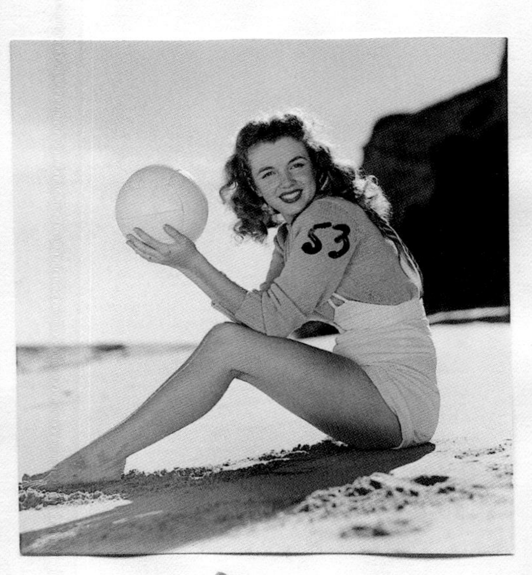

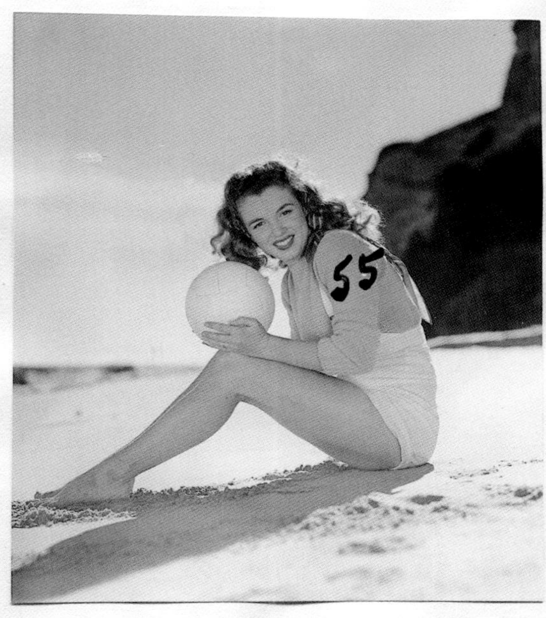

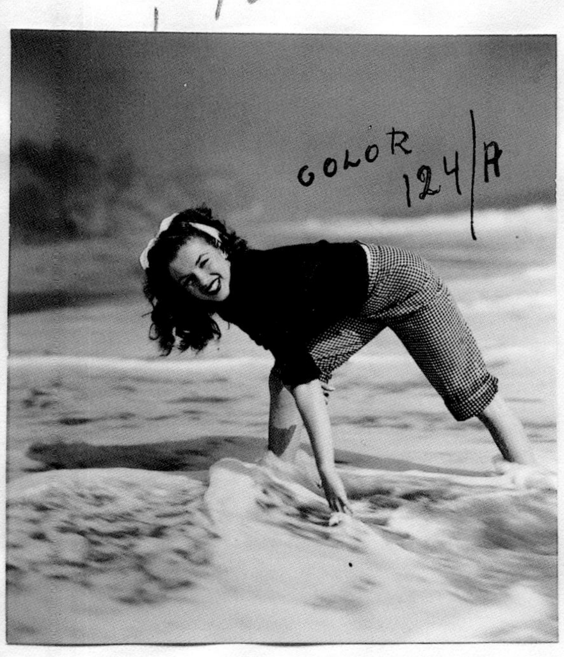

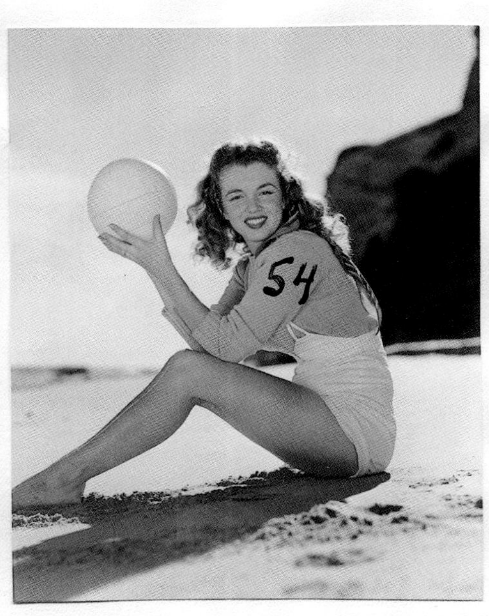

ANDRE DE DIENES
1401 SUNSET PLAZA DRIVE
HOLLYWOOD, CALIF. 90069

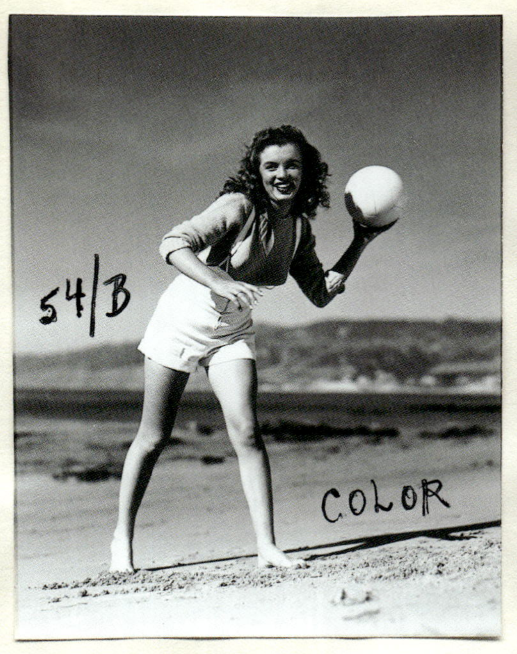
54/B
COLOR

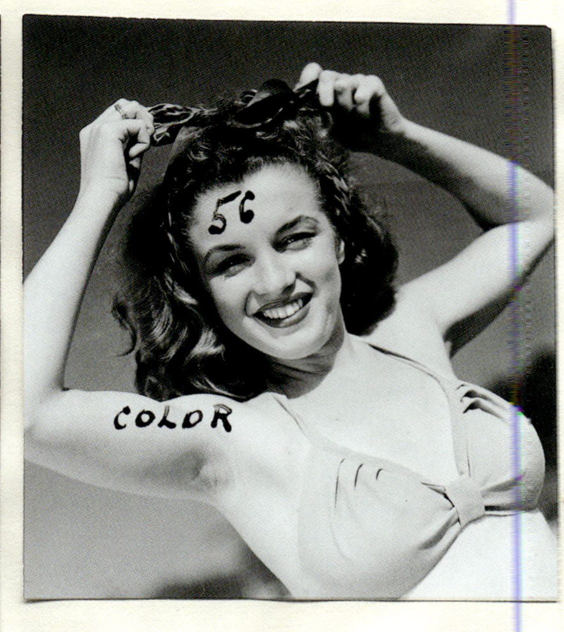
56
COLOR

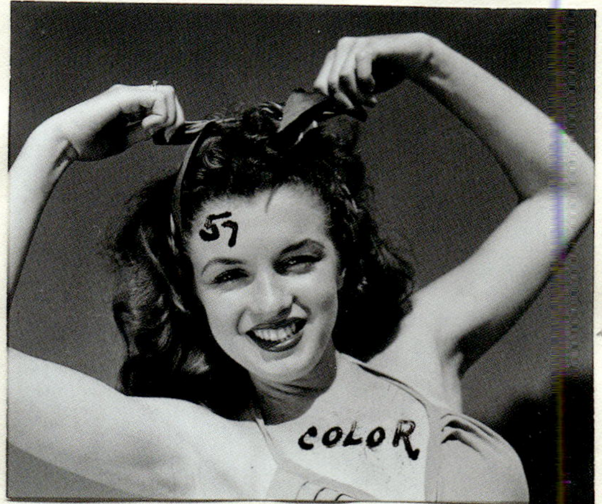
57
COLOR

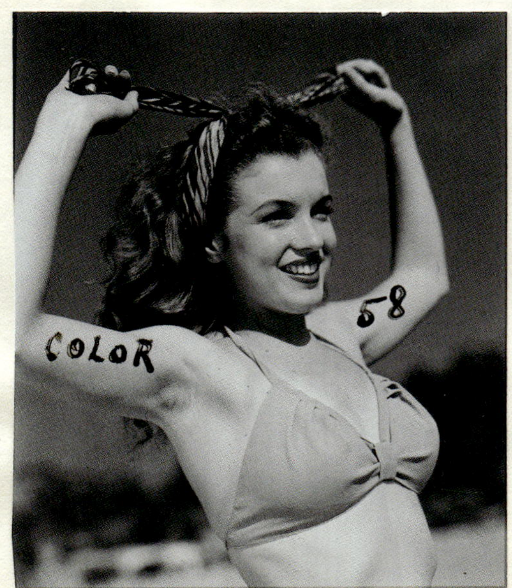
58
COLOR

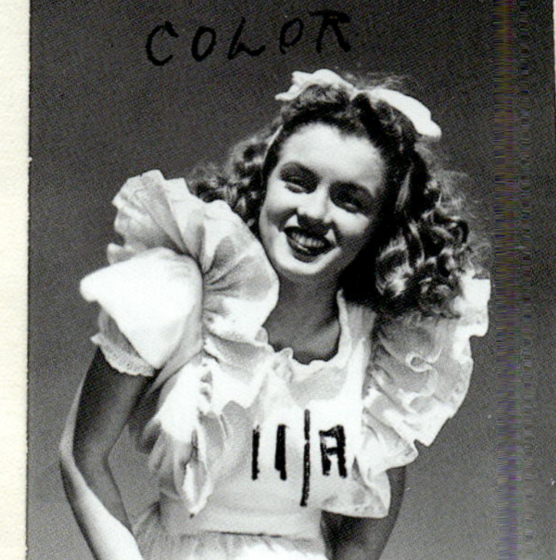
COLOR
11/A

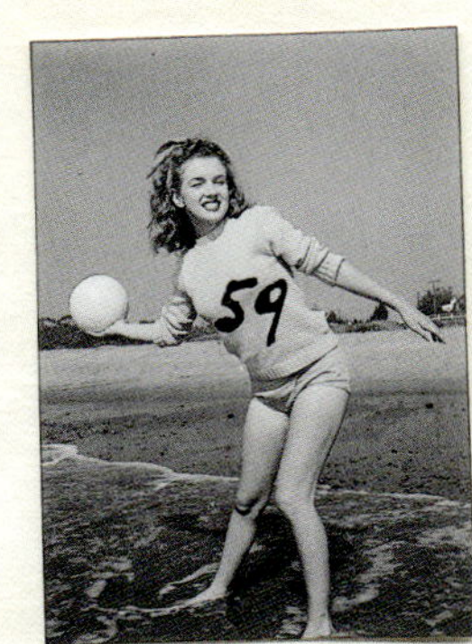

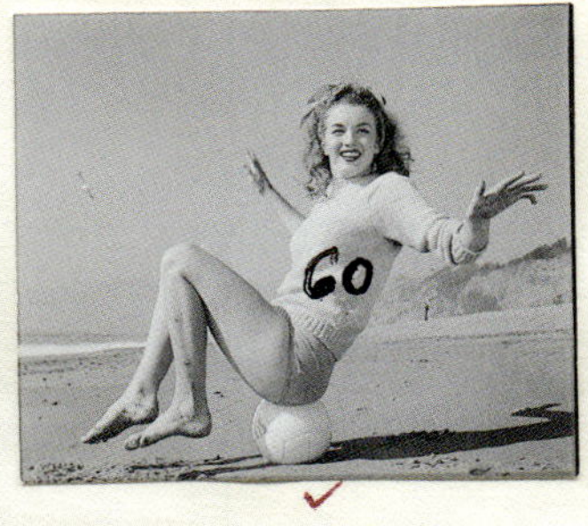

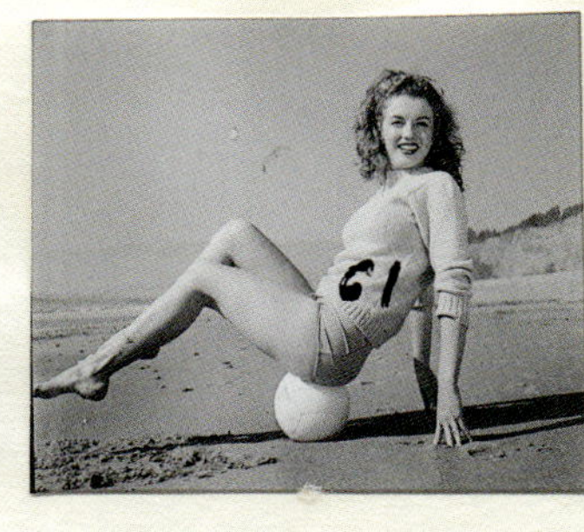

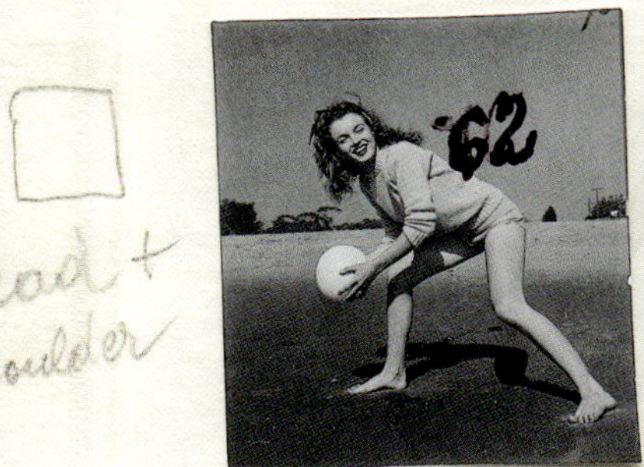

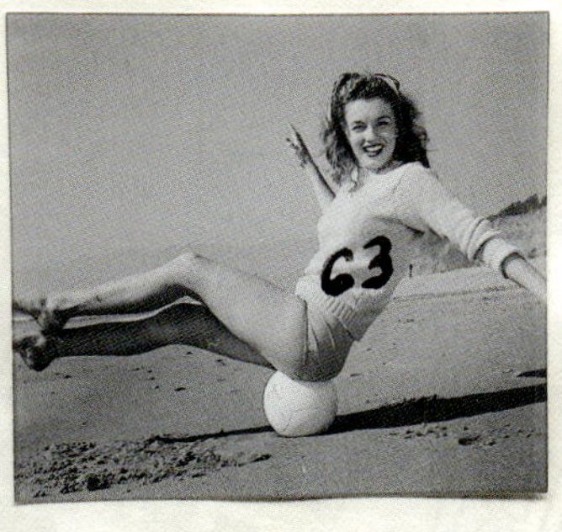

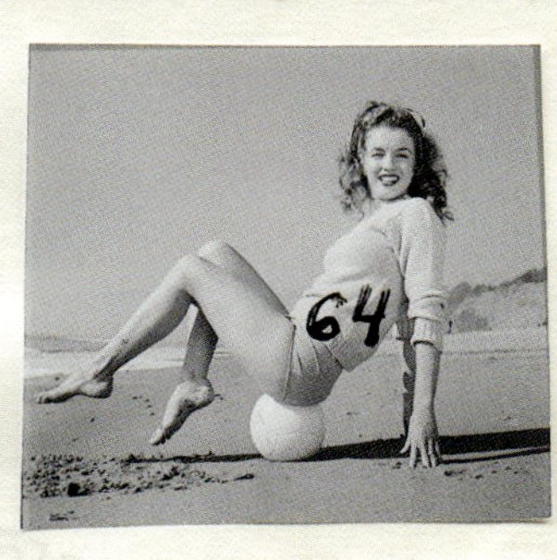

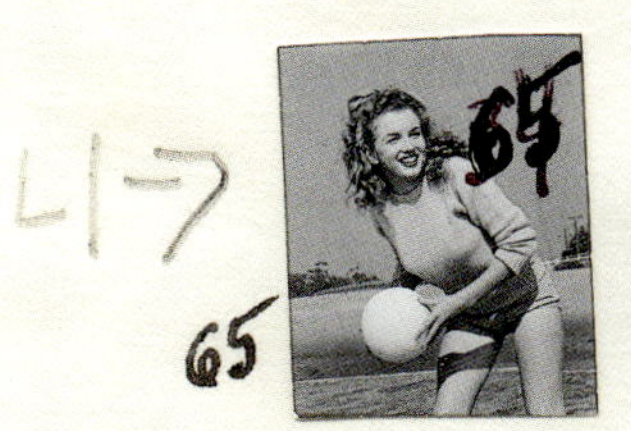

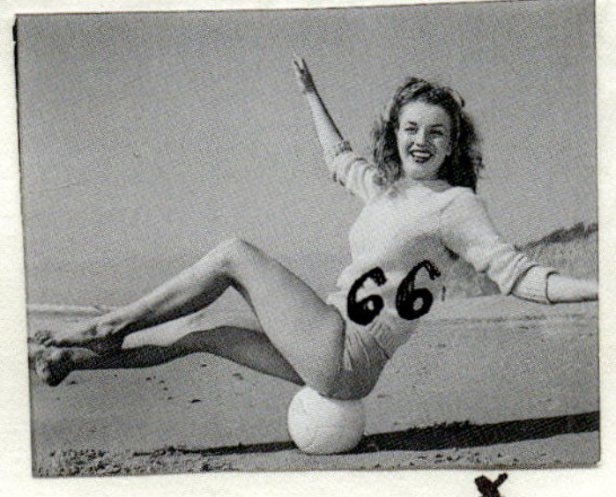

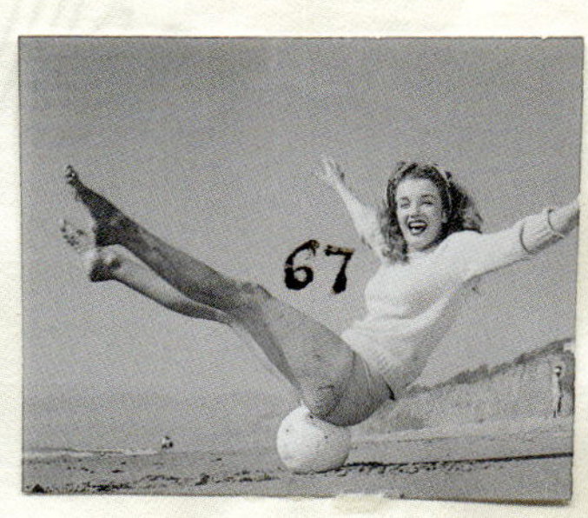

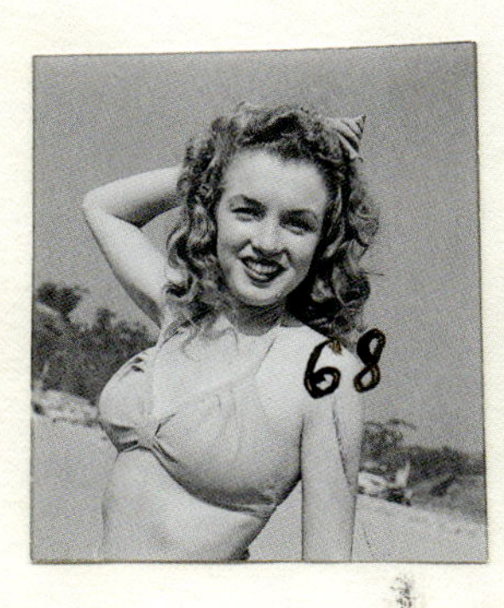

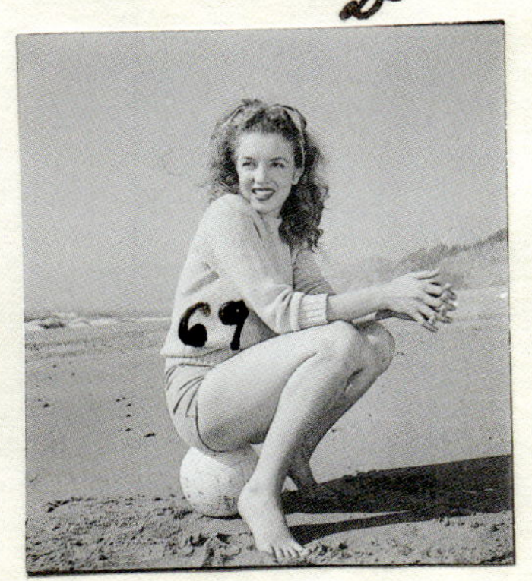

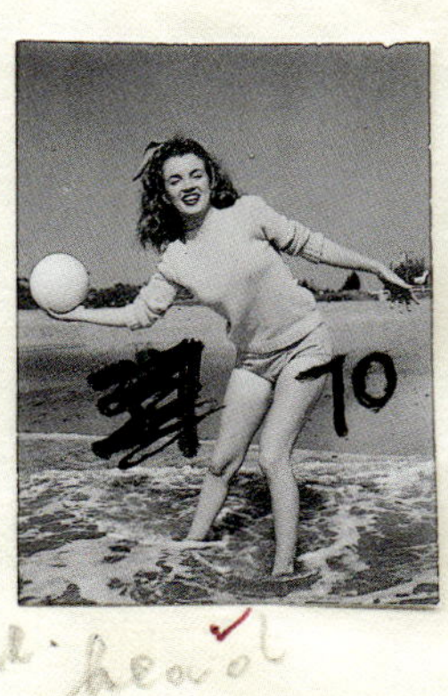

ANDRE DE DIENES 9
1401 SUNSET PLAZA DRIVE
HOLLYWOOD, CALIF. 90069

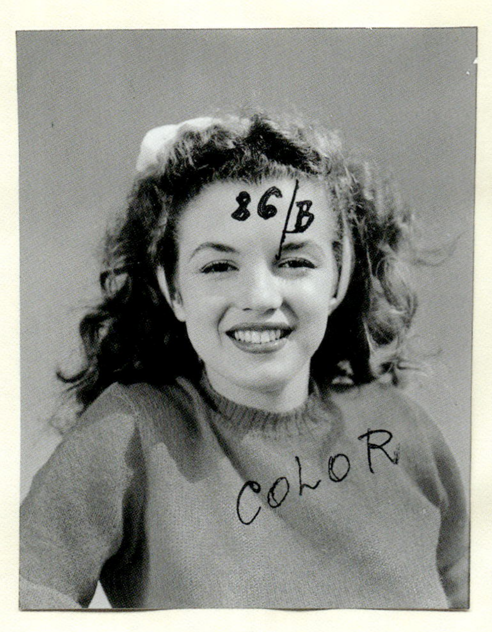

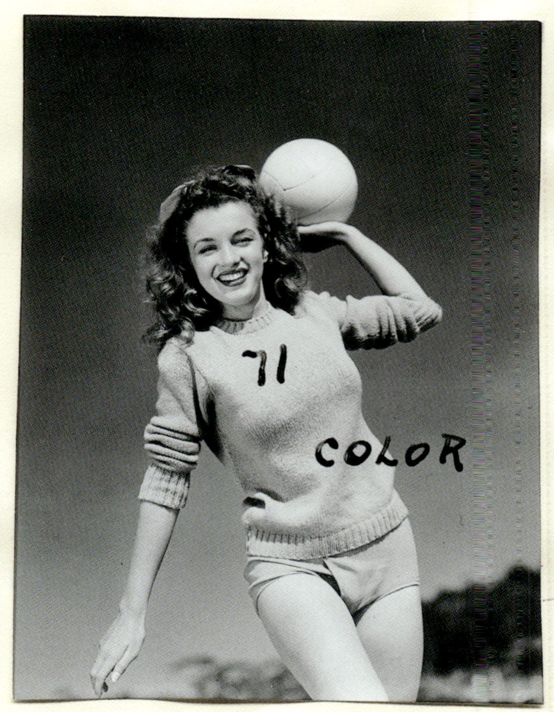

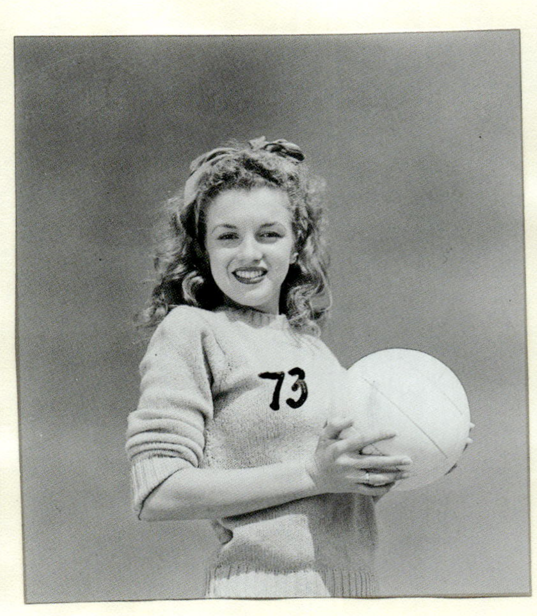

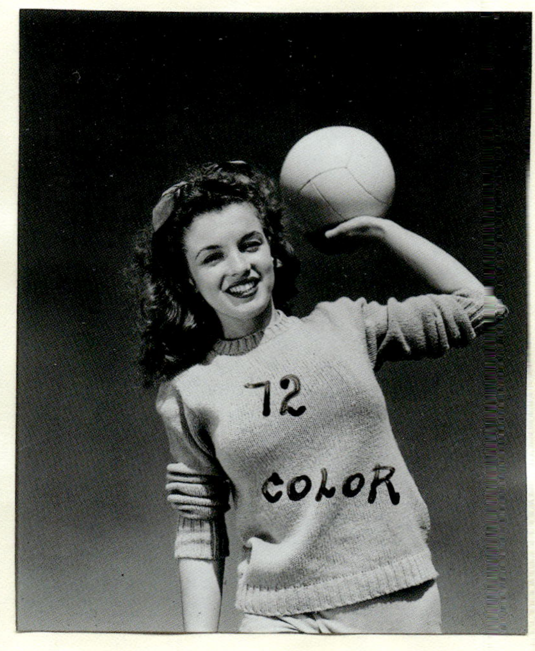

ANDRE DE DIENES
1401 SUNSET PLAZA DRIVE
HOLLYWOOD, CALIF. 90069

"The girl
from the Golden
"West

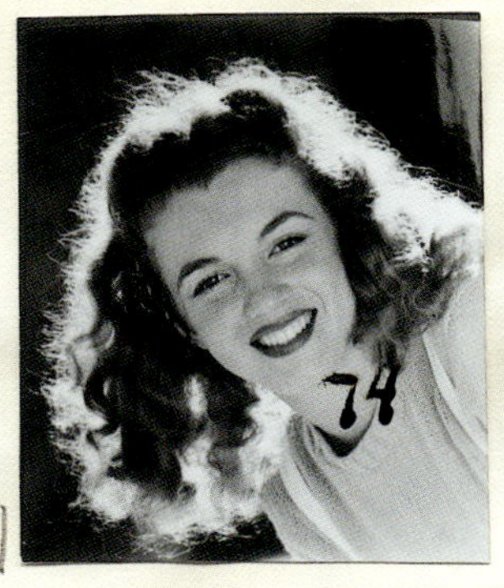

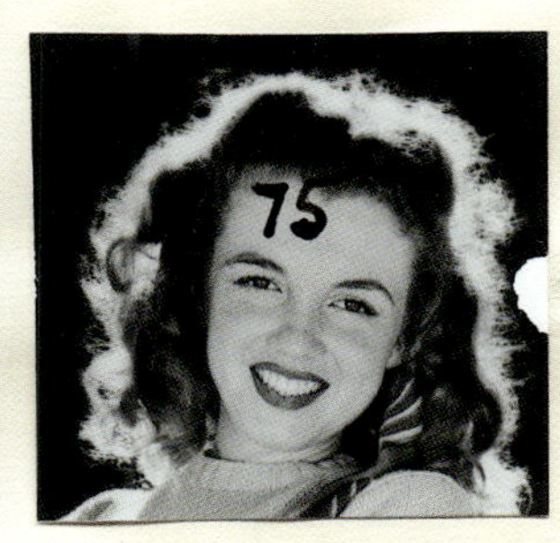

LI

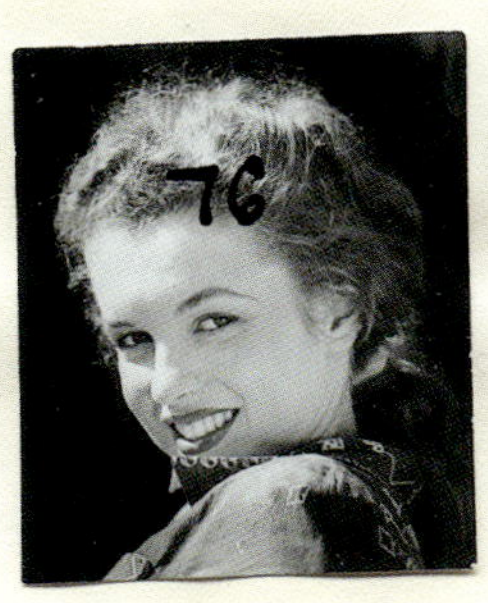

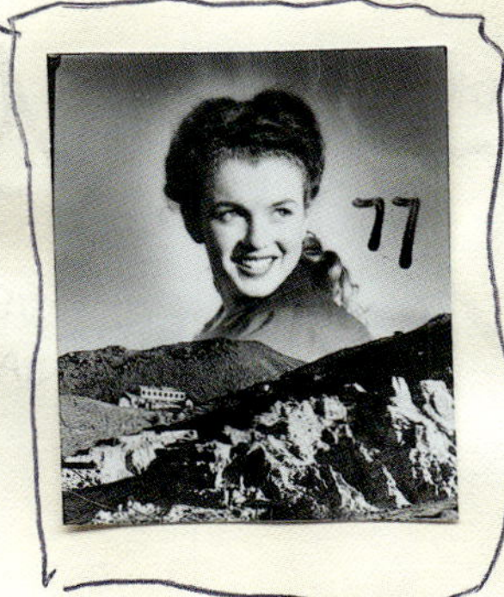

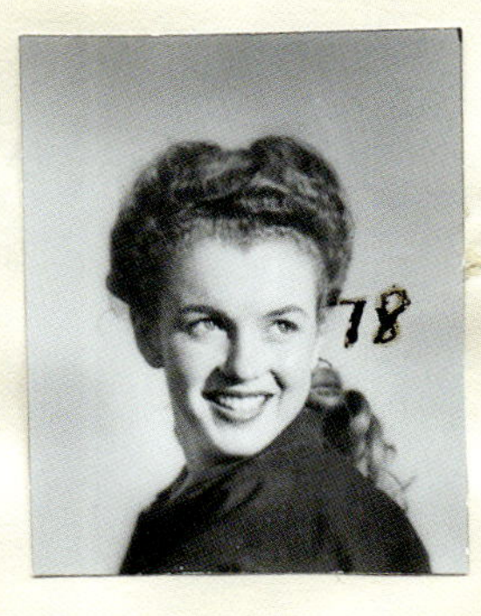

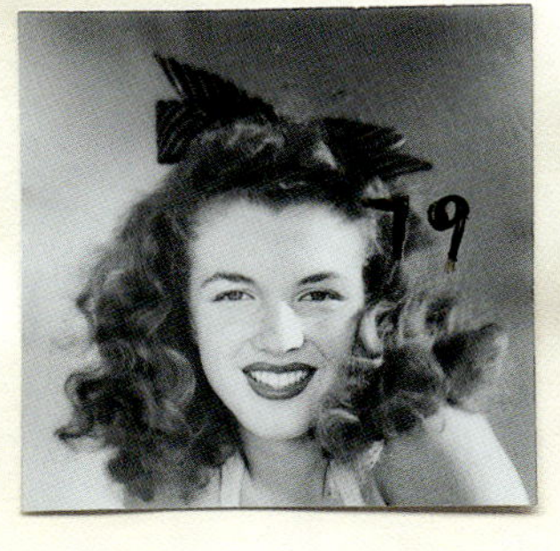

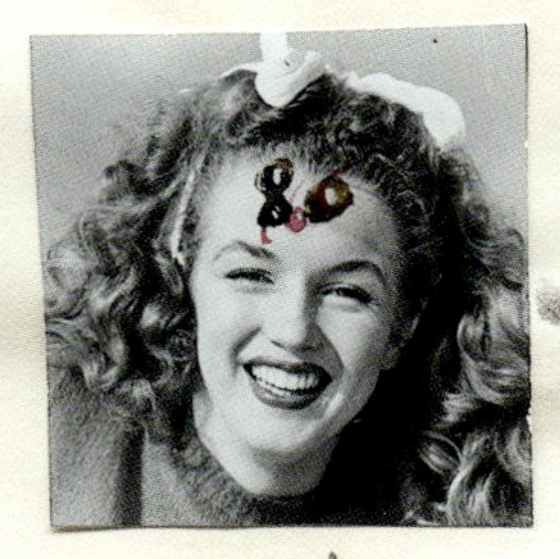

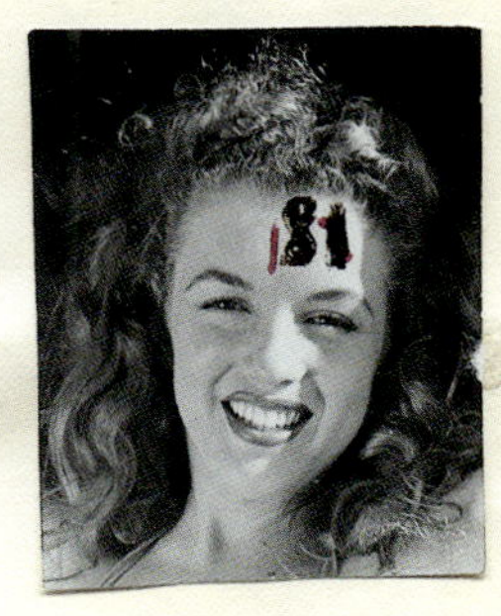

LI

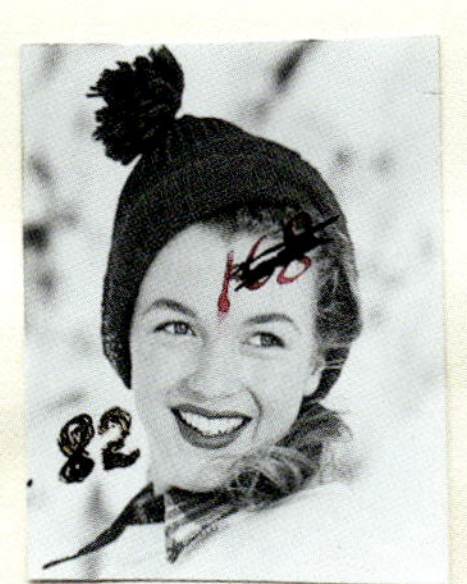

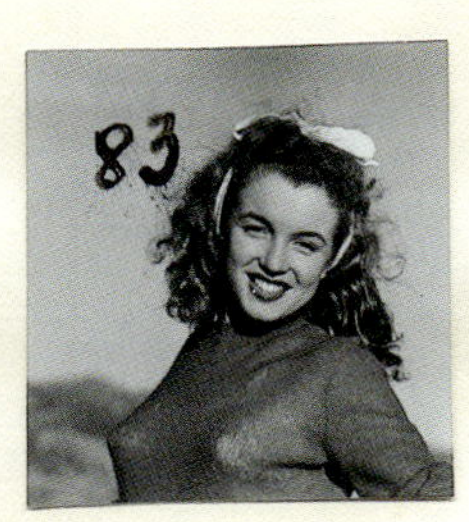

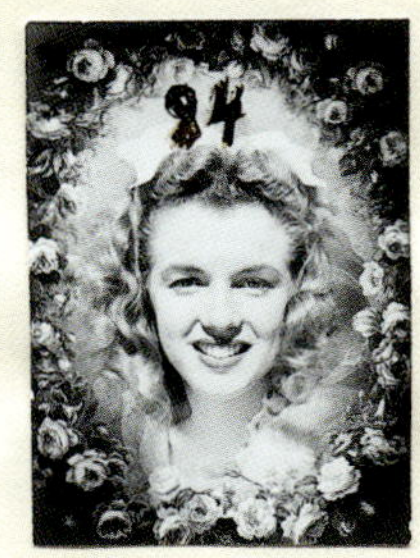

11

ANDRE DE DIENES
1401 SUNSET PLAZA DRIVE
HOLLYWOOD, CALIF. 90069

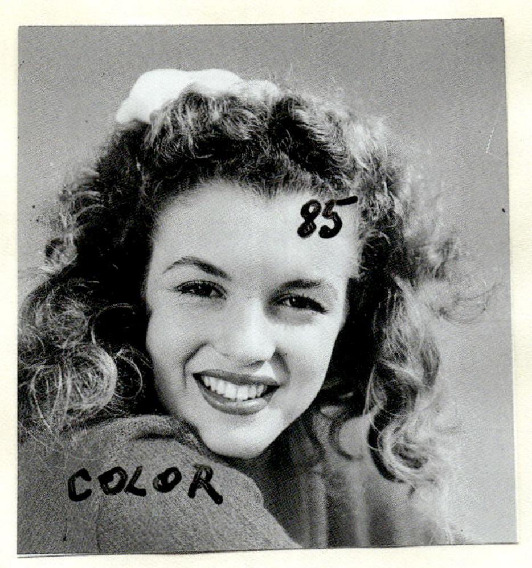

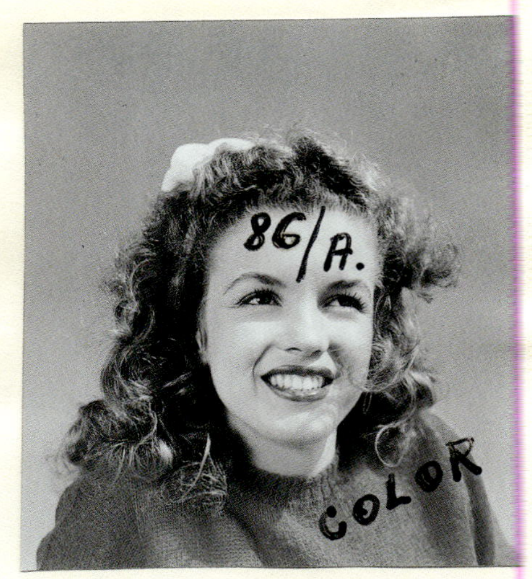

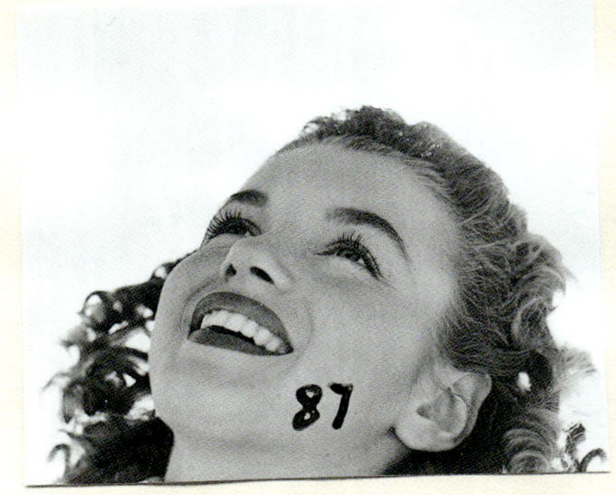

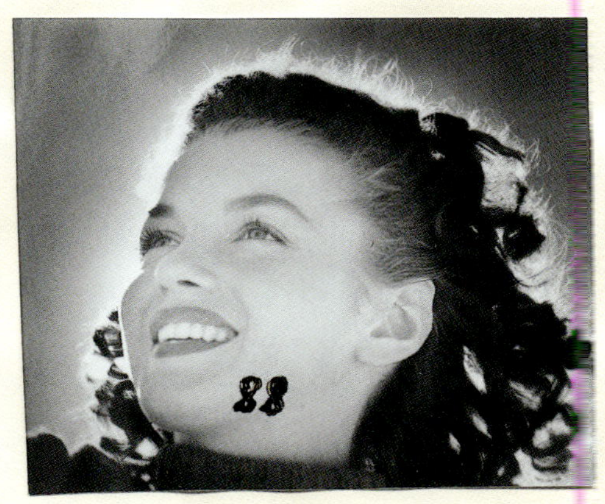

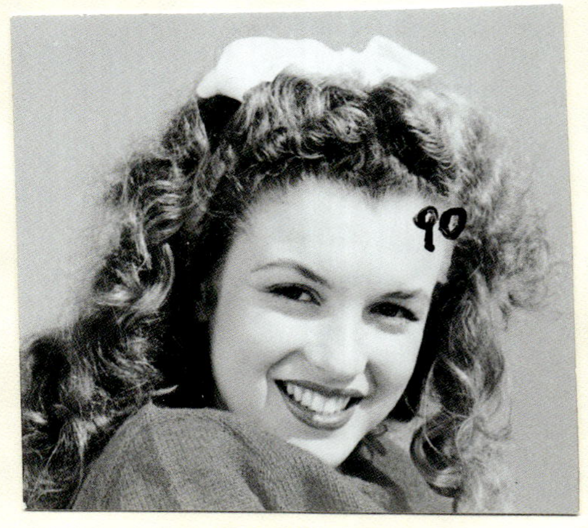

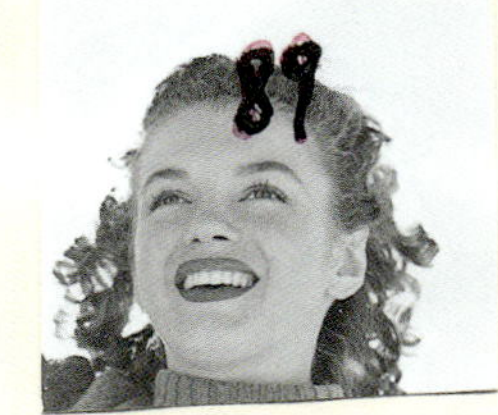

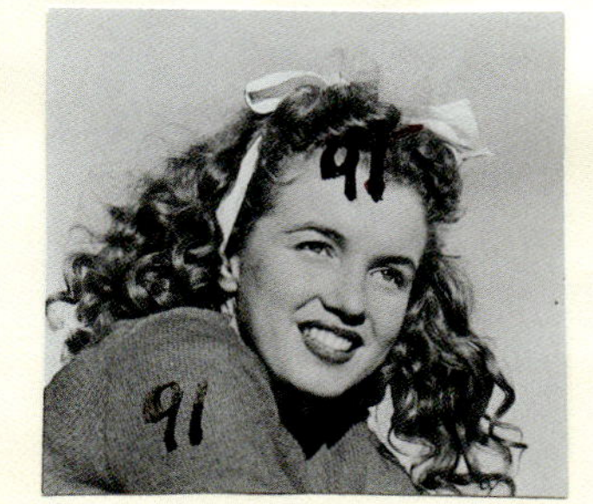

12

ANDRE DE DIENES

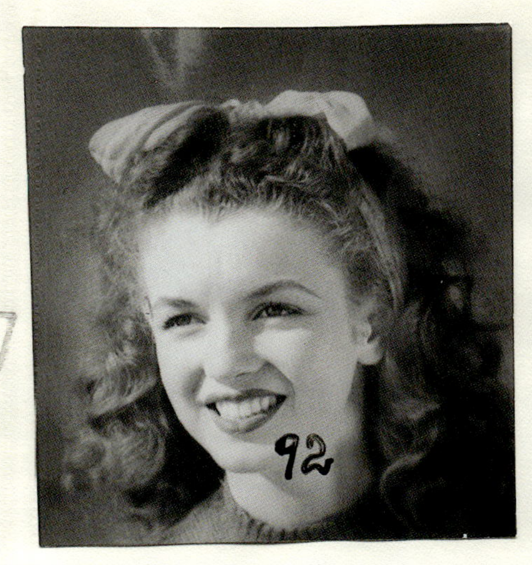

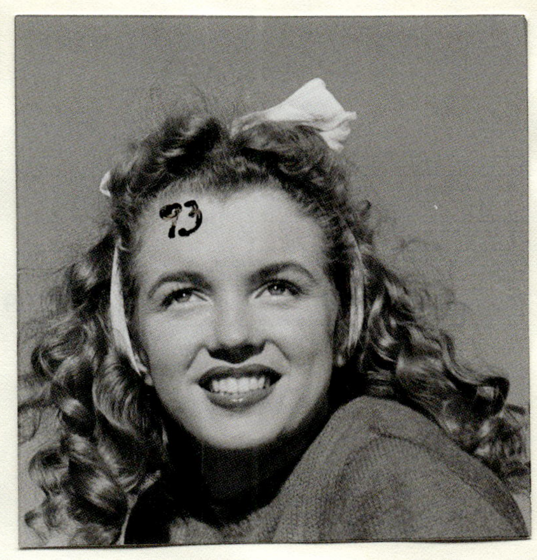

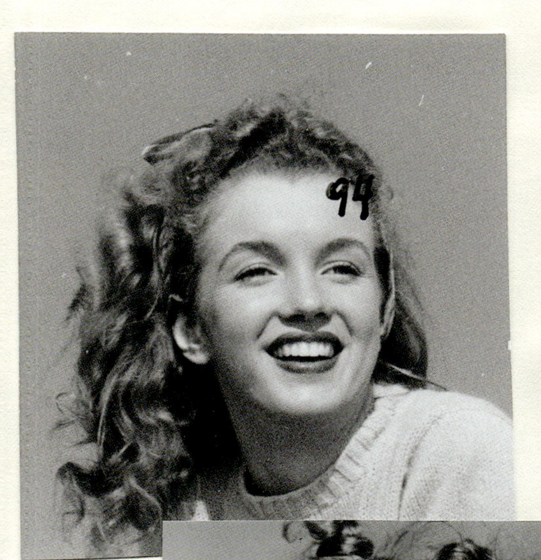

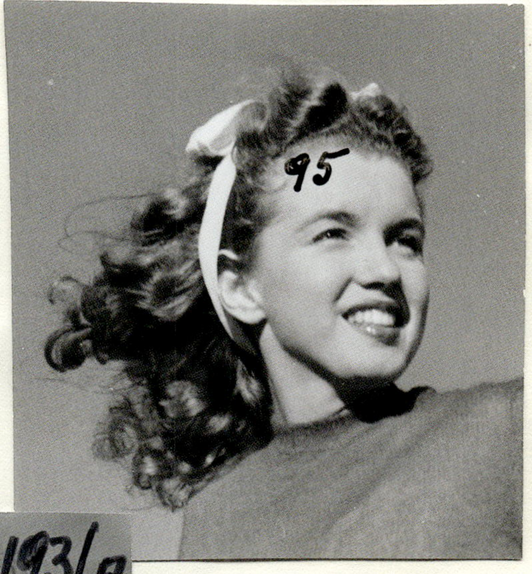

193/A

ANDRE DE DIENES
1401 SUNSET PLAZA DRIVE
HOLLYWOOD, CALIF. 90069

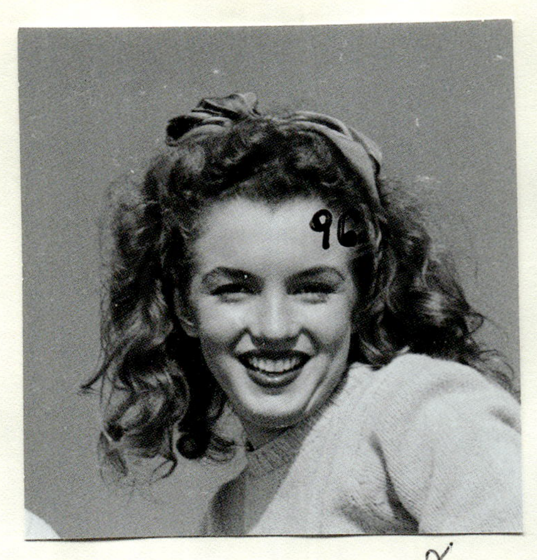

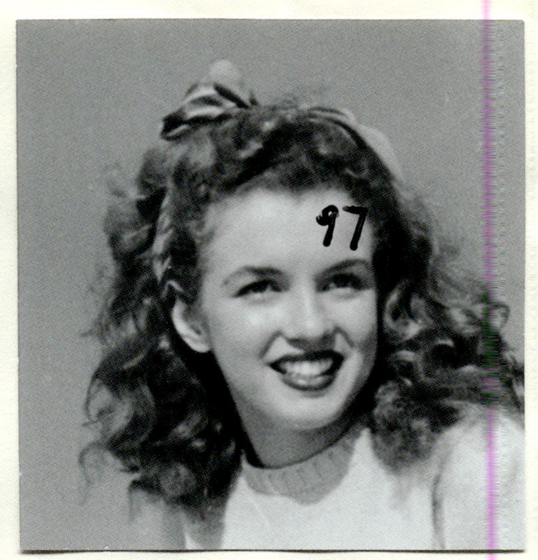

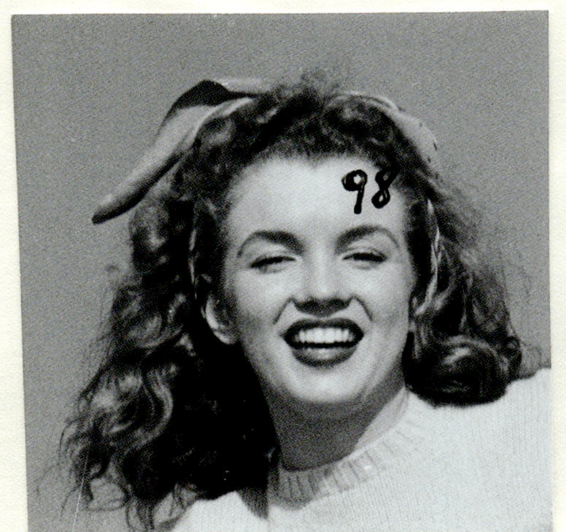

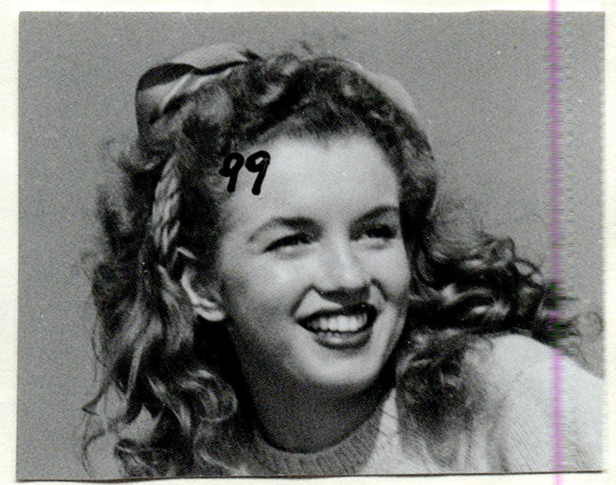

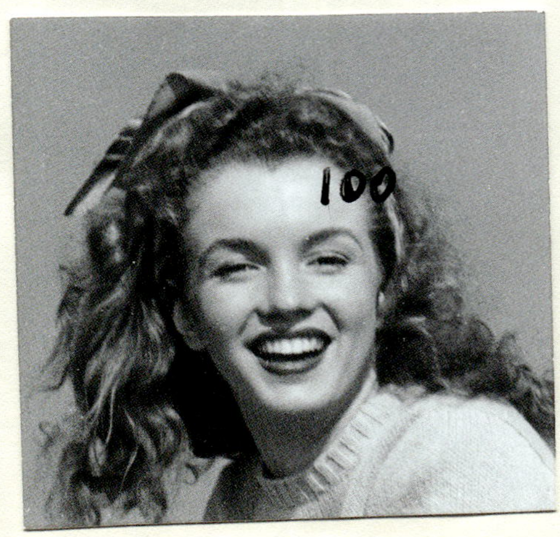

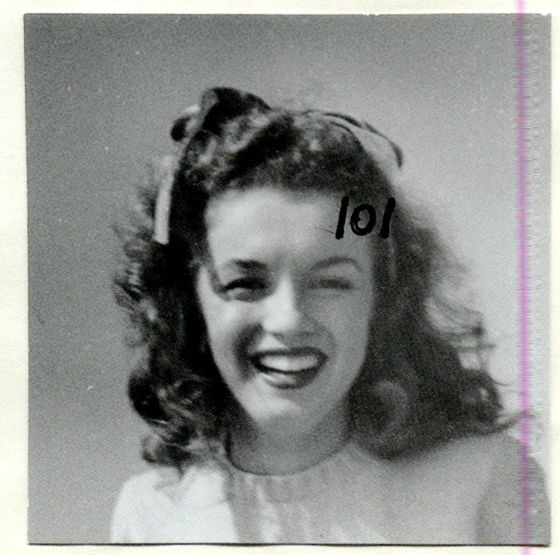

ANDRE DE DIENES

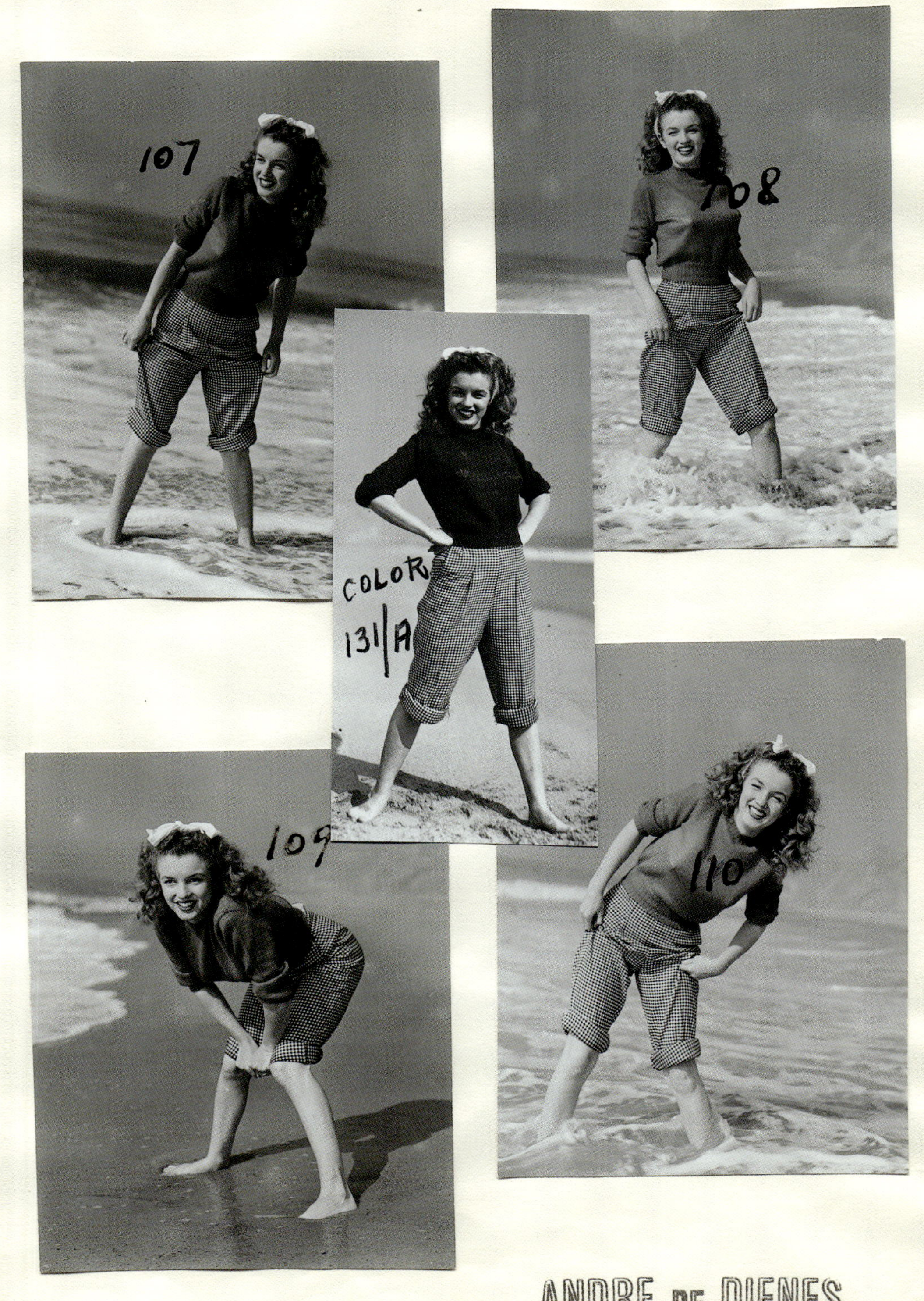

ANDRE DE DIENES
1401 SUNSET PLAZA DRIVE
HOLLYWOOD, CALIF. 90069

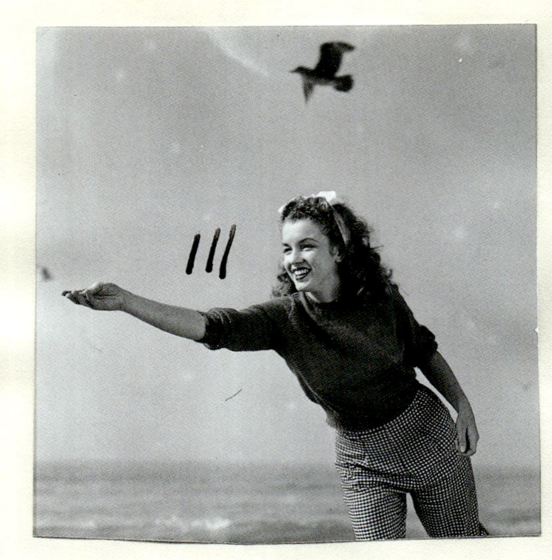

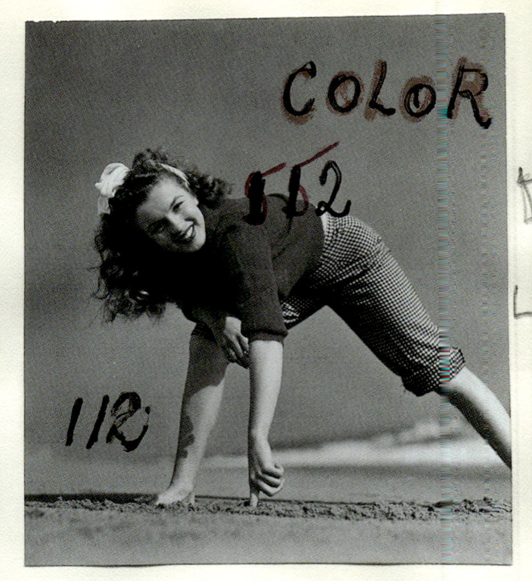

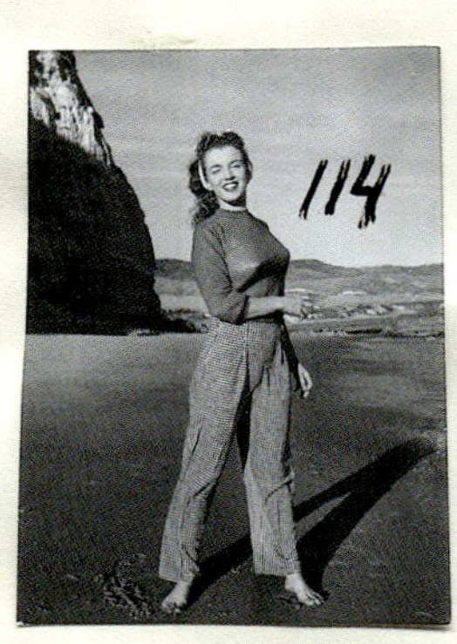

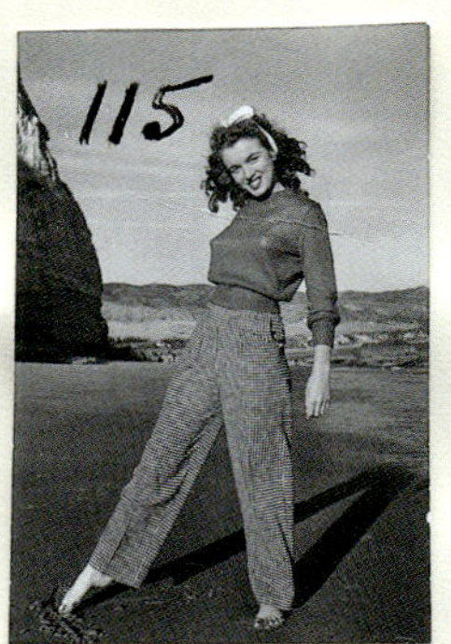

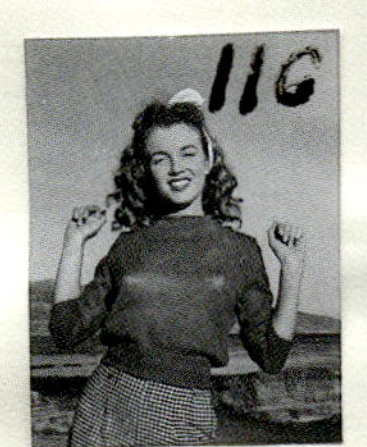

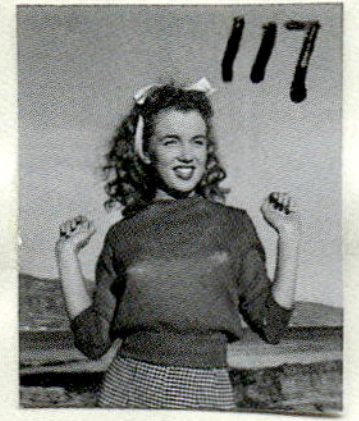

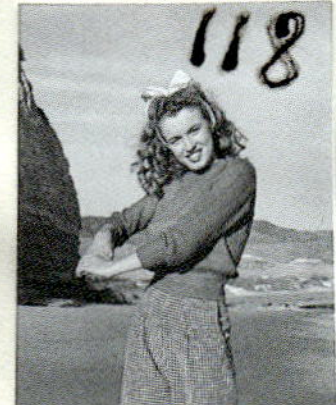

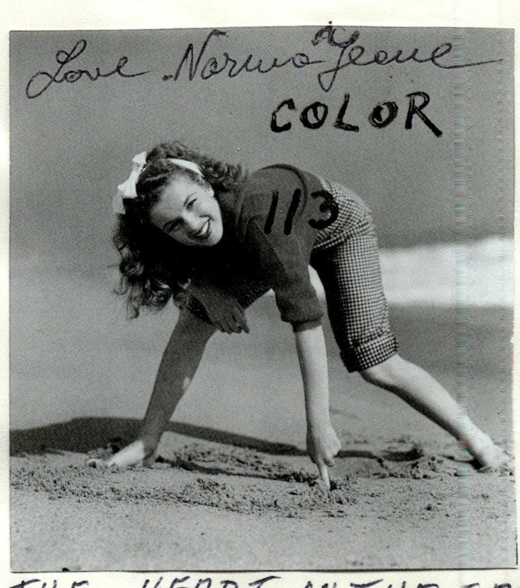

THE HEART IN THE SAND

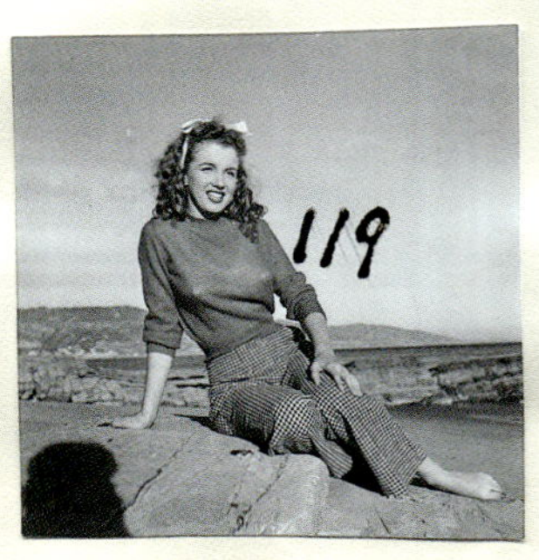

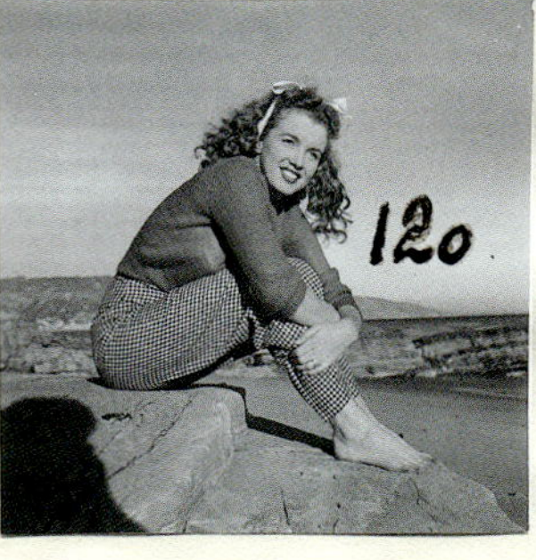

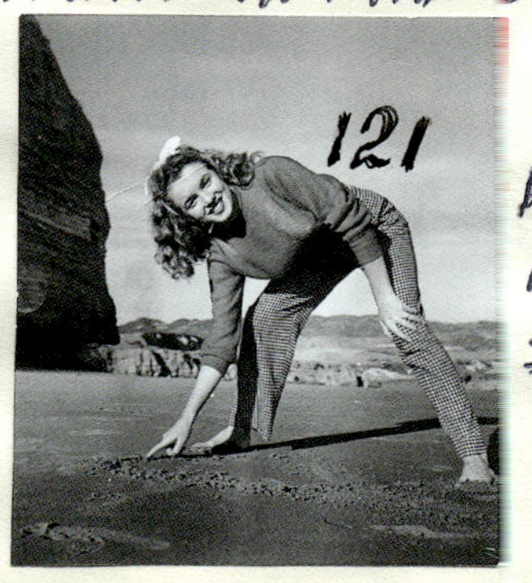

IS FOR ME

17

ANDRE DE DIENES

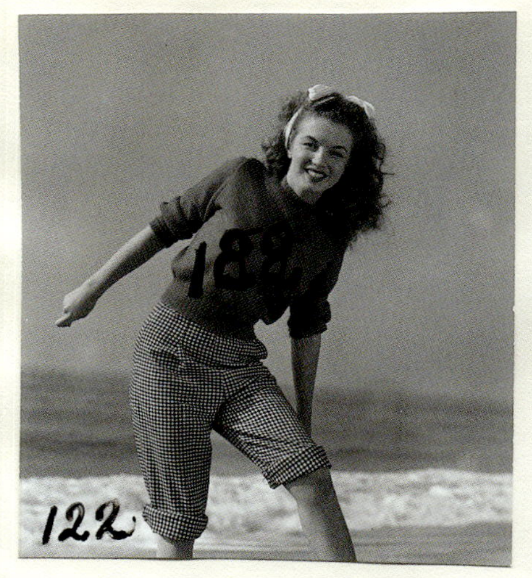

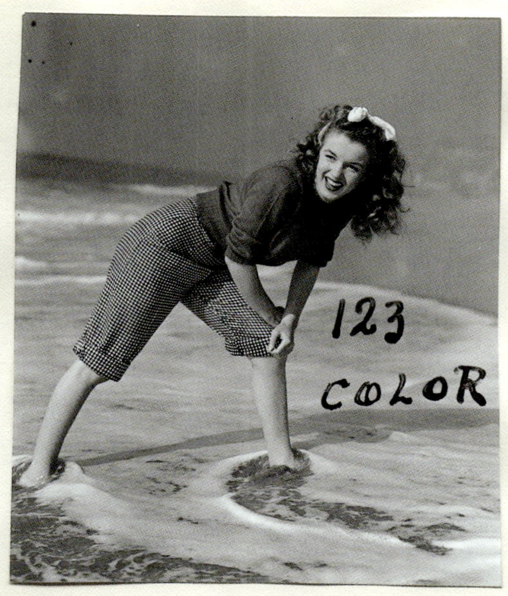

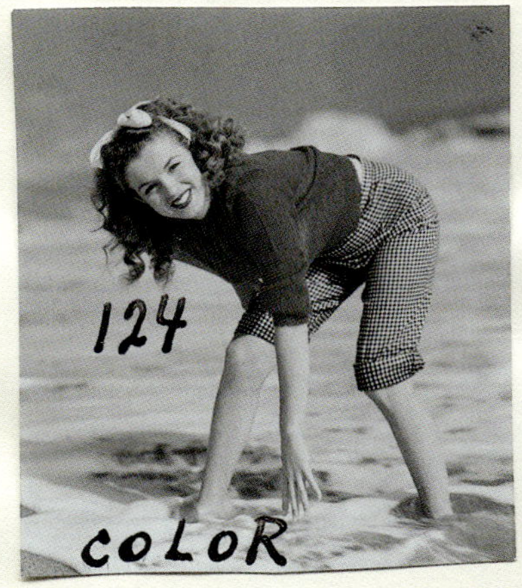

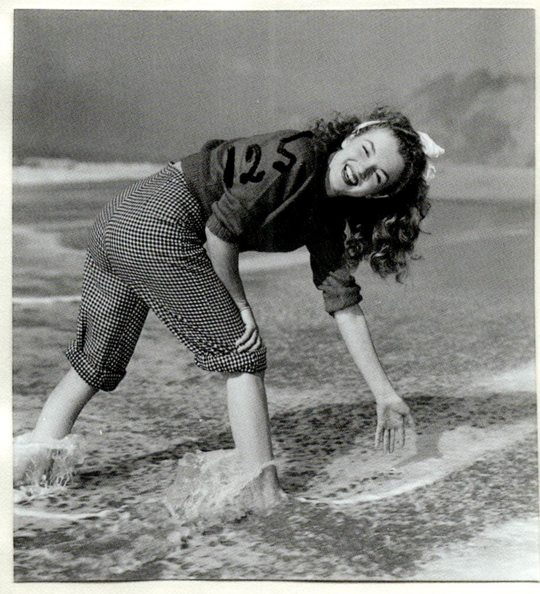

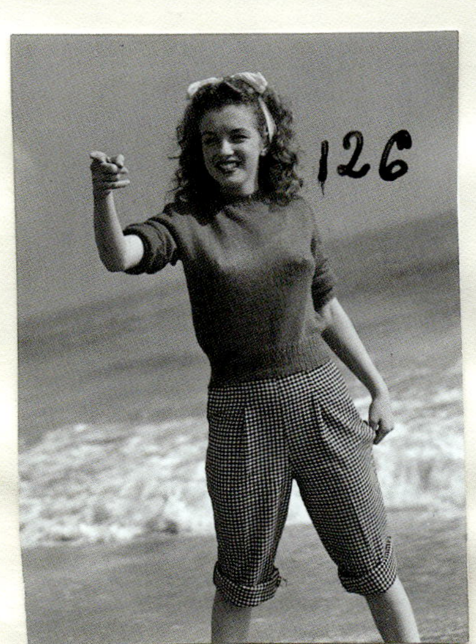

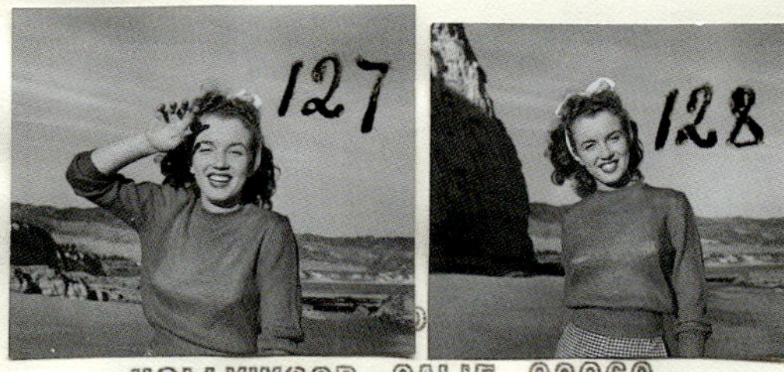

HOLLYWOOD, CALIF. 90069

to make color posters of these

132 or 133

129

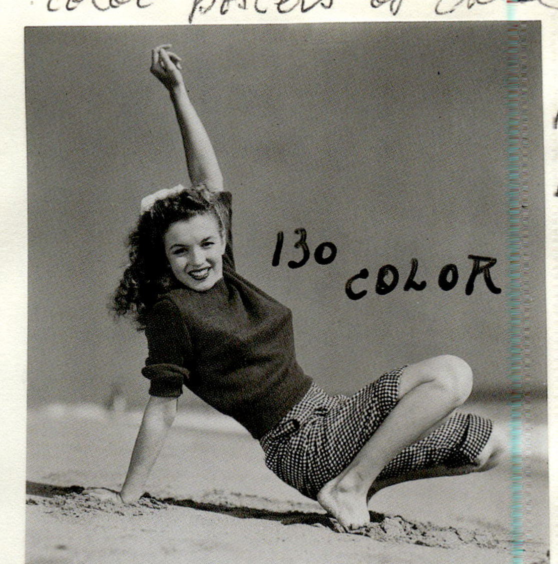

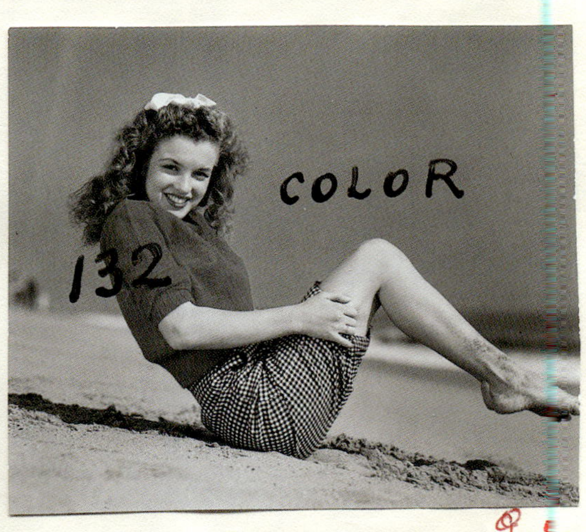

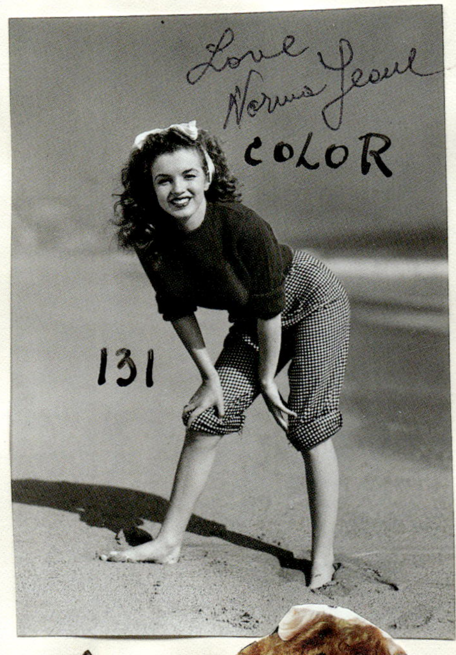

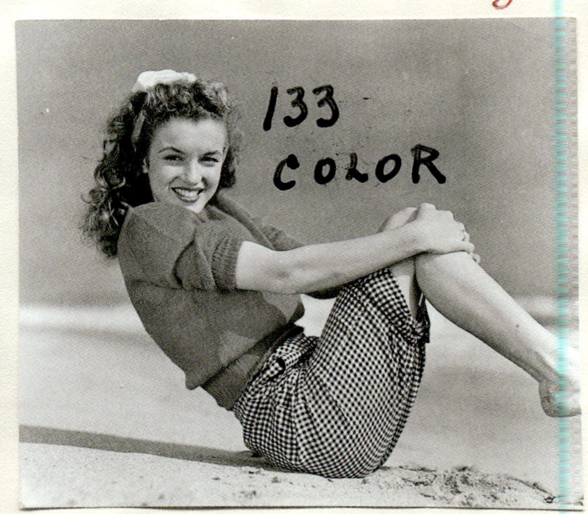

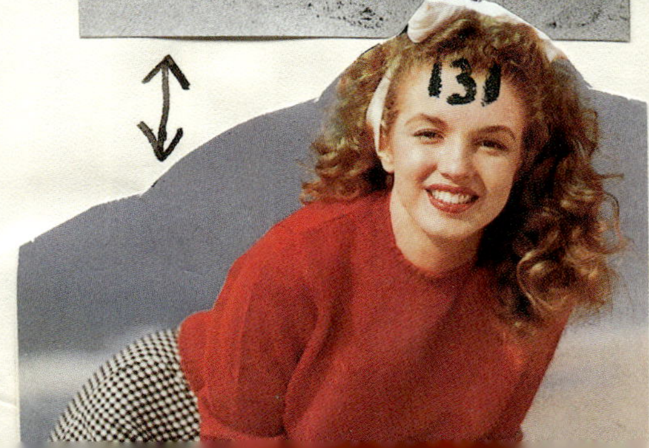

ANDRE DE DIENES

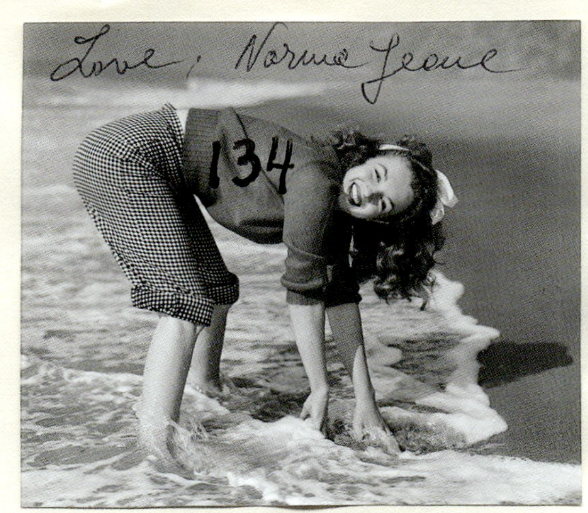

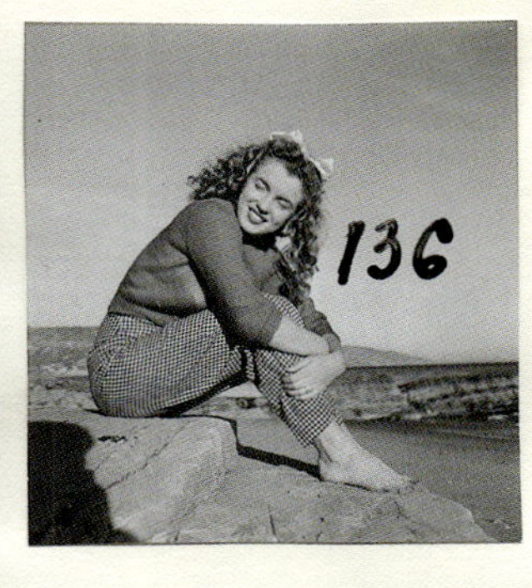

L

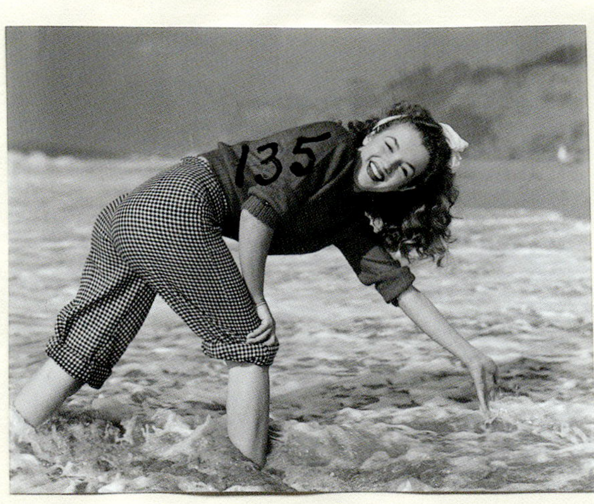

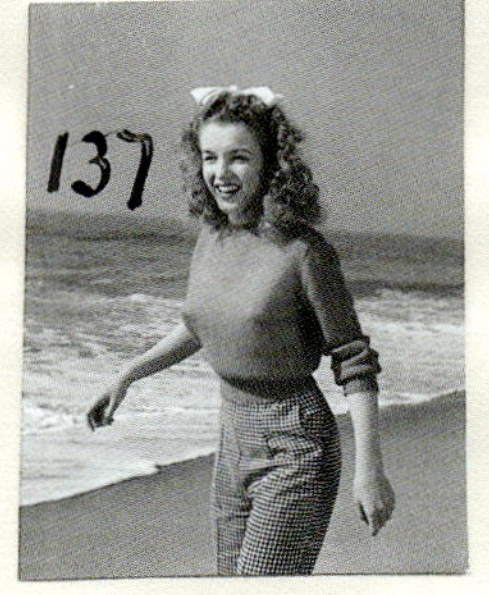

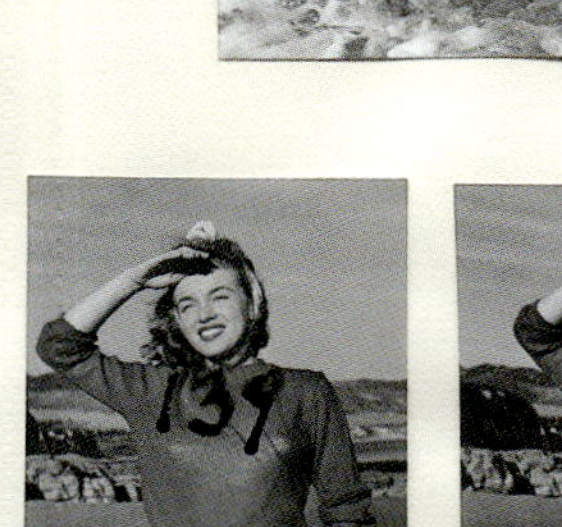

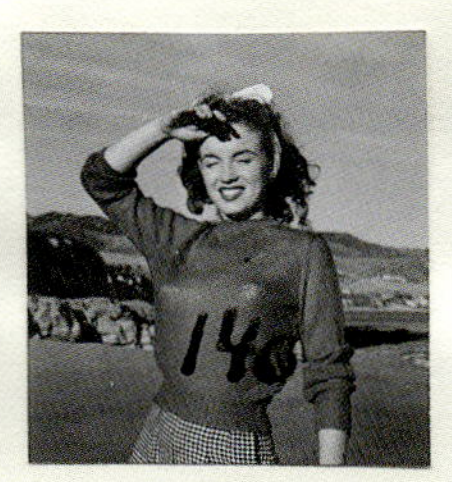

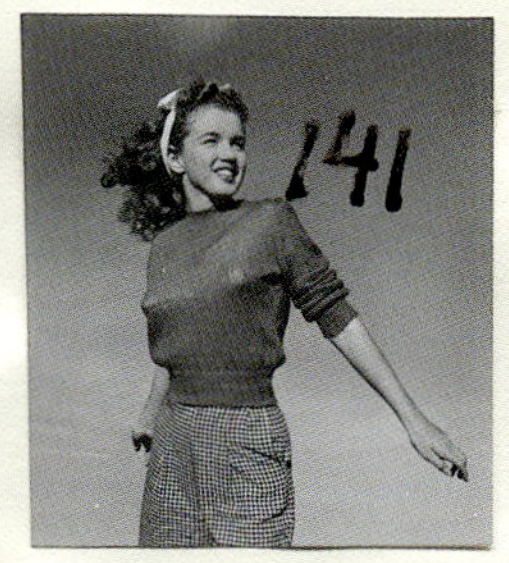

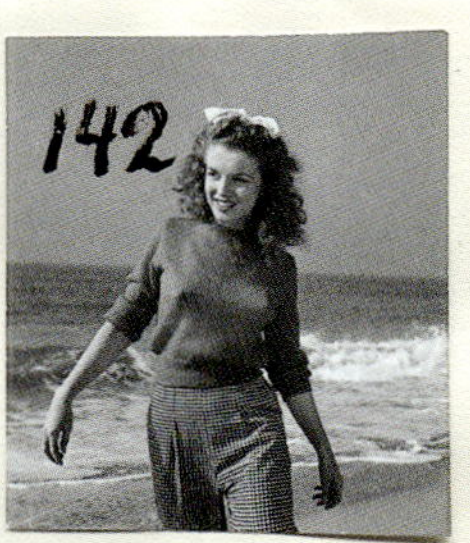

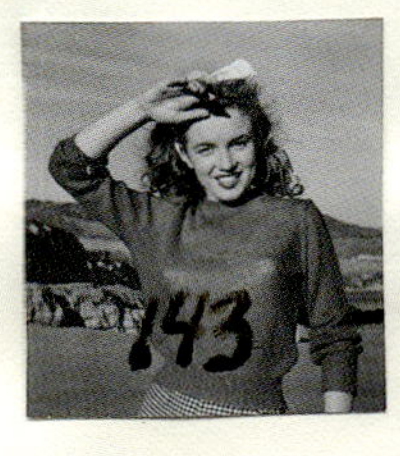

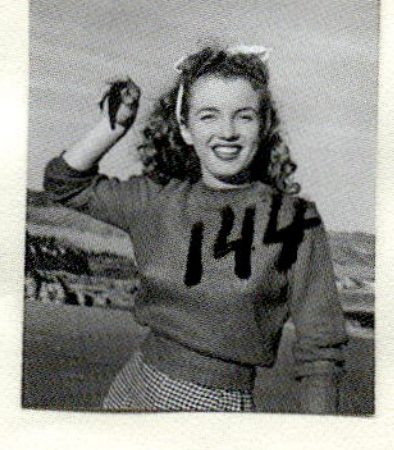

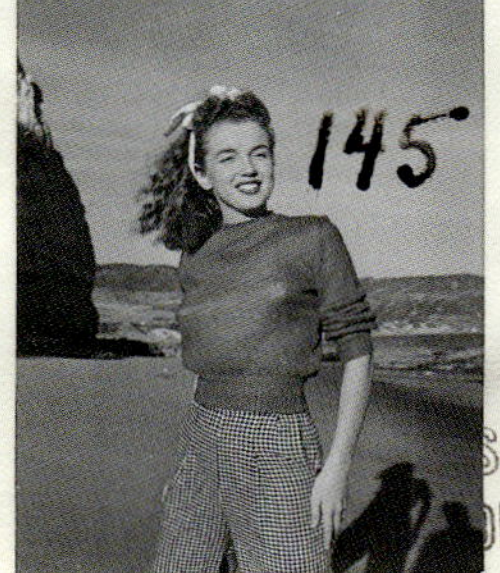

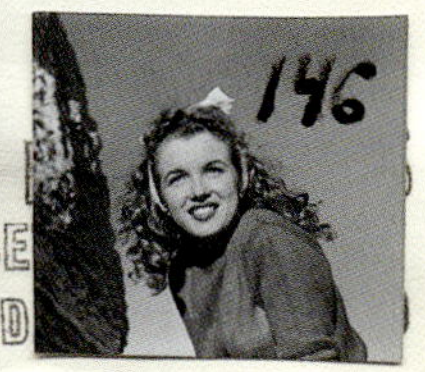

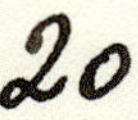

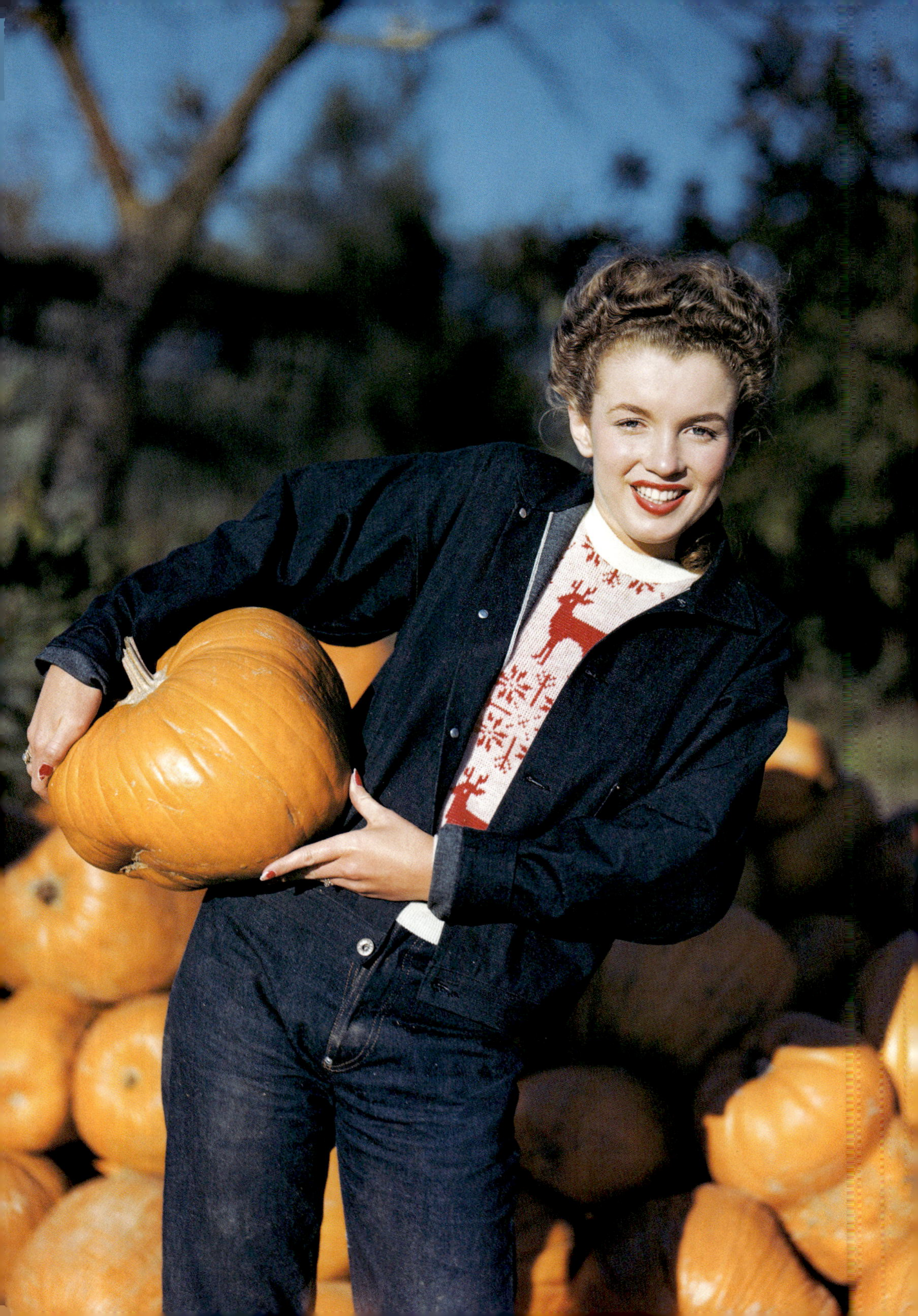

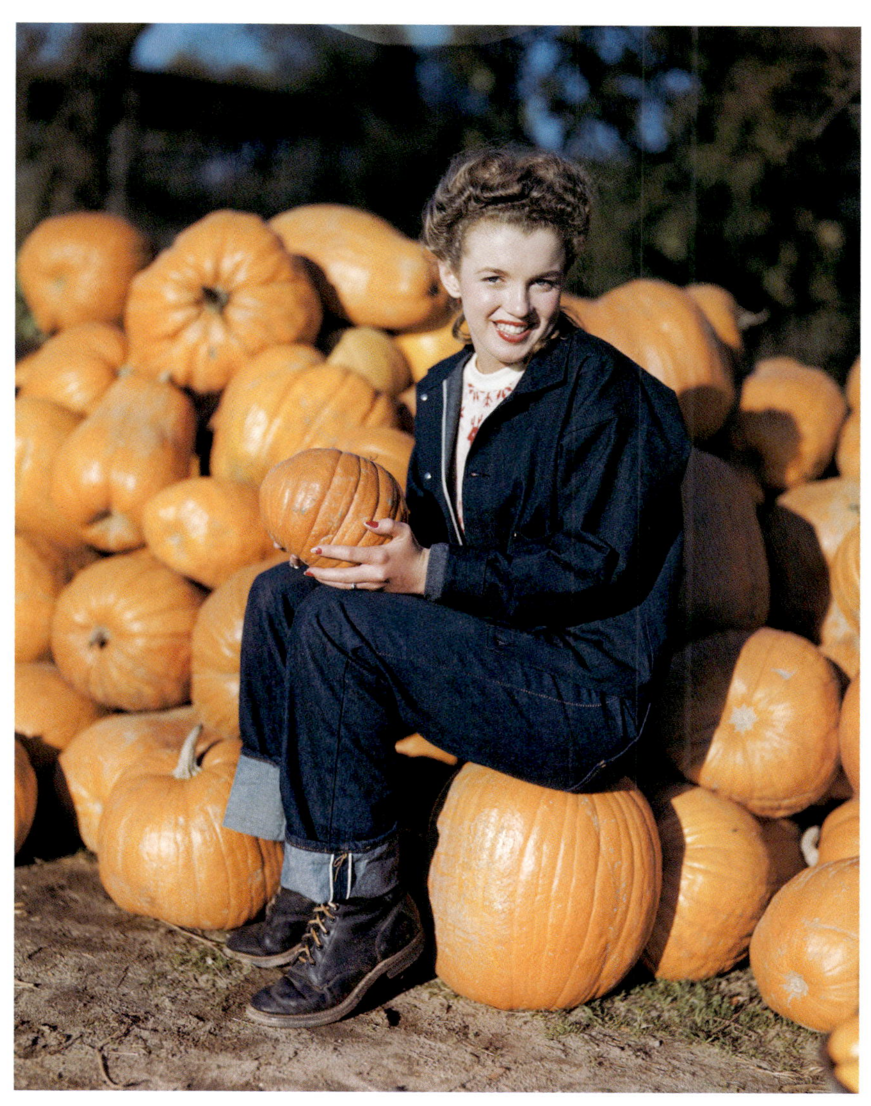

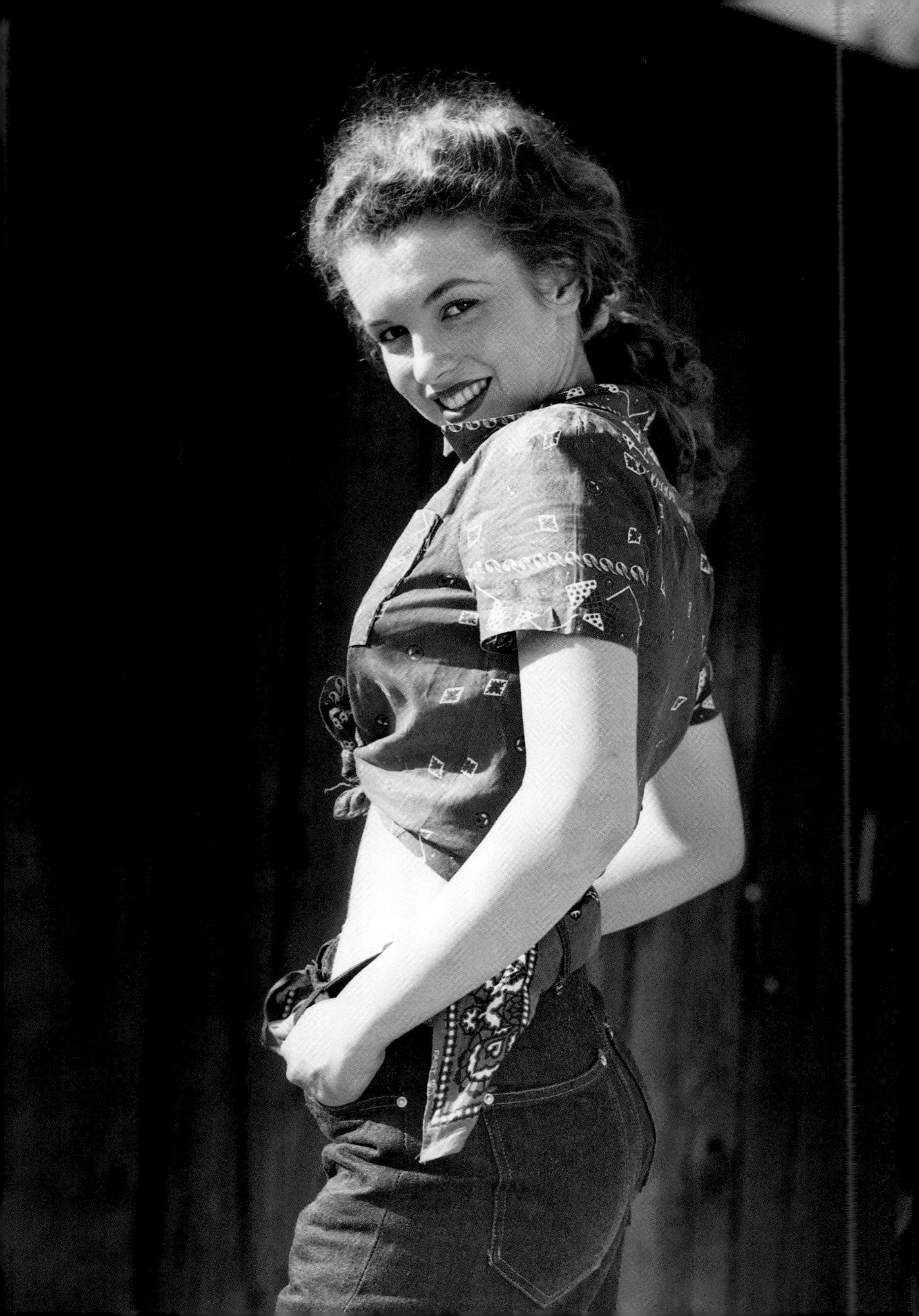

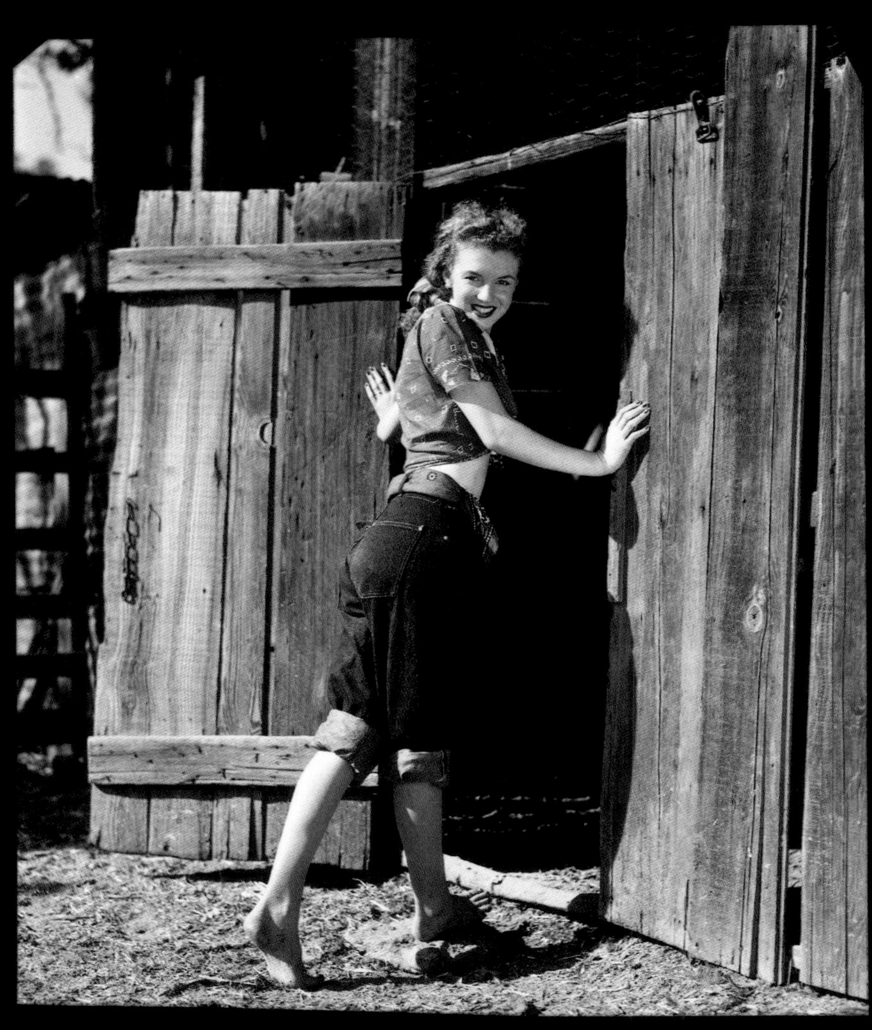

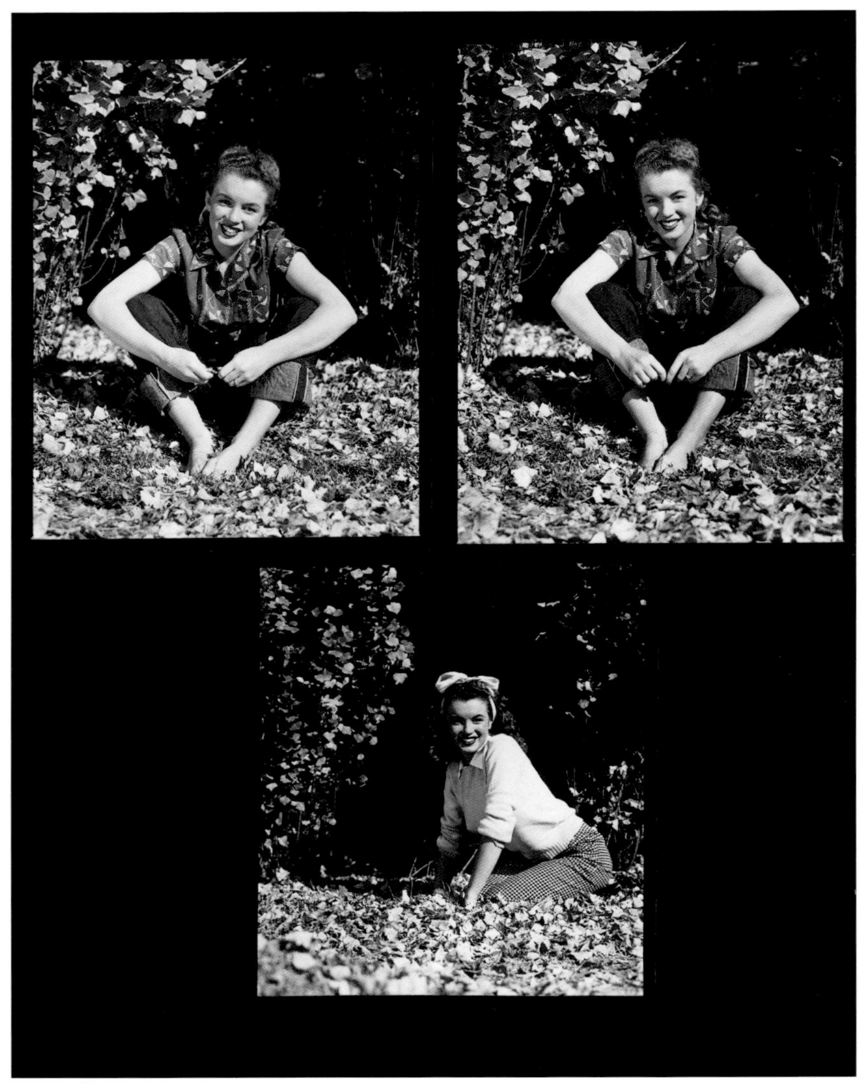

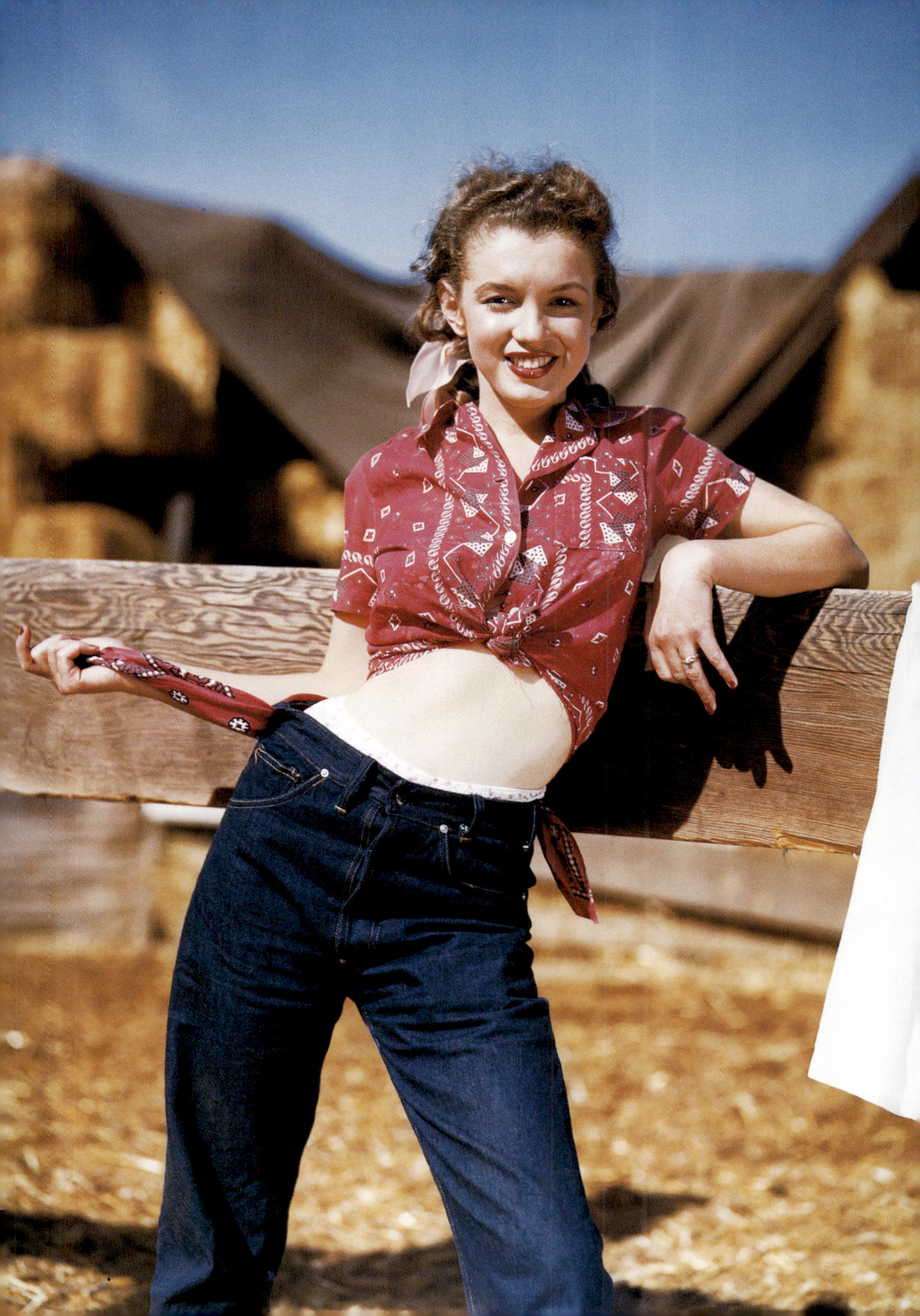

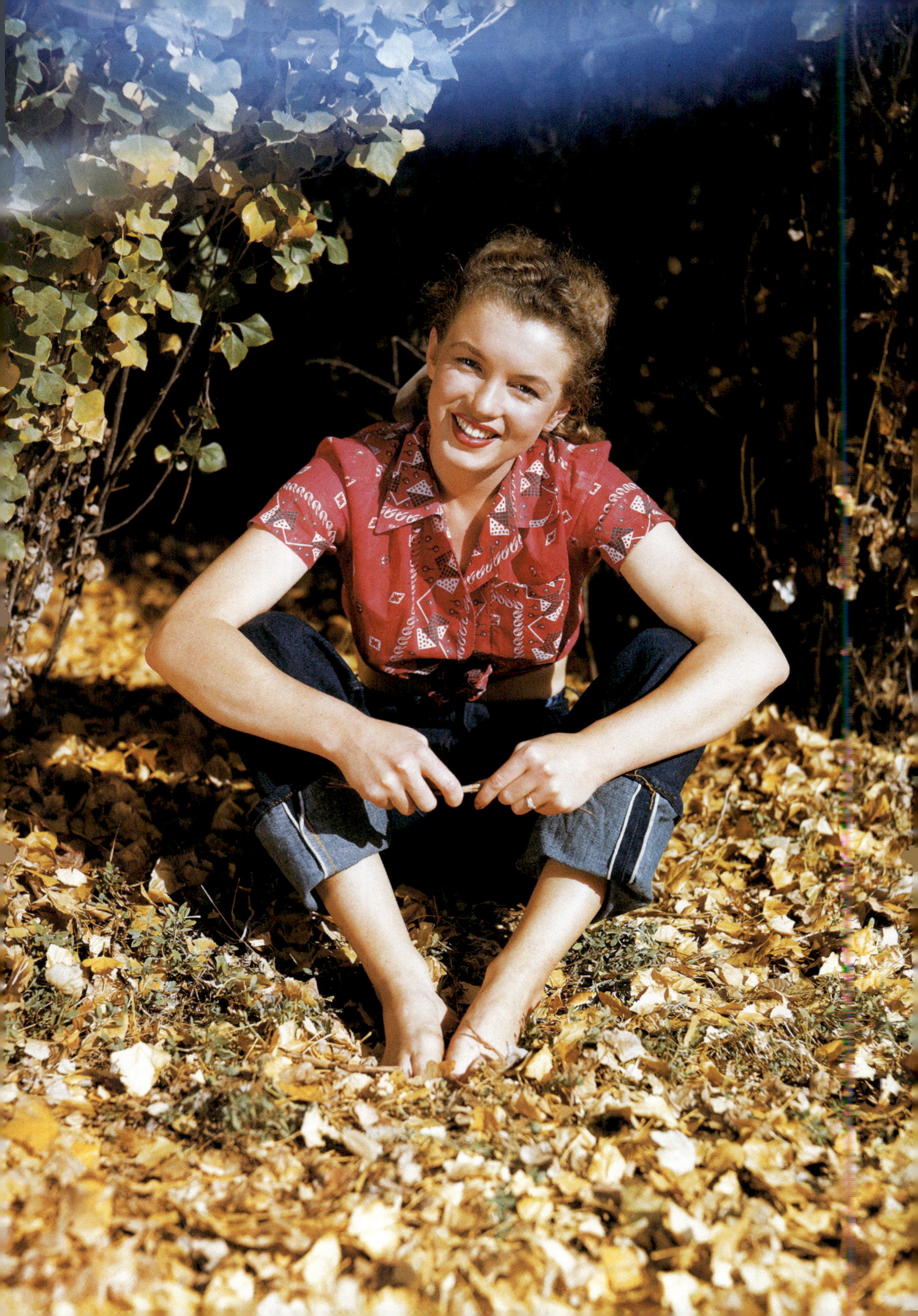

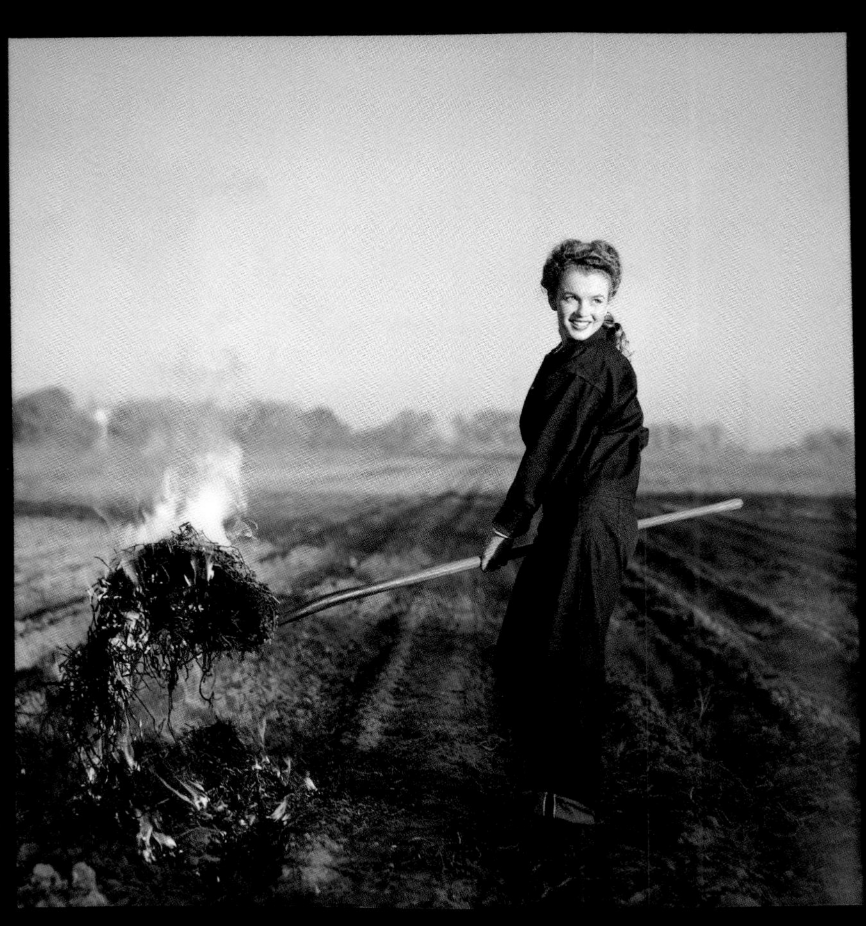

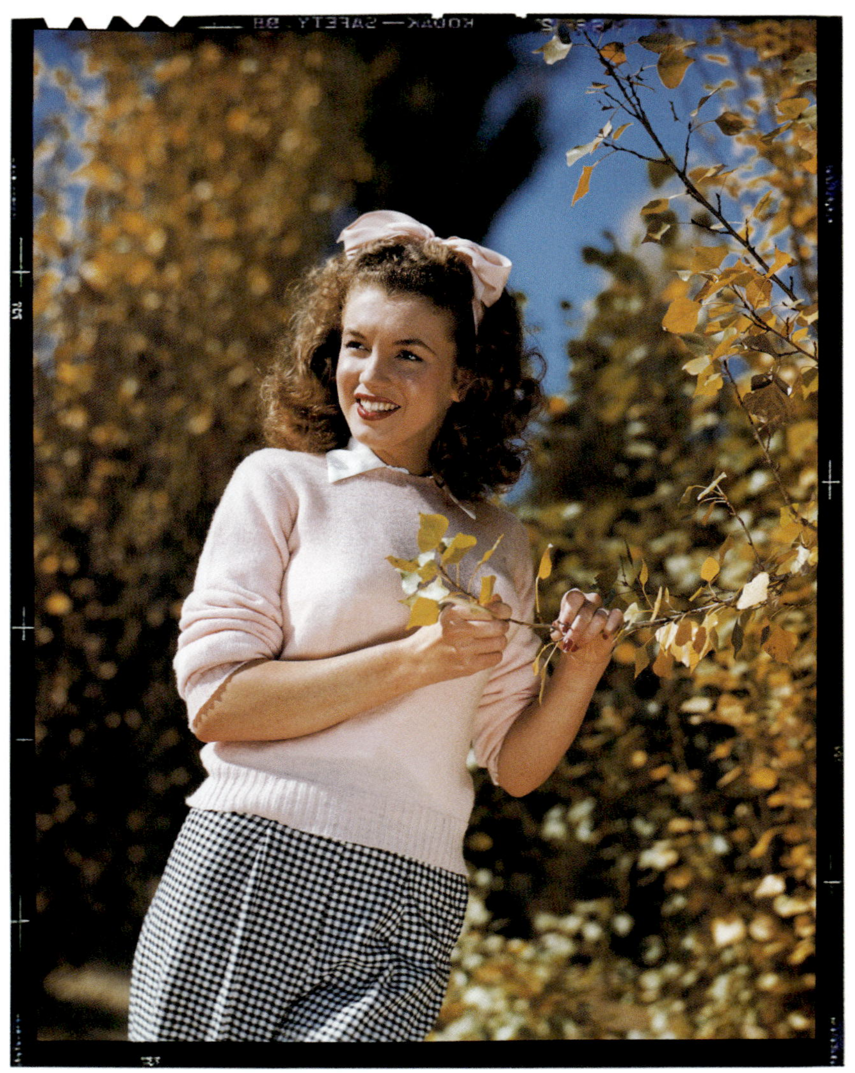

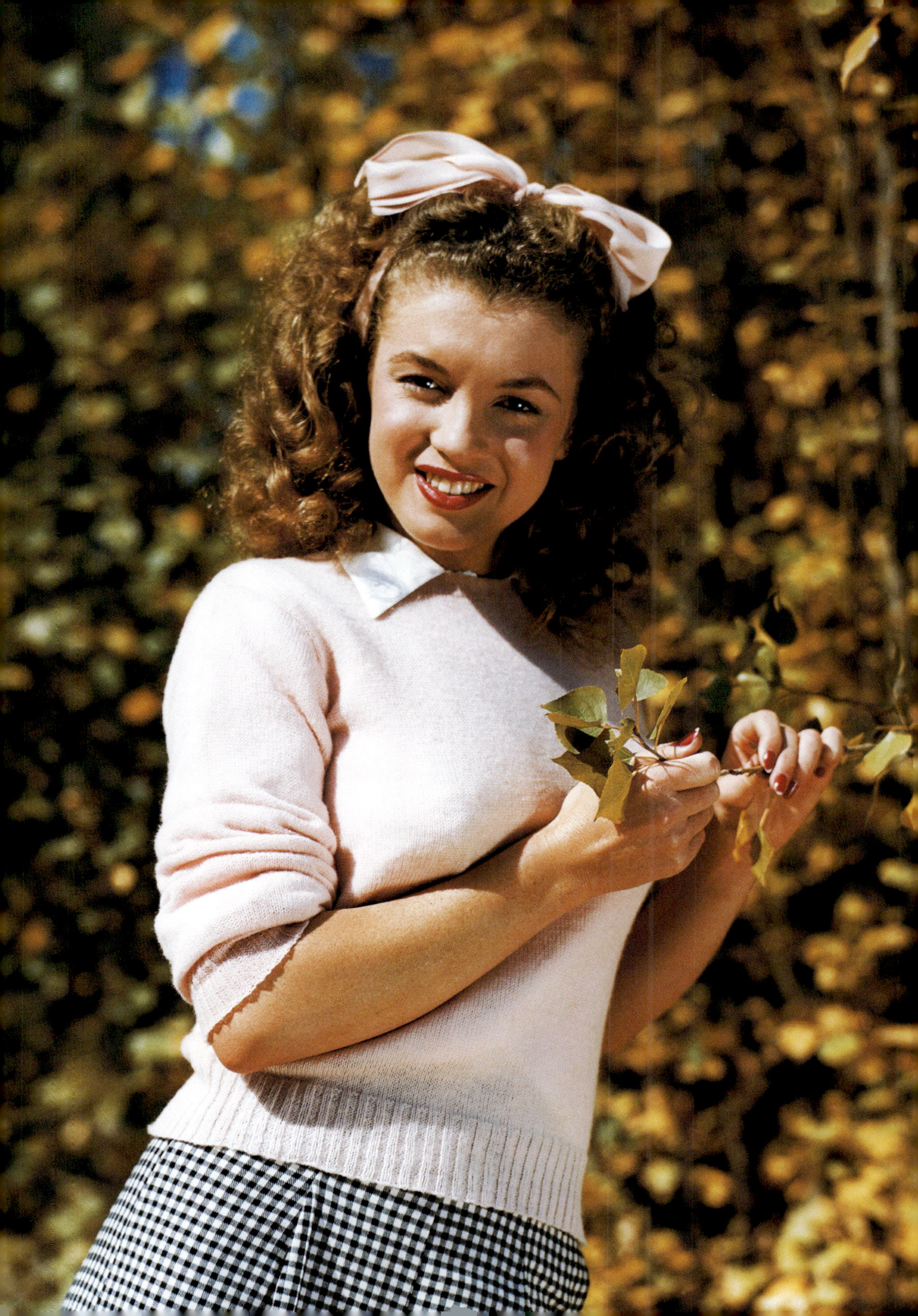

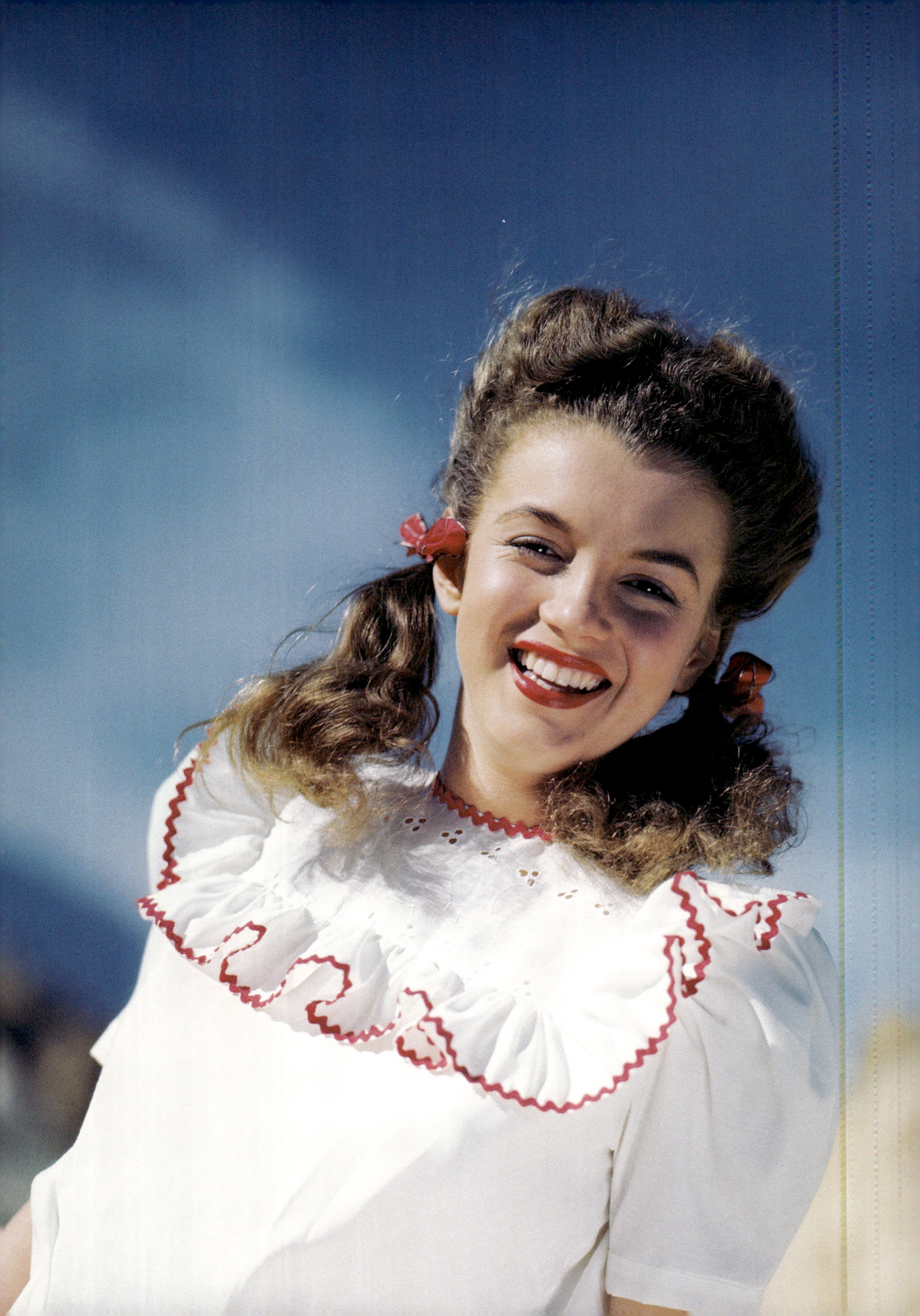

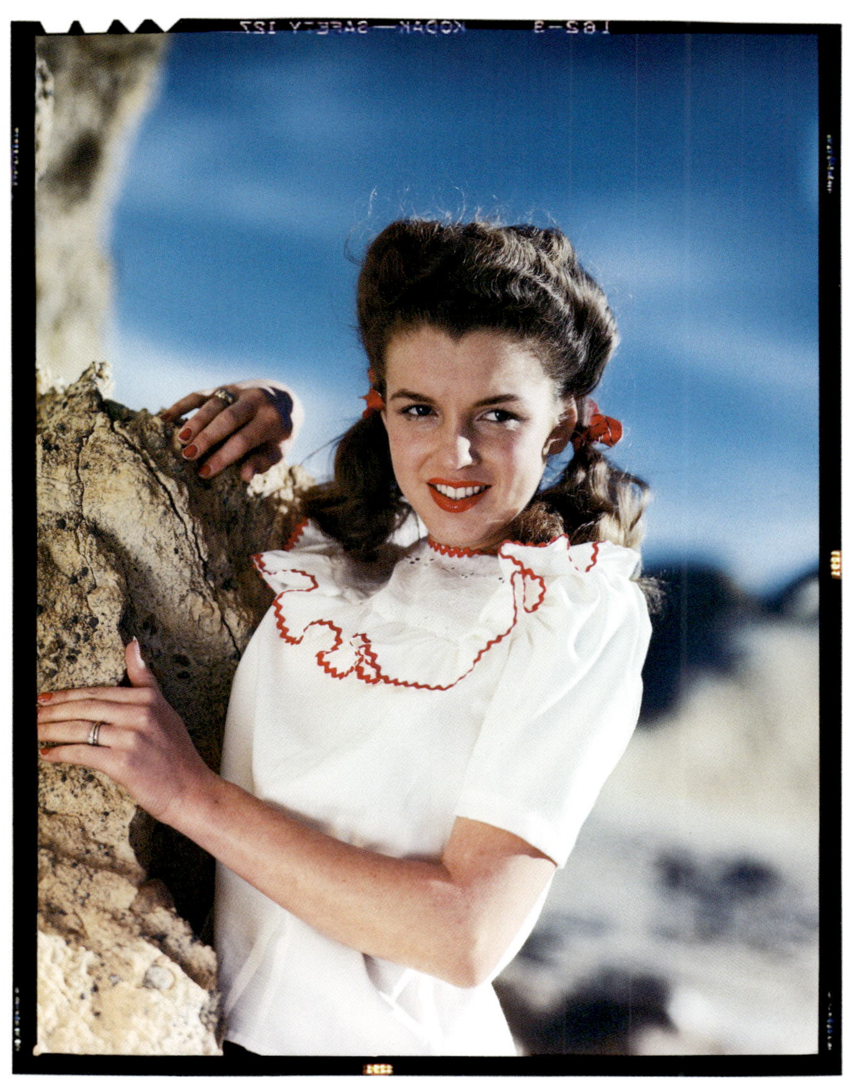

Next time, when I phoned, Norma Jean invited me for lunch, at her home, in West Los Angeles. I never forgot the impressions I had from the first moments I arrived, and parked my car in front of a small frame house in a quiete, surburbean street (in West Los Angeles): Norma Jean was leaning out from the window on the second floor-- waving happily and shouting joyfully " Andre, Andre, so nice of you to come ! Come upstairs ! " Nobody ever before greeted me with such joy and sincerity ! Again, she reminded me Krisztina, the maid, whom I loved so much, who used to lift me up in her arms with the same sincerity!

The apartment upstairs was small, but neat-looking, very clean, with religious pictures on the walls. Norma Jean was still wearing the same outfit as the day before: the pink sweather, and tight fitting slacks. Her aunt, " Aunt Ana " was a well-fed, grayish-haired, elderly lady, acting pleasant, but rather serious. After we found a vase for the flowers I brought, we set down at a beautifully set table, and they both said a short prayer before the meal started.

It was a long, long lunch, for I let myself go and told them all sorts of things about myself; where I was born, about my life in Europe, and in America, about the Indians in the West, but mostly about the previous year I spent in Hollywood, photographing many beautiful girls and movie stars. And I told them Norma Jeane's curly hair reminded me of Shirley Temple, whome I photographed on a farm in San Fernando Valley -- with a price winning-cow who got to be named, also, " Shirley Temple " And I told them how I insisted Shirley should remove her boots and walk barefeet in the mud, and in the cow-dung, as peasant girls do in Transylvania! And how shocked Shirley was at first! She, the great movie star, how could I even imagine her doing that ! Yet she obeyed, and removed her boots, and I photographed her barefeet. And what a nice person Shirley was! And sometime later, she sent me a box of fine candy, delivered to my bungalow by her chauffeur ! It was Shirley Temple's Christmas present for me.

(12/1944)

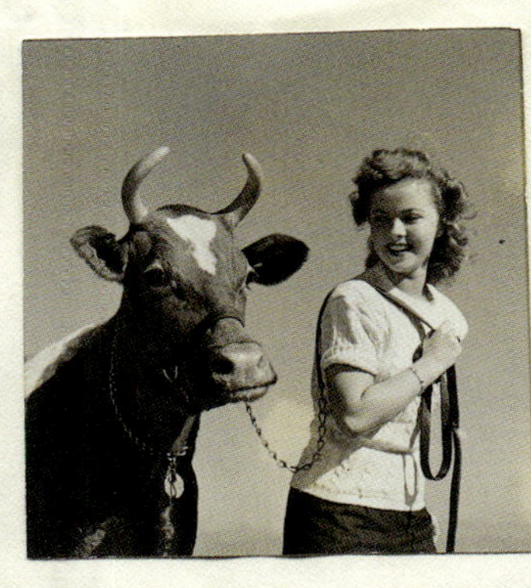

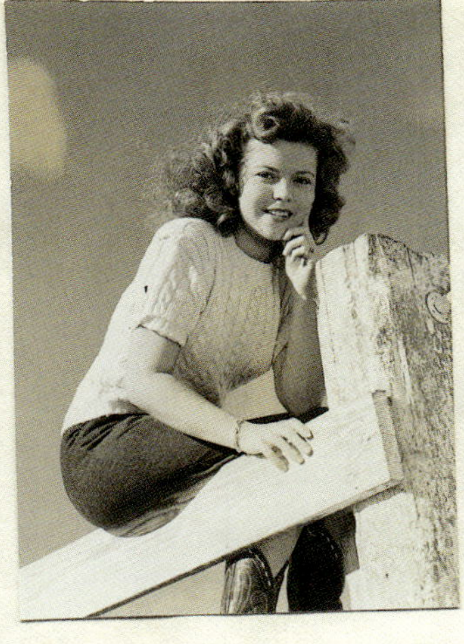

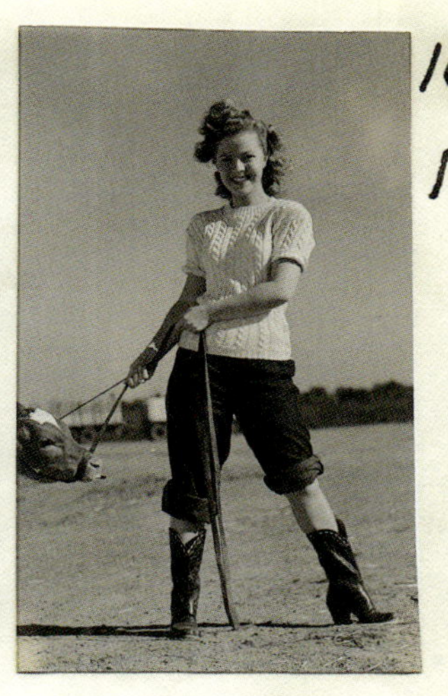

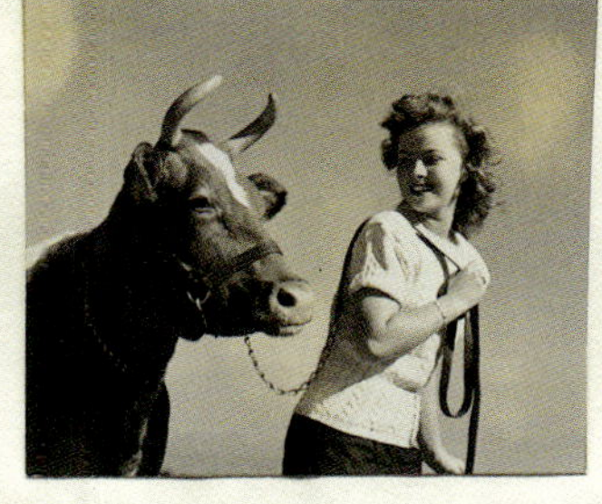

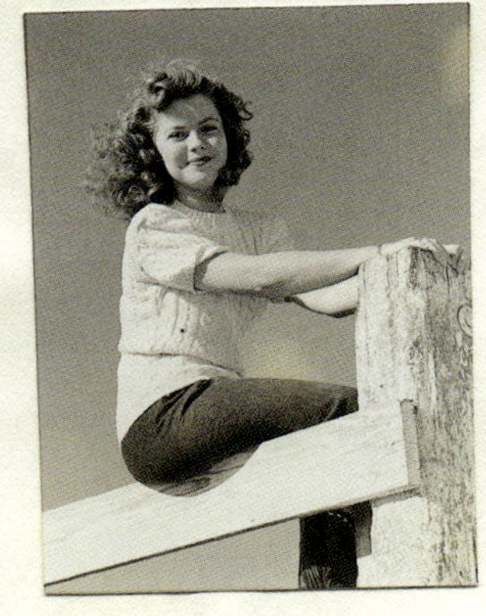

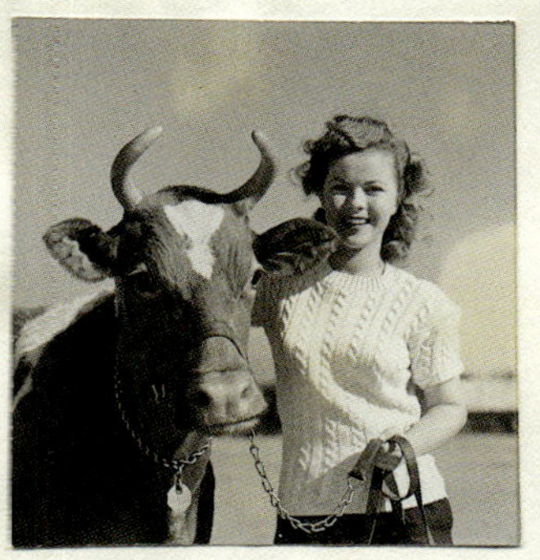

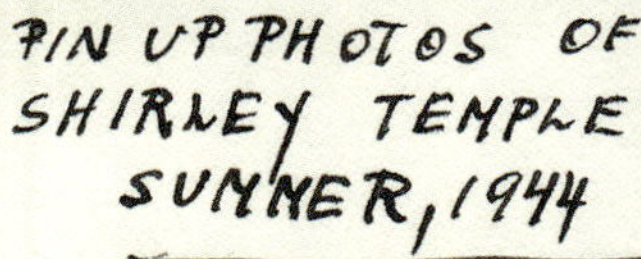

PIN UP PHOTOS OF SHIRLEY TEMPLE SUMMER, 1944

(THE BEAUTIFUL PRIZE-WINNING COW WAS NAMED "SHIRLEY TEMPLE." THAT'S WHY I TOOK HIRLEY OUT TO THAT FARM)

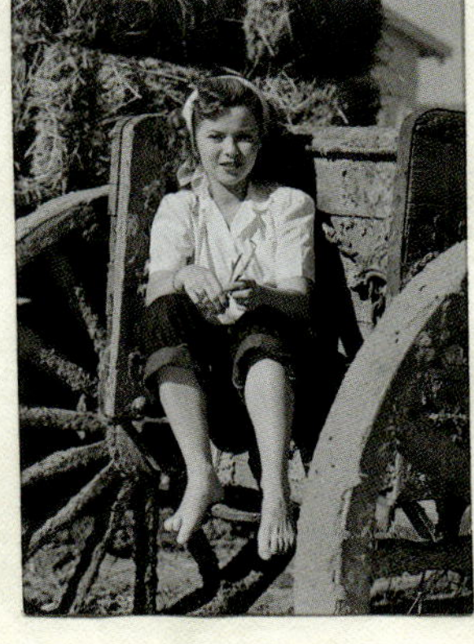

SHIRLEY WAS VERY COOPERATIVE, BUT SHE WAS QUITE SURPRIZED WHEN I ASKED HER TO GO BAREFEET ON THE MUDDY GROUND! NO M.G.M. STAR WAS EVER REQUESTED TO DO SUCH A THING!

I still remember well how Norma Jeane was amused when I told her the rest of my story about Shirley Temple; that I knew Shirley liked me very much from the very beginning of that sitting we had out at the farm where I photographed the cow with her (or, vice-versa) and Shirley I kissed inside the barn. A few days later Shirley was posing for the famed commercial photographer Paul Hesse, (in his studio on the Sunset Strip, corner of La Cienega Blvd.) and while she was sitting in front of the studio camera, when for an unknown reason, Shirley scribed on a piece of paper that "ANDRE DIENES was the best photographer in Hollywood"! Both, Hesse and his assistant were startled by this brief and strange message. Than, the assistant walked over to my bungalow, at the Garden of Allah, just two blocks away, to tell me this story. The flattery Shirley manisfested for me, went into my head, I said to myself, "Shirley must really like me! She is still very young, lovely, unmarried, perhaps very restless to be loved; so I am going to ask Shirley to marry me !" I was quite serious about it ! A few days later I gathered courage, and bought a nice bouquet of flowers, and drove out to her home in Brentwood, on Rockingham Avenue (a large estate, with a big iron gate in front) to ask her to marry me ! The gate was closed, I reng, a large black and white Dane-dog spreng our from the bushes, and charged to the gate where I stood outside. He just barked and barked furiously, but nobody came out from the house. I fetched my camera from the car and took pictures of the dog through the gate, than I left, and never returned to ask Shirley's hand ! I did not have the courage! maybe So I failed to marry Shirley Temple ! — I STILL HAVE THE PHOTO OF THE DOG!

Norma Jeane loved hearing my story ! The funny coincidence was that Norma Jeane had her hair in curles, and ringlets, and looked almost like like Shirley! And I told her so. She loved my comment ! I excused myself for a few minutes, dashed down to my car, in front of the house, and brought up my portfolio of beautiful photos of beautiful girls I photographed, including Shirley, to show them I wasn't lying.

And I entertained Norma Jeane and Aunt Ana with stories about Ingrid Bergman sweathing in the wheatfields when I took her pictures on a hottest summer day and that the farmer ren to us swearing, cussing, cursing, ordering us out of the fields -- in fear I might set his crop on fire with the large silver-foil reflector I was using. (to fill in the dark shadows on Ingrid's face in the brilliant sunshine) And how I made Dorothy Mac Guire climb high on a cliff overlooking the ocean because I wanted her to pose with the beautifully polished rocks the winds have carved out on that cliff. And what a lovely person Carole Landis was, so obligingly changing dress after dress, at least ten in one afternoon, because I was instructed by her studio to photograph her in as many different outfits I could, for that high fee the studio was paying me for a day of my time! And that Carole Landis insisted we go to her beautiful house in Beverly Hills after all that picture-taking hassle was over with, and she fixed strong drinks for me, to calm my nervousness down......

I suppose all those stories might have sounded and sound even now like braggings, but they were true! After the lunch was over, Aunt Ana told me I can take Norma Jeane away on the trip I was planning. And she recommended I should take good care of her! I felt she must have been impressed by my stories, and my enthusiasm for doing many things, and I felt that she had confience in me. There was no business-like talk about how much I would pay Norma Jeane, or for how long a time would we be away. As I think back to it all, maybe Aunt Ana felt Norma Jeane needed a new man, and me, Andre, might be right for her, one way or another. And perhaps she was glad to see Norma Jeane go on her own, and to embark on a new life, since her marriage with Jim Dougherty was over with, or was going on the rocks.

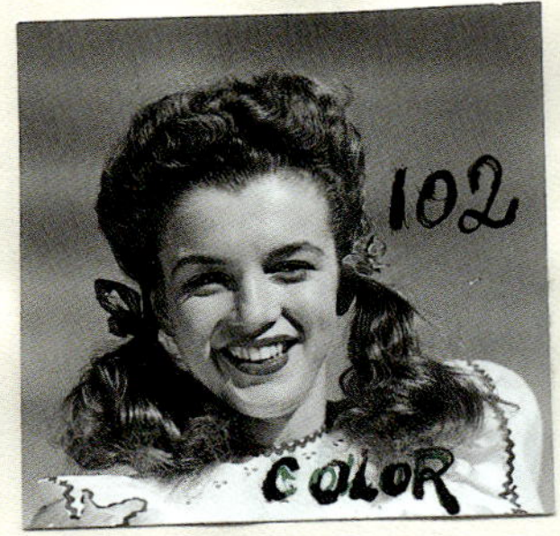

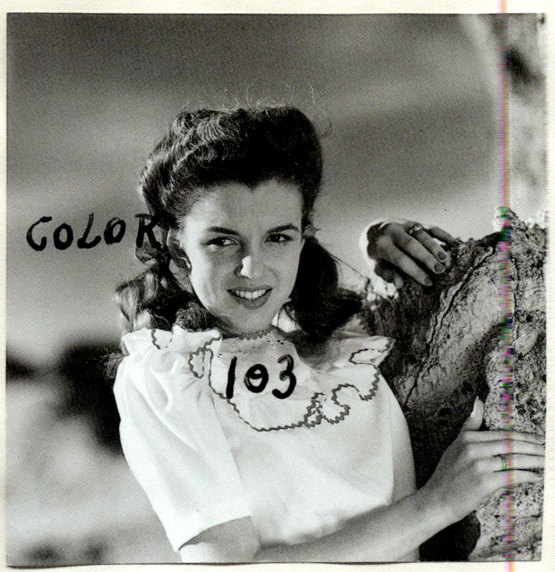

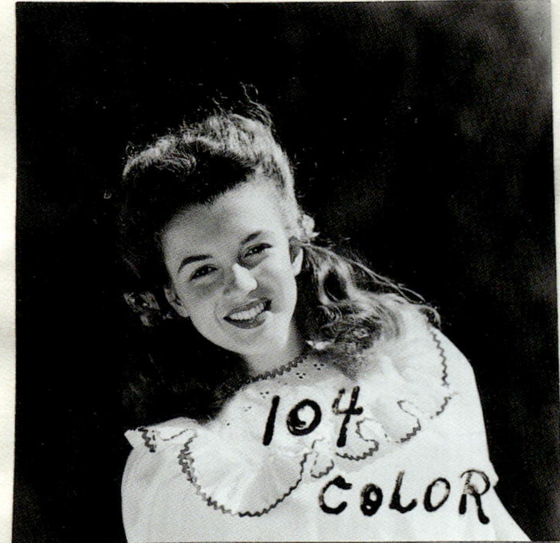

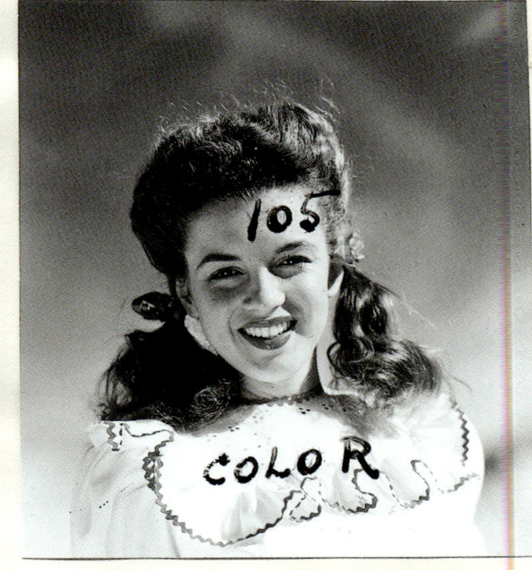

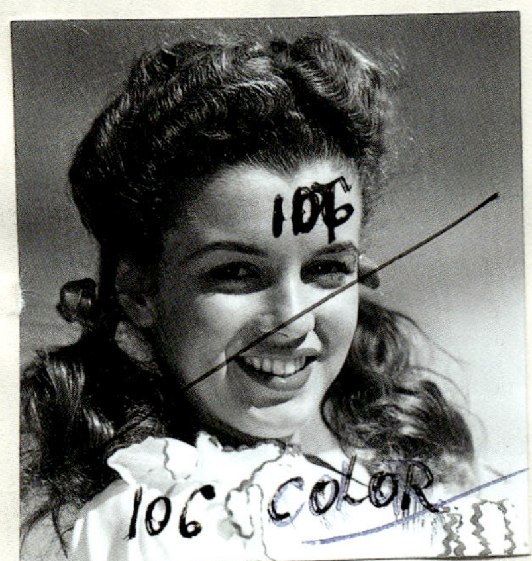

ANDRE DE DIENES
1401 SUNSET PLAZA DRIVE
HOLLYWOOD, CALIF. 90069

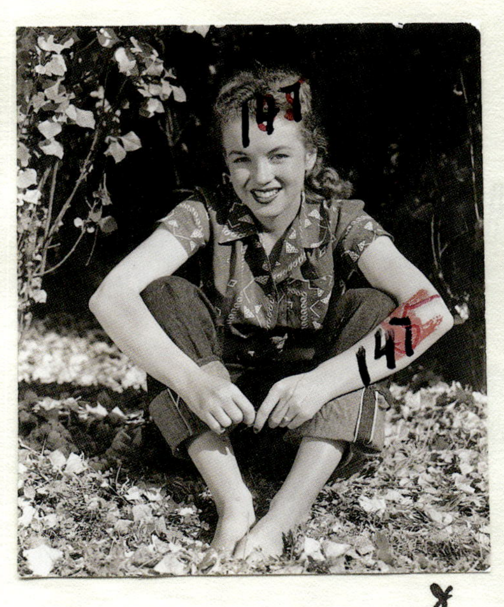

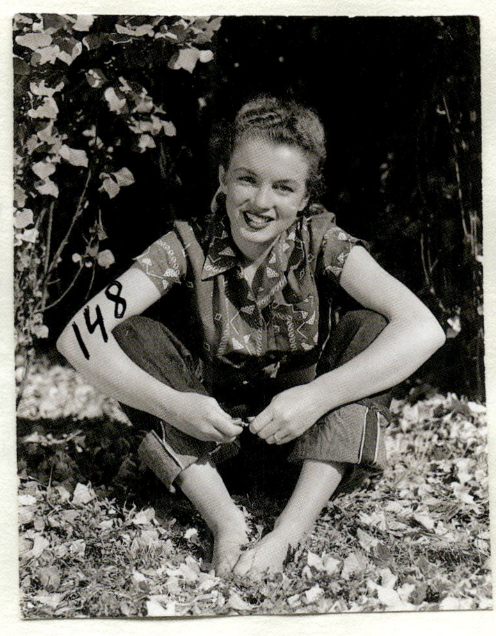

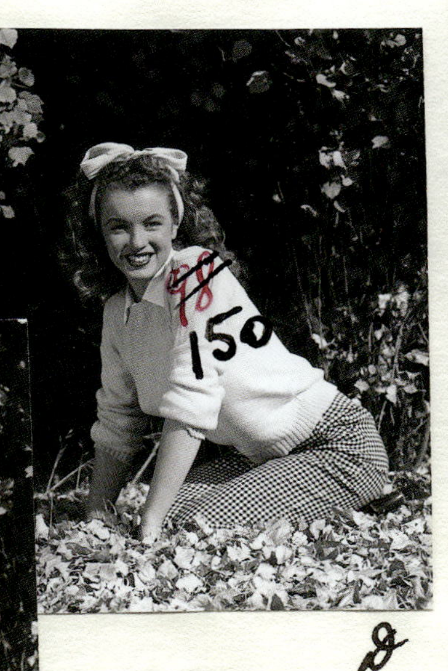

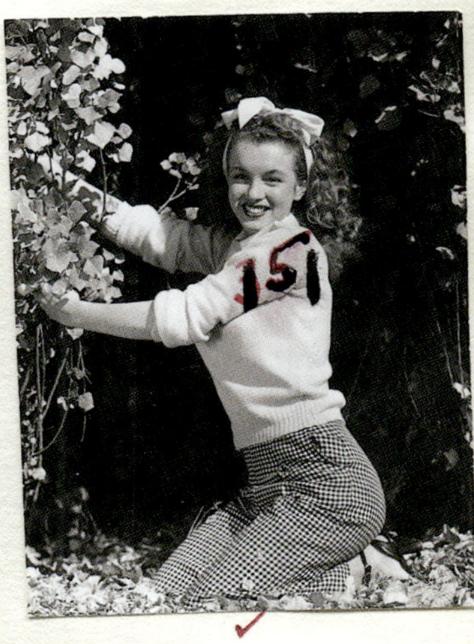

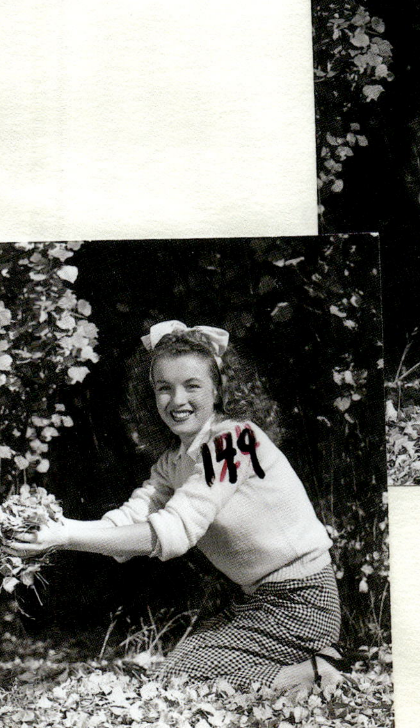

ANDRE de DIENES
1401 SUNSET PLAZA DRIVE
HOLLYWOOD, CALIF. 90069

21

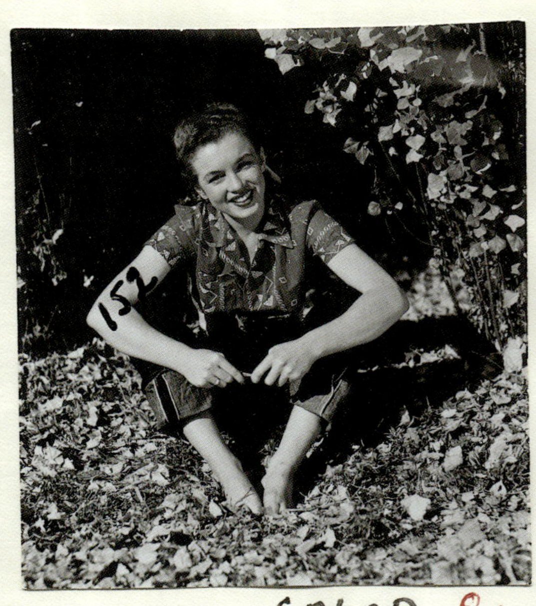

COLOR g.

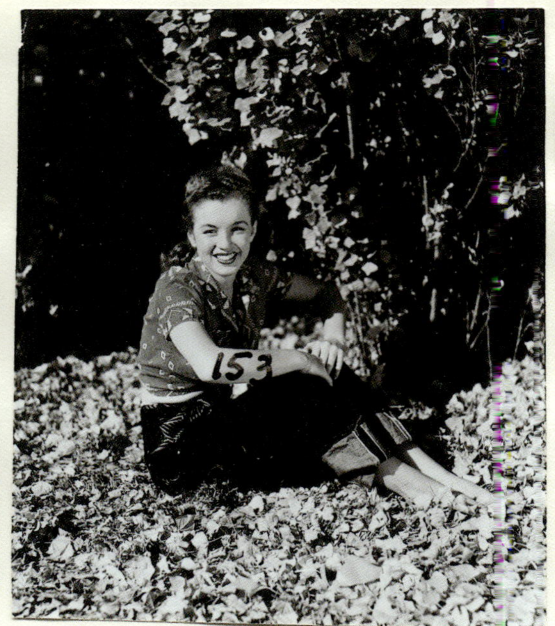

COLOR

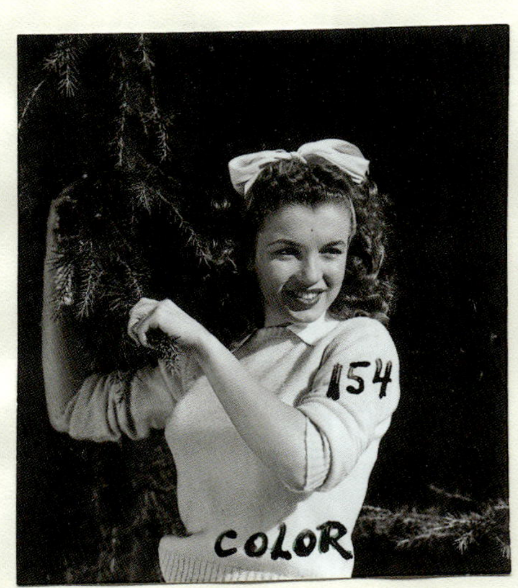

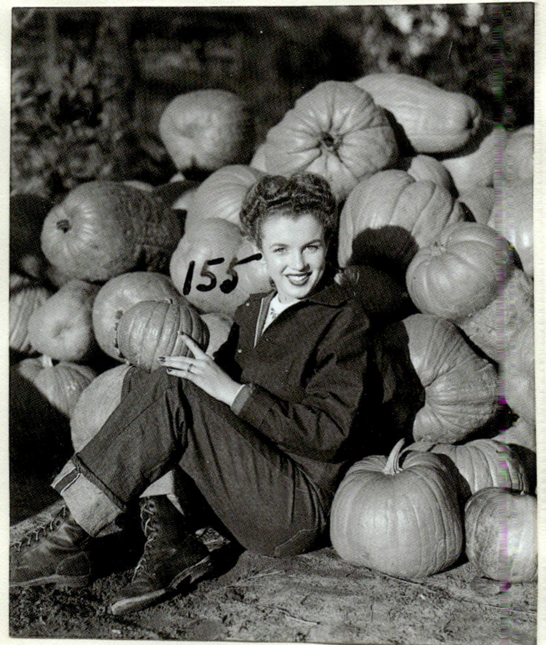

6

ANDRE de DIENES
1401 SUNSET PLAZA DRIVE
HOLLYWOOD, CALIF. 90069

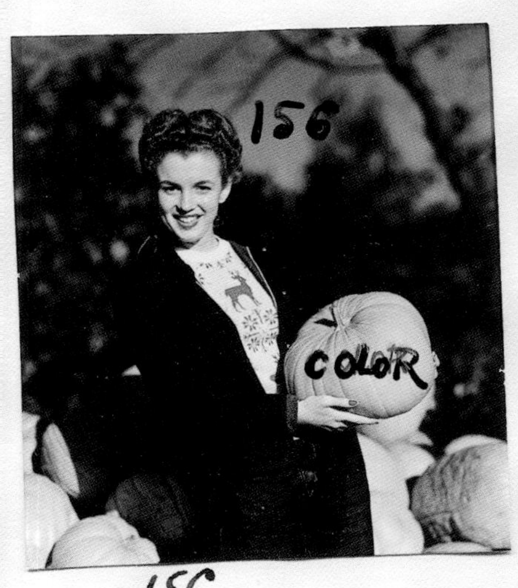

156

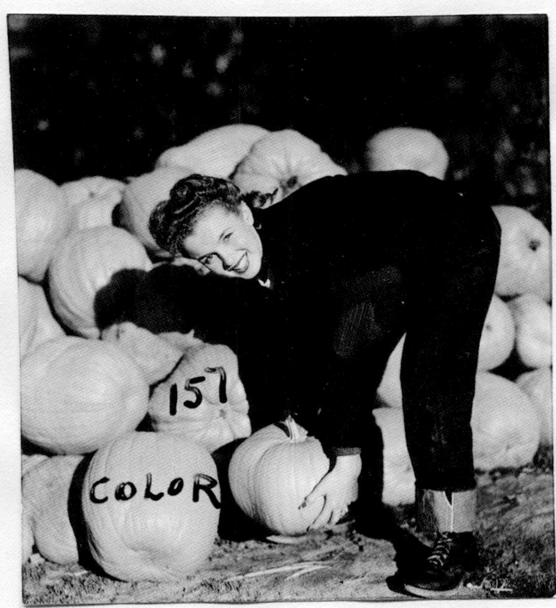

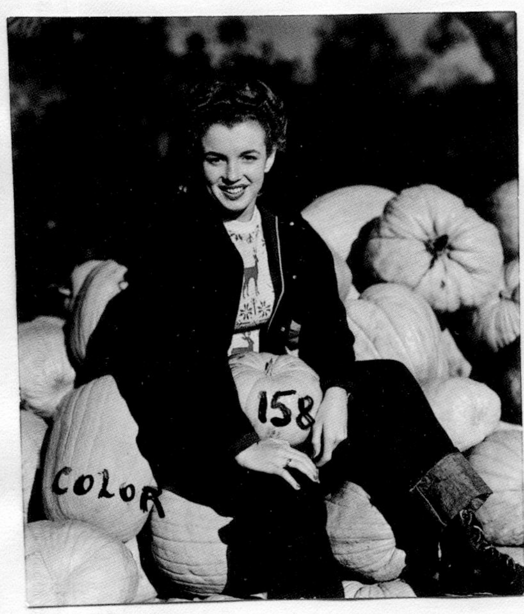

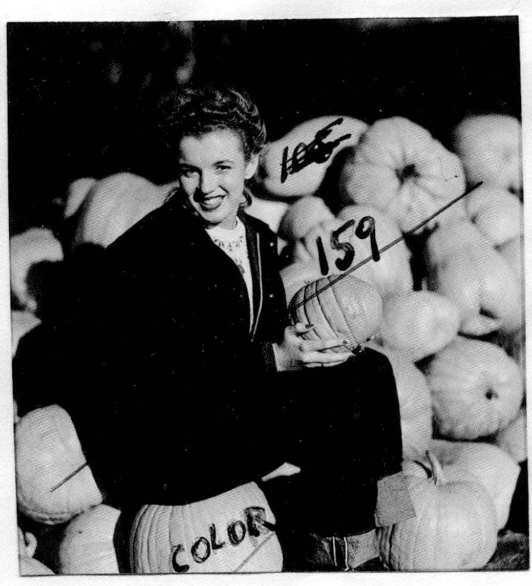

ANDRE de DIENES
1401 SUNSET PLAZA DRIVE
HOLLYWOOD, CALIF. 90069

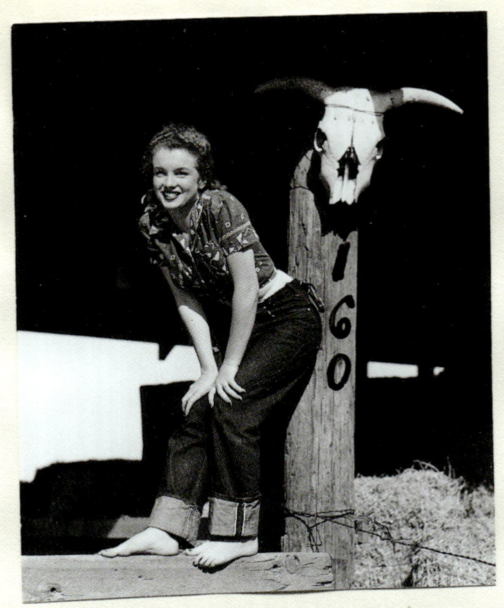

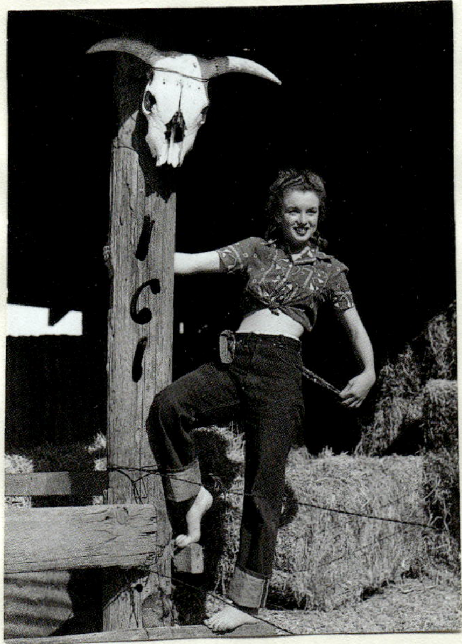

L-7

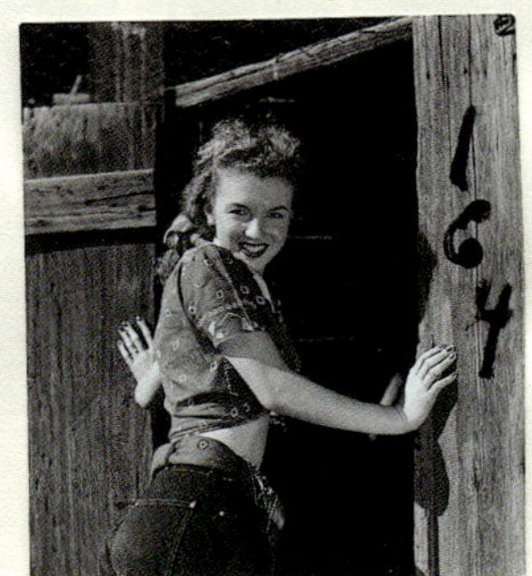

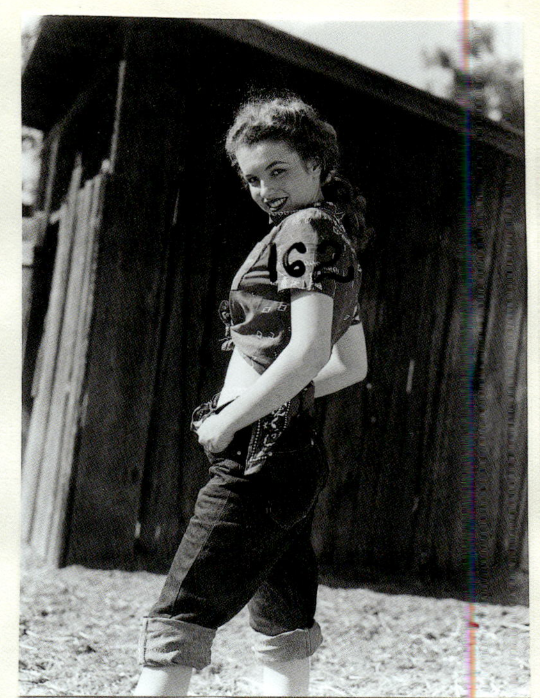

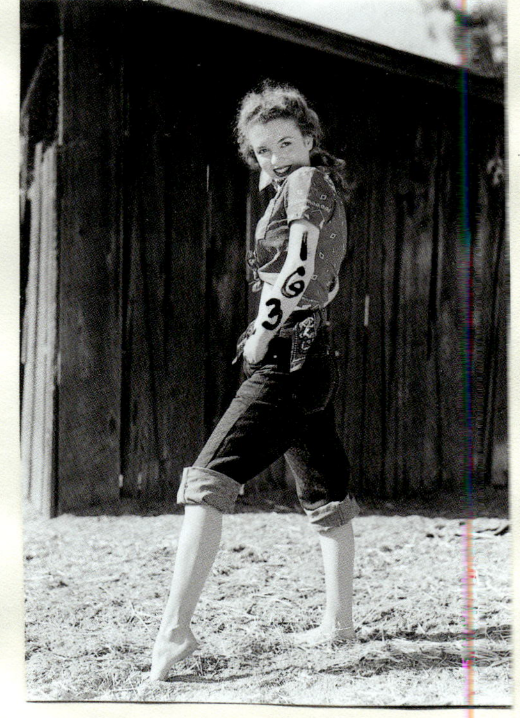

ANDRE DE DIENES
1401 SUNSET PLAZA DRIVE
HOLLYWOOD, CALIF. 90069

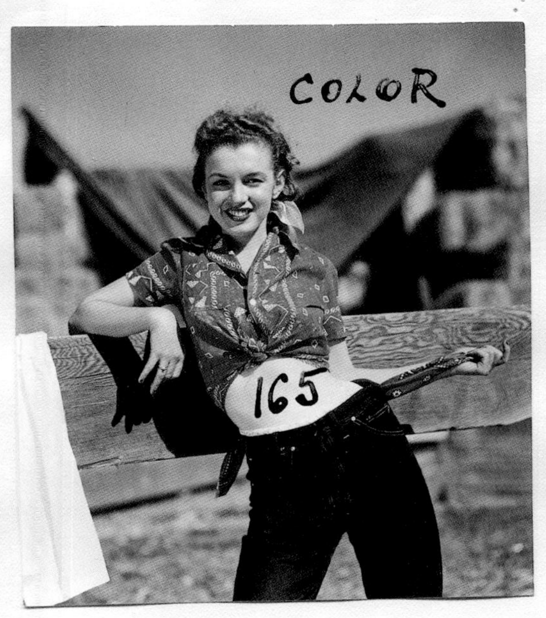

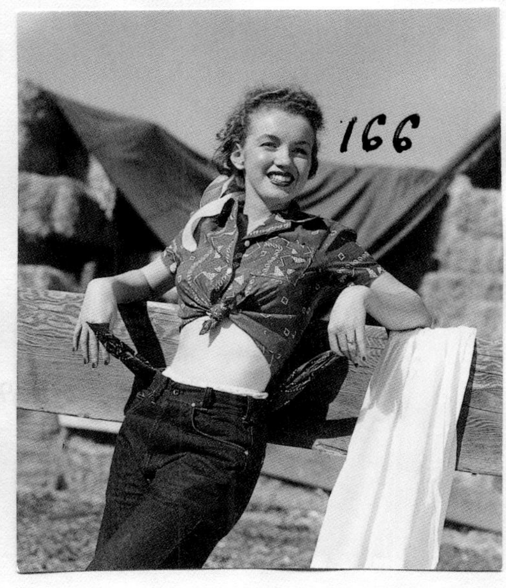

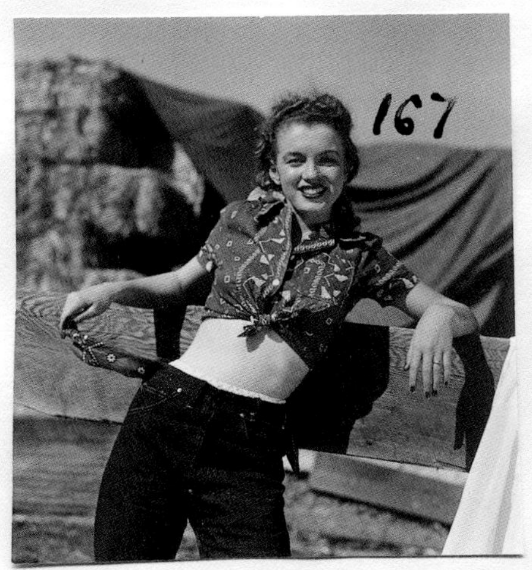

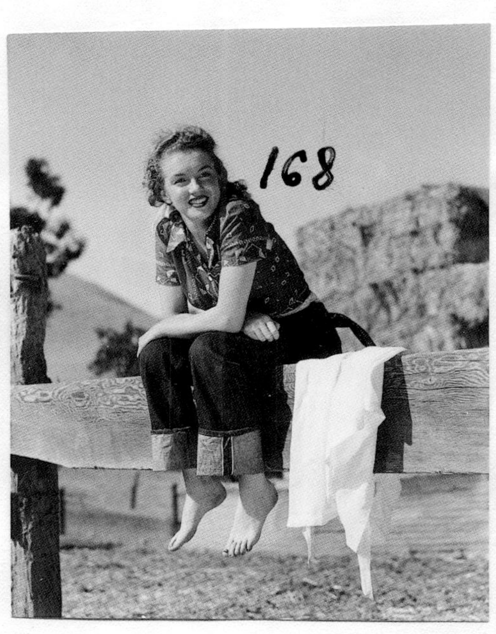

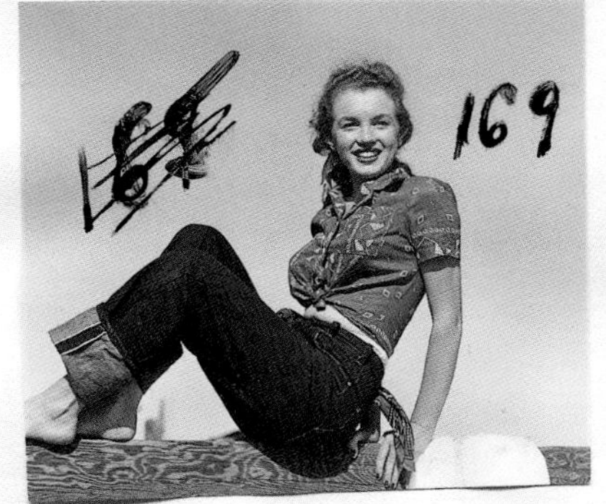

ANDRE DE DIENES
1401 SUNSET PLAZA DRIVE
HOLLYWOOD, CALIF. 90069

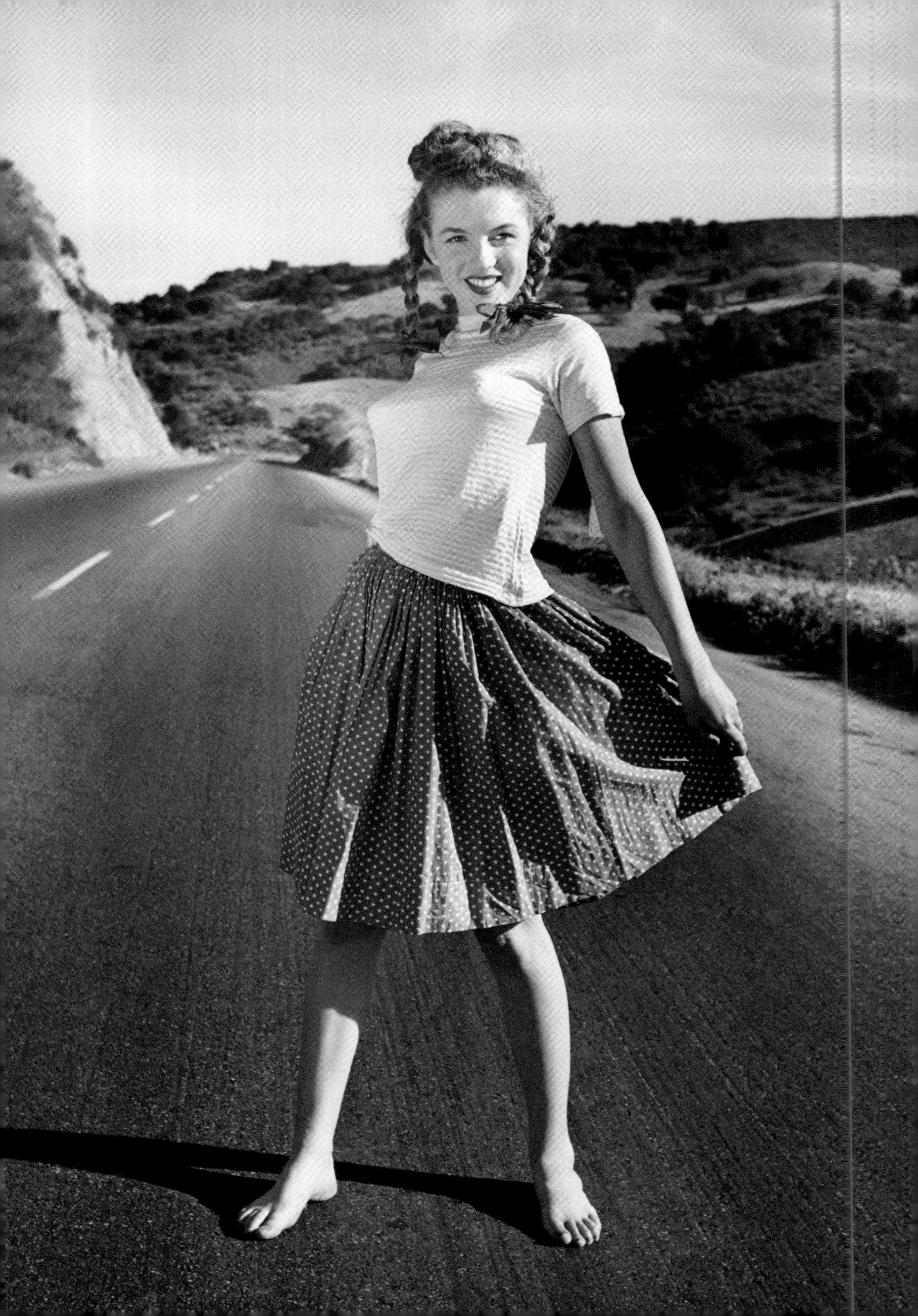

SHE STARTED HERE

1945

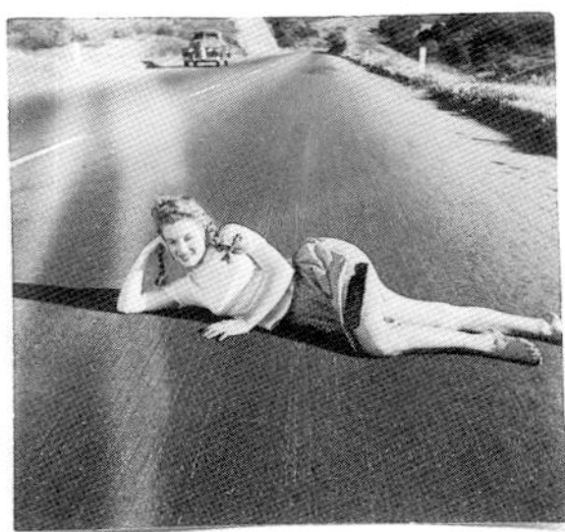

<u>The Journey Begins</u> In the days that followed, I bought Norma Jeane various clothes to wear for my pictures and to keep her warm because it was December and my plans were to visit the desert, the mountains, everywhere in California, Nevada, Arizona, anywhere my fancy would dictate going. I removed the back seat of my big Buick Roadmaster automobile and laid down a sheet of thick foam rubber with blankets on top and pillows all around, so Norma Jeane could sleep whenever she wished during the long drives I was planning. That was her little "cage" as I called it. She laughed like crazy when I told her she would become my little slave and prisoner, that I might even buy a long thin chain to attach one end of to her ankle and the other end to the car! Her hatbox full of her things and a small suitcase were also placed in her "cage," plus a basketful of food and thermos bottles for milk and coffee, etc. The trunk of the car was for my equipment and the front seat was also for her, with pillows against the door to give her as much comfort as possible. And thus the long journey began.

We were hardly on the outskirts of Los Angeles when the police patrol stopped me for faulty driving. Norma Jeane was sitting close to me and the policeman might have felt jealous! She felt very indignant. In her sweet voice she riposted to the policeman that he was a crook and that we had done nothing wrong. The man, part seriously and part joking, said to Norma Jeane that if she cared to stay there for the night he would not make us pay the fine. I paid twenty dollars and we

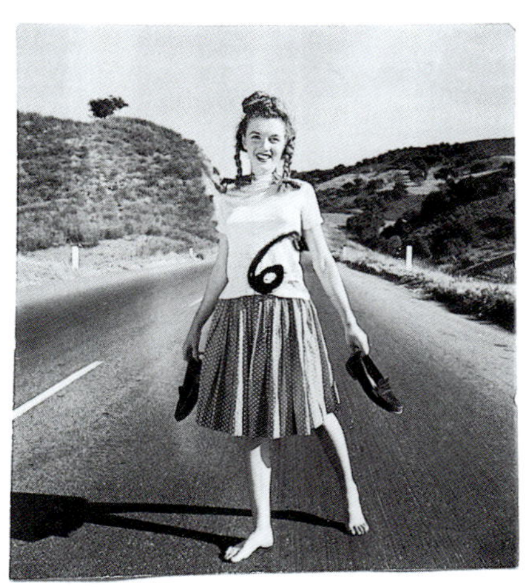

continued the trip. That was only the first proposal she got on that trip. Amazingly, at various places we stopped, people began proposing to her. A garage mechanic said he would give his left arm if she would stay and become his wife. A miner in the mountains said he wanted her and would give her everything he had. A young farmer said he was looking for a woman of her beauty! The owner of a motel proposed to her! And the haberdasher where I stopped to buy her jeans went nearly out of his mind wanting to see Norma Jeane try on various garments in the little dressing closet. Like a magnet, she attracted all men! I became reluctant, even cautious, stopping wherever there were men around. She good-humoredly laughed every time and gently apologized to the men that she was unable to stay…. She did not tell me so, but I knew she was very pleased. So that's how the legend of Marilyn Monroe began – every man was crazy about her!

After we left the police station, I asked her to stand on the highway, barefoot, fixing her hair in pigtails. While taking her picture like that, in a sudden, strange, psychic revelation, I began pointing at the small white stars on her red skirt, prognosticating that those stars meant that some day she would become a very famous movie star! For a while I was talking, babbling about a future fabulous life, foretelling almost incoherently that the road behind her symbolized life, and that those were the first photos of her future successes to come!

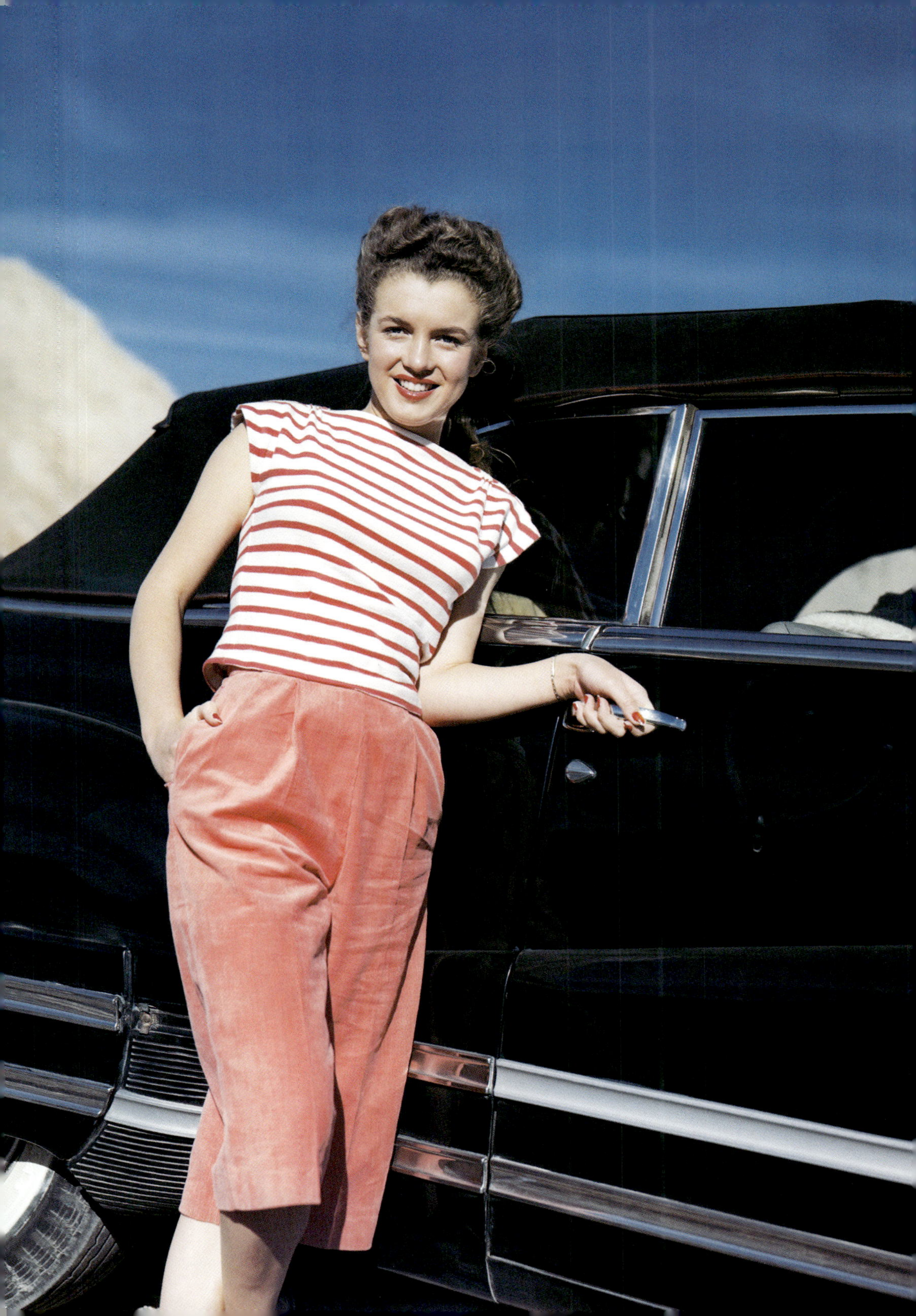

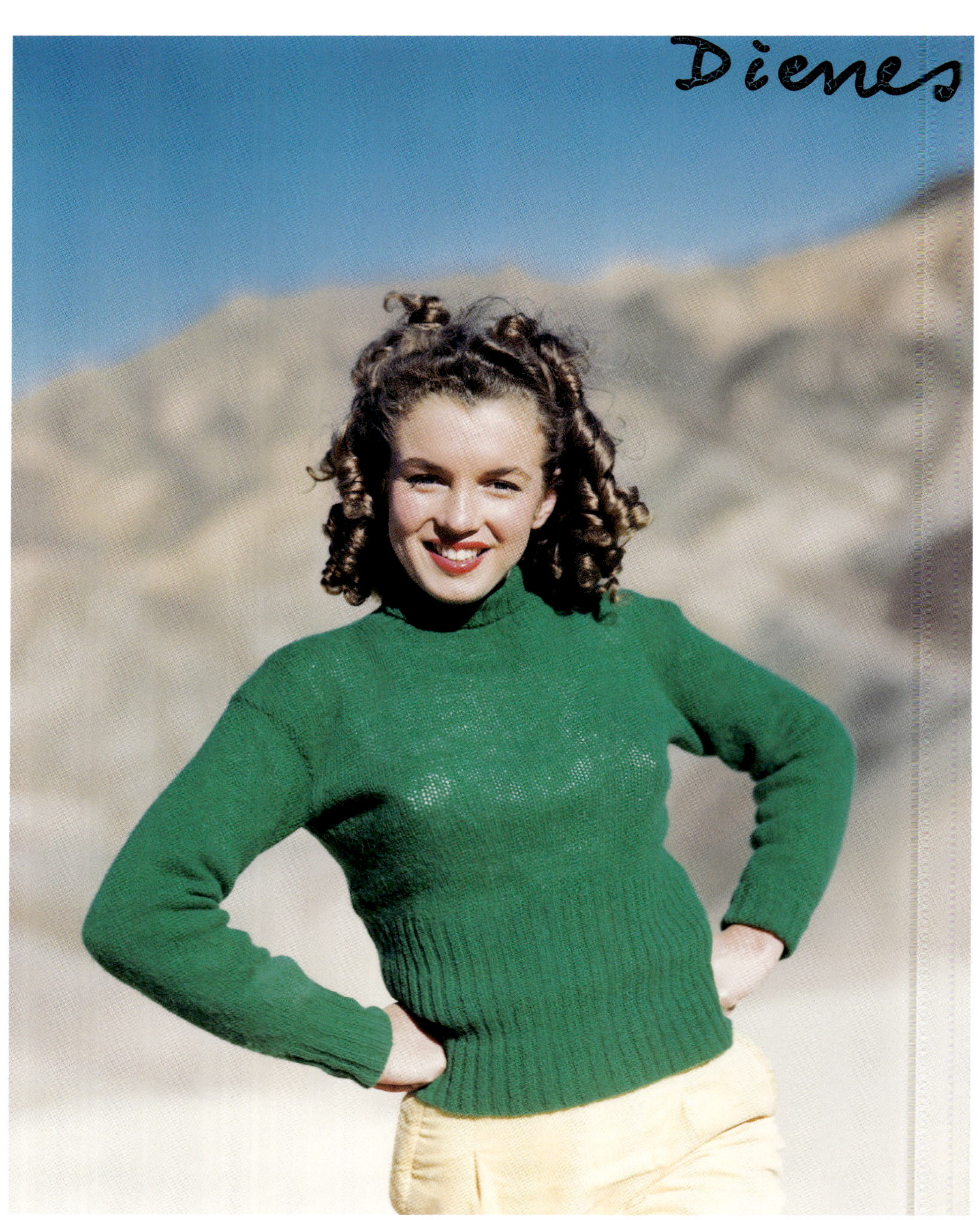
Dienes

in Death Valley, Calif.

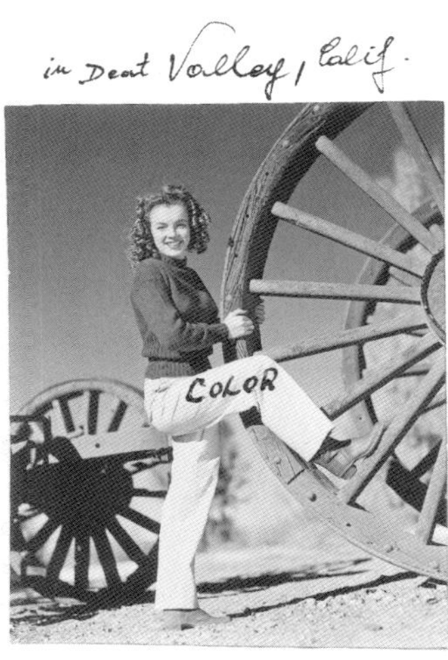

Death Valley My first destination was Death Valley, California, where I wanted to visit places connected to finding gold. Also, I had in mind to take nude photos of Norma Jeane at a place called "Darwin Falls" in the western region of Death Valley, which I imagined to be a large, beautiful waterfall. As it turns out, imagination and reality are two different things. After a long drive, and some hiking, we found only a small waterfall with a little bit of water coming down, and even if I could have taken nudes against that, I simply could not go through with it. I was too much in love with her to ask her crudely to undress and expose herself. I knew that if I really asked her to undress, or insisted on it, she would have done it, but it seemed to me a heartless, tactless procedure to make her shed all of her clothes all of a sudden. I could not go through with it! I just began adoring her; I did not want her to show herself to me in the bright sunlight, I was too idealistic and shy!

It was evening when we got to Furnace Creek Inn, in the heart of Death Valley, and I asked Norma Jeane whether she would like to sleep in the same cabin, with me, or would she prefer a separate one. Sweet, darling Norma Jeane calmly explained her sentiments to me – that she liked me very much, but she was only separated, not divorced, and she would feel far better if she had her own cabin. Besides, she loved to sleep well and if we were together she would not be able to get her rest. She got her wish! We had separate cabins. But I could hardly sleep all night – I felt the torment of wanting her! Toward dawn,

TRAVELLING THROUGH CALIFORNIA

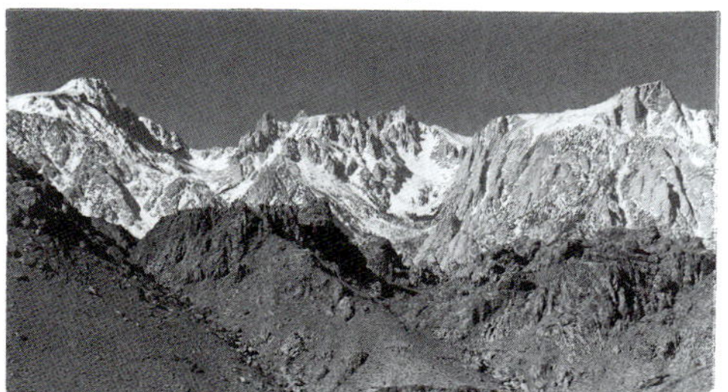

Mt. WHITNEY, WEST OF DEATH VALLY, CAL.
THE HIGHEST PEEK IN THE U.S.

I ventured to knock on her door. She opened it, and laughingly, like someone who is accustomed to handling men in those kinds of situations, she asked me to remain a "good boy" and to return to my cabin. I did.

A few hours later, when I woke up, the sun was just rising from behind the mountains. I was ready to start on the trip again, and to my great surprise, when I went to knock on her door again, she was already made up and taking the curlers out of her hair. The sunlight shone right into her cabin and she was cheerful, exuberant, and eager to go to the dining room for her breakfast. It was a very chilly morning and still, she was eager to pose for pictures as soon as she got dressed. Any other model would have still been in bed, or would have wiped her sleepy eyes, complaining about having to get up, saying what a "sadist" I was to wake her up so early… to "slave" for me for pictures! But not Norma Jeane! She was the sweetest darling I have ever met!

Again, instead of photographing her nude, I took pictures of her dressed, sitting on rocks. Since the desert seemed so beautiful, so tranquil to both of us, I spread out a blanket and I was reading to her from a quotation book I had brought along with quotations about most everything that touches spiritual life. Norma Jeane listened attentively, and then she took from her handbag her Christian Science prayer book and she, too, read for me.

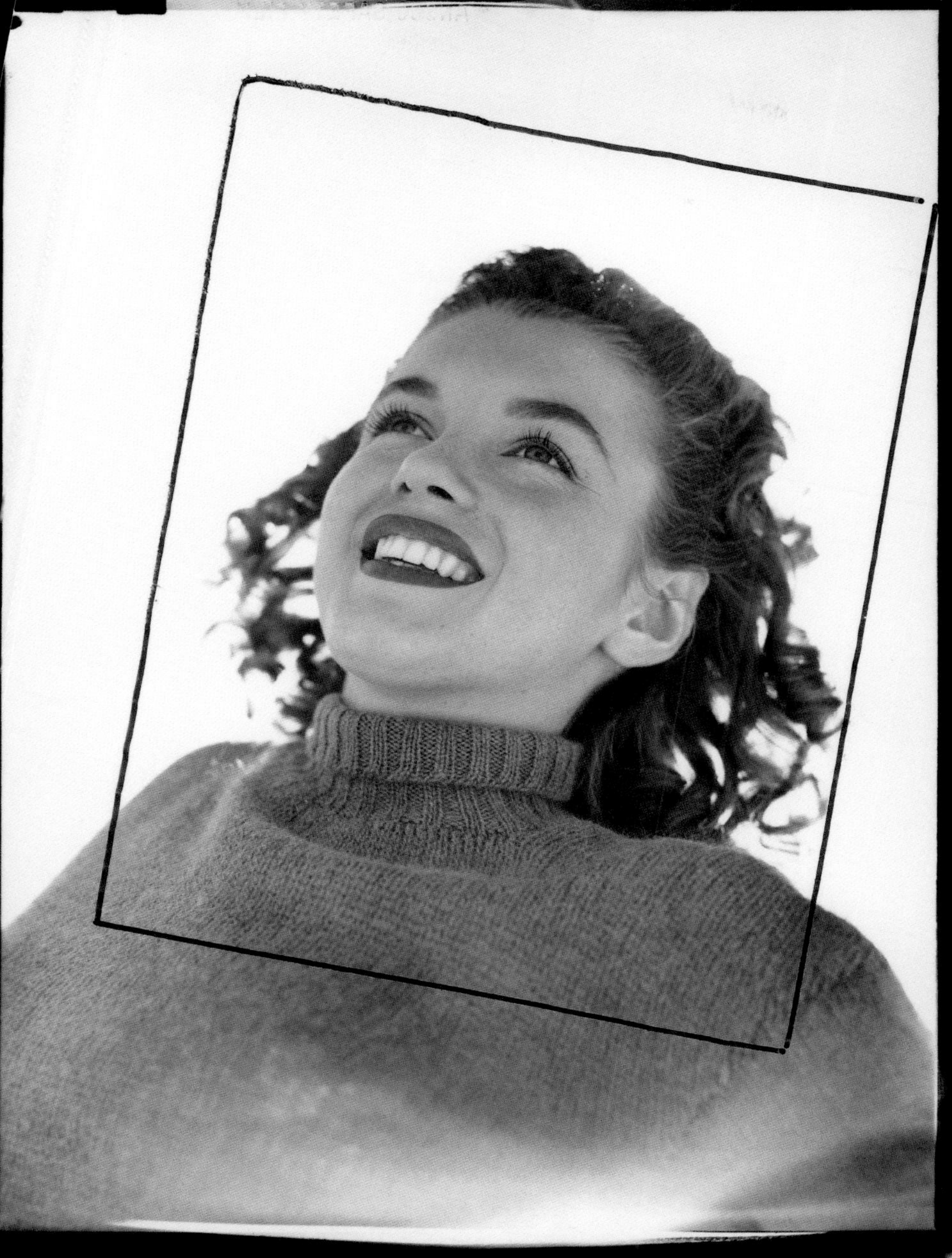

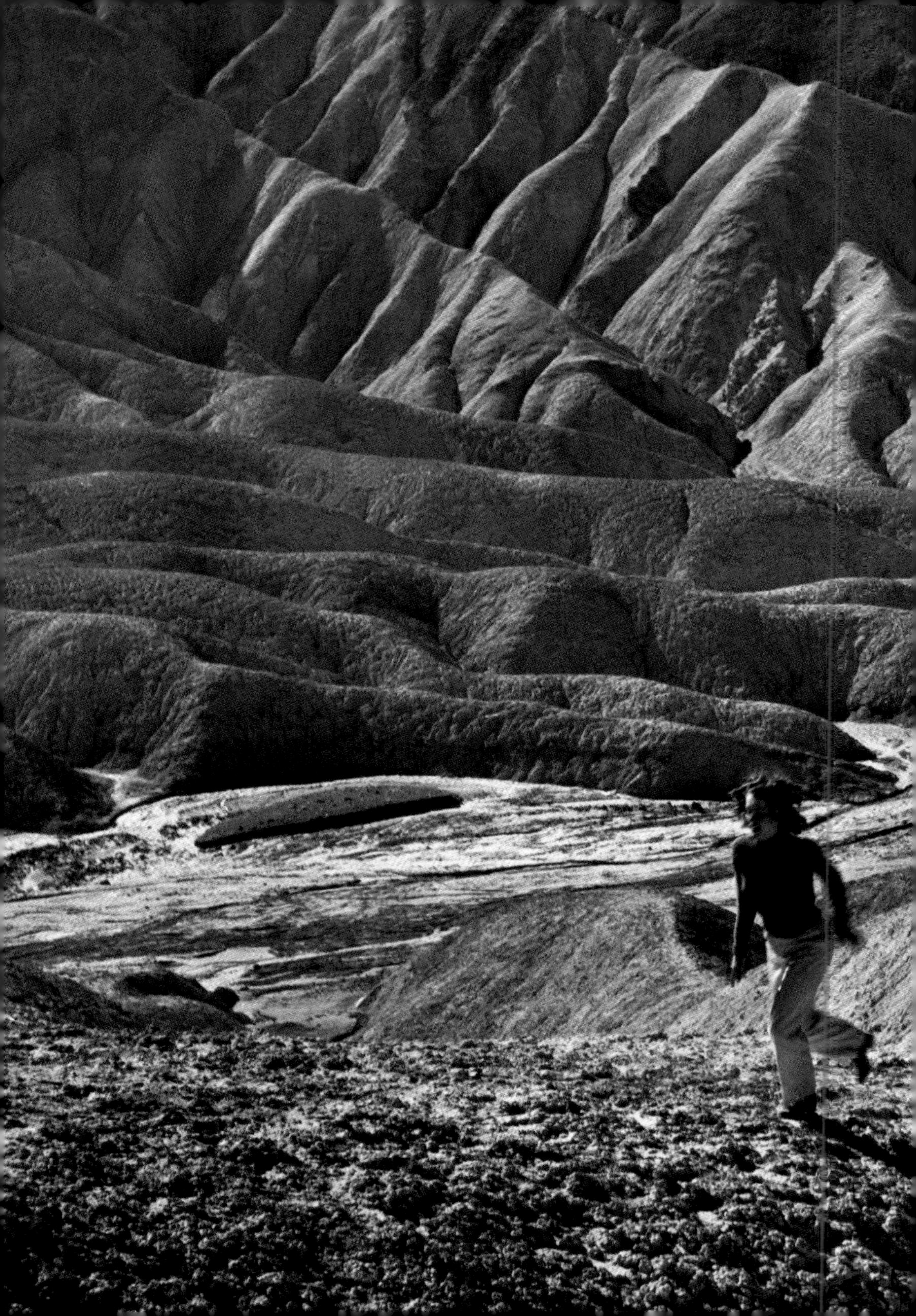

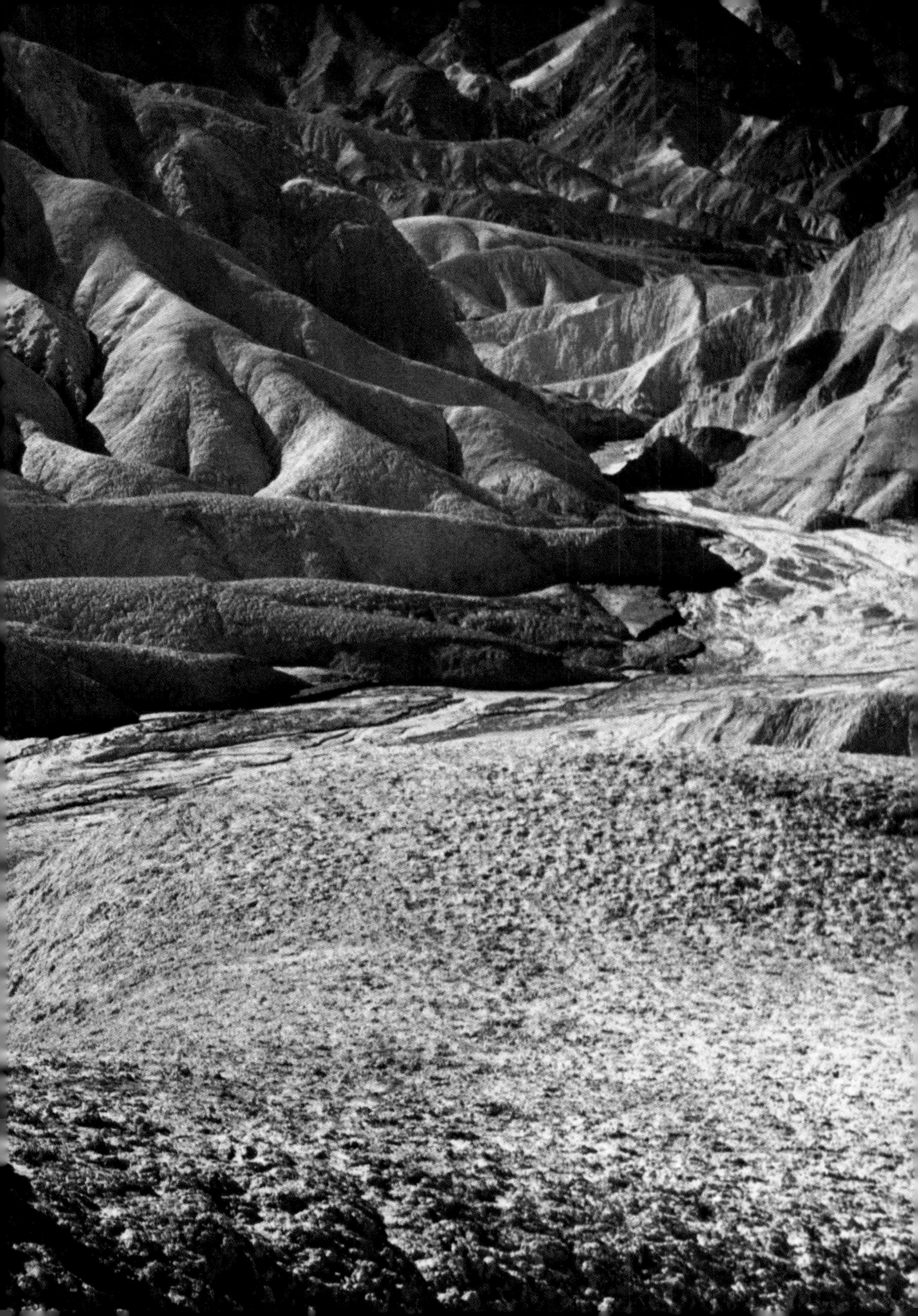

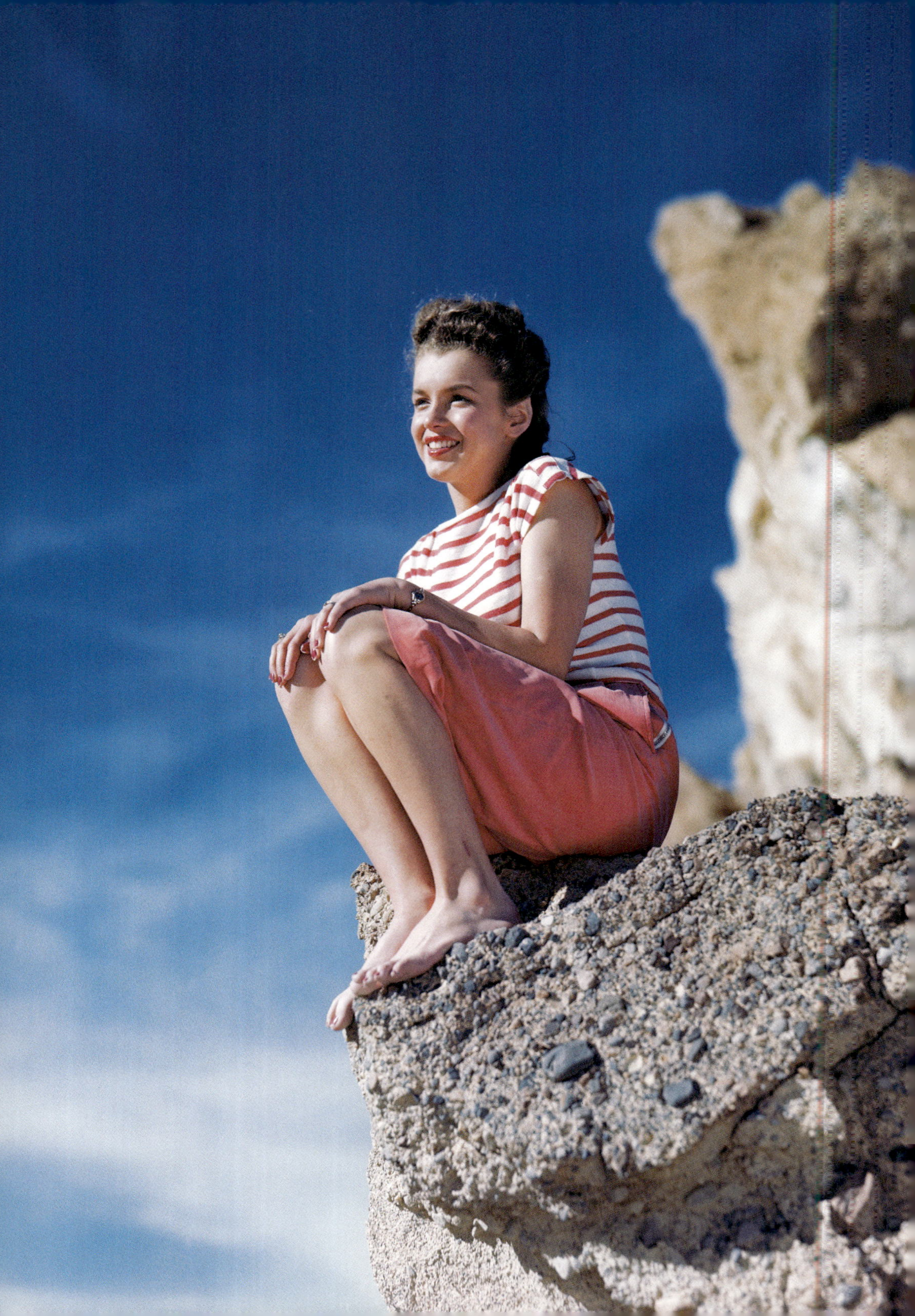

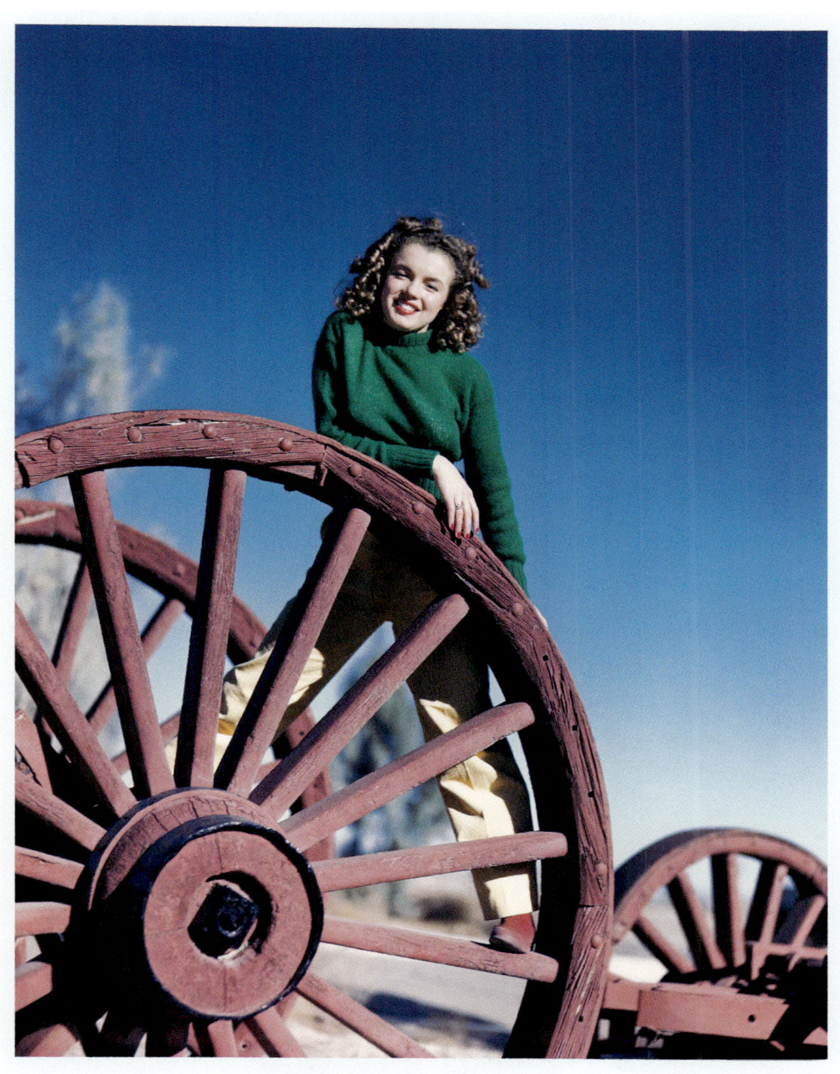

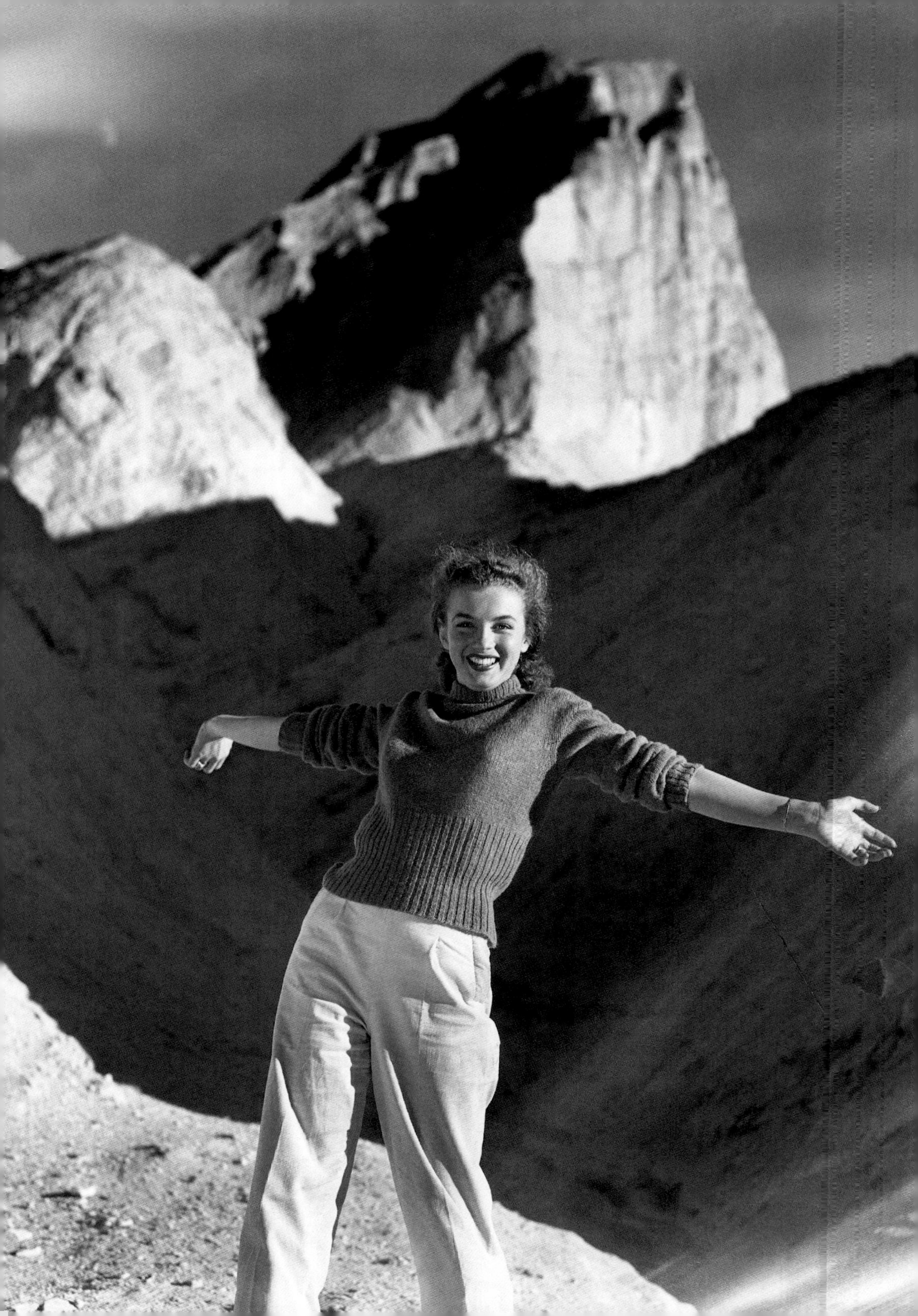

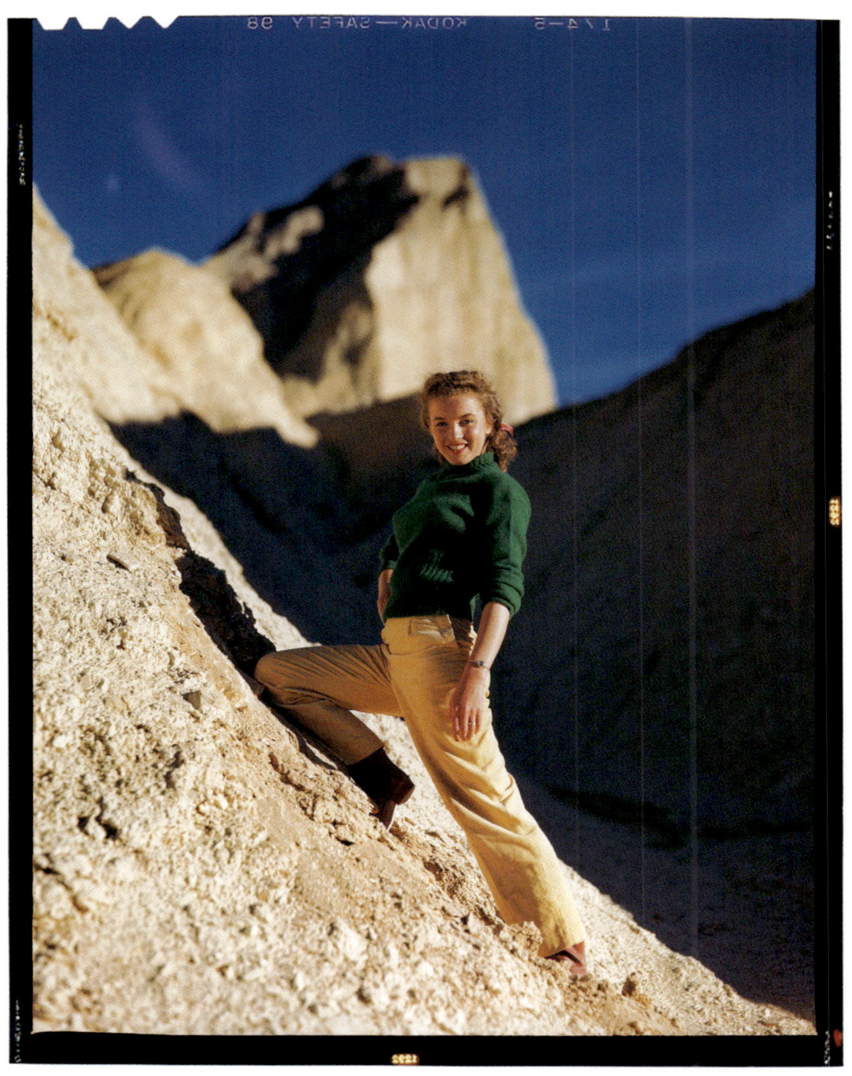

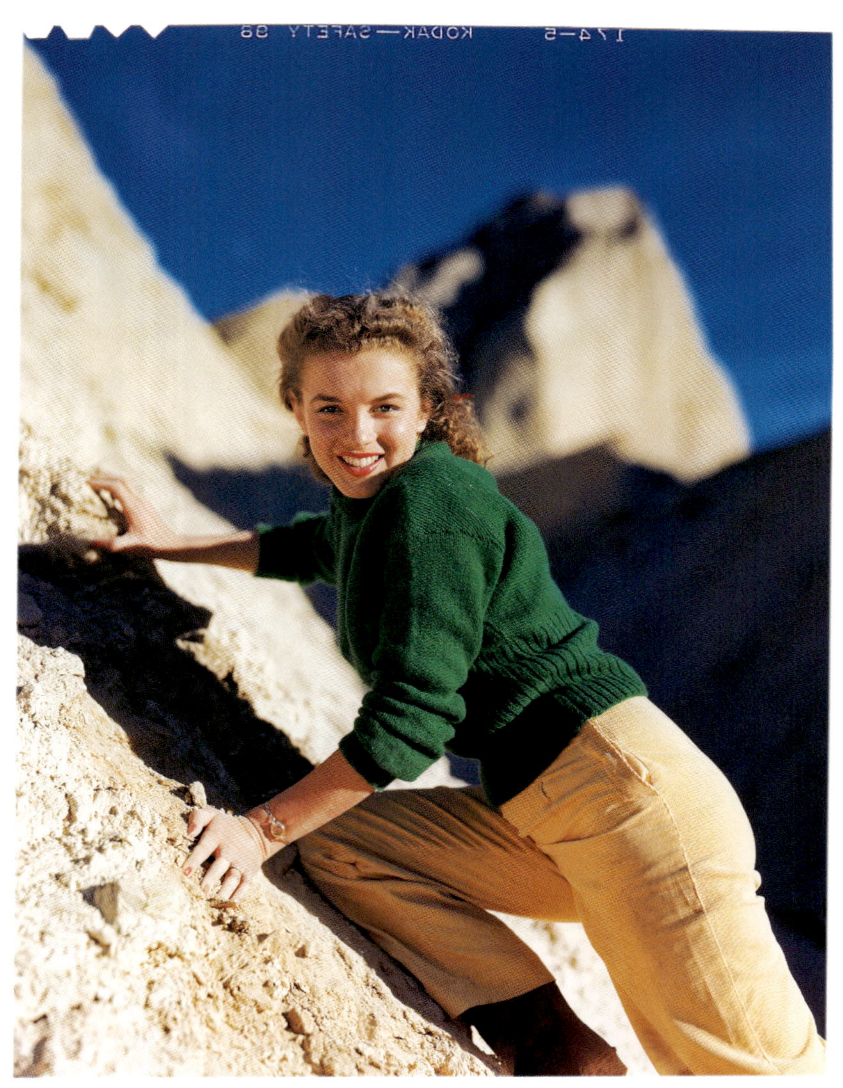

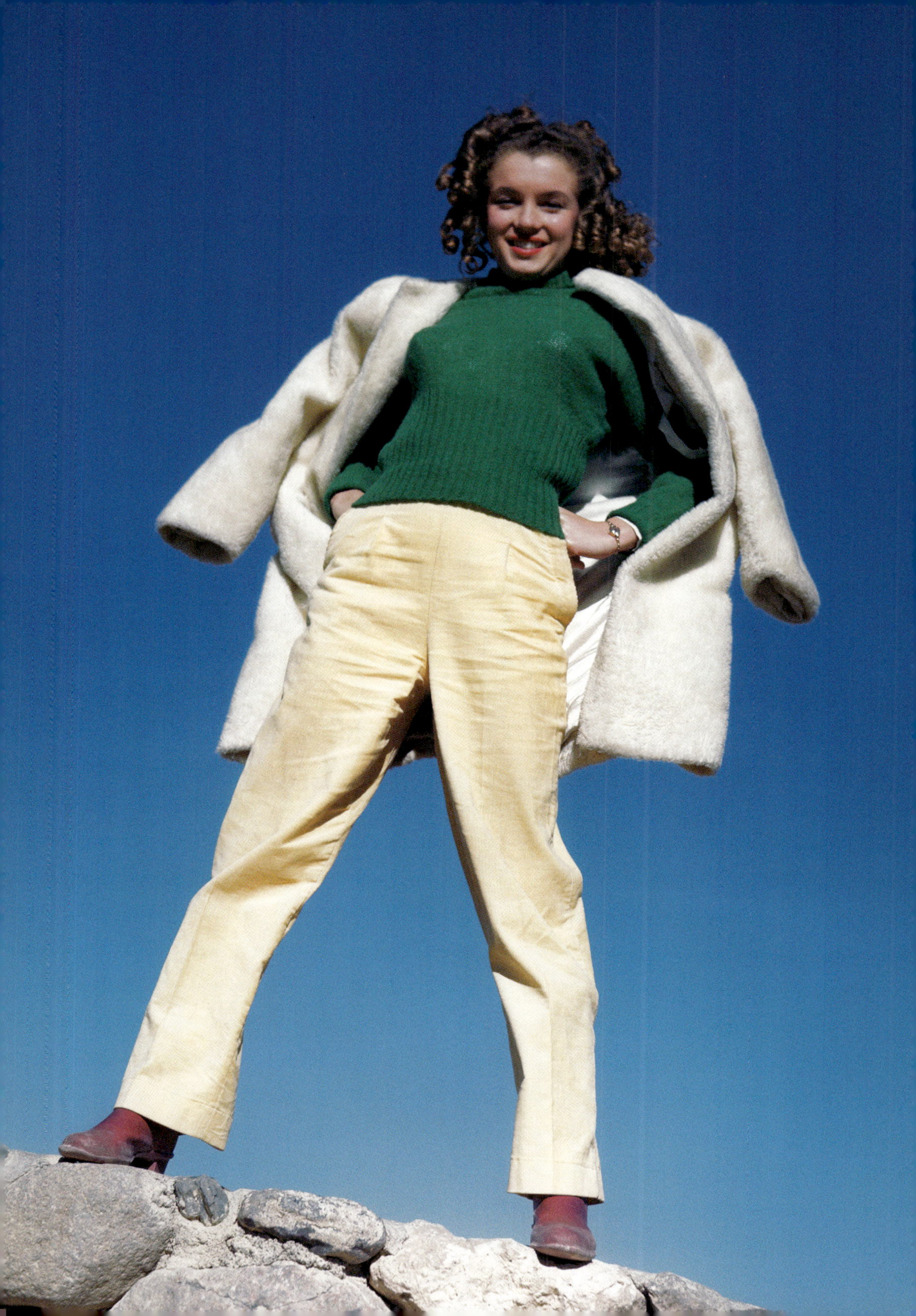

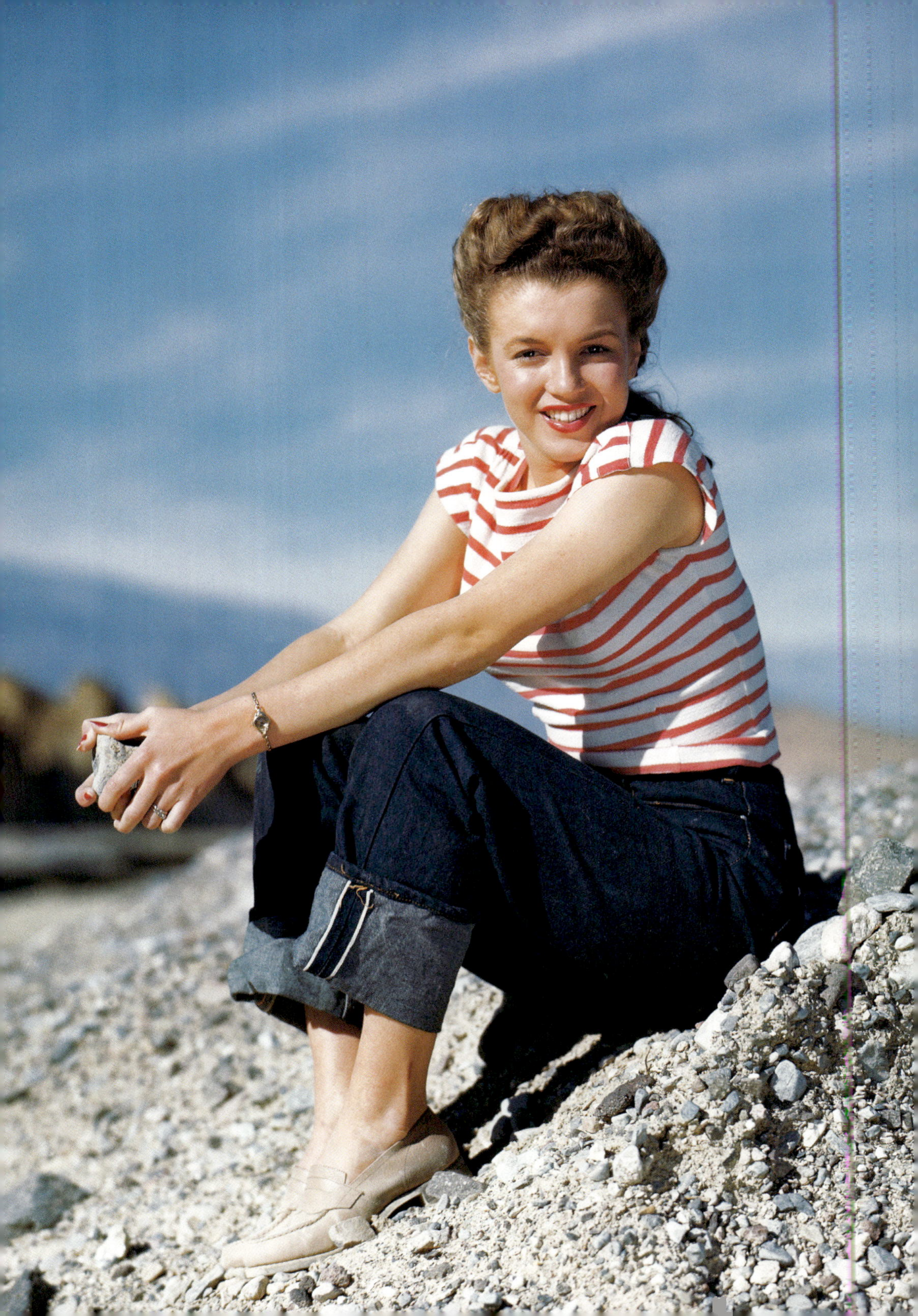

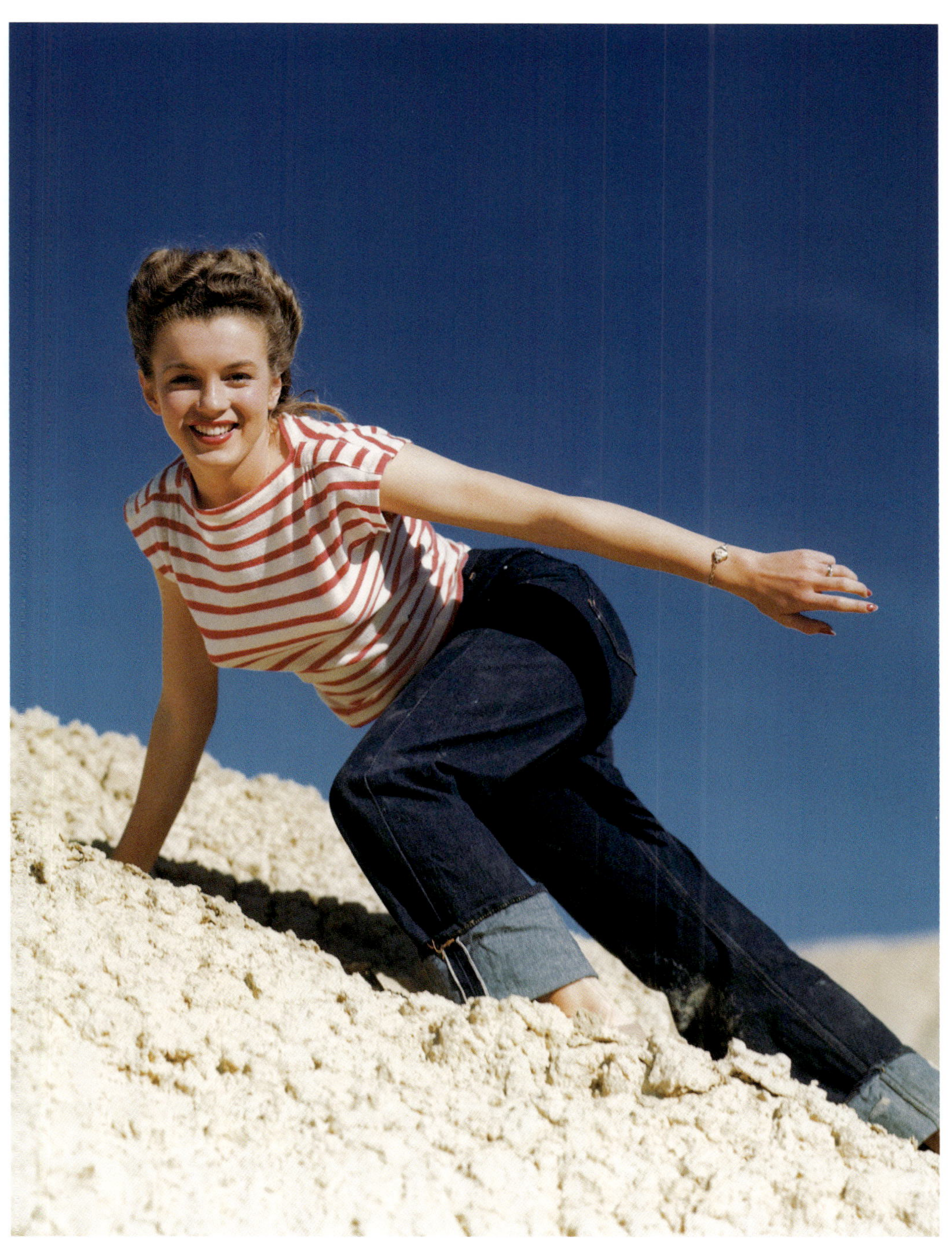

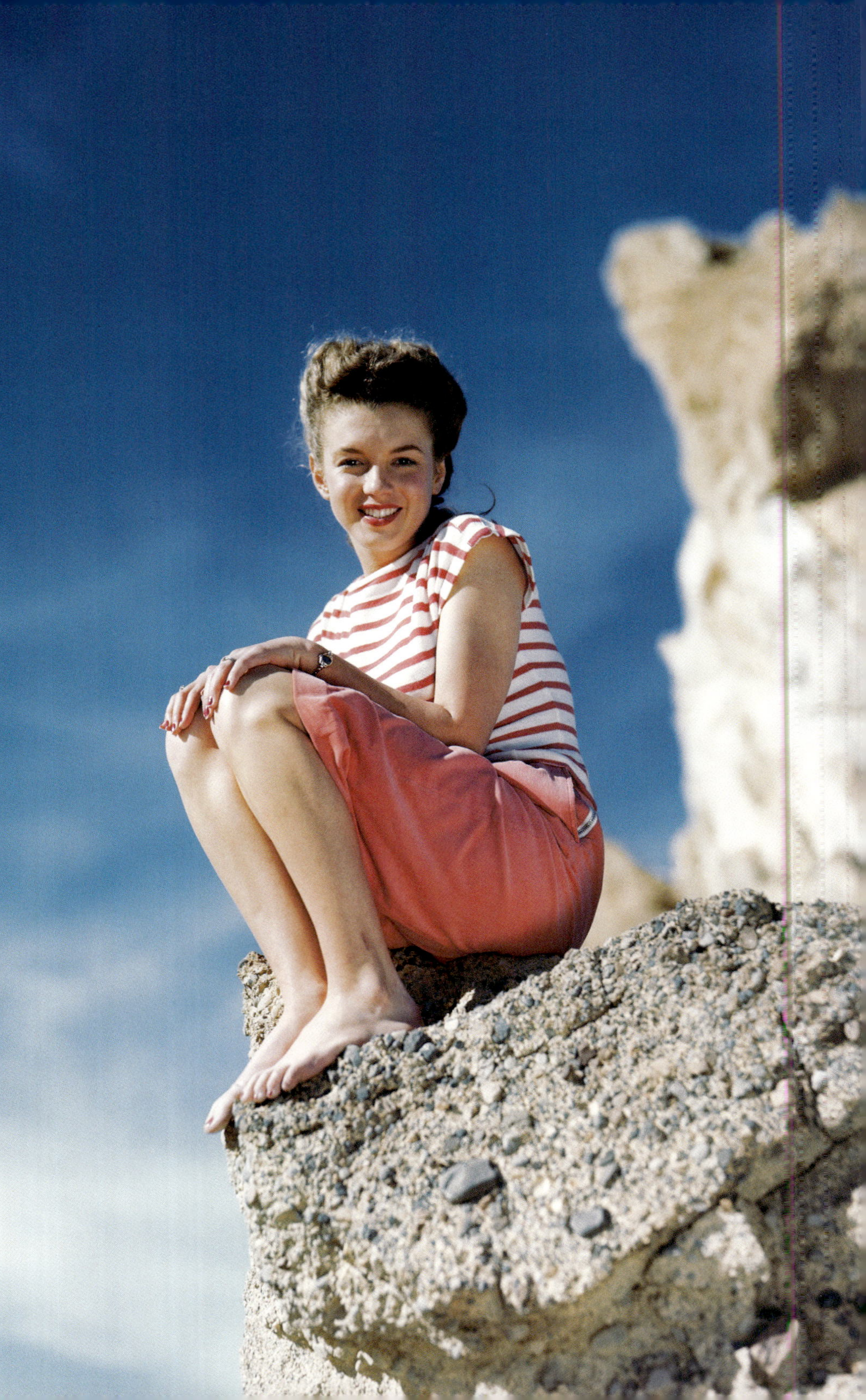

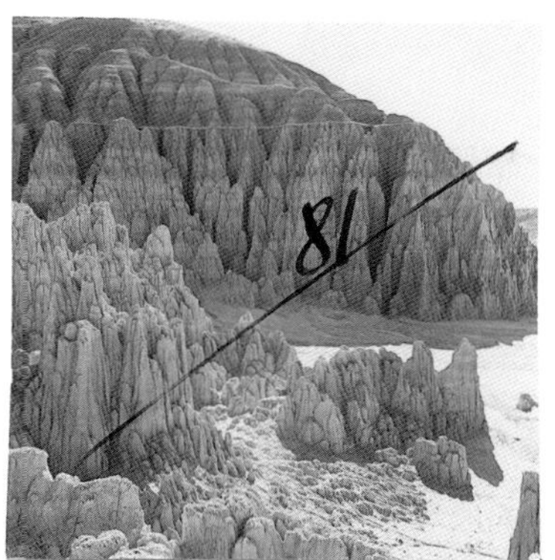

We were parking right here

<u>Cathedral Gorge</u>   I decided to visit a scenic wonder, far north of Las Vegas, called Cathedral Gorge State Park. It turned out to be a fantastic place, an incredible maze of mountains eroded by thousands if not millions of years of rainfalls and windstorms, eroded in such a curious way that only the photographic camera can prove. There I thought I might take nudes of Norma Jeane, because that unusual scenery fascinated my imagination. But it turned out otherwise.

As I was unloading my photo equipment, two hoodlum-looking characters approached us, offering us guidance to some of the most unusual and remote places there, that few visitors would ever be able to visit otherwise. But I was no fool; I sensed danger. I declined the offer, saying I came to take a few pictures and that I loved photographing the morning sunlight, and that I did not need any guides. The two fellows were examining Norma Jeane with envious eyes while directing jealous and hostile glances at me, but they walked away to a nearby outhouse.

Since we had parked in the very center of that amazing canyon, I did venture to take a few photos. For protection, I always had a sharp old sword underneath the front seat of the car, and I handed it to Norma Jeane to carry. In my camera case, I also had an Indian hunting knife, so with those in our possession I felt somewhat protected while I was snapping a few pictures. But then we saw the two fellows coming toward us. Norma Jeane and I ran to the car as fast as we could. I pushed her in, threw my equipment in, and we took off just in time to escape from something frightening – rape, or murder! The men were running toward us when we escaped. Even now, I shudder thinking of it.

Norma Jeane did not think much of the incident. As usual, she just laughed with lots of humor, from her heart, and she said I just worried too much. I insisted that we had escaped being murdered, and I made her swear she would never tell her Aunt Ana that I had exposed her to such danger.

I really laugh now, thinking how, all of a sudden, I took off from Hollywood with a pretty girl and engaged into facing the most rugged desert territory of the western part of the U.S., where I was a total stranger and my automobile tires were all worn and gas was not easy to find. Yet I adore laughing about it because when one is in love, one can be nearly insane! I am astonished now, while thinking back to all that: me, a young man, under some hypnotic influence, enamored of a 19-year-old pretty young girl, traveling, driving around, willy-nilly in the wilderness, having not the slightest sure idea of what he wants to do, where he is traveling to, and for what purpose!

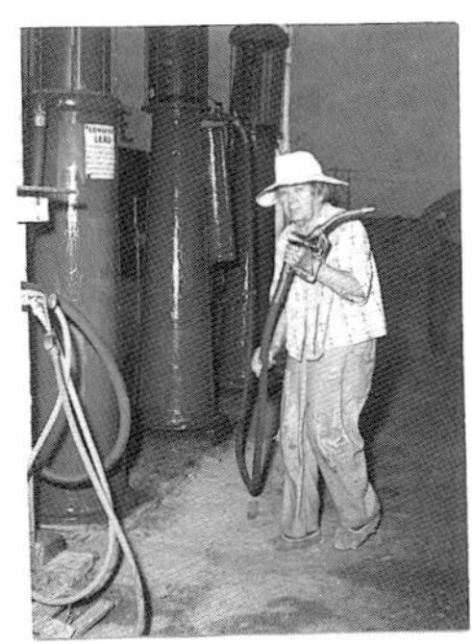

THE OLD LADY AT THE GAS STATION, IN THE DESERT

<u>A Change in Plans</u> In the next twenty-four hours, I drove hundreds of miles south, all the way along the Colorado River, sometimes on terrible roads where only foolhardy people travel. But the desert was absolutely magnificent everywhere! A tire blew out on the main highway to Yuma, just before we would have driven through many miles of sand dunes.

To our great surprise, the person who owned the gas station was an old woman, very western looking, with a cigarette in her mouth. When I told her I planned to visit Picacho Camp, north of Yuma, and explore Superstition Mountain up in Arizona to look for gold, she said I was insane! Furthermore, she said the weather was changing; the windstorm would create a fantastic dust storm across the sand dunes, and if I tried to go across, we would never emerge alive!

While I was installing an old, recapped tire I purchased (World War II had just ended and new tires were still almost impossible to find), the two ladies got acquainted. She was interrogating Norma Jeane about who she was, where from, etc. and Norma Jeane divulged to her that she had a mother who was just released from a sanatorium for mental disorders, who was staying in a hotel in Portland, Oregon. At that, the old lady began lecturing me: "Never mind the childish, foolish ideas to search for gold" – I had the gold right there with me (Norma Jeane) and she instructed me: "Young man, take your girl up to Portland to see her mother!"

Norma Jeane was looking at me with questioning eyes, as if to ask me if I would drive up to Oregon to see her mother. But I said, "No, let's not chicken out! Let's go to Arizona!" Then she confessed that she was scared to go, and she was scared the day before, too, when the two hoodlums were running after us. But she did not want to spoil my happy, adventurous plans, so she kept silent.

I decided we would not go to Arizona to roam the mountains, but we would take pictures in the sand dunes which were just a few miles from the gas station. And then, afterward, we would go to Oregon. The old lady was right: we had hardly entered the region of the sand dunes when the wind began to blow stronger and stronger. The road was just a one-lane, unpaved road, winding like a snake. Luckily, I could make a U-turn and we returned before the wind created an immense dust storm.

I had consumed a few bottles of beer after we left the old lady and rented a motel room, begging Norma Jeane to take a shower and to relax. And there she was, stark naked, reclining on the bed, reading a newspaper, but our thoughts were extremely perplexing. Neither she nor I wished to start out on a sexual venture. There was a short period of silence, mute nervousness in us both, and I asked her to get dressed. I did not want her to do any favors for me! Love ought to be mutual!

Yosemite From the lowest part of Southern California, where we started the trip, to Portland, Oregon is easily at least 1,200 miles of driving; for the love of Norma Jeane, and to earn her respect, I was driving day and night toward the north. Fantastic what one can endure when young and enthusiastic! I drove all night long in steady pouring rain toward Yosemite, and at daybreak it was snowing very hard as we were slowly driving down into the Yosemite Valley. The large hotel and the lodge in Yosemite were all filled with skiers; no rooms were available. No beds in the dormitory either. Not even cabins nearby; the only cabins available were unheated log cabins, much further away in the woods. Of course, I rented two. I had no choice; we were exhausted. The cabins were simple, small, with just a bed and a small table, but everything was very clean. No bathroom. Her cabin was a few feet away from mine. The outhouses were a few hundred feet away. It was very cold, and although it was only afternoon, we went to bed fully clothed.

During the night, I was awakened by banging on the cabin door. She had something to ask me. She said she was afraid to go to the "john" by herself; she was afraid of the bears, and would I please accompany her there? I remembered my uncle telling me, when I was a child in Transylvania, that wolves, bears, and all wild animals hated loud noises, so I emptied a large can of tomato juice and while Norma Jeane walked with the flashlight to the outhouse, I walked behind her, beating the empty can furiously with a spoon to make as much noise as I could. I chuckle every time I think of that funny "procession" through the snow to the "john" and back to the cabins!

The next morning, she told me she felt very embarrassed. I took her in my arms, hugged her, kissed her, and promised I would make up for it, make her forget that awful night. We went to the lodge and while she took a shower in the dormitory, I bought her a complete winter sports outfit at the gift shop. Two sweaters, ski pants, bright red woolies for undergarments, several kinds of ski bonnets to keep her ears warm, wool socks, ski boots, ski gloves, and a beautiful Indian silver and turquoise concho belt, the kind you only find in the Indian trading posts, way out on the reservations.

By the time she was back from the shower, there was a heap of merchandise on the counter, all for her. There were nearly tears in her eyes, she was so happy! As soon as she put those things on, in her cabin, we left Yosemite. It was much too cold there. Her hands were purple from the cold. It was a great adventure, and funny. I love to reminisce about it.

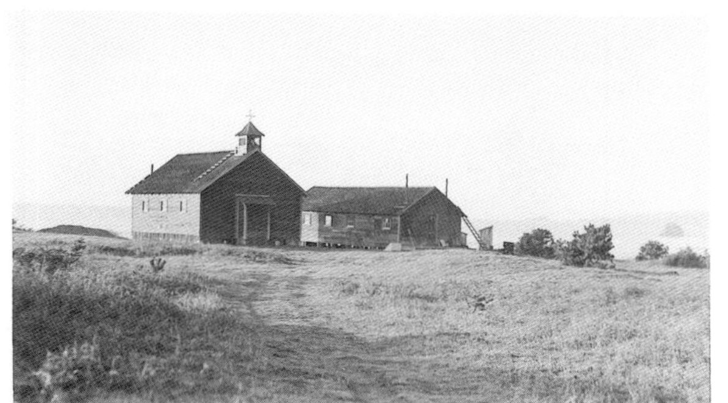
RUSSIAN CHURCH, NORTHERN CALIF.

Your Crazy Hungarian A very funny thing happened on the seacoast, somewhere north of San Francisco. I was going to photograph Norma Jeane against an old church built of unpainted wood, but by the time she got ready with her makeup, an old woman ran to us screaming that we were on Russian territory! I could not believe what she was talking about, yet she was dead serious. I thought she must have been drunk or crazy. She was going to whack at me and at Norma Jeane.

The unpleasant behavior of the furious old woman did not abash us for too long. Norma Jeane was laughing in disbelief; I felt I needed some wine to calm myself, and by the time we stopped at a motel, I was rather tipsy. I asked the lady manager in the office for a pair of adjoining single cabins, connected! The lady looked at me, surprised. She looked out the window where my car was parked, and she saw Norma Jeane waiting in it. And she asked me, "Are you two married?" I could not lie, I said, "No". Domineering like a mother, she yelled at me, "Separate cabins!" And she handed me the keys and asked me to register our names. The cabins were five dollars each.

And again, from wanting her, I felt tormented all night and I could hardly sleep. During the night, I sprang to my feet and wrote Norma Jeane a letter, and went to slip it under her door. It amazes me how vividly my mind can remember certain details; I think these were almost the exact words I wrote to her:

TRAVELLING WITH NORMA JEAN. (Dec. 1945)

In the days what followed, I bought Norma Jeane various clothes to wear for my pictures, and to keep warm, because, it was December, AND my plans were to visit the desert, the mountains, everywhere in California, in Nevada, in Arizona, anywhere my fancy would dictate going. I removed the back seat of my big Buick "ROADMASTER" automobile, and layed down a sheet of thick foam-rubber, and blankets ON TOP, and pillows all around, so Norma Jeane could sleep, there whenever she wished to lay down to rest, during the long drives I was planning to do. That was TO BE her little "cage"..as I called it. And she loughed like CRAZY when I told her she shall becаome my little slave, and my prisoner; and THAT I might even buy a long thin chain, to attach one end to her ankle, and the other end to the car ! Her hatbox WAS full of her things, and a small suitcase was placed also in her "cage," plus a basketful of food, and thermos bottles for milk, and for coffee, etc. The trunk of the car was for my equipment, and the front seat, next to me, was also for her, with pillows against the door, to give her as much comfort as possible. And thus, the long journey began.

We were hardly OUT in the outskirts of Los Angeles, when the police patrol stopped me for faulty driving. Norma Jeane was sitting close to me, AND the policeman might have felt jealous! He said, I was zig-zagging across the center dividing line, and thinking I might BE have been intoxicated, he ordered me to follow him to the police station. I wasn't intoxicated at all! Nor have we zigzagged accross the center line! In those times the procedure was that the motorist STOPPED must follow the police to the POLICE headquarter, and pay the fine, cash, and will be freed again.

Norma Jeane felt very indignent. In her sweet voice, she riposted to the policeman that he was UNJUST, AND HE WAS a crook; we had done NO FAULTY DRIVING nothing wrong, and I told the PATROL man it was my policy never to argue with the police. The man, part seriously, part jokingly, said to Norma Jeane, that if she cared to stay there for the night, he would not make us pay the fine. I paid the twenty dollars, and we continued the trip. The reason I care to mention

1945

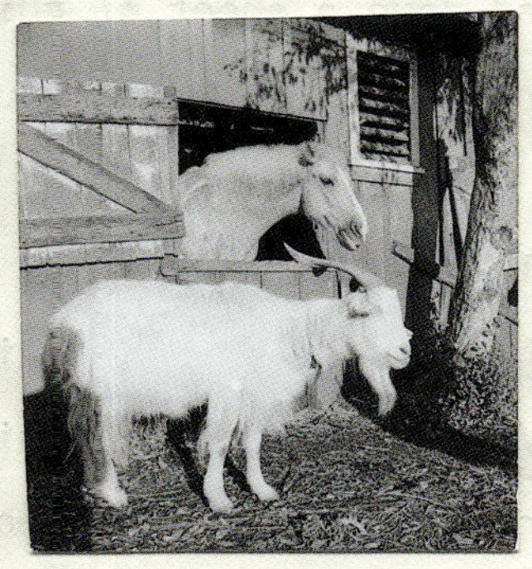

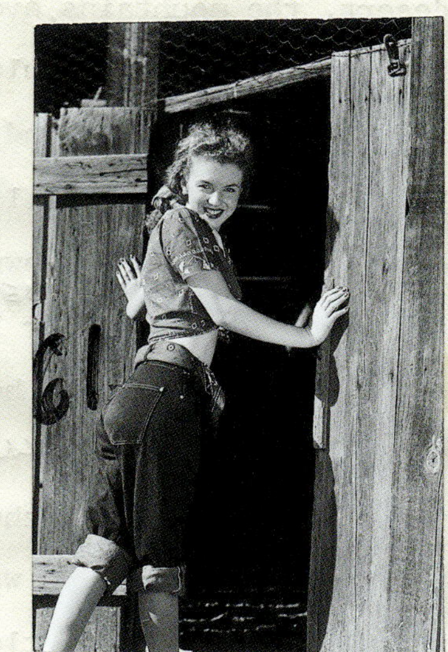

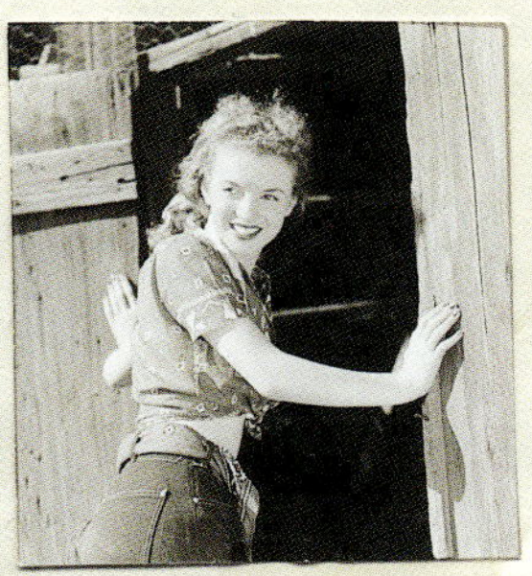

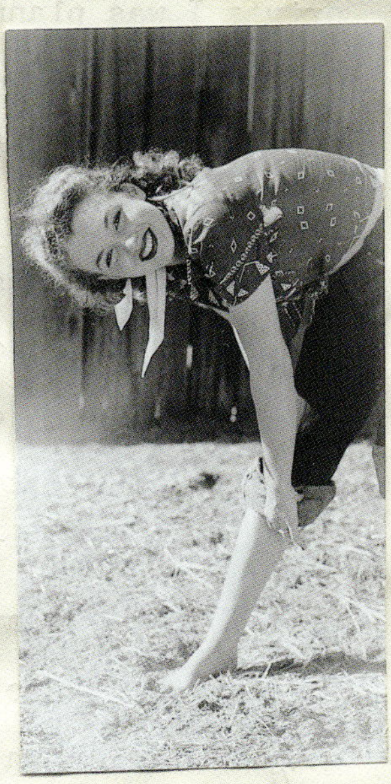

ON A FARM,
NORMA JEANE WAS
FEEDING THESE
ANIMALS

Nov-Dec. 1945

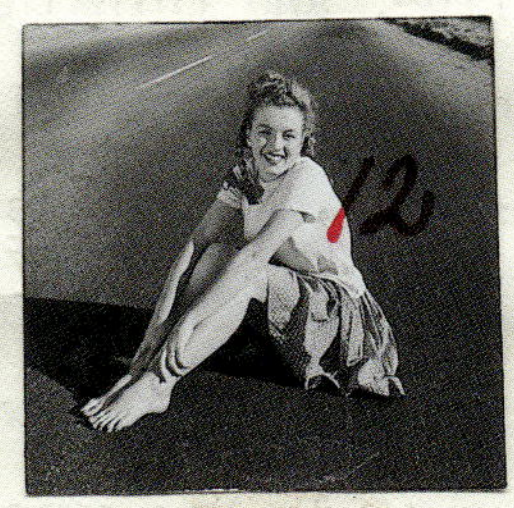

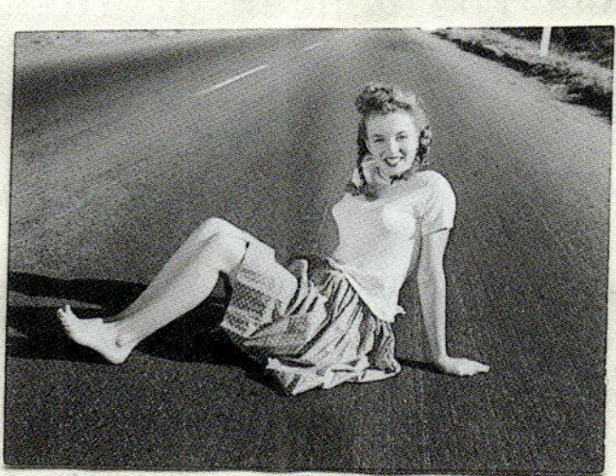

this insignificant incident is that that was only the first proposal she got on that trip! Amazingly, at various places we stopped, people began proposing something to her! A garage mechanic said he would give his left arm if she would stay and become his wife! A miner in the mountains said he wanted her and he would give her everything he had! A young farmer said he was looking for a woman of her beauty! The owner of a motel proposed to her! A grocery store clerk also! And the haberdasher where I stopped to buy her jeans, and rugged shoes, which she would need in the wilderness, went nearly out of his mind wanting to see Norma Jeane try on various garments in the little dressing closet where people tried on things before buying them. He wanted to see Norma Jeane in that warm, "long-John" country style long underwear, I bought for her one the cold nights in the mountains. Like a magnet, she attracted all men! I became reluctant, even cautious, stoppping wherever there were men around! She good humoredly loughed everywhere, and gently apologized to the men that she is unable to stay..... She did not tell me so, but I knew she was very pleased! So that's how the legend of Marilyn Monroe began right away! Every man was crazy about her! Strange, how fate works!

But, I better start again describing the trip in chronological order. After we left the police station, I asked her to stand on the highway, barefeet, fixing her hair in pigtails, to impersonate Krisztina, the maid, in my childhood. While taking her pictures like that in a sudden, strange phsychic revelation, stemming from my unconscious, over which I had absolutely no command, I began pointing at the small white stars on her red skirt, and began prognosticating that those stars meant that some day, she shall become very famous! A famous movie star!! For a while I was talking, babbling about a future, fabulous life for her, telling almost incoherently that the road behind her symbloizes life, and those moments I took the pictures of her, were the first photos of her future success to come! Yet, after I spoke, I asked myself why have I said those things? What possessed me to say those things, and

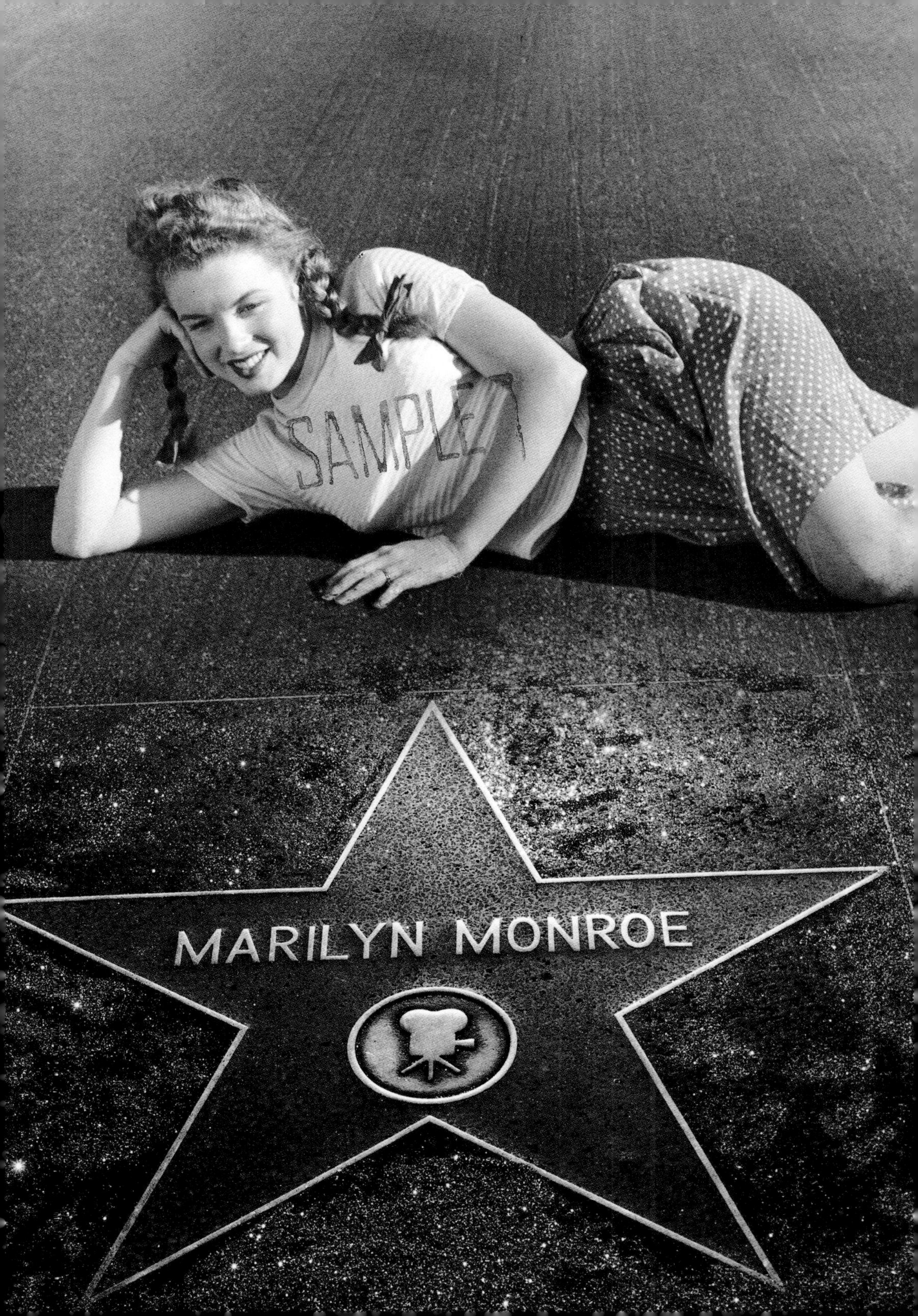

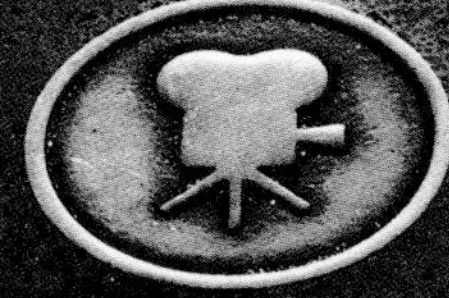
SAMPLE
MARILYN MONROE

predict to her that some day she shall become famous, and the photographs we shall take of her will become part of Hollywood's history ! I suppose, in those moments of excitement, unconsciously, I followed the mental suggestions of my friend in New York, who prognosticated to me that with the second girl I shall meet on that trip to Hollywood -- I shall make history ! And I just kept repeating, what my friend have predicted a few week before !

I did not tell anything about the to Norma Jeane, nor did she seem to take my words seriously. That was the first day she started to pose for me on that trip; she was on a modelling job with me, and all she probably cared for was the hundred dollars I promised to pay her for each week of travelling with me, and posing for photographs, nude or otherwise ! Neither me, nor her had the faintest idea that, indeed, year later she shall become so famous! Or maybe I did, because some of the pretty girls I photographed the year before had made name for themselves in the movies. And my photographs of beautiful girls were much in demand by the magazines. (Again, this sounds like braggings; But I can't help it; those were the facts !) And having pictures on magazine covers and having write-ups and pictures inside the magazine were almost a sure beginning to success in those days when glamour photography was only in its beginning stages, and millions of soldiers were admiring my photographs of pretty girls. In fact, the formula for success have not changed at all. If a girl wants a career in the movies, the first things she needs is pictures and write ups in magazines, lot's of sex - appeal, and lots of exposure to men who love beautiful women ! The more guts she has to do it, the better ! Men will always favor women who appeals to them ! That's only natural !

I was a good photographer, and Norma Jeane took the chance to pose for me, travel with me, and her picture appeared on the cover of a magazine a few months later.

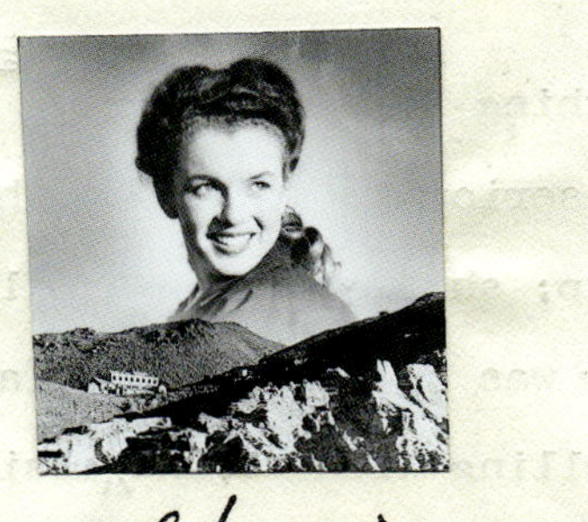

at a gold mine in the desert
(but Norma Jeane was my gold!)

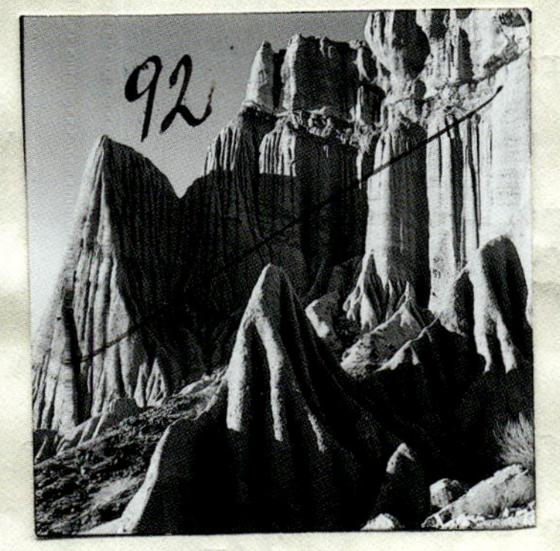

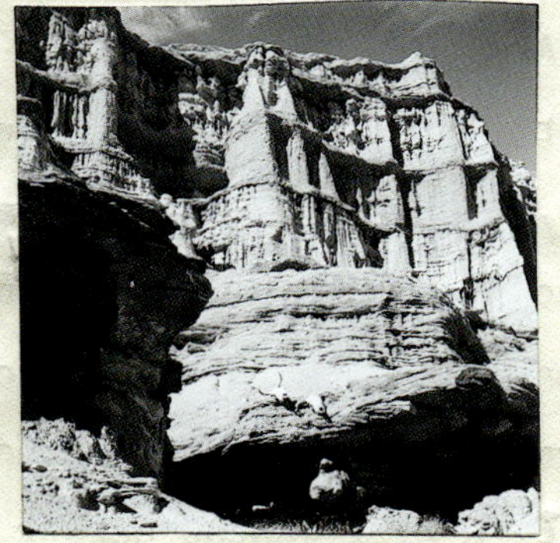

Red Rock canyon.

Again, instead of photographing her nude, I took pictures of her dressed, sitting on rocks etc. And, since the desert seemed so beautiful, so tranquil to both of us, I spread out a blanket, and I was reading to her from a quotation book I brought along, quotations about most everything what touches spiritual life, all sort of philosophical thoughts by great men, long dead already. Norma Jeane listened attentively, and than she took out from her handbag her Christian Science prayer book, and she red for me too. While she was reading, I had the urge to push her hair away from her forehead, and to remark that she had a "great forehead" -- large, wide, something like Beethoven's ! And I said, there must be a great deal of brain inside it ! Did she know who Beethoven was ? I did not ask her. I just kept gently rubbing her forehead, and she seemed very pleased, smiling at me with a birarre, enigmatic smile.

Later that day, after I took more photos of her, something peculiar happened to me, again, what I never forgot: I began prognosticating to her that she shall become one of the world's most photographed woman; and that some day, when I shall be old, I shall write a book about myself, and about many women I photographed ; and I shall be writing about her, in a cave, in the desert; because I love the desert, and I love solitude. And I was telling her that when I will become old, I shall live in a cave, and write my memoirs, and much of what I shall write will be about her. And I kept telling her over and over again that she shall become very famous !

MEMO: The reader might think I am making up this story, but I am not ! It happened as I tell it ! And the funny thing is, that, when I began writing this book, I took a trip to the desert, where I stayed in a cave-like opening in the wall of a mountain, I stayed there two nights, sleeping on blankets, and I was sitting for two days on a rock, writing the first pages of this book, just to make my prognostications come through! Otherwise, I am not too fond of living in caves! I love hot and cold running water, I love to take two showers each day; I love a full refrigirator, and I love to get lots of mail. And I love to be in my drakroom finishing beautiful photographic enlargments of my best photos. Actually, being all day in my darkroom is almost like being in a cave. If there wasn't a radio to listen to, I would feel completely isolated from civilisation. And during the months I am writing this book, and preparing the photo illustrations for it -- It's like living in complete isolation. And to make it even more realistic, and true, I gathered at the seashore AND IN THE DESERT tons of rocks and brought them home to my backyard, in many installments. And now, I am typing this story among rocks, lots and lots of rocks, to have the feeling that I am out in the wilderness, as I have told to Norma Jeane that it will happen — SOME DAY..

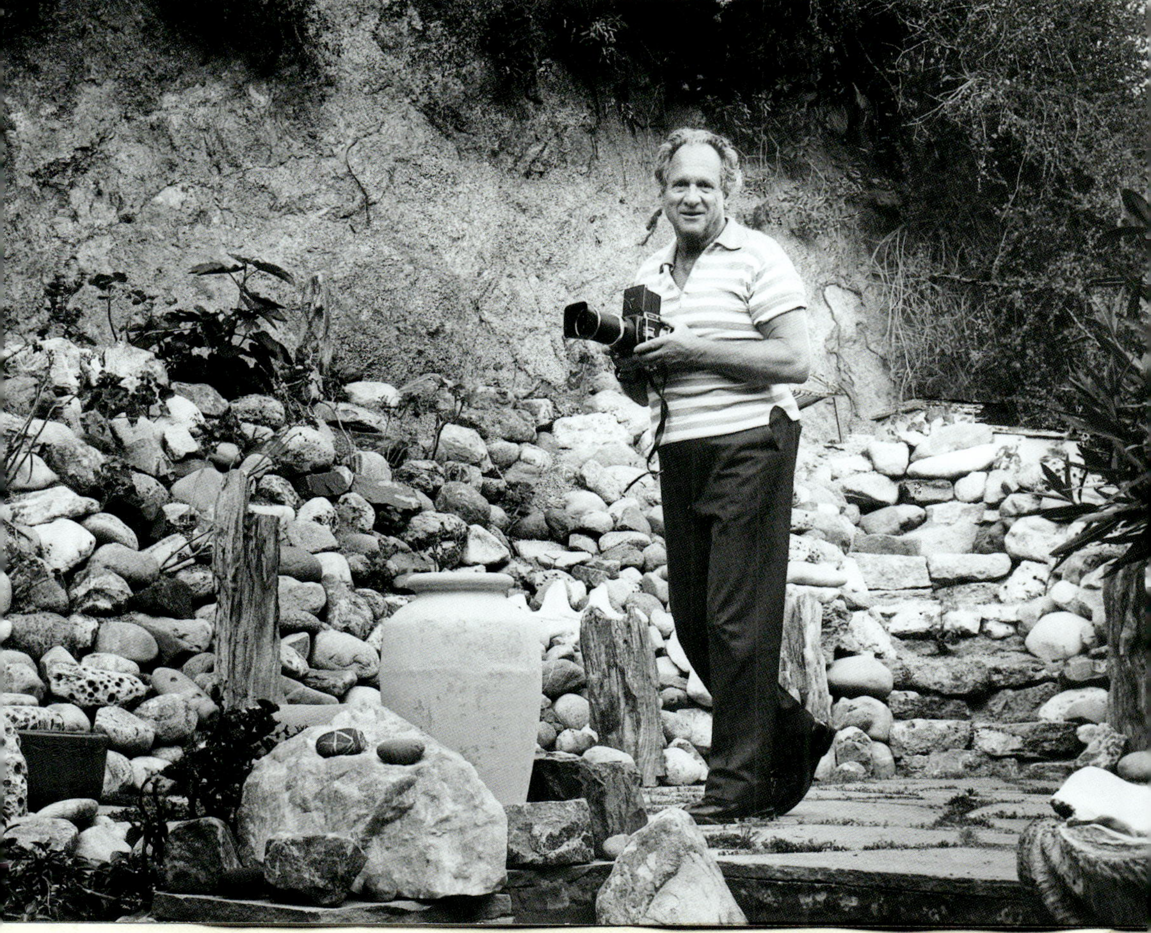

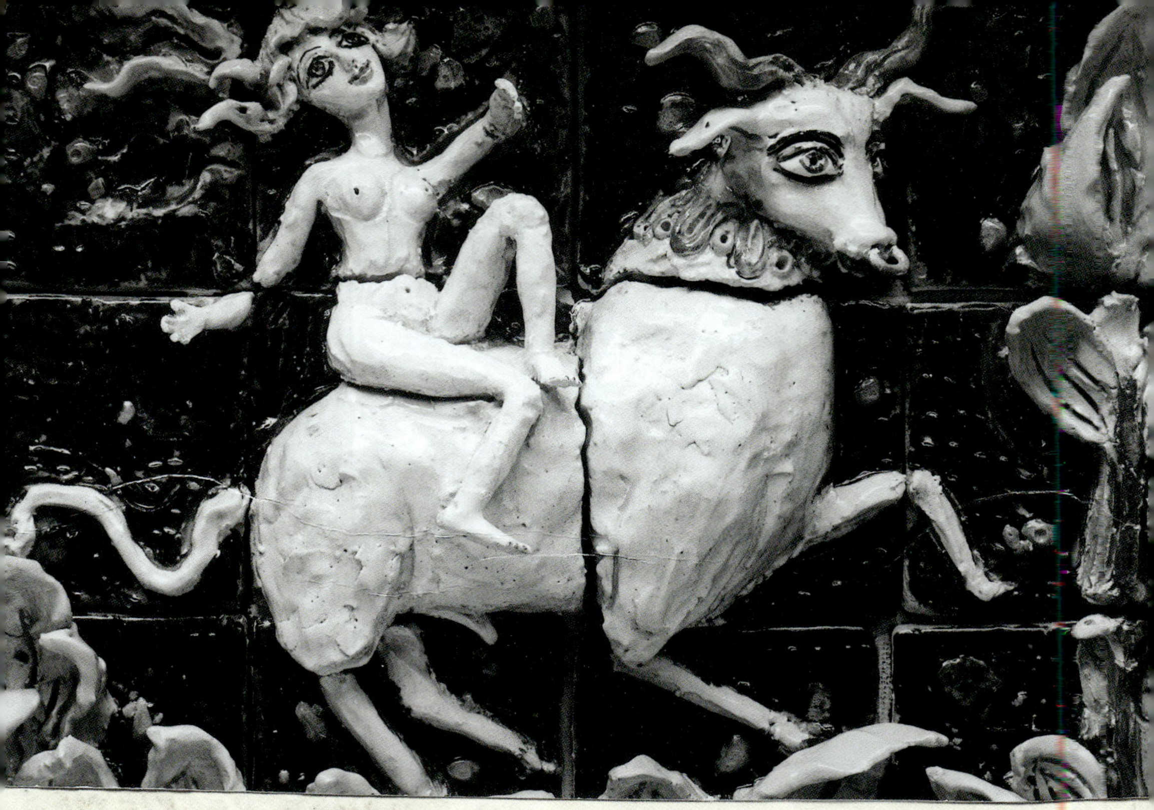

"EUROPA"

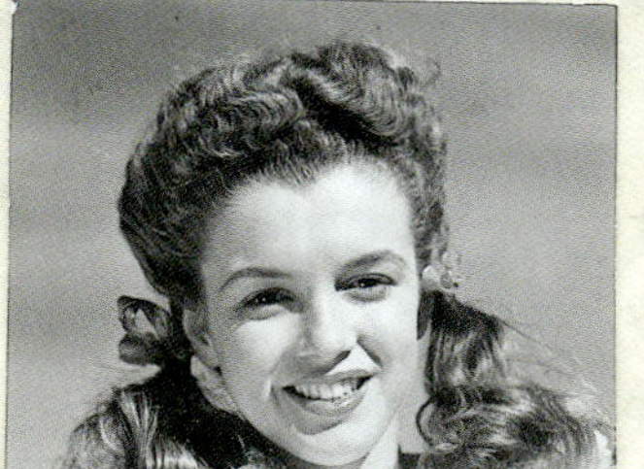

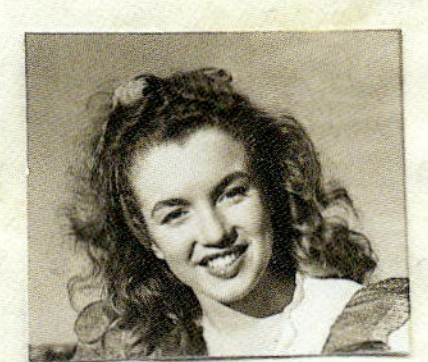

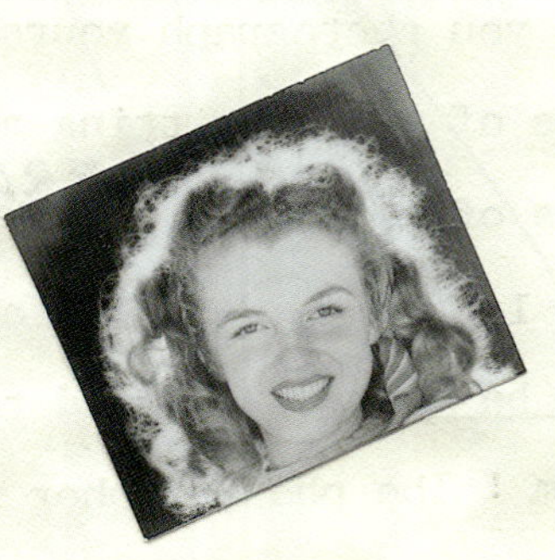

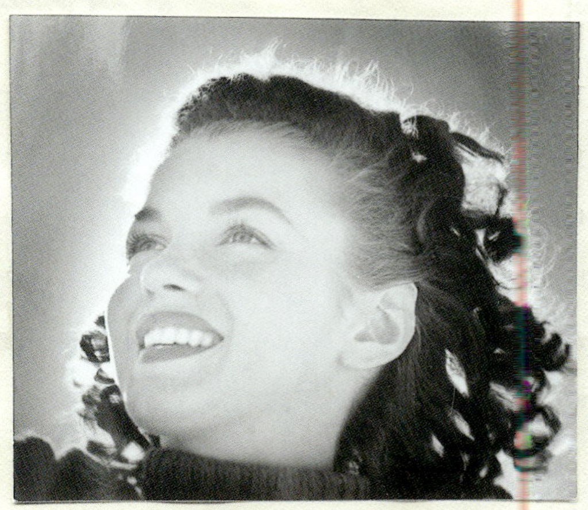

Just as I left Transylvania on foot when I was fourteen years of age, to cross Europe, because I wanted to end up in the american West, this time, all my past comings and goings, and doings culminated in that trip with Norma Jeane. I felt that, that mysterious prefixed goal in the crux of my mind came to reality for me with Norma Jeane. Driving to Death Valley was only the first day's fancy of my mind. The second night with her, was like fleeing into the future; I drove all night through an extremely desolated section of southern Nevada; —

I was in a delirium of complete happiness. I told Norma Jeane I felt like God "Zeus," from the Greek mythology, who, having observed from heaven a beautiful young shepherdess tending her flock, on a beautiful, flower-covered field, disguised himself into a bull and pleaded gently the pretty shepherdess to mount on his back. Than, abducted her by flying accross the oceans, to an island, where he made her his mistress, and she bore children by him. (THE LEGEND OF EUROPA)

I still remember vividly hom much Norma Jean loughed, because I said something, that all those Greek gods and goddesses were most probably ordinary mortals, the elites, the notables of those times, about whom Greek authors and poets invented stories to amuse the public; representing them as deieties, but probably God-Zeus was nothing more than a very wealthy, important man -- who was a crazy "sex-maniac," and abducted the sweet little shepherdess! And now, I was Zeus, I was abducting her, Norma Jean! I never heard Norma Jean lough so hard!

She wanted to hear more mythological stories. I think I told a few more, but the converstaion drifted to ourselves, to our own lives, and mainly about myself. She wasn't too talkative a person, She told me stories about her childhood, most of what I do not remember -- to be frank, And some, I remember, but they were written up by various writers and newspaper reporters, much slanted, and probably very much exagerated. She preferred to listen to me. I have always been a good talker, when some one who inspires me to open up my mind...

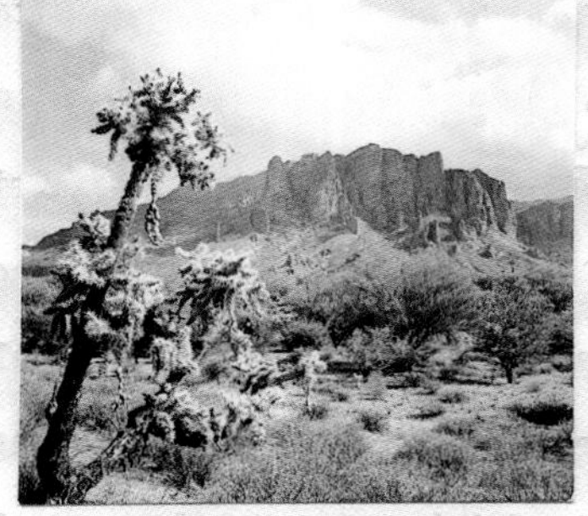

THE SUPERSTITION MOUNTAIN, ARIZONA.

THE SOUTH SIDE.
BEHIND IT IS A FORBIDDING TERRITORY
WHERE MANY ADVENTURERS LOST THEIR LIVES IN THE 1800'S
(AND STILL DO! EVEN NOW!)

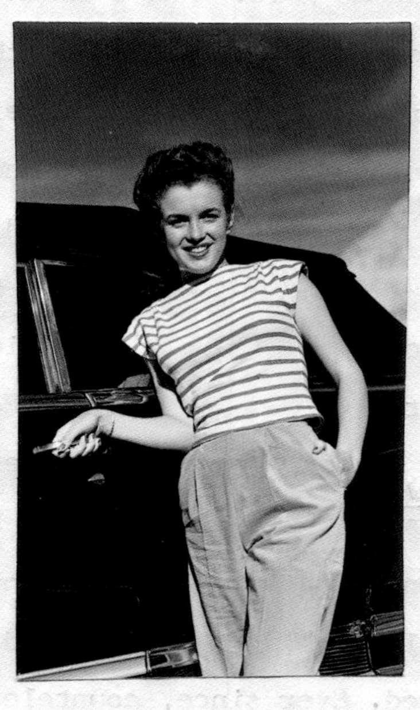

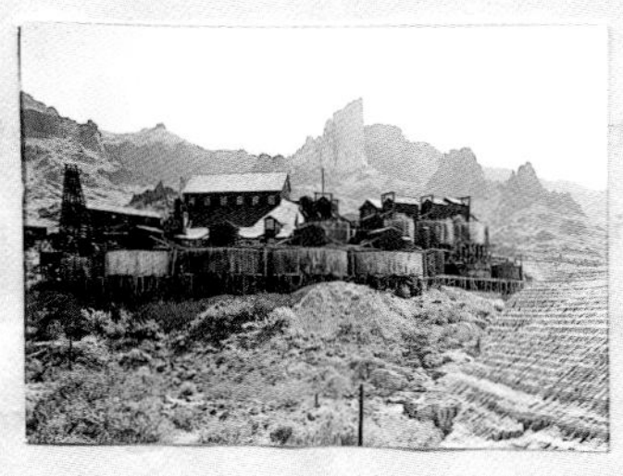

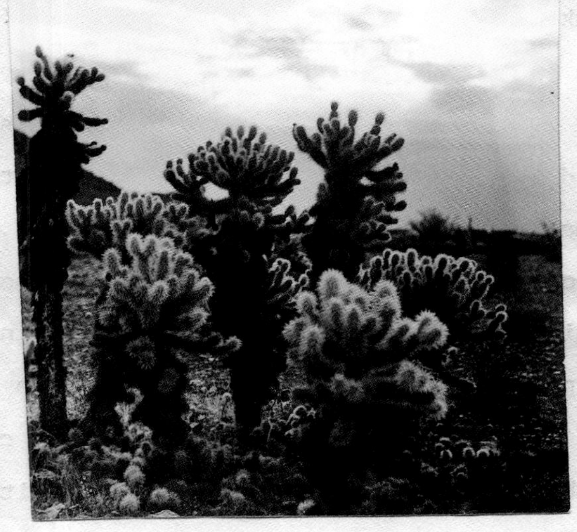

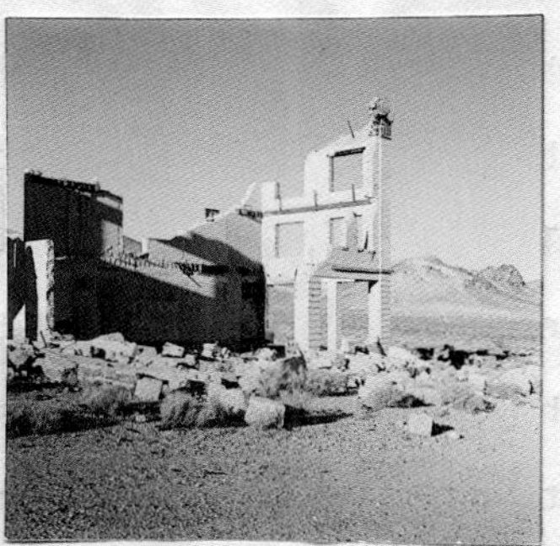

Nevada, ghost town

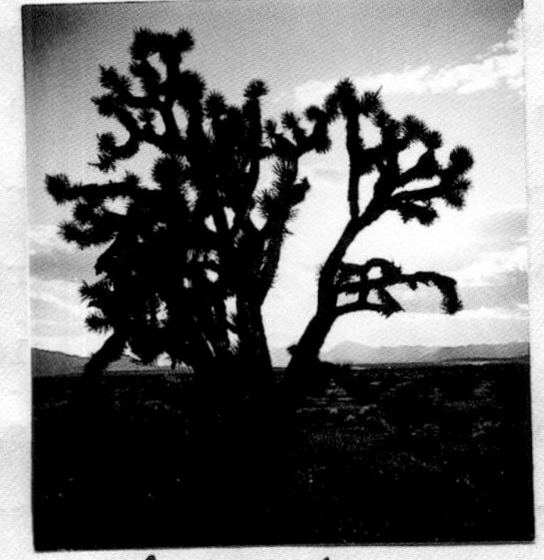

Sunset, the wide open desert

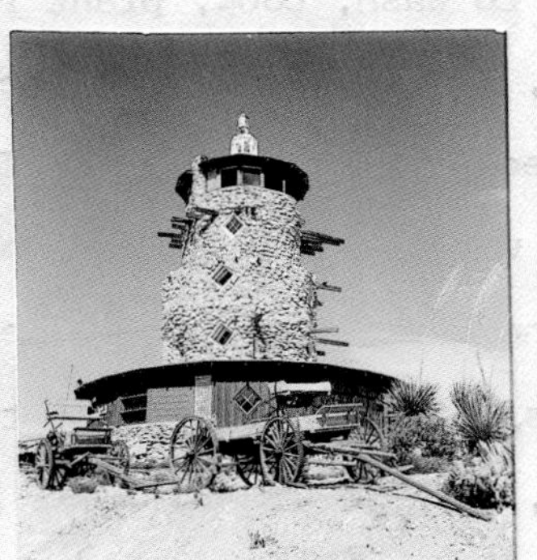

One of my "dreams" was to build my own "castle"!
This one, too, is one, overlooking the desert.
Some one built it for fun!

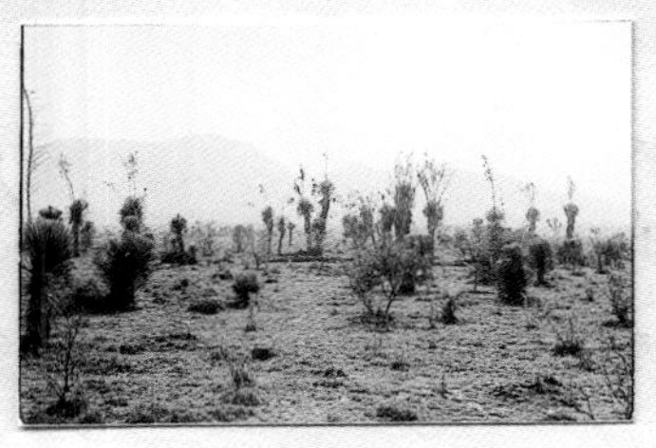

While Norma Jeane slept, I was thinking that America was still far too unexploited from its rich ore deposits all throughout that immense expanse of land throughout the entire western sates; the gold rush a century before, was just a fast, passing event, there must be much more gold yet to be found, if only one takes the pain and effort to look for it ! And what an incredible thing it IS that there ARE, literrally, millions of people idling, not knowing what to do with their lives, when the desert is still so unexploited. I was driving more than a hundred miles without seeing a single sign of human inhabitation, while Norma Jeane was sleeping, I could not see even a trace of mankind inhabiting that region, except the paved highway, AND the scenery was breathtakinly beautiful! The sun went down, the sky was purple, it was like driving through a totally unexplored region of the globe ! A Complete desert all over ! Vast, beautiful land ! (Could have been bought for very little.)

And while driving through all that, I was day-dreaming, I shall become rich, and build for Norma Jeane another castle like the one "Scotty" built in Death Valley. (Walter Scott, an ex rodeo rider, built the castle with a multi-millionaire's money) It took fifteen years to build it)

But my mind wondered away into another direction, thinking I ALSO shall photograph her for years to come, while travelling with her, world over, and publish her photos in magazines, and in books I would publish. And there WOULD BE no end to what we COULD do together through our lives. I had these kind of " dreams" in New York. I even spoke to a lovely young lady about that, whom I liked. (but she married another photographer, Eliot Elisofon, who worked for LIFE magazine) But now, I had Norma Jeane: I would realize my dreams with her ! So were my thoughts, while the future Marilyn Monroe slept, and dreamt of who knows what, and awoke later, and ate some cottage cheese from the food basket she had in the car nearby. SHE handed me coffee from the thermos bottle, while I was speeding through the wilderness in the dark of the night. And she did not EVEN ask where were we, what time was it, AND she did not complain it was getting very chilly in the car. (the heater did not work) She did not light a cigarette, she did not wish she could have a "drink," or champagne, AND Sweet, darling, Norma Jeane, was willing and happy to step into the cold night, and gaze at the sky with me for a little while, and she, too, was breathless by the beauty of the universe, as we pointed at the various big stars (in " ORION", the wonder of the sky, the most splendid of all heaven) Not a word came out from her mouth about Hollywood, about career in the movies, about movie stars. She was LIKE an angelic little female! She did not even ask where shall we sleep that night!

It was night when we stopped at Las Vegas to gas up. The town was dazzling with lights, but Norma Jeane wan't interested to see the town. She must have been there before, because she mentioned she knew a darling little chapel there, where she would like to marry again -- some day. (And I felt,she was thinking about me !)

A funny thing happened there before we left. At a slot machine, I told her to stretch her sweather under the machine, because a jackpot will be gushing out. To impress her, I told her I was psychic. And she believed it! After I put in the quater, and she pulled the handle, ten dollars worth of quarters fell into her sweather. She wanted another try, but I told her, no! Next Time! Intuitive feelings must not be abused ! She has to wait until I am ready for such a thing, again!

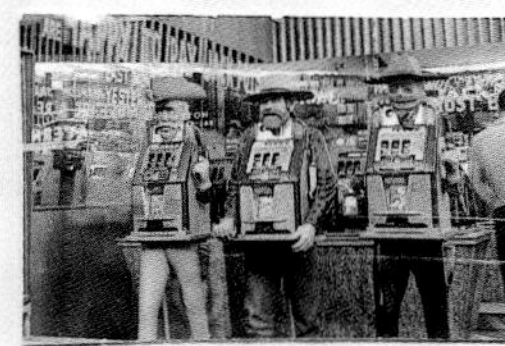

LAS VEGAS DOWNTOWN 1945

It would have been far better to stay in Las Vegas to enjoy our-selves, and luxuriate in a big Hotel, and sunbath at the poolside, but I was too young to waste my life away like that, though I had regrets about it a few hours later that night, I felt so exhusted, I just pul-led up near a gas station, and we slept in the car until dawn, and than the adventure continued. I decided to visit a scenic wonder, far north of Las Vegas, called " Cathedral Gorge State Park ", and It turned out to be a fantastic place, an incredible maze of mountains eroded by thousands if not millions of years of rainfalls and windstorms, eroded in such a curious ways what only the photographic camera could prove. There, I thought I might take nudes of Nudes of Norma Jeane, because that unusual scenery fascinated my imagination, after all, that very strange part of the western scenery what really excited me ever since childhood, when in books I have seen drawings, paintings of the weirdest rock formations and lo, there was I, with a beautiful girl ! So why not ! I must take nudes ! But it turned out otherwise.

As I was unloading my photo equipment, two hoodloom-looking cha-racters approached us, offering us guidance to some of the most unusual and remote places there few visitors would ever be able to visit other-wise, unless guided by experts. (There was no ranger station there at all, only a delapidating outhouse for men and women.) But I was no fool. I sensed danger. I declined the offer saying I came to take a few pictures, I loved photographing in the morning sunlight; and I was in a great hurry, and I did not need guides. The two fellows were examining Norma Jeane with envious eyes, but they walked away to that nearby outhouse.

Since we had parked in the very center of that amazing canyon, I did venture to take a few photos. For self-defense, I always had a sharp old sward underneath the front seat of the car, and I handed it to Norma Jeane to carry it, while in my camera case I had a hunting

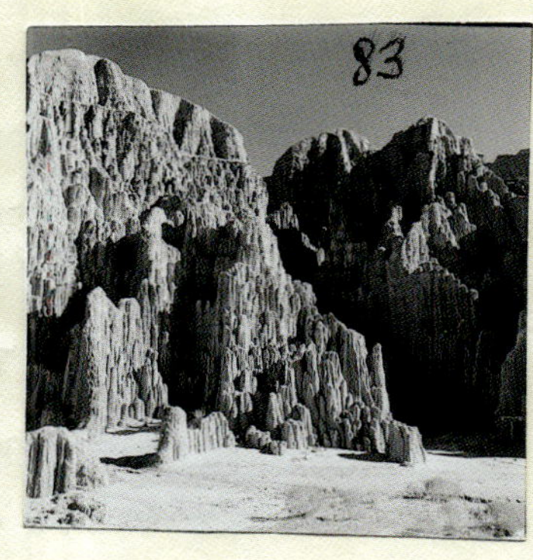

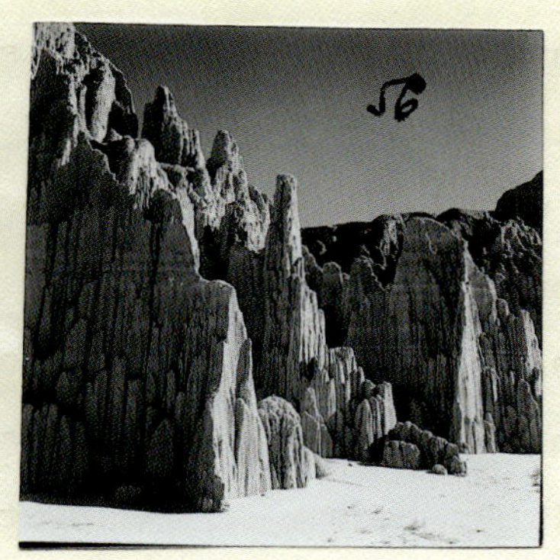

CATHEDRAL GORGE STATE PARK, NEVADA.
(SOUTH OF ELY – EASTERN NEVADA.)

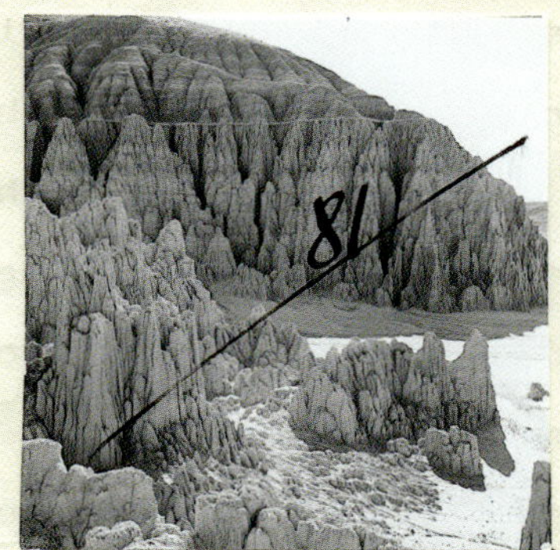

We were parking right here

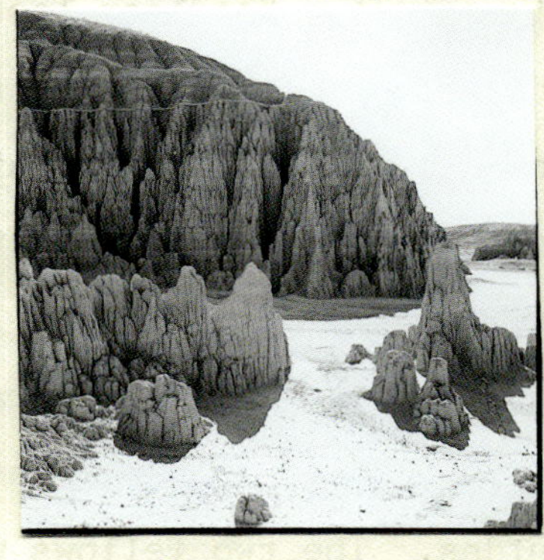

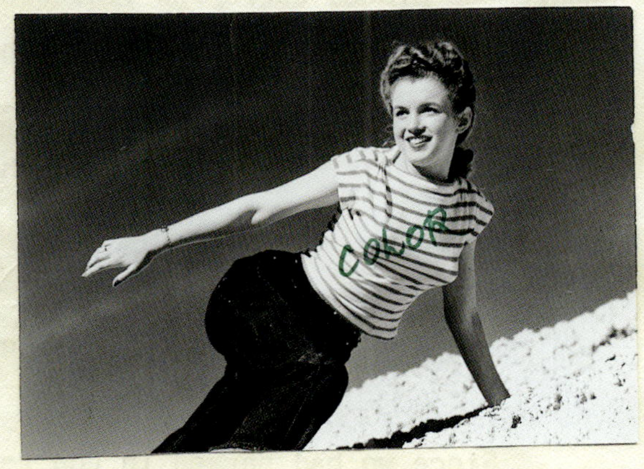

knife from India, strong and real sharp, so with those in our possession I felt somewhat protected while I was snapping a few pictures. But than, we sow the two fellows coming toward us. Norma Jeane and I ren to the car as fast as I could, I pushed her in, threw my equipment in, and we took off just on time to escape from something frightening even to think for. Rape, and murder ! The men were running toward us when we escaped. Evan now, I shudder thinking of that incident. Our bones would be still there, burried in a remote canyon; and if in a century or two, some one might have found the remains, they would have thought we were primitive Indians killed perhaps by ferocious animals.

Norma Jeane did not think much of the incident, as usually, she just loghed with lots of humor, in her heart, and she said I just worried too much, and overexagerated my suspicions and feas. I insisted we escaped being murdered ! And I made her swear she would never tell to her aunt Ana, that I had exposed her to such a danger ! I no longer cared to visit my friend's ex wife, and the mines further up north; At the intersection of the main highway, I decided to go down to Southern California, and through the immenses sand dunes near Yuma, over to Arizona. To the reader this might sound nothing at all, but if you took a trip like that, you would know what an immense adventure that is, or was, especially for me, than, when the roads were just primitive, paved and unpaved; riding down along the Colorado River where a century ago before, only explorerers cared to venture; and adventurers, and misionaries, some, who got massacred by the Indians.

I really lough now, thinking of it, that all of a sudden, I took off from Hollywood, with a pretty girl, and I engaged into facing the ruggedest desert territory of the westen part of the U.S. where I was a total stranger, my automobile tires were all worn, and gas was not easy to find. It almost seems to me as if there was a little bit of "insanity" mixed into my quest for adventure. Yet, I adore loughing about it because when one is in love, on can be nearly insane ! I am astonished now, while thinking back to all that ! It all happened with the future, famed Marilyn Monroe ! It's really something to lough about. And shake one's head in disbelief! A young man, under some hypnotic influences, enamored with a 19 years young pretty girl, travelling, ~~running~~ driving around willy-nilly in the wilderness, having not the slightest sure idea of what he wants to do, where is he travelling to, and for what sure purpose !

I am glad I can lough at my own doings ! It was lots of fun ! AND I AM STILL HERE, **TO DO SOME MORE !** GOD, I THANK YOU ! HUMBLY, WITH ALL MY HEART !

When I shall have this book finished, I shall fall in love again ! Maybe even more than ever before !

Even an aging man has the right to start over and overagain. If you can fall in love, it means there is still lot of life left in you !

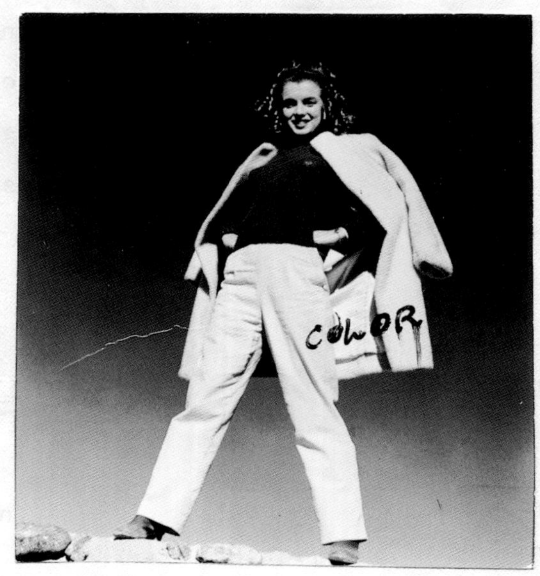

"MY GODDESS"

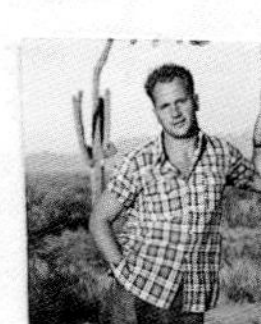
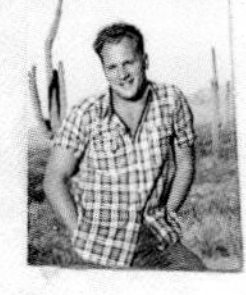

ANDRE DIENES

~~First~~, As I was speeding on the unpaved road, suddenly a tire blew out, and we came to a halt on the side of the road, and we were stuck in the soft sand. The shovel and the pick I brough along for "gold digging" proved to be extremely useful right away, I was shoveling, gathering rocks, smashed down dead MESQUITE TREE branches ~~of bushes~~ with the pick, AND jacked up the car, put on the spare tire, WITH THE BRANCHES I build a short solid track for the car to reach the road. It was a miserable job to do. Norma Jeane wanted to help, but I urged her not to, I suggested she should stay clean and pretty, becuase I wanted to photograph her. She was sitting on a boulder, reading her small Christian Science prayer book, and sometimes watching me, Suddently, I became very emotional, I went to her, AND knelt down in front of her, hugged one of her legs, I kissed it, and I asked her to marry me as soon as possible ! I was pleading her in a soft-spoken manner "- Norma Jeane, get your divorce; please be my wife! I shall be the best husband you could ever find ! Let's start a new life together !" But instead of answering anything to just what I just told her, her eyes got fixed on a large tarantula spider what was slowly crossing the dirt road, just a few feet away from us. It was the most amazing thing that fate had to create that scene for me, exactly at the moment when I was nearly in tears because of my great emotions, But it turned out to be a rather comical event. Norma Jean was much amused by the tarantula. Unafraid, she examined it rather closely, as it finally crossed the road and settled on a large rock. I ren for my camera and took pictures of of her while she was watching the spider from the opposite side of me. The spider was in the center, a perfect foreground for my photo composition of close ups of Norma Jeane. She even dared to lift her hand as if to wanting to pick the spider up with her fingers. The photos I took made me jubilant ! And I was justifying the mishap of the morning with the two hoodlums-- that, if we hadn't gone to see that amazing canyon, we would have never met the tarentula on the road, AND thus, I would not have had the pictures I took of her with THE SPIDER !

186

and I took many beautiful, and exclusively satisfying photographs of nudes. And I did encounter sand storms several times, So bad, that the windshield of the car had to be replaced twice, and the insurance Company refused to insure me [illegible] And once, I did make the trip to the Superstition Mountains [illegible] to explore, but I sort " chickened out ". I [illegible] ped territory. I had a nude model with me [illegible] not to expose her to danger. Just prior to [illegible] remote desert region, the car got stuck in the [illegible] a winding dirtroad inside a canyon. While the [illegible] all night long, I walked about ten miles to the main [illegible] Finally, the highway patrol summoned help for us. The model was a newly married girl, her husband was worried sick for [illegible] why hasn't she come home ? So that's one of the [illegible] what can happen in the wilderness. Still, I [illegible] escapades. No sooner my girl recovered from the [illegible] back again and again to take pictures, for [illegible] The heat, the dryness, and the lack of enough drinking water was [illegible] problems!

The models squandered the water by noon, or early afternoon, and by mid afternoon, or evening, [illegible] until we reached the car. Once, an inexperienced girl [illegible] with the entire supply of drinking water (a two gall [illegible] carried along on the dunes. One hour later, the heat [illegible] we could not take any photos. The entire trip was a total loss, as far as picture taking was concerned. I had to return to L.A. the next day.

COLOR

As for nudes of Norma Jeane, had it not been to the meeting the old lady, and the windstorm what arose, I might now posses some beautiful photos of her, taken in the sand dunes. (I even took pictures of nudes of my wife, there, in 1956) But it is possible also that had we gone into the Superstition Mountains, we might have run out of gas, or the car might have stuck somewhere, and we would have perished !

Nature's will; the Sex-drive, is an enormously powerful force in all of us! Simply because Norma Jeane's breasts were protruding in her sweather, I went completely erractic in my desire to have her. I WAS taking her TO LIVE into the wilderness, or driving her to New York, never to return to Hollywood; I had aboslutely no fixed plans, various plans popped into my mind, but all I wanted was to have her to be mine in bed! And than, to own her, AS WIFE. And to do with her whatever I pleased ----(giving her ten children !) Many men, after me, went "nuts" about her; and I often wondered ever since -- just why ? What did she have ? Or was it all just hysteria ? I can not tell ! It could not have been hysteria from my part, because at that time, she was unknown, a nobody, JUST PRETTY. But there was something about her, or something in my mind, what compelled me to want to flee with her. Just flee, away from everything and everybody, so that I can be alone with her. But I do not think that feeling is abnormal. In fact, I think it is very normal; LOVE IS LIKE THAT! In this incredibly complex, american way of life -- human nature does not know any more what is normal ! Our lives in America have gradually became a chaos ! Or, perhaps it was like that before, too, all over the world, but on a much smaller scale ! As the population grows all over the world, so problems increase, get magnified by leaps, now. NOW

I have known her only about three-4 weeks, AND I have lost my head completely! But it's nothing compared to how many other important men in Hollywood have done the same, after I was through with her ! Not really through, but MY real romance was over with, NEXT YEAR. (1946) I apologize for having gone into philosphical thinking, but this is a quite normal, natural thing for me! I can't just tell a story without reflecting on the real issues of life ! Because the real issues are always everpresent in everything we do, from hour to hour, from day to day, except that we all play games -- most of the time ! We deceive others, and we deceive even ourselves ! The two main issues in life are the sex drive, and to be secure ! (self-preservation) SO Becuase of sex drive

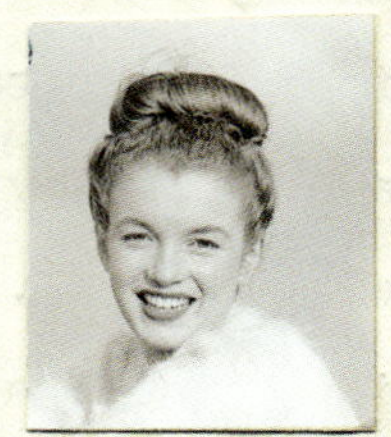

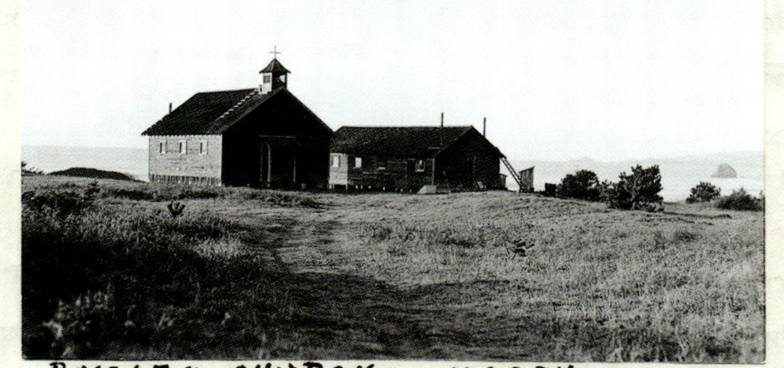

RUSSIAN CHURCH, NORTHERN CALIF.

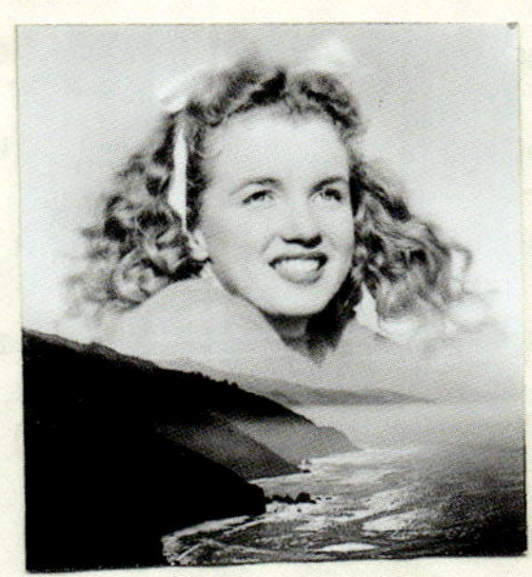

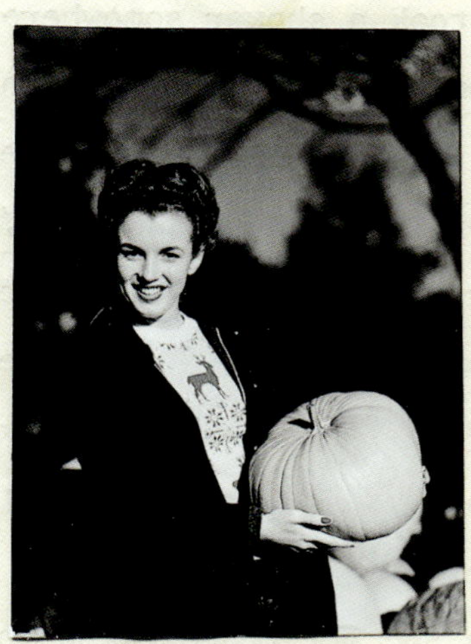

ANDRE DE DIENES
1401 SUNSET PLAZA DRIVE
HOLLYWOOD, CALIF. 90069

A very funny thing happened on the seacost, somewhere north of San Francisco. I was going to photograph Norma Jeane against an old, old church, built of unpainted wood, dry as can be, but, by the time Norma Jean got ready with her make up, an old woman ren to us screaming, shouting we must get out from there. I asked her why ? She said we were on foreign territory! That land was not part of the United States ! It was Russian territory ! I just could not believe what she was talking about. Yet, she was dead serious. I thought she must have been drunk, crazy! She was going to whack at me, and at Norma Jeane. Norma Jeane was aghast; I was confused. I could not take picture there of Norma Jeane, the woman chased us away ! But at least, I took this picture of the church before the woman appeared.

Since than, I LEARNT there used to be Russians settlements on the northern coast of California. (I do not know where the exact location is.)

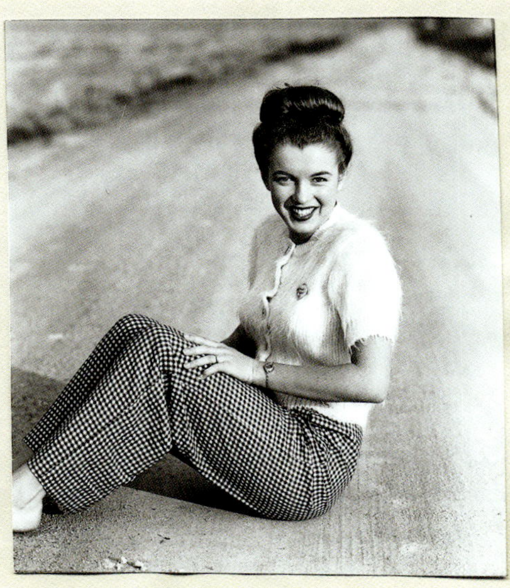

The unpleasant behaviour of the furious OLD woman did not abash us for too long. Norma Jeane was loughing in disbelief; I felt I needed some wine (perhaps due to the influence of the old woman who chased us away) to calm myself, and by the time we stopped at a Motel, I was rather "tipsy." I asked the lady-manager in the office for a "pair-of-adjoining-single-cabins", connected ! The lady looked at me a, surprised. She looked out the window, my car was parked right there, and she saw Norma Jeane waiting in it. And the lady asked me : " Are you two married ? " I could not lie. I said, No ! Domineeringly, (something like a 'mother.') She yelled at me " Separate Cabins ! And she handed me the keys, and asked me to register our names. The cabins were five dollars each. (only ! What a fantastic change has taken place in the U.S. since the past 35 years!)

And, again, from wanting her, I felt tormented all night, and I could hardly sleep. During the night, I spreng to my feet and wrote Norma Jeane a letter, and went to slip it under her door. It amazes me how vividly my mind can remember certain details, though it happened 35 years ago; I think these were almost the exact words what I wrote to her. It went something like this, or written with far more faulty sentences :

in the dead of the night,
December, 1945.

Dear sweet Norma Jeane:

It is so painful for a man to stay away from making love, especially when the beloved is right nearby! And maybe she, too, suffers from the same self-denial? But she is too shy to let herself go....

What a pity we are created so shy ! What pleasurable, glorious nights we could spend if only we would dare !

The cemeteries are full of corpses, and bones, who once were ALIVE, also too shy, too strict, too religious, too morally inclined, and too avaricious, even with themselves, to please and to satisfy their true instincts. And they spent perhaps even a life-time tormenting themselves with lack of loving! Something Nature did not wish them to do ! Billions of people had died without having had enough earthly pleasures !

Norma Jeane! Love is the only real thing in life. The only thing what really matters ! Please come to knock on my door. Please let me love you ! I shall never forsake you ! I shall always love you !

Your crazy Hungarian ~~lover,~~ Andre!

I pushed the note under her door, knocked a few times to wake her up, and I rushed back to my cabin. But she did not come to knock on my door. BUT the good providence arranged it differently, two nights later.

"Norma Jean's breakfast"

That night, after I slipped the note under her door, I noticed the windows of my cabin didn't have gook enogh latches to lock the windows tight and since there was a tavern nearby full of merry, drinking men, carousing, singing loudly, I was afraid while I sleep, some drunk might try to rob me. As a precaution, I put my billfold -- full of money-- under my pillow. But in the morning when Norma Jeane woke me out of my deep sleep with strong knockings on my door, I got dressed in great haste, grabbed my things in haste, and left. She looked so pretty, so refreshed, prettier than ever before, and I complimented her for it. In the haste and excitement I forgot about the billfold under the pillow. We took off, drove for an hour or so in the dismal rainy, foggy winter weather, and finally stopped in a small cafe, somewhere on the highway, where Norma Jeane could have a good, hearty breakfast. She loved te eat in small cafes where home-cooked meals were served for simple people. Her breakfast consisted of Orange juice, a bowl of hot oatmeal, or cream of wheat, with butter and syrup on top of it and eggs, with ham, or bacon, or sausages, and a large glass of milk. And even a side-order of pancakes with genuine Maple Syrup ! I always insisted she eat should eat well. And she took good advantage of it. And She ate the breakfast with the happiest expression on her face as if it were the greatest thing in life. (It sure is ! One of them !) As I was reaching for my billfod to pay the bill, I nearly got a heart attack from the shock. The billfold was still under my pillow. Hastily I untied my "money belt ", unzipped it, handed her a hundred dollar bills, one of the several ones I kept there as emergency money; and I left the cafe in a hurry, instructing her to wait for my return right there.

To my utmost relief, the cabin wasn't cleaned up yet, I found my billfold, but I drove back to the Cafe with such joy that I passed it in the misty, foggy weather which blinded my judment. And I could not find the Cafe. I, who travelled world over! Who could locate even a needle in a haystack a thousand miles away, if I were told to do it, I was driving nervously miles and miles, back and forth, on the busy highway, for almost two hours, exasperated by my stupidity !

Finally, I found the Cafe around noon-time, but Norma Jeane wasn't there. She went to the BUS Depot, the owner of the cafe told me. I found her there, outside, in the phone booth. She spoke for one more instant, than hanged up and ren to me shouting, Andre, Oh Andre, and we embraced with hysterical joy. She thought I had an accident, or I have deserted her; left her stranded in the Cafe, with a hundred dollars, probably disappointed and disillusioned because I wasn't able to sleep with her, or because she did not come to my door at night. Thus, she was on the phone, talking to her 'Aunt Ana', consulting the lady what she ought to do, to alert the Highway Patrol to search for me, or whether she ought to return to Los Angeles. Norma Jeane was palpitating in my arms, telling me what a distressful time she had waiting for me in the Cafe.

Afterward, she called her aunt again, to explain what had happened, and that I found my vallet under the pillow.

I sure arrived to the Bus Depot right one time! Ten more minutes, and Norma Jeane would have taken the bus, back to Los Angeles !

I wondered ever since; what if I had misssed her, and she had gone back to Los Angeles! How each of us would have continued life ? Would she have become a Marilyn Monroe ? It is impossible to tell. Even small incidents like that, could have completely altered our lives!

L #1 LOVE

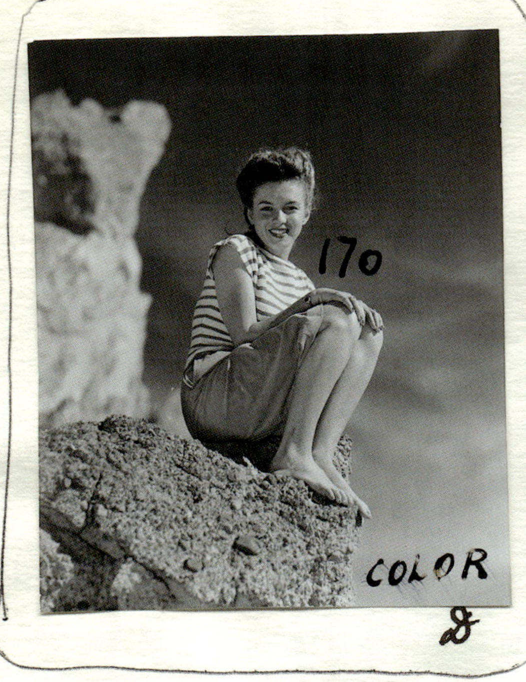

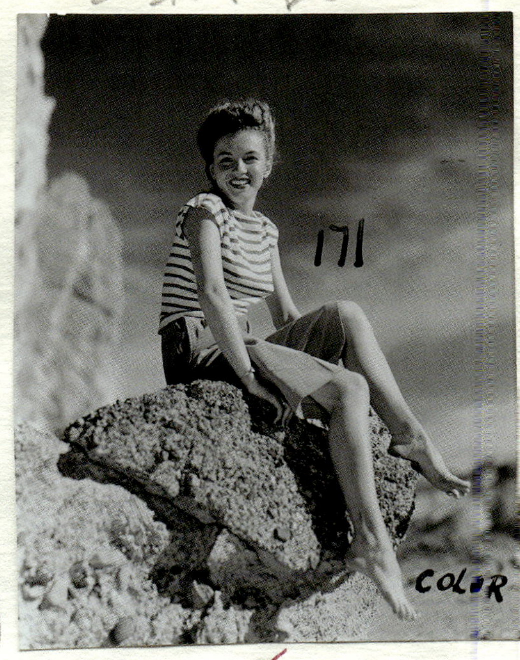

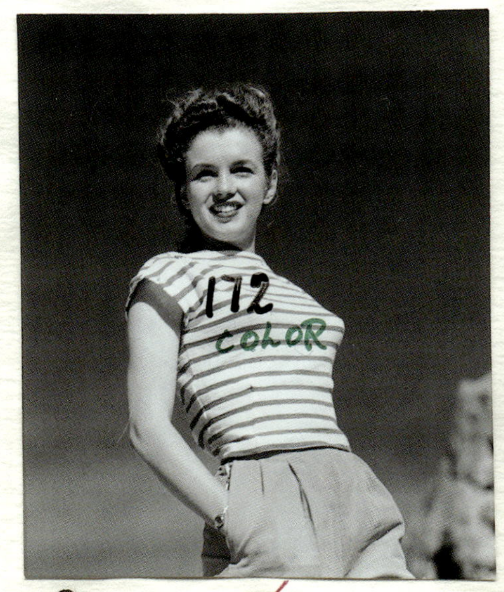

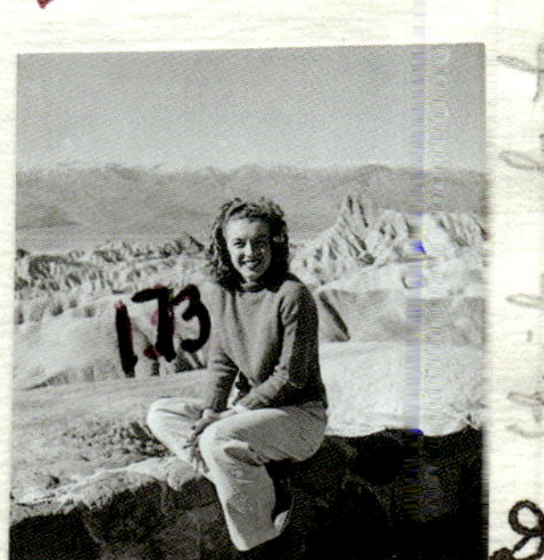

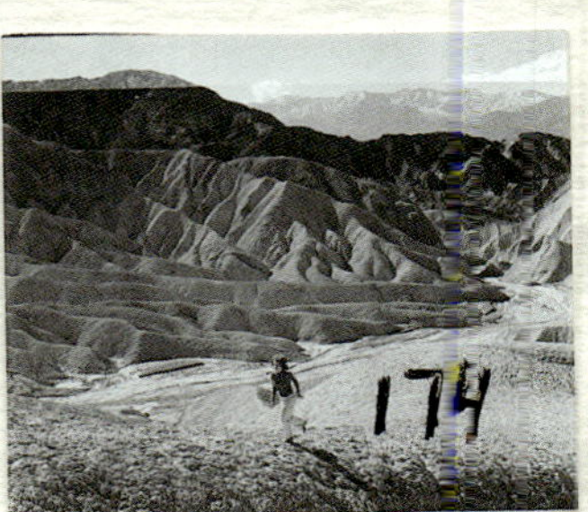

DEATH VALLEY, CAL.
DEC. 1945

ANDRE DE DIENES
1401 SUNSET PLAZA DRIVE
HOLLYWOOD, CALIF. 90069

26

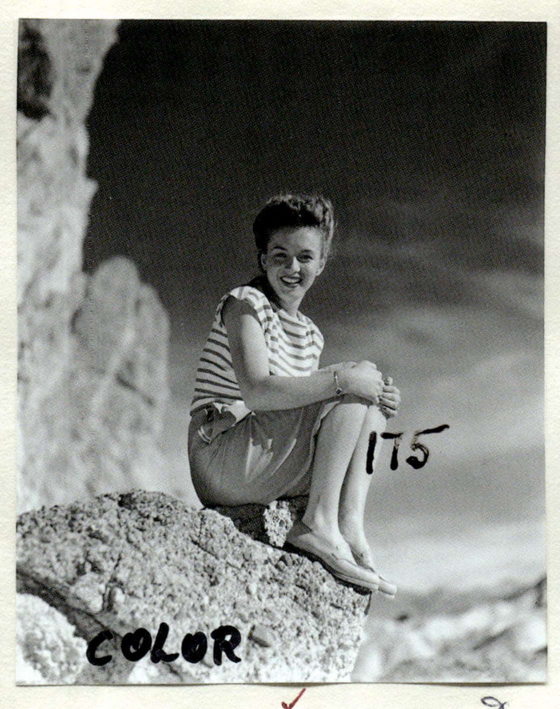

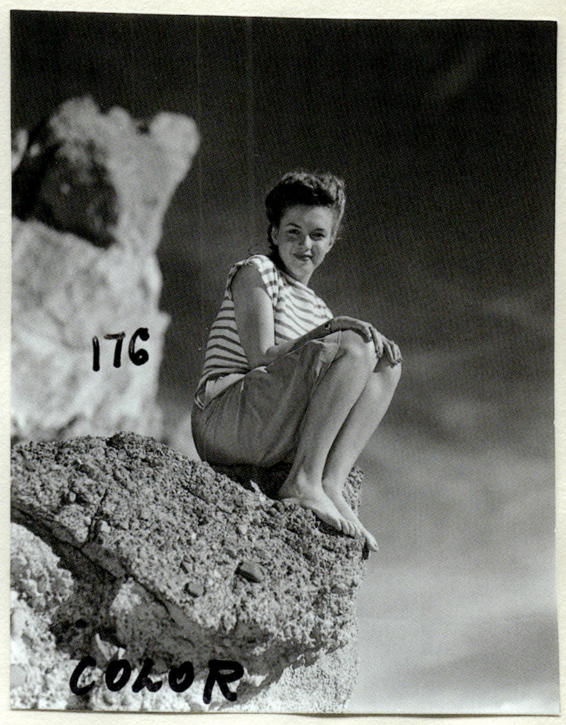

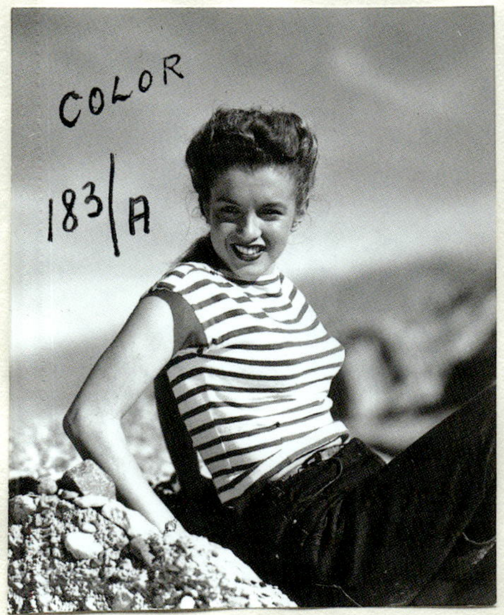

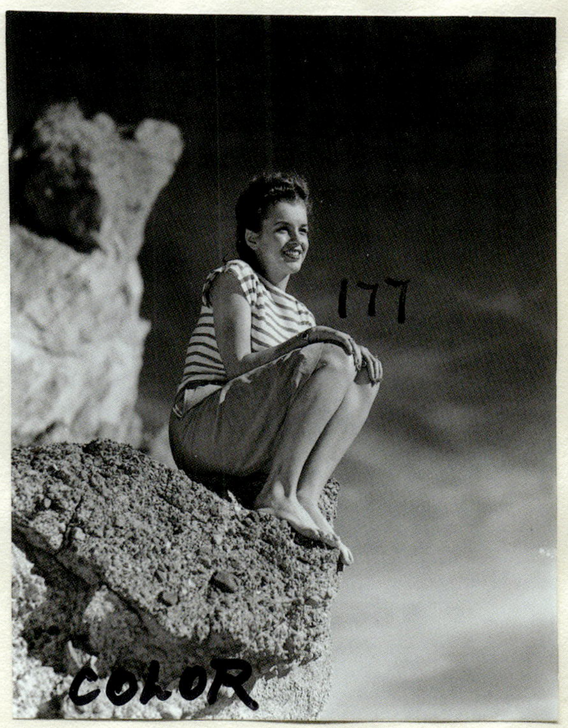

ANDRE DE DIENES
1401 SUNSET PLAZA DRIVE
HOLLYWOOD, CALIF. 90069

27.

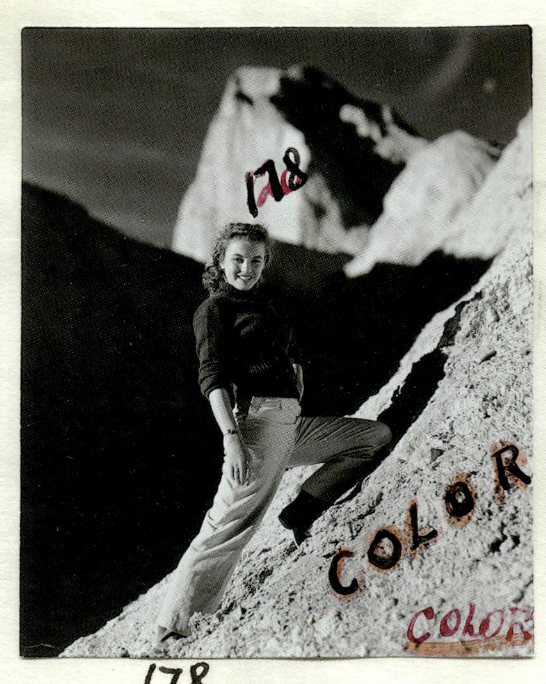

178

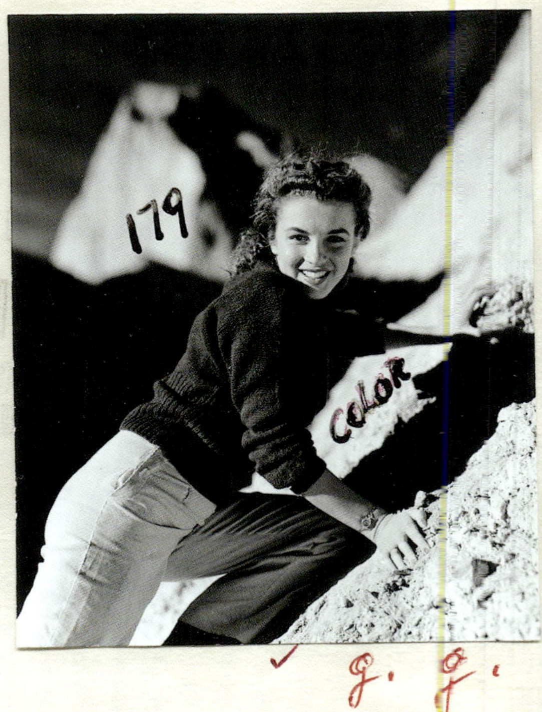

✓ g. g.

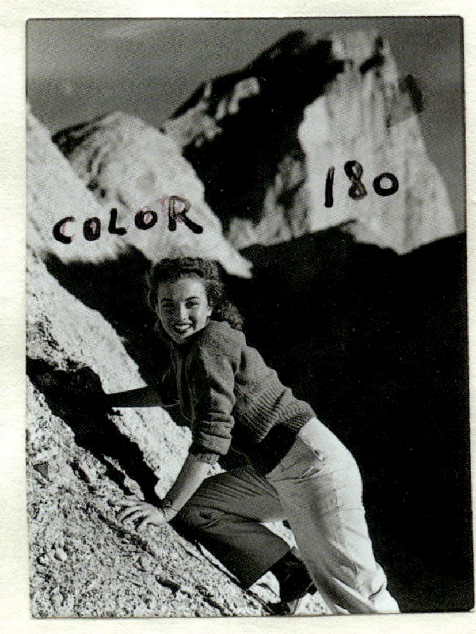

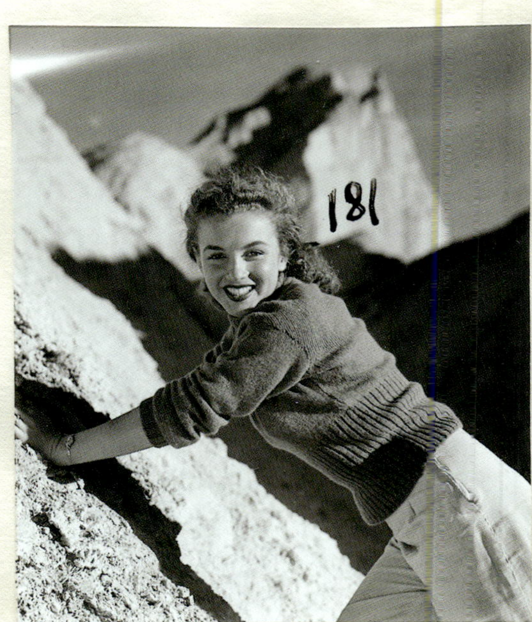

DEATH VALLEY, CAL.
1945

ANDRE DE DIENES 28

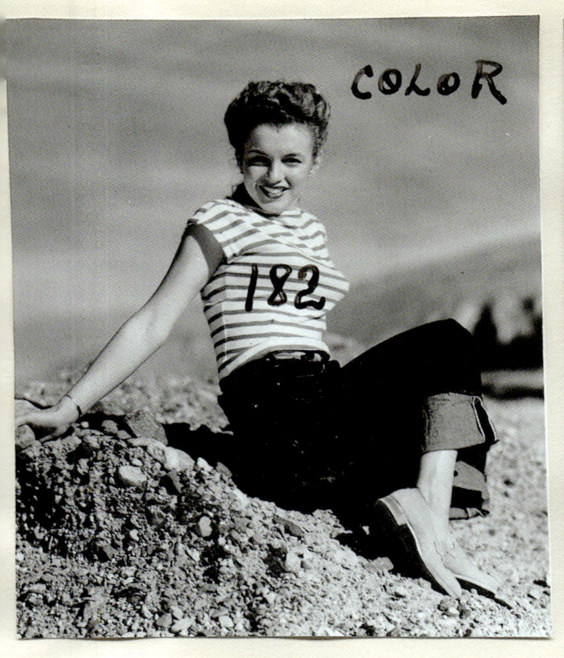

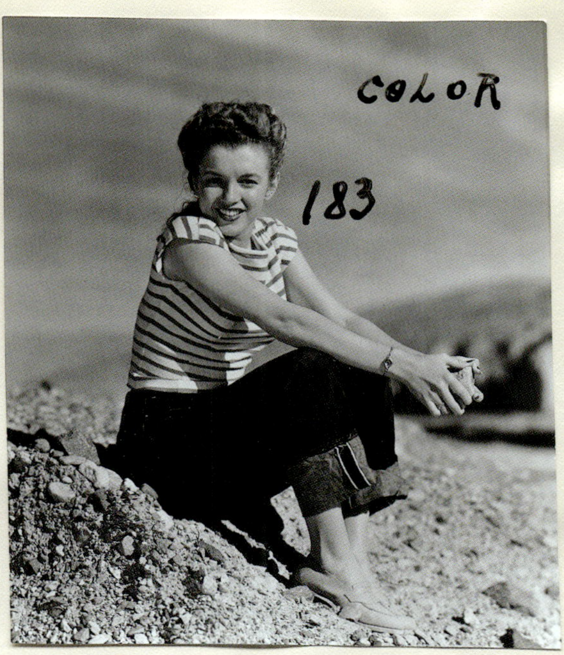

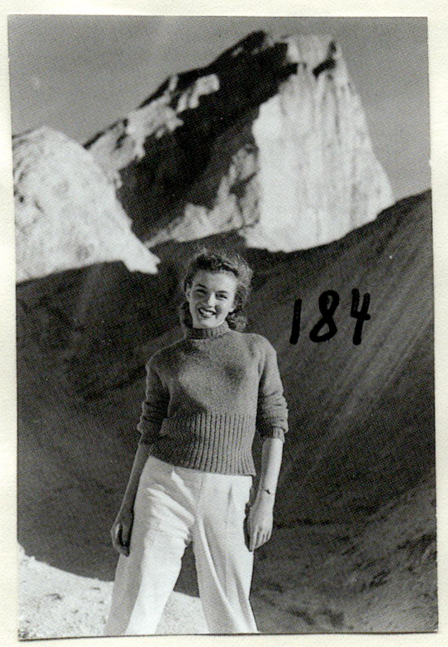

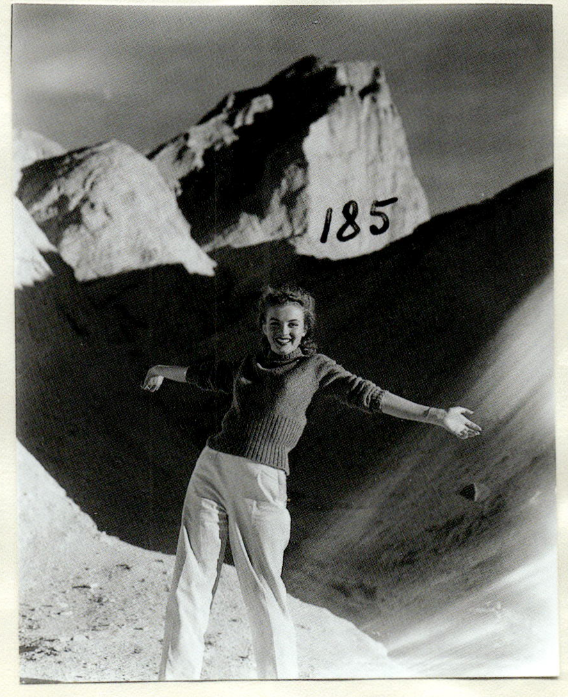

ANDRE DE DIENES
1401 SUNSET PLAZA DRIVE
HOLLYWOOD, CALIF. 90069

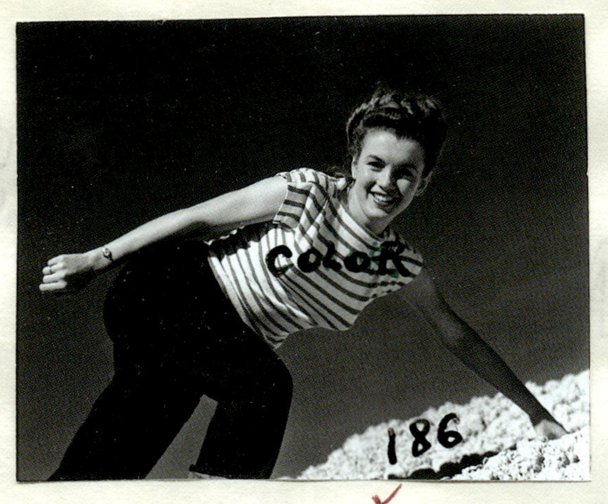

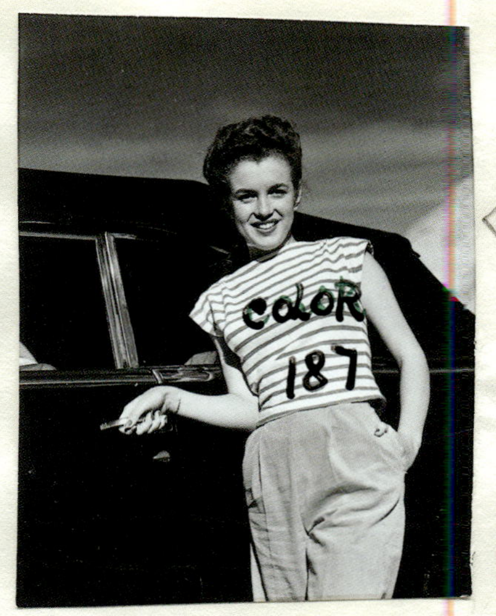

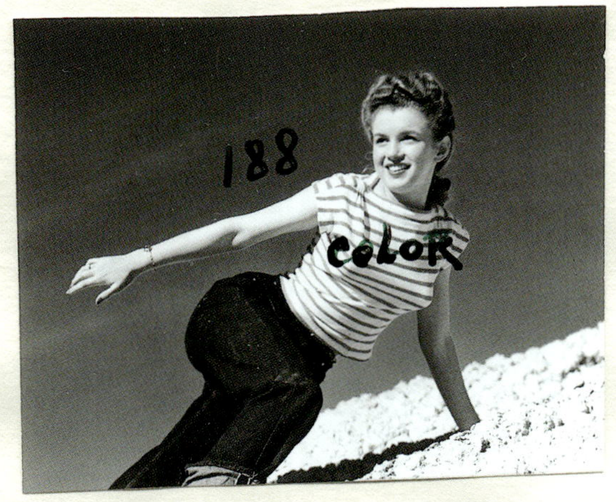

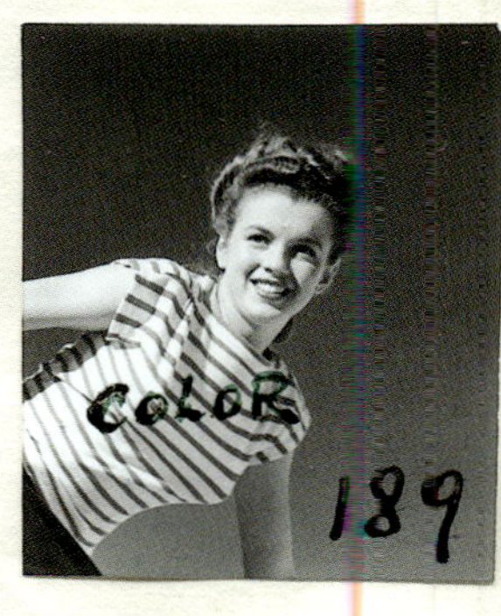

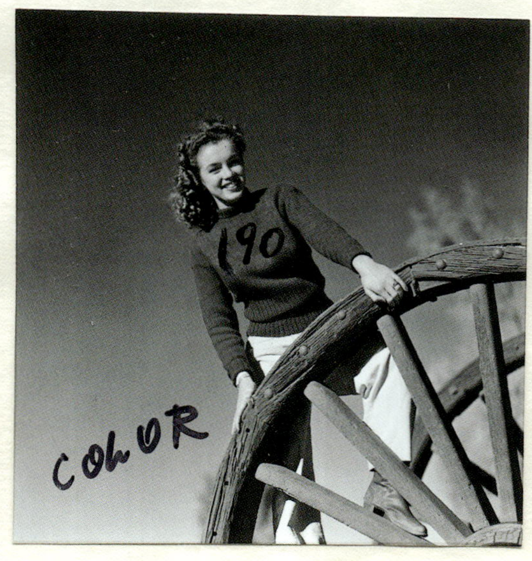

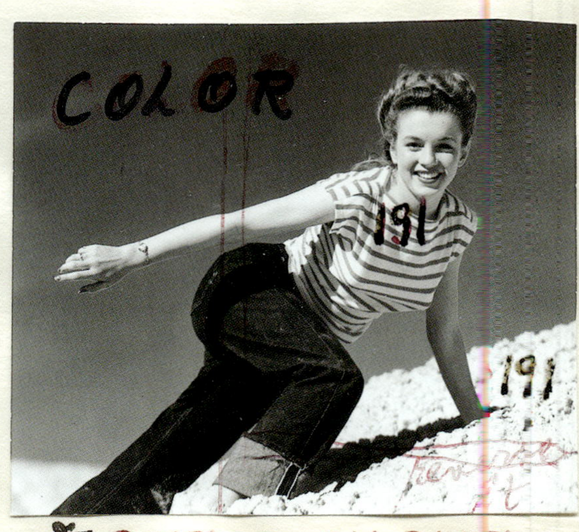

REVERSE ALL THESE SHOTS

ANDRE DE DIENES

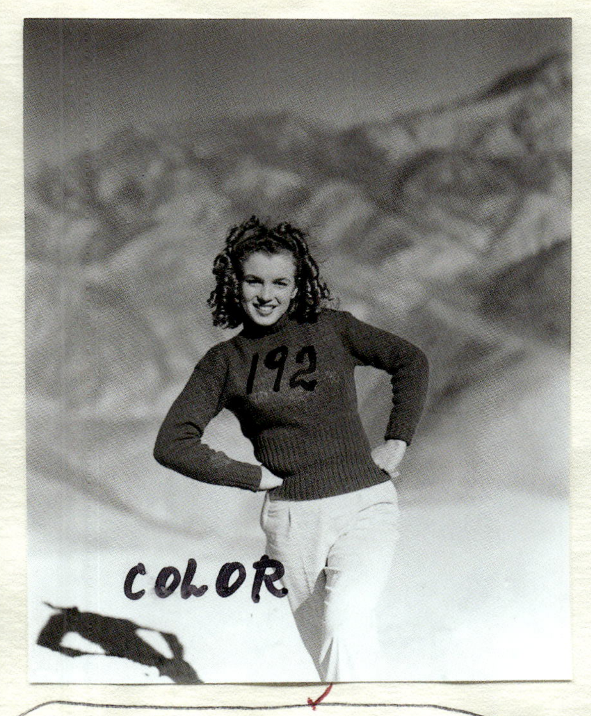

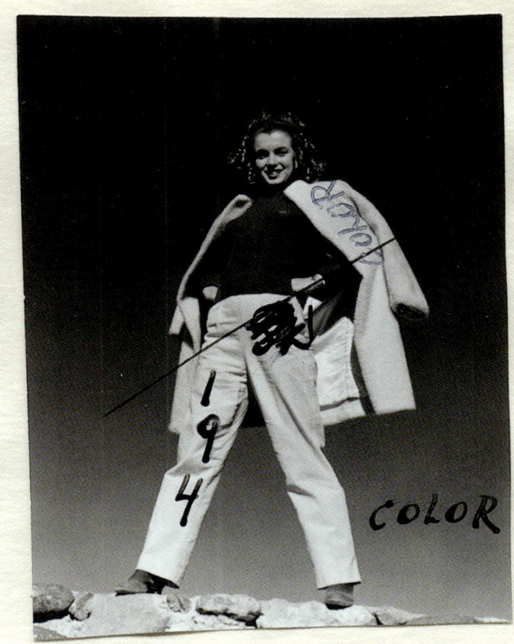

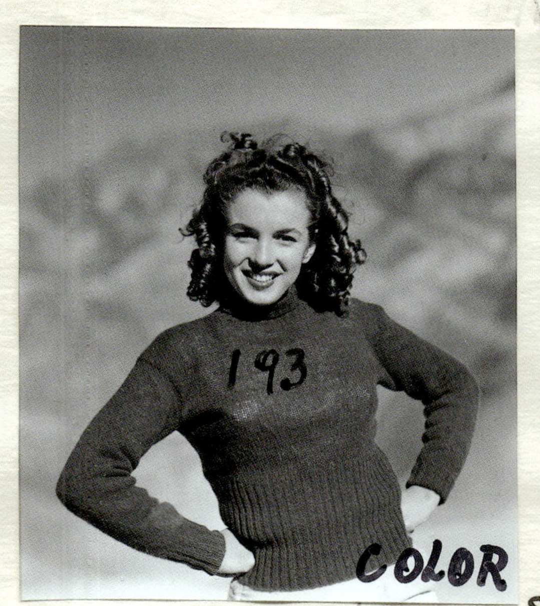

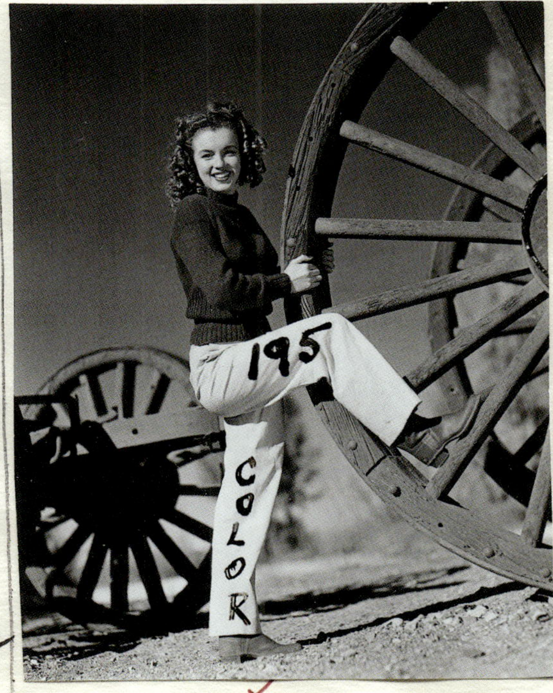

(green sweather) &

IN DEATH VALLEY, CAL

ANDRE DE DIENES
1401 SUNSET PLAZA DRIVE
HOLLYWOOD, CALIF. 90069

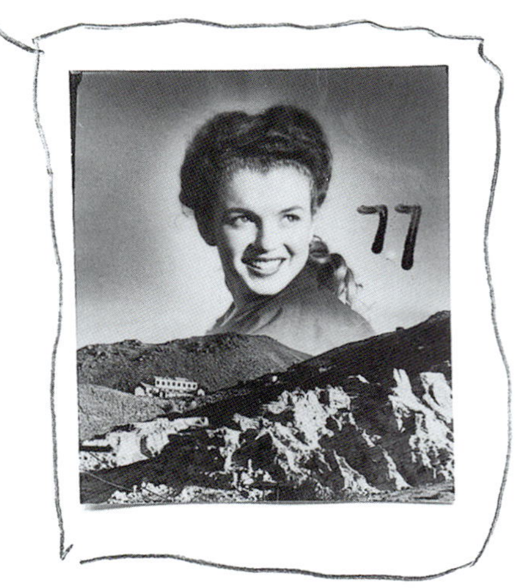

In the dead of night, December 1945

Dear sweet Norma Jeane:

It is so painful for a man to stay away from making love, especially when the beloved is right nearby! And maybe she, too, suffers from the same self-denial. But she is too shy to let herself go....

What a pity we are created so shy! What a pleasurable, glorious night we could spend if only we would dare!

The cemeteries are full of corpses and bones who were once alive, and also too shy, too strict, too religious, too morally inclined, even with themselves, to please and to satisfy their true instincts. And they spent perhaps even a lifetime tormenting themselves with lack of loving! Something Nature did not wish them to do! Billions of people have died without having had enough earthly pleasures!

Norma Jeane, love is the only real thing in life. The only thing which really matters! Please come to knock on my door. Please let me love you! I shall never forsake you! I shall always love you!

Your crazy Hungarian, [André]

I pushed the note under her door, knocked a few times to wake her up, and I rushed back to my cabin. But she did not come to knock on my door. The good providence arranged it differently, two nights later.

Inner Norma Jeane We stopped in Sacramento for an hour to pay a fast visit to a relative of her Aunt Ana and then we headed north to Eureka and into Oregon. Norma Jeane was completely awed, spellbound, when we made stops in the various redwood forests in northern California. There in the forests, that pretty Hollywood model's Nordic ancestral instinct awoke. I noticed a great change in her there; she became alive to the surroundings. It seemed to me as if those were the places where she belonged. She noticed and pointed out to me the smallest details, like miniature bugs she picked up or the smallest little flowers hardly visible in the vegetation and the patterns of the ferns and little brown mushrooms growing at the feet of the giant Sequoia trees. She went to take a long, solitary walk among the giant trees, despite the fact that it was raining. Her hands turned blue and purple. She walked away so far, I was worried she would get lost. By late afternoon I found her sitting at the base of a giant tree, praying.

Norma Jeane did not pretend to be spiritual – she did not have to; she was absolutely nobody at that time, just a 19-year-old girl who had just started out modeling a few weeks before that trip. She was completely sincere and natural. And it was there, in the forest, that I really fell in love with her. I saw the perfect kind of wife to last for a lifetime. She was easy to get along with! She was a delight to travel with! It was wintertime and daytime was short; I told her we must start early each morning, so she had an alarm clock and she was up before me every morning! She was constantly in a good mood, very cheerful. She was completely content having just a basketful of food in the back of the automobile, where she slept sometimes. Her happiest moments were when she ate cottage cheese with pineapples right out of the container. The food basket was her little kitchen and if I did not feel like stopping in a restaurant, it was completely okay with her. She was a completely uncomplicated young lady!

Alternately, she was quiet and reserved, sometimes very serious, but never pretentious, never trying to impose her ego on me. And certain little things impressed her, struck her as so funny that she could hardly stop laughing. She was no movie star at that time, and never even dreamed she would be some day.

In the forest, I started singing loudly "I love you as I have never loved before, since first I met you at the village green." Norma Jeane took over the song from me and sang loud. She had a rather lovely, natural voice. It became like our team-song, from then on. Ever since, when I sing it, I think of her and get tears in my eyes each time. When I am in the mood to get sad, I start singing the song and the vision of sweet Norma Jeane comes back to me, walking through the cathedral-like beautiful forests in northern California. And from that afternoon on, I called her "Little Mushroom," a nickname for her admiring the mushrooms on the bark of the trees.

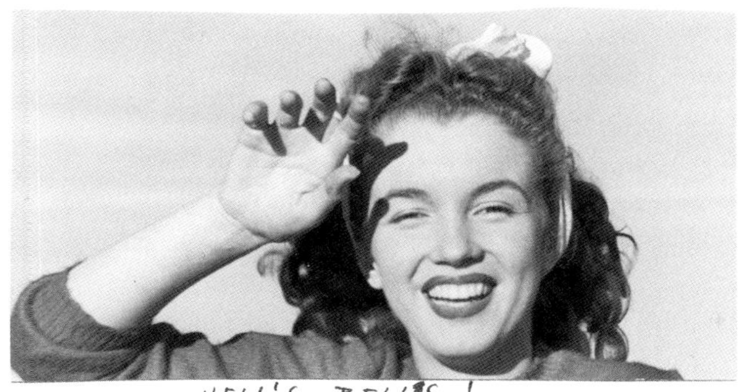

HELL'S BELLS!

Hell's Bells! The idyll in the forest with my "Little Mushroom" turned into a small disaster a couple of hours later. We were both soaking when we resumed the drive, and soon we got to a large group of cabins in the midst of a forest grove. I promptly rented two cabins, side by side, as usual, and unloaded part of the luggage and told Norma Jeane to stay there while I would drive to the nearby service station to take care of the car.

It was already dark when I got back and Norma Jeane wasn't there. The luggage was gone from both cabins, except her toothbrush and a few things in the bathroom. The man in the office could not tell me anything. He said that no dishonesty ever happened there and that they did not even have locks on the cabin doors, only to bolt the lock from the inside!

I was nearly out of my mind. How could she desert me after such a beautiful afternoon in the forest? I was about to drive to the sheriff's when a car drove up, driven by a young fellow, and out hopped Norma Jeane with a large paper bag on her arm, from which she pulled out one of the two bottles of red wine she'd bought. I was shouting at her angrily, asking where she was and why the hell she had left the cabins. And she looked at me horrified as she saw my angry and rude disposition. Then she explained that she walked to the village to buy me wine, cheese, and salami and the grocery clerk drove her back.

The fact was that part of my photo equipment and part of our luggage was stolen from our cabins, the negatives of the beautiful photos

I took of her in the forest were gone – forever! And other lovely photos of her – all gone! And one of my valuable cameras also! It seemed like a disaster. I was angry at her for not staying in the cabin until I returned. I spent a tormented night; I did not even think of trying to sleep with her. But in the morning, she greeted me with a cheerful disposition. She never seemed sweeter; she was telling me not to be concerned with the value of the camera lost, nor about the negatives gone, or anything. She kept emphasizing that only half of the luggage was unloaded and stolen, so I still had the rest in the car! And she shouted at me, "Hell's bells, André, cheer up!" I loved hearing her cheerful loud shout, "Hell's bells!" She laughed, because she knew her exclamation seemed funny (otherwise, she would not have used the word "hell"). She was enjoying her own wit, and her laugh was beautiful

The sheriff took down the case, but the questioning was too embarrassing to answer! I knew the case was hopeless, so there was nothing else to do but leave and not to worry about the loss anymore, nor to blame Norma Jeane. She had nice intentions when she walked to the store to buy me the wine…. The love letter I left under her cabin door the night before must have done something to her mind; the wine she brought back must have been an invitation to something! And fate arranged it that the two bottles of wine she bought were mighty nice to have the next night, and the night after…. Her intuitions were right! We needed the wine; days and days of driving were beginning to be too much.

Portland Anticipating a happy reunion between Norma Jeane and her mother, we bought various presents (for which I paid, of course), but the actual meeting was a let-down – a dull, rather gloomy event. The hotel was an old mediocre place in the center of Portland. We found her mother in a small room on the top floor. She greeted Norma Jeane with a sad expression, then she sat in the chair near the window and they carried on a slow-paced conversation in a very low, monotonous tone. The lady was aged, thin, expressionless, and void of any emotions while the conversation went on. Norma Jeane was in good spirits and she tried to cheer up her mother, unsuccessfully. Before we went to visit her, I'd failed to question Norma Jeane about her mother, so I had no idea why she was just released from some institution for her mental problems. I recall that during the conversation, her mother put her head into her hands and bent down; there were many rather painful moments like that. It was a dark, cloudy afternoon, the room seemed very gloomy to me, and Norma Jeane looked at me with painful embarrassment. Then, since there was little else to do, we departed. My mind was on my trip and I was eager to reach Timberline Lodge, a wonderful big hotel east of Portland at the foot of Mount Hood.

I am sorry I did not take any pictures of Norma Jeane with her mother, but since I have never liked to get mixed up in other people's relationships, I did not even think of snapping pictures of them in that darkly lit, sad room. I was a young, amorous man! I wanted to be with Norma Jeane; I wanted to be happy!

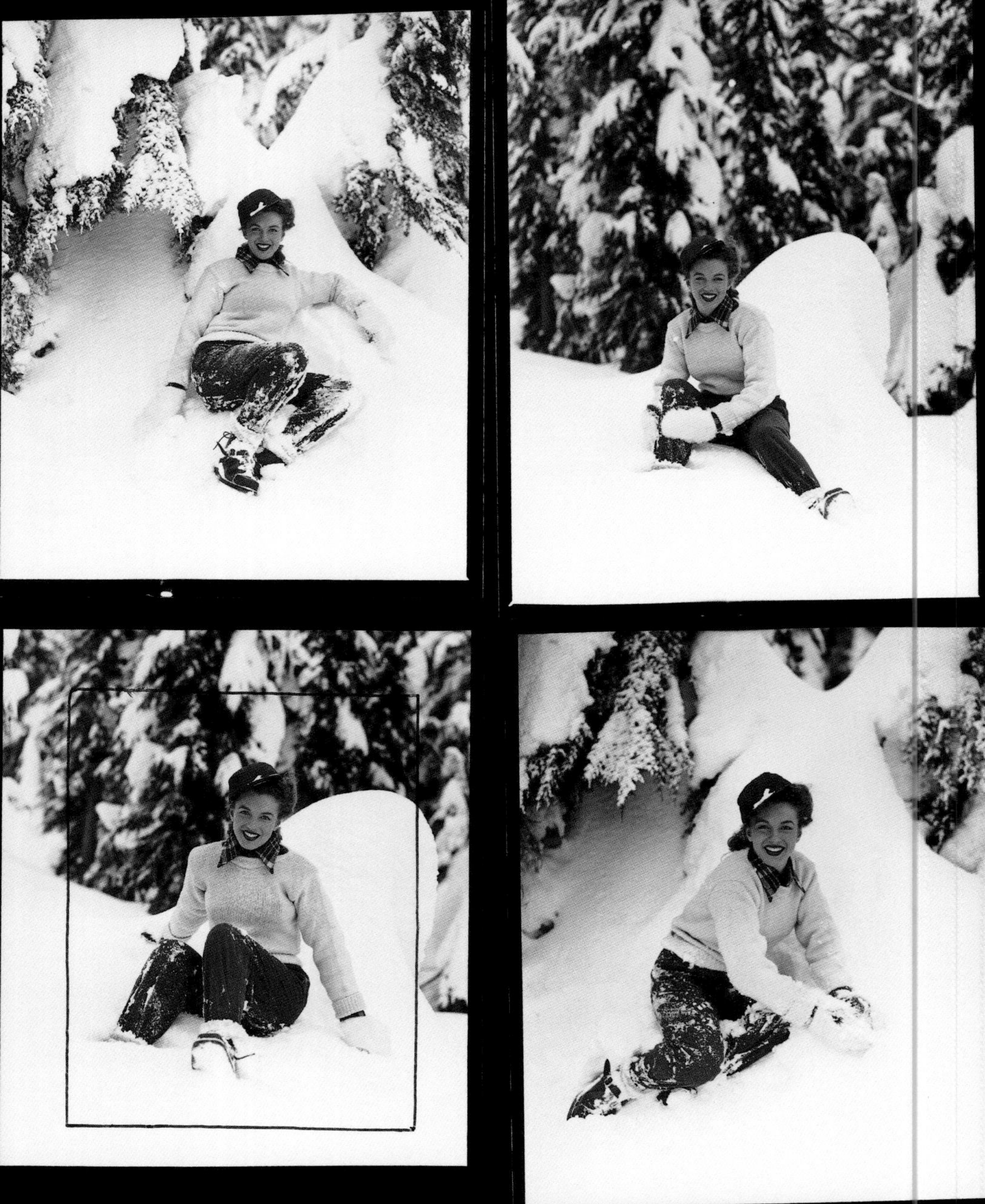

AT MOUNT HOOD,

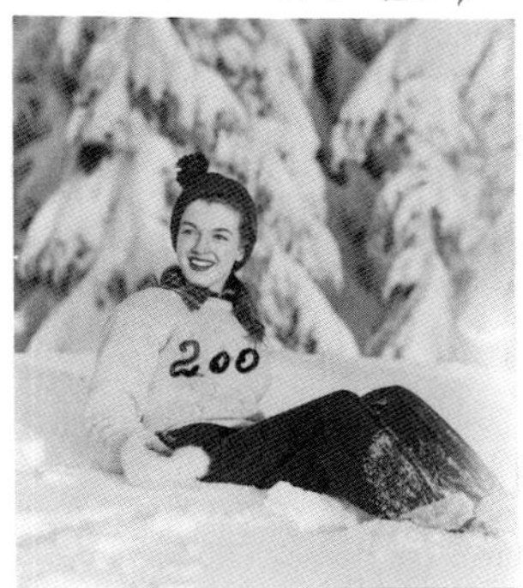

IN OREGON,
DEC. 1945

Marry Me! It was raining while we drove to Mount Hood, Oregon, and the rain turned into snow when we got to the Timberline Lodge. I went to inquire for accommodations and there was only one room available, with a double bed. I went out to the car where Norma Jeane was waiting; she was in a rather serious mood. She said she could prefer it if we would drive on and find cabins somewhere in the woods… separate cabins. I felt disappointed, because I liked that hotel and wanted the comfort there. The opportunity would have been extraordinary to take pictures of Mount Hood – a beautiful, extinct volcano – and it's a fantastic place for good skiing. But I obeyed Norma Jeane and drove down on the narrow, curving road while it was snowing really hard and dusk was coming. At the junction of that narrow road and the main highway, there was a place called Government Lodge. The snow was already too deep and my car could not go any further. We got stuck right in front of the hotel, as if fate's hand had guided us there purposefully. And in that hotel, too, there was only one room left available – a room with one double bed and a bathroom at the end of a long corridor. I came out to inform Norma Jeane that we had to stay there! It was already darkening. Norma Jeane smiled at me. She said, "Okay, let's take the room. Let's not worry anymore about anything!"

A funny thing happened there almost as soon as I registered. On the ground floor there were slot machines everywhere. I pointed at one slot machine out of the many and told Norma Jeane in a loud voice that she needed pocket money for Jergen's lotion (that she loved for her skin) and I commanded the slot machine to provide a jackpot for it. The bartender and everybody at the bar were staring at us, perhaps thinking I had gone nuts. I told Norma Jeane to stretch out the bottom of her sweater under the machine. I put the quarter in and pulled the handle, and out gushed a flood of quarters! Everybody cheered.

We had a good dinner and afterward we flipped a coin to decide who would occupy the bathroom first. It wasn't much of a bathroom, just a lousy shower and a toilet. Then we went to bed without the slightest nervousness, as if what was happening was the most natural thing in the world. It was a strange contrast to all the days of amorous emotions I had to fight, and the frustration I went through every night. Finally, we spent the night together, in the same bed! When the lovemaking was over with, Norma Jeane cried in my arms. She was happy, satisfied. And I was holding her, and she was holding me as if I were her child.

You might say, "André, let's hear what it was really like to make love with the future Marilyn Monroe!" But to respect Marilyn's memory, I prefer not to discuss sex. She was a divine, lovely young woman. And said she was never as happy before! She was crying. It was a fantastic, almost supernatural feeling when I fell asleep in bed with Norma Jeane. She was hugging me, I was kissing her tears; she said she had never had an orgasm before in her life. And I felt greatly satisfied also, having waited for at least two weeks to make love with her — more than I could possibly endure! Why didn't or couldn't I have made her pregnant? I've asked myself ever since….

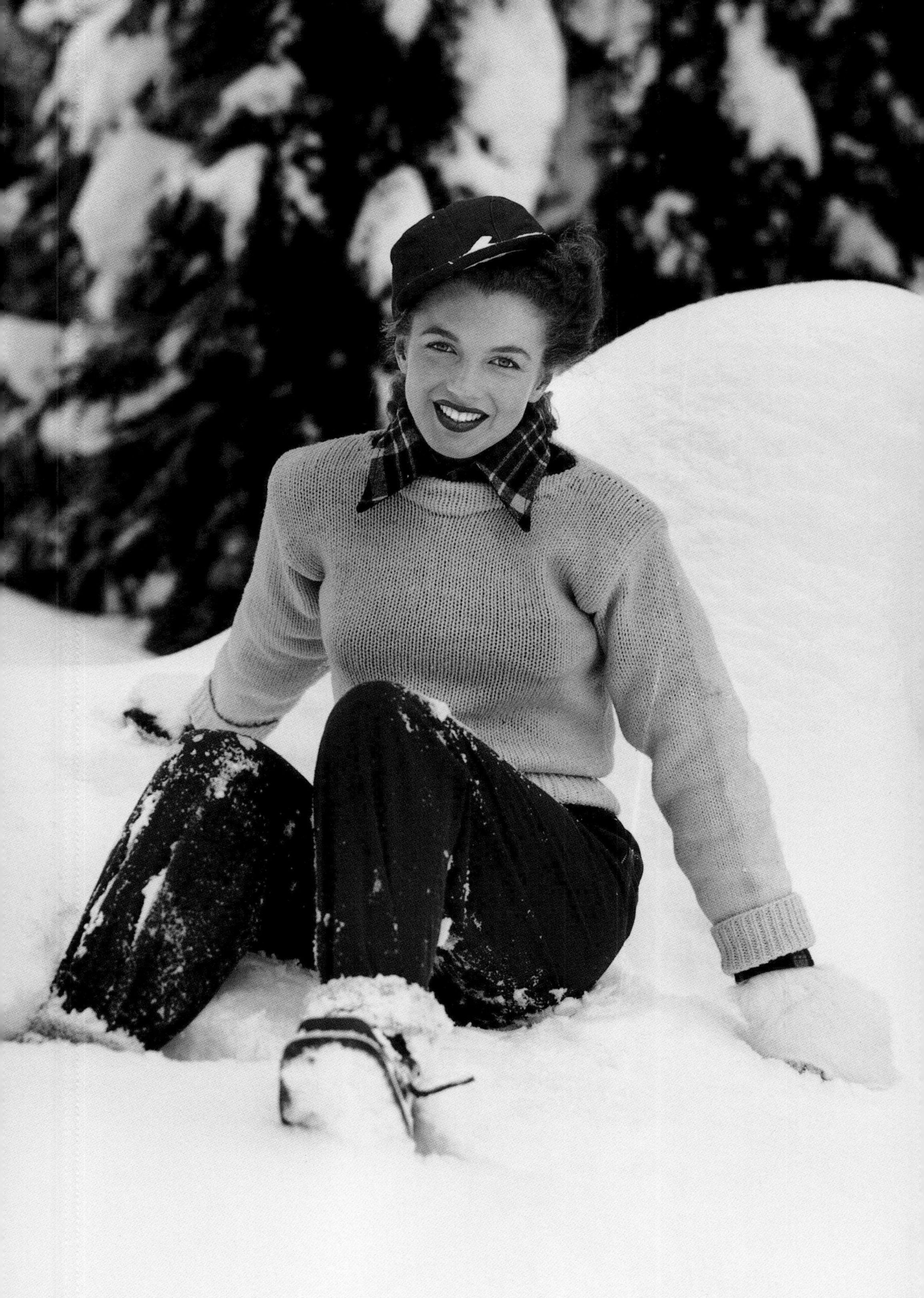

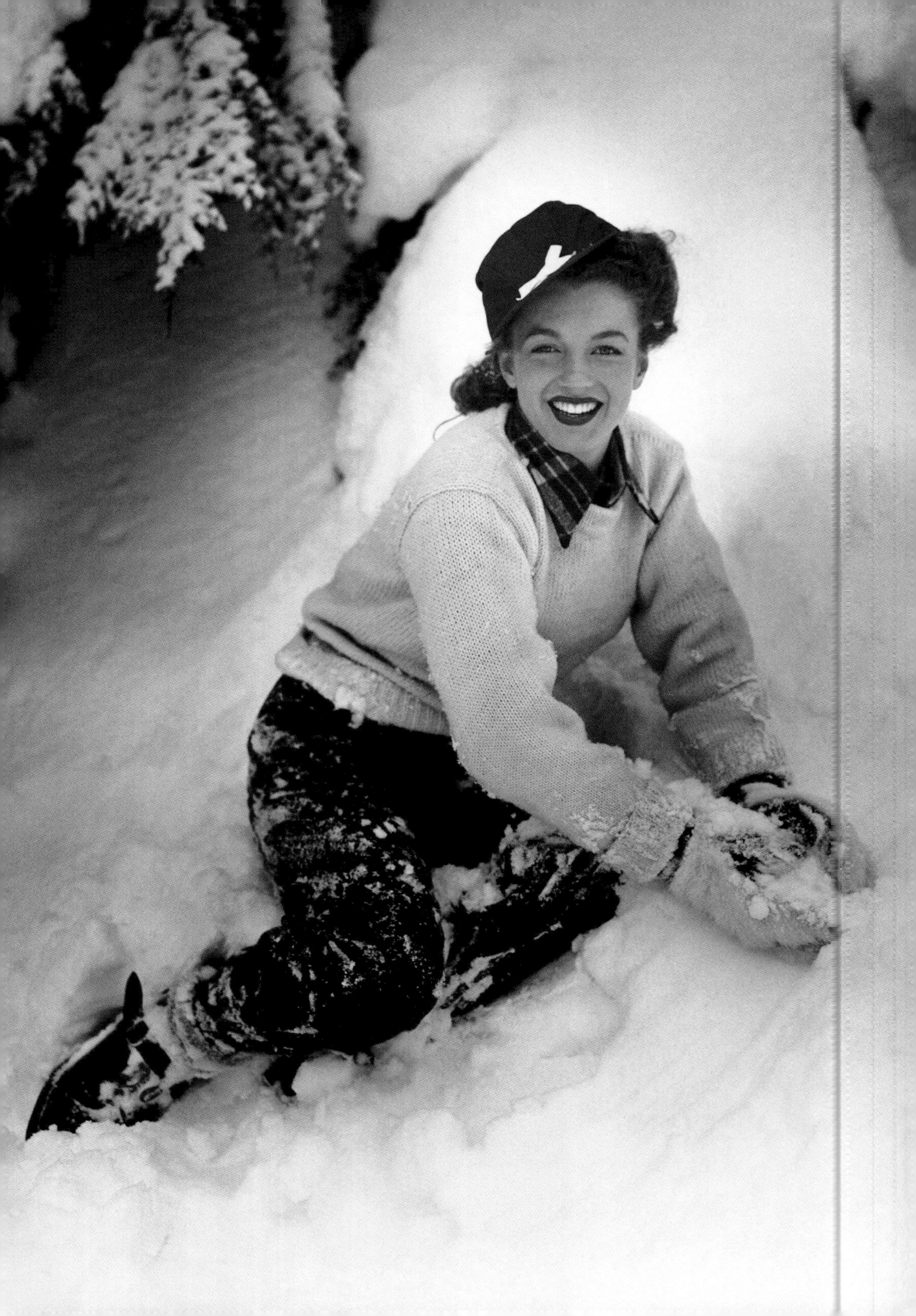

Next, when we went down for lunch, it was still snowing hard, and my car was covered with snow. The wife of the owner of the hotel took us for honeymooners, and offered us the best room they had, on the first floor – a wood-paneled wonderful cozy room. We stayed in there for two days while it was still snowing relentlessly. Our short stay there was like being in paradise!

A bizarre event happened there in that room during the first day of our stay. Norma Jeane was manicuring and putting nail polish on her toenails and she lifted her hands in the air to show me her palms, observing how curious it was that in each palm there was a large M. Somewhat childishly, we compared our palms, looking at the lines in them. And there, I told Norma Jeane the story of an old bell-ringer in Transylvania who, in my childhood, had predicted that the two letters "MM" would mean a great deal to me when I grew up. And I told Norma Jeane the story about my meeting the old man while reading a strange old book, and how the old man was preoccupied with one of the pages where the writing began with the two words "memento mori." Norma Jeane was fascinated by my story, and we discussed again and again the two Ms in our palms. I told her jovially that the Ms had nothing to do with death – to the contrary, they meant "marry me!" And we pressed our palms together. We hugged and kissed and decided we shall get married as soon as she would get a divorce from her husband. We decided she would go to Las Vegas to get the divorce and we would get married there, right after. From those moments onward, we felt we

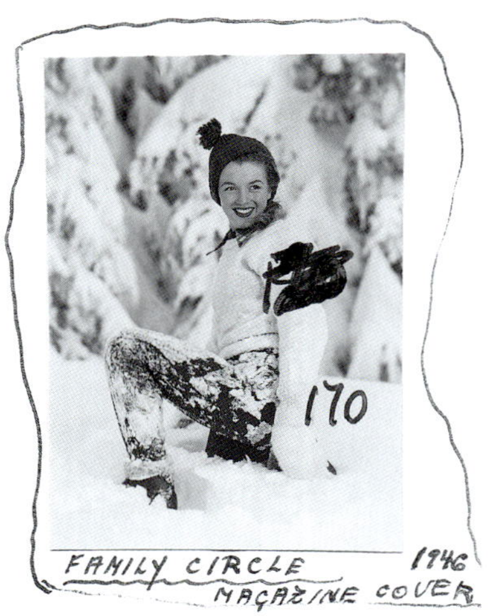

FAMILY CIRCLE 1946
MAGAZINE COVER

were engaged. I told Norma Jeane about my wanderings through Transylvania on foot, and having carved many times in the bark of trees the two initials "M.M." I promised her that when we got married, I would buy her a thick, heavy, gold wedding ring, and have the two initials engraved inside the ring, as a memento to remember the prediction of the old bell-ringer. I even took a picture of her palm.

While it was snowing, we stayed in the room all day long, except for a brief hour when I took her out to photograph her in the snow, reading. She was pampering herself, combing her curly hair out again and again at the mirror, and draping herself in the bed sheet, while examining the results in the mirror. A sexy little "vampire" she was, glamorizing herself with the bed sheet, as if it were an expensive evening gown! If only I had the foresight to photograph her in that room as she was glamorizing herself on the bed naked, quite uninhibited. The future Marilyn Monroe was there, in that room! A sex symbol was incubating that afternoon!

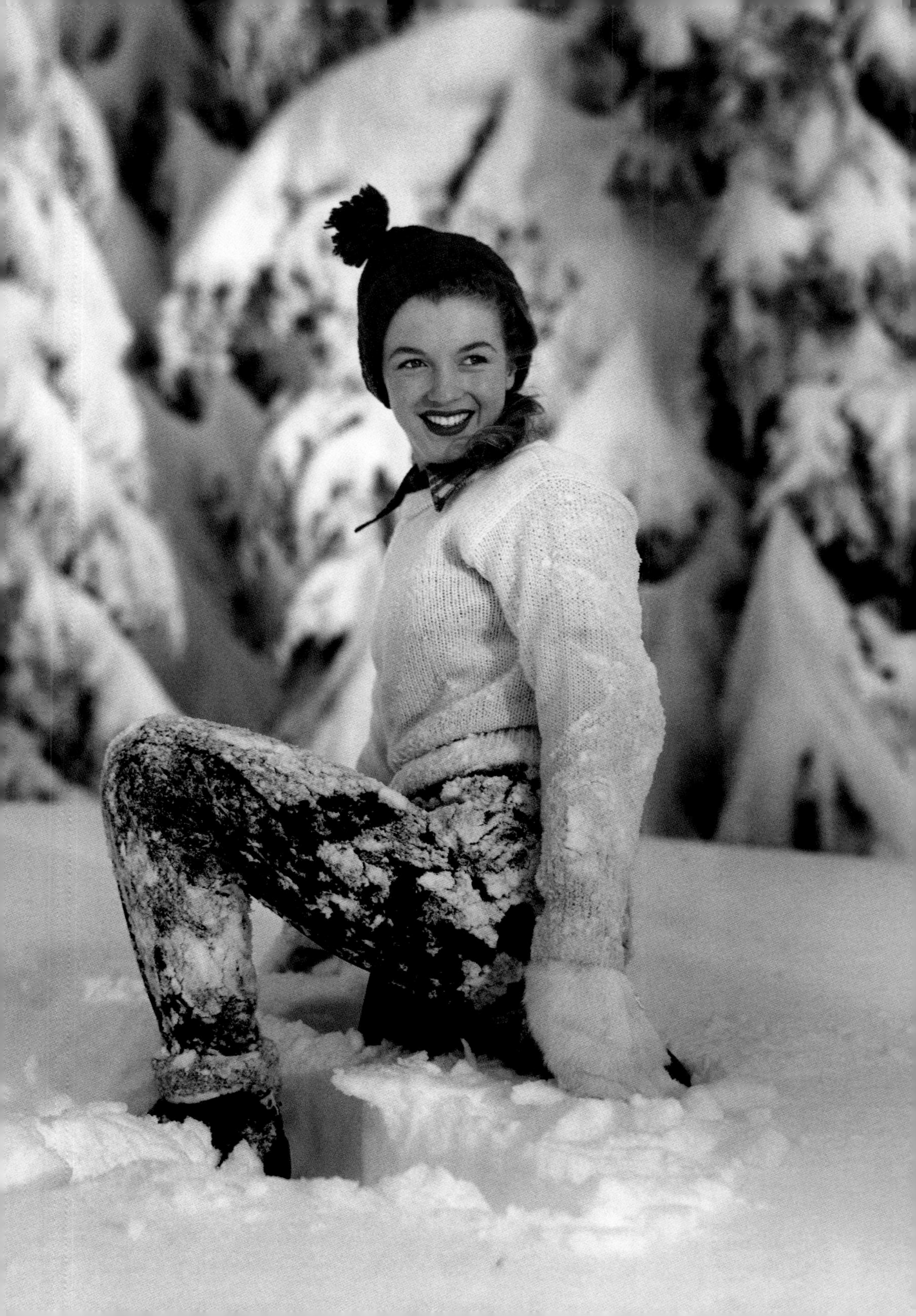

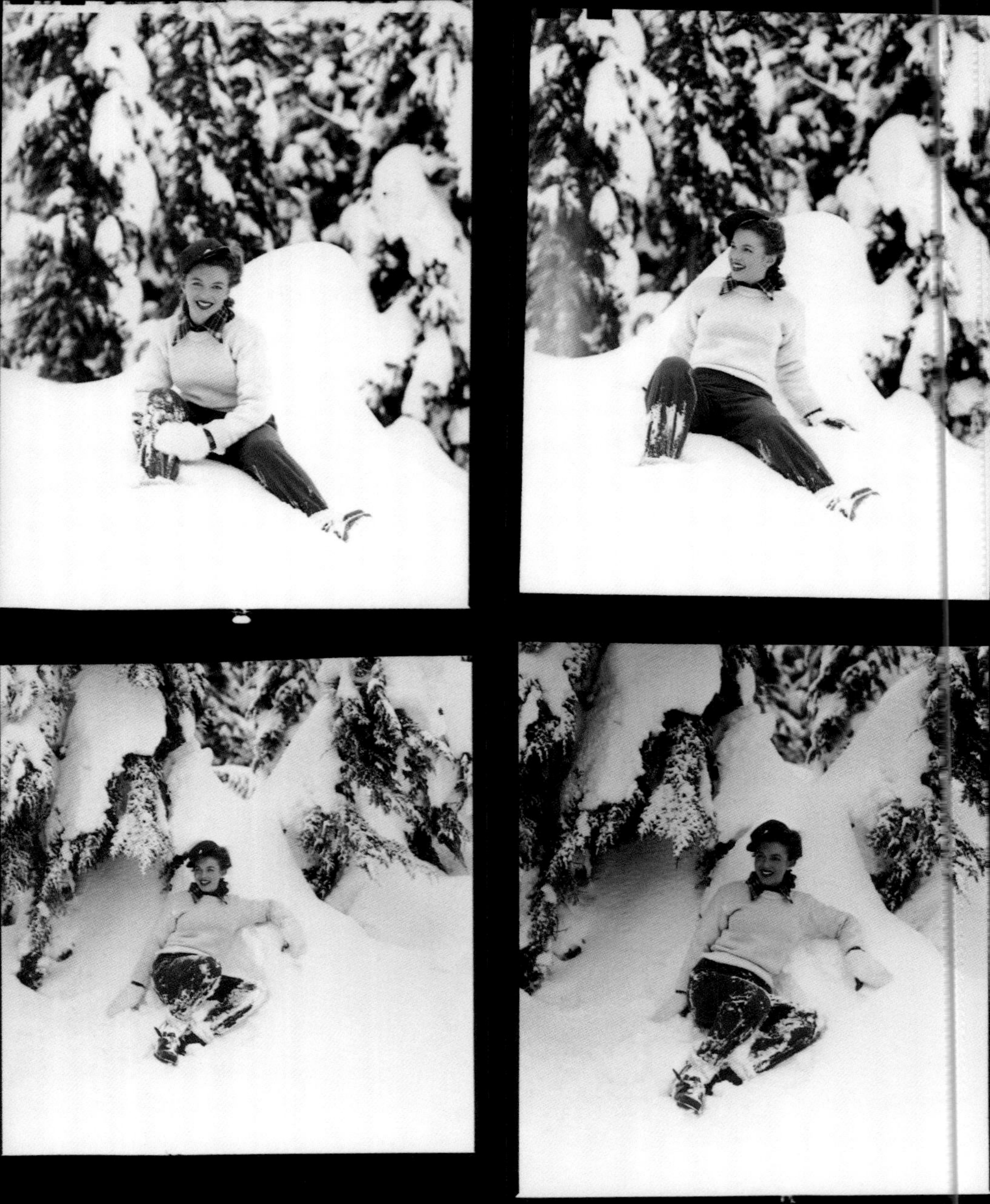

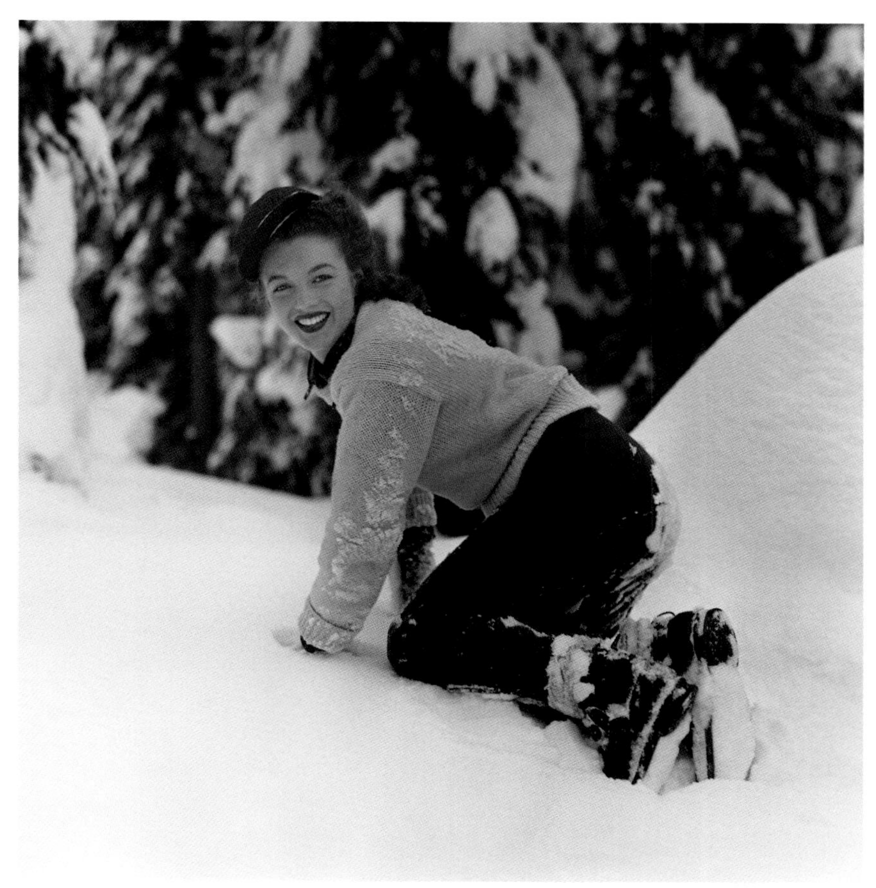

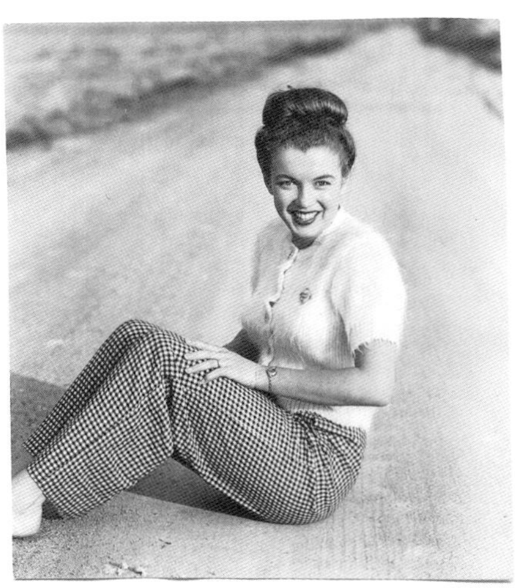

<u>Idyll Interrupted</u> I had the strong urge to call my fortune-teller friend in New York, to tell him about Norma Jeane – that I got all of a sudden engaged to that girl he predicted I would meet and fall in love with in Hollywood! I called and called my studio all night, without luck. When I called him at his other place, I got the shocking news, the surprise of my life. The man at the desk told me that my friend was killed in an automobile accident while speeding on a rainy night. He died instantly.

The idyll, the romance between Norma Jeane and me was drastically interrupted, even severed. If I had not phoned New York, who knows where else I could have taken Norma Jeane and where the trip would have ended. If only I hadn't made that phone call so soon, I could have continued photographing and loving Norma Jeane!

The last thing I remember of her in that hotel room is that while I was on the phone to New York, she was painting her fingernails and her toenails bright red. And she was showing me her beautiful legs in a very enticing way, not like a girl who is ready to get married to a man who loved the rugged outdoors and shunned the phony façade of Hollywood.

The news about the death of my friend changed my plans immediately. I was worried about leaving my studio in New York unattended. It was fortunate that the snow stopped, the road got cleared by the big snow-plows, and we were on our way back to Los Angeles, to take Norma Jeane home. The trip was long and Norma Jeane was often carsick and dizzy.

She had to sleep a lot to fight it! Later in her life, when she became Marilyn Monroe, constantly in demand for work or to give interviews, and was late to show up to work at Fox, she used the excuse that she was ill. Nobody believed her. I did believe it! Because I remember and still remember, that despite her cheerful, enthusiastic attitude to life, sometimes her moods changed. The long drives tired her mind; she said she was carsick and needed sleep.

I suppose I must have confused Norma Jeane on that trip. Sometimes the issue was that we would get married, travel and do things together, and other times it was my boasting that I would find gold and become very rich, and then I contradicted all that with my predictions that she would become famous and successful in the movies. So all that must have been confusing to her. Then, on occasion, when we discussed the future, I asked her what she would really like to become. To my surprise, she said a lawyer! I asked why, and she said she would like to do good, to defend the helpless and victimized! That was a beautiful statement.

We discussed that she would come to live with me in New York, in my studio on 58th Street and 5th Avenue which I would decorate beautifully starting as soon as I returned to New York, and she would go to Columbia University to study law. This wasn't just talk – we meant it!

PAIN....

IN PORTLAND OREGON,

Anticipating of a happy reunion between Norma Jeane and her mother, we bought various presents to bring (for which I paid--of course) but the actual meeting was a great let-down. A dull, rather gloomy event. Or, so it seemed to me. The Hotel was an old, mediocre place, in the center of Portland. We found her mother in a small room, on the top floor. She greeted Norma Jeane with a sad expression, than she set in a chair near the window, and they carried on a slow-paced conversation, in very low, monotonous tone. The lady was middle aged, or a little older, thin, expressionless, void of any emotional ups-and-downs while the conversation went on. I can not remember what they talked about. Norma Jeane was in good spirit, she tried to cheer up her mother, but unsuccessfully. Before we went to visit the lady, I failed to question Norma Jeane about her mother. So I had no idea why she was just released from some institution for serious mental problems, or insanity, or whatever, so I did not know exactly what the circumstances were between the two. I recall only, that, during the conversation, her mother put her head into her hands, bent down, and there were rather painful silent moments like that. It was a dark, cloudy afternoon, the room seemed very gloomy to me. Norma Jeane looked at me with painful embarassment, than, since there was little else to do, we departed. My mind was on my trip, I was eager to reach Timberline Lodge, a wonderful big Hotel, some sixty miles eat of Portland, at the foot of Mount Hood, where I was planning to do some skiing.

I am sorry I did not take any pictures of Norma Jeane with her mother, but, since I have never liked to get mixed up in other people's family relationships, I did not even think of snapping pictures of the two in that darkly lit, sad room. I was a young, amorous man; I wanted to be with Norma Jeane; I wanted to be happy! But now, I have great regrets for not having captured with my camera that pathetic sadness I witnessed, in that Hotel room.

PLEASURE.... "Marry Me!"

It was raining while we drove to Mount Hood, (Oregon,) and the rain turned into snowing when I got to the TIMBERLINE LODGE. I went in, inquired for accomodations, there was only one room available with double bed. I went out to the car where Norma Jeane was waiting, she was in a rather serious mood, she said she would prefer it if we would drive on, and find cabins somewhere in the woods, among snow-covered pine trees.... separate cabins..... I felt disappointed, because I liked that hotel, I loved the comfort there, the opportunity would have been extraordinary there to take pictures of Mount Hood, that beautiful, extinct, snow-covered volcano, when the sun would come out, And, it's a fantastic place for good skiing ! But I obeyed to Norma Jeane and drove down on the narrow curving road -- while it was snowing real hard, and dusk was coming. At the junction of that narrow road and the main highway, there was a place called Government Lodge, with a few homes and Hotel; an old brick building; and right there, the snow was already deep, my car could not go any further. We got stuck right in front of the Hotel, as if fate's hand had guided us there purposely, and in that Hotel, too, there was only one room left available, a room up on the fourth floor, with one double bed, The bathroom was at the end of a long corridor. I came out to inform Norma Jeane, to tell her we have to stay there! It was already darkening, nearly evening, Norma Jeane smiled at me; She said o.k., let's take the room, Let's not worry any more about anything!

A funny thing happened there almost as soon as I registered. On the left side of the ground floor there was a long bar, on the right side the restaurant, and slot-machines everywhere. Intuition is a baffling, amazing thing; I pointed at one slot machine out of the many, and said Norma Jeane, in loud voice, that she needed pocket money for Jergen's Lotion, (what she loved for her skin) and other cosmetics, and I am commending the machine to provide the "jackpot" for it ! The bartender, and everybody at the bar was staring at me, perhaps thinking I have gone nuts, and again, like in Nevada, I told Norma Jeane to stretch out the buttom of her sweather under the machine. I put the quarter in, pulled the handle, and outgushed a flood of quarters ! Everybody cheered. Norma Jeane was counting the money, and she put it away in her purse. For a minute I watched, and jokingly I said to her, " don't I deserve a commission ! " But instead of answering, she turned to the bartender, saying " Serve him a drink ! But just one drink ! " And they all loughed But I had at least two drinks ! She didn't have any !

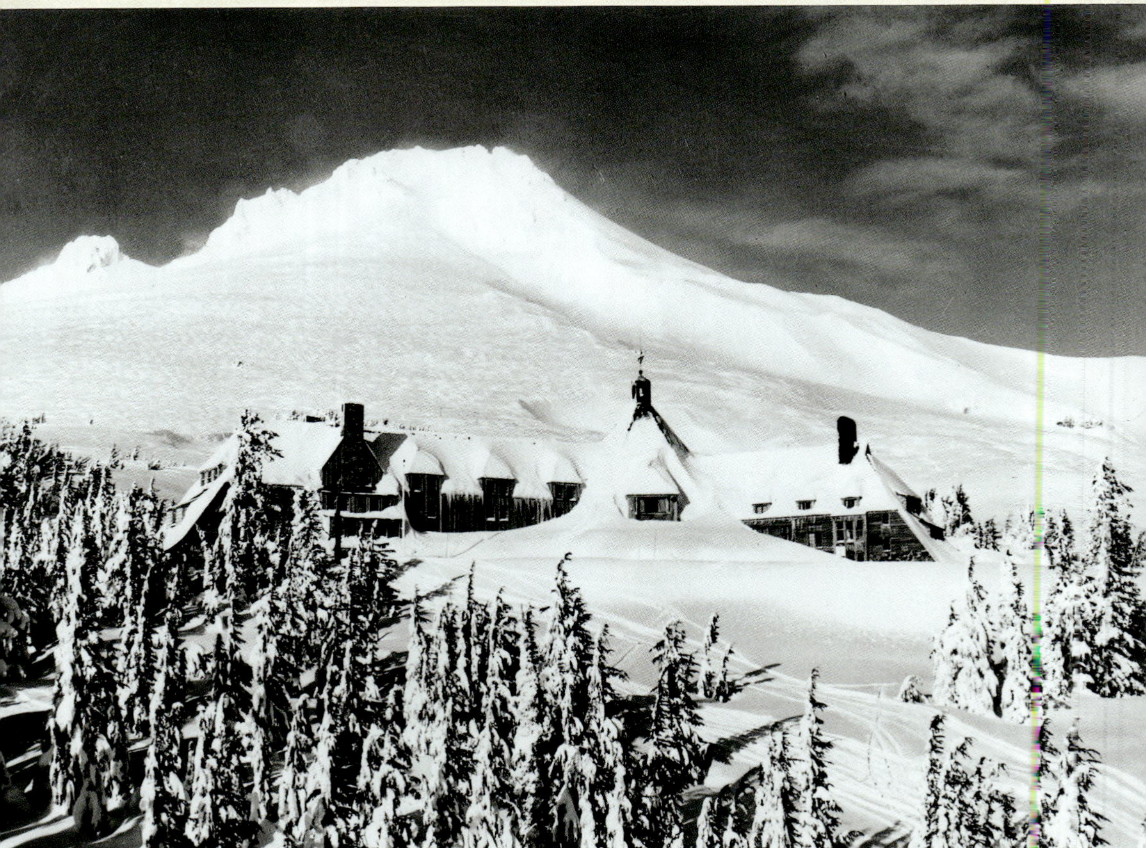

This is the view of Timberline Lodge. Snowed in, like the time Norma Jeane spoiled it for us to stay there. (in the background, Mt. Hood)

(COURTESY, TIMBERLINE LODGE)

We had a good dinner, and afterward we flipped a coin to decide who will occupy the bathroom first. It wasn't much of a bathroom, just a lousy shower, and the toilet, at the end of a dismally lit, long corridor.

We went to bed without the slightest nervousness, as if what was happening was the most natural thing in the world... A strange contrast to all the days of amorous emotions I had to fight, and the frustration I went through every night. Finally, we had to spend the night together, in the same bed! When the lovemking was over with, Norma Jeane cried in my arms. She was happy, satisfied. And I was holding her, and holding her, and my thoughts drifted back to my childhood, to ten years before, when Krisztina, the maid, took me in her arms one night. I felt that it was an amazingly similar feeling to be in Norma Jeane's arms, and she in my arms. I felt her face, wet with tears, exactly like Krisztina's tear-drenched face, while she was holding and embracing me. Norma Jean, too, was holding me as if I were her child. I think, to a woman, a man is always half child, half man. At long last, being unified with Norma Jeane was an unbelievable experince for me, as if all the 10 years gone by were just a few days, and love. I felt as if the two women were the same, just one woman. Norma Jeane's body was the same, her hair felt the same, her voice was the same, her loughter sounded the same as Krisztina's. I had to spend ten years, and travel ten thousand miles to find another Krisztina... I felt like being in heaven !

But you, the reader might not be interested in these sentimentalities. You might say, "Andre, don't give us this sentimental hogwash, let's hear what was really like to make love with the future Marilyn Monroe !" To that, I can only answer that love-making depends greatly on the man. Generally, the man is the leader ("the orchestra leader") the woman submits, follows, contributes. A woman is usually as exciting as the man feels about her. And vice versa. But to respect Marilyn's memory, I prefer not to discuss sex. She was a divine, lovely young woman! She said she was never as happy before! She was crying

I fell asleep with the feeling that, at long, long last, remembering the sight of Krisztina's beautiful body; there was somebody, a young,beautiful young woman, with her body completely naked, like once, Krisztina, having shown to me the body of a woman completly naked, given to all my masculine desires, an immense, masculine desire, an immense desire for the feminine body, mixed with poetic feelings.......
Sensuality, sexualtiy, idealisme,-- all mixed in a tension, a complete idealisation of body and soul; a marvellous combination of the self and the mind; a fantastic sensouous poetic feeling of sensuous desires and mental processes of the soul, until the untimate climax of an orgasme; a passion what lasted for several hours ! It was poetry and reality all mixed ! The result of an immense storm of one's being frustrareted for weeks beforehand, and stemming back to my childhood, seeing in my mind the maid's body,Krisztina's body, strong, feminine, sensuous, in all the nakedness of nature , bathing nude, standing naked in the sunlight's complete radity, large-breasted, her hair combed out; her hips curvacious, and the sunshine spreading beautiful feelings all around......
It was a fantastic, an almost supernatural feeling when I fell asleep in bed, with Norma Jean......... Norma Jean was hugging me, I was kising her tears; she said she had never had an orgasm before in her life; And I felt greatly satisfied also, having waited for at least for two weeks -- to make love with her, was for more than I could possibly endure !
Young love, clashed in complete sincerity, was the end result-- that night !
Why haven't or couldn't I made her pregnent; I asked myself ever after.......
~~Or was it just oral-sex; I don't remember for sure...... to be honest.~~
But when I fell asleep, I felt that she was the only girl I ever loved, and I could love ever after,until my dying days.......
HOW IRONIC, HOW INCREDIBLE, that so many years have gone by since those years in 1945, and to this days, in 1983, I have not found a female I could be so attached to emotionally -- as to Norma Jean!....

Next noon, when we went down for lunch, it was still snowing hard, and my car was covered with snow. The wife of the owner of the hotel took us for honeymooners , and offrered us the best room they had, on the first floor, a wood panelled wonderful cosy room, which just got freed. We stayed in there for two days, while it was still snowing relentlessly. Our short stay there was like being in paradise !

A bizarre event happened there in that room during the first day of our stay; Norma Jeane was manicuring, and putting nail-polish on her toenails, and she lifted her hands in the air to show me her palms, that she observed, how curious it was that in each palm there was a large M. Somewhat childlishly, we compared our palms, looking at the lines in them. And there, I told Norma Jean the story of the old bell-ringer in Transylvania, who, in my childhood, predicted that the two letters M.M. will mean a great deal to me when I shall be a grown-up man. And I told Norma Jeane the story about my meeting the old man while reading a strange old book, and the old man was most preoccupied with one of the pages where the writing began with the two words MEMENTO MORI. Norma Jeane was fascinated by my story, and we discussed again and again two M-s in our palms. And I told her jovially, that the M-s had nothing to do with death, well to the contrary, they meant " Marry Me!". And we pressed our palms together. Than, we hugged and kissed, and decided we shall get married as soon as she would get a divorce from her husband. We decided she would go to Las Vegas, Nevada to get the divorce, and we would get married there, right after.

From those moments onward, we felt we were engaged. I told Norma Jeane about my wonderings through Transylvania on foot, and having carved many times in the bark of trees the two initilas M.M., I promised her that, when we will get married, I shall buy her a thick, heavy, gold wedding ring, and I shall have the two initials M.M. engraved inside the ring ! -- as a memento for ever, to remember the amazing prediction of the old bellringer. I even took a picture of her palm.

While it was snowing, we stayed in our room all day long, except for a brief hour, when I took her out to photograph her in the snow. I was reading; she was pampering herself, combing her curly hair out, again and again at the mirror, and draping herself in the bedsheet, while examining the results in the mirror. A sexy little 'vampire' she was(!) as she was glamorizing herself with the bedsheet, as if it were an expensive evening gown! But I was too much in love with her, the Norma Jeane.... the vision of my childhood idol, Krisztina, the peasant girl !

If only I had the foresight, to photograph her in that room, while she was glamorising herself, or photograph her on the bed, naked, quite uninhibited ...

The future Marilyn Monroe was there, in that room! A sexy Hollywood beauty! A sex-symbol was incubating that afternoon ! Perhaps I was too tired to VISUALIZE it (!), And now I live to regret my negligence !

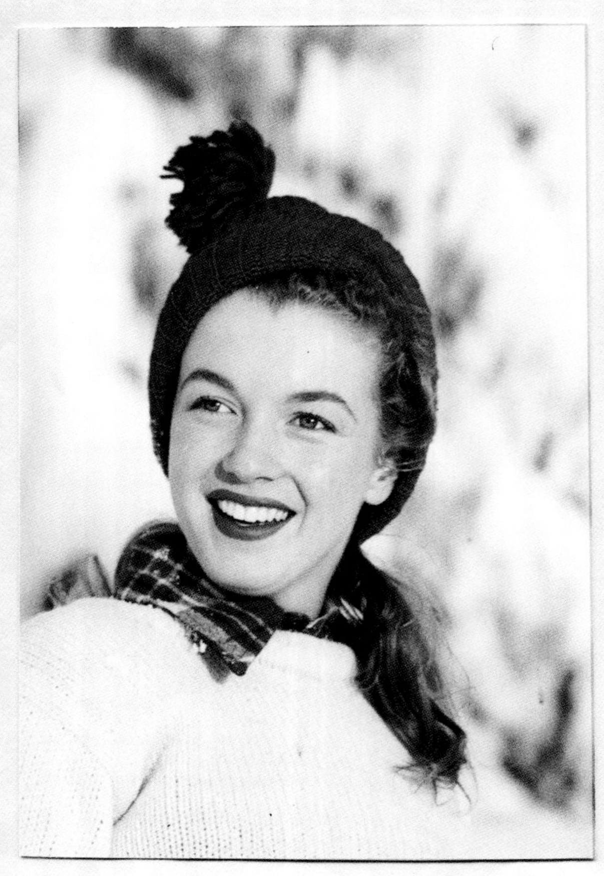

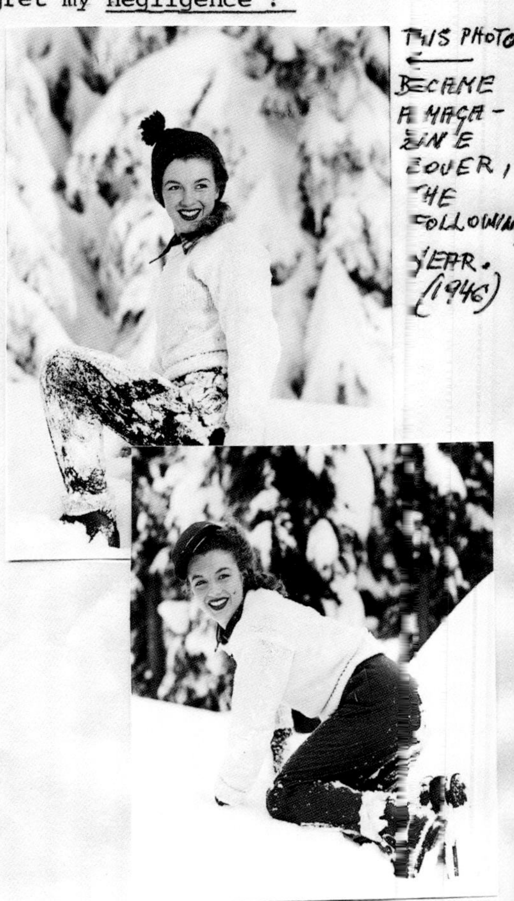

THIS PHOTO ← BECAME A MAGAZINE COVER, THE FOLLOWING YEAR. (1946)

I had the strong urge to call my mind-reader, fortune-teller, card-reader friend in New York, to tell him about Norma Jeane! That I got all of a sudden engaged to that girl he predicted I shall meet and fall in love with in Hollywood! I called and called my studio all night, without luck. And when I called him at his other place, I got a shocking news, the surprise of my life! The man at the desk told me, that my friend was killed in an automobile accident. While speeding on a rainy night, he didn't stop at a red light, and another car hit his car, broadside, and my friend died instantly.

I was stupefied and Norma Jeane was recalling the old lady's prognostigation about the tarantula spider predicting misfortune! The idyll, the romance between Norma Jeane and I was drastically interrupted, even severed. If I had not phoned New York, who knows where else I would have taken Norma Jeane, and where and how the trip would have ended. Life depend always on those little if-s, which are like cornerstones in the labyrint of events in the lives of all people. If only I hadn't made that phone call so soon, so I could continue to enjoy photographing, and loving Norma Jeane!

But what if I had climbed Mount Hood, as I told Norma Jeane I wanted to, and I would have frozen to death!

Or what might have been our later lives like, if Norma Jean would have gotten pregnent by me, on that trip! ? IFS... IFS... WHAT IF....

I think everything happened as it was meant to be! Norma Jean was destined to become Marilyn Monroe. The last thing I remember of her in that hotel room, that, while I was on the phone with New York, she was painting her finger nails, and all her toe-nails, bright red. And she was showing me her beautiful leggs, in a very enticing way, not like a girl who is ready to get married to a man who loves the rugged outdoors, and shunns the phony facade of Hollywood, and night clubs, and evening gowns.

L-7

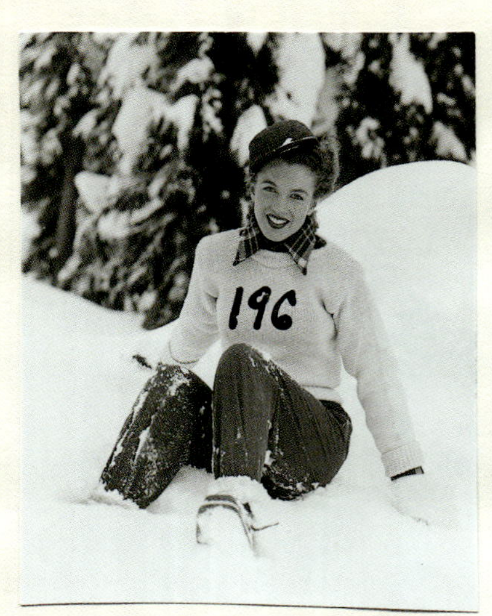

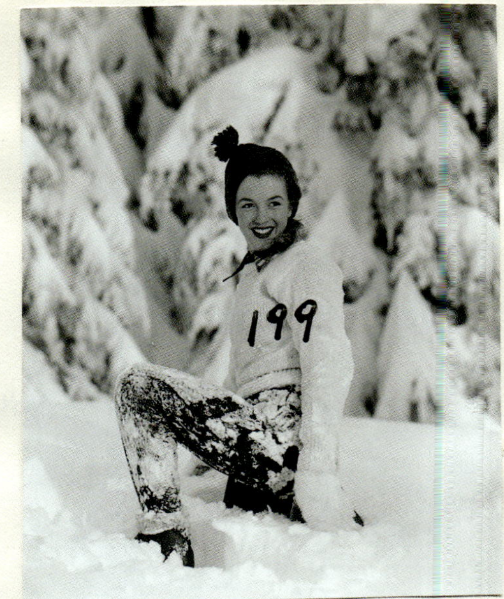

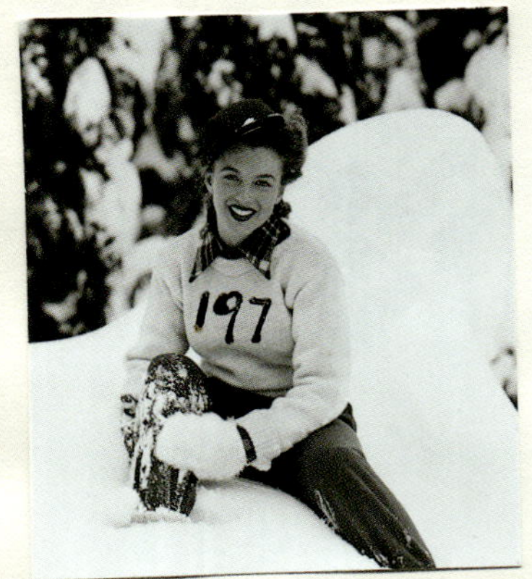

AT MOUNT HOOD,

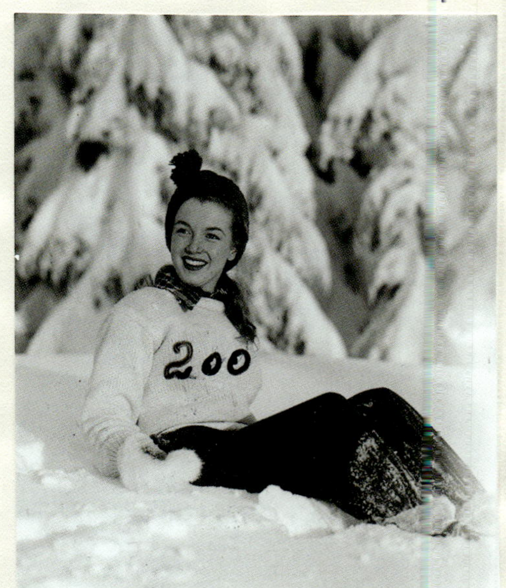

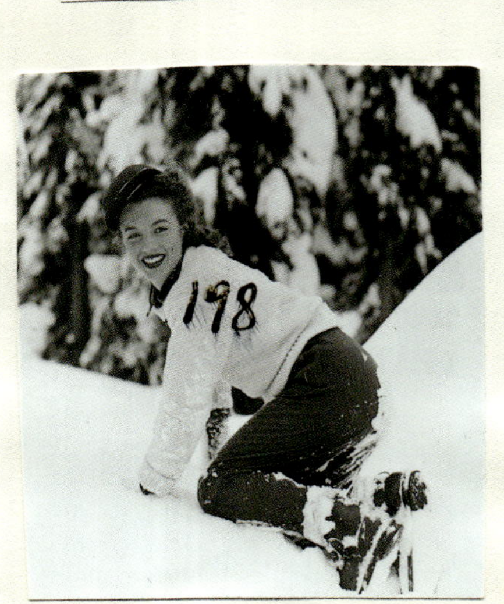

IN OREGON,
DEC. 1945

3

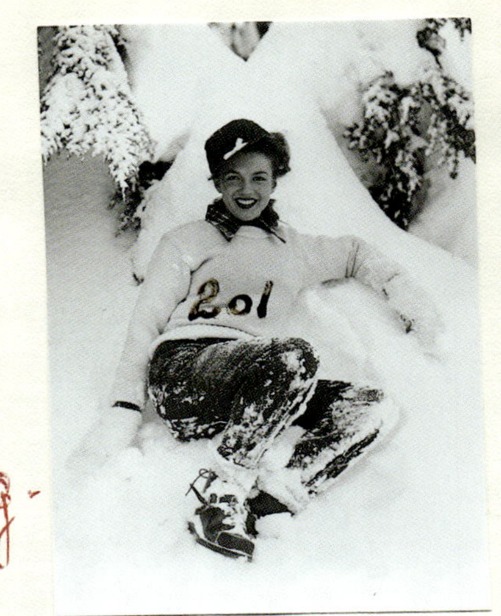

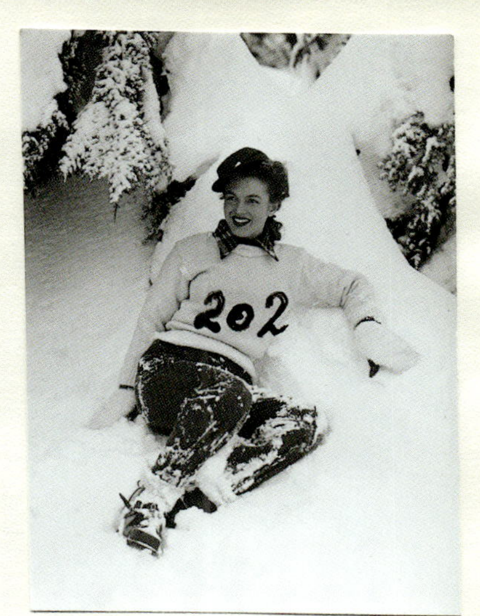

g-

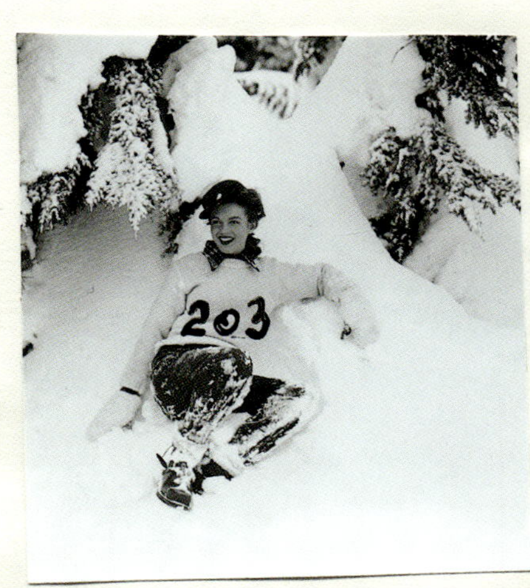

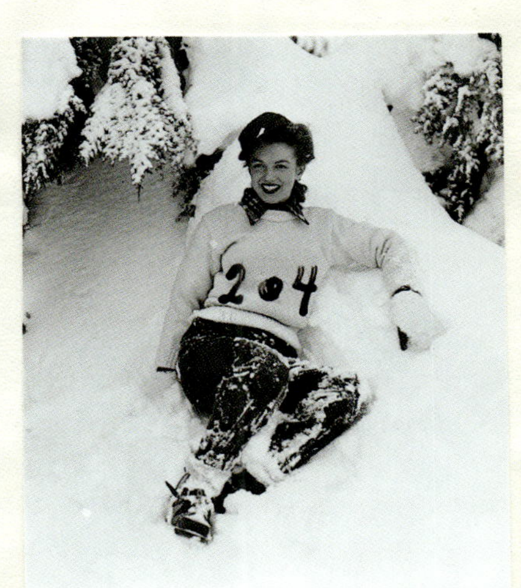

L-7

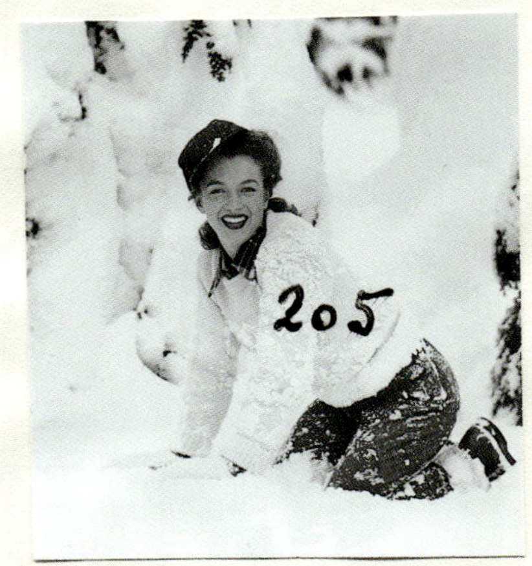

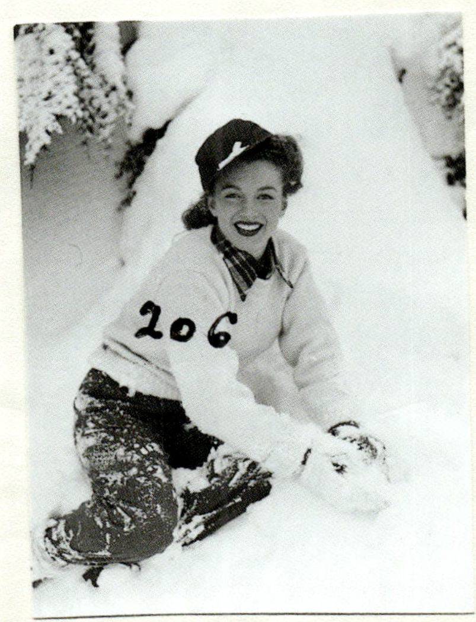

ANDRE DE DIENES

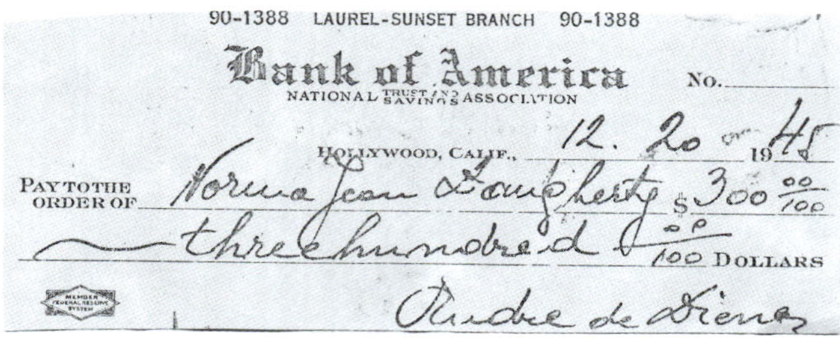
90-1388 LAUREL-SUNSET BRANCH 90-1388

Bank of America
NATIONAL TRUST AND SAVINGS ASSOCIATION

No.

HOLLYWOOD, CALIF., 12. 20 1945

PAY TO THE ORDER OF Norma Jean Dougherty $ 300 00/100

three hundred 00/100 DOLLARS

Andre de Dienes

<u>Hollywood</u> As I look back, indeed it was confusing, sort of making plans for our future marriage. But what happened an hour later gave a good blow to it all. We were approaching Los Angeles and entered Hollywood by Laurel Canyon. It was evening, and we reached Sunset Boulevard at the 8000 block, where the Garden of Allah was, where we had first met a month before. I suggested having coffee at Schwab's Pharmacy, a famous drugstore which was like a landmark in Hollywood. For nearly fifty years, it was the gathering place of a potpourri of movie personalities in Hollywood, and show biz people who came here to try their luck in Hollywood; movie extras, male and female, young actors and actresses, talent scouts, agents, handsome wolves, etc. Even the famous columnist Sidney Skolsky stopped by every day; the place was his information-gathering source for several decades. To Norma Jeane, I suggested going to Schwab's because I was going to write a check for the two weeks she traveled with me, a hundred dollars a week, plus I added a hundred dollars more to be nice to her. And she would sign the usual model's release. That way of doing business was a routine, customary thing for me. Even with my new fiancée it had to be so!

Norma Jeane didn't know anything about Schwab's drugstore, as she had never been there before, and I thought it would be nice to take her there. But it turned out that I took my darling little "lamb" right into a lion's den. Hardly a few moments passed after I gave her the check and she signed the release, when a photographer I knew came over to us saying something like this: "André, I must congratulate you! You know how to pick pretty girls! Who is this delightful creature, would you please introduce me to her? I would like to photograph her someday." And the photographer and Norma Jeane engaged in conversation. The photographer started bragging about what a great photographer he was and what beautiful photographs he would take of her. The truth was that as a photographer, he was just okay, but as a seducer of women he had a great reputation in Hollywood. Norma Jeane was smiling, happy, very nice to him, and willingly wrote down her phone number for him. She told him she would call him in a few days and would be very happy to pose for him!

It was like a thunderbolt had struck me. I got a fantastic shock, seeing my beloved Norma Jeane nearly flirting and giving her phone number to the photographer so willingly. Of course, I felt jealous, but controlled my rage and revulsion. I was shocked that my newfound sweetheart, my future wife, was so delighted to give her phone number to a total stranger! The shock awakened me from the dream, from the illusion… from the puppy-love we built on the trip…. We were back in Hollywood! And the reality was that she was just a model whom I hired to pose for me! And then, at the drugstore, she was free again to pursue her career, to do as she pleased! Indeed, even though she had said nothing to me about wanting to be in the movies, Norma Jeane was just another pretty girl in Hollywood who wanted to make it in the movies, and I was just a girl-crazy photographer who fell in love with her!

Suddenly, my mind got illuminated by the truth, that certain relationships are like castles of cards, collapsing at any moment, by the slightest touch. But now, thinking of it, I realize that the trip home was a long ordeal and we were both tired from driving a thousand miles without interruption, so Norma Jeane found it refreshing to be greeted by a man who flattered her so strongly! Besides, I know it was meant to be so. She was nice to me, too, from the first moment she met me. So she was nice to that photographer, and nice to many, many people she met afterward. That is the natural course of life! It was a good thing I did not show my jealousy. I took her home to Aunt Ana in West Los Angeles, and we parted in good spirits, agreed to write, and planned to get married after her divorce sometime in the middle of the following year, 1946.

Nothing Would Stop Her During the months that followed my engagement with Norma Jeane, through the first part of 1946, she and I corresponded regularly and spoke on the phone also. But it was she who phoned most of the time – collect, of course – and usually the conversation ended with her letting me know that she was broke. I remember her crying in the phone, loudly enough for me to hear, about being broke, and the conversation always ended with me promising to wire her by Western Union – right away – twenty-five or fifty dollar sums. I did that quite a few times. Poor thing, she had a hard time getting started in her career as a model.

Then summer 1946 was approaching, and Norma Jeane went to Las Vegas to get divorced from her husband, James Dougherty. I contributed some money to her expenses, and it was agreed that we would get married in that little chapel she liked in Las Vegas.

I phoned Norma Jeane in Los Angeles to tell her she could leave for Las Vegas and instructed her in which hotel to meet me. I told her how wonderfully happy I felt that at last we were getting married. Disaster struck me in those moments: in a sweet, apologetic voice, Norma Jeane said, "André, please don't come, I can't marry you! I want to become an actress!" She said she had thought it over and her career was more important! She wanted to get into the movies! The news shocked me, but I took it calmly and told her I would come to Los Angeles anyway and that I would phone her when I arrived.

I drove hundreds of miles without rest to reach Hollywood and when I arrived, I phoned Norma Jeane again. She said she would meet me at Sunset and Vine, in front of the NBC studios, at 1 p.m. I waited there at least 2 hours but she didn't show up. Then, jealous, enraged, disillusioned, and feeling cheated and betrayed, I drove to her apartment on South 3rd Street in Santa Monica. As I was parking the car in front of the building, I saw a man coming out and I had a strong, intuitive feeling that he had just left Norma Jeane's apartment. I backed my car away a short distance and watched the man drive away, then I waited a few minutes or so and then went to ring her doorbell. Norma Jeane opened the door and gazed at me, ashen white and speechless. She wore a black lacy sort of nightgown – somewhat torn – and there were empty wine bottles and empty glasses on the table behind her, movie scripts, phonograph records in confusion, the bed all messed up, and a large bouquet of flowers in a vase. I stood there, smiling, sizing up the delightfully disorderly room and sensing what must have been going on there during the previous hours. Norma Jeane was extremely embarrassed. I took her tenderly in my arms, kissed her cheeks, pressed my cheek against hers, and I consoled her, asking her not to be so embarrassed….

I felt guilty for surprising her. She was sniffling for a while, her cheeks were wet with tears, but she regained her composure and soon she was in her usual cheerful mood. We agreed that our marriage was over with. But so what? We would remain friends! I promised that

I would never be jealous or possessive in any way from then on, and that I would never come to visit her unannounced! My sweet Norma Jeane was smiling again. I even made her laugh, when I told her she made the right decision not to marry a domineering sex-maniac Hungarian like me!

I remained in California for a few more months after that afternoon in 1946. I remember I did ask Norma Jeane whether that man who left her apartment when I arrived was any use to her, to advance her career. And she said, "YES!" I knew who the man was, someone very important in Hollywood who slept with many beautiful girls. So I asked Norma Jeane what he had done for her. She handed me a clipping from the newspaper. In the photo, she sat at his side in a nightclub. It was then that I felt nothing would stop Norma Jeane from getting ahead in her career. It became clear to me that she was a true product of Hollywood; her mother worked for the movie studios, she was born and raised there and she had no other culture than what she absorbed in her childhood from the atmosphere of Hollywood. Her destiny was not at all with me.

ANDRE DE DIENES
1401 SUNSET PLAZA DRIVE
HOLLYWOOD, CALIF. 90069

Copy
The model release
Norma Jean signed
12/1945

EXHIBIT B

For a valuable consideration, the receipt whereof I hereby acknowledge, I hereby grant, sell and transfer to Andre de Dienes, 18 East 58th Street, New York City, his successors and assigns, my photographs and the right to use my said photographs for advertising purposes, for the purposes of trade, for the purpose of illustrating any story or article in any magazine, periodical or newspaper, or for use in connection therewith or for any other purpose whatsoever, without any claim of any nature by me, whether said claim be for libel, for violation of my right of privacy or otherwise, and whether arising out of any statute or otherwise, and I do hereby specifically waive and release any claim that I might otherwise have by reason of the use of my photograph or photographs for any purpose whatsoever, and I agree not to bring any suit or other proceeding by reason thereof.

Norma Jeane Dougherty (L.S.)
(Signed)

1134 Nebraska Ave.
(Address)

563-32-0764
(Social Security No.)

Dated:

Reader: Note the e at the end of Jeane

Norma Jeane didn't know anything about Schwab's drugstore, she had never been there before, and I thought it would be nice to take her there, but as it turned out to be, I took my darling little lamb right into the lion's den. Hardly a few moments passed after I gave her the check, and she signed the release, when a photographer I knew came over to us saying something like this: Andre, I must congratulate you ! You know how to pick pretty girls ! Who is this delightful creature with you ? Would you please introduce me to her ! I would like to photograph her some day " And the photographer and Norma Jeane engaged into conversation, the photographer bragging what a great photographer was, and what beautiful photos he will take of her. The truth was that as photographer he was just o.k. but as seductor of women, and lover, he had a great reputation in Hollwyood. Norma Jeane was smiling, happy, very nice to him, and willingly wrote down her phone number to him, and he gave her his card, Norma Jeane told him she will call him in a few days, and will be very happy to pose for him !

It was like if thunder had struck me! I got a fantastic shock seeing my beloved Norma Jeane nearly flirting, and her phone number to the photographer so willingly ! Of course I felt jalous, but controlled my rage and revulsion, but I was shockd that my newly found sweetheart, my future wife was so delighted giving herphone number to a total stranger ! The shock awakened me from the dream, from the illusion....from the poppy-love we built up on the trip..... We were back in Hollwyood and the reality was that she was just a model whom I hired to take pictures of, and than, at the drugstore she was free again to pursue her career, and do as she pleased. Indeed, even though she had said nothing to me about wanting a career in the movies, Norma Jeane was just another pretty girl in Hollwywood who want to make it in the movies. And that I myself was just a 'girl-crazy photographer' falling in love with one girl after another! And whoever falls in love with a girl who is a model, or an actress -- is looking for nothing but trouble ! Suddenly my mind got illuminated by the truth, that certain relationships are like castles of cards, collapsing at any moment, by the slightest touch.... Like when Norma Jeane and the photographer smiling at each other..... And her, being so nice to him !

But now, thinking of it, I realized the trip home was a long ordeal; we were both tired driving a thousand miles without interruption, so Norma Jeane found it refreshing to be greeted by a man who flattered her ego so strongly ! Besides, I know, it was meant to be so! She was nice to me, too, from the first moment she met me the first time, when she came for the interview. So she was nice to that photographer, and nice to many many people whom she met afterward. But that is the natural course of life ! We smile, we are pleasant, we turn out our best, when self-interest dictates it. Self-interest is the greatest driving force in us ! Completely understandeable to an enlightened mind !

It was a good thing I did not show my jealousy. I took her home to her Aunt Ana, in West Los Angeles, and we parted in good spirit, agreeing we shall write, and planned to get married after her divorce, sometimes in the middle of the following year. (1946)

How absurd, how monstruously stupidly we man behave when in pursuit of " LOVE "! Our minds are propelled ONLY by sex hormones ! We lose all reason! We hardly know what we are doing ! We are completely under the influence of our animal urge ! Yet, at the same time, I am asking myself, who is the wiser? The one who chases after ~~great~~ achievements, fortune, or the one who seeks to satisfy his romantic inclinations, or the libido...SEX! Who is really the judge of it all ?

(Anyway, the reader might as well know how the great Marilyn Monroe, my darling -- Norma Jeane -- began her career ! Partly at my expense !)

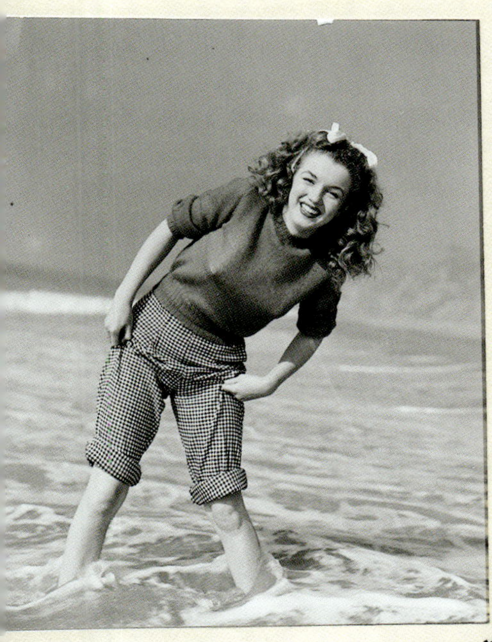

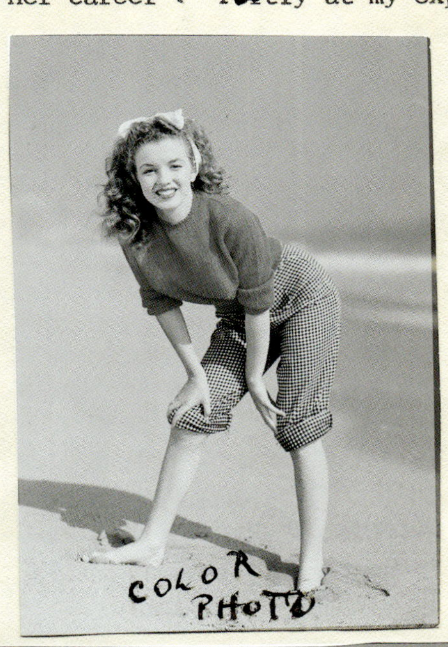

"SEX-APPEAL"
1945

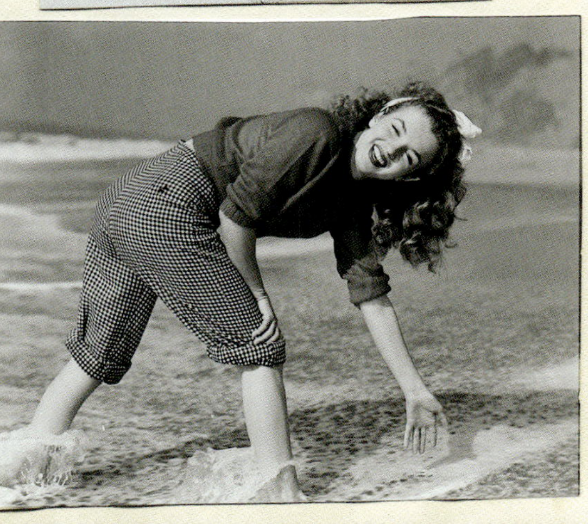

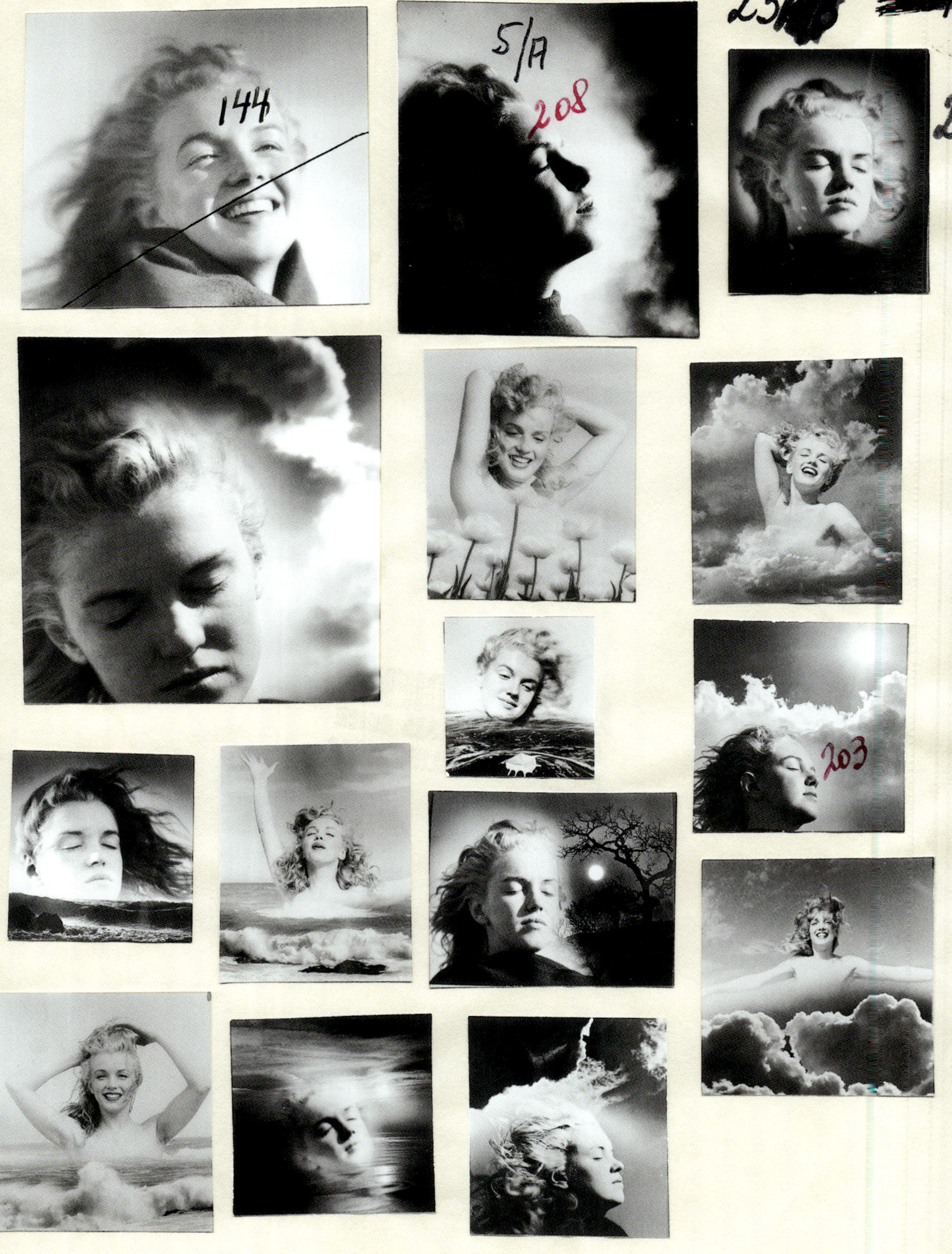

I keep creating a wide variety of similar photos, but I have not shown them to any publisher -- yet.

I remained in California for a few months after that afternoon in 1946, when I nearly killed myself, because Norma Jeane let me down, and I remember I did ask her whether that man, who left her apartment just when I arrived --was of any use to her-- to advance her career. And she said YES ! I knew who the man was. Some one very important in Hollywood, who slept with many beaufiful girls. And I asked Norma Jeane, what did he do good for her? She handed me a clipping from the newspaper. In the photo, she set on his side in a nightclub. I saw that photo already weeks before. But she wasn't Marilyn Monroe yet. It was than, that I felt that nothing shall stop Norma Jeane to get ahead in her career. I became clear to me that she was a true product of Hollywood; her mother worked for the movie studios, she Norma Jeane was born in Hollwyood, raised there, she had no other culture than what she have absorbed from childood onward the athmosphere of Hollwyood. Her destiny was "Hollywood", not at all with me. What are the main ingredients necessary for a young lady to try a career in show business ? A few very elemental things: To have something to offer! (sex appeal, talent, if possible both combined) To be where the action is! And to have guts ! Norma Jeane had all that ! Only eight months have gone by since I had first met her in Novermber 1945, yet the change was already very apparent. Her hair was blonder, she dressed with more sex-appeal, and she was freed from her marriage completely. She lived in a small apartment, and she did with her life as she pleased! Having been a very independent person myself, her new status struck a sympathetic feeling in me, and from than on, I began to boust her ego constantly. I used to do that to most of the models whom I knew, whom I photographed even before I met Norma Jeane, The case was always the same: young girl models, becuase she needs money, and wants a career of some sort -- to become famous, or to marry some one very rich.

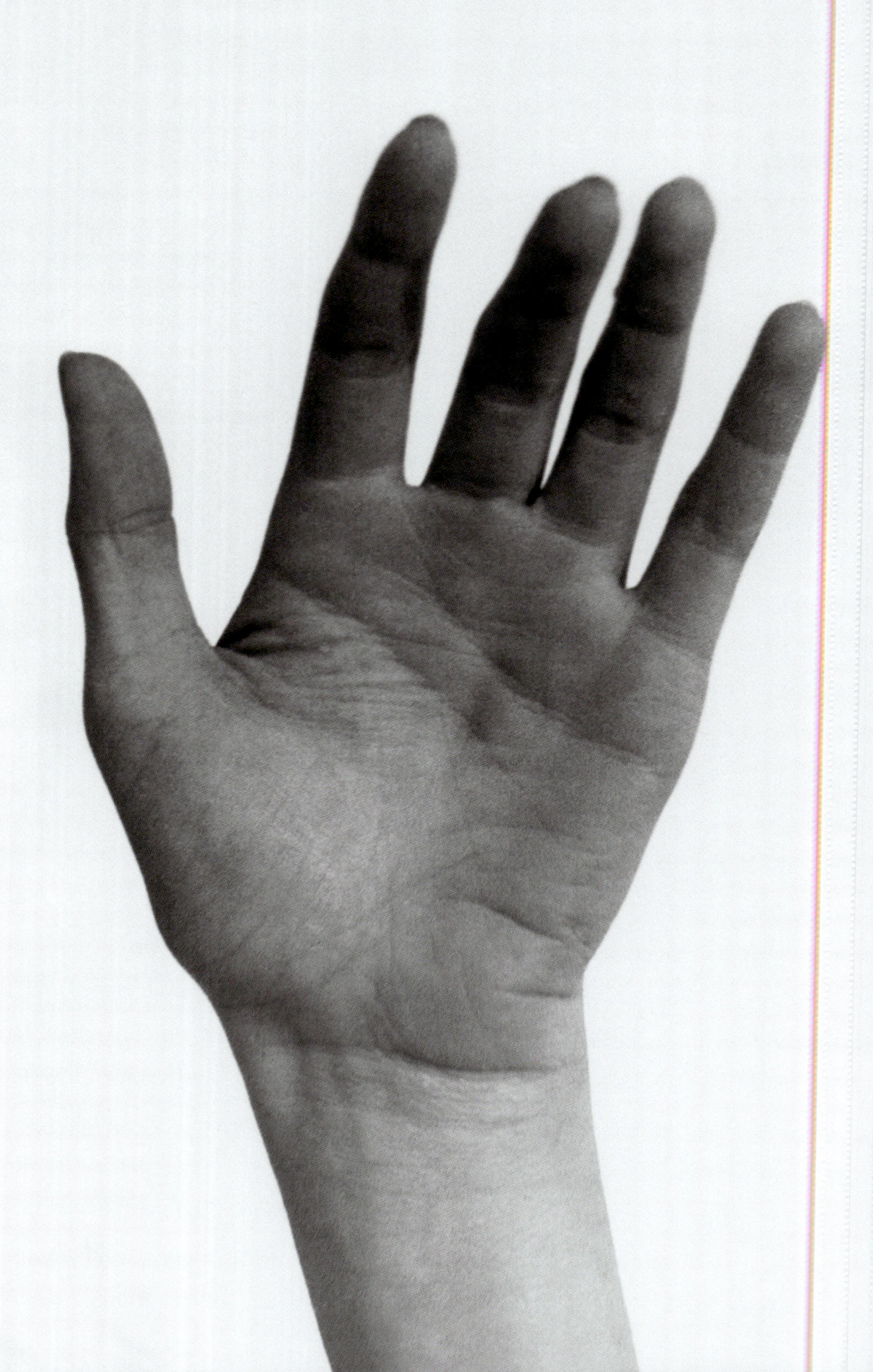

M. M.

M.M. During the summer of 1946, just at the onset of Labor Day, again, Norma Jeane called me to say she had important news to tell me, and she asked me to come to her apartment. When I got there, she came right to the subject: "Guess what, I have a new name!" With a pencil, slowly, carefully, she wrote her new name on a sheet of paper: MARILYN MONROE. And she emphasized the twoM initials in an almost calligraphic way! I have never forgotten, through all these years, my big surprise when I stood there, behind her, watching her writing her name…. There was something almost supernatural about how beautifully she wrote the large capitalMs. How much I've regretted since that day when Norma Jeane, or rather Marilyn, wrote down her name for me, that I did not have the foresight to keep that sheet of paper.

From now on, I shall refer to Norma Jeane as Marilyn. I had to get used to her new name right away. After she signed her new name, the conversation went on for a while about certain mysteries of life one cannot explain, like she so cleverly finding a name with two Ms, especially the name "Marilyn," because in Portland, Oregon, just a half year previously, I'd told her that the two large Ms in her palm meant "Marry Me," and now, even that resembles her new name – "Marry" became "Marilyn!" We were discussing how amazingly the subconscious mind goes to work and concocts decisions, because of previous impressions or suggestions!

I remembered that there was a long weekend ahead, and I suggested that we visit a few of the beautiful California Missions. Marilyn had

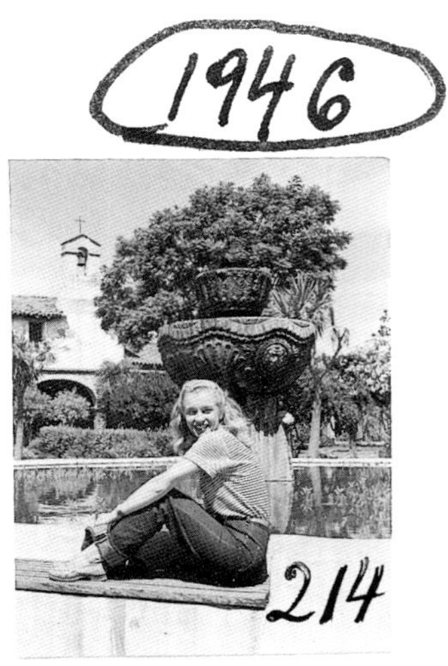

nothing better to do for the weekend. So we took off in my car to visit, first, the Mission in San Juan Capistrano, and afterward others, further down, and one in San Diego.

Marilyn loved the missions. She got exalted everywhere, and whenever we passed by a small cell, where padres once slept on primitive wooden beds with just a thin mattress, jokingly I remarked to Marilyn that we should remain in the mission after it closed, and we could bathe in the fountains outside and sleep in the beds the padres slept in a hundred or more years before! And I said to Marilyn rather loudly, "Let's stay, let's go to bed here tonight!" People around heard me and smiled, making some funny remarks; but sweet Marilyn did not get angry at me, she laughed good-heartedly and remarked, indeed, how lovely it might be to spend a night in an old adobe room by candlelight.

That evening, all the way down to San Diego, all the motel cabins were filled up. None available! Marilyn, exhausted, was sleeping in the back seat of the car. She did not care where she slept; she always trusted me, and I never failed to take good care of her.

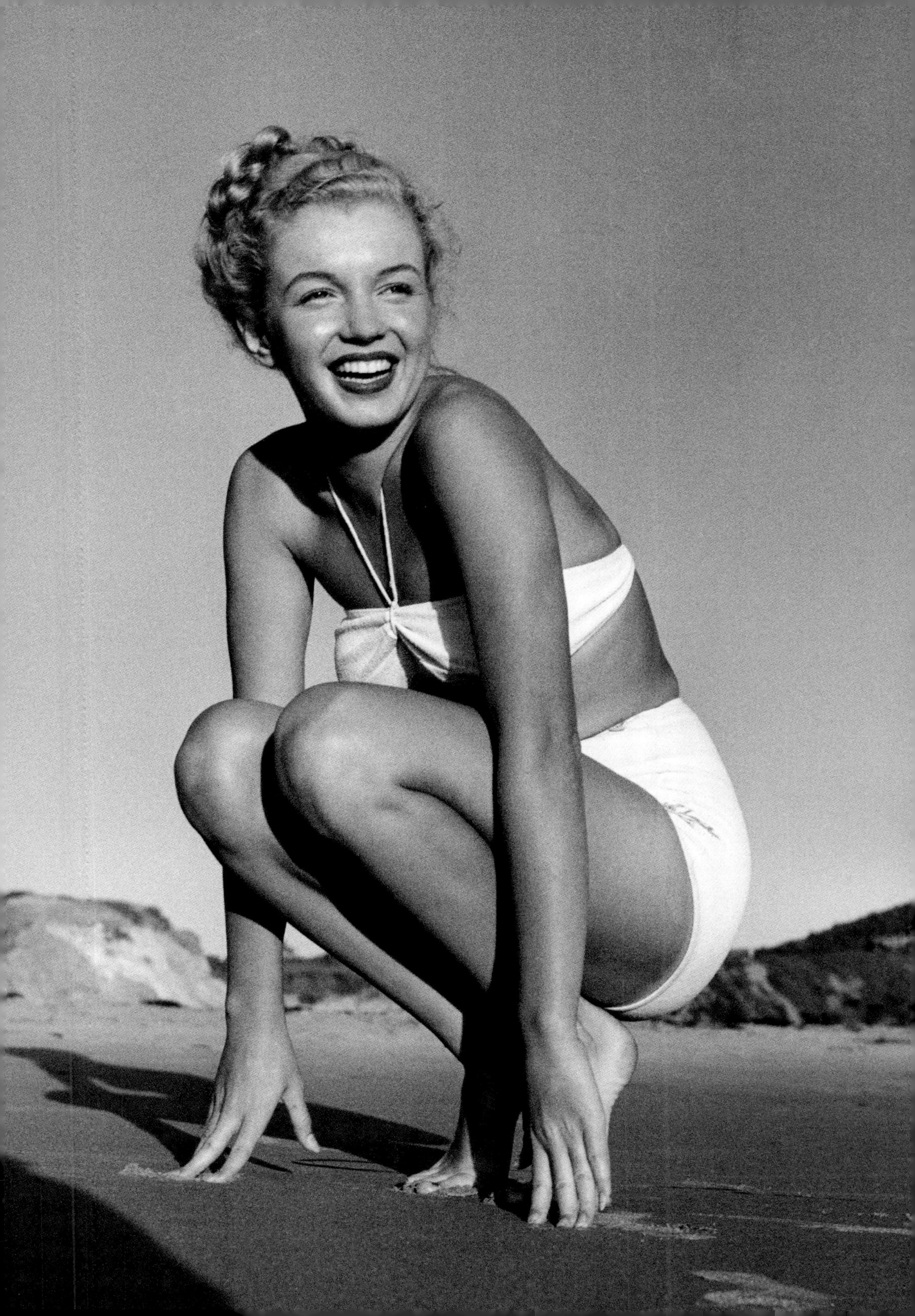

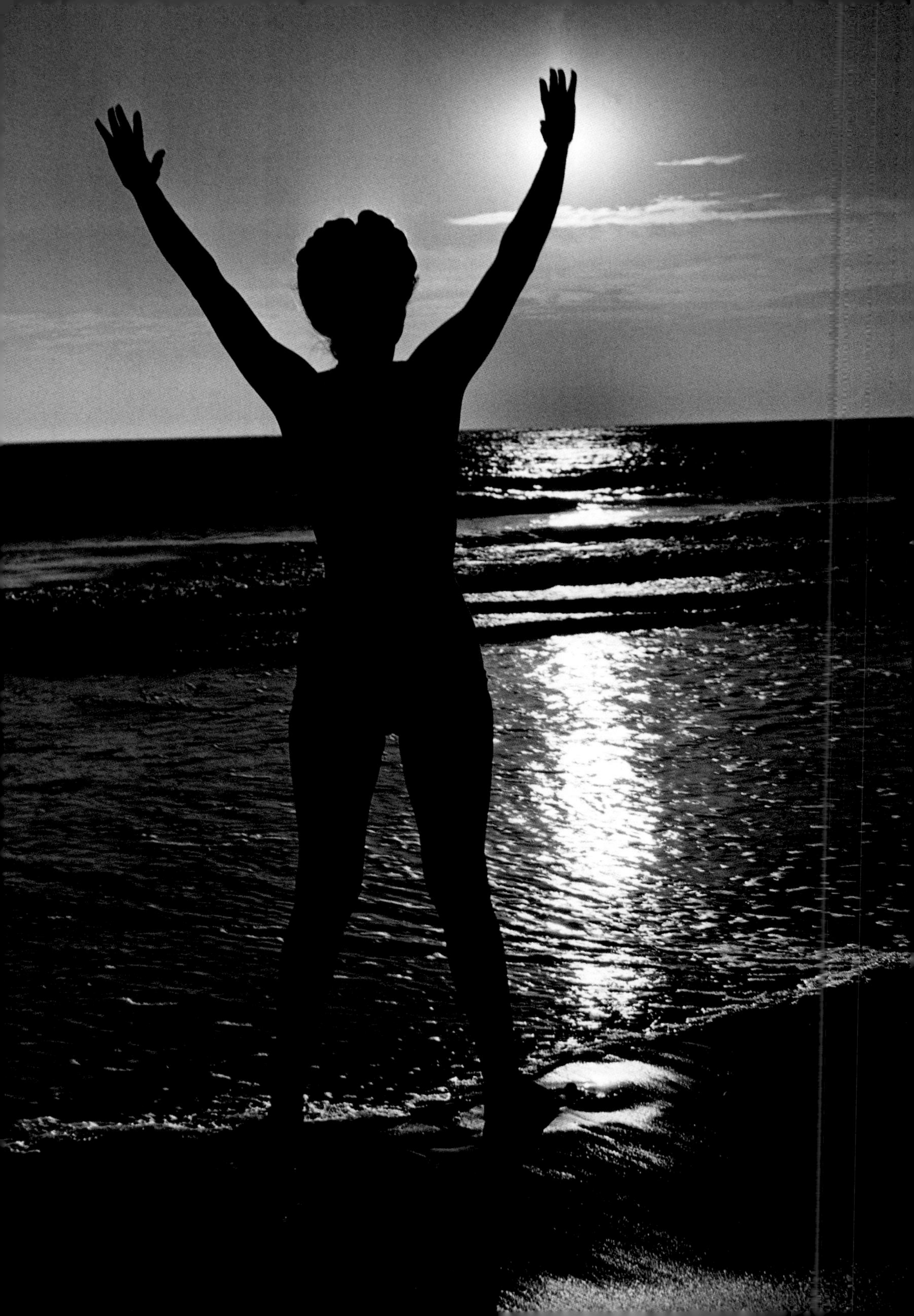

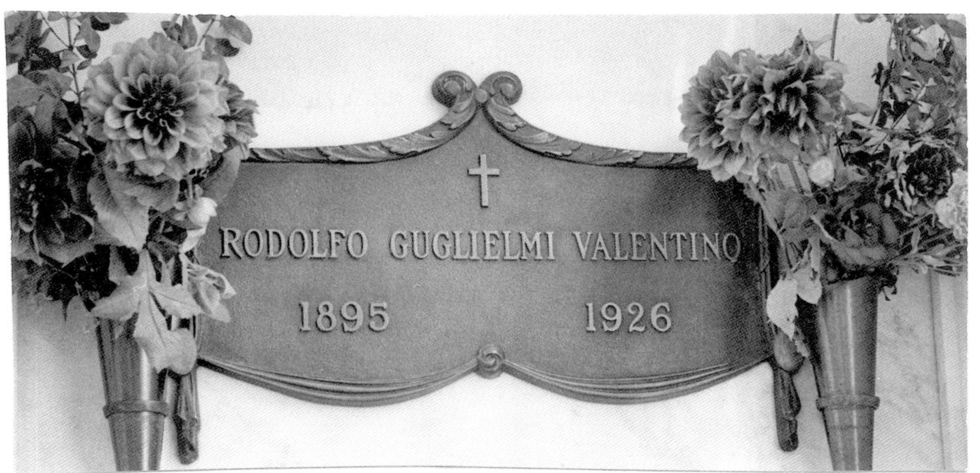

<u>Hollywood Memorial</u> One day, still in 1946, I was driving through Hollywood, taking Marilyn to a movie studio on Gower Street and as we passed the Hollywood Memorial Cemetery on Santa Monica Boulevard, I suggested we ought to make a quick tour inside the cemetery where many famous movie personalities were buried, such as Rudolph Valentino, Norma Talmadge, Marion Davies, Douglas Fairbanks, Sr., and many others. Marilyn didn't particularly care for the suggestion, but when I told her that the cemetery was just behind Paramount Studios on Melrose Avenue and that Rudolph Valentino was resting in his coffin just a few hundred feet away from where she might be making a film someday, her interest was aroused.

Marilyn became very silent when I guided her through the marble corridors of the vast mausoleum to the place where Rudolph Valentino was resting entombed in the wall behind a white marble slab. And we discussed what fantastic fame he achieved and what a fantastic event his sudden death became in 1926. I remarked to Marilyn that she was born the same year, 1926, and maybe she was born to replace and continue his legendary career! And maybe she, too, will become famous!

I recall Marilyn answering something to the effect that since he died so young, it wasn't worth it at all! And I said to her, "What more can you ask? He became immortal!" And Marilyn responded that she would prefer a long, happy life. Then she lifted a rose out from one of the urns on both sides of the bronze plaque bearing his name, and I recall having chided her that it wasn't a nice thing to steal flowers from the dead…. And Marilyn answered something like: "I am sure he would be very pleased to know that a lonesome girl took the flower home to keep it next to her bed." (Strange thing is, now I'm the one who goes to visit Marilyn's remains in the cemetery, and steals flowers from her to bring home and have them in a glass next to my bed.)

After we went out, I suggested that she ought not to go to her appointment at the studio, but instead I would read to her from a large quotation book which was always with me in the trunk of my car. We sat on the lawn, right at the spot where Tyrone Power is buried. We read about life, love, happiness, fame, vanity, women, death, and other things, but it was the word "fame" that caught her attention the most. She made me underline some quotes she liked most. I still have the book, and I copy out a few she liked and include them here:

"A woman's fame is the tomb of her happiness." – L.E. Landon

"Live for something! Be good and leave behind you a monument of virtue that the storm of time can never destroy. Write your name in kindness, love, and mercy on the hearts of the thousands you come in contact with, year by year, and you will never be forgotten. Your name, your deeds will be as legible on the hearts you leave behind as the stars on the brow of evening. Good deeds will shine as the stars of heaven." – Chalmers

"What is fame? The advantage of being known by people of whom you yourself know nothing, and for whom you care as little." – Stanislaus

Then she suddenly decided that she'd had enough poetry and philosophy and she should go to her appointment, even if she was already very late. I'm sure it was the word "fame" that prompted her to leave me! A pang of jealousy gripped me, and I yelled at her something like, "Are you going to lay that producer?!" And she angrily answered, "Yes! Why not?" And we hurled at each other a few more angry words. But the bad mood was over soon and I dropped her on Gower Street. It was agreed maybe we'd go to the seashore some day, and read some more…. She said she needed to educate herself and that I ought to bring along some unusual books.

But in my mind it was otherwise. I was thinking of going back to New York to mind my business…. I was still in love with her, but I felt the relationship became hopeless for me. She just liked me to sustain her ego, to feed her with my constant enthusiasm for life, and for all the pep talks I gave her.

THIS was during Summer of 1946, just on the unset of Labor day, when, again, Norma Jean called me to say she has important news to tell me, and she asked to come to her apartment. When I got there, she came right to the subject: " Guess what, I have a new name ! " With a pencil, slowly, carefully, she wrote her new name on a sheet of paper : MARILYN MONROE. And she emphasized the two M initials in an almost calligraphic way ! I could never forget through all these years gone by, my big surprise, when I stood there, behind her, watching her writing her name... It was something almost supernatural how beautifully she wrote the large capital M letters....and my mind drifted again to my childhood years, how hypnitozed I always was by those two M initials. And again, I spoke to Norma Jean about the old man in Transylvania, and how often I carved those initials in tree barks before I took a good sleep under some tree in the countryside, all over Europe.

How much I regretted ever after that day when Norma Jean, or rather, Marilyn, wrote her name down for me, and I did not have the foresight to keep that sheet of paper. We still did not know to what great fame she shall rise! In fact, we had no idea yet !

From now on, I shall refer to Norma Jean as Marilyn, I had to get used to her new name right away. After she wrote the name down carefully, she began to sign her new name, again and again, under the first signature. She was taking the liberty to sign her name as fast as she could. If only I would have kept that sheet of paper ! What a precious document it would be now for me to show ! And to have !

But let me fast go on with my story, a precious memory of those early days with Marilyn Monroe. After she signed her name, the conversation went on for a while about the certain mysteries of life one can not explain, like she, so cleverly finding a name with the two M-s. Especially the name Marilyn, because, in Portland, Oregon, just a half a year previously, (12/1945) I told her that the large M-s in her palm meant " Marry Me",

THIS SANCTUARY IS INTACT, AS IT WAS BUILT IN 1806.

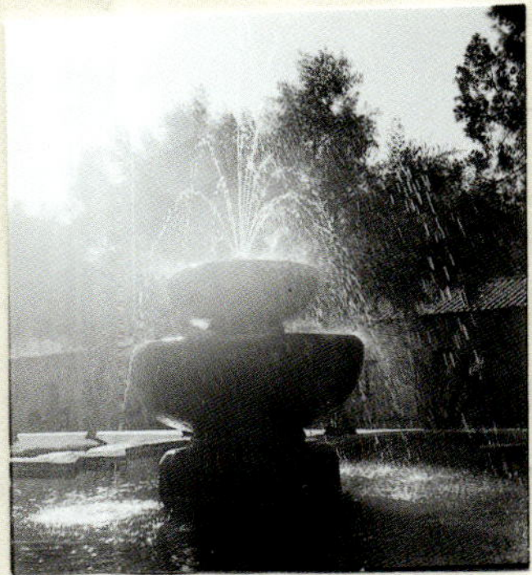

SAN FERNANDO
ST. LOUIS REY.

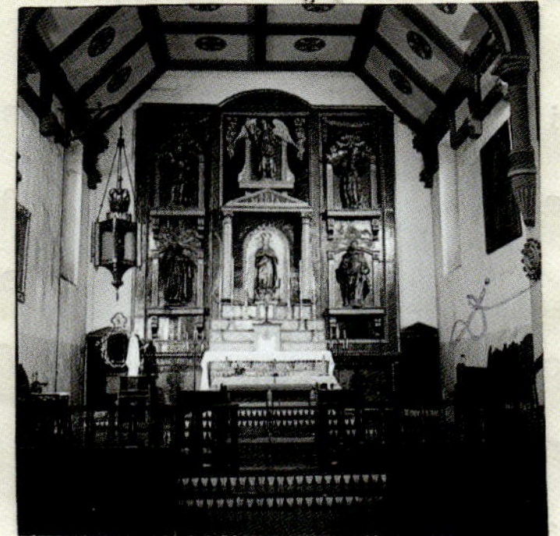

SAN GABRIEL

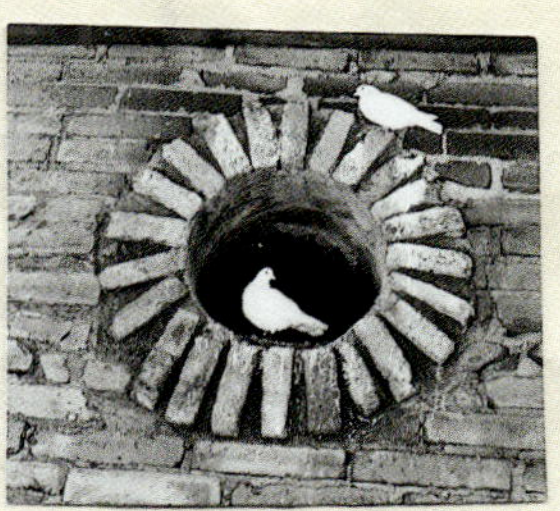

CAPISTRANO

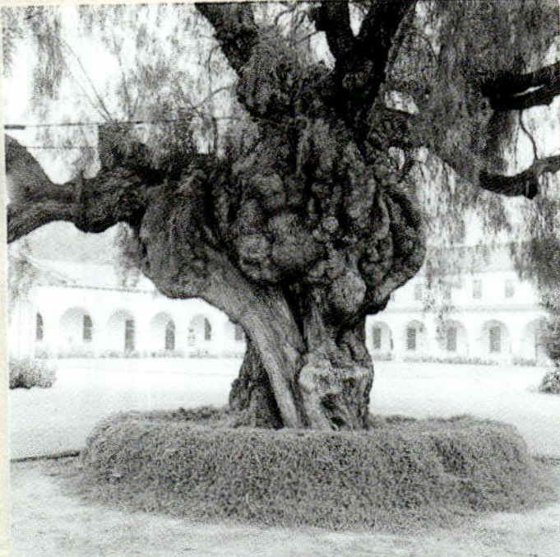

THE OLDEST TREE IN CALIF. FROM SPAIN.

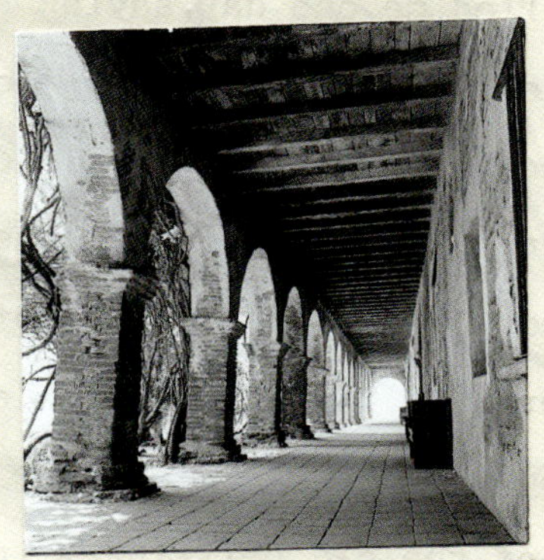

SAN JUAN CAPISTRANO

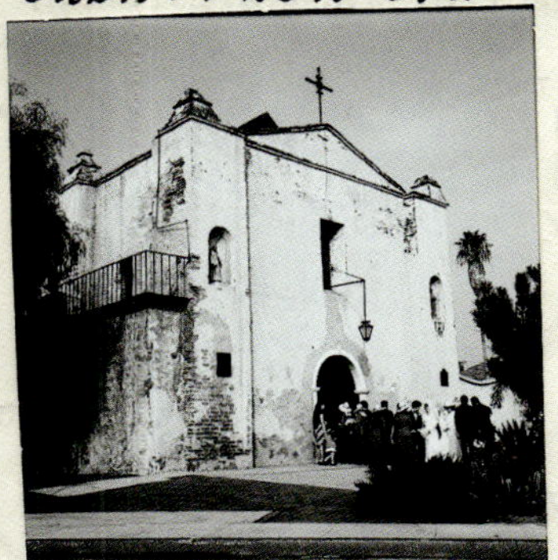

SAN GABRIEL
FOUNDED IN 1771

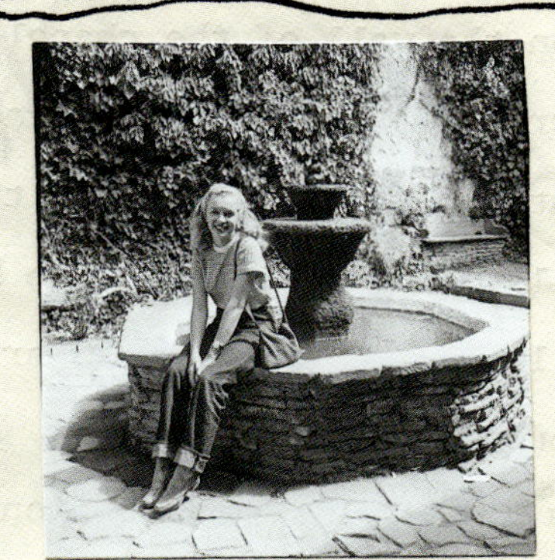

THE NEW MARILYN MONROE. 1946
AT CAPISTRANO MISSION

ANDRE DE DIENES
1401 SUNSET PLAZA DRIVE
HOLLYWOOD, CALIF. 90069

I opened the windows of the room to let the warm breeze go through freely, lit some lamps to create a subdued, semi-dark athmosphere, the bellboy brought me two candles to light, and when everything was the way I wanted it, I left the door open, and went back to the car what I left parked in the dark street, only about fifty feet away from the room which was on the ground floor, section. The distance between the room and the car was all surrounded up with tall bushes, and exotic trees, gently lit by subdued lighting. It was a dark place, but romantic, magnificent. I took out a bottle of wine from the trunk of the car, and quickly gulped down at least half of it, because what I was going to do needed courage. Than, I woke up Marilyn, and in a very serious tone of voice, I told her I drove everywhere but could not find any cabin available, and in desperation I drove back to one of the Missions and forced the gate open, drove the car in, and there we were, and it was up to her whether she wants to continue sleeping in the car, or she would come with me, and sleep in the cell which she saw that afternoon, where a candle was placed on the table, 150 years before, when the padres slept there. Marilyn sleepily crowled out of the car, and I saw her worried, almost horror-stricken face lit by the dome-light of the car. And when she stood up in the dark street, under the palm tree, I quickly grabbed her arm and led her through the alley, half way to our room, where I stopped, to ask her whether she was afraid to sleep in the cell? Was she afraid to come ? She answered, "We will be arrested"! Not saying anything further, I pulled her toward the open door of our room, and there I burst into loughter, and mumbled that once I have shown her the Bridal-veil waterfall in Yosemite Park (Dec.1945) and now, instead of an ice-cold log cabin, or the padre's cell, a "bridal suit" was waiting for her! And dinner shall be served in our room! It was a large room, furnished in Spanish, and Mexican style. The rest I hardly remember. The wine completely hit my tired mind after that long, long day's travelling and sightseeing. And, I wouldn't tell about it anyway!

Nex day, we went down to the basement to visit the catacombes. The tunnels were filled with old oriental antiques, accumulated by the builder and owner of the Hotel. And they were all for sale. Marilyn found a small wooden Buddha she liked. She was rubbing its stomack--wishing it were hers, to bring her good luck. Next to the Buddha was a chinese statue, a woodcarving about three feet high, redish brown, and guilded here and there, representing a chinese GODDESS slighly raising the bottom of her robe with one hand, and holding a scroll-like object in the other hand. Marilyn found the Buddha far more TO HER LIKING, interesting for "luck" puposes; I was intrigued by the sexual implications of the chinese lady holding the scroll. Both pieces were about the same price, eighty or ninety dollars. I knew Marilyn wanted me to buy the Buddha for her as a souvenir of our get-together, but I found the GODDESS far more old and valuable, and beautiful, and artistic. Never mind the good luck she was wishing for -- I said to her, and being very practical, I proposed, almost insisted THAT I should buy the statue of the lady for her, — because, some day, she shall have a beautiful apartment, or house, and the statue will look great on A coffee table ! My pointing out the beauty of the statue, compared to the not-so-good-looking Buddha won her approval. SO I bought if for her.

Outside, when I was putting the heavy statue into the trunk of the car, I heard a clicking sound inside the statue. I lifted it up again, shook it, shook it again, with all my strenght, and the strange clicking sound bacame stronger. We bacame VERY perplexed and excited, and I suggested we should go to San Francisco, where I used to buy ivory statuettes of naked Chinese ladies (reclining) from a repu-

CHINESE GODDESS "KUAN YIN" (SYMBOL OF THE "WORLD MOTHER")

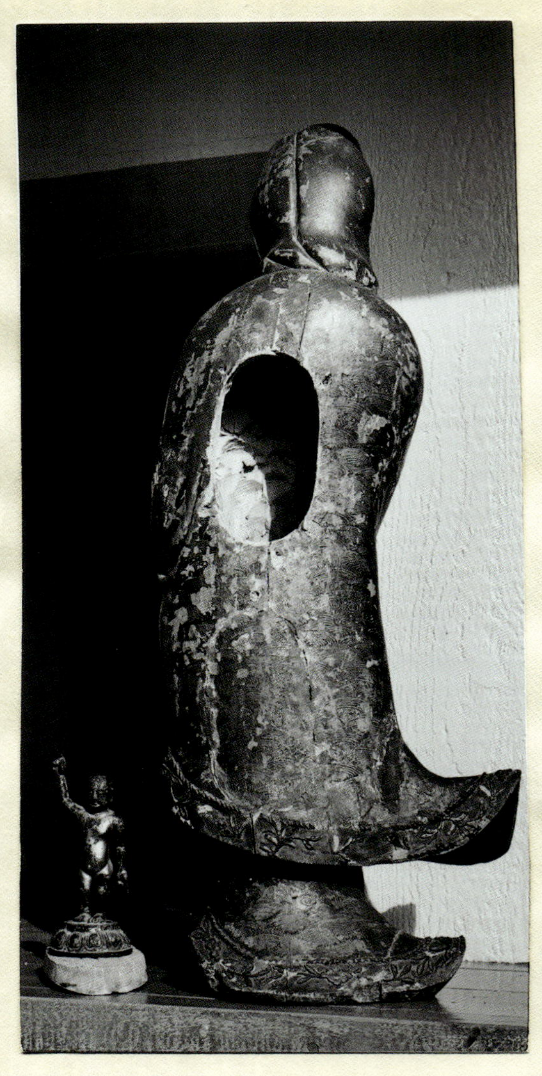

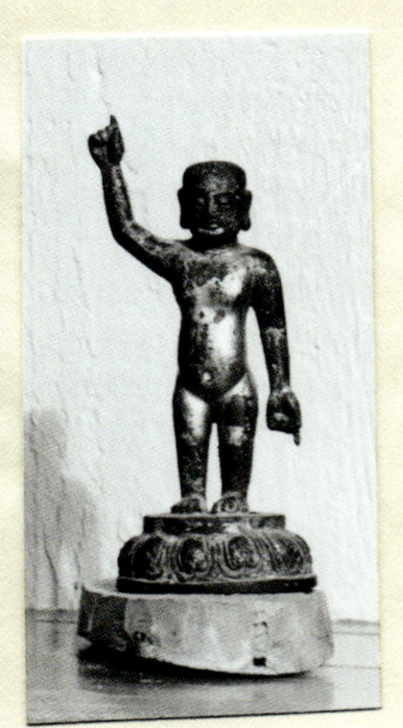

table Chinese art dealer of Oriental arts, and the dealer would be glad to examine the sculpture, and tell us what was clicking inside, and why ! We were mystified by the noise.

Two days later we were at his store, when he opened it in the morning. The man politely asked my permission to do a small 'operation ' on the sculpture, and with a sharp instrument, HE delicately peeled off the thick layer of paint, and OLD guilding, from the back side of the statue, and SOON, revealed an oval shaped lid. He slowly removed IT with the insturment, and to our utter surprise, there was a cavity carved out inside the statue, from what the dealer removed a blue silken bundle, AND unbundled it, and to our utmost amazement there were two small Buddhas, ABOUT 6 INCHES HIGH, one of wood, in sitting position, and the other of bronze, guilded, but the guilding slowly disappearing by the wear of times. (The second little statue represented a chinese man, Conficius the chinese philosopher and teacher) Both pieces were very old. The Buddha perhaps 500 years old, the Bronze CONFUCIUS statuette about a thousand years old, said the dealer. She listened to the dealer's tales with attentiveness, and her mood turned to extasy while learning things she did not know.

The dealer wanted to buy the statue and the small statuettes, but we refused to sell them. He offered five hundred dollars. I said nothing doing! For a while he insited buying the things, but Marilyn's sincere and affectionate handling of the stauettes melted the stern expression of tha merchant's face, and he ceased insisting to buy the things from us. The treasures -- I should say ! The merchant became completely taken by Marilyn's beauty and sweetness, and he invited us to come back later in the afternoon, when he closes the store, and he would take us for dinner. We gratefully accepted the invitation, I took my PRECIOUS merchandise with me, and put them in the trunk of the car.

I made another trip with Marilyn which I can never forget. It happened about a month after we have visited the Missions.

I was reading in bed one evening, and the phone reng; it was Marilyn who called, and asked what was I doing. I said to her, first, she has to listen to a song I loved, which I learnt when I was a young boy. And I seng to her in Hungarian RAMONA, the lovely song (which was created sometimes in the 1920s). Than, I told her I was reading the novel RAMONA (by Helen Hunt Jackson) a beautiful, immortal story, and that I was in tears because something terrible has happened in the story. She became very curious about the story, so I told her over the phone about the very touching love story what took place in Southern California in the middle part of the 1800s. Ramona, a half-breed Indian girl, with black hair and steel-blue eyes, (an orphan) was working on a Ranch as servant. She fell in love and eloped with a handsome, young Indian boy named Alessandro, and together they fled, and went to get married in one of the missions Marilyn and I just visited a few weeks before. After the marriage, during a series of hardships and wonderings on Indian territory, Ramona's young husband, Alessandro, allegedly stole the horse of a Deputy Sheriff. The Deputy went to the pursuit of Alessandro, who pulled a knife on the Deputy, and the Deputy shot him dead by self defense. Ramona, broken-hearted and frightened, fled accross mountains, to go to find refuge again at the Ranch where she once worked as servant.

I was explaining Marilyn on the phone that I was exploring, and taking pictures on that territory, north of San Diego, where that true story once happened, and I was planning to go back again to find the cemetery where Ramona was burried in 1922, when she died an old woman.

Marilyn insisted she wanted to go with me. In fact she said she phoned me because she was lonesome! She suggested we ought to go right away! So we went. We left Los Angeles in the middle of the night !

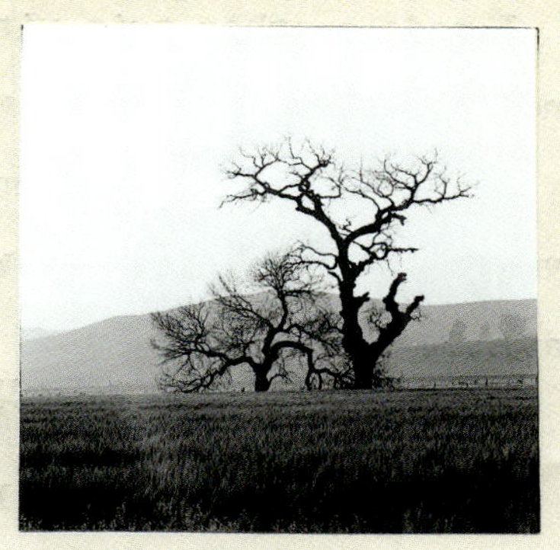

OLD TREES
NEAR TEMECULA

"ALESSANDRO" AND

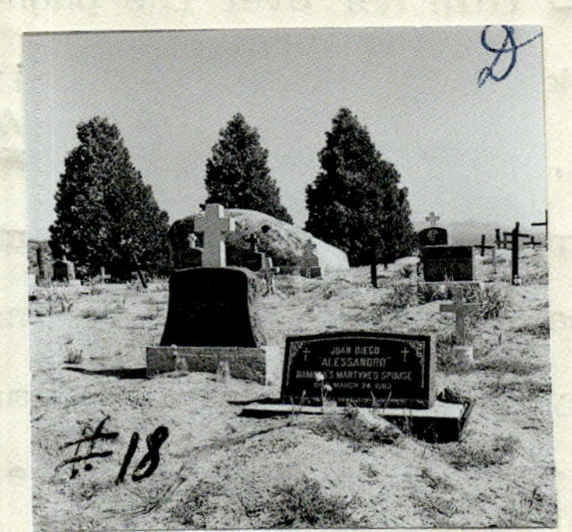

"RAMONA"

RAMONA'S GRAVE. (SHE WAS RE-BURRIED A FEW YEARS AGO)

A Beautiful true story in the history of California. It will live for ever!

By morning we were at TEMECULA, in the very heart of that Indian territory where once Ramona and Alessandro found refuge. In the midst of a large open field, we spotted two big oak trees standing side by side, and Marilyn made some touching remarks about the trees, something to the effect that they only had each other in that immense wilderness. There were hardly any other trees around there, so most probably Ramona and Alessandro must have known those trees, and even rested in their shade. We spent a few hours under the trees and Marilyn was reading for me from the pages of RAMONA. Sometimes her eyes were full of tears when she was reading the descriptions of Alessandro's love for Ramona, whom he called "Majella", meaning "wood- dove."

Later that afternoon, we found the cemetery in the midst of an immense, blaak desert, a small Indian cemetery, with lots of simple, wooden crosses. And there, again , Marilyn read for me at Ramona's grave, and she tried to hold her tears back when she read how Alessandro was shot to death up in the San Jacinto Mountains, where the two had fled from the white men. Sweet Marilyn, she swore there, that some day, she shall dye her hair black, and she shall play Ramona's part in the play "Ramona," which is being played every year, in memory of that beautiful love affair.

But Marilyn forgot all about it in later years. She often mentioned wanting to play the part of Grushenka, the beautiful, tantalizing girl in Dostoyevsky's Brothers Karamazov, but Ramona, went into forget, perhaps because it wasn't the glamorous kind of story what Hollywood wanted her to play. Neither she, perhaps, because Ramona wasn't a frivolous girl.

As for me, more than thirty year later, I still go back to re-visit some of those places in the desert where once I took Marilyn, went to Ramona's grave, also. The small Indian cemetery is closed to visitors, but I was lucky, there was a funeral the day I went to revisit it. It's an inspiring, beautiful place, surrounded by solitude and complete peace, and silence.

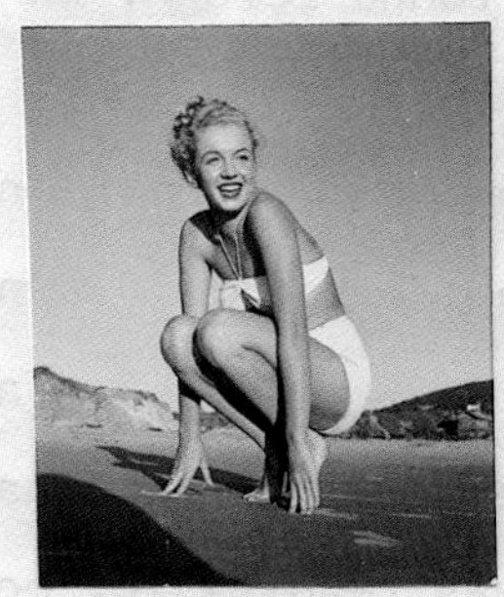

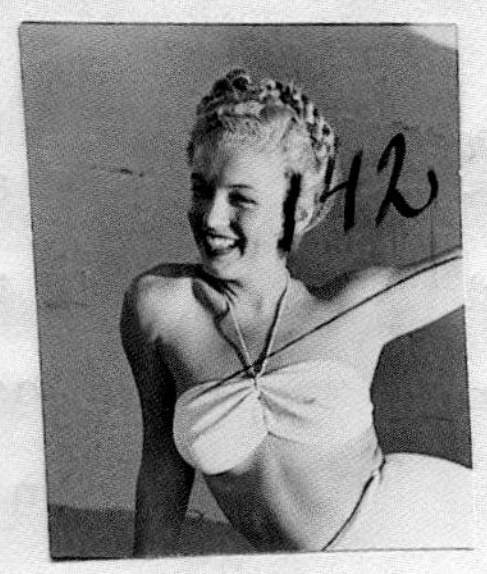

FALL 1946. NOT NORMA JEANE DOUGHERTY ANY MORE;
THIS IS MARILYN MONROE! FIRST PHOTOS!

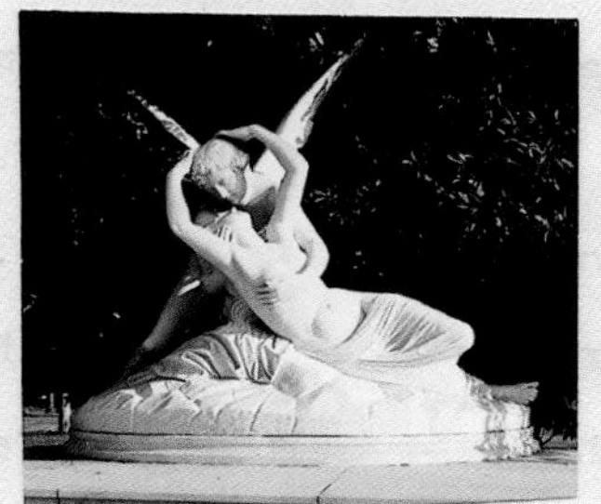

"CUPID AND PSYCHE"
HOLLYWOOD MEMORIAL CEMETERY

ON — "FAME"

LIVE FOR SOMETHING ! DO GOOD AND LEAVE BEHIND YOU A MONUMENT OF VIRTUE THAT THE STORM OF TIME CAN NEVER DESTROY. WRITE YOUR NAME IN KINDNESS, LOVE, AND MERCY ON THE HEARTS OF THE THOUSANDS YOU COME IN CONTACT WITH, YEAR BY YEAR, AND YOU WILL NEVER BE FORGOTTEN. YOUR NAME, YOUR DEEDS, WILL BE AS LEGIBLE ON THE HEARTS YOU LEAVE BEHIND, AS THE STARS ON THE BROW OF EVENING. GOOD DEEDS WILL SHINE AS THE STARS OF HEAVEN. (Chalmers)

WHAT IS FAME ? THE ADVANTAGE OF BEING KNOWN BY PEOPLE OF WHOM YOU YOURSELF KNOW NOTHING, AND FOR WHOM YOU CARE AS LITTLE.

(Stanislaus)

A WOMAN'S FAME IS THE TOMB OF HER HAPPINESS.

(L. E. Landon)

Lives of great men all remind us
  We can make our lives sublime,
And departing, leave behind us
  Footprints on the sands of time;--
Footprints, that perhaps another,
  Sailing o'er life's solemn main,
A forlorn and shipwreck'd brother,
  Seeing, shall take heart again.

(Longfellow)

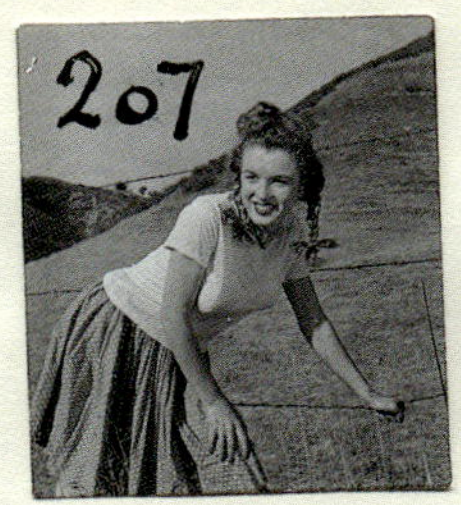

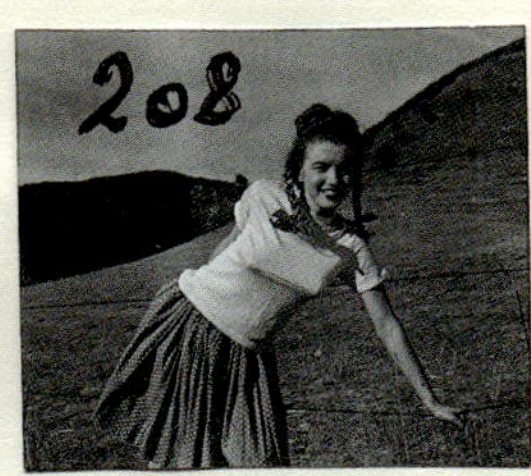

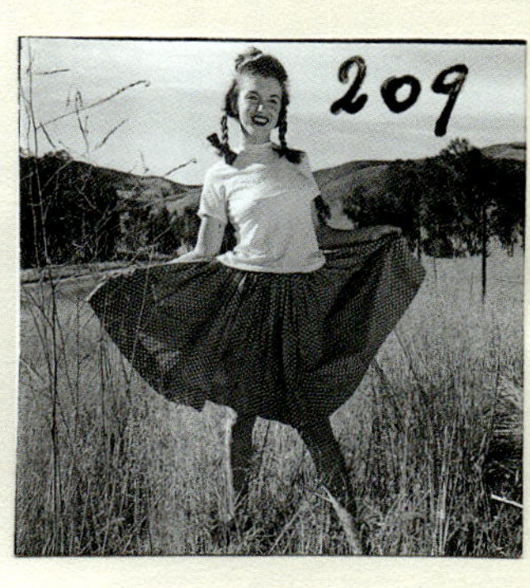

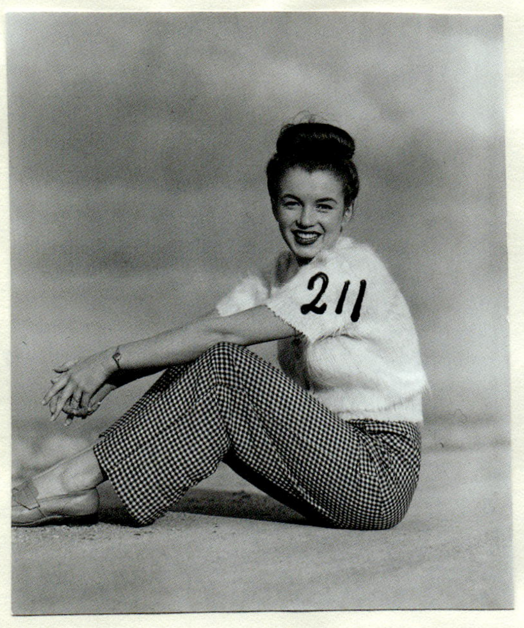

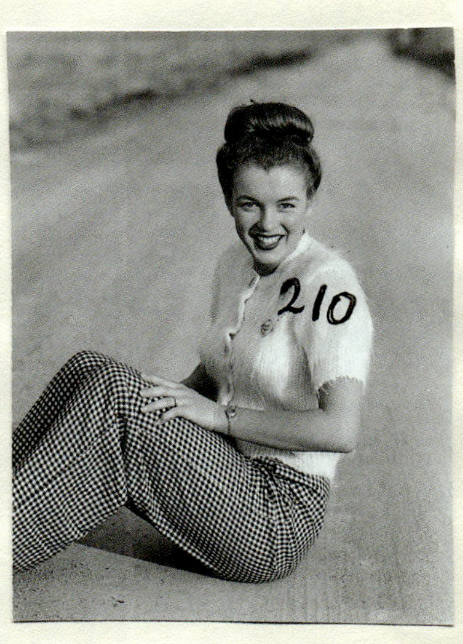

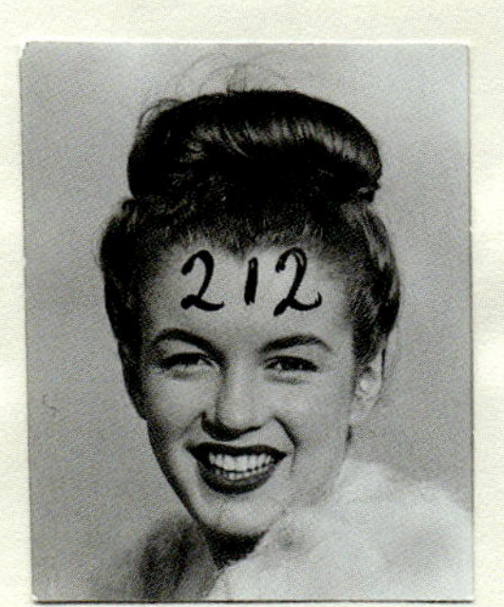

These above pictures, of Norma Jean sitting on the ground, on a country road — are her last pictures as a professional model. Next year, in 1946, she elected herself to become an actress ! She was determined, strong - willed ! She wished to succeed !

1947

NORMA JEANE

"SHOWING OFF" WITH HER FIRST MAGAZINE COVERS.

(ALL 3 COVERS WERE THE PHOTOS I TOOK!)

(THE FOURTH MAGAZINE'S "LAFF"'s COVER IS <u>NOT</u> HER PHOTO. SHE HAD PHOTOS OF HER ON THE INSIDE PAGES)

A.D.

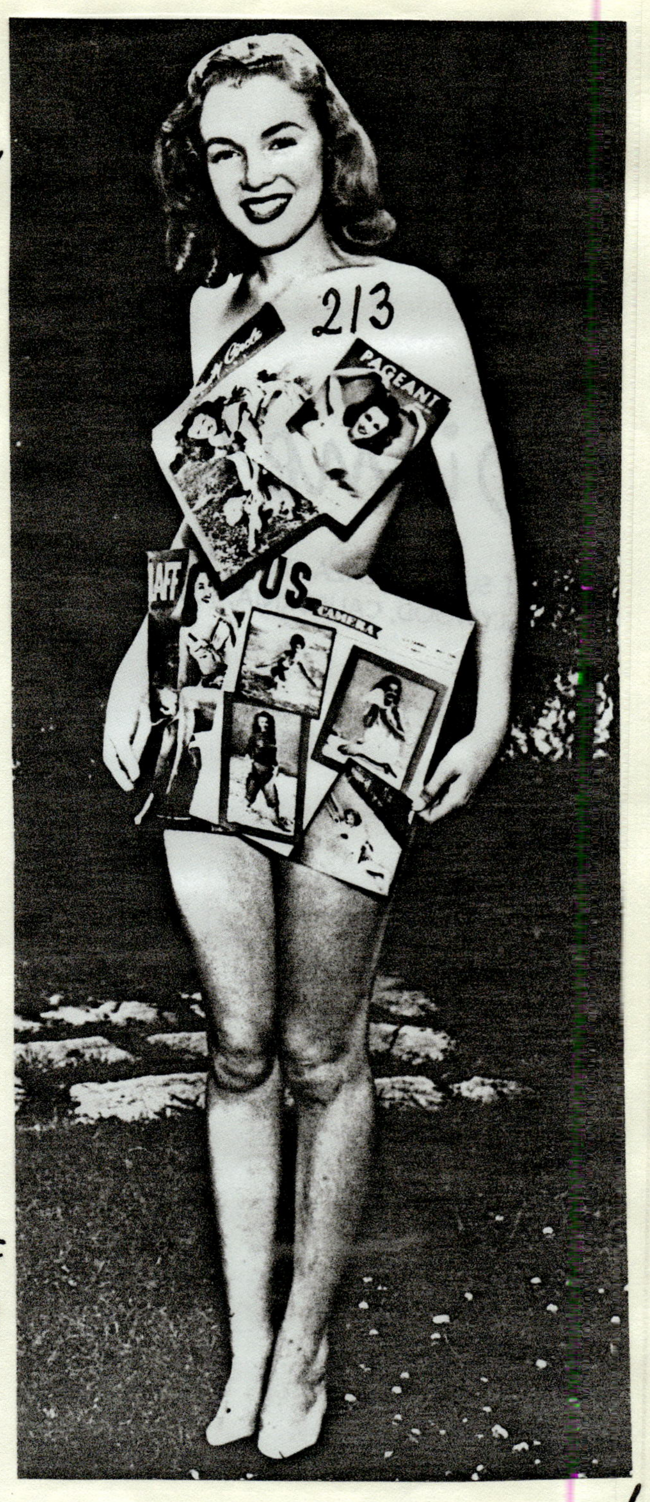

1946

MARILYN MONROE

FIRST PHOTOS. 1946

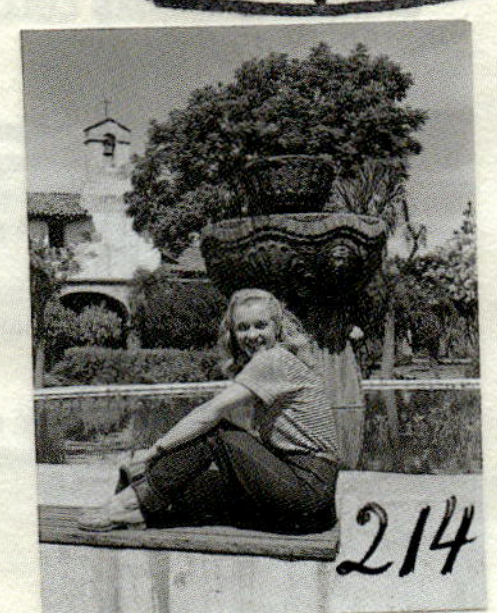

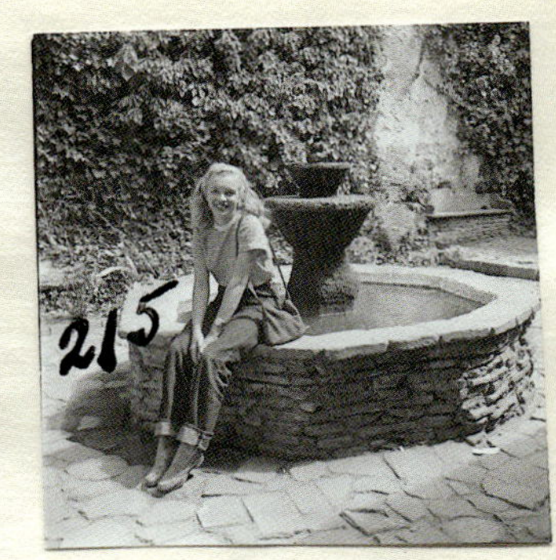

HERE, SHE IS NO LONGER "NORMA JEAN"; SHE JUST ACQUIRED THE NEW NAME M. M. (WE WENT ON A TRIP TO CELEBRATE IT.)

L-1

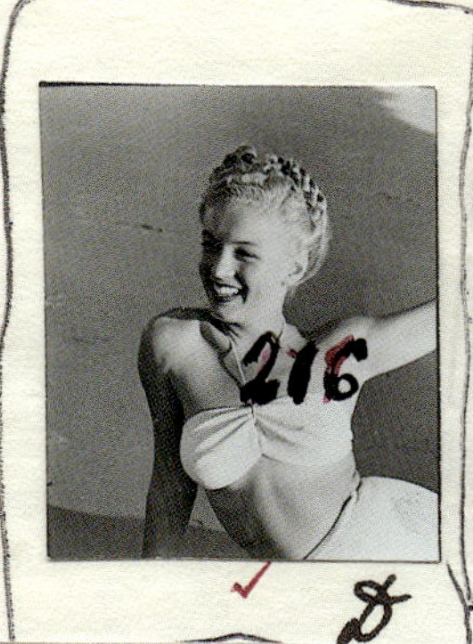

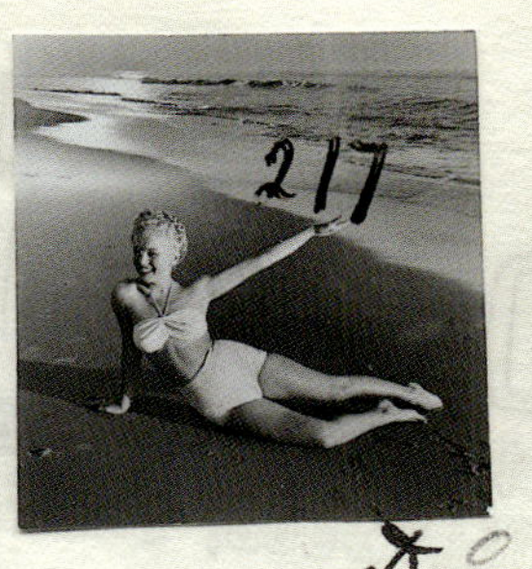

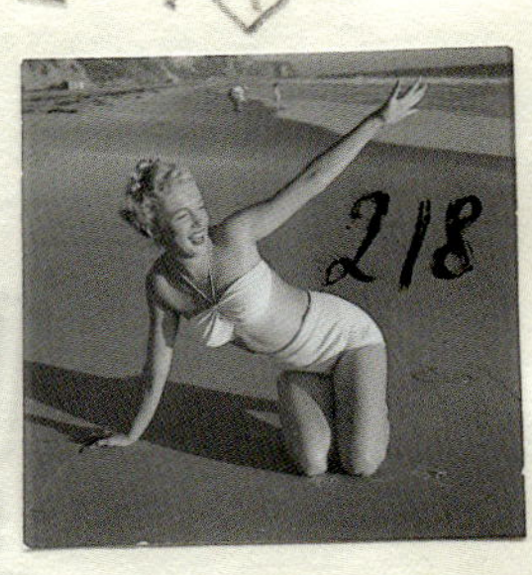

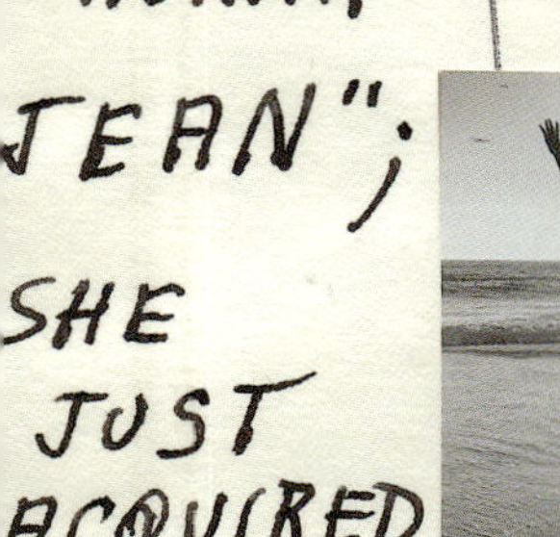

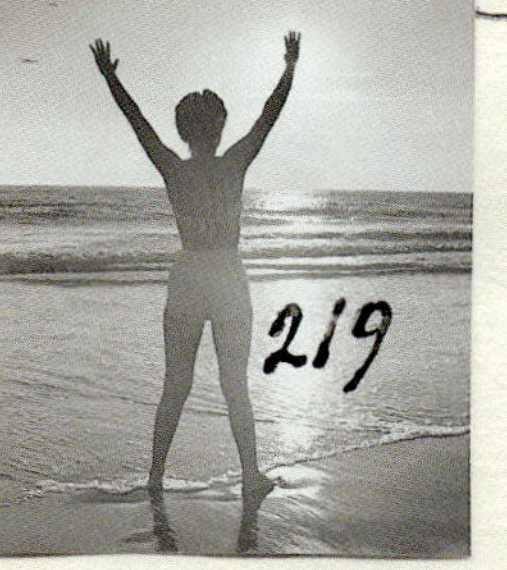

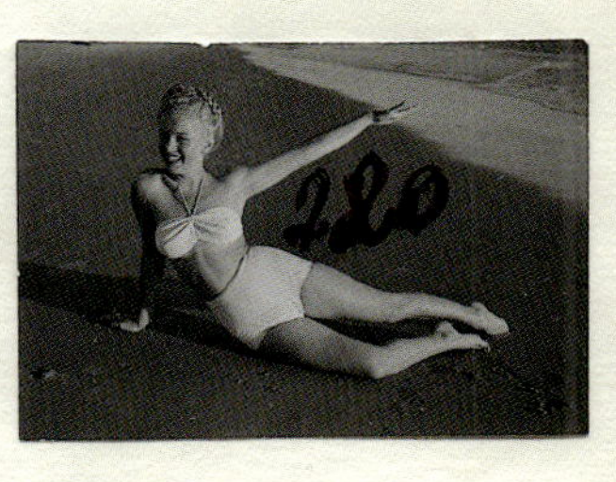

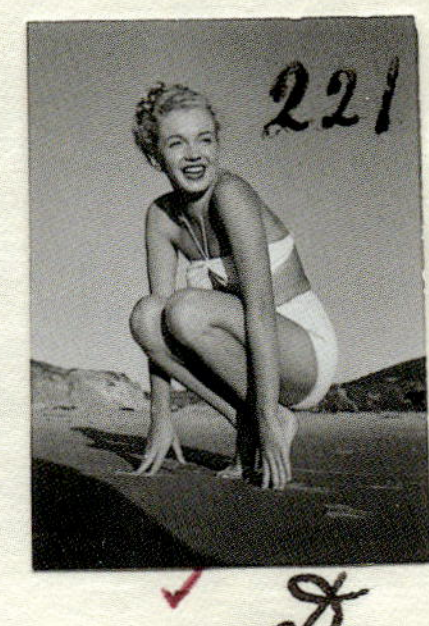

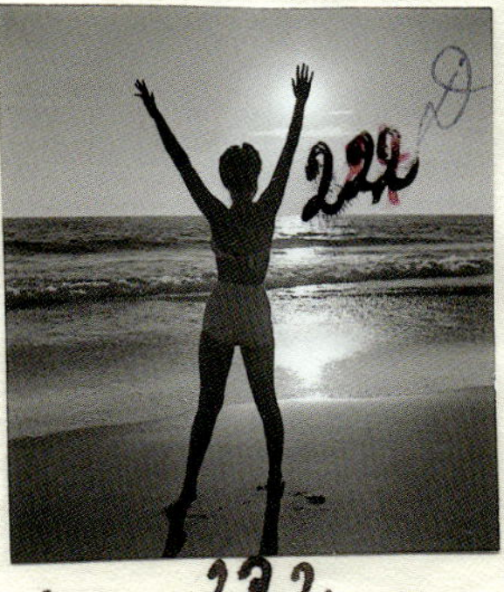

222

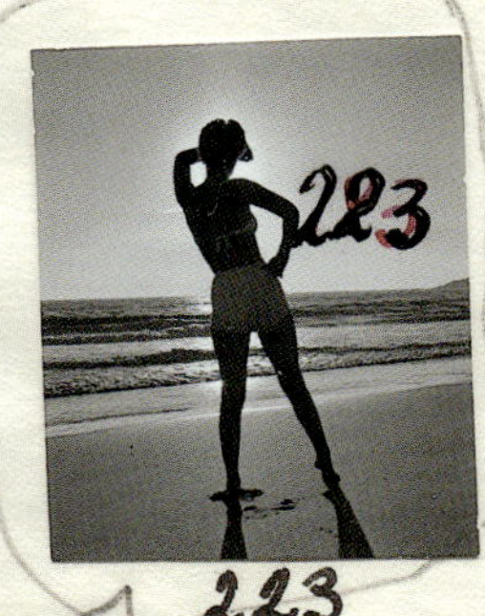

223

L

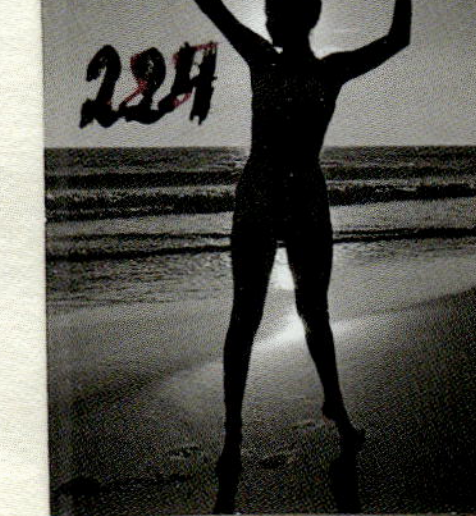

224

3

ANDRE DE DIENES
1401 SUNSET PLAZA DRIVE
HOLLYWOOD, CALIF. 90069

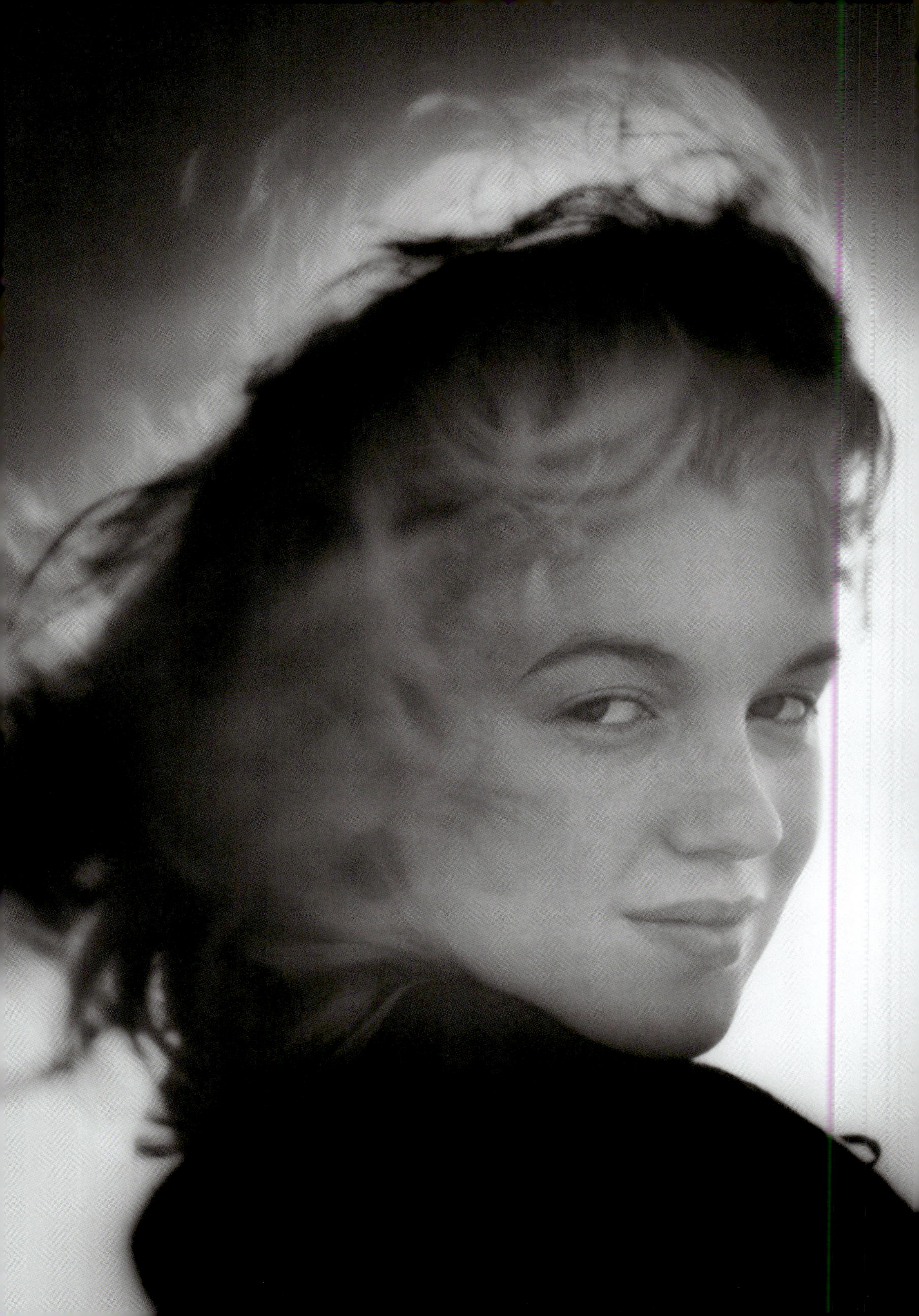

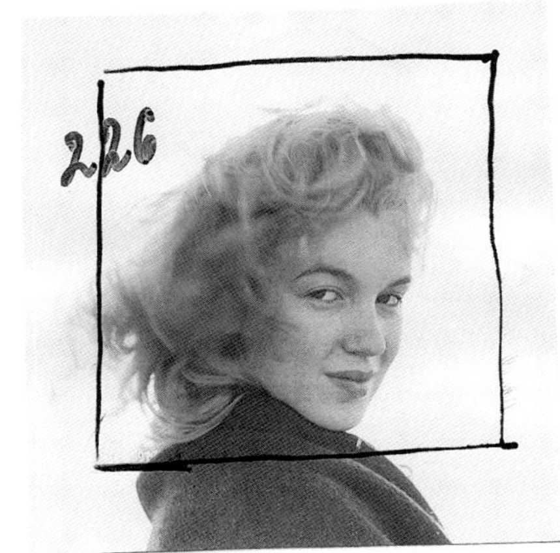

"THE SPRINGTIME OF LIFE"

The End of Everything Soon after that day in the cemetery, I entered a second-hand bookshop I passed by. I suppose I reacted to Marilyn's suggestion that I ought to bring an unusual kind of book! I was browsing from shelf to shelf, having absolutely no fixed idea of what I wanted. I was about to leave when my eyes fell on an old leather-bound volume. I pulled it out. The cover looked worn and torn, and handwritten pages were loose and about to fall out. There were small, very old engravings pasted on the pages here and there of famous people, like Pascal, Boccaccio, Tennyson, Edgar Allan Poe, and small engravings of landscapes from Italy and Germany and Scotland. The book dealer, with a gesture of nonchalance and lack of concern, said that I could have the book for fifteen dollars. I paid and hurriedly left, fearing he might change his mind, declaring he had made a mistake; the book was worth far more!

I went to a restaurant to sit and sit and study what I had bought. I read the beautiful, handwritten poems and studied the pictures. It was an album a lady started in Scotland around 1830. In it, she wrote her thoughts, her own poems, and poems she'd copied of famous people. I called Marilyn to tell her I'd found something very unusual, a book I must show her, share with her, so we can read it together. That agreement we had made in the cemetery that we would go out to the seashore and read some more could come through, due to the book I'd found. A few days later, Marilyn and I were far out at the seashore, north of Malibu on a deserted beach, where we read the pages of the book with a magnifier to decipher the small but beautiful handwriting.

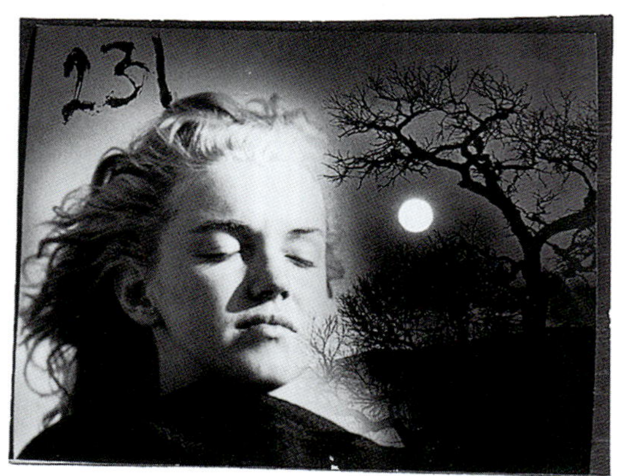

"TIME"

I remember so well which poems Marilyn loved. She was nearly in tears several times. Marilyn wasn't the kind of person who would have tears in her eyes easily, no matter how deep the emotion. But the poems touched her immensely. She was holding herself back from bursting into sobs while she was reading a poem entitled, "Lines on the Death of Mary." She told me that it fit her, but the lady who wrote it forgot to put the "lyn" after the name "Mary!" I remarked that a few days before in the cemetery she told me she preferred a long, happy life and now she was saying she would not live long…. The poem we were reading about the death of Mary was a prediction for her that she would die young!

The reading ended and I began taking pictures of her, one by one, depicting the moods she interpreted for me. An entire spectrum of life, depicting happiness, pensiveness, introspection, serenity, sadness, torment, distress – I even asked her to show me what "death" looked like in her imagination. She threw a blanket over her head; that was how she interpreted it.

The photo that followed was her own idea. She told me to get ready with my camera because she was going to show me what her own death would look like – someday. She looked down with a very sordid expression, pointing out to me that the picture's meaning would be "THE END OF EVERYTHING." I quickly snapped the photo. I asked her why she pictured her death so sordid, so gloomy, instead of giving me an expression of calm smile as if dying was nothing more than going from one

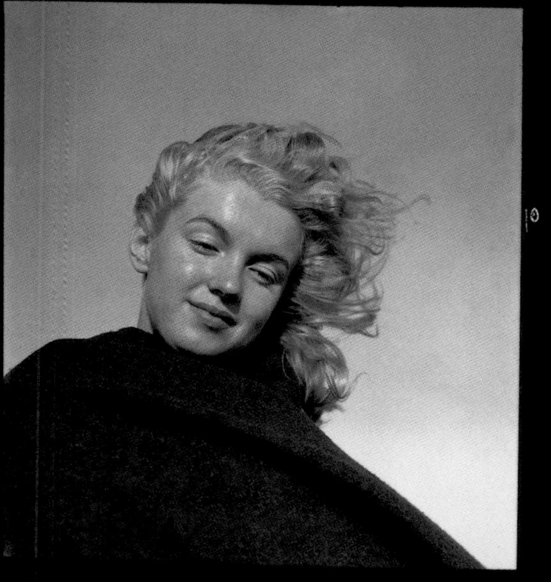

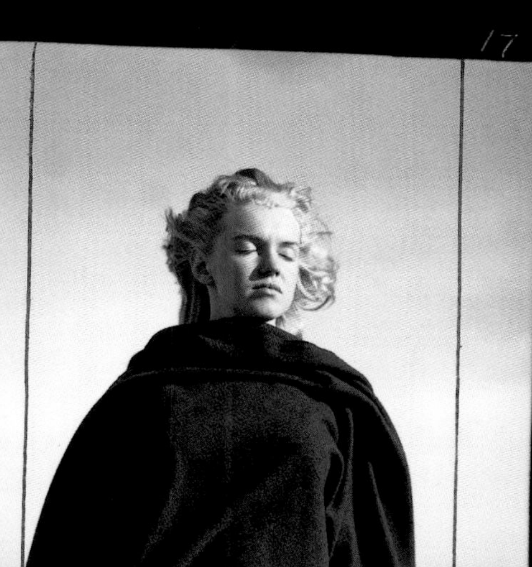

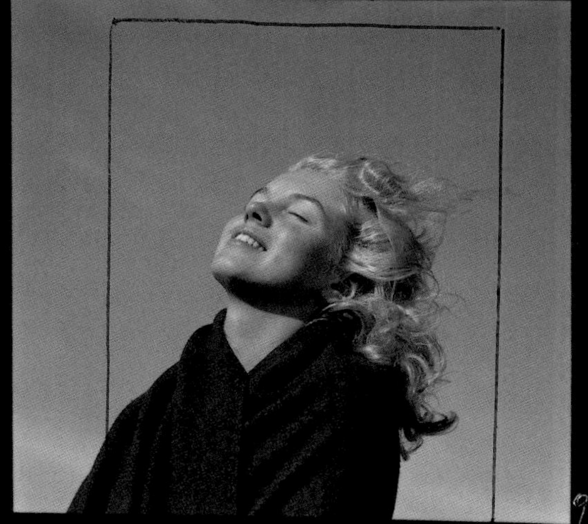

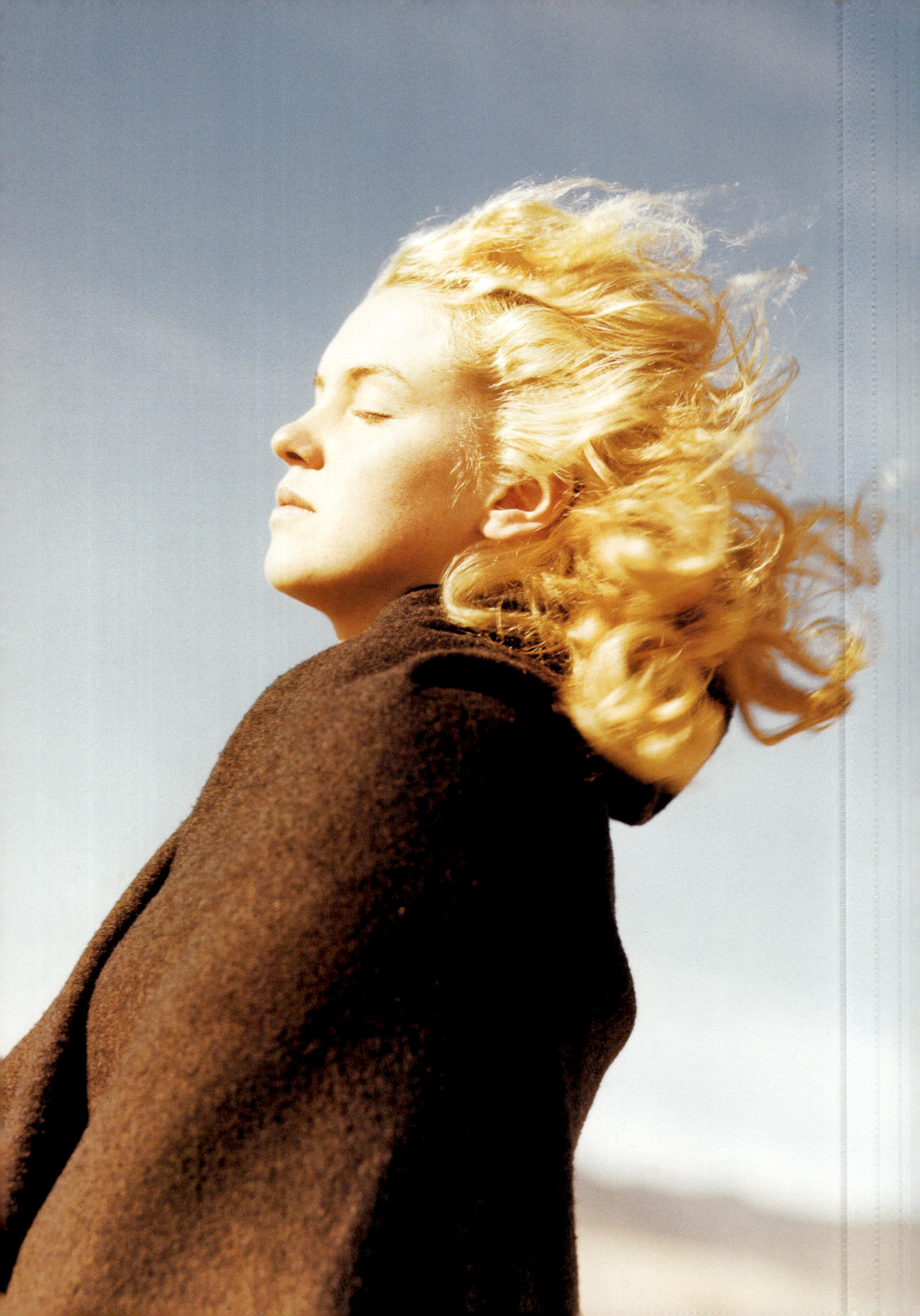

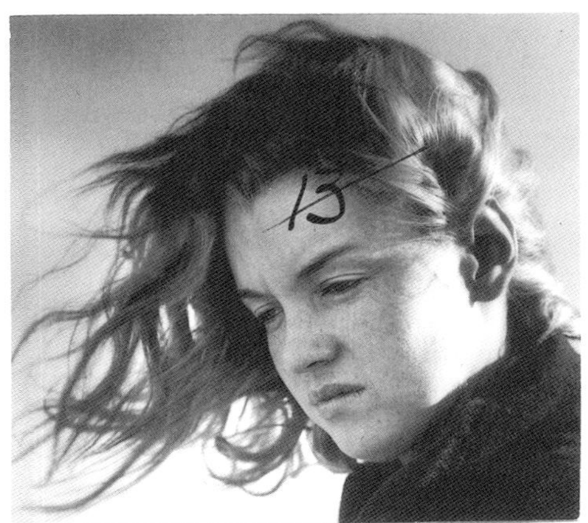

"THE END OF EVERYTHING!"

world into another, a beautiful transfiguration. But Marilyn insisted that was the way she imagined her death.

The next photo was my idea. I asked her to lie down on the ground to show me what she would look like when dead and again, I snapped the photo. It was already late afternoon; we were taking photos on the top of a cliff, overlooking the ocean. The scenery and the light of the setting sun were magnificent; I was in the mood to take many more poetic photos of her, but after I took the photo of her face simulating death, suddenly she sprang to her feet and, part seriously, part wittily, she began shouting, screaming at me, "Hell's bells, look what you've made me do to my hair! I have a date tonight!" And she was shaking her head and taking out the pieces of straw that stuck in her hair. I calmed her down by promising that someday I would do a beautiful album with her pictures, accompanied by all kinds of lovely quotations from my book, and even some of the poems she liked in that album we'd just read together. She made a strange remark, saying, "André, do not publish those photos now, wait until I die!" And I asked her, how does she know she will die before me? After all, I was 12 years older than her. And in a sad, low-toned voice, she said she thought she would die before me. But that took only moments; soon she was gay and cheerful again, looking forward to her dinner date, and she was urging me to hurry, hurry, pack everything into the car and leave!

I can't forget how sad I felt that evening while driving back to Hollywood – to be on time for her dinner date. Marilyn was no longer

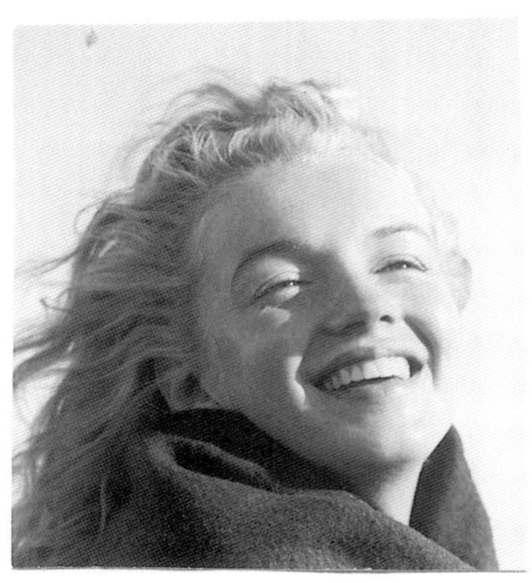

"HAPPINESS"

the lovely Norma Jeane I once knew, only a few months before! She was going out to have dinner at Romanoff's in Beverly Hills, and I felt terribly, terribly put down, belittled, and left behind.

I was packing my bags that night to return to New York, when the phone rang. It was her! She said she had a miserable evening with a lousy guy – a swindler, someone who wanted her to pay for the dinner! But we reasoned that since she had exposed herself toa career in Hollywood, she ought to be strong enough to cope with everything that comes along – good or bad. But I did not inquire as to what happened. Instead, she suggested we ought to go out the following night and that I ought to photograph her during the night. In a vindictive mood, I told her, "No. I am leaving for New York," and that I wasn't interested in her anymore! I did go back to New York the next day.

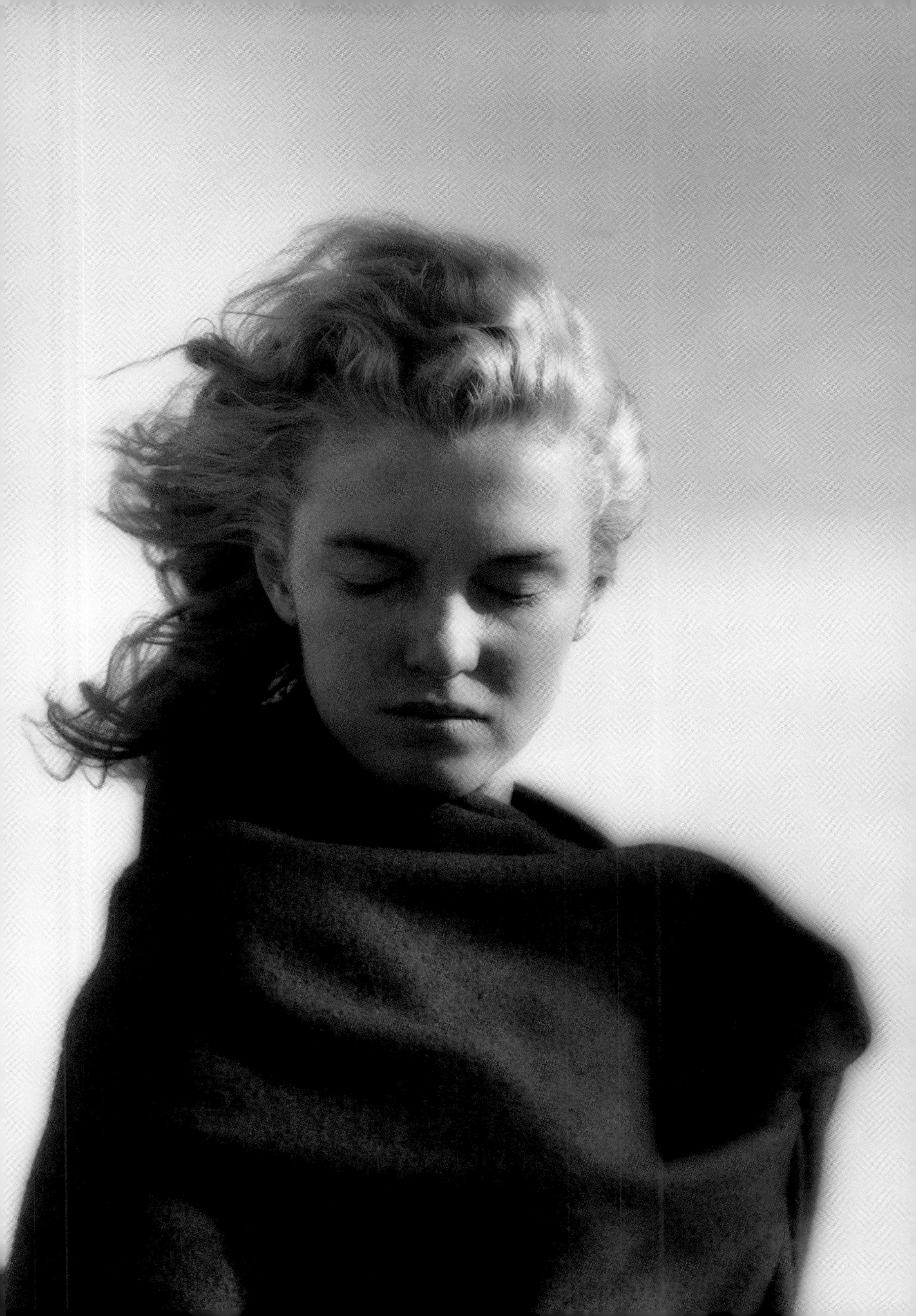

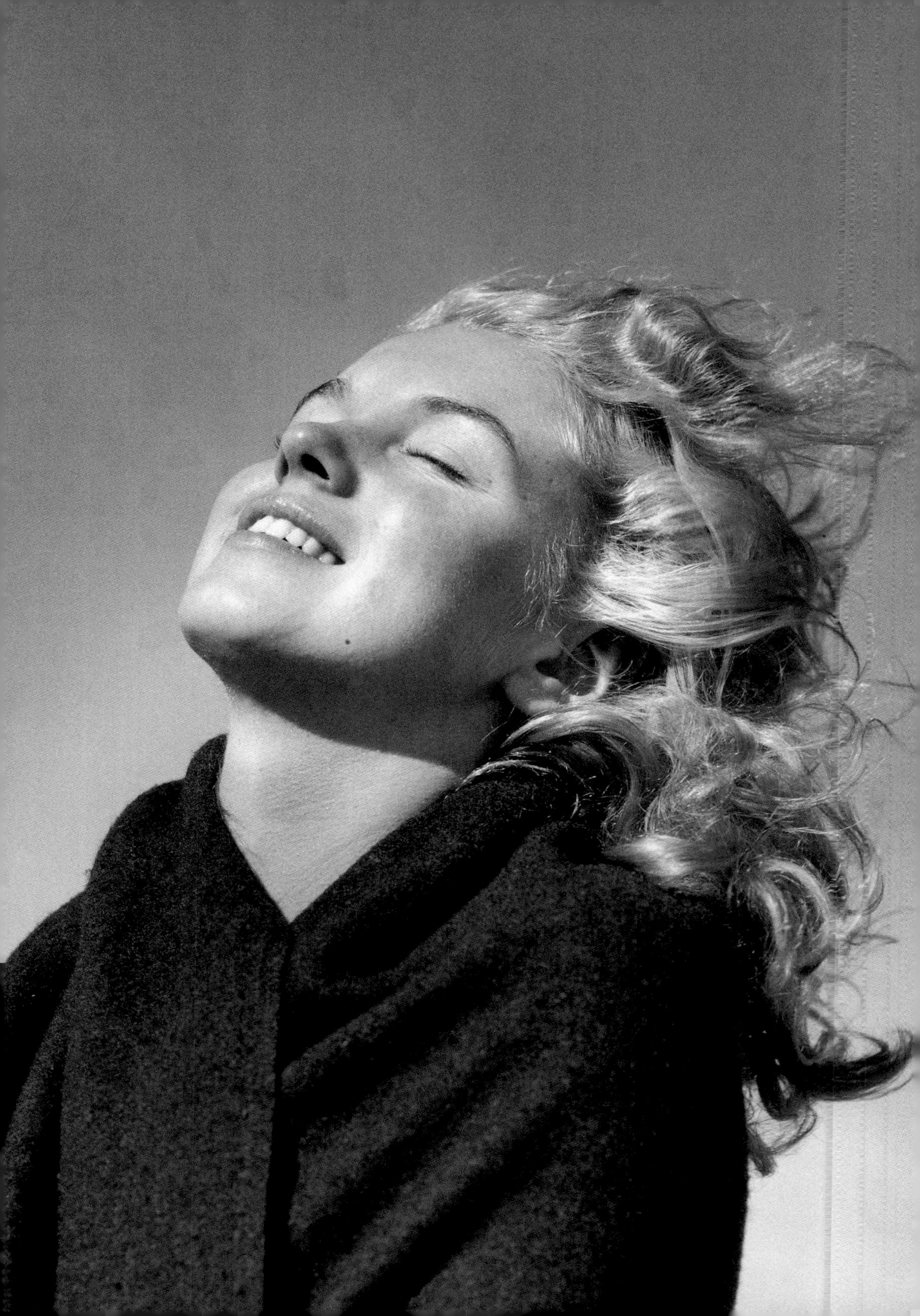

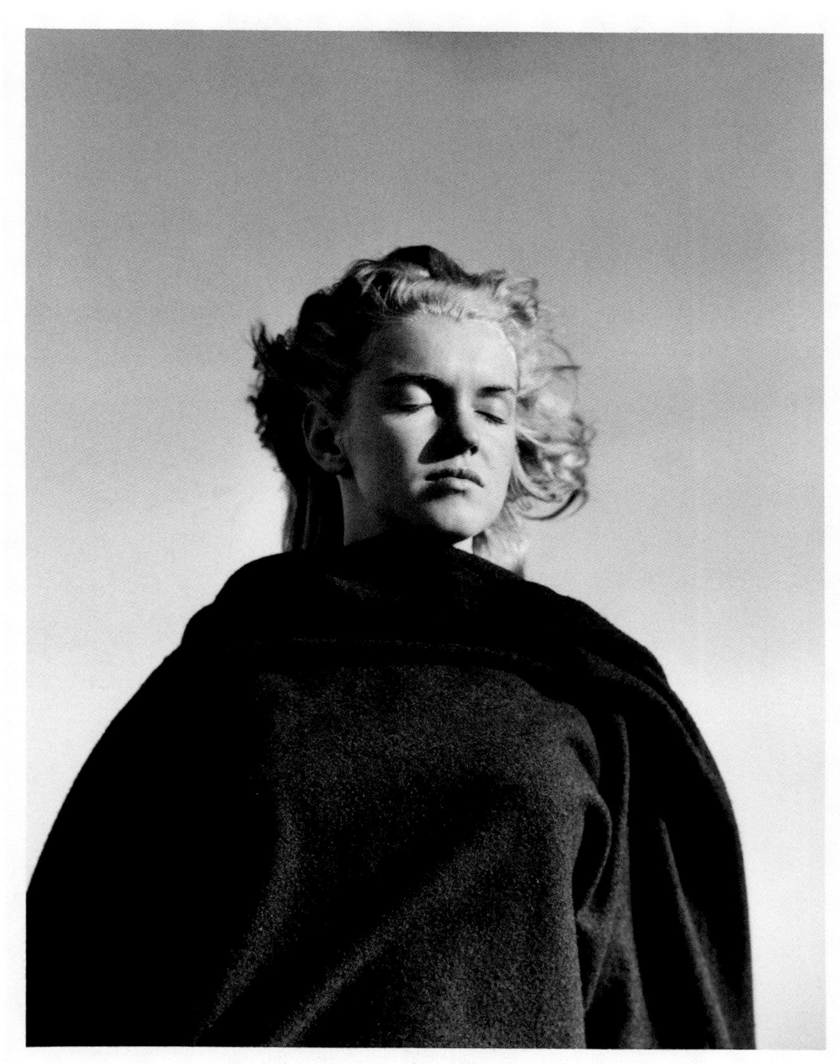

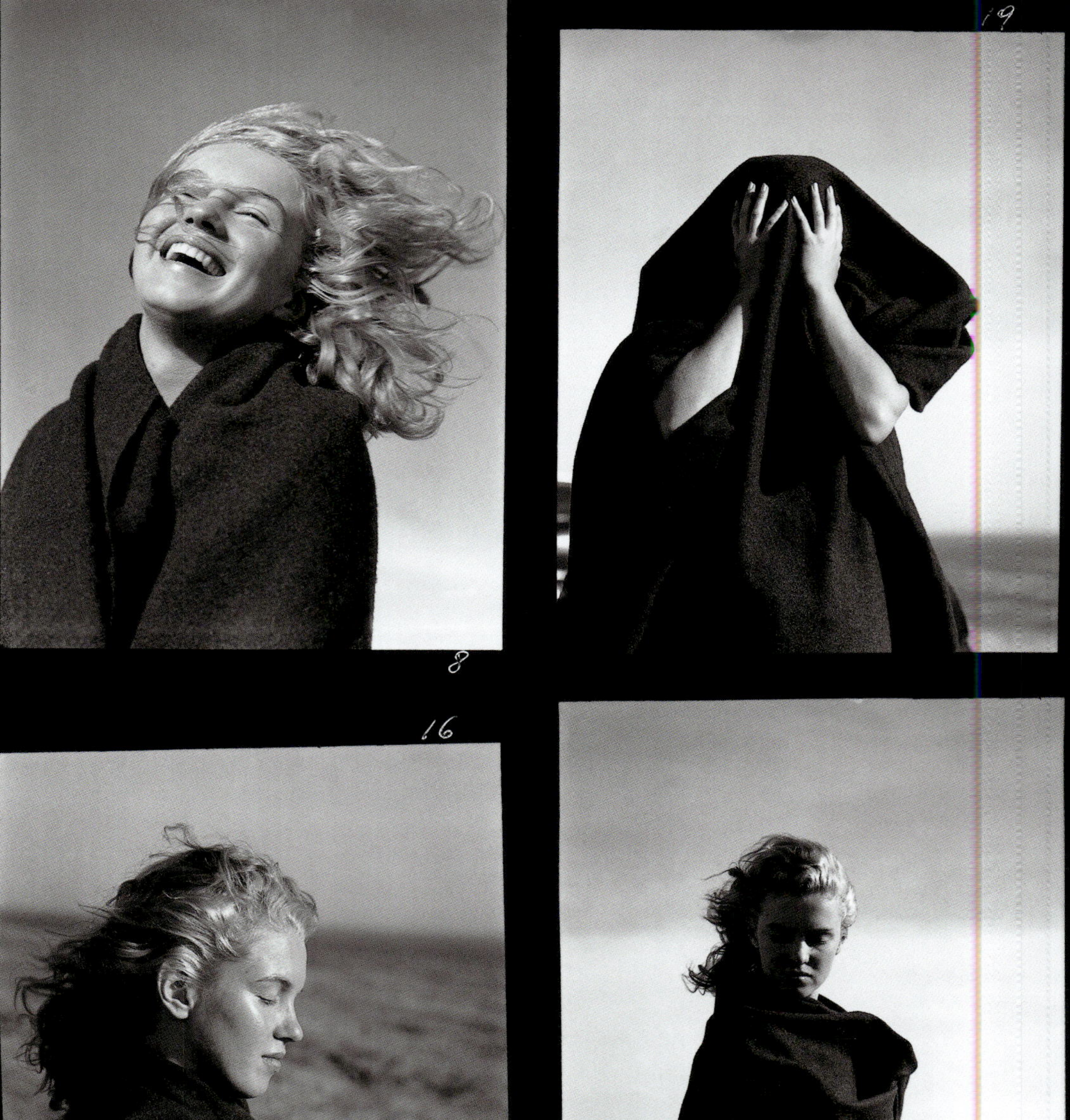

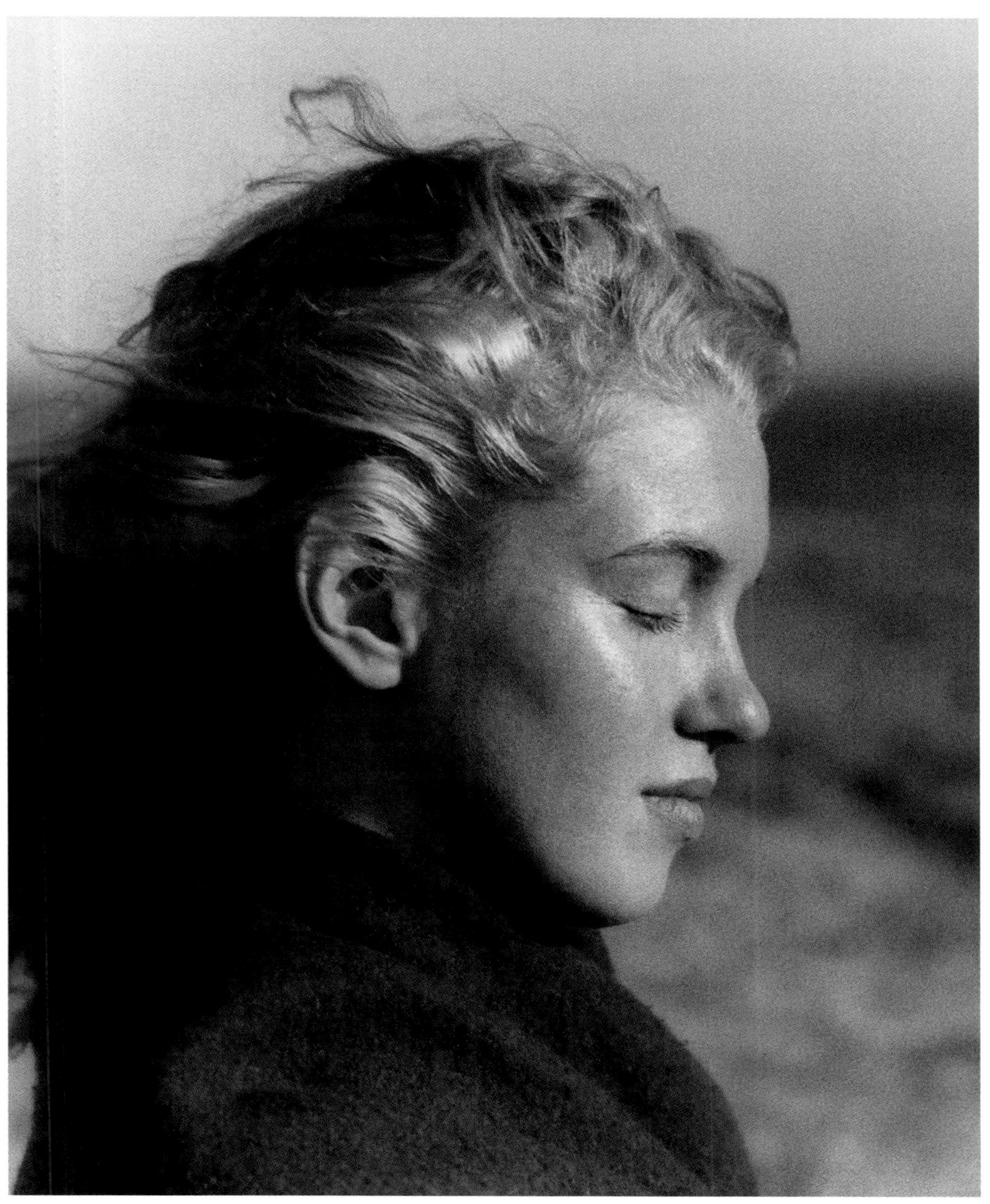

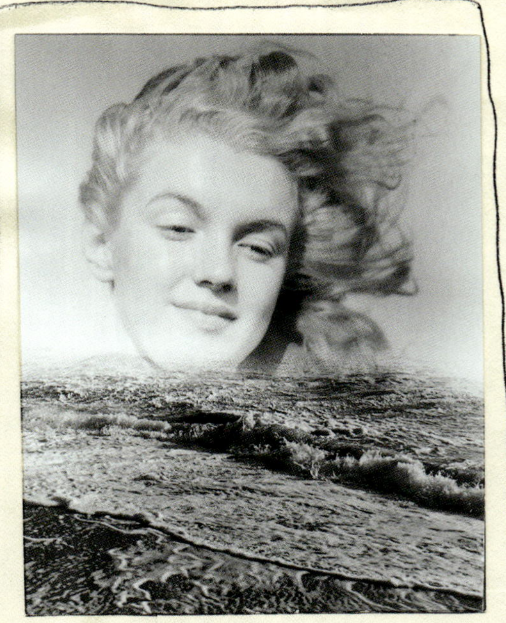

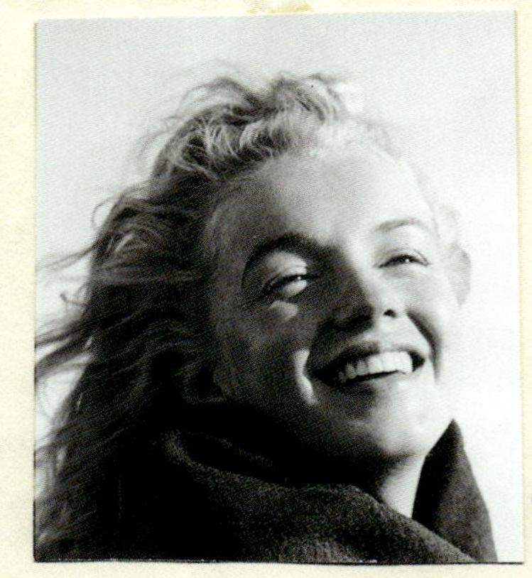

"HAPPINESS

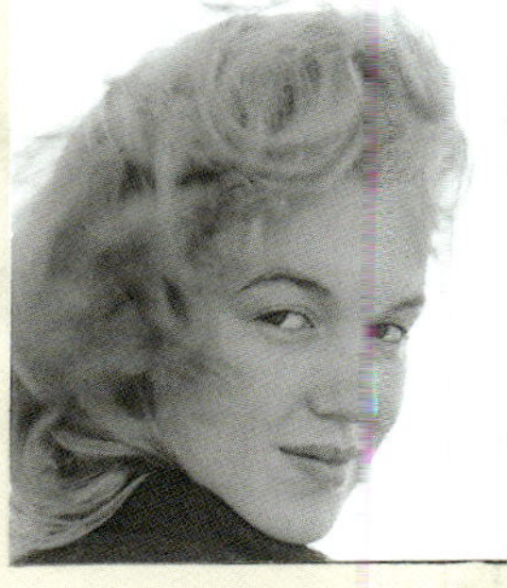

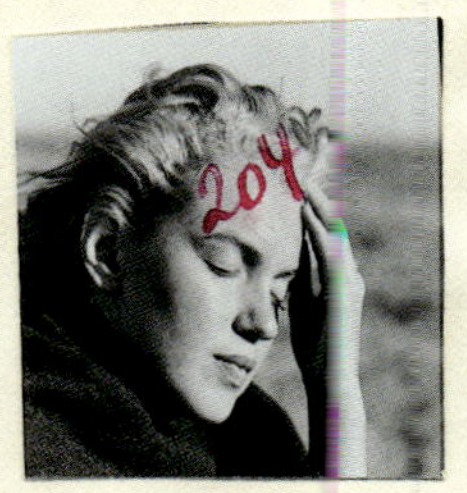

ONE OF THE MANY HANDWRITTEN POEMS IN THE ALBUM

WHAT IS LIFE ?/'TIS A DELICATE SHELL
THROWN UP BY ETERNITY'S FLOW,
ON TIME'S BANK OF QUICKSAND TO DWELL,
AND A MOMENT ITS LOVELINESS SHOW.
GONE BACK TO ITS ELEMENT GRAND
IS THE BILLOW THAT BROUGHT IT ON SHORE
SEE ! ANOTHER IS WASHING THE SAND
AND THE BEAUTIFUL SHELL IS NO MORE !

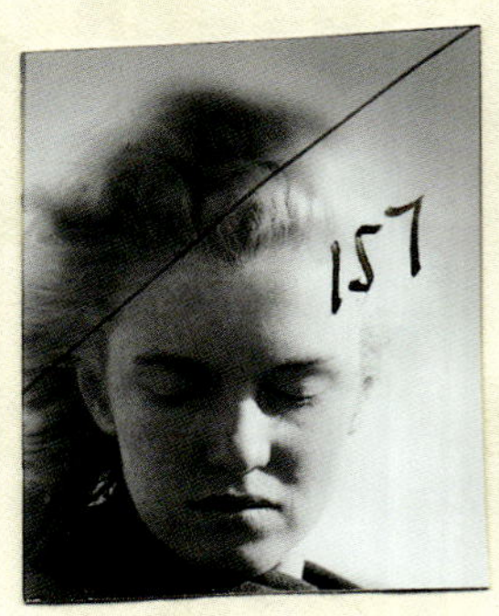

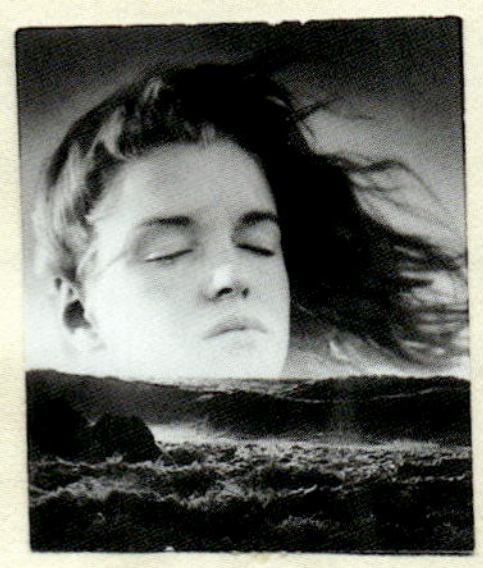

MARILYN, WITHOUT MAKE UP.
1946

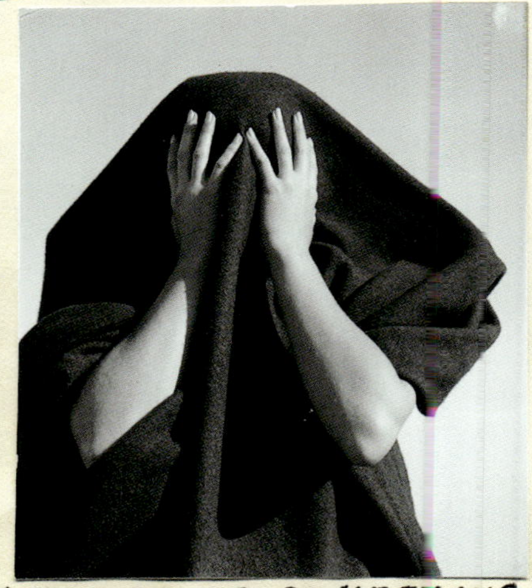

"DEATH IS SOMETHING FRIGHTENING !"

her, share with her, so we can read it together. That agreement we made in the cemetery that we shall go out to the seashore to read some more -- have come through-- due to the book I have found, THE lovely ALBUM I bought at the antiquarian... And A FEW DAYS LATER, Marilyn and I were far out at the seashore, north of Mailbu, on a deserted beach, where we read the pages of the book with a magnifier, to decipher the small but beautiful handwritings.

I remember so well which poems Marilyn loved. She was nearly in tears several times. One poem is about the futility of life. I quote it here, hoping the reader will find it lovely also. The title is :

WHAT IS LIFE ?

Marilyn wasn't the kind of person who would have tears in her eyes easily, no matter how deep the emotion. But the poems touched her immensely. She nearly weeped. She was holding herself back from bursting into sobs while she was reading another poem entitled :

LINES ON THE DEATH OF MARY ----"

She SAID it fits her. But the lady who wrote it forgot to put the---LYN after the name Mary ! And I REMARQUED, saying that a few days before she told me in the cemetery in Hollywood, that she prefers a long, happy life, and now she says she will not live long. The poem we were reading about the death of Mary was a predicament for her ! THAT she shall die young !

The reading ENDED, AND I BEGAN taking pictures of her, one by one, depicting moods she interpreted for me. An entire spectrum of life, depicting happiness, pensive, introspection, serenity, sadness, torment, distress, I even asked her to show me what "death" looked like in her imagination. She threw a blanket over her head, and this is how she interpreted it.

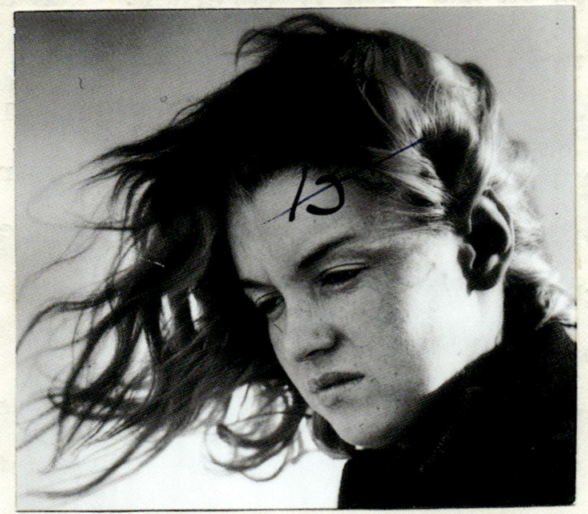

"THE END OF EVERYTHING!"

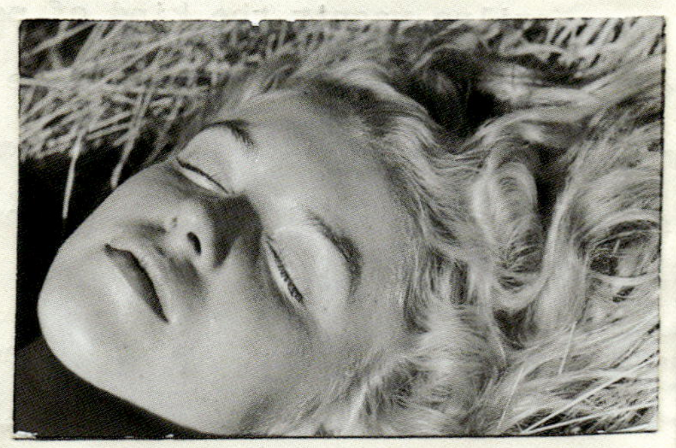

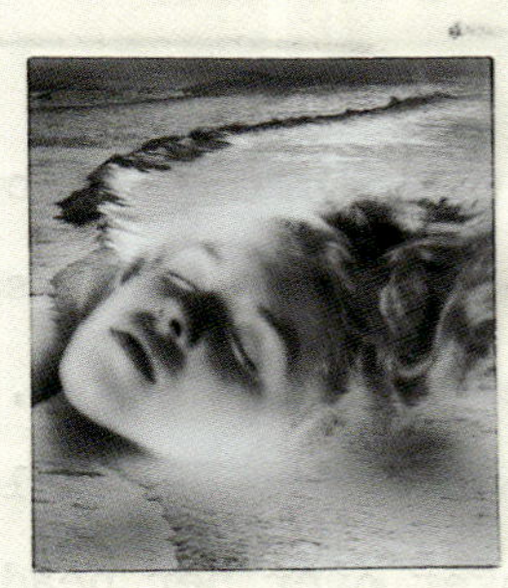

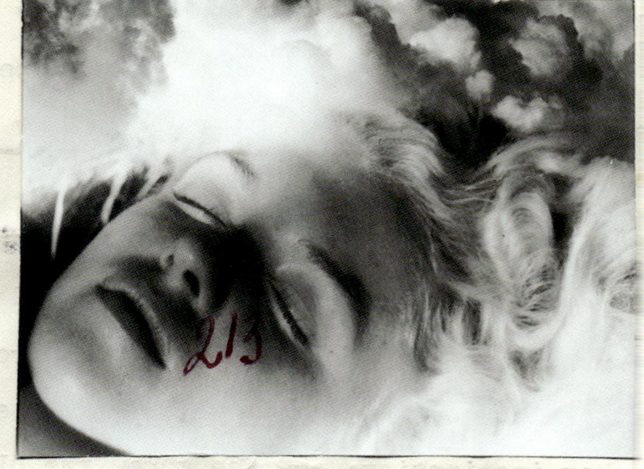

"DEATH AND TRANSFIGURATION"

The photo that followed was her own idea. She told me to get ready with my camera! She was going to show me what her own death will look like -- some day. She looked down with a very sordid expression, pointing out to me, that that picture's meaning will be " THE END OF EVERYTHING " And I quickly snapped the photo. I asked her why does she picture her death so sordid, so gloomy, instead of giving me an expression of calm smile, as if dying was a going from one world into another, a beautiful transfiguration....like the music by Richard Strauss-- Death and Transfiguration," so melodious, so beautiful .....But, Marilyn insisted that's the way <u>she</u> imagines HER DEATH!

How interesting it seems to me now, that in those moments in 1946 she was enacting, prohesising to me her own tragic end which came 16 years later in 1962. And that the poem she read with me from the ALBUM, was, as if it had really been written for her memory ! Were such feelings simply coincidences, or were they true premonitions of things to come ?

The next photo was my idea. I asked her to lie down on the ground, to show me what will she look like when dead ! And she lied down and pretended she was dead, and again, I snapped the photo. It was already late afternoon; we were taking these photos on the top of a cliff, overlooking the ocean. The scenery, and the light of the setting sun was magnificent; I was in the mood to take many more poetic photos of her, but after I took the picture of her face simulating being dead, suddenly she spreng to her feet, and part seriously, part wittily she began shouting, screaming at me :"Hell's Bell's, Look what you have made me do to my hair ! I have a date tonight ! " And she was shaking her head, and taking out the pieces of straws what stuck in her hair from having lied on the ground where the hay was cut, I calmed her down by promising some day I shall do a beautiful album with her pictures, accompanied by all kinds of lovely quoatations from my book, and even some of the poems she liked in that Album we just read together. She made a strange remark, saying, Andre, do not publish these photos now, wait until I die ! And I asked her, how does she know she will die before me? After all, I was 12 years older than her. And in a sad, low-toned voice she said she thinks she shall die before me. But ~~all~~ that took only moments. She was gay and cheerful again, looking forward to her dinner date, and she was urging me to hurry, hurry, pack everything into the car and leave the place !

I can't forget how sad I felt that evening while driving back to Hollywood-- to be on time for her dinner date. My ~~romantic attachment was over with her~~. Marilyn was no longer the lovely Norma Jean, I once knew -- only a few months before ! She was a changed woman; ambitious, calculative. She was going out to have dinner at Romanoff, in Beverly Hills. And I felt ~~terribly~~ (terribly -- put down, and belittled, left behind.....

I was packing my bags that night to return to New York -- when the phone reng. It was her ! She said she had a miserable evening, with a lousy guy, a swindeler ! Some one who wanted her to pay for the dinner! But we ~~agreed~~ REASONED that since she had exposed herself to a career in Hollywood, she ought to be strong enough to cope with everything what comes along, good ~~and~~ OR bad. But I did not inqure what had happened, why was she so upset, what had the man done so wrong? Instead, she suggested we ought to go out the following night, and that I ought to photograph her during the night. [illegible]

In a ~~vengeful~~ vindicative mood, I told her, No, I am leaving for New York, and I wasn't interested any more in her ! I did go back to New York the next day.

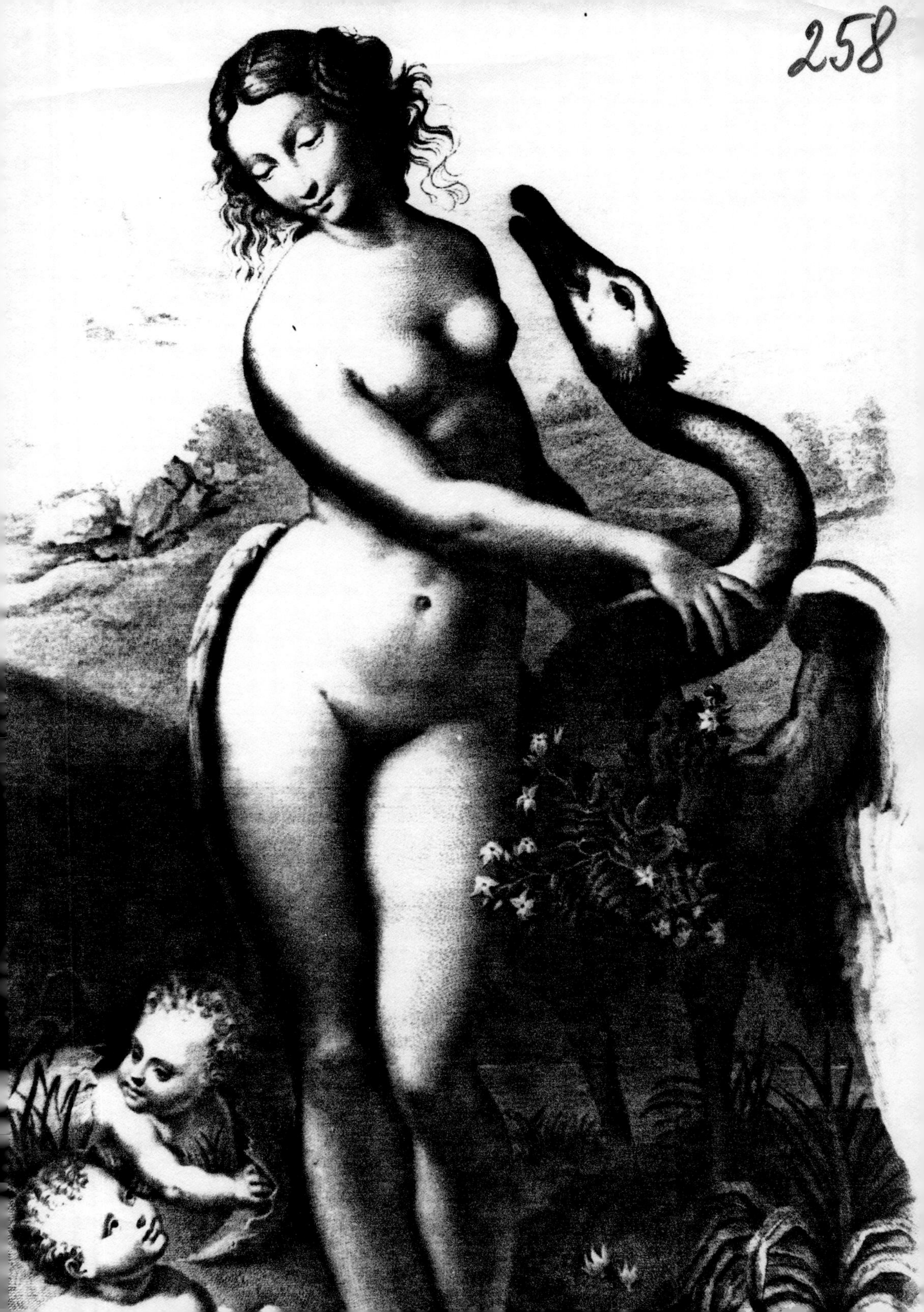

incident happened I created a few beautiful pictures by skillfully combining photography with very old engravings I collected, and I showed the prints to Marilyn, sincerely hoping that she will be inspired by them to pose for me nude, standing, or coming out from the surf like the goddess of beauty, Aphrodithe. We were driving and dicussing the issue, but she wasn't in a very good mood that morning, and I felt hurt that she snobbed my artistic ideas and sneared at me for suggesting nudes of her. I became peeved, and shouted at her in anger that she was stupid she didn't even know who Leonardo de Vinci was, or who Sandro Botticelli was, the simple little Italian monk who painted the famous " Birth of Venus " which was one of the treasures in the Ufficci Museum in In Florence, I guess, I wanted to hurt her, to get even and show my superiority and I shouted at her angrily " You are a fake, a phony, a hypocrite ! You will never become an actress ! And I told her to go to hell and I swore to her that I shall find models far more beautiful than her, to pose for me ! And that I shall find models by the dozens, and photograph all the nudes I wanted !

A thundering , explosive protestation burst out of her " You will see ! I will show you ! Just wait and see ! I will make it !" But suddenly the fight came to a halt. At the next stop light she jumped out of the car, slammed the door with all her strenght, and without looking back snobishly walked away. I yelled after her to come back, but she turned her face away, and me, by pride I drove on.

That happened on a Sunday morning, in Culver city, not too far from the Fox studios, where 15 years later she swemm in the nude for her last movie, in 1962, SOMETHING's GOT TO GIVE, the film which was never made, because she died.

Fortunately, the argument about nudes was just a minor clash between us, it was neither the first, nor the last. But as I vowed, I found many pretty models to pose for me, nude, and my photos met with much success. And while my career was blossoming, hers,--too, began to show great hopes. She did her best to show me she wan't joking when she swore she shall become an actress ! But she had gone through very hard times, at least twice, when her contract, which guaranteed her a small weekly salary was cancelled.

I do not want to discuss Marilyn's career. There are several VERY well-written books about all that. I would prefer to recall an amusing story about her, that happened sometimes between 1947 and 1949. She was spreading a story about herself in Hollywood, that she might marry a millionaire, An old millionaire ! And people thought it might be Johnny Hyde, Hyde was the executive vice president of the William Morris theatrical agency, the most reputable and influential agency in Hollywood's movie business. Hyde began doing many wonderful things for Marilyn, He was very wealthy, but not that old ! Not an old man ! The story what she spread around about perhaps marrying an old millionaire have started with me in New York. Occasionally, she and I exchanged letters. She was always very considerate, inquiring about me, about my cat, about my girlfriends. Unfortunately, in a stupid, short period of anger toward her, I sent her back those letters she wrote to me. It's an old Hungarian custom, that when a romance is over, even the correspondance is given back to the concerned ones. Anyway, I was stupid, I sent back a bunch of nice letters she wrote, so I have nothing to substantiate my story WITH. But this is what have happened :

One day, just as I was parking my car in front of my studio at 18 East 58th Street, I got into conversation with an old gentleman who was walking his dog. After I told him I was a photographer, and my principal subjet matters were pretty girls, he came up to my studio where the walls of my office were covered with enlargments of my best glamour photos, and many photos of Marilyn. He carefully examined all the photos, and curiously, it's at Marilyn's pictures he came to a halt, and inquired who she was. He liked her. He said he would like to meet her ! I told him the story, that she was a model in Hollywood, and perhaps she might become a future actress; and that I almost married her, but her career was far more important; still, she writes and phones me from time to time. That our friendship continued. And I told the old man that Marilyn wasn't doing too well neither financially, nor in her career, and she was often broke.

The old man came back again, to ask me to be good enough to sell him some of those prints he has seen on my walls. I replied-- nothing doing-- I will not take the pictures off the wall, Than he pleaded to make some new prints for him, and he will pay any price I wish. I obliged, and a few days later brought to him the print to the address he gave me, a very good address, just off Park Avenue. I think I asked a hundred dollars per print, But he was a dear gentleman! He asked me whether that was really enough, and if not, he would gladly pay more

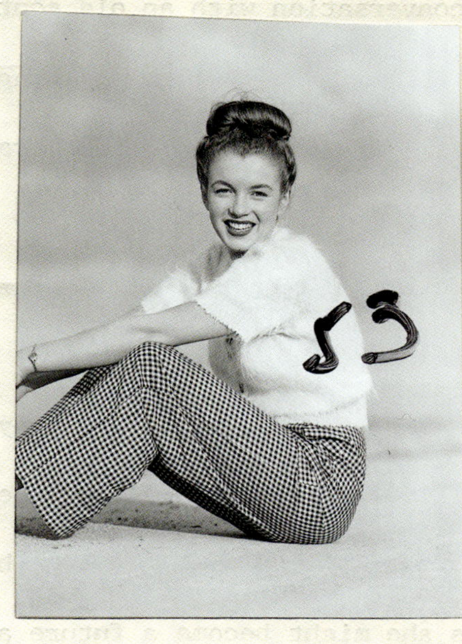

THE VERY LAST PHOTO I TOOK OF "NORMA JEANE"

1946
MY FIRST PHOTOS OF MARILYN MONROE

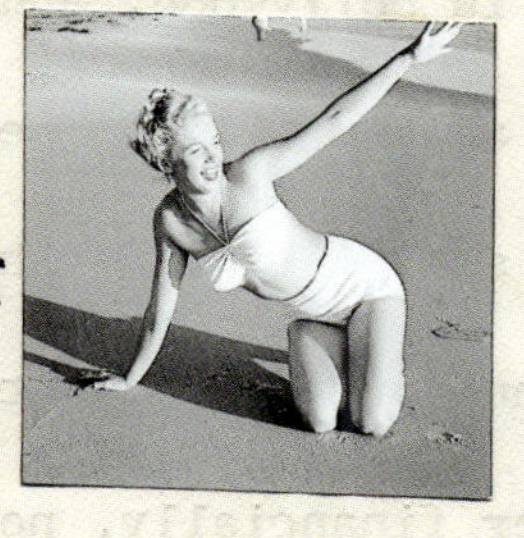

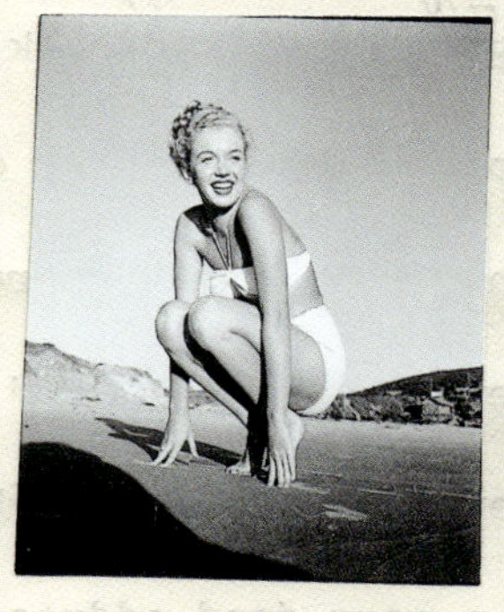

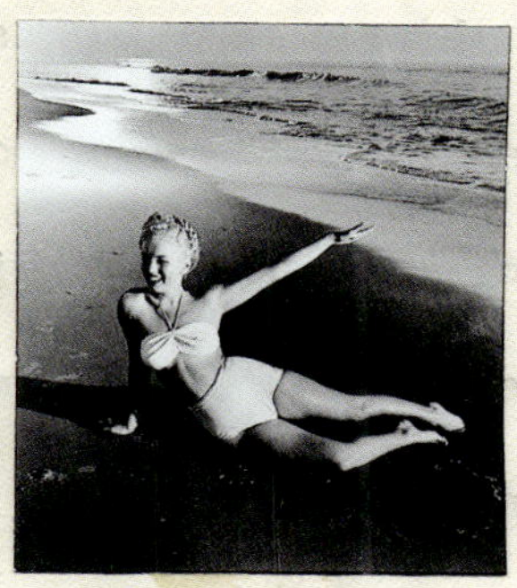

(I BOUGHT THE BATHING SUIT)
AND I ASKED HER TO BRAID HER HAIR

Than, THE MAN opened his heart to me, He lived in HIS big, five story building all by himself, with his servants, and that he was very wealthy, BUT knowing his life will end soon, he wanted a little happiness. He wanted Marilyn's address and phone number. He wanted to send her money to come to New York, because he wanted to marry her ! He bousted he will leave a million dollars for her, and the building, and various business interests. He had only one son, just killed in the war IN JAPAN, which ended the year before. Day after day THE MAN phoned me, asking for Marilyn's phone number, Marilyn did not believe me, She asked me not to give NEITHER ADRESS, NOR PHONE NO to the man, Nor her real name ! She said the man was much too old, and probably a luny ! To tell the truth, I was jalous, AND DIDN'T EVEN CARE that the man promised me a "big commission" for the good deed, after Marilyn would come to New York! The man was already old, living too comfortably and peacefully in his brownstone building, He didn't want to take the effort to travel to Hollwyood to meet Marilyn. LATER ON, Occasionally he visited me, but slowly the issue died down. Meanwhile, Marilyn might have been bragging in Hollwyood that an old millionaire was in love with her ! And indeed, HE was ! He died two years later. I haven't got the vaguest idea what have happened to his vast fortune ! I wonder what would have happened if the two had met ? I did propose the man that I shall make him meet some other models whom he might like; but he was an obstinate man, saying, all girls were prostitutes, AND DISHONEST, AND pushy as hell! But Marilyn was an exception for him He has decided that SIMPLY BY LOOKING AT my photographs ON THE WALL ! Strange !

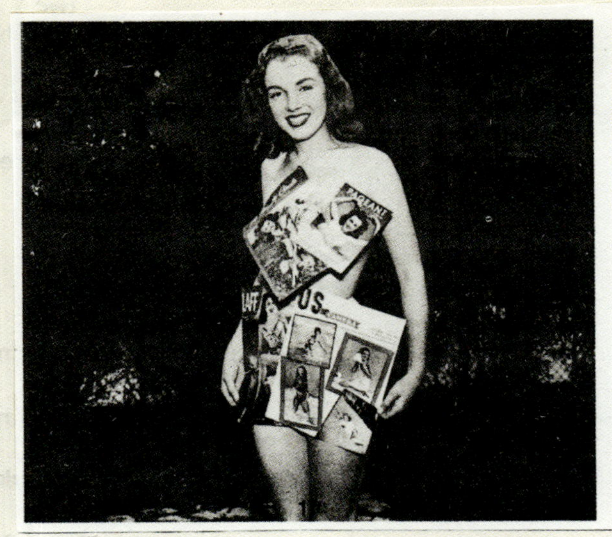

MARILYN PUBLICIZING HERSELF
WITH 3 OF MY MAGAZINE COVERS.
U.S. CAMERA
FAMILY CIRCLE
PAGEANT

There are various versions in existance of the story how Howard Hughes, the billionaire who owned R K O Studios spotted a picture of a pretty blonde on a magazine cover, and instructed his aids to find the girl -- Marilyn Monroe -- and arrange a screen test for her. It is impossible to know the exact truth. There are many myths going on in Hollywood about everything; I would like to show three evidences here; Marilyn Monroe's first magazine covers, the photographs I took of her in 1945. Whether it might have been one of these photos Howard Hughes liked -- I can't tell, but I can tell a story what is true. Sometimes in the late 1946 or early 1947, a man came to my studio, asking me to be good enough to make some enlargments from some of his 35 mmtr. negatives. He heard about me, that I was an artist, and make wonderful enlargments. And he, too, loved photography. He was Jack Frye, the ex president of Trans World Airlines (TWA), an early pionner in the history of commercial aviation in America, and a partner or associate of Howard Hughes, way back when they first started carrying mail and passengers from the West coat to the East coast. I really do not know much about all that; all I know is that Jack Frye, liked my photographs of pretty girls, and liked my photos of Marilyn what he noticed on my walls, and he advised me to send a selection of Marilyn's photos to Howard Hughes, to promote my photography, and that he -- Jack Frye warmly recommends me for any future assignments Howard Hughes might care to give me. I did send Marilyn's photos, if to an address ~~on Romaine Street (4000 Romaine~~ ?) ~~where he had an office in incognito~~. Howard Hunghes aid sent me back the photos, thanked me kindly, and promised that if opportunity arises to use me,they shall keep me in mind. But they kept one magazine cover, which I sent along with the photographs. This one here: PARADE Sunday Picture Magazine February 16, 1947

And inside the magazine there was a double page spread with my first magazine cover of Marilyn, and a couple of the first photos I took of her.

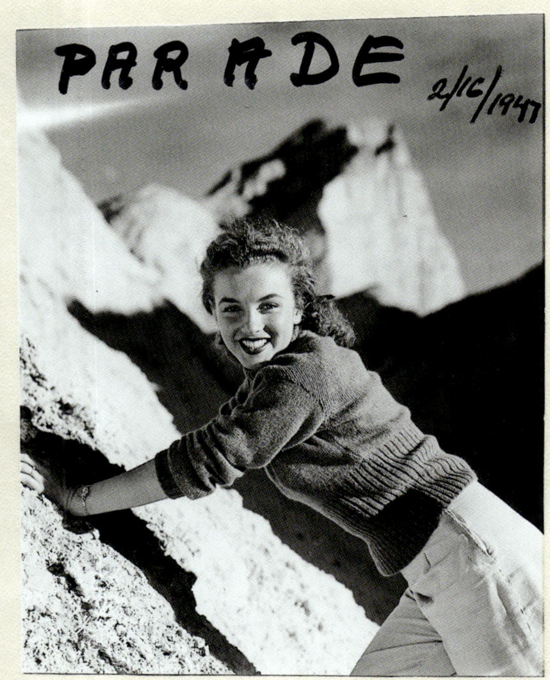

Between 1947 and 1949, Marilyn had a very hard time getting started in Hollywood with her carreer. Nobody knows for sure how she had managed existing through those years, but she was a go-getter, and was plugging herself all the time, and meeting a great many people, what really is the most essential thing to do, to start on the ladder of success. In January 1947 she sent me a small present; a nice little leather-boud book I still treasure having:

1947

SCIENCE and HEALTH
with
Key to the Sriptures
by
Mary Baker Eddy

On the first leaf of the page she wrote this

(This was sort of a " Dear John ", the proverbial — letter, after she decided she will not marry me.)

1/15/48

Dearest Andre,

Line 10 and 11 on page 494 of this book is my prayer for you always.

Love,
Norma Jeane

and I quote here line 10 and 11 from page 494

" Divine Love always has met and always will meet every human need...."

I think the present was sort of a farewell present to me, Sort of a last word to our love-relationship. From than on, I got away from thinking about her. I got thoroughly absorbed in photographing one pretty girl after another, nude and not nude, simply for my own pleasure, for self-expression, AND I made great efforts To have the photos published.

My artistic nudes met with instant appreciation in France; during the latter part of the 1940s. I had several Albums published in , under the title NUS (Nudes) and these albums were sold also in the U.S. but "under the counter" only, because publication of such photos books -- even if artistic -- was absolutely prohibited yet in those years. The distributor who brough my albums from France to America made a great deal of money with them! That was the birth, the CAUSE, CREATING THE IMPETUS TO PUBLISH nudes in the United States.

In 1948 I took the train to Chicago, carrying a briefcase full of the most beautiful nudes I photographed thus far, I went to see the owner, publisher of PUBLISHERS' DEVELOPMENT CORPORATION, George von Rosen, who published a couple of small-size, very mediocre looking nudist magazines, and a magazine named ART PHOTOGRAPHY, and also various other magazines. I convinced von Rosen right away, that my photos of nudes were far superior to those few he was publishing. He was so impressed, he called in his business manager, who came in with a large book to show VON ROSEN the prifits and assets of his business. Than VON ROSEN called into his office all his editorial staff. Withing a few hours, they selected a couple of hundred of my photos. George von Rosen was a gentleman; he gave me a check immediately for nearly five thousand dollars. When he handed it to me, he said he could have decucted 2 % REBATE for paying me right away, but since I took the initiative to come to see him, he would not deduct that 2 % rebate. He even took me for a steak dinner, and drove me at midnight to the Airport where I took the plane back to New York.

I am not patting myself on the shoulder, but that trip I made to see GEORGE von Rosen was the real birth of the the publishing of magazines with nudes, nothing but nudes. It SOON became a new "industry" in America, producing billions of dollars

ENTERTAINMENT FOR **MEN**

PLAYBOY

JANUARY, 19

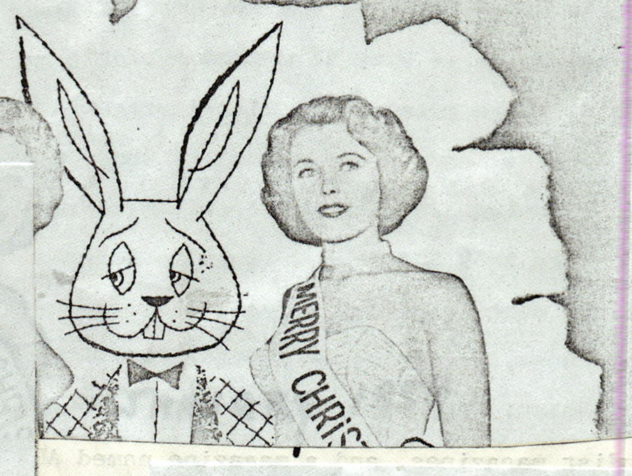

SOME say you can judge a man by the way he furnishes his home. If that's true, photographer Andre de Dienes is just about the most interesting guy we've ever heard tell about. He has one of those modern ranch-style houses stuck up on a hill in sunny California, and he sent us some pictures of it the other day. We've got to admit, we approve of the decor and we'd like to furnish our own apartment in a similar style if Andre will just send us the names and phone numbers.

at home with DIENES

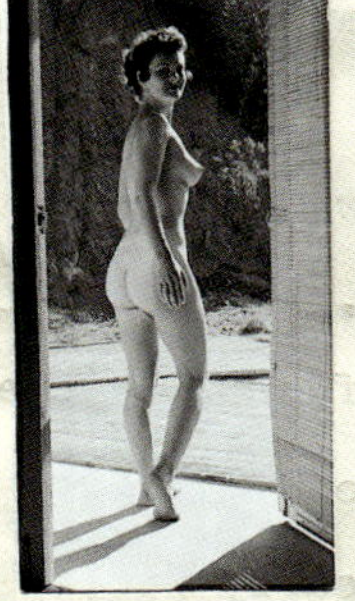

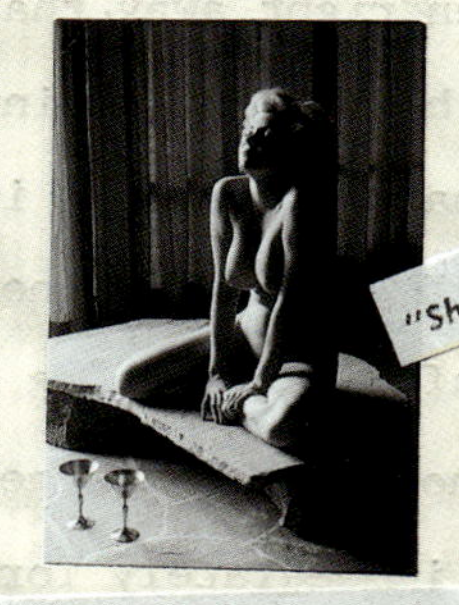

"Shay, Andre, what's in this drink?

The living room features two stone tables—ideal for the casual get-togethers so popular in California. And Andre's get-togethers are apparently casual in the extreme.

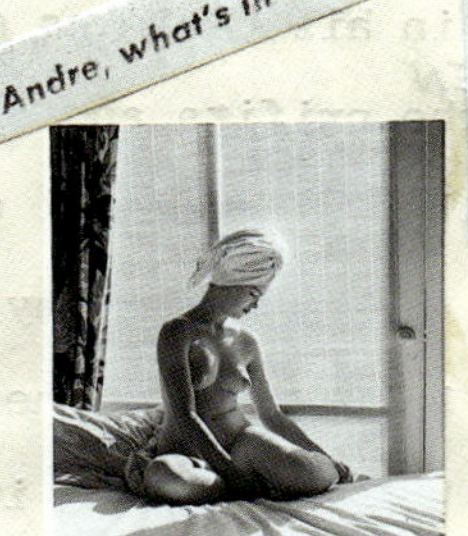

Andre's sun-porch—complete with sunbather, of course.

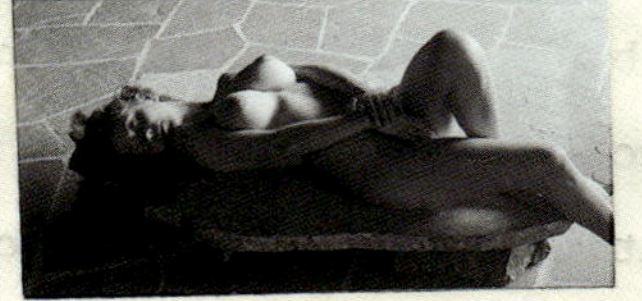

The bedroom includes, of course, a bed—and a very attractive young lady, too. Andre explains that shooting pictures like this is strictly business with him. Believe we'll dig up our old brownie and go into business for ourselves this weekend.

HOLIDAY ISSUE

THE SECOND ISSUE OF PLAYBOY Jan. 1954

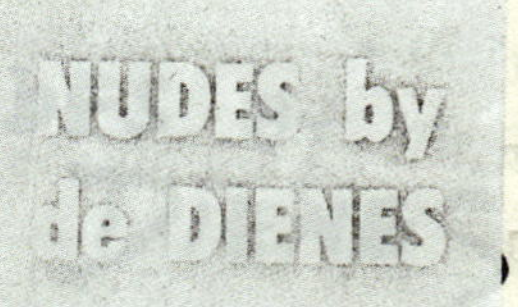

of revenue to PUBLISHERS, to the paper manufacturers, to the distributors of the magazines, to Eastman Kodak, etc. who produce the photographic supplies, and a little, very little, only minuscule part of the money going to the photographers who take the pictures, Me included.

As soon as Von Rosen began publishing my nudes, other publishers cought up with the idea, and other photographers began photographing nudes, and an ever-increasing variety of magazines started to be published. Hugh Hefner, publisher of PLAYBOY, worked as sales promotion manager for Von Rosen's PUBLISHERS' DEVELOPMENT CORPORATION. That's where he got the idea to publish his own magazine, PLAYBOY, probably inspired by my nudes, AND OTHERS', though he never acknowledged it publcily; never made even simple remark about that, through his entire fabulous rise to fame-and-fortune, WITH PLAYBOY. His job at Publishers' Development Corp. gave him the insight into the secrets of successful publishing, because, Von Rosen was a great businessman, and was doing real well ! Hefner became even better than VON ROSEN! A Genius! I am fortunate to be able to mention here, if not brag, that I contributed to his first successes with my nudes. My name is on the cover of the second issue of PALAYBOY magazine, January 1954 " Nudes by de Dienes ", and inside the magazine, I had a three pages layout of a few of my lovely photos of nudes, all beautiful, well-endowed, PRETTY GIRLS. The layout's title " at home with Dienes " This is one of the photos published in the layout. The young lady is one of the many very lovely girls I photographed, (to get even with Marilyn, when I swore to her, one day in 1947, that I shall find as many models for nudes as I wanto to) And than, I HAD the girl put on the towel, to make a turban of it. A couple of years later I repeated the same idea with Marilyn, in the bedroom of

MARILYN'S FIRST MAGAZINE COVER. 1946

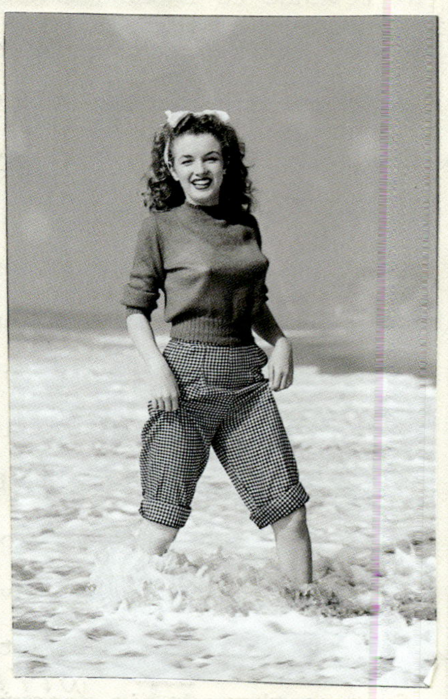

THE FAST-ACTION DANCE SHOTS I HAVE SHOWN TO U.S. CAMERA MAGAZINE. in 1946

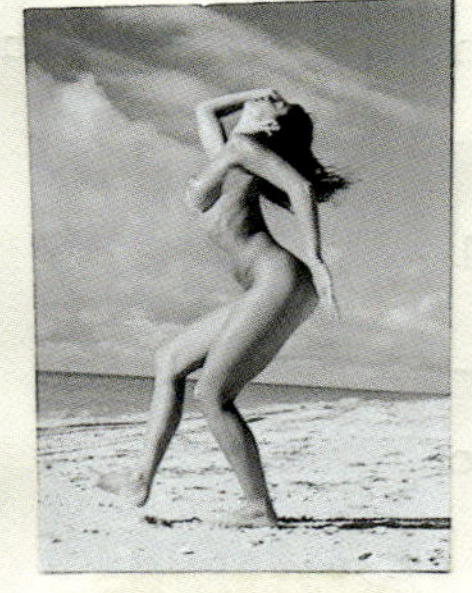

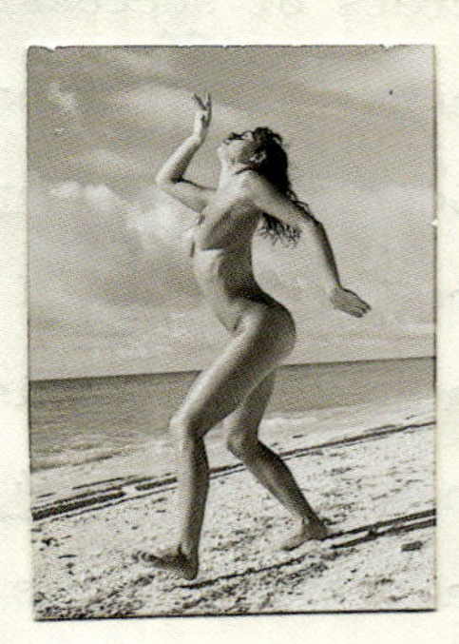

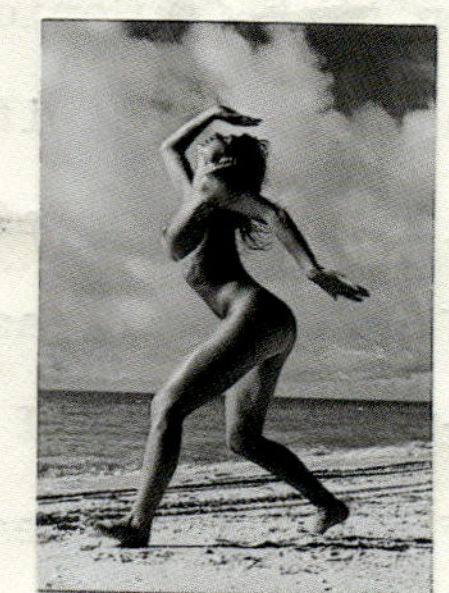

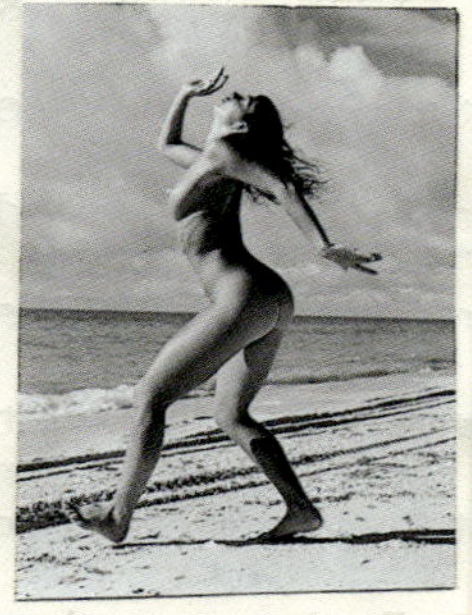

THE EDITOR FELT IT WAS "PORNOGRAPHY"!

her b~~ungalow in~~ the Bel Air Hotel, ~~in Los Angeles~~. But ~~more about that later; let me first~~ I continue NOW with my rambling about nudes and magazines.

This happened in the late 1940s, but I never forget it. I went to see the editor of a photographic magazine, U.S. CAMERA, (a than prestig~~ious~~ photo magazine) who, in 1946, published the very first picture ever published of Marilyn Monroe (than only Norma Jeane Baker,--this photo I took of her in 1945) on the cover of a magazine. I wanted to sell the man some of my nudes to be published in his magazine. But THE EDITOR ~~he~~ became awfully indignant, scornful, rebuking me,how do I dare to show him "pornographic photographs !" ~~And~~ Truthfully, I felt ~~rather ashamed~~, abashed, crushed by those remarks he made about my photograpphs. (so unjustly. [...]t only because NUDES were a novelty to him !) For the benifit of the reader, I enclose here a few of those photographs I showed to the man in those late 1940-s.

I will not give the reader a false image that photographing nudes were all fun, happiness and LIKE "paradise",being associated with girls who posed nude ~~for me~~! Occasionally, yes, it was heavenly FEELING, partly because I loved creating pictures, and because I was free to do with my life as I pleased, but most of the time the work was just hard work, NEEDING endurance, much expenses,a~~nd not a good income~~, and much irritations, troubles and heartackes with the girls I met. My nudes were a novelty to the publishers, the photos got published, but the photos served only as visual entertainment to the readers, BUT ~~and~~ Most captions TO ~~with~~ the photos had to deal with photographic, technical explanations how the photos were taken, in what kind of lighting, and with what film, what exposure,etc., because, those were the only legitimate excuse for the photos to be published in ~~most~~ magazines,or in books, But the stories what lie behind the photos, the truth about how I took the photos, and who were the models ARE ~~is~~ yet to be told by me. I would not be a succession of romantic Casanova-like autobiographical confessions, but ~~rather~~

1946

*

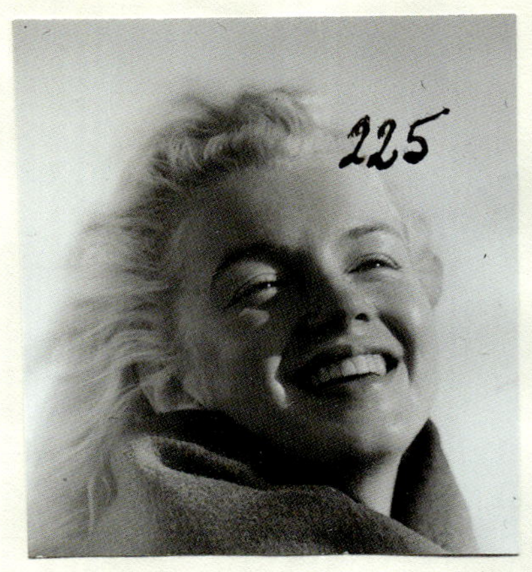

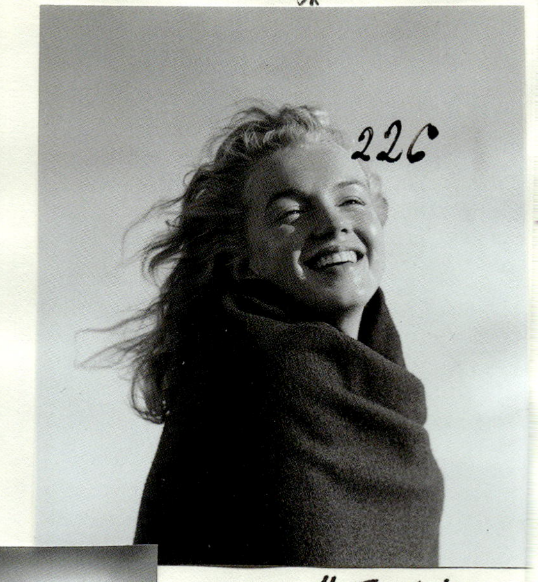

"JOY"

227/A

227/B

228

MARILYN MONROE WITHOUT MAKE-UP. I PAID HER TO POSE FOR THESE PHOTOS ALSO. I WANTED TO ILLUSTRATE A BOOK OF POETRY AND PHILOSOPHY I HAD IN MIND TO PUT TOGETHER.

ANDRE DE DIENES
1401 SUNSET PLAZA DRIVE
HOLLYWOOD, CALIF. 90069

46

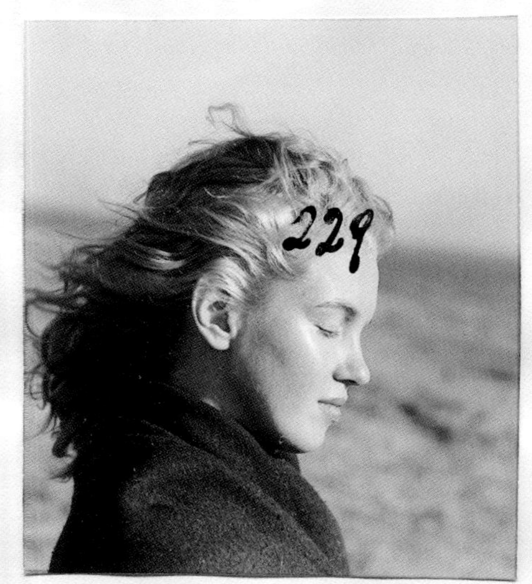

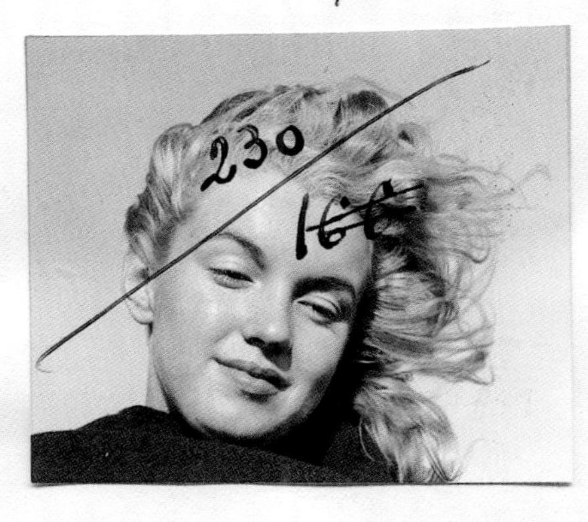

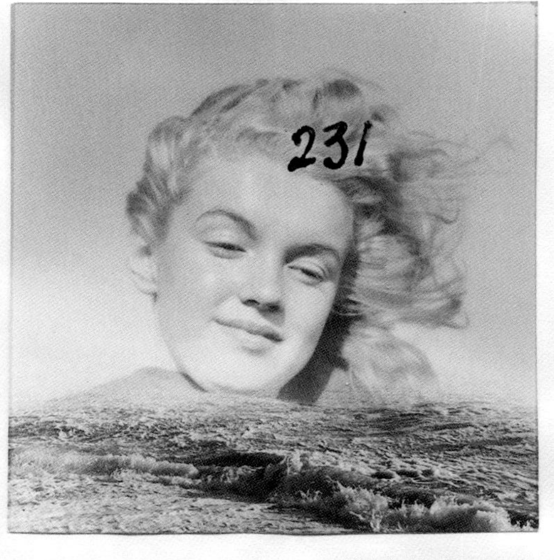

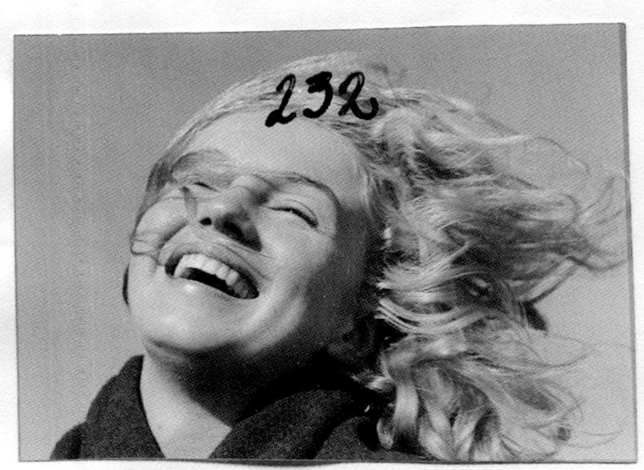

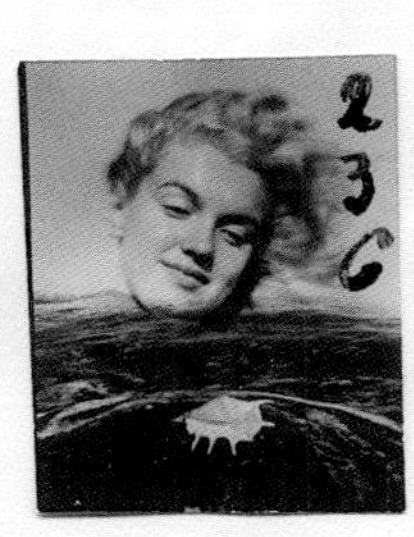

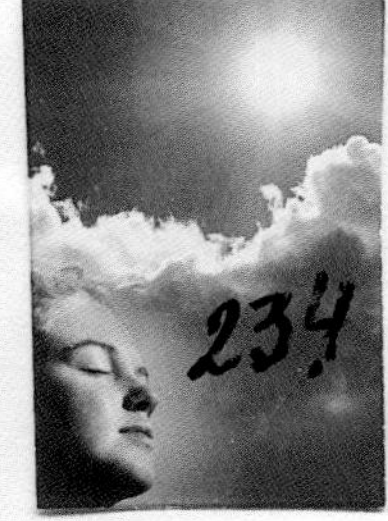

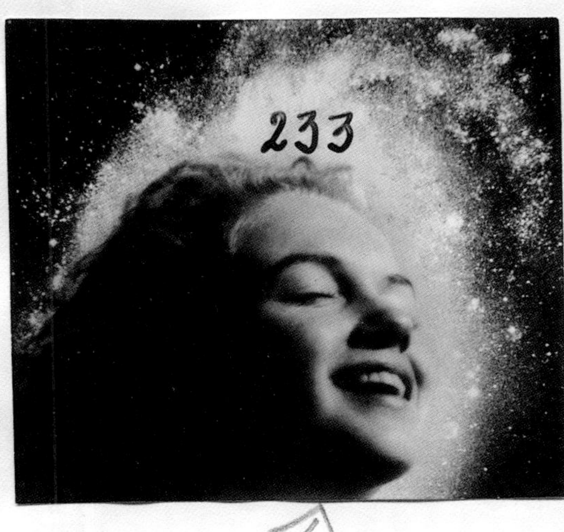

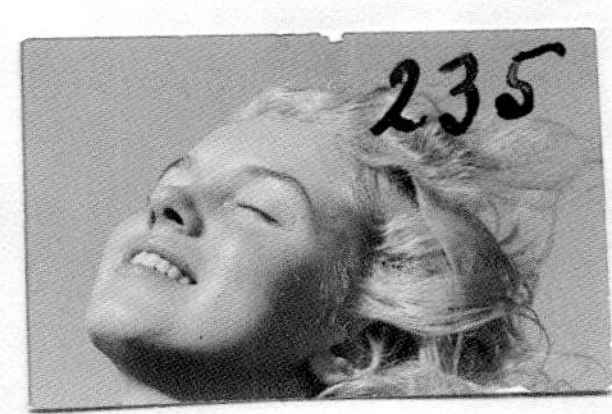

ANDRE de DIENES
1401 SUNSET PLAZA DRIVE
HOLLYWOOD, CALIF. 90069

37

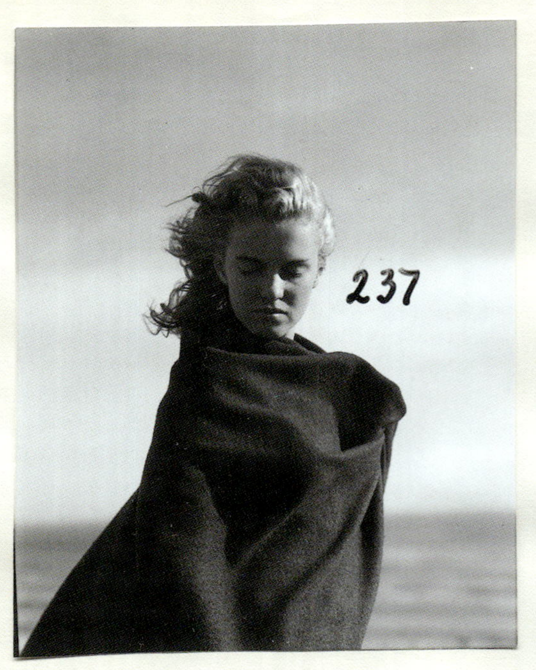

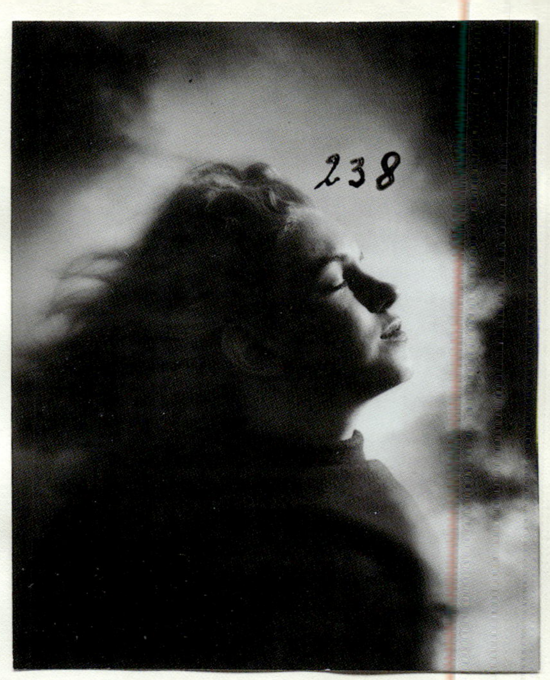

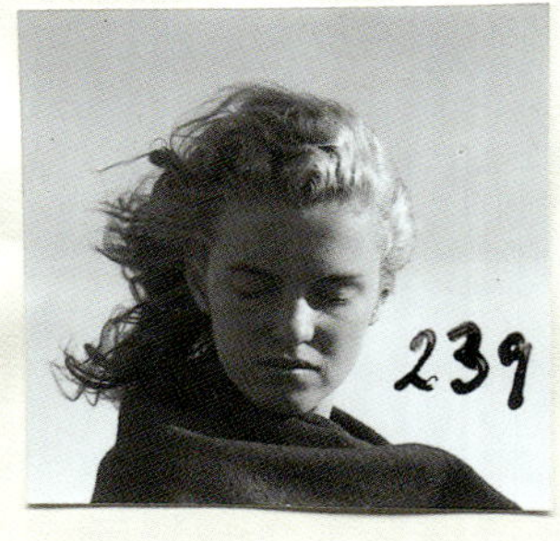

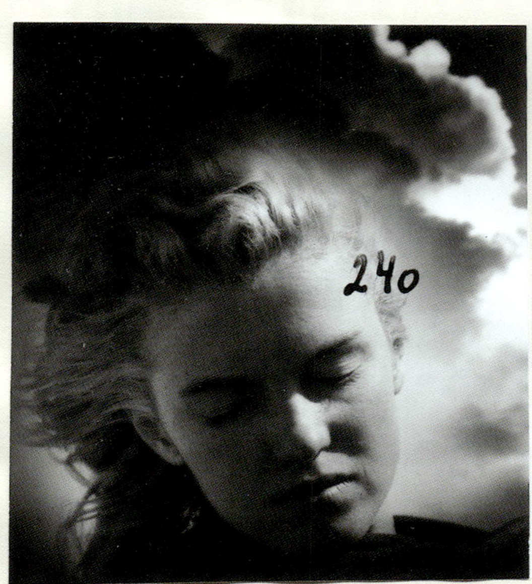

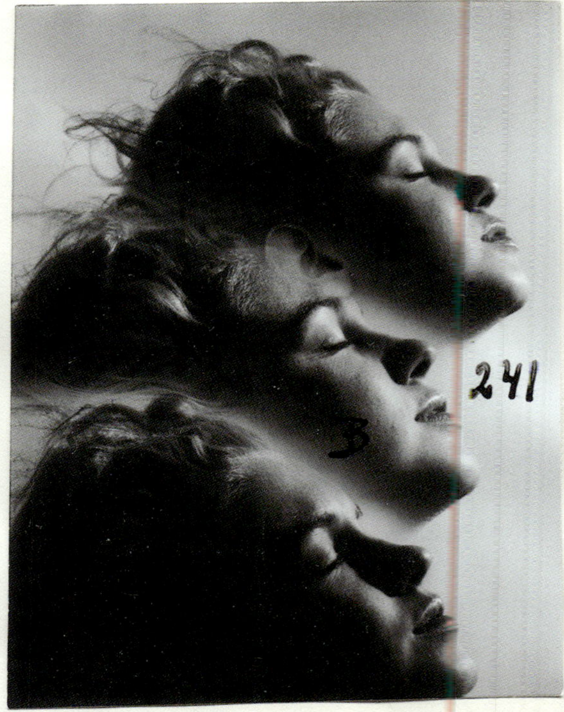

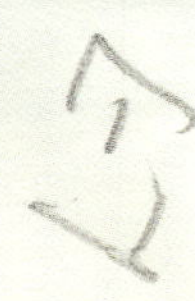

ANDRE DE DIENES
1401 SUNSET PLAZA DRIVE
HOLLYWOOD, CALIF. 90069

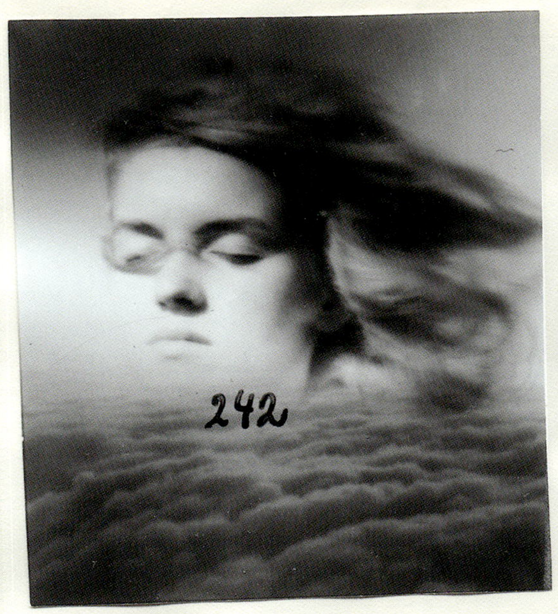

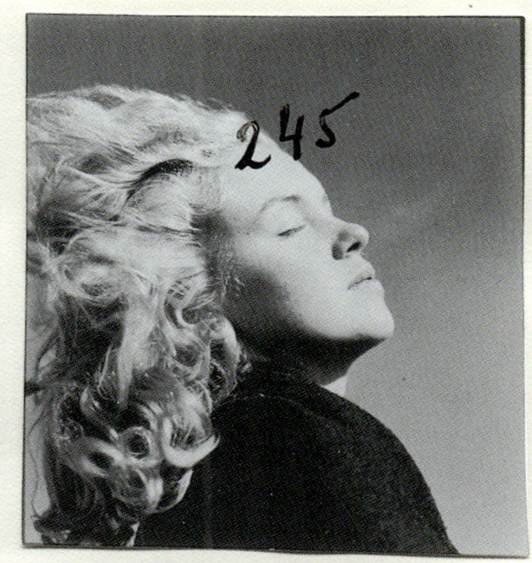

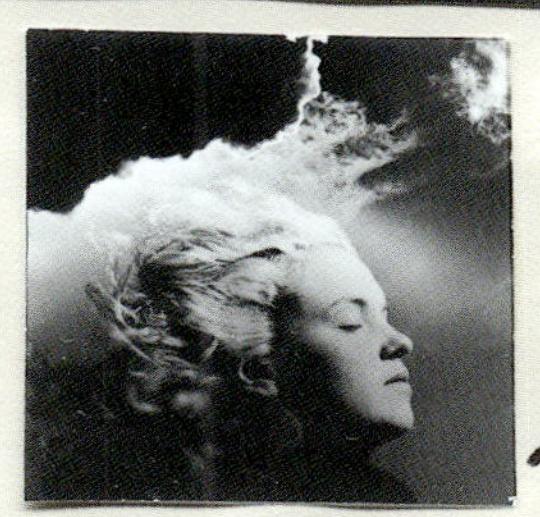

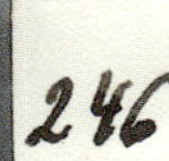

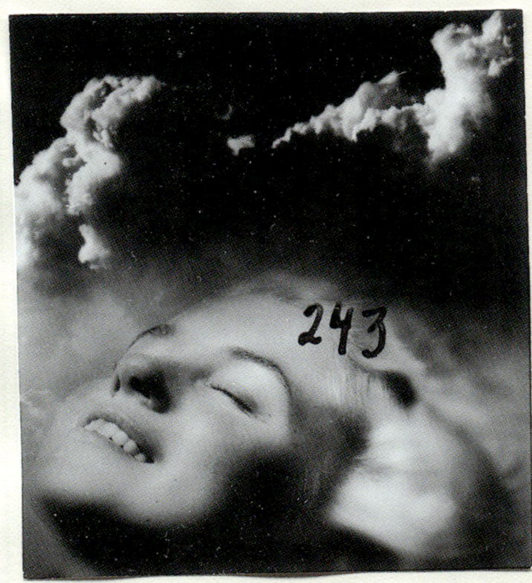

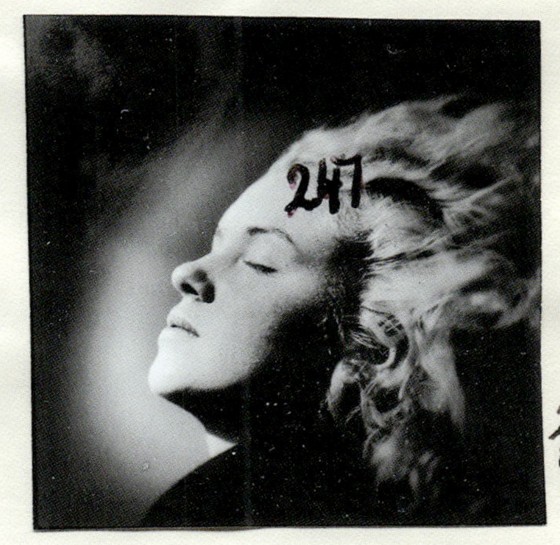

247

244

244

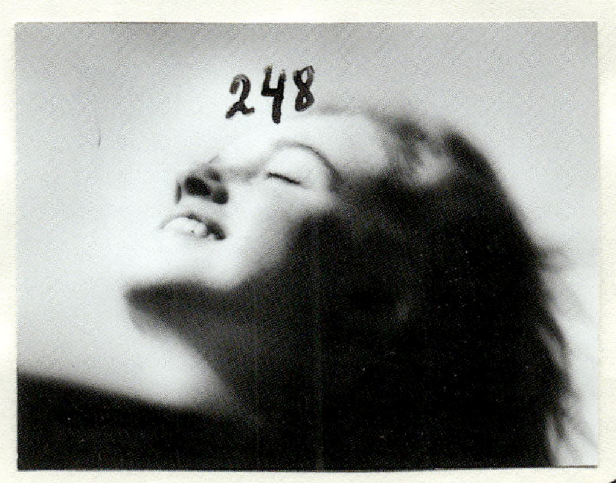

ANDRE DE DIENES

L-7

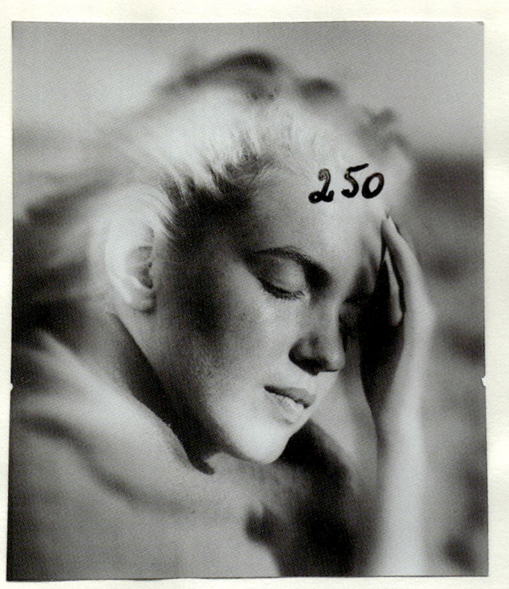

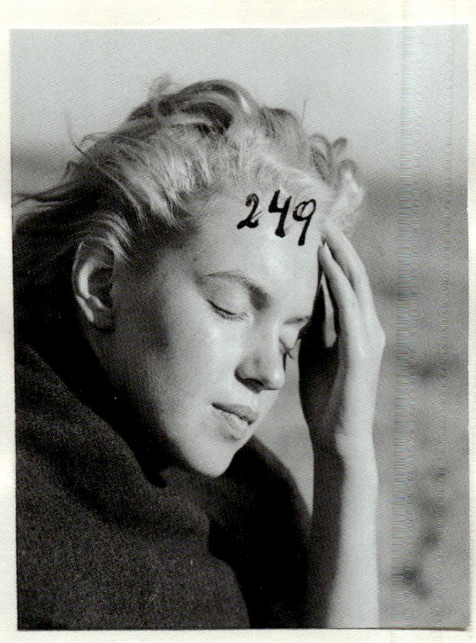

"INTROSPECTION"

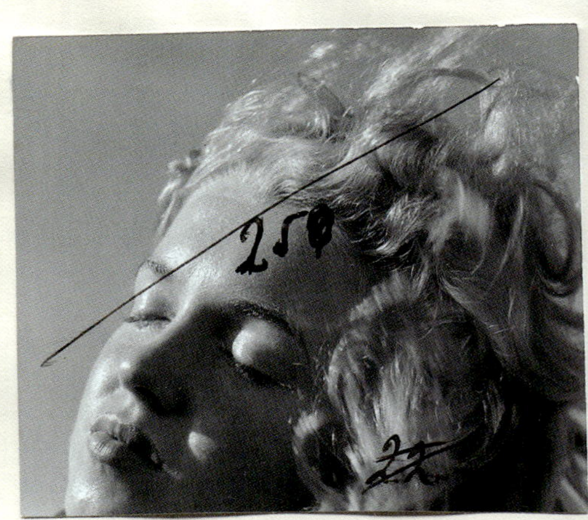

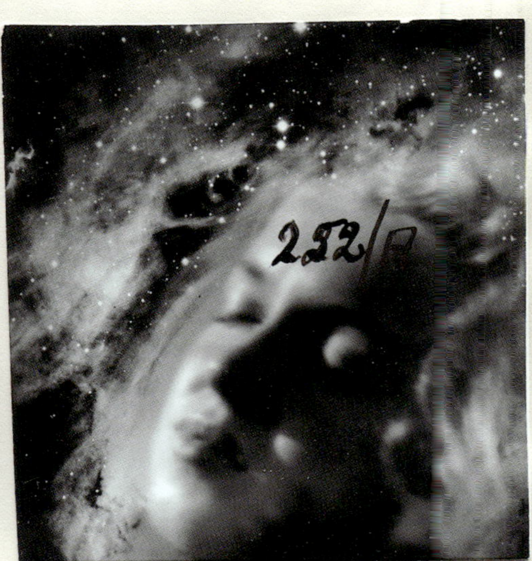

L-1↗ 252

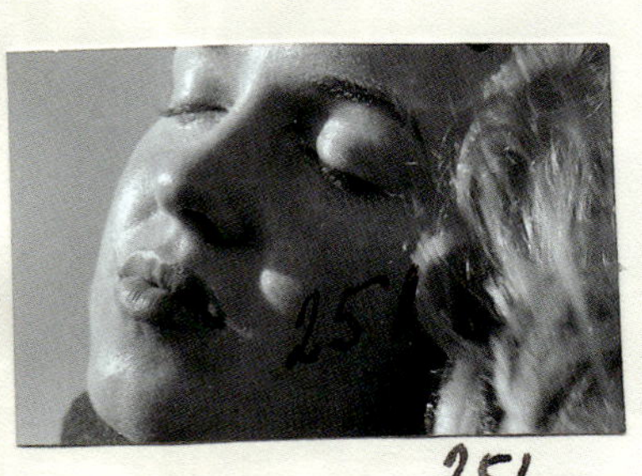

251

ANDRE DE DIENES
1401 SUNSET PLAZA DRIVE
HOLLYWOOD, CALIF. 90069

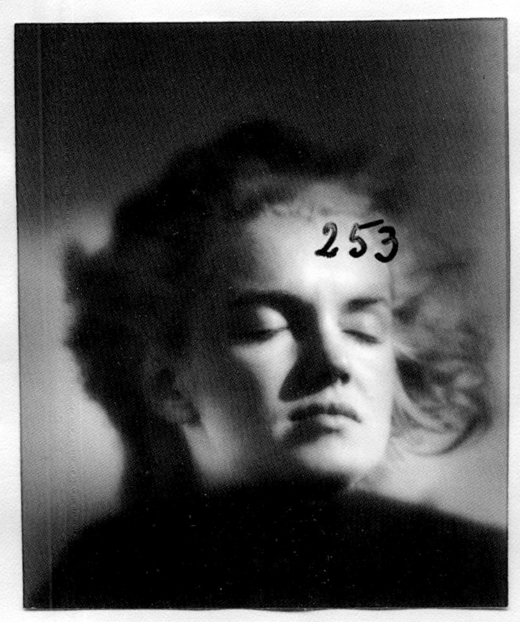

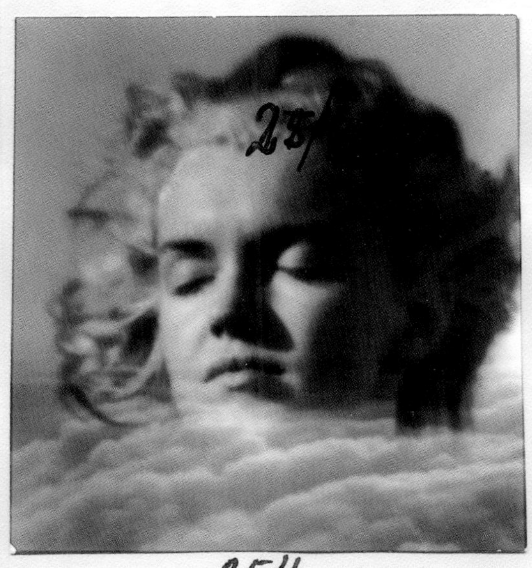

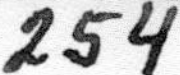

254

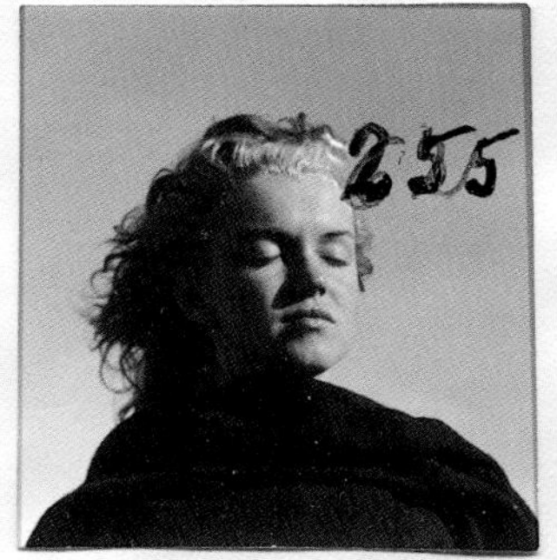

255
"THE THINKER"

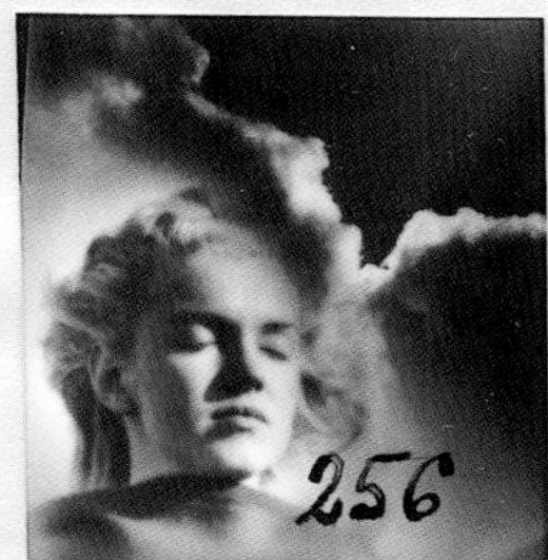

257

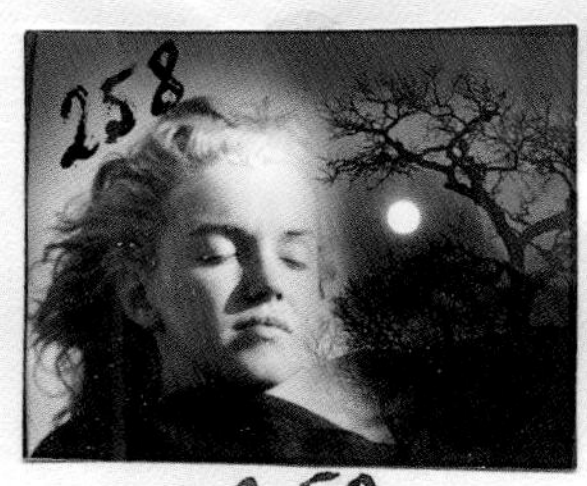

258

ANDRE DE DIENES
1401 SUNSET PLAZA DRIVE
HOLLYWOOD, CALIF. 90069

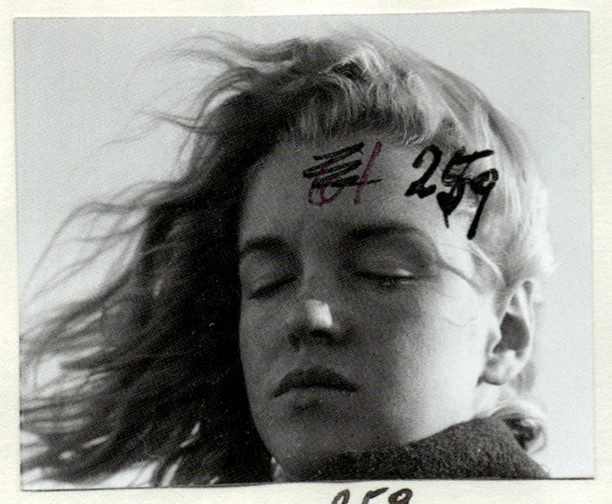

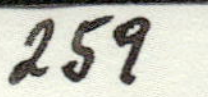

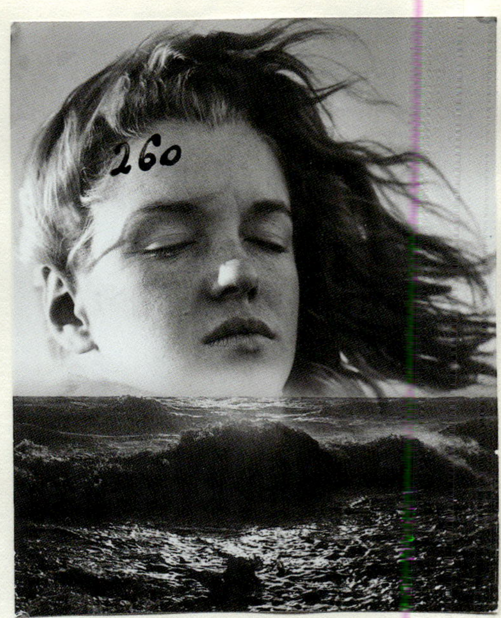

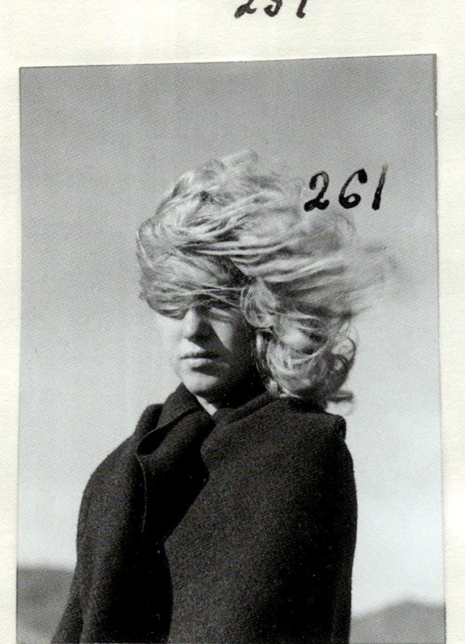

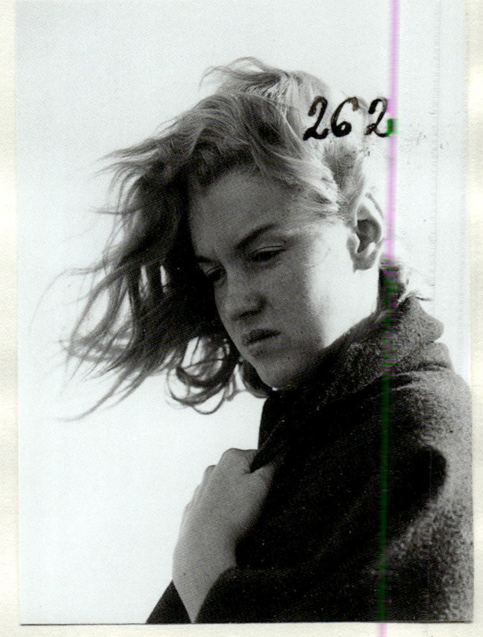

L-7

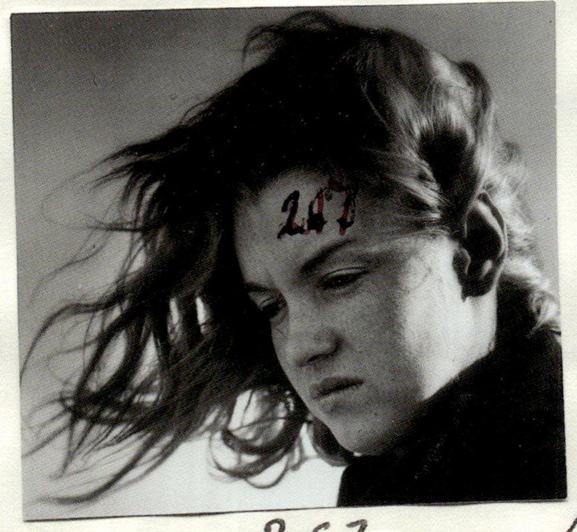

263

"SADNESS" OR "THE END OF EVERYTHING"

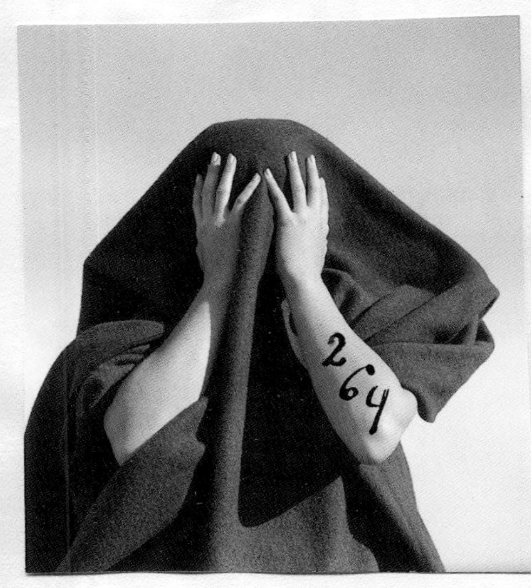

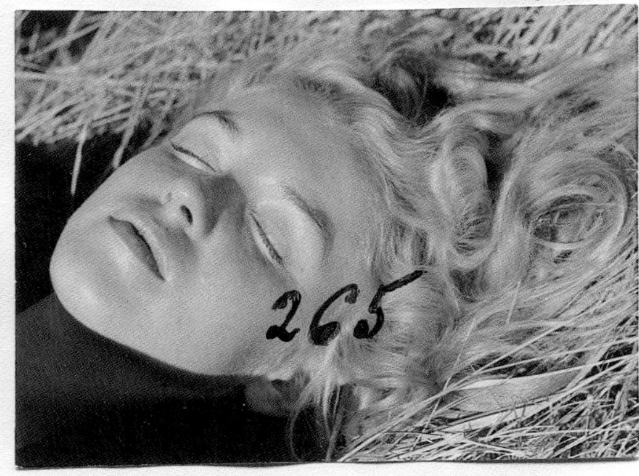

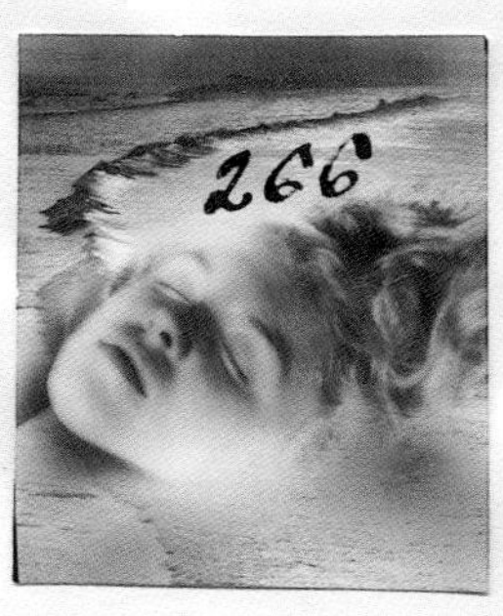

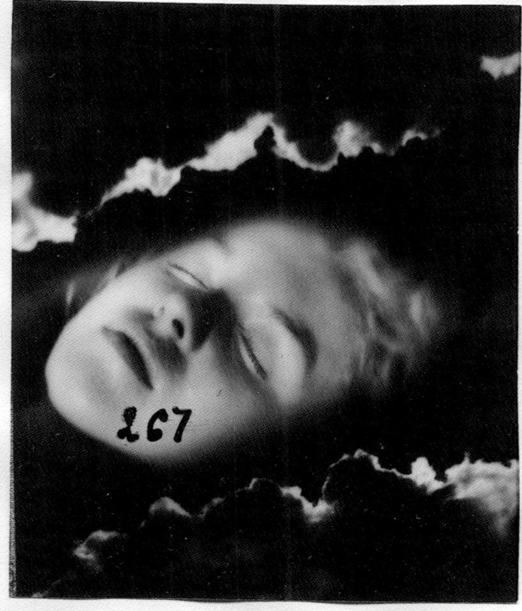

L 7

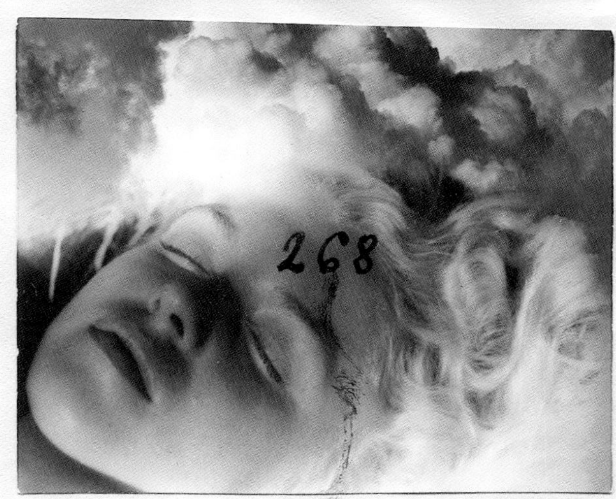

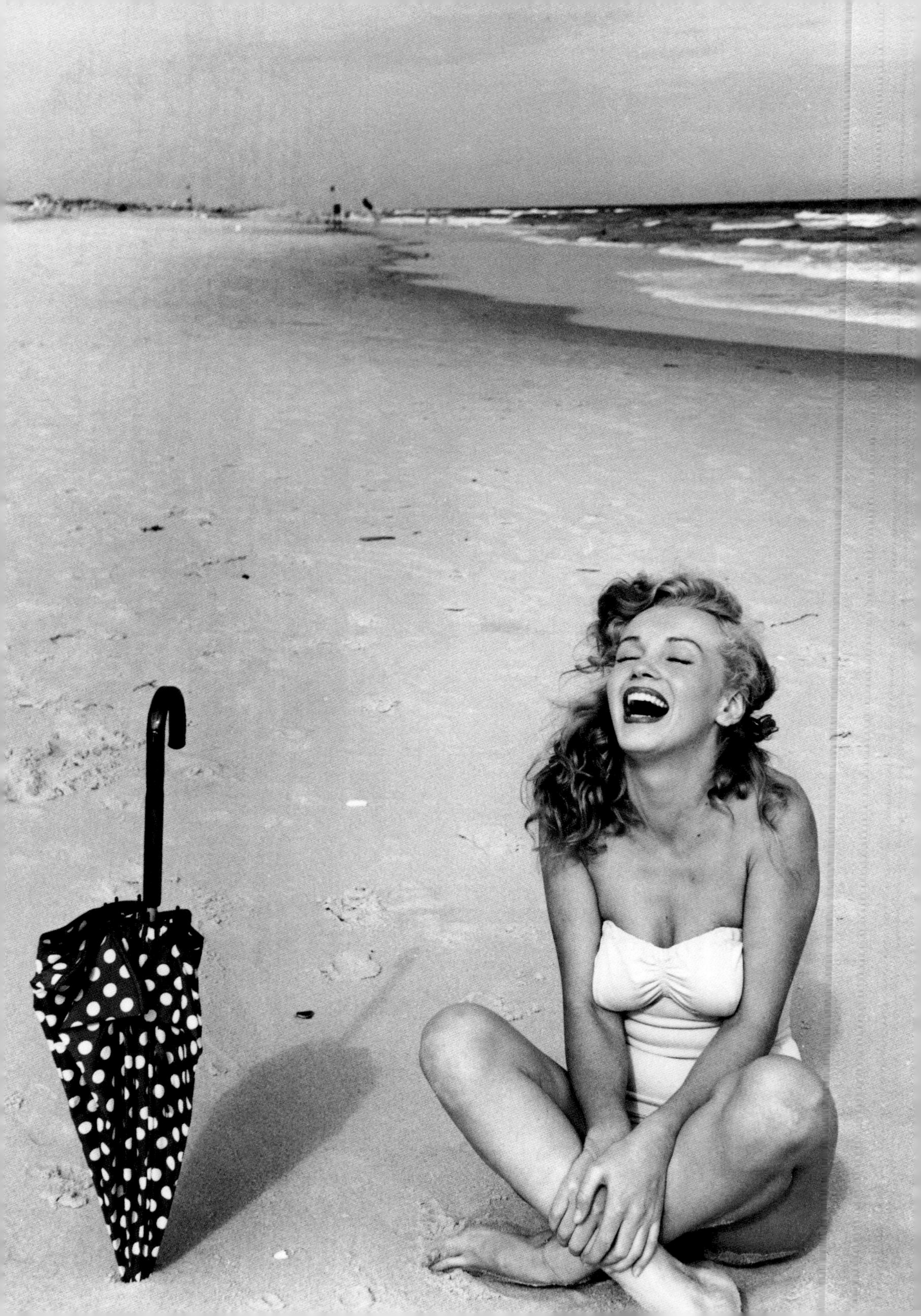

<u>Tobey Beach</u> After a long time away from Marilyn, I suddenly spent an extremely happy and productive day with her during the summer of 1949. This is what happened:

I was driving from New York to Binghamton, NY to see a client. Before I reached Binghamton, I drove through a lovely wooded section of Pennsylvania and decided to stay the night at a motel near the woods. But for some reason, I did not sleep well; bizarre dreams woke me up in the middle of the night and I simply could not go back to sleep. After a while I said to myself "heck, I'll get up and drive to Binghamton where I can continue to sleep in a hotel."

When I stepped out from my cabin in the dead of night, thick fog shrouded everything around me. I started to drive, and drove and drove slowly and cautiously. After a couple of hours I realized I was driving in the wrong direction – back to New York! Tired and exasperated by my mistake, I found the excuse that it was fate's will! And I drove home to New York, thinking I would make the trip again soon.

Was that just a coincidence, or was it a premonition or telepathic communication with Marilyn back in New York? No sooner than I woke up from a good long sleep, the phone was ringing, and without any preliminary greetings of any kind, Marilyn was shouting on the phone, "André, let's take pictures again! Let's make history!" And she explained that she had just arrived, her first ever trip to New York. She was on a nationwide trip to publicize "Love Happy," in which

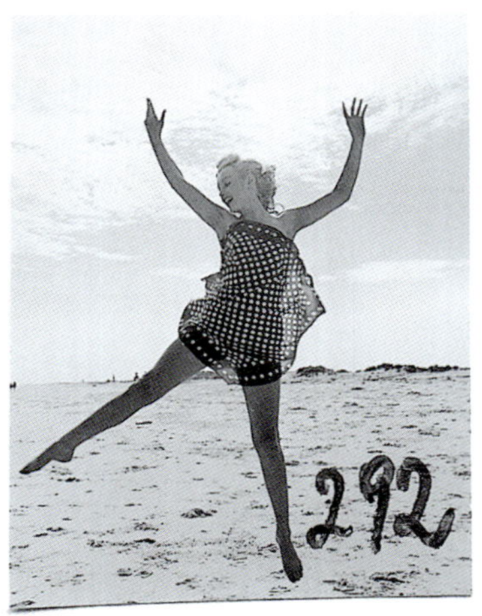

she had a small but nice part with Groucho Marx (who liked her very much), and now, at long last, her career as an actress was really, really going to begin the right way! I could tell by her voice that she was happy, very excited, exhilarated! She was shouting, "Let's take pictures tomorrow! I give you my entire day!" And she asked me, "Do you have a nice bathing suit I can wear?"

She was staying at the Hotel Pierre, only a few blocks from my studio. The Pierre is one of the classiest hotels in New York. I knew she could not afford such an expensive place; she had a small contract guaranteeing about 100 dollars per week, and she'd only had two bit parts in movies…. So whom did she come to New York with, to stay at the Pierre? But I wasn't nosy, I could not have cared less who she stayed with at the Pierre or who she made love with! The important thing was that she asked me to photograph her again – in a bathing suit. It was, in fact, bathing suit pictures of pretty girls that I had been going to sell in Binghamton! The coincidence was amazing! Marilyn had arrived just in time! And she insisted I photograph her! And my sweet darling love, Norma Jeane, because of whom I once almost killed myself, was on the telephone, almost ordering me to spend the day with her on her first day in New York City! We agreed to spend the following day at the seashore out on Long Island on a deserted beach.

I rushed to the department stores and bought two bathing suits (one white, one pink), two parasols (one white, the other red with white

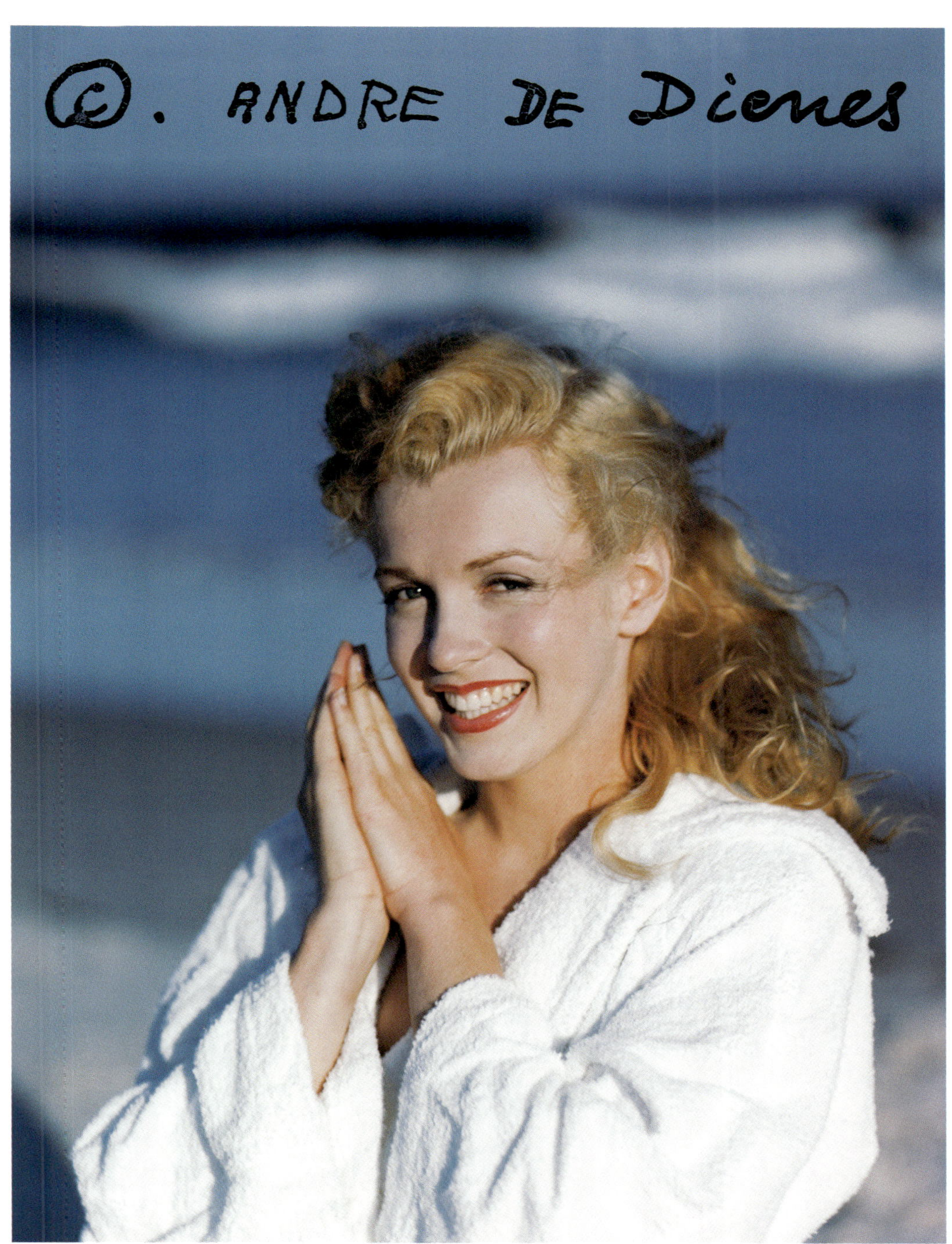
©. ANDRE DE Dienes

polka dots), and several silk scarves, with the express idea that after we were through with the bathing suit pictures, I would make her take off the bathing suit and cover herself with the scarf and dance for me with the scarf tight against her body in the wind; while shooting the fast action pictures, the wind would blow the scarf away and I could capture a few fantastic action shots of her in the nude! I also prepared a basketful of food and included a bottle of brandy which was strictly for me – to calm my nerves after the picture-taking session was over.

It was only 6 or 7 o'clock in the morning when she called again the next day, saying she'd slept really well and was full of energy and ready to go! I can never forget those moments when my sweet, innocent Norma Jeane stepped out of the elevator at the Pierre that morning. She was transformed into a magnificent, elegant young woman, with great poise! Sophisticated like I had never seen her before, her eyes were sparkling with happiness. She was the most dazzling beauty in the world! And I could feel that she wanted me to know that the magical times of her life were about to begin.

It was a really hot, humid summer day and Jones Beach was already crowded when we got there. I always hated taking pictures of models when there were people around, but to work among a crowd, that was impossible for me! I felt dismayed and we drove on further to a place called Tobey Beach, which was also full of people. I was pondering what to do when luck came to my help. The wind began to blow, clouds

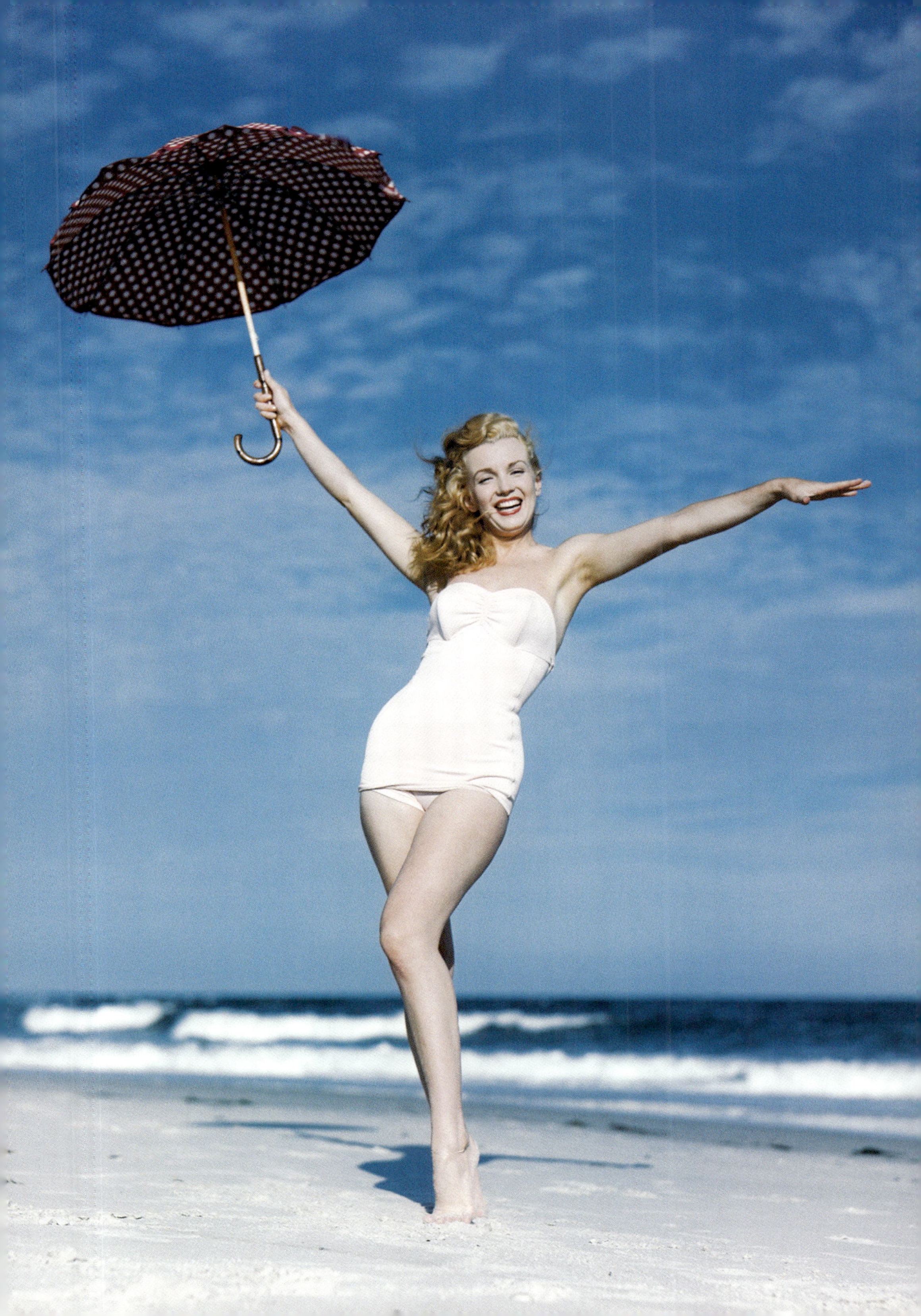

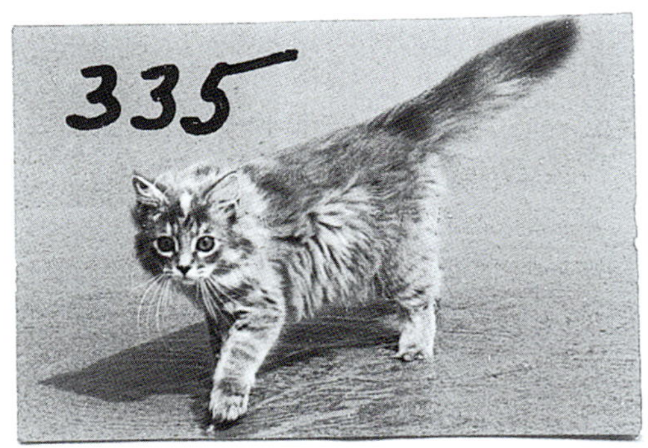

were billowing, lightning struck, and the crowd, fearing the coming of an immense storm, hastily packed up and left the beach. Honestly, it was as if God had swept the beach clean just for Marilyn and me. Hardly anybody remained, yet it hardly rained at all, then the storm calmed down and disappeared completely and by mid-afternoon the entire beach was nearly deserted. It was like a miracle! Nobody came back. I could take pictures in peace for a few hours in the late afternoon sunlight I loved so much for my photography.

I had taken along my small, gray Persian cat because Marilyn had insisted the kitty cat would be lonesome in my studio. The little cat was roaming around on the wet sand, amused by the waves of the ocean, and Marilyn was dancing gaily for the cat. I directed her to pretend the cat was a handsome young man and she was to entice him. And to look right into my lens, because the whole world would be looking at her later! When I photograph somebody, I talk a great deal, almost continuously; I give directions, I relentlessly invent stories to keep up the interest of my subject. With Marilyn, I asked her to flirt with my camera, to entice me with all her sex appeal and to move as fast as possible, without any posing, while I was clicking the shutter over and over. And I spoke to Marilyn about her being a new Lillian Russell and I began teaching her how to walk onto a stage. She was holding the parasol and I told her that she was Lillian, the great stage actress, and over and over I made Marilyn walk towards me with more and more self-assurance and sex appeal,

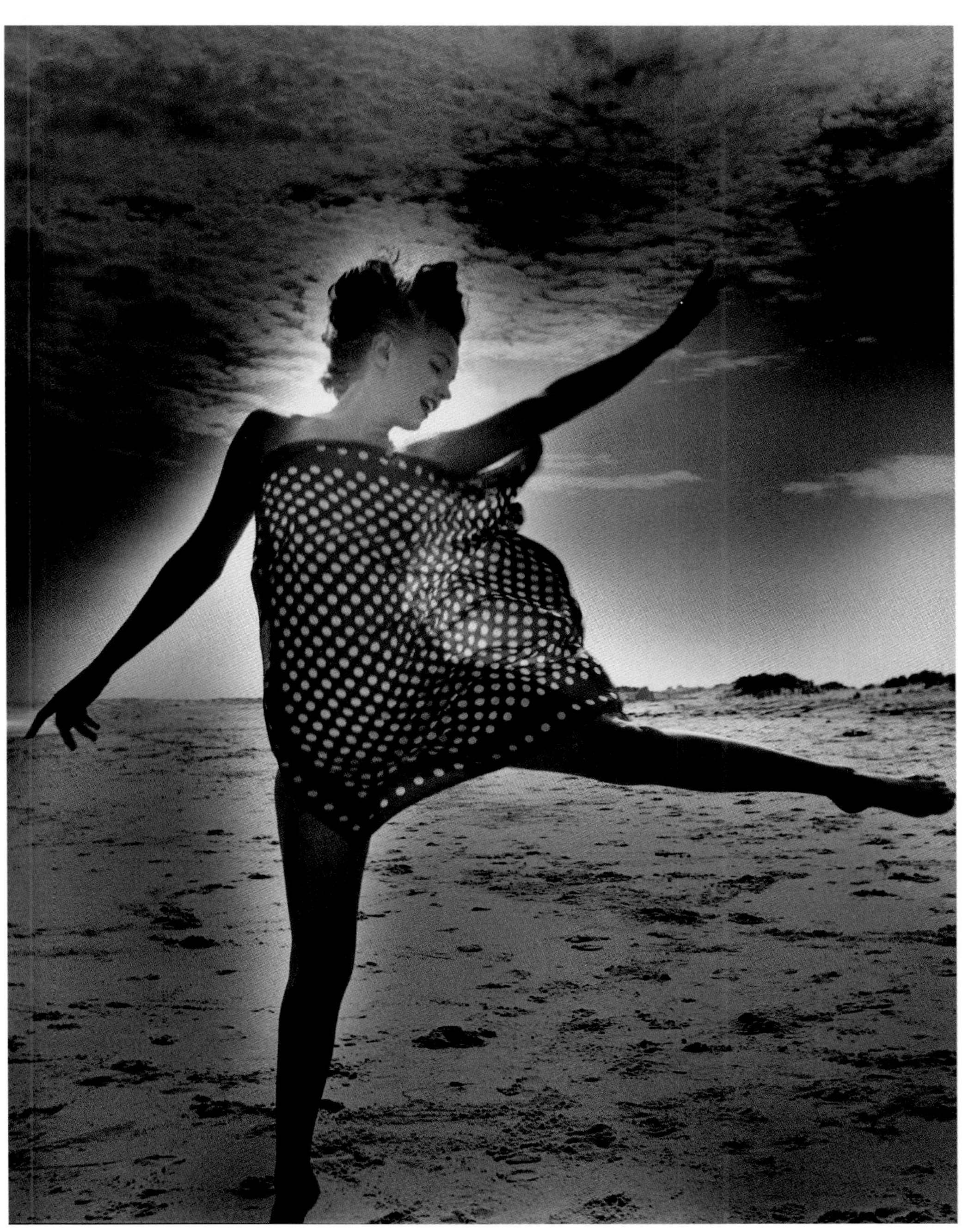

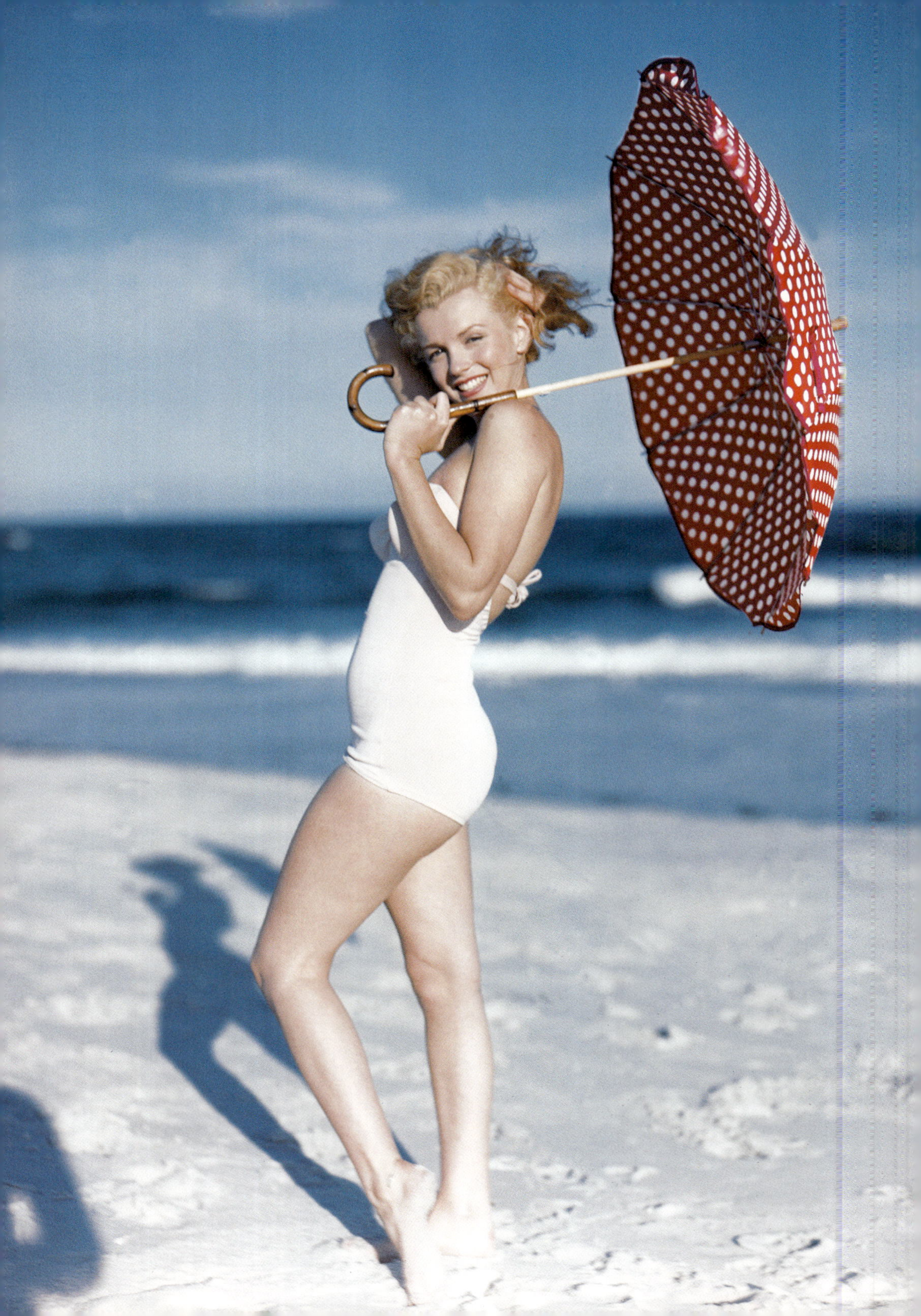

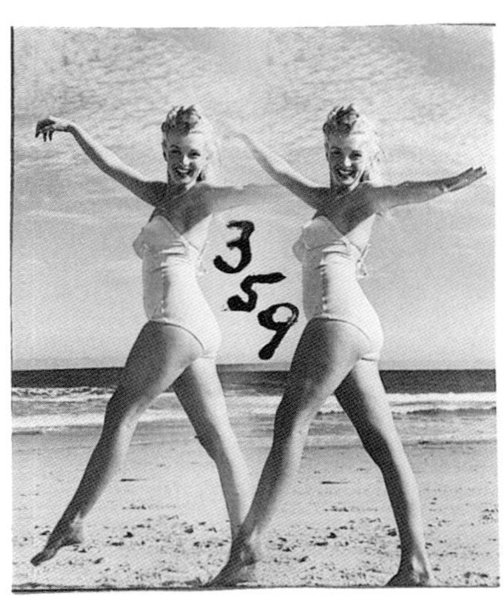

pretending she was walking onstage! I took at least two dozen shots of her like that. Marilyn was extremely cooperative, patient, eager to please me and eager to learn! Out of a little idea and imagination I created an enormous enthusiasm for both of us that afternoon, and repeatedly we told each other that we were going to make history! And I told her my pictures of her would last forever. It was a happy afternoon for both of us.

There was only one minor little problem – the cup of the bathing suit had wire in it and it was badly scratching Marilyn's bosoms. Her skin was all red on her breasts. She suffered a lot, but did not complain at all, and she danced in the scarf too, as I had planned it, but the wind did not blow it away from her body. I did not mind not taking nudes of her; I knew I could find plenty of other models for that purpose. We felt happy; there was no way I would have wanted to change the mood of that gloriously happy day – by wanting to photograph her nude. I had love and respect for my beautiful Marilyn. I felt fortunate and grateful that she chose me to be with, for a full day, before she began her publicity appearance in New York City.

The photographs I took of her that day in 1949 represent a young Marilyn. The poses are casual, because that was the kind of photography I was very active in creating in those years. I did not care how the wind blew her hair; I even liked her hair to be all messed up. But her image as movie star became different. It became how the

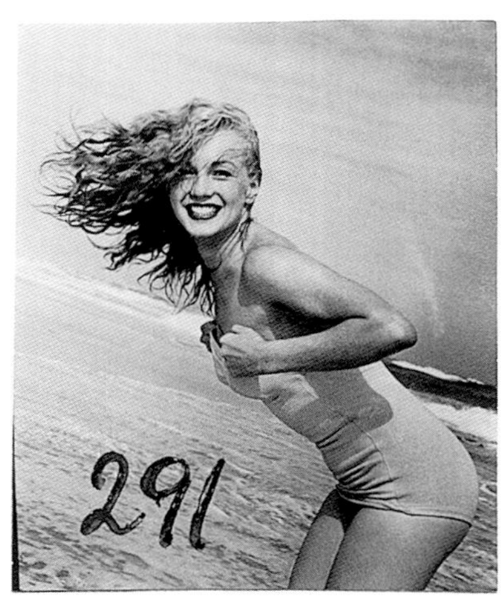

public had seen her on the screen, in her movies. That image was created at the Hollywood studios, done by hairdressers, make-up men, etc. A far more glamorized kind of photography, sometimes too artificial for my taste. I preferred – for my pictures – a very casual Marilyn.

The next day Marilyn gave the first and most important interview of her career. The press literally mobbed her, adored her! And from that day onward, her name was mentioned almost every day in the newspapers all over the world – the craze for Marilyn Monroe had started!

a fast-moving succession of crazy, silly, sometimes very funny, sometimes harrendous experiences and adventures, AND delightful experiences, unexpected, crazy incidents, almost ridiculously funny at times. And horrowing experinces also, and much hardships with it, ALSO for there was plenty of that, too, because, when you travel to far away locations into the mountains, or to deserted beaches, or into the deserts, on sandy dirtroads, to photograph AT remote places where I could find complete privacy, unexpected troubles COULD happen, and did happen, plenty of times. Thinking back to all what have happened to me, I can't help chuckling THINKING TO entitle my imaginary future book, or a fast-sequence comedy movie, like the kind they used to make in the early 1900-s, I would entitle the book " A PERVERSE SORT OF PARADISE " because all what had happened to me was, indeed, something like that. Unique, delightful experiences and unpleasant experiences all intermingling in rather rapid succession, because, year after year, I did nothing but photograph pretty females. Looking back to it all, I think I did the kind of work most man can, or could only dream about.....

However, occasionally, in tired, pessimistic moods, I consider my life was sort of a blunder, a waste for having photographed so many girls, hundreds of them, and having taken many thousands of photographs for which I have little or almost no use at all now. I just made a living with the work, AND amassed no fortune. To make a great deal of money with photography, one have to do commercial work! BUT I turned my back to all that ! I preferred artistic work. I spent several decades photographing and spending most of my time in my laboratory creating nice photographinc prints. Nudes superimposed with the ocean, with clouds, with flowers, ETC., and NOW I repeated

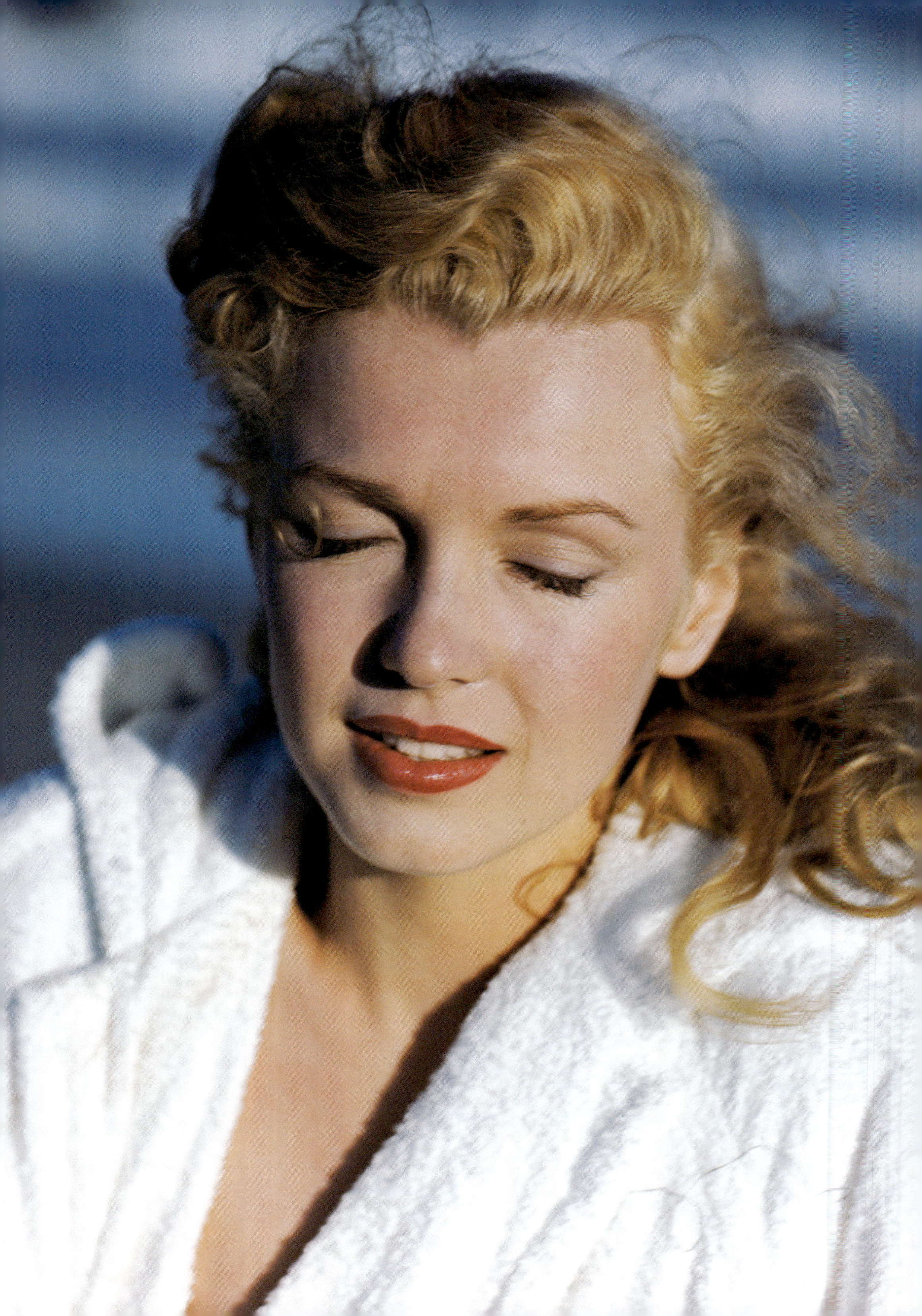

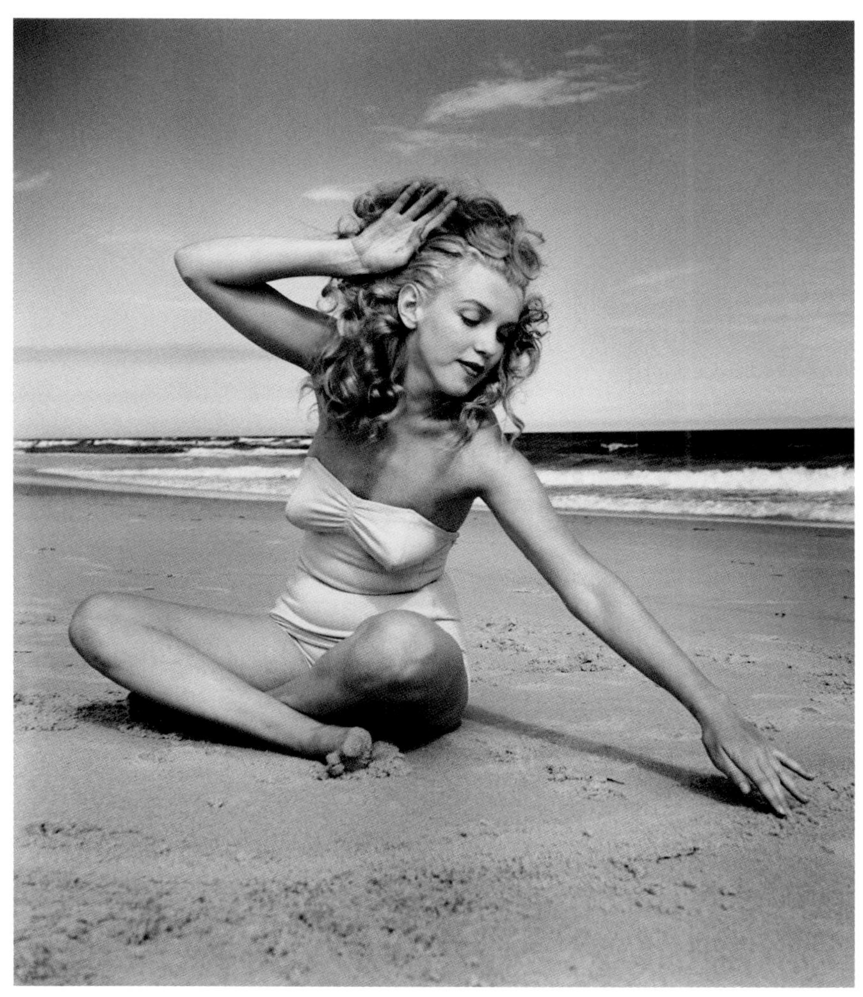

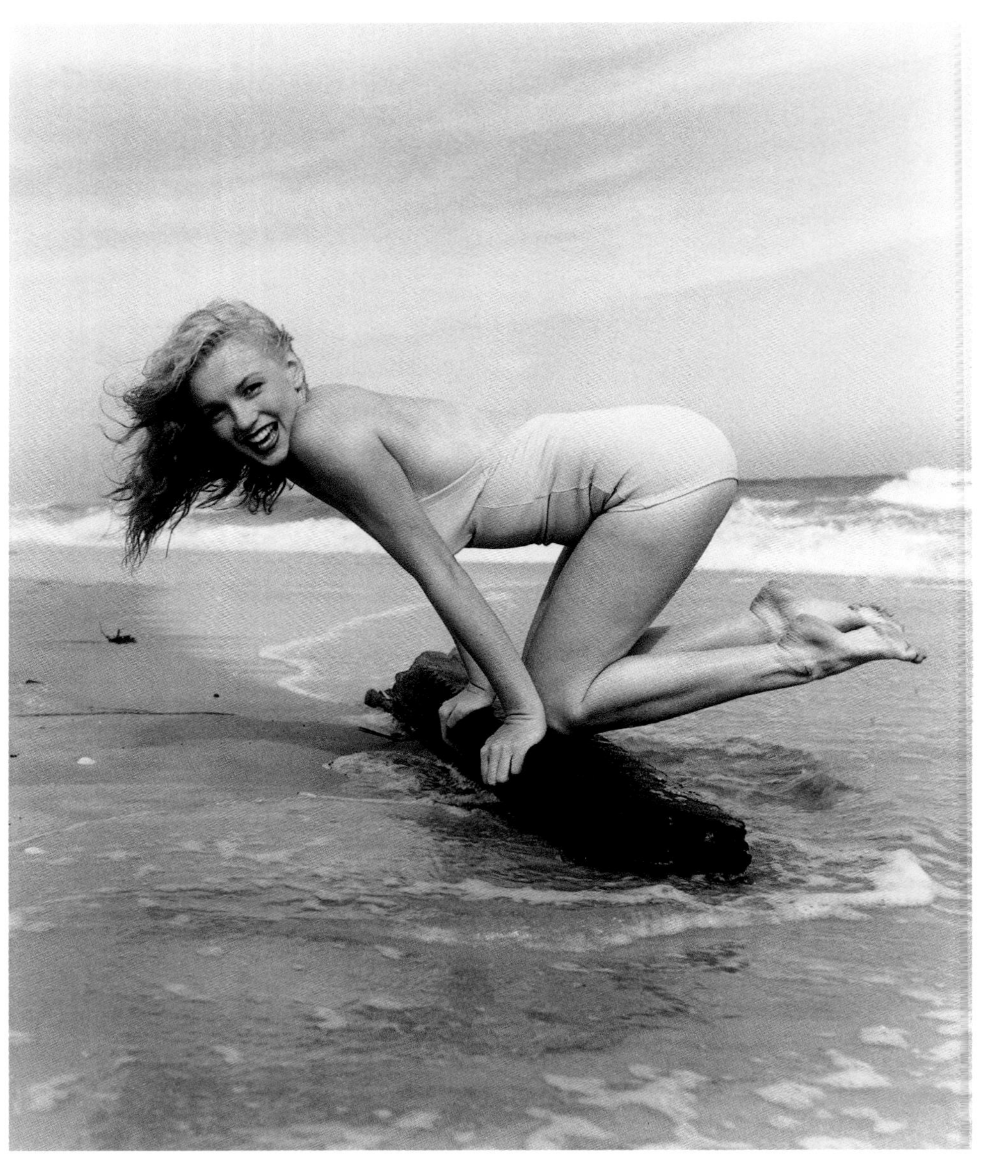

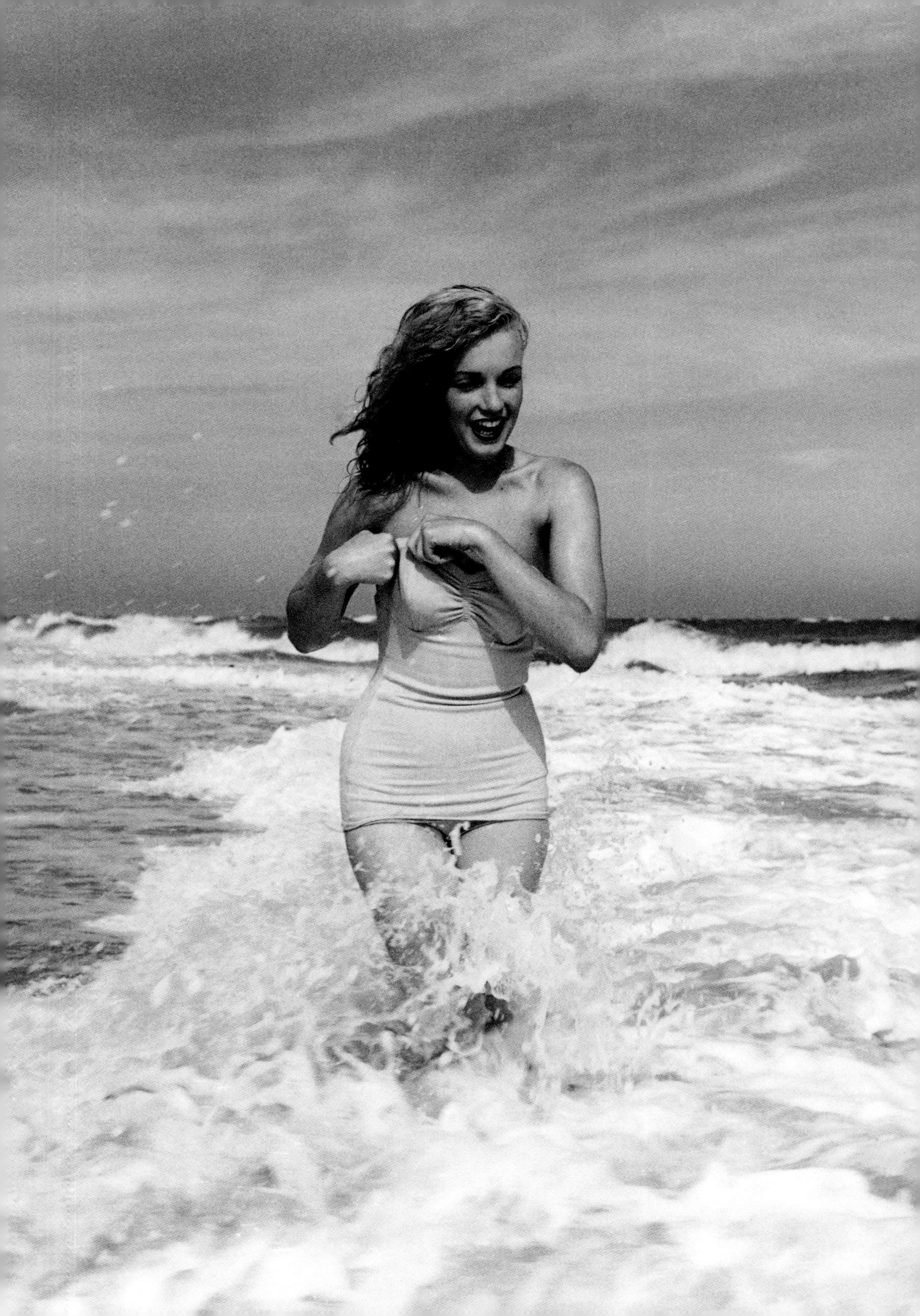

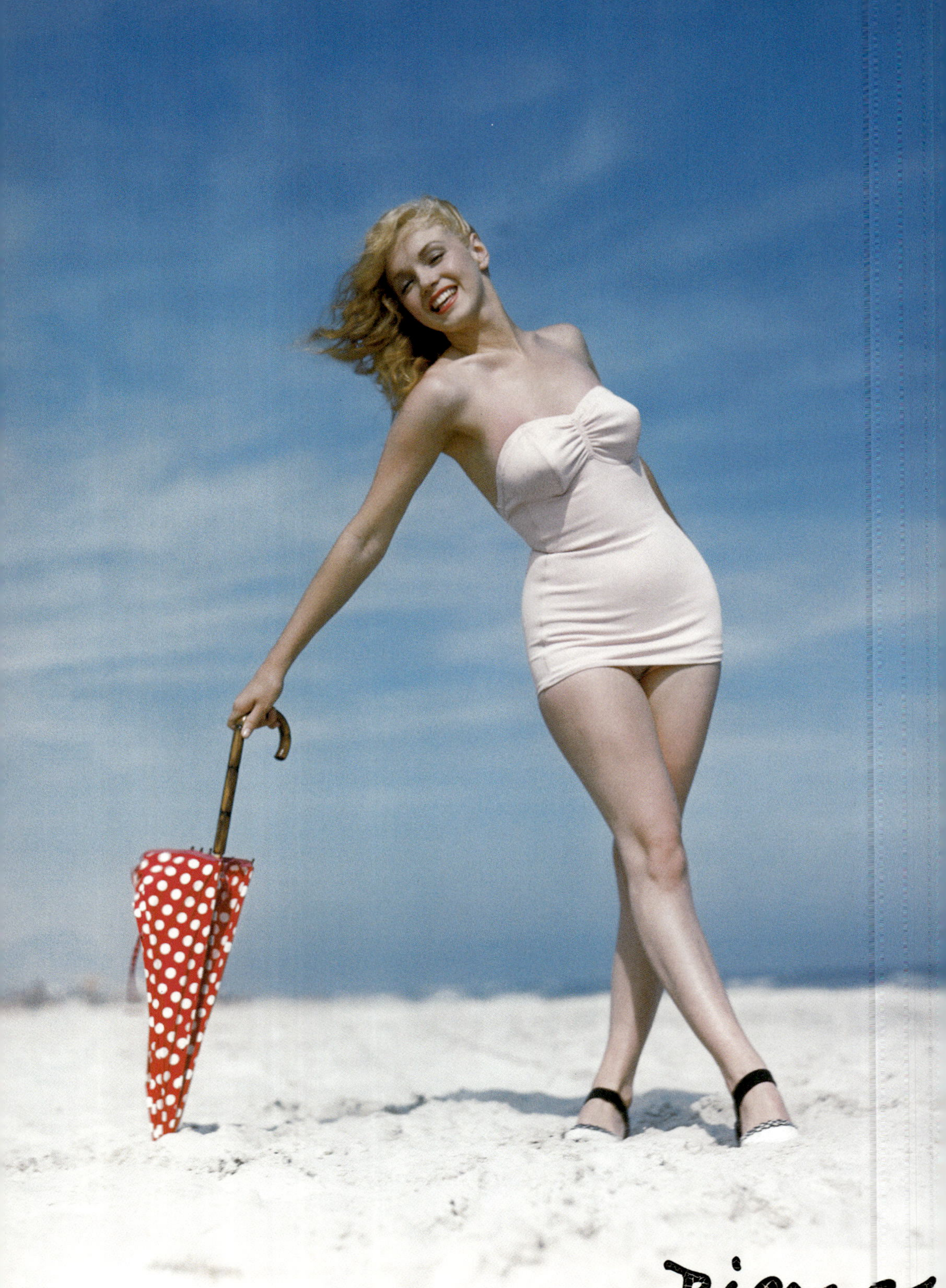

Dienes

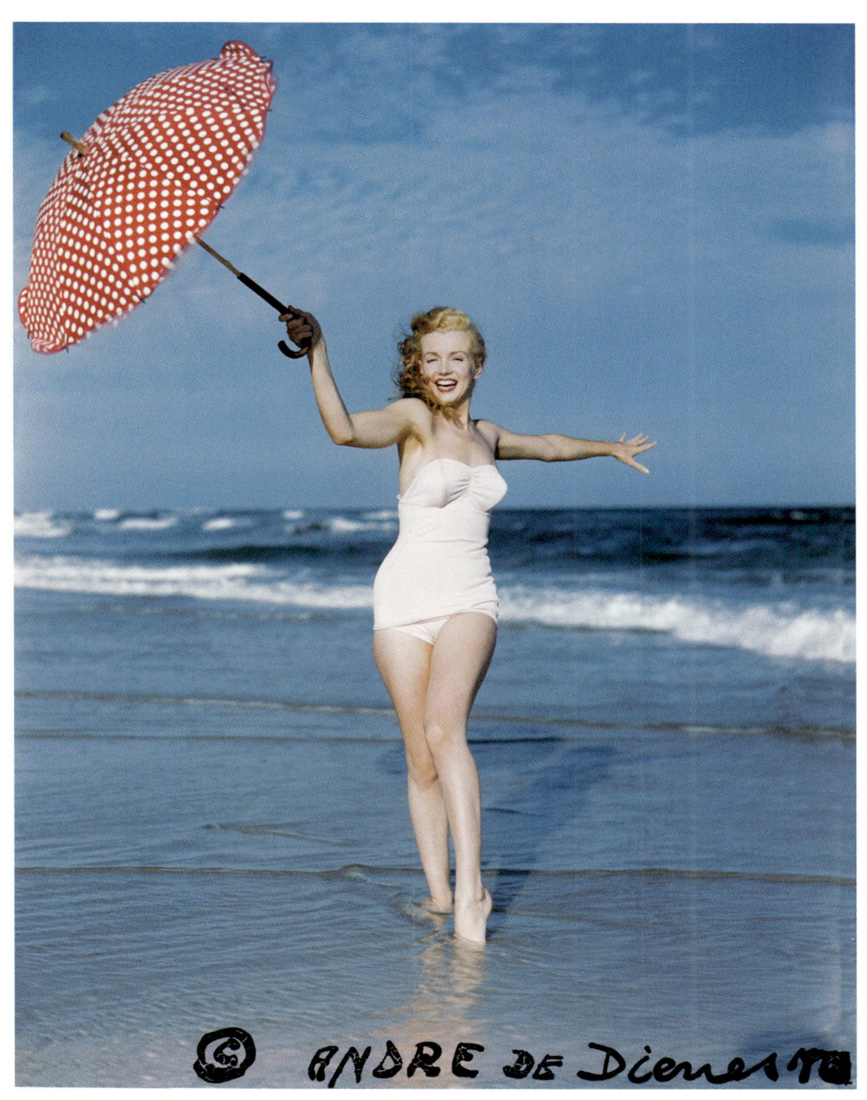
© ANDRE DE DIENES

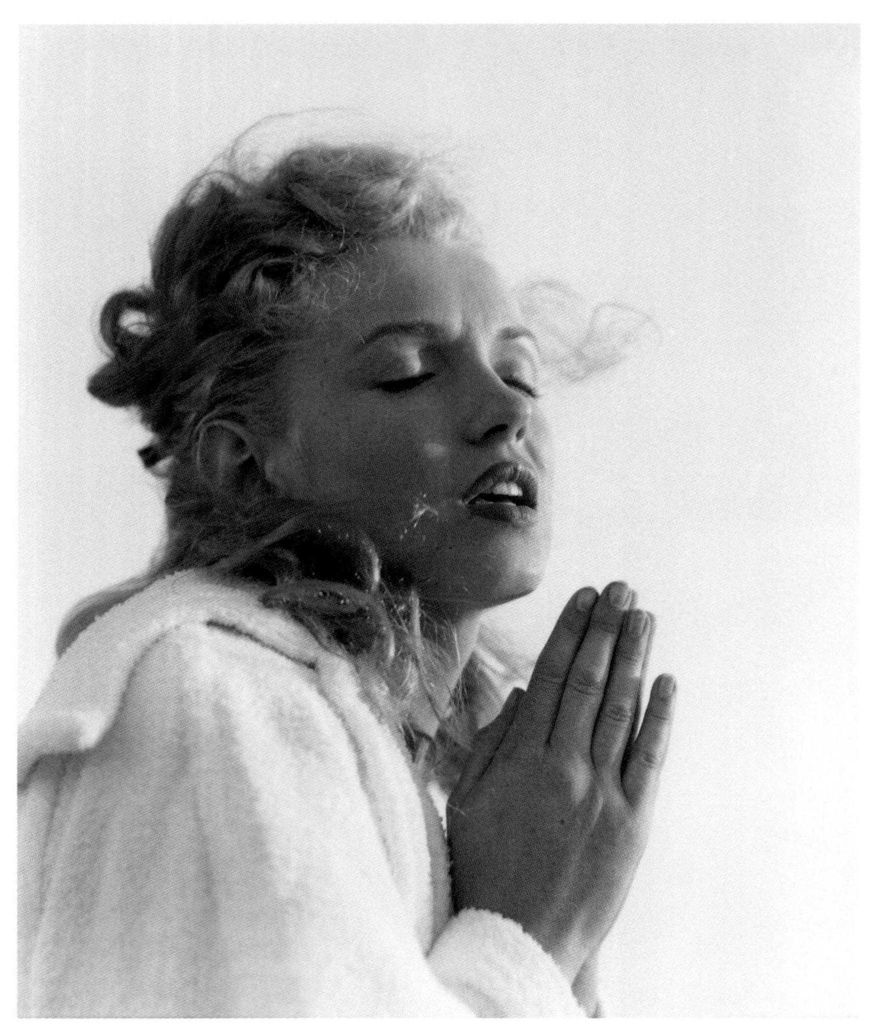

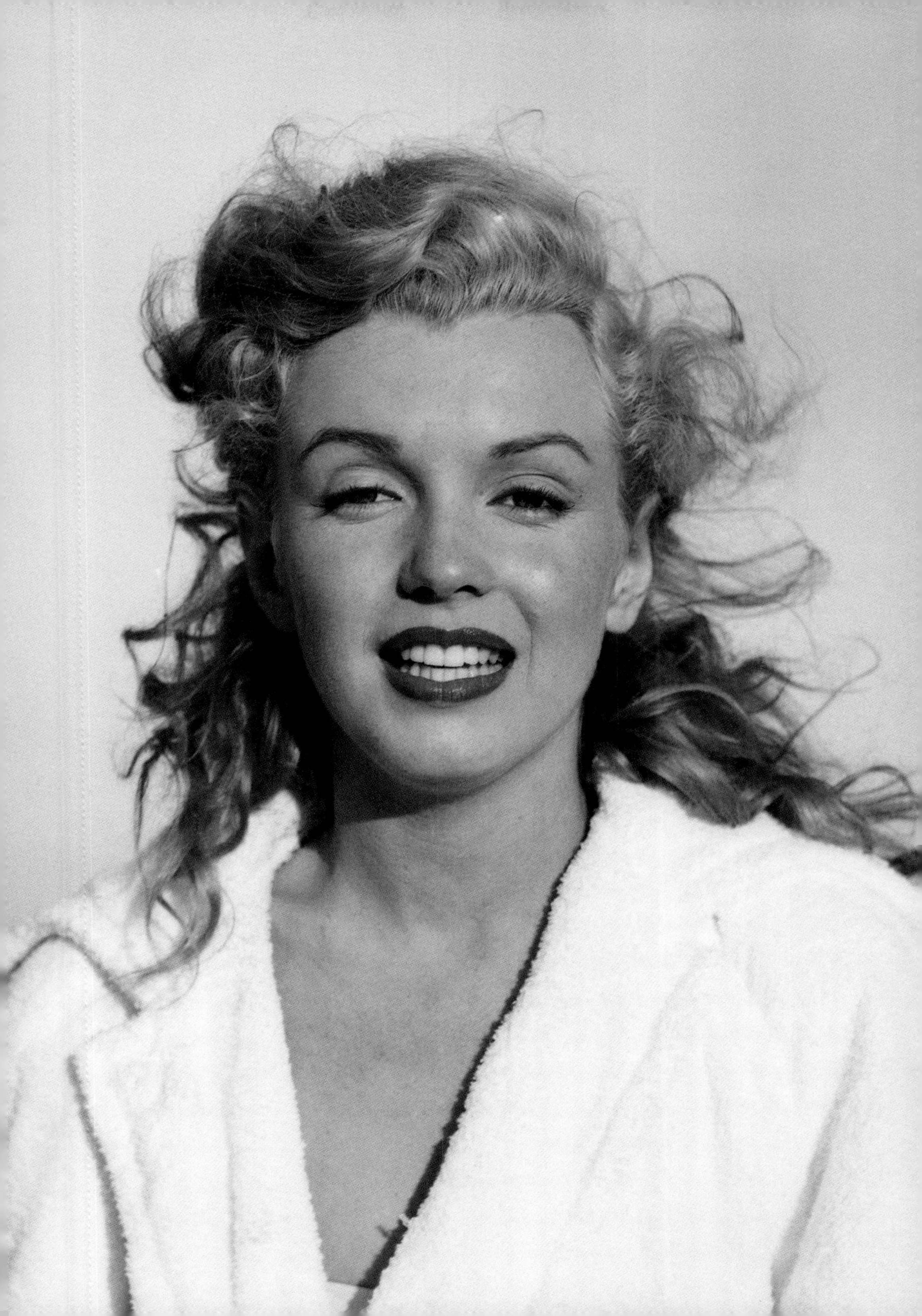

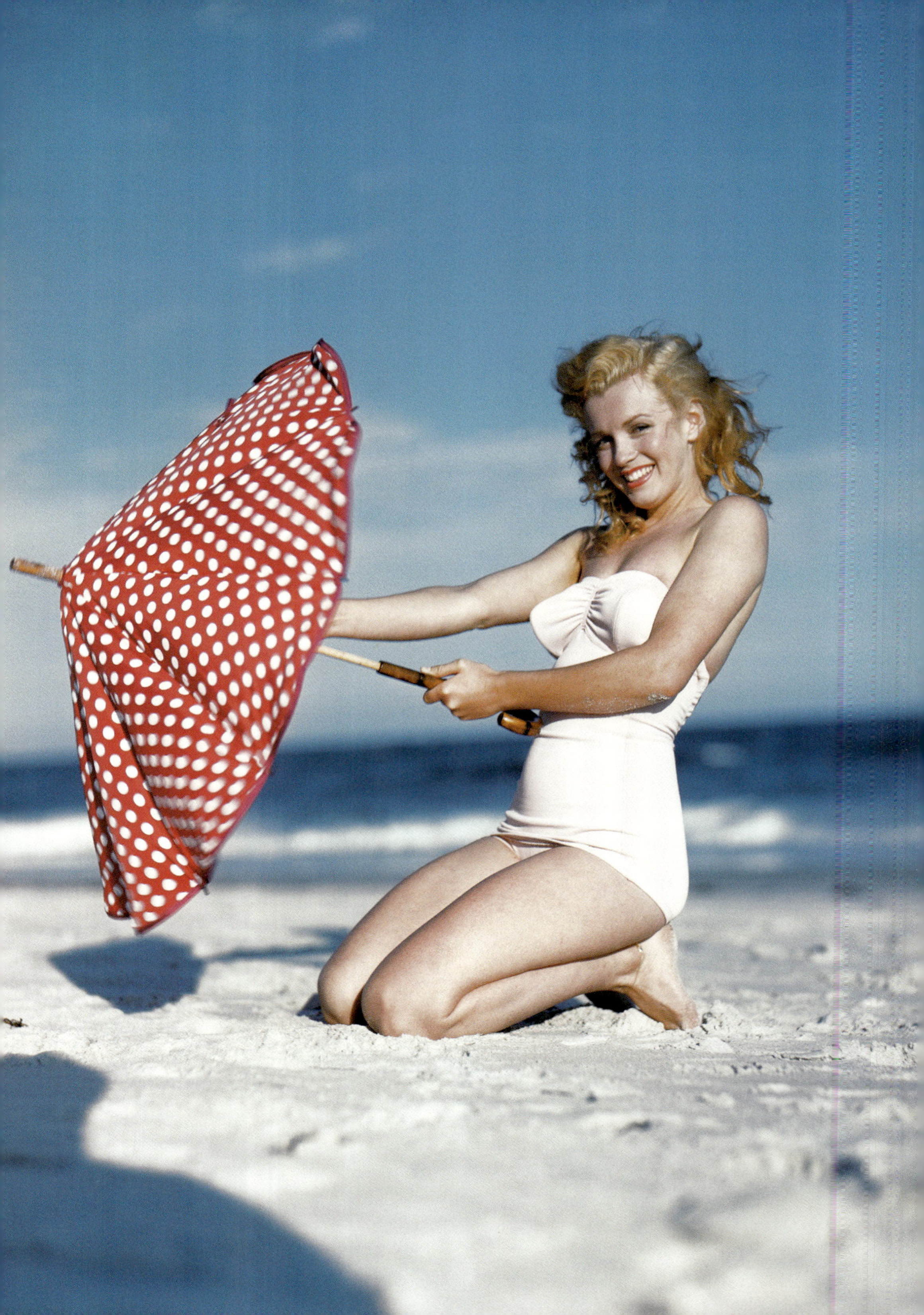

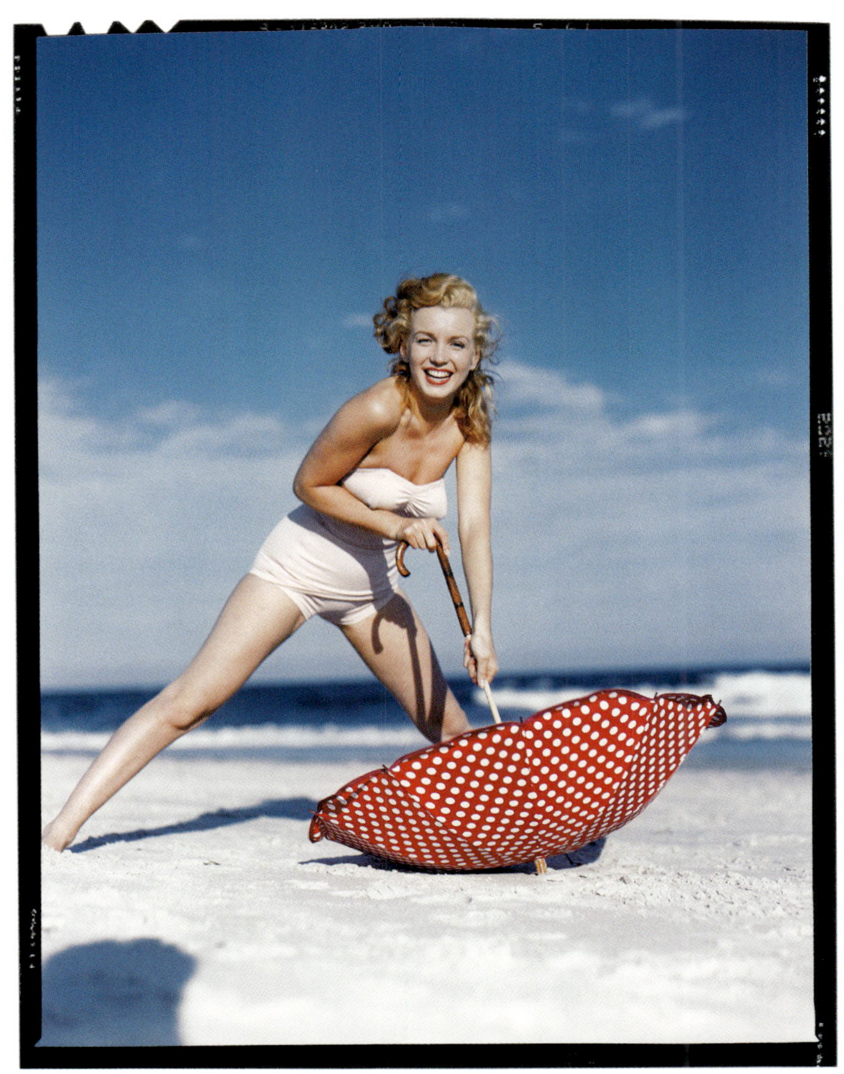

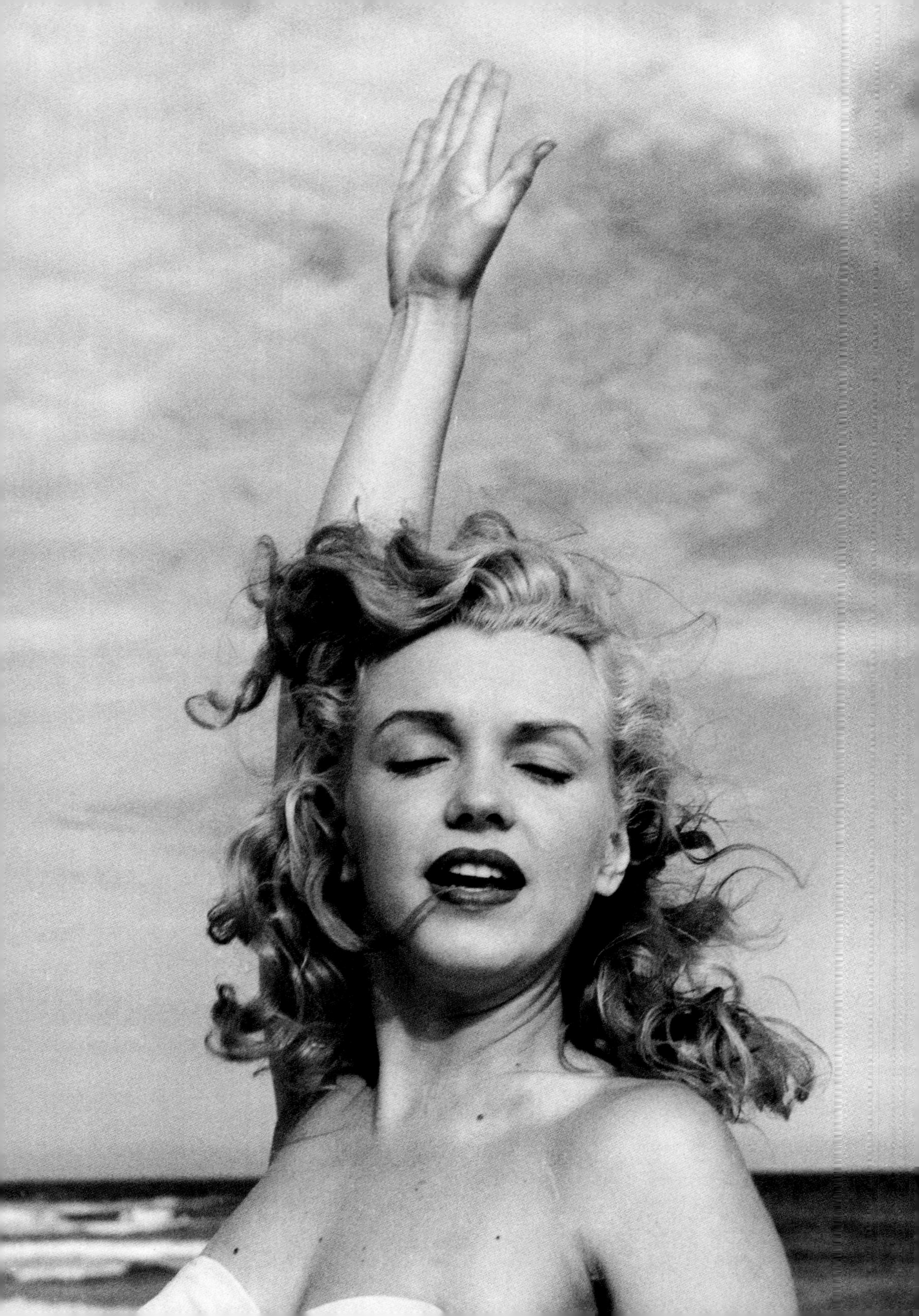

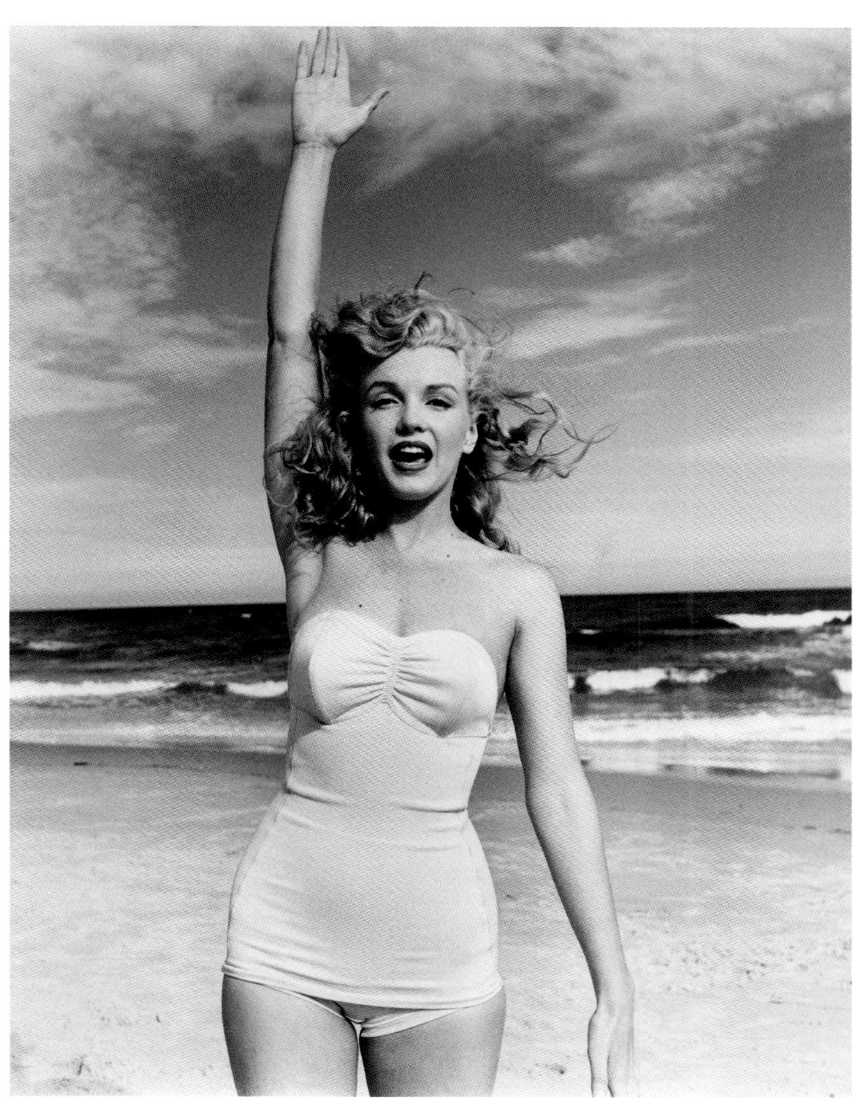

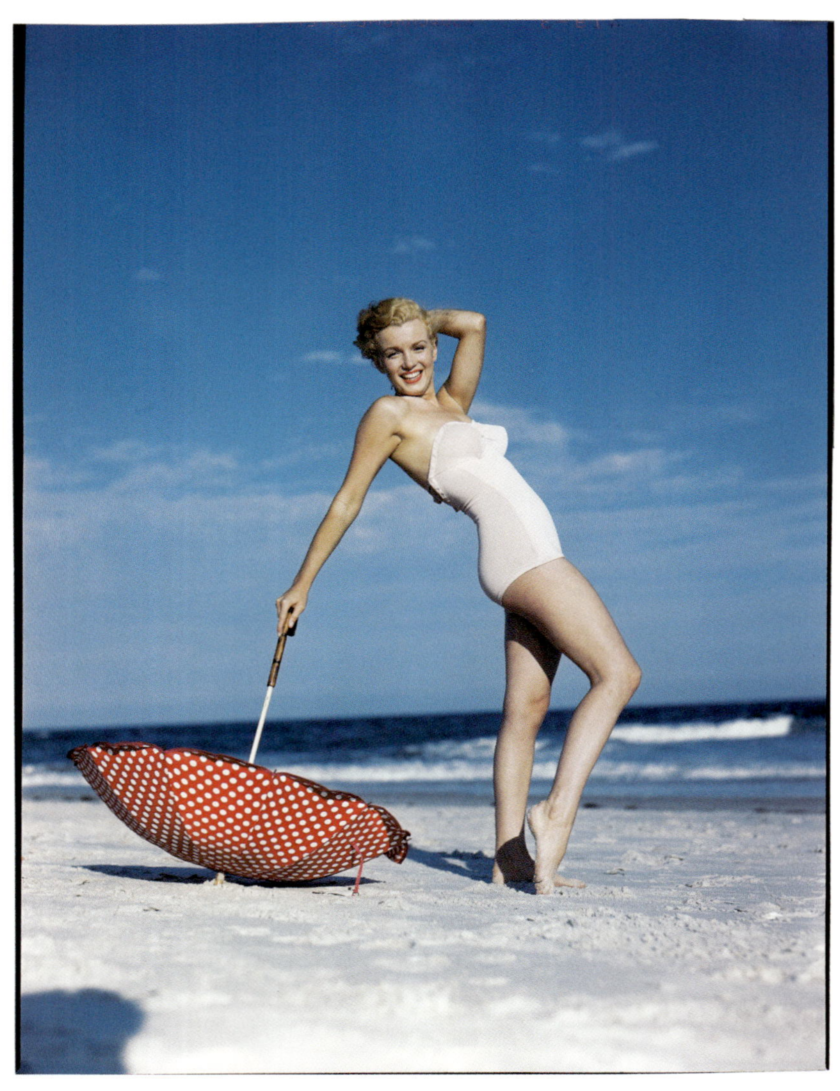

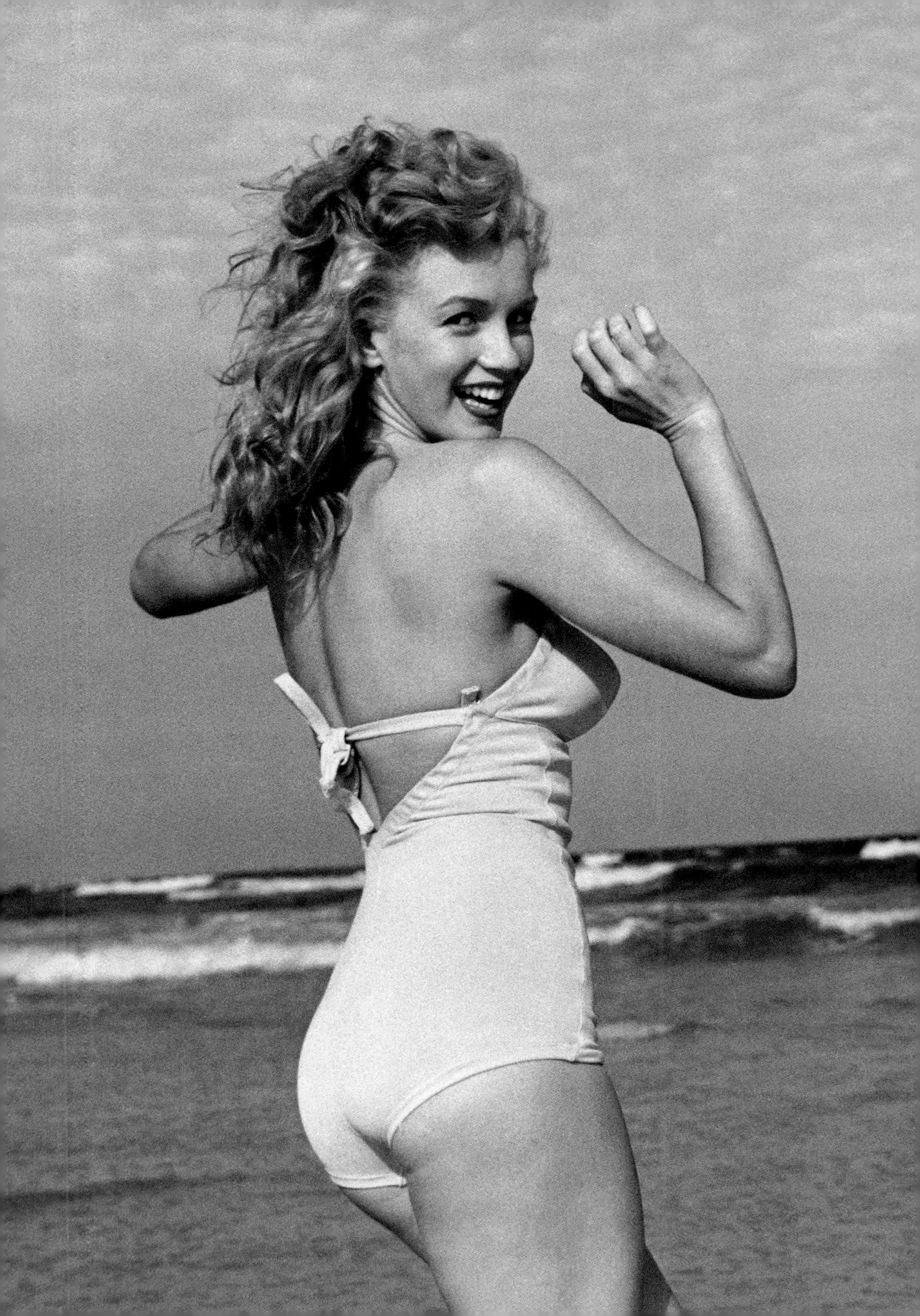

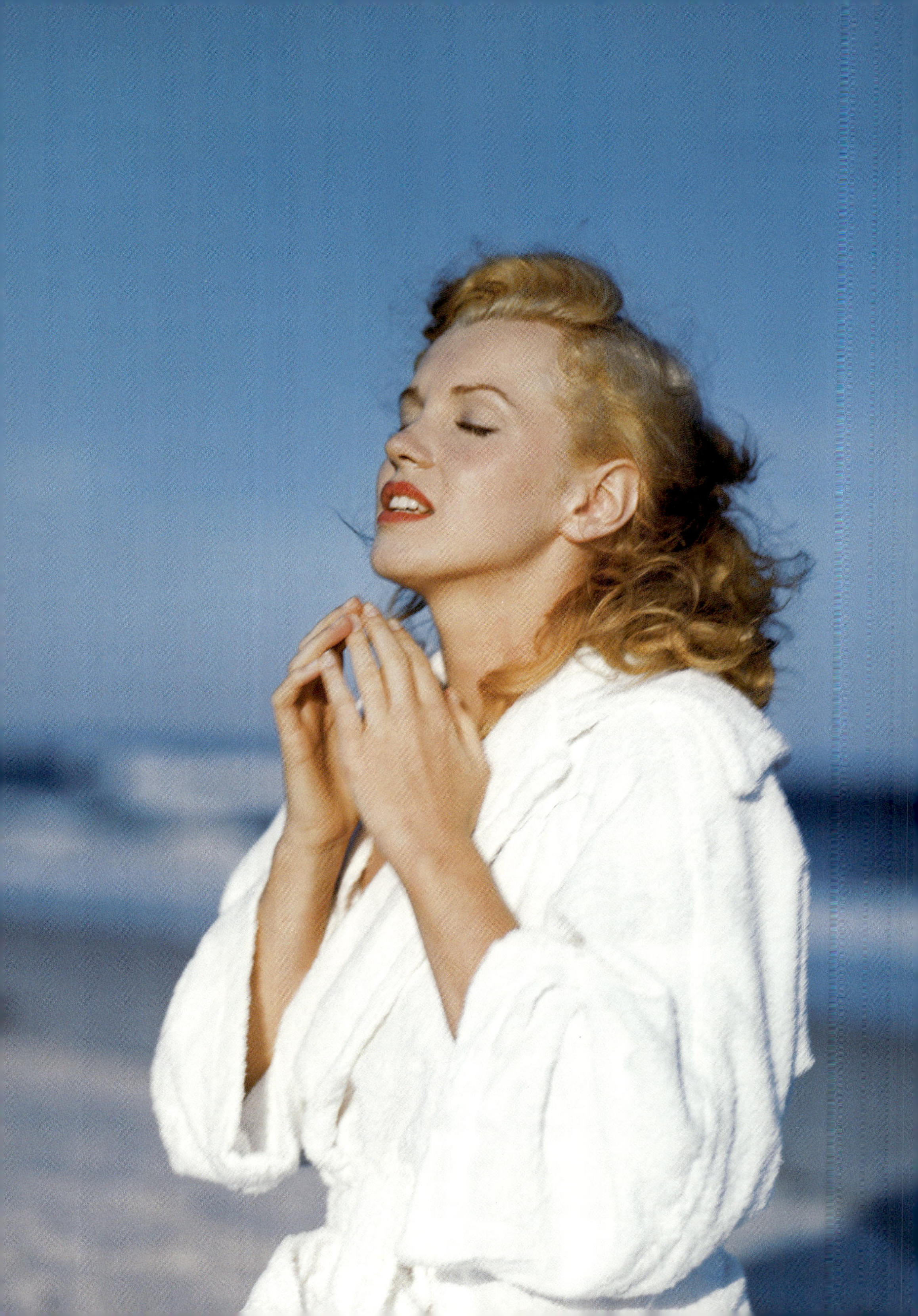

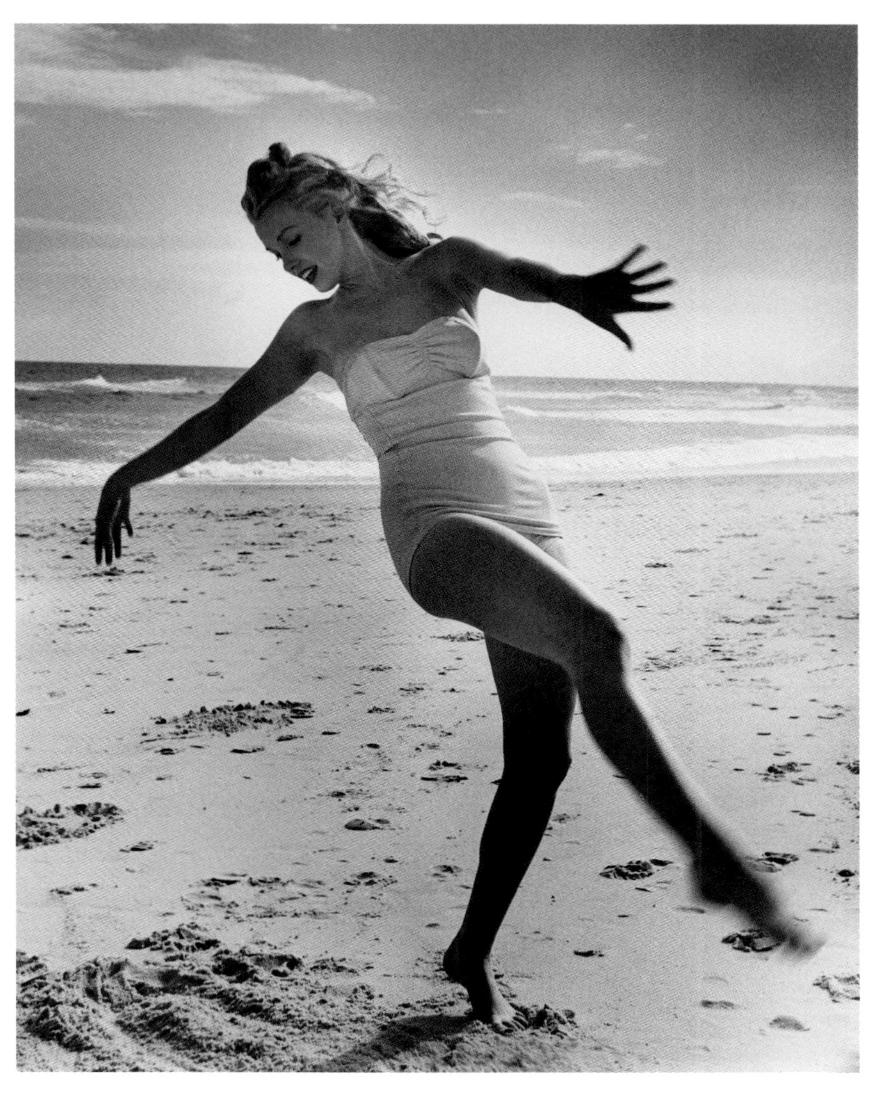

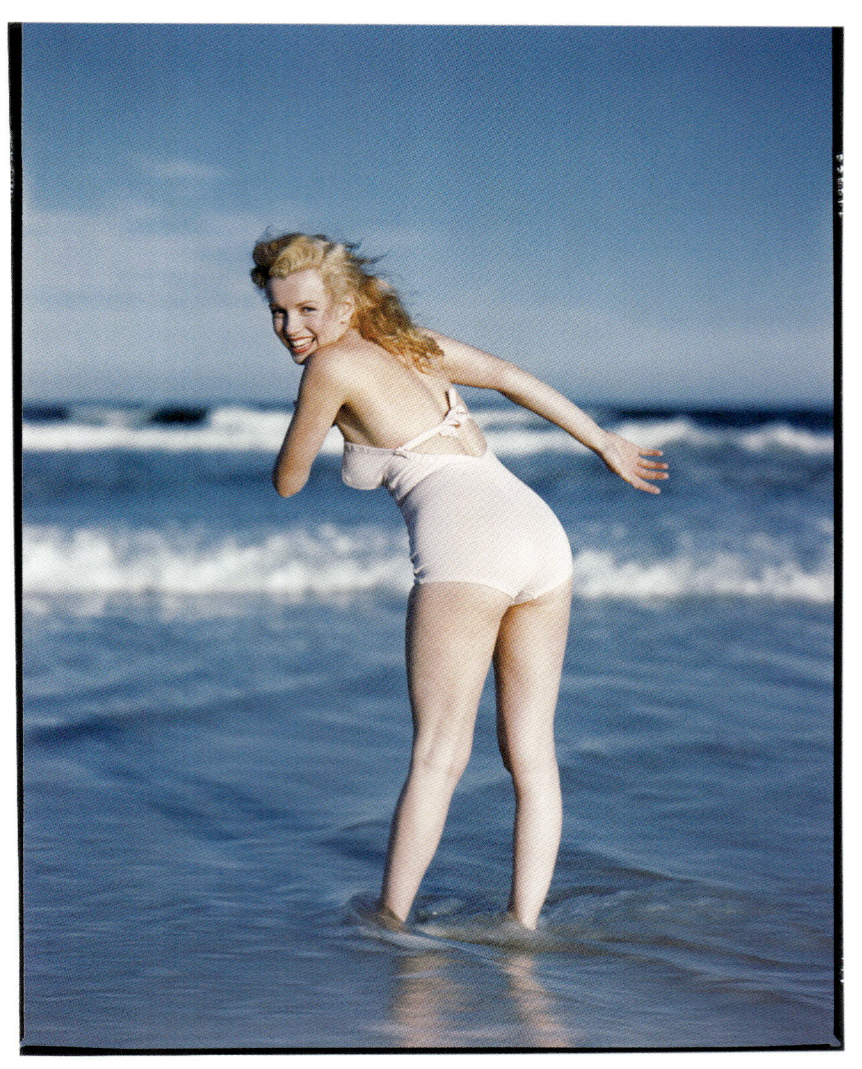

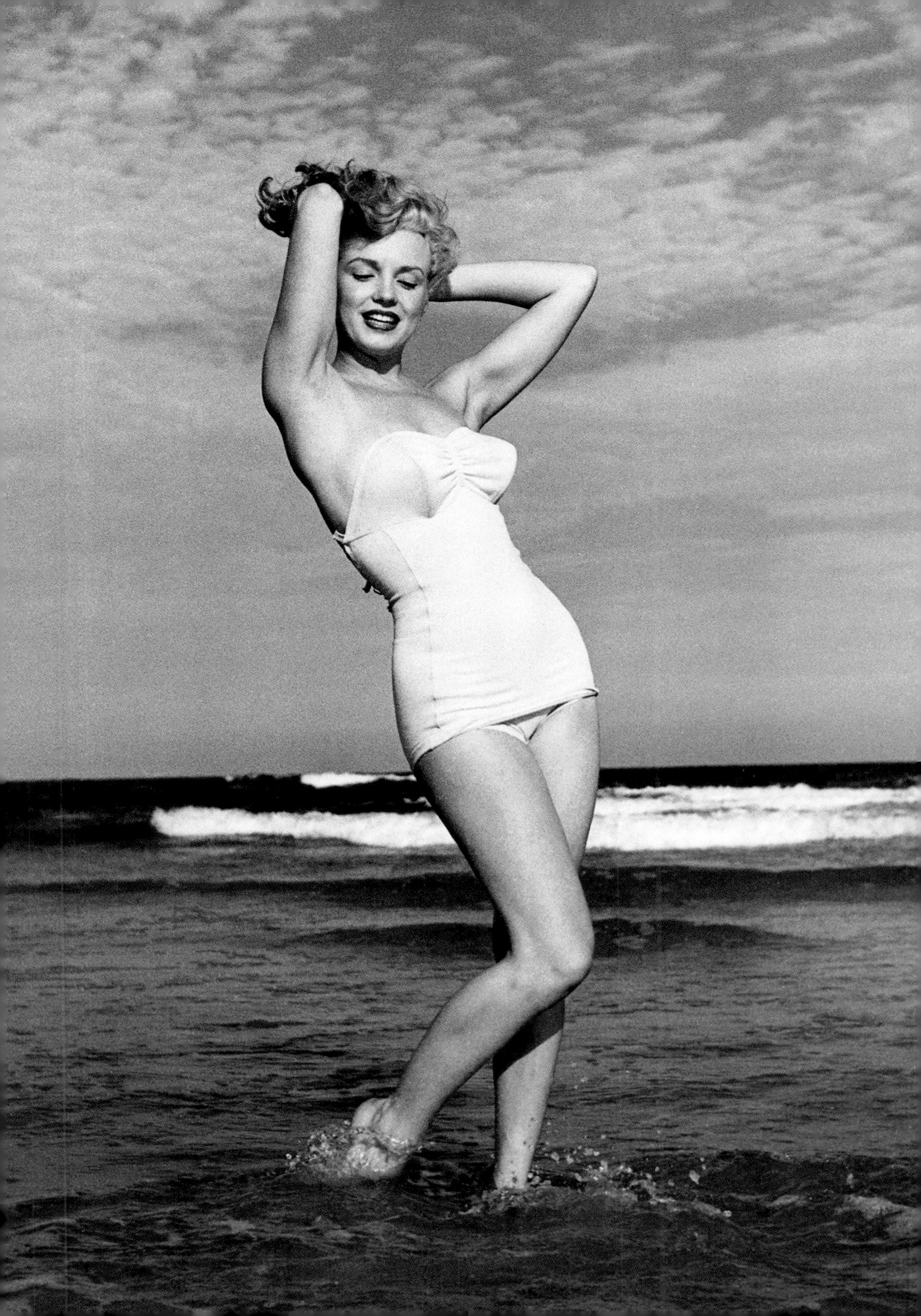

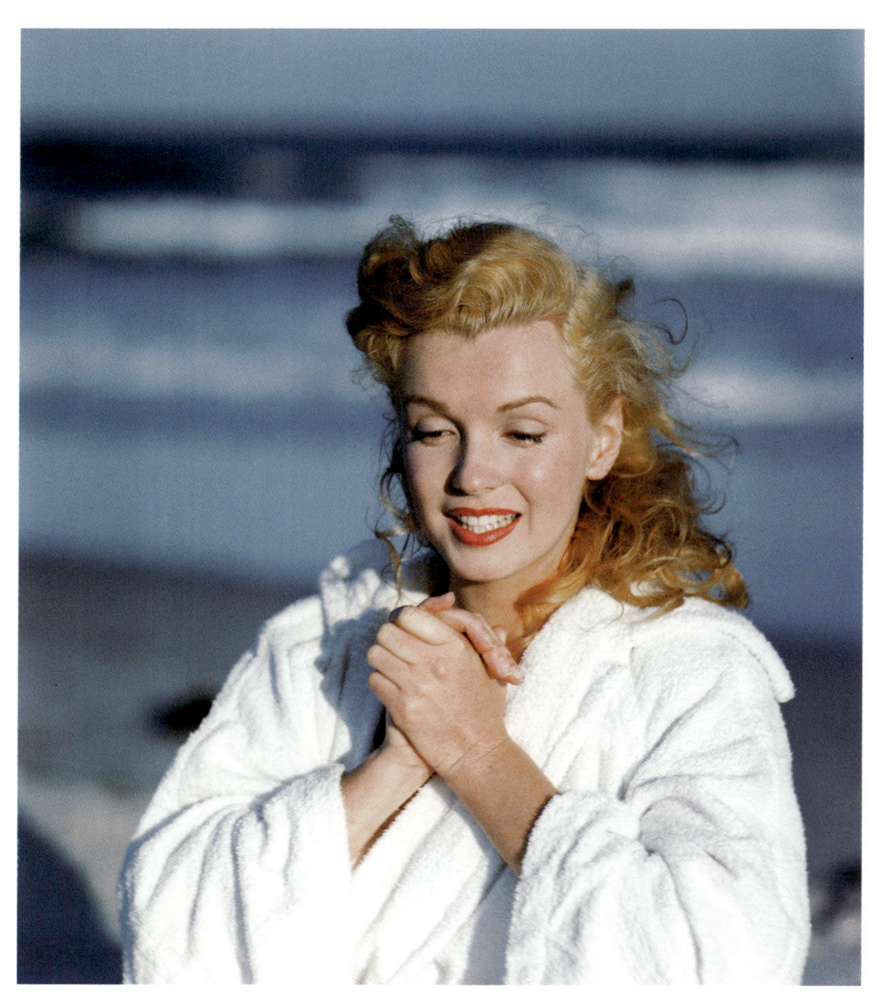

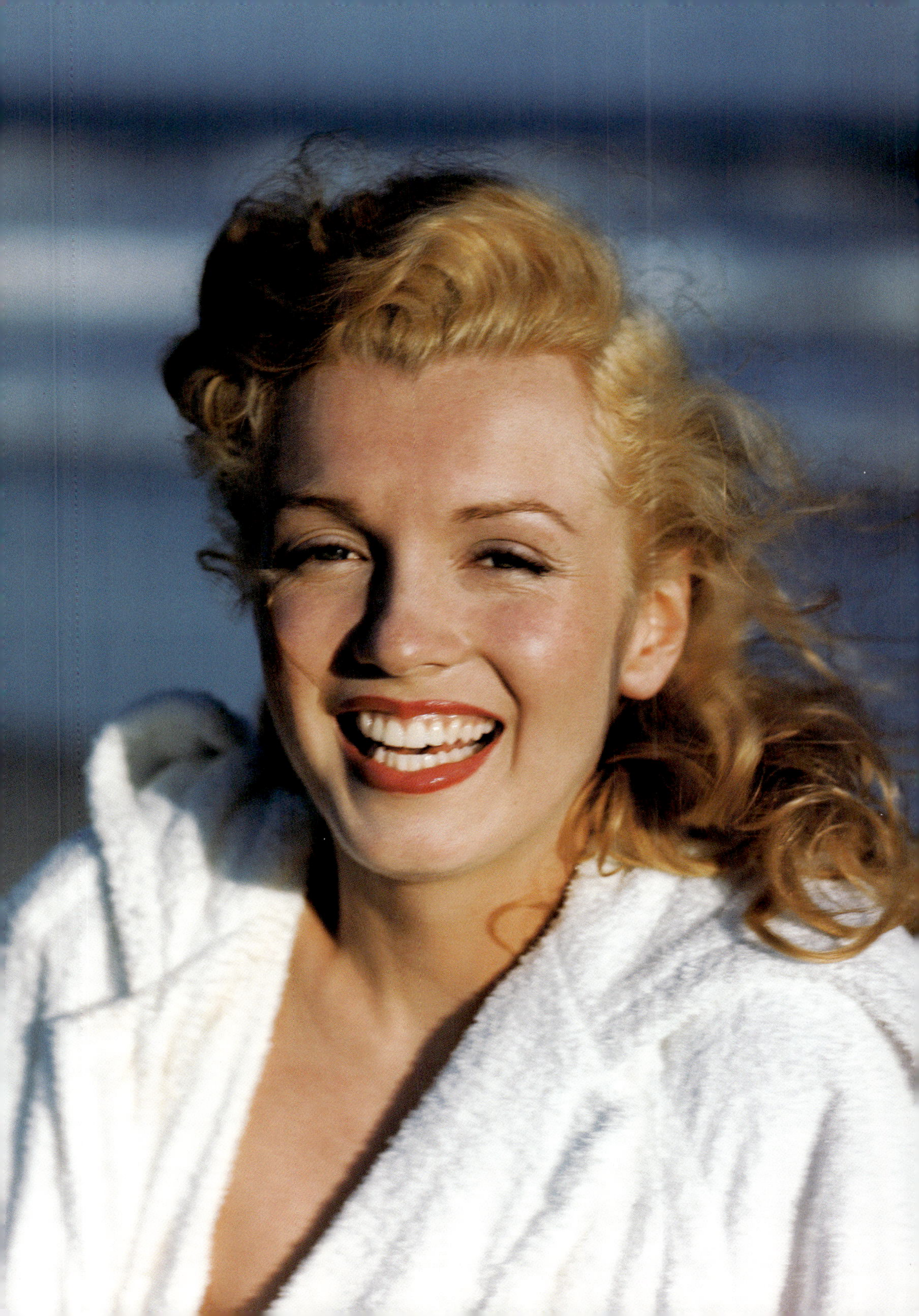

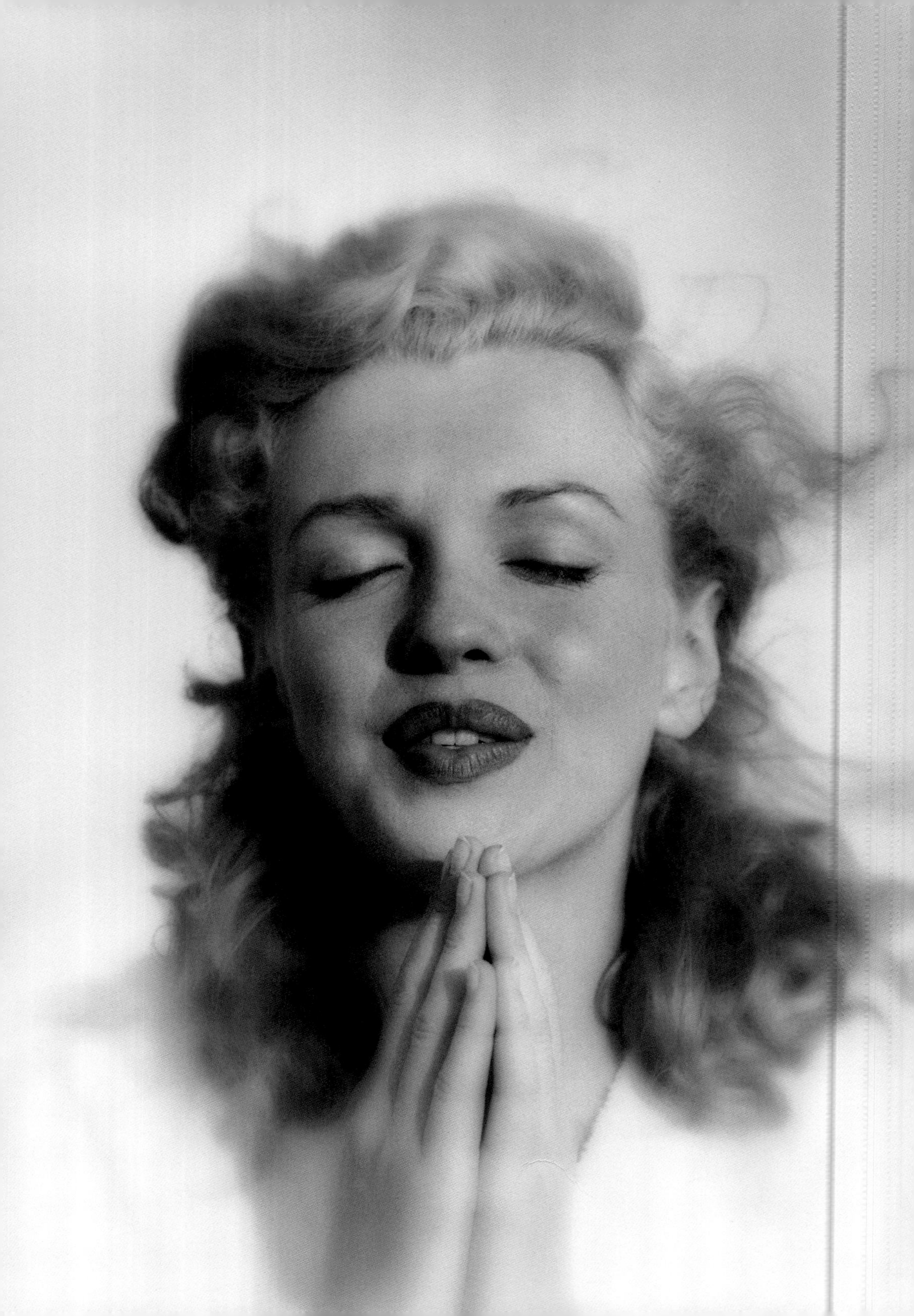

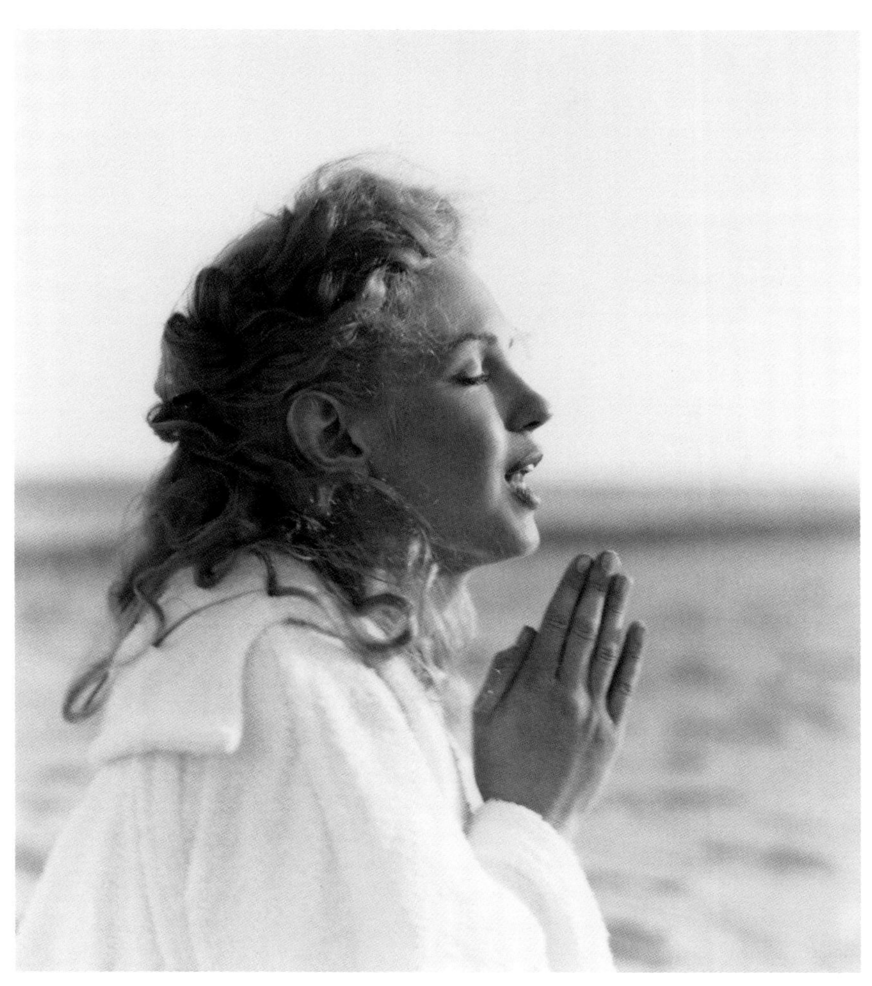

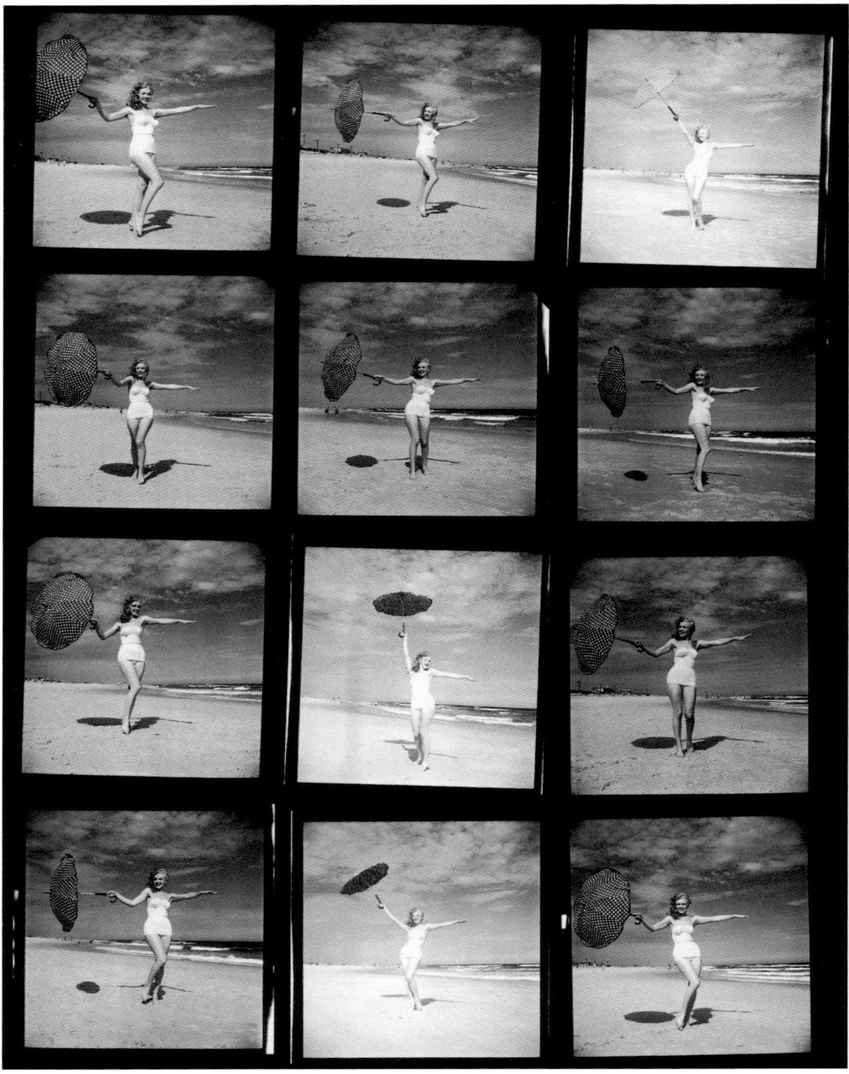

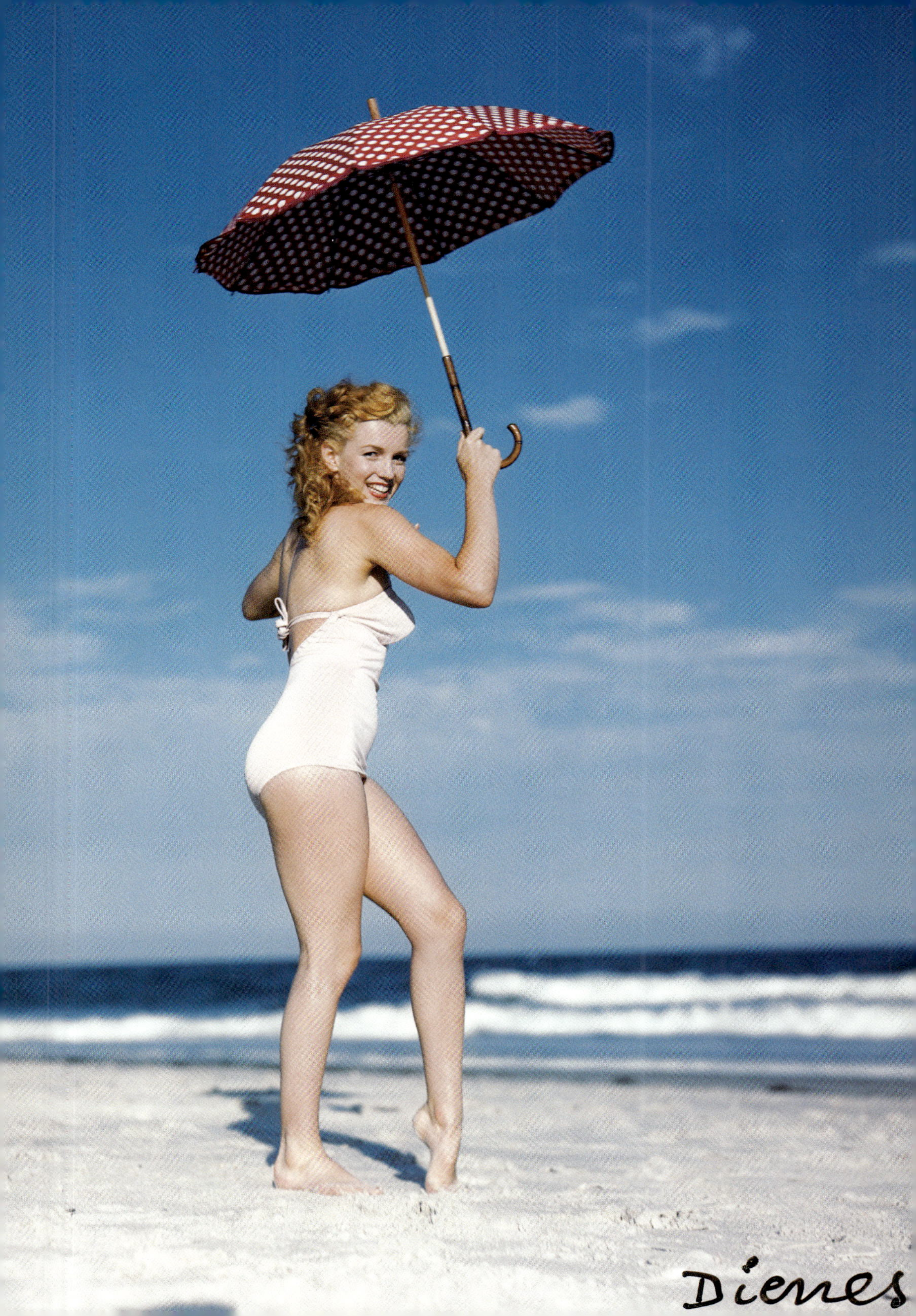
Dienes

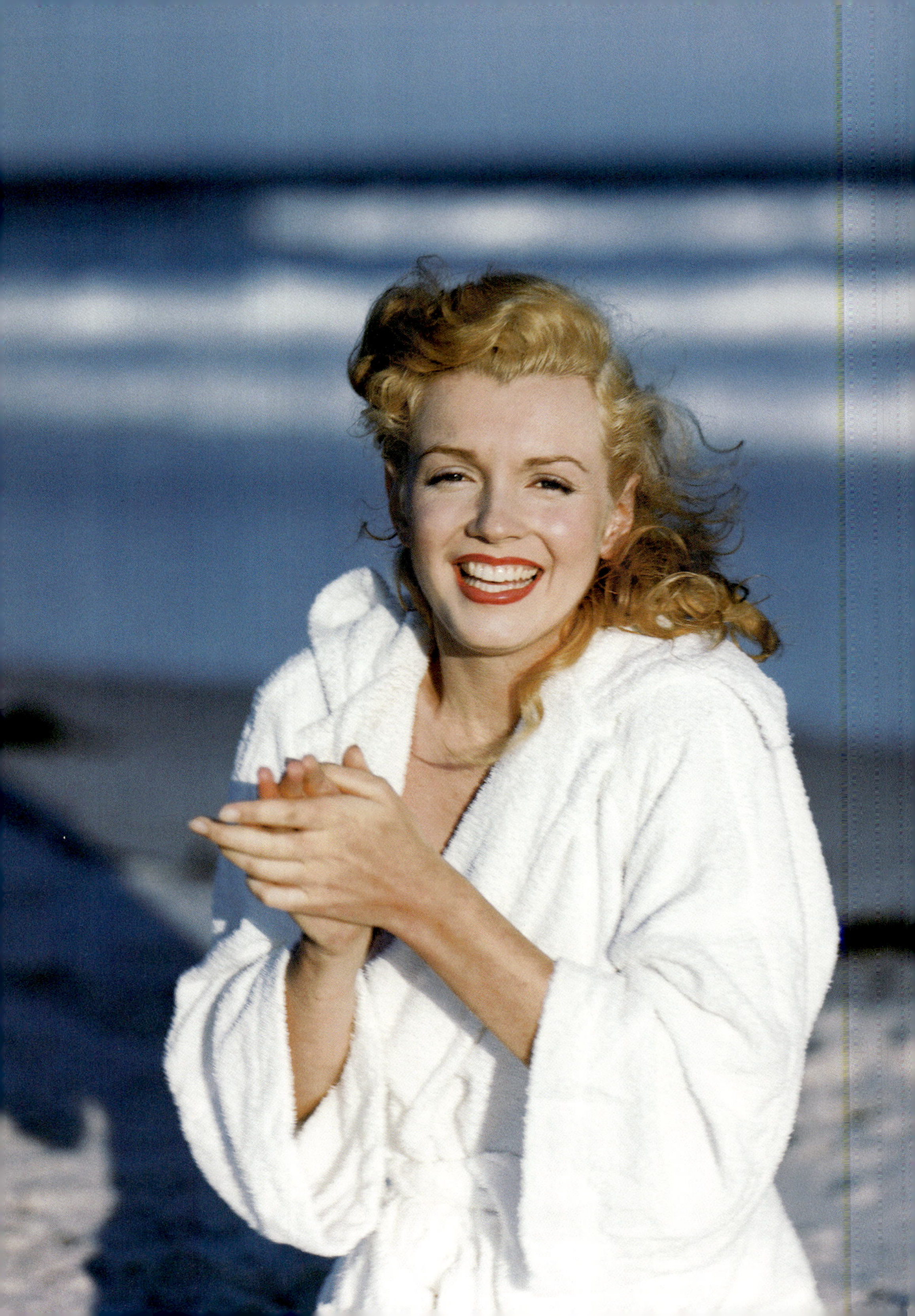

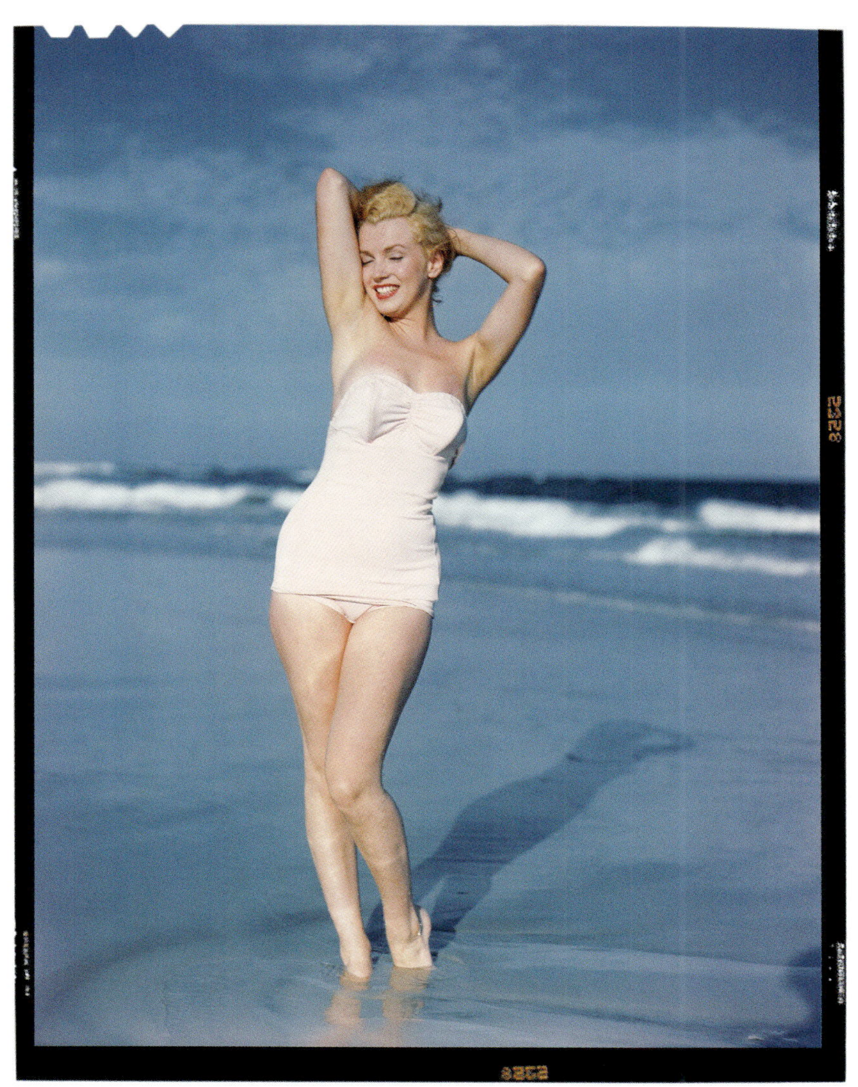

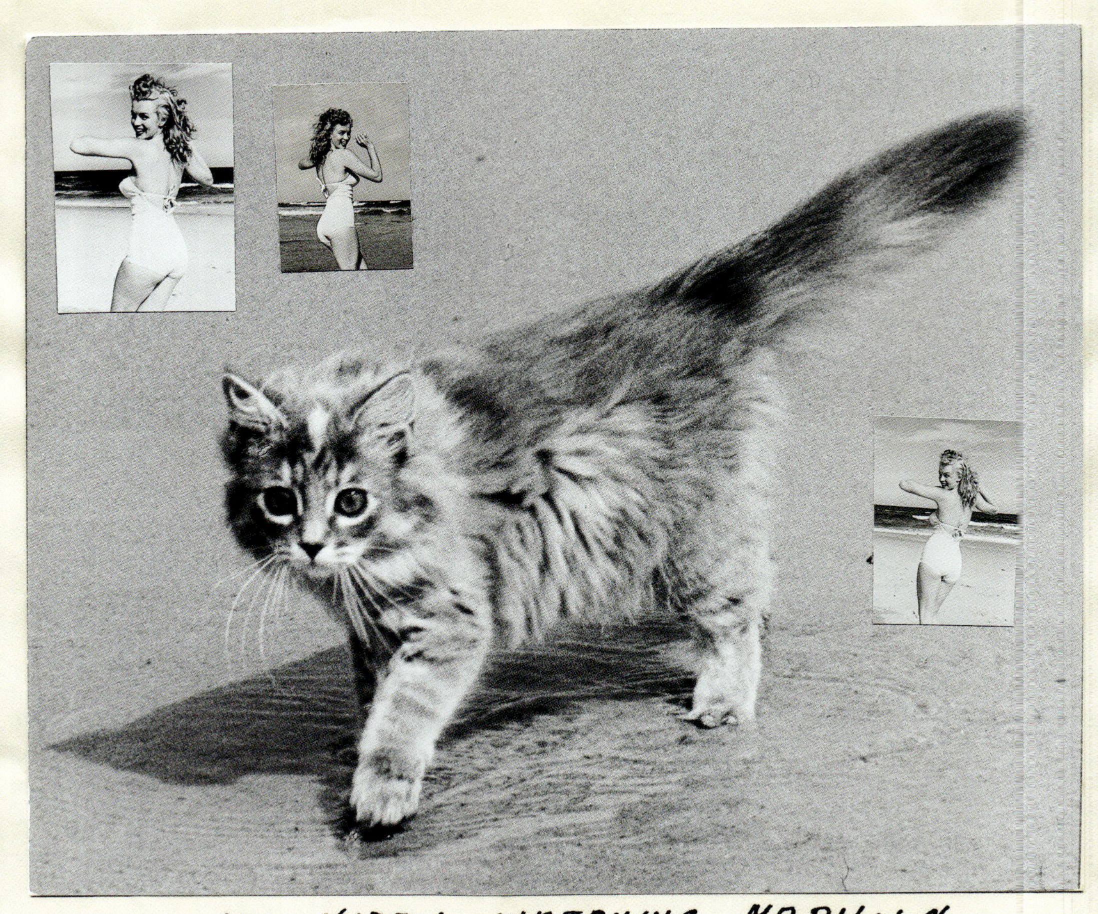

MY KITTY, WATCHING MARILYN SHOW OFF HER FANNY, AND DANCE.

AUG. 1949

MARILYN NEVER TOLD THE WORLD THAT IT'S ON THAT DAY, AT THE BEACH, SHE GOT THE FIRST LESSONS FROM ME, AND FROM THE CAT — TO WIGGLE HER DERRIÈRE. (BOTTOCKS). SHE ALWAYS CLAIMED ALL CREDITS TO HERSELF!

(P.S MARILYN: YOU ARE FORGIVEN!)

It was a real hot, humid summer day, Jones Beach was already crowded when we got there. (some 60 miles from New York) I always hated,hated taking pictures of models where there were people around, but to work among a crowd, that was impossible TASK for me ! I felt dismeyed, and we drove on,further away to a place called TOBEY beach, which was also full of people. I was pondering what to do, where to go TO FIND PRIVACY! every minute was important -- I was eager to photograph her again Than, luck came to my help. The wind began to blow, clouds were billowing, lightnigs struck in the dark clouds, and the crowd fearing the coming of an immense storm, hastily packed up and left the beach. Honestly, it was like as if God had swept the beach clean just for Marilyn and I. Hardly anybody remained, yet it hardly rained at all, THAN the storm calmed down, and disappeared completely, and by mid afternoon the entire beach was nearly deserted ! It was like a miracle ! Nobody came back . I could take pictures in peace for a few hours, late afternoon, IN sunlight I loved so much for my photography.

I took along my small grey Persian cat, because Marilyn insisted THE KITTY CAT would be lonesome in my studio. The little cat was roaming around on the wet sand, AMUSED by the waves of the ocean, AND Marilyn was dancing gayly for the cat. I directed her,to pretend the cat was a handsome young man, and she was to entice him. Or to look right into my lens, because the whole world will be looking at her later ! When I photograph somebody, I talk a great deal, almost continuously; I give

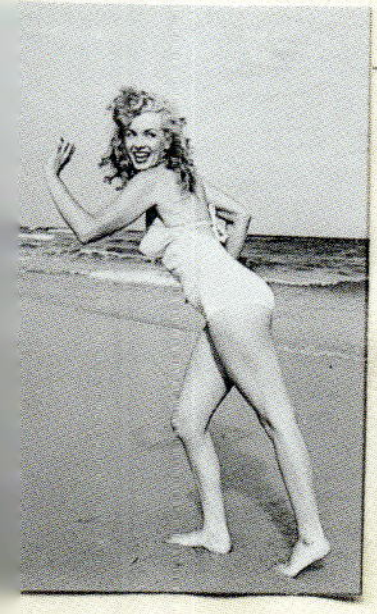
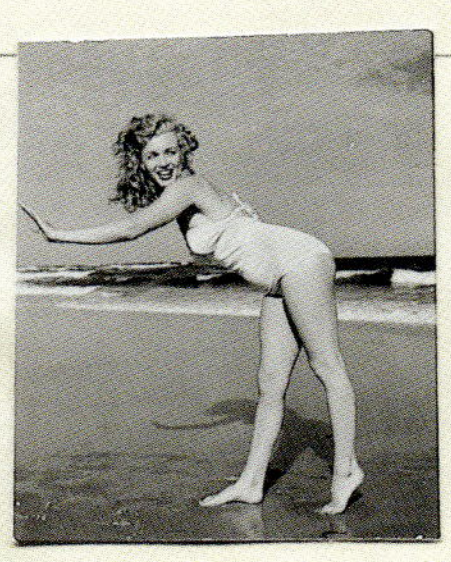
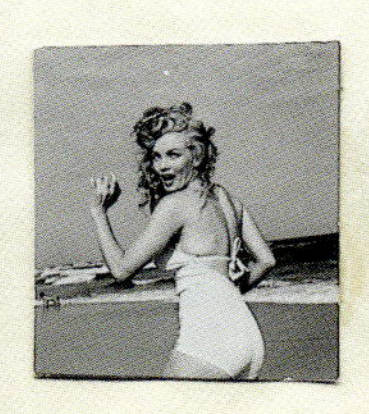
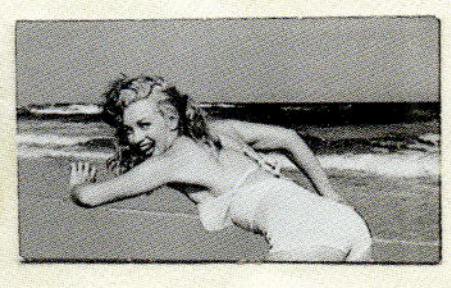
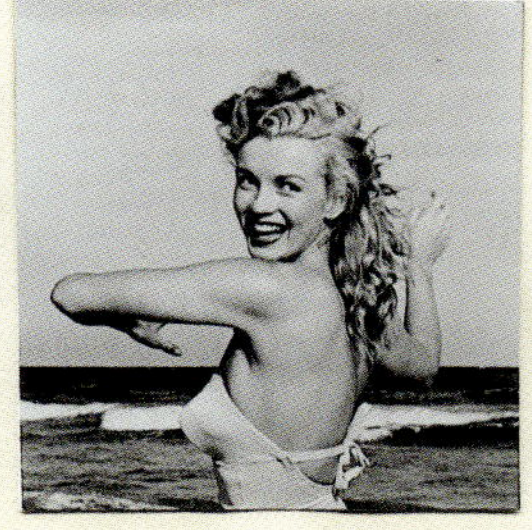

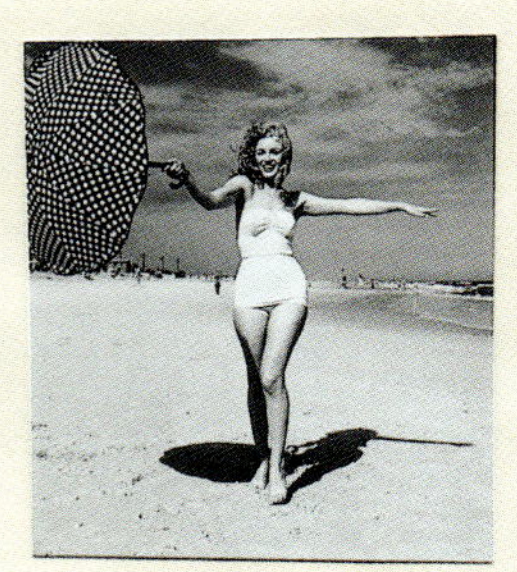

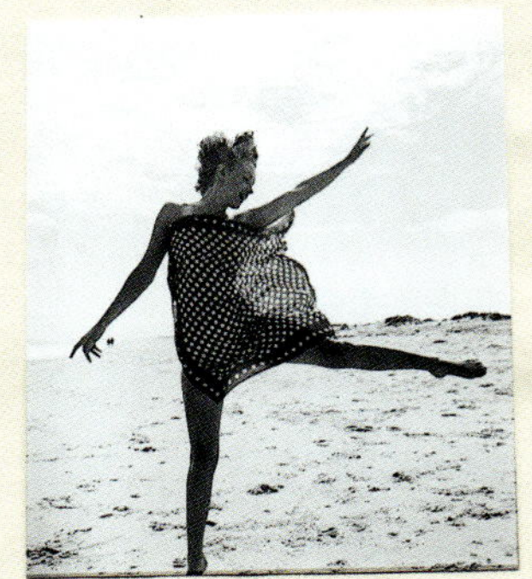

directions, I relentlessly invent stories to keep up the interest of my subject. With Marilyn, I asked her to "flirt" with my camera, to entice me with all her sex-appeal (to be sexy, but not corny), and to move as fast as possible, without any pose, while I was clicking the shutter on and on. And I spoke to Marilyn about she being a new "Lillian Russell;" I began teaching her how to walk onto a stage. She was holding the parasol, and I told her she was Lillian, the great stage-actress, and over and over I made Marilyn walk--toward me-- with more and more self assurance, and sex-appeal, pretending she was walking, entering onto A stage ! I took at least two dozen shots of her like that. Marilyn was extremely cooperative, patient, eager to please me, AND eager to learn ! To tell the truth, I hardly knew anything ABOUT Lillian Russell, And neither did Marilyn. I was still just sort of "green" in America, but the name reng familiar to me, and I knew she was ONCE famous, So, I was thinking that Lillian Russell having been so famous, Marilyn ought to follow her example! Out of a little idea and imagination, I created an enormous enthusiasm for both of us that afternoon, And repeatedly we ENCOURAGED each other THAT we are going to make history ! And I told her my pictures of her shall last for ever! And again and again she was frollicing around on the sand, and I was clicking the pictures, convinced, reassured, determined, that she shall become famous ! It was a happy afternoon for both of us.

There was only one minor little problem, but ennoying; The cup of the bathing suit had wire in it, and it was scretching badly Marilyns bosoms, Her skin was all red on her breast. She suffered MUCH, but did not complain at all, she danced in the scarf too as I planned it, but the wind did not blow it away from her body. * I did NOT mind NOT taking nudes of her. I could find plenty of other models for that prupose, We felt happy; no way would I have wanted to change the mood of that gloriously happy day -- by wanting to photograph her nude. I already had thousands of negatives of nudes in my files; I did not need any of her. And I did not wish to take a chance, TO maybe make her angry at me. I had love and respect for my beautiful Marilyn. I felt fortunate and grateful that she chose me to be with, for a full day, before she began her puclicity appearance in New York city. Otherwise, I could not have been able to take all those lovely photos of her that day.

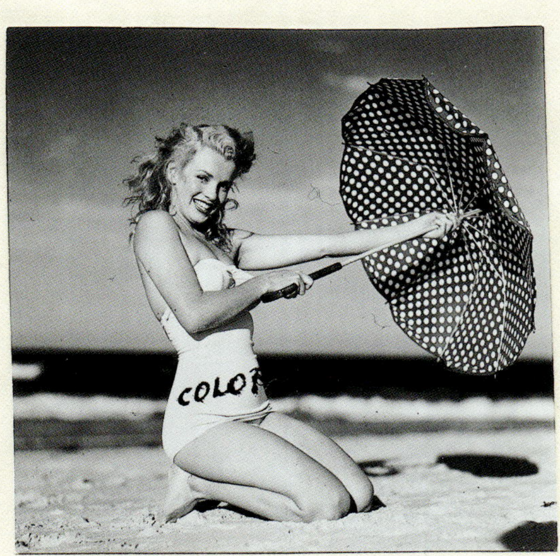

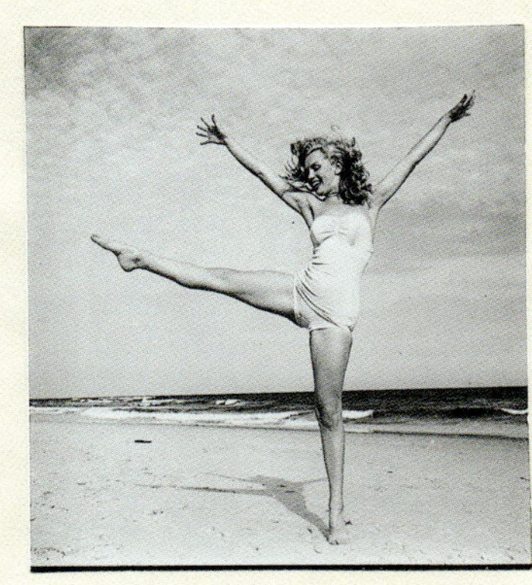

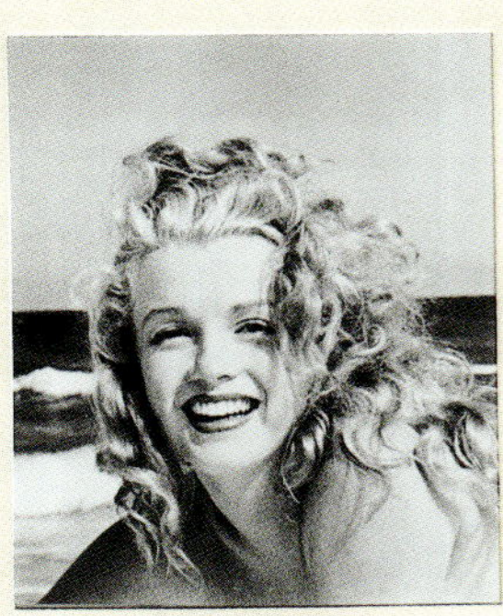

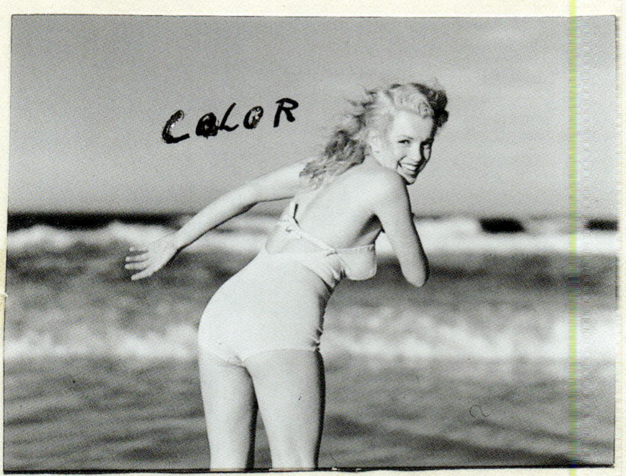

ANDRE DE DIENES
1401 SUNSET PLAZA DRIVE
HOLLYWOOD, CALIF. 90069

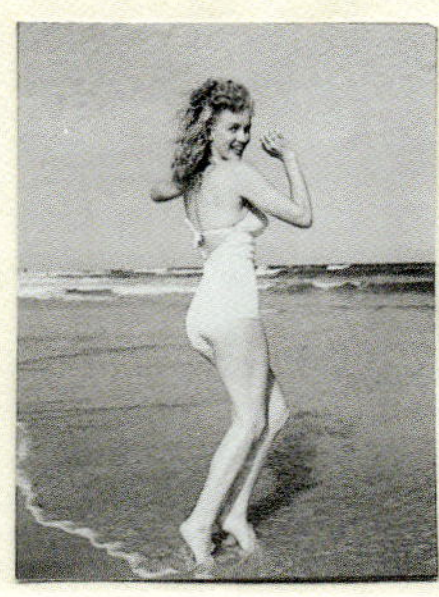

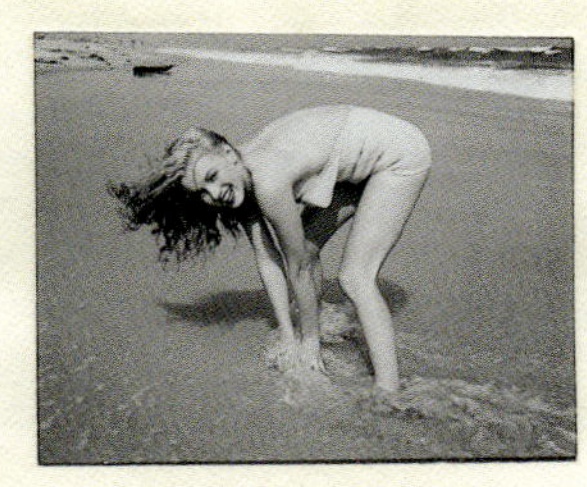

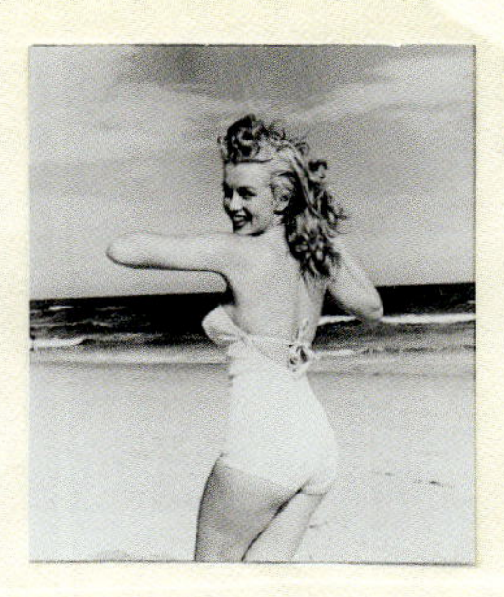

TRASITION. These photographs I took of her in 1949 represent a young Marilyn. The poses are casual, because this IS THE kind of photography I was very active in creating in those years. I did not care how the wind blew her hair, the more natural, the more messed up by the fast movements, the better I liked her hair to be all messed up. But her image as movie star became different. It became how the public had seen her on the screen, in her movies. That image was created at the Hollywood studios, done by hairdressers, make up men, etc. A Far more glamorised kind of photography, sometimes too artificial for my taste. I never liked a hairdo what looks too prepared by the hairdresser, and hair-sprayed to remain stiff, strong like wire,so it can't move--so it would remain glamorous looking. Even NOW, I dislike women who's look depend on WHAT the hairdresser dictates, except for certain FESTIVE occasions, when a beautiful hairdo is essential. Good hairdoos are essential SOMETIMES, in fact, some CAN BE works of art. But I preferred -- for my pictures-- a very casual Marilyn.

As a postscript, I should add, that, when I returned to Binghampton to sell photos to my client, this is the photo which got sold, of Marilyn. The client did not know at all,that soen,the young lady will become THE very famous MARILYN MONROE.

The care ride from the seashore, back to Manhattan, was a real comical event. Having mixed my joy, my happiness, and the cognac I brought along, I got a bit intoxicated, and some place, I took the wrong road and was heading out toward north, instead of toward New York. At a gas station where we stopped, my kitty cat, sick of the car ride, wanting her freedom, leaped out of the open window, and ren into a garden; and me after the cat, accross a fallen fence, and Marilyn too, AFTER US, loughing hysterically. I cought the cat, Meanwhile in the garden, Marilyn was touching, caressing a large bronze sculpture of a faun, playing the flute. Alas, it was getting dark, and I had no more film left, I could not take pictures of her hugging the faun. Both of us were very enthralled by it, and by the surrounding garden itself, SO enchanting, falling into decay by neglect. .....
As a footnote to this story, I must mention that, a few days later I returned to take pictures of the faun. I took along a beautiful model, to photograph her nude, hugging the faun, like Marilyn did. First, I was looking for the ownner of the place. Total silence, nobody was home. I wasted no time; while the model was taking off her clothes, I just snapped a couple of pictures of the sculpture, when a woman ren out from the house, shouting, SCREAMING at us, to get out of the garden ! With a branch in her hand, lifted up to strike me, she looked like a fury ! It would have been a perfect scene for an artist to paint a painting, my bautiful model, nude, caressing the faun, and the fury ready to strike ! " Jealousy " would be the right title for it. But the lady did not strike me, just kept shouting at us to get out.

****

It's a good thing Marilyn did not have any of THE Cognac
Safe and sound, I drove her back to the Hotel Pierre that evening. And how lucky it was that it happened that way, and Marilyn probably slept real well that night ....
The next day, Marilyn gave the first, the most important interview of her career. The Press literally mobbed her; adored her ! And from that day onward, her name was mentioned almost every day in the newspapers all over the U.S., and world over ! Suddenly, she became world famous ! The craze for Marilyn Monroe have started

Insert:

I must add that, Besides Marilyn's great charm, sweetness, honesty, captivating personality, and her will to want to become somebody famous and important, the key to her sucess and fame was the exceedingly well-planned publicity she got, all figured out, and carried out by very competent people at the Publicity and Publica-relations department of the 20th Century Fox Studios! Her reception in New York was fantastic ! Publicists, and people from the press, and people themselves, got very excited about her ! She received a tremendous amount of publicity and adulation! It just kept coming. And she cooperated beautifully ! No wonder so many women were jealous of her, and so many beautiful girls wanted to follow her footsteps.... and still do now, so many, many years since. Yet, none succeeded, yet, to rival with her fame...... I don't think there is a civilized place in the world, where they do not know the name Marilyn Monroe ! Her name became completely synonimous with AMERICA !

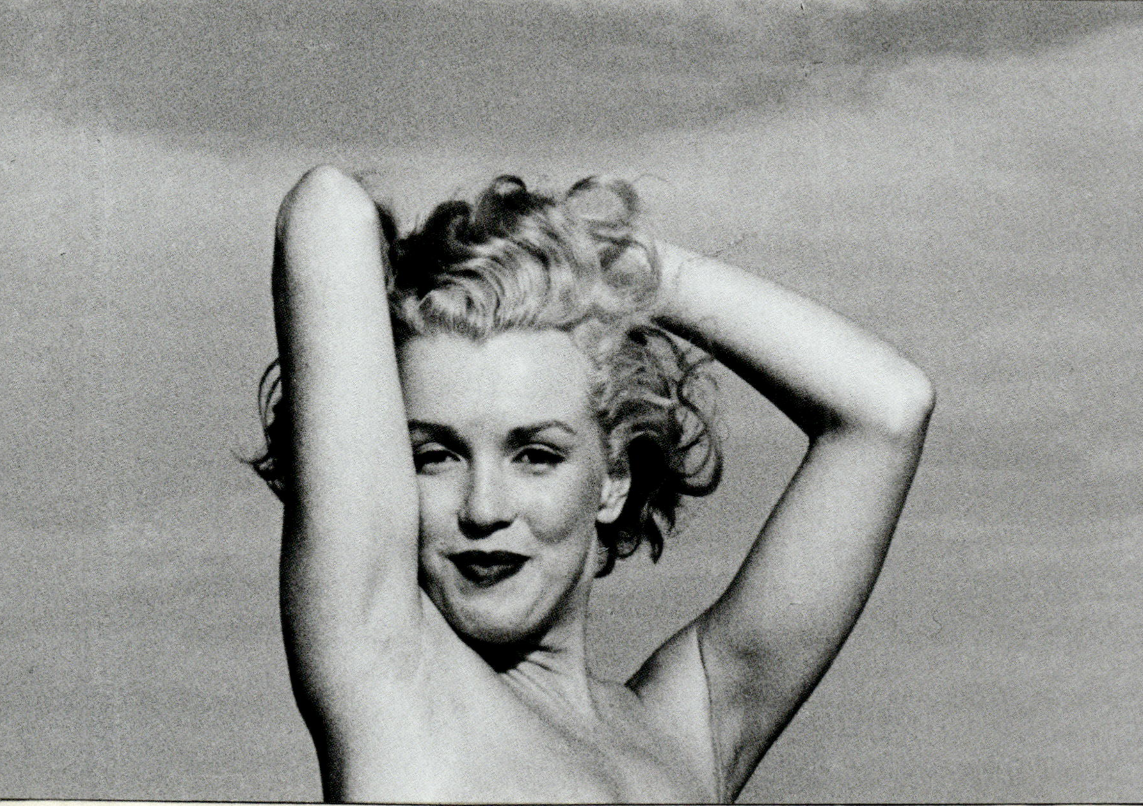

The beautiful imp ! 1949

1949

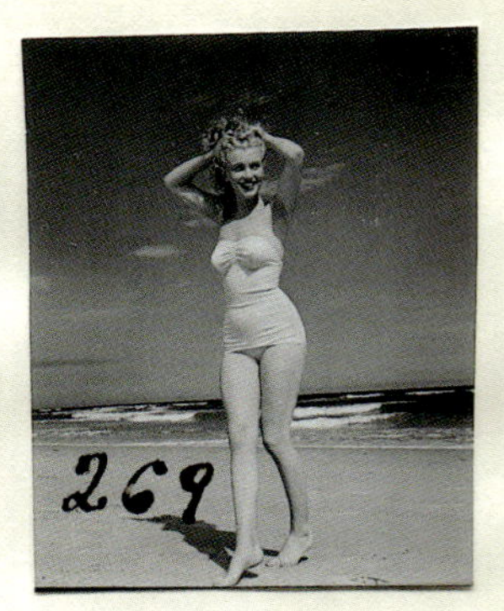

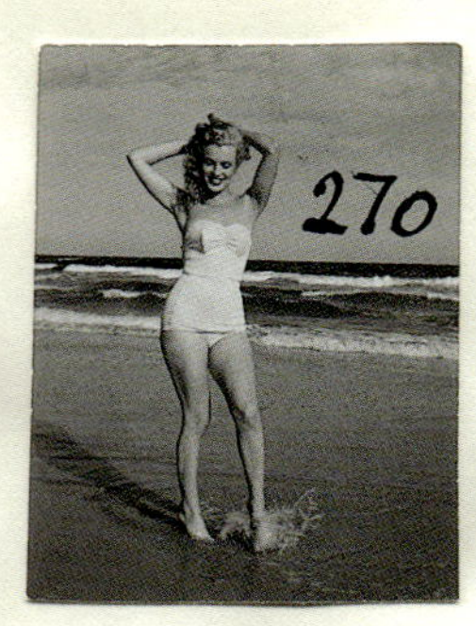

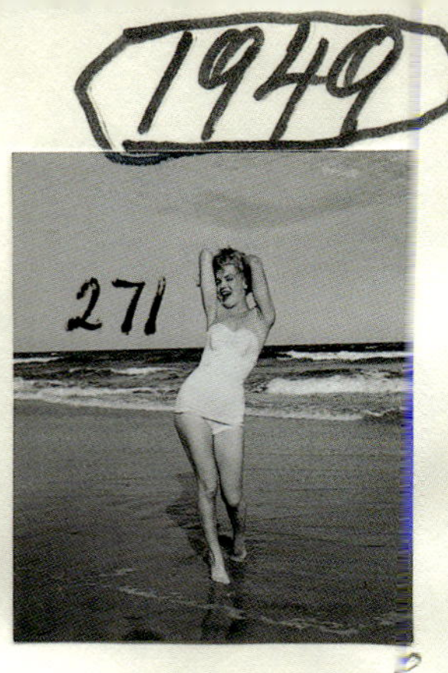

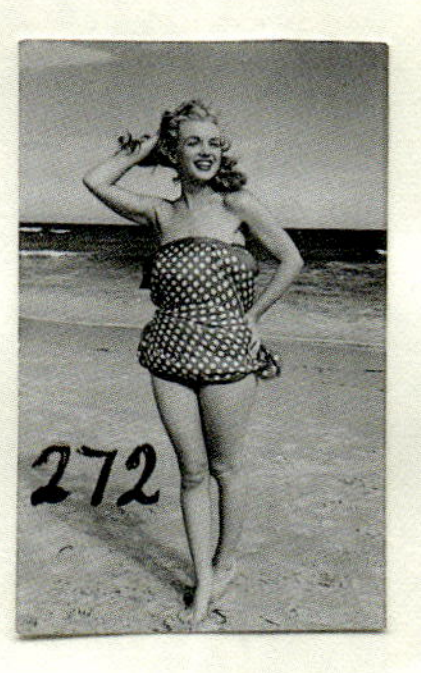

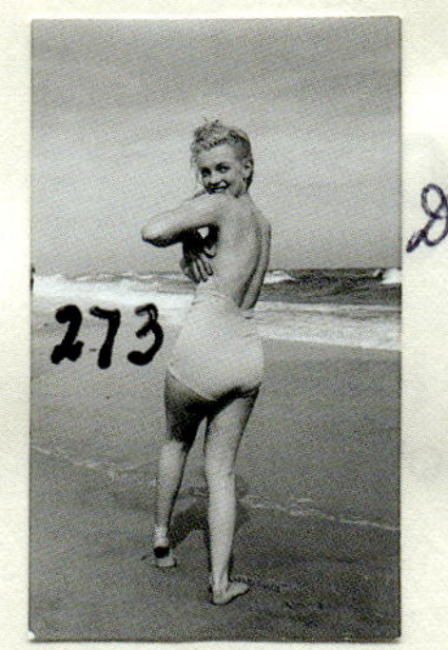

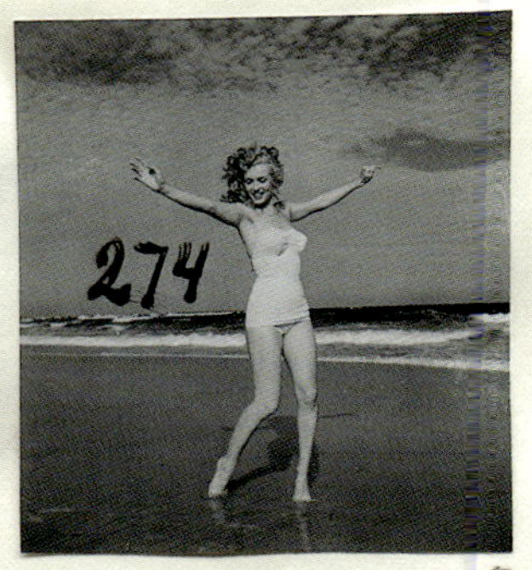

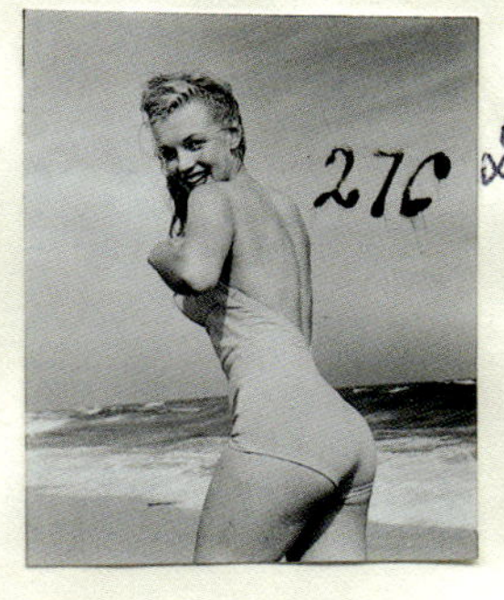

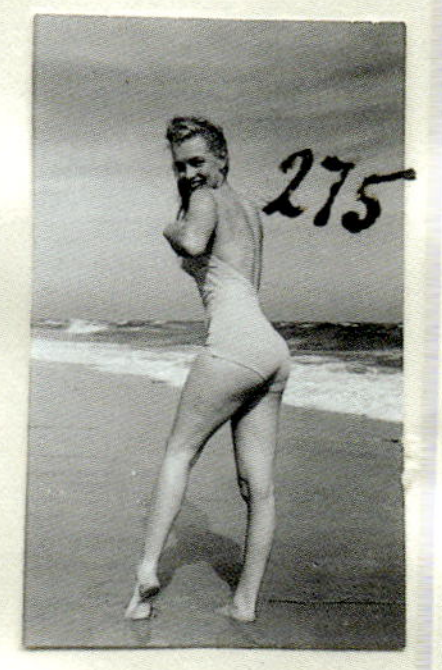

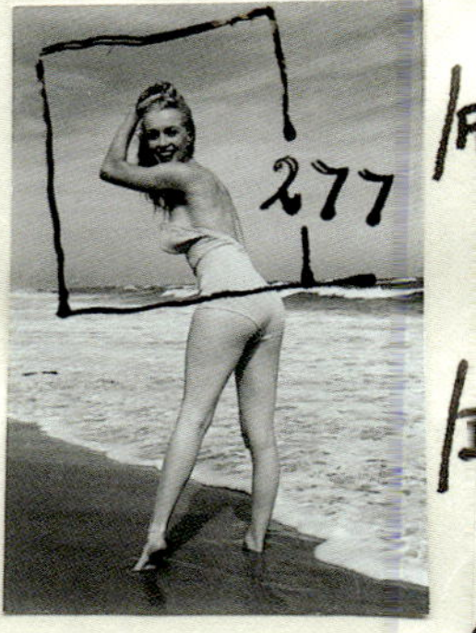

44

ANDRE DE DIENES

1949

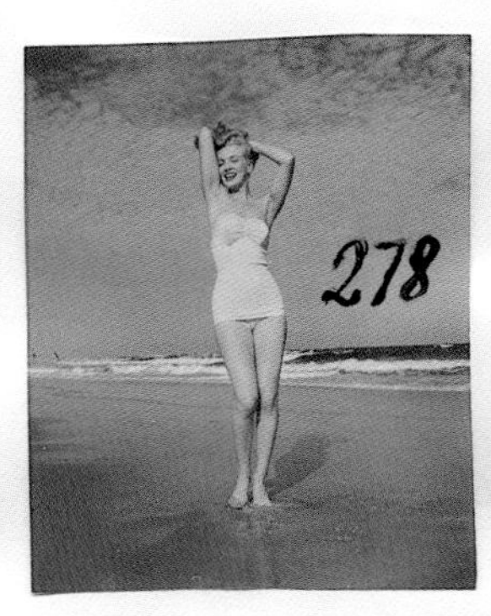

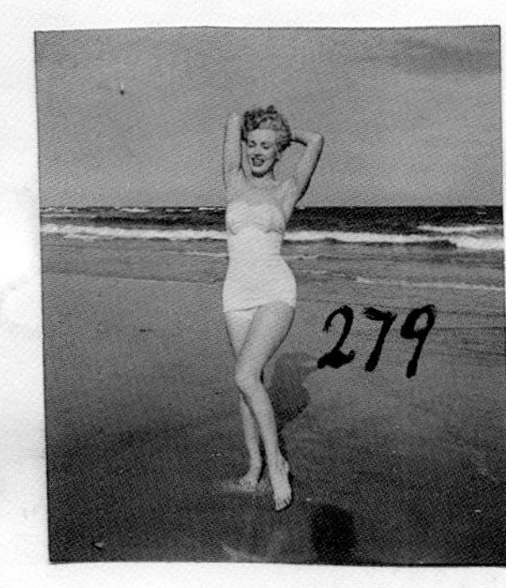

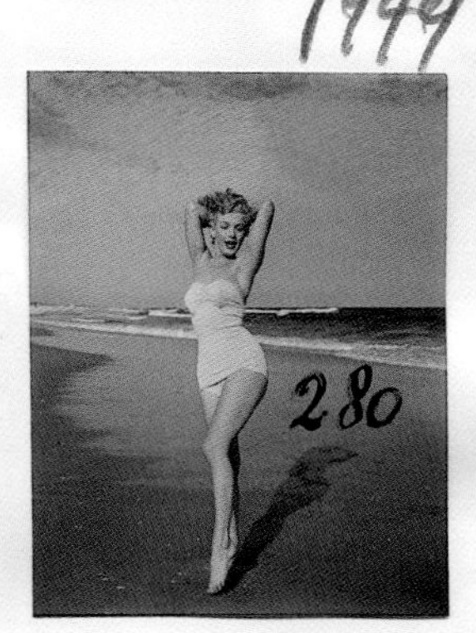

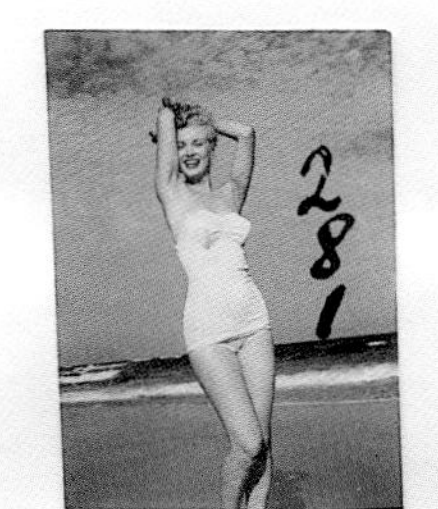

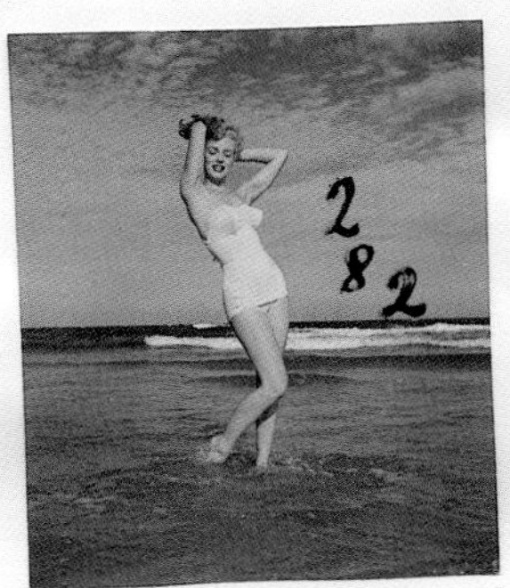

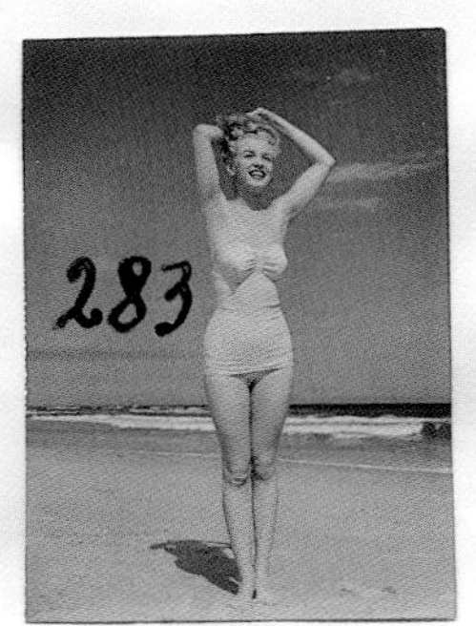

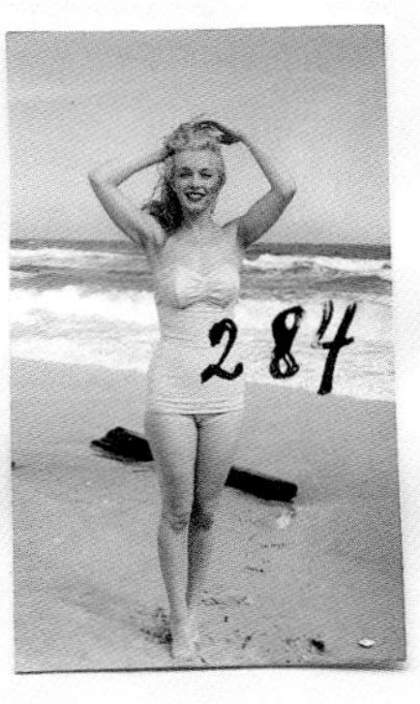

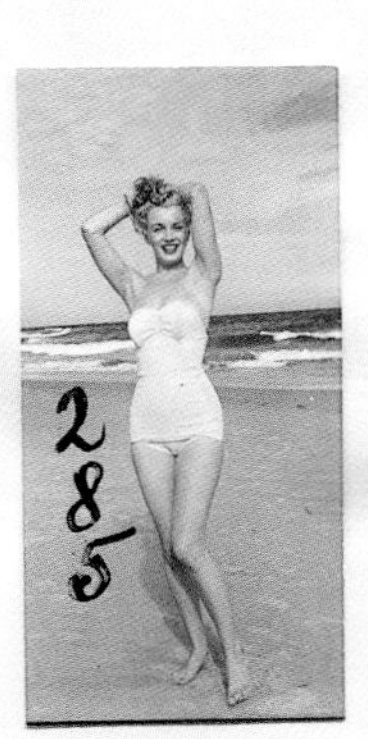

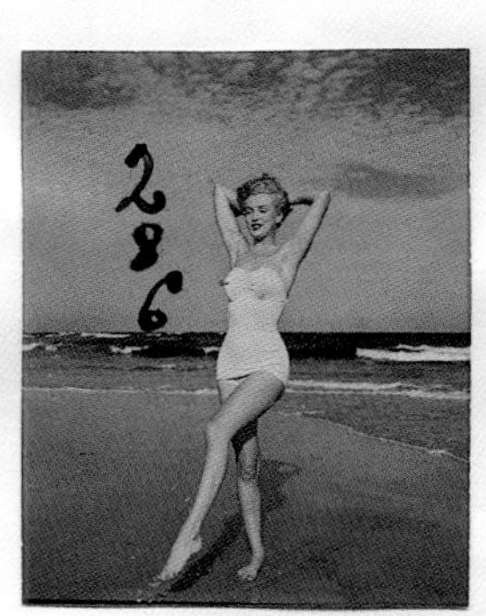

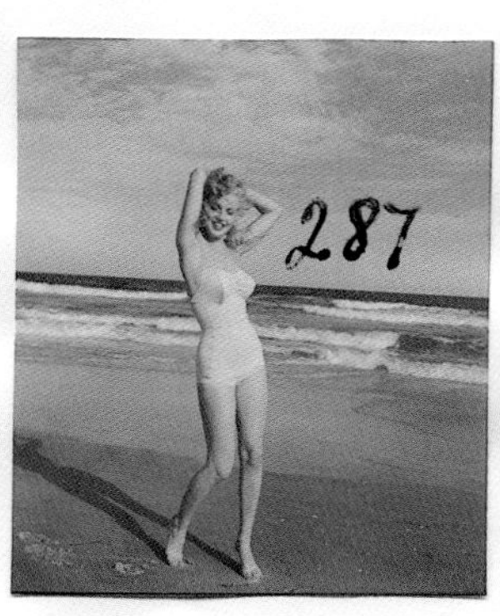

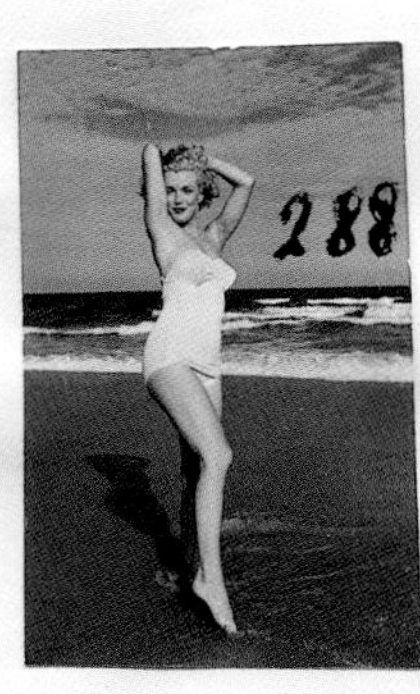

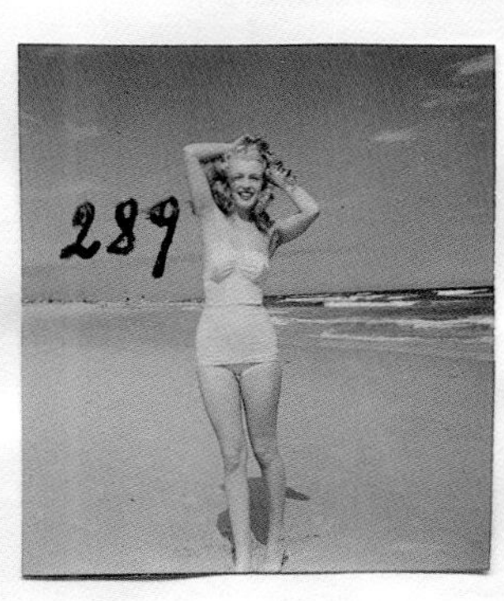

ANDRE DE DIENES

1949

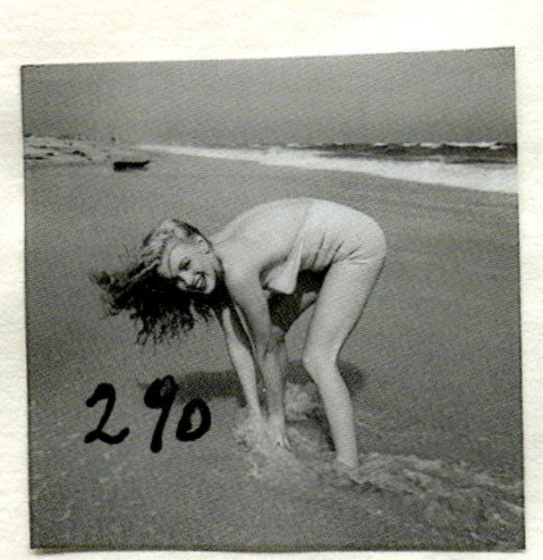

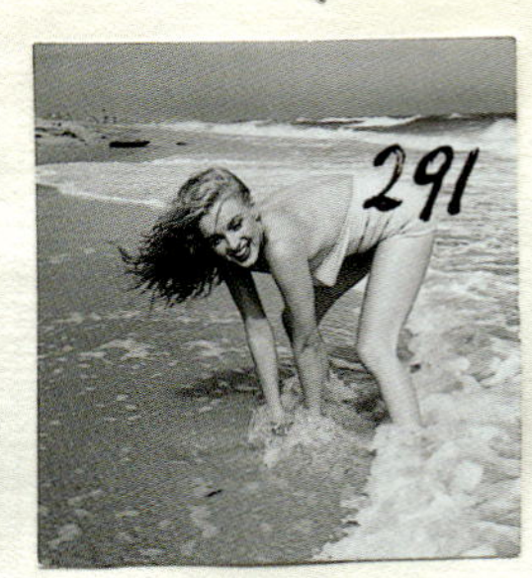

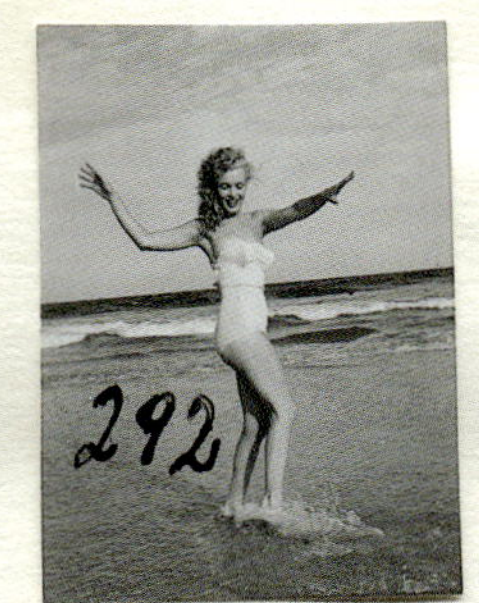

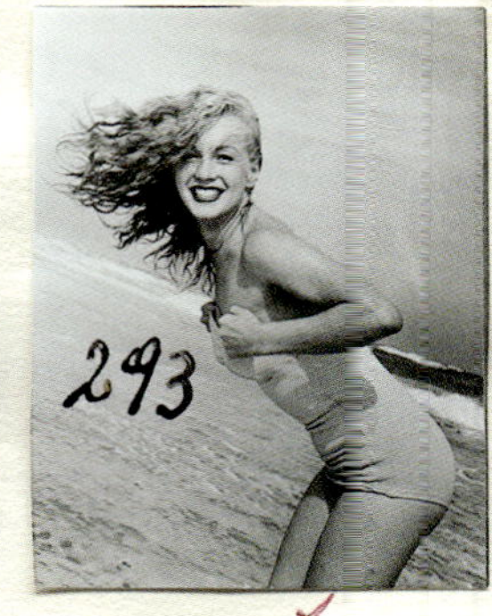

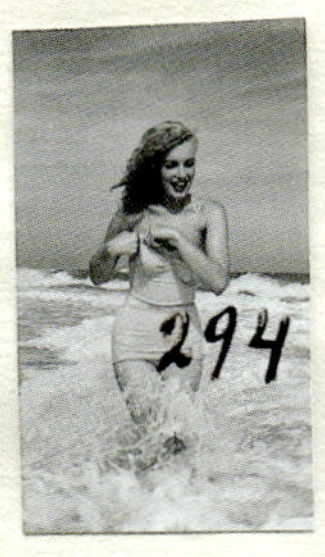

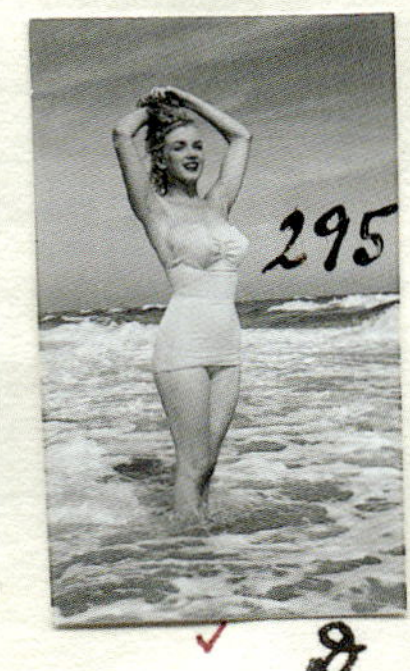

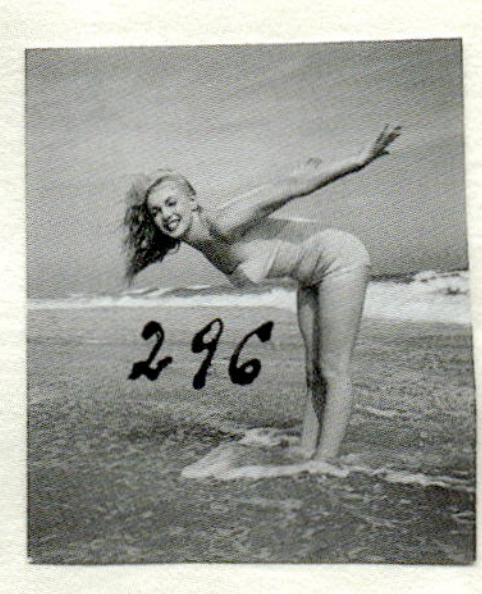

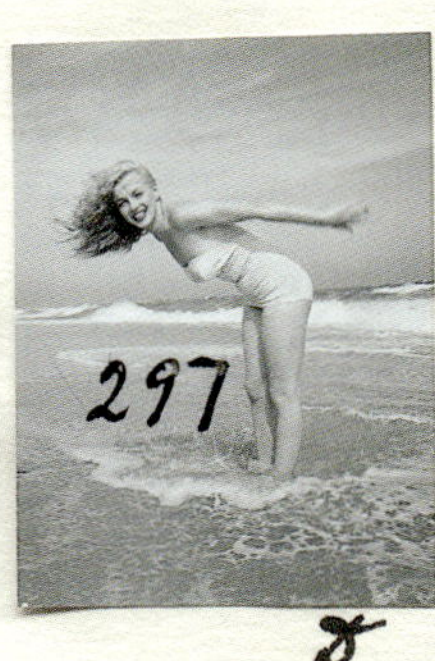

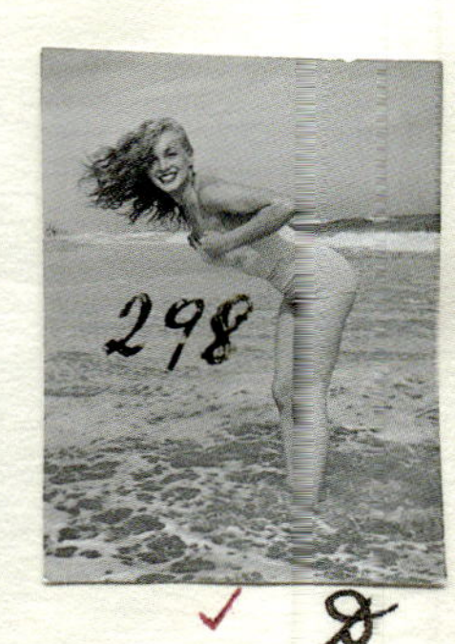

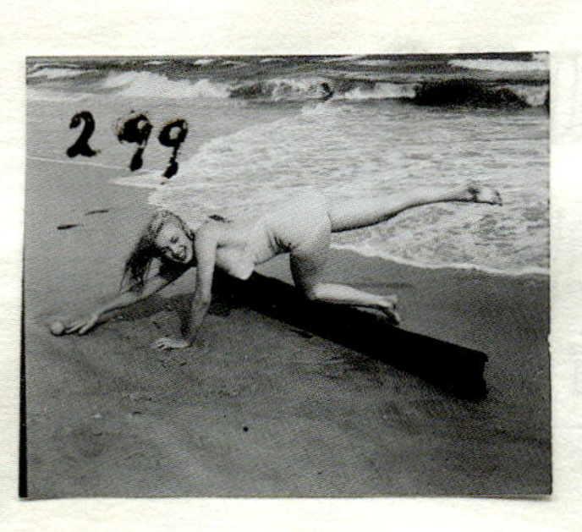

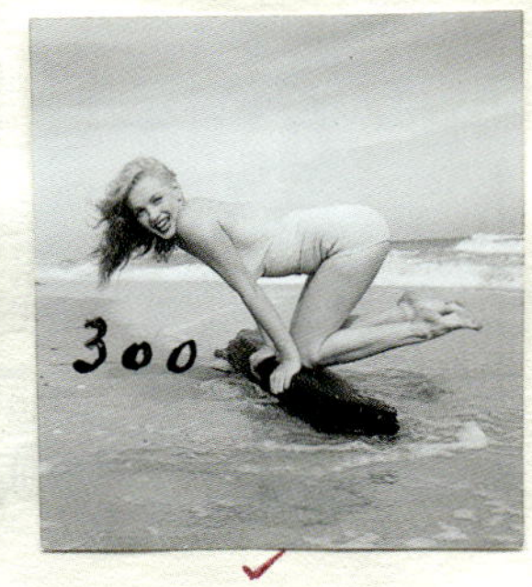

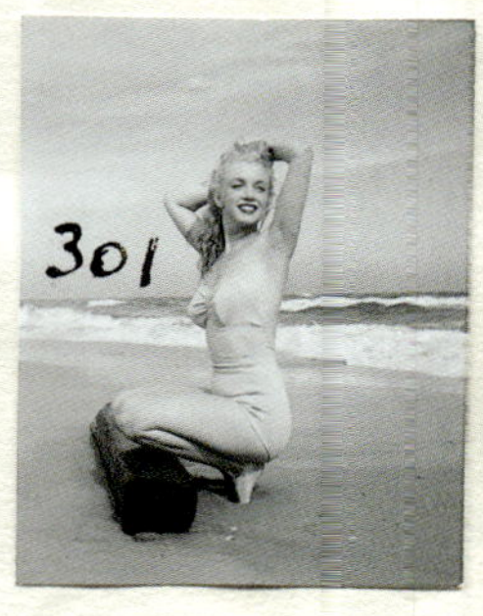

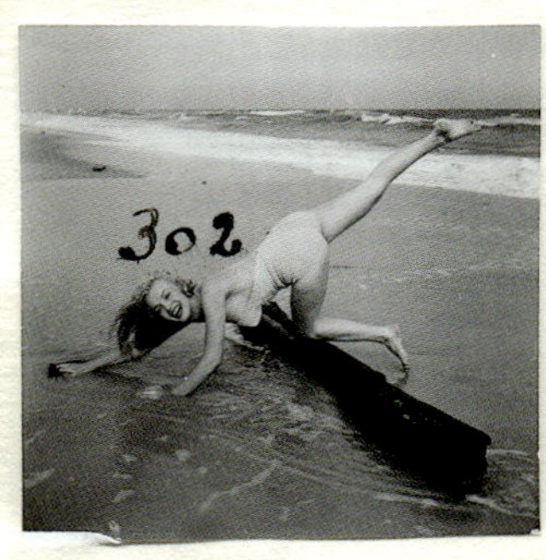

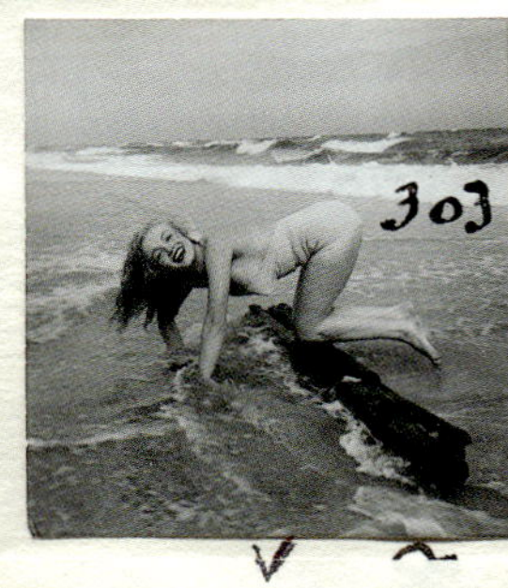

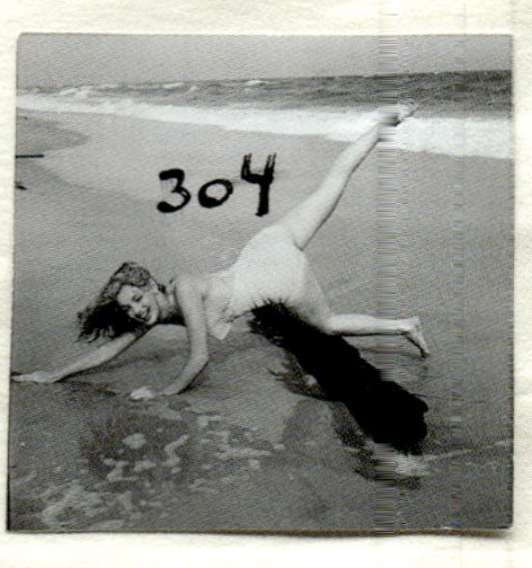

ANDRE DE DIENES
1401 SUNSET PLAZA DRIVE
HOLLYWOOD, CALIF. 9006

46

1949

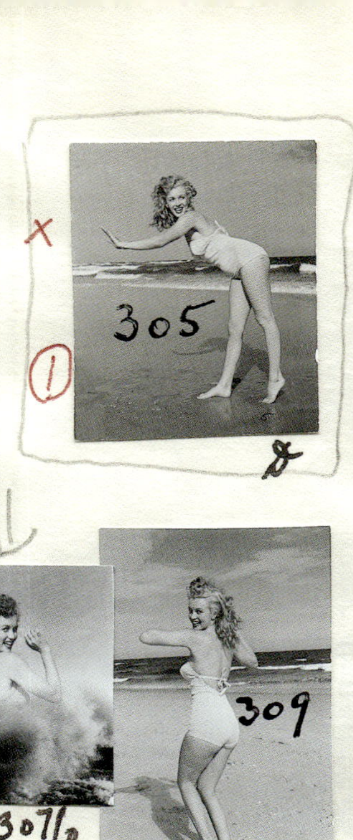

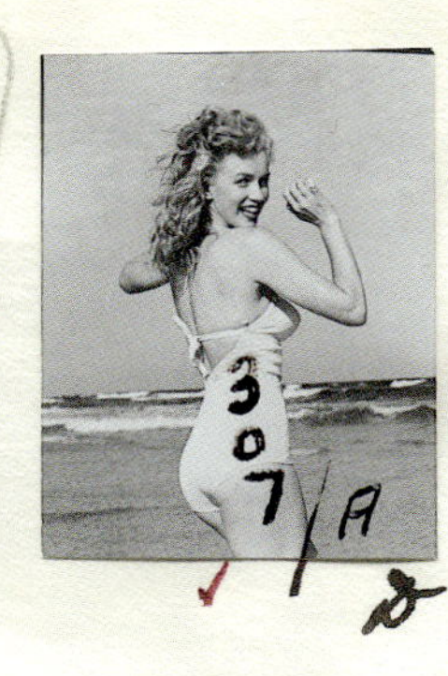

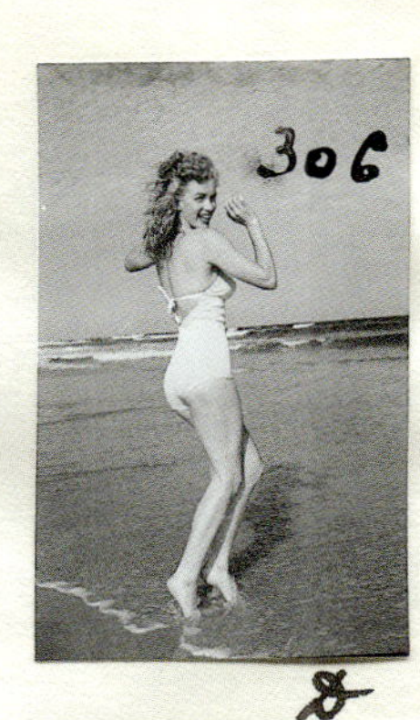

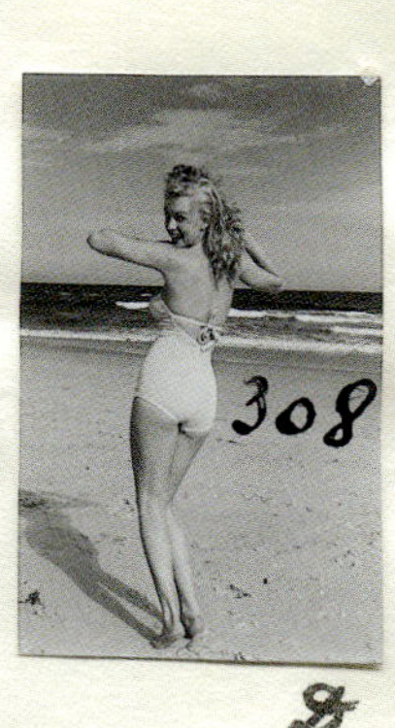

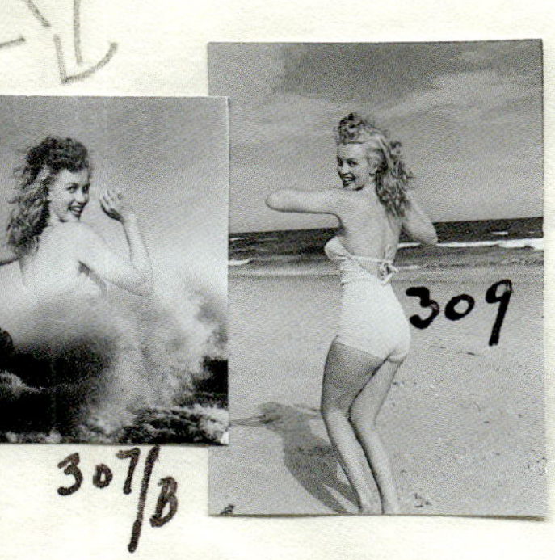

307/B

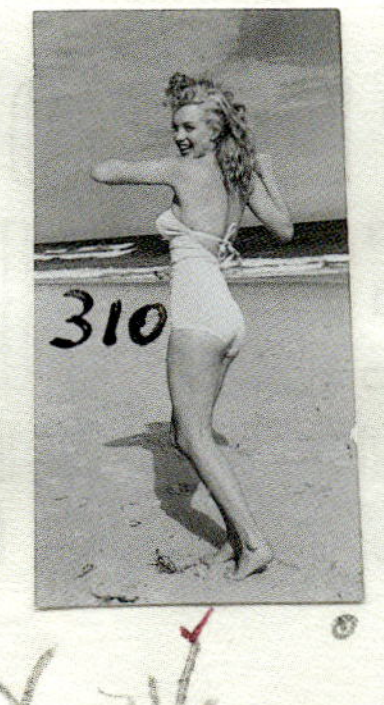

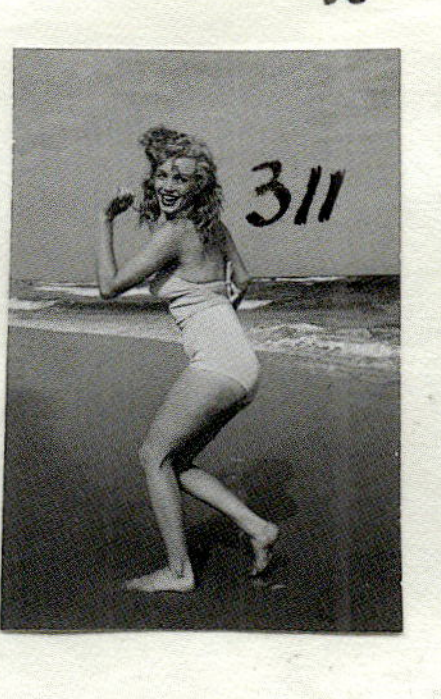

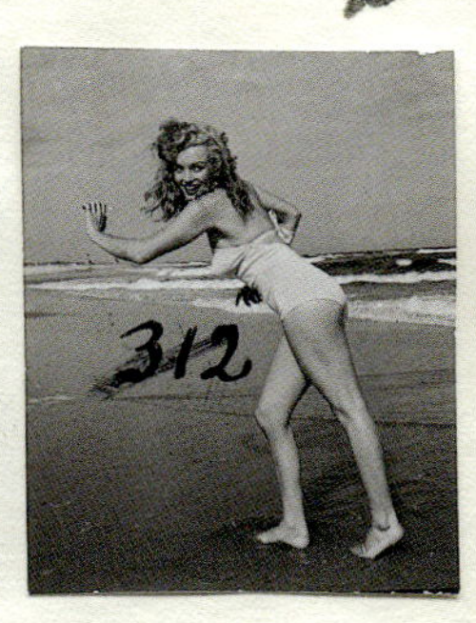

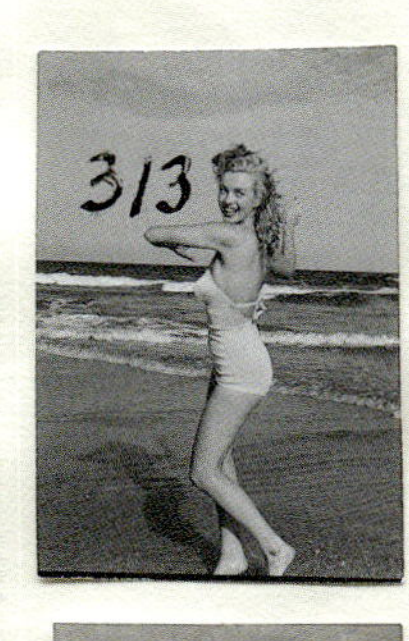

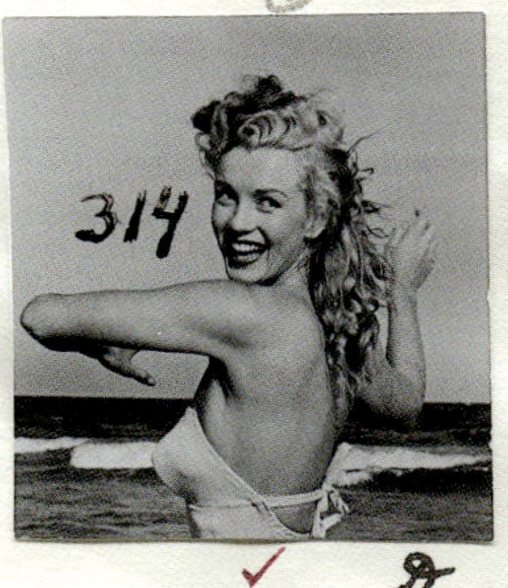

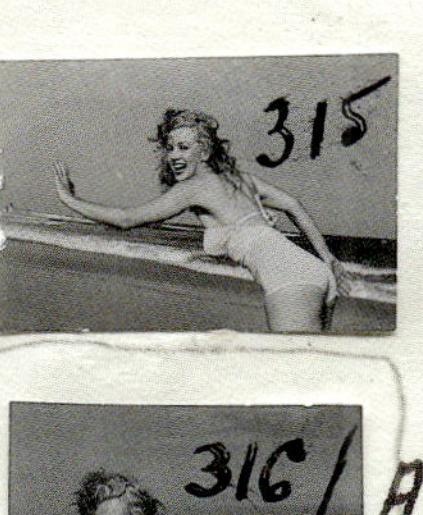

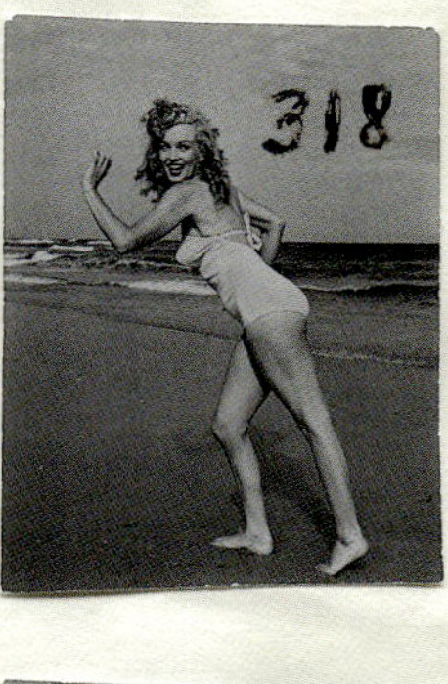

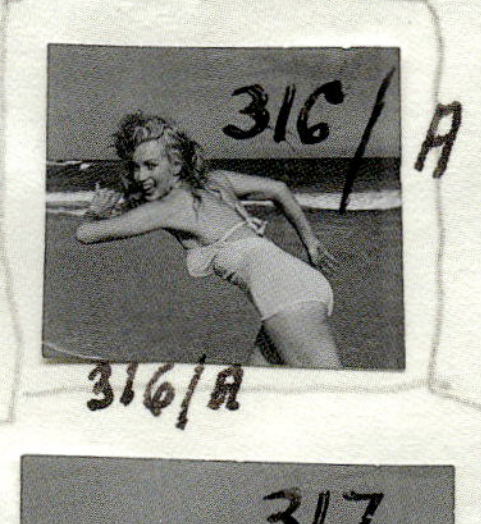

316/A

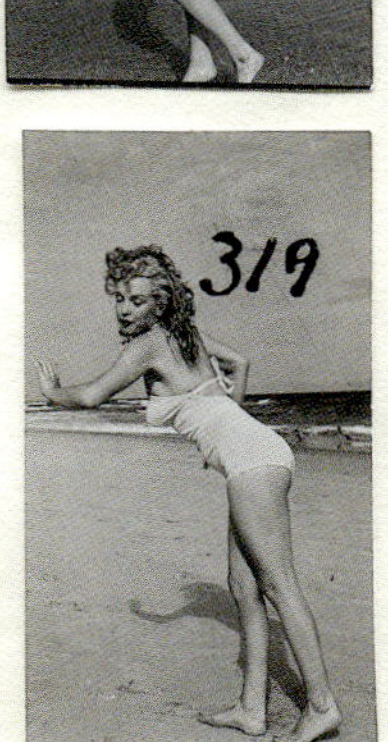

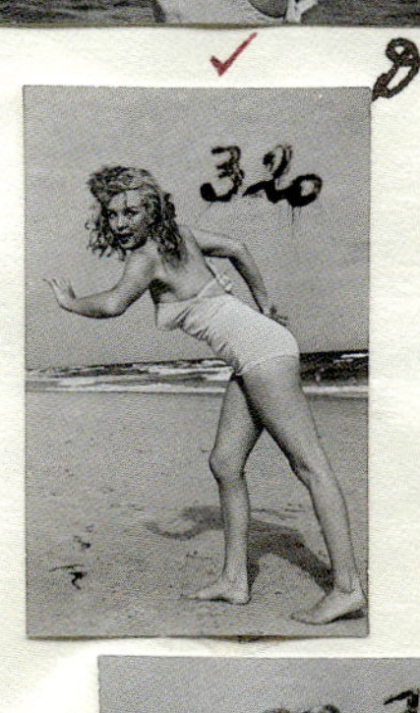

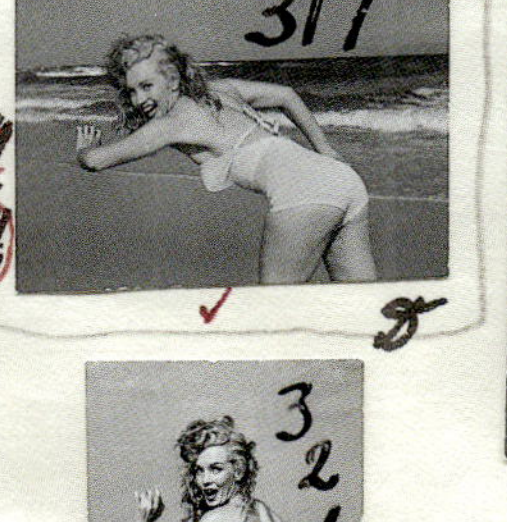

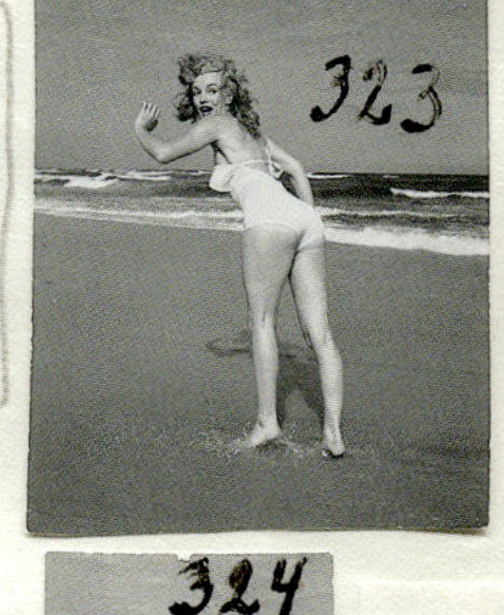

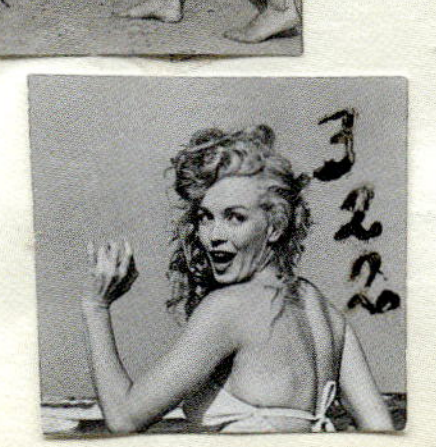

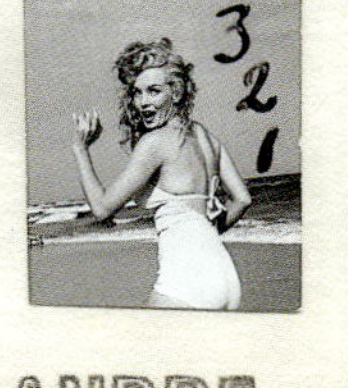

324

ANDRE DE DIENES

47.

1949

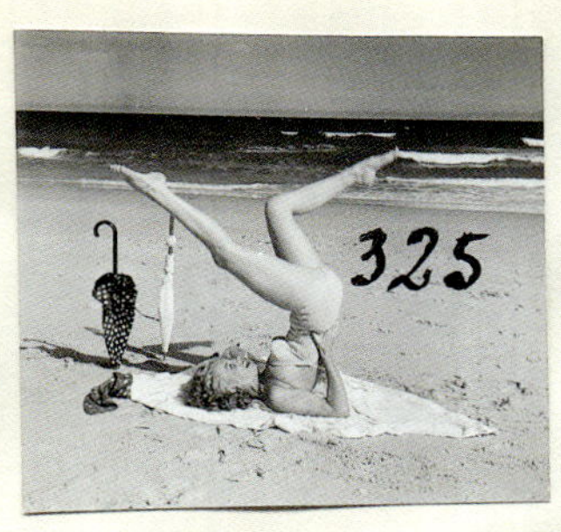

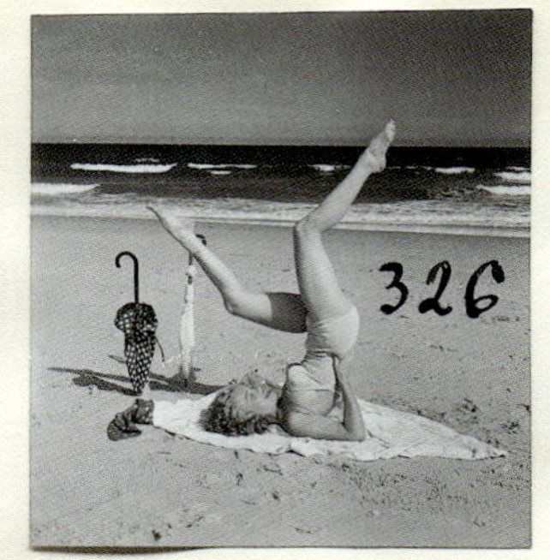

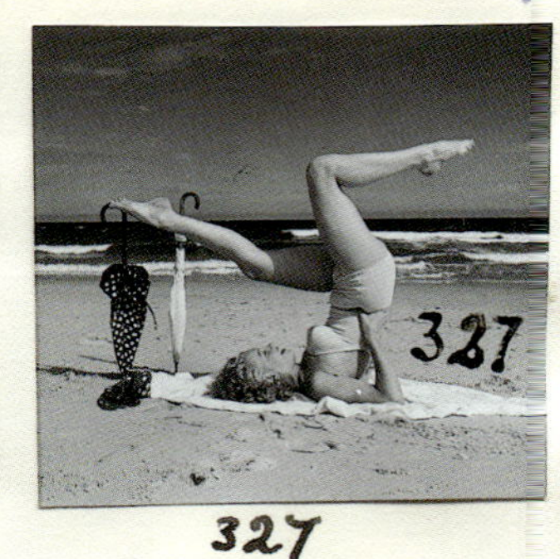

327

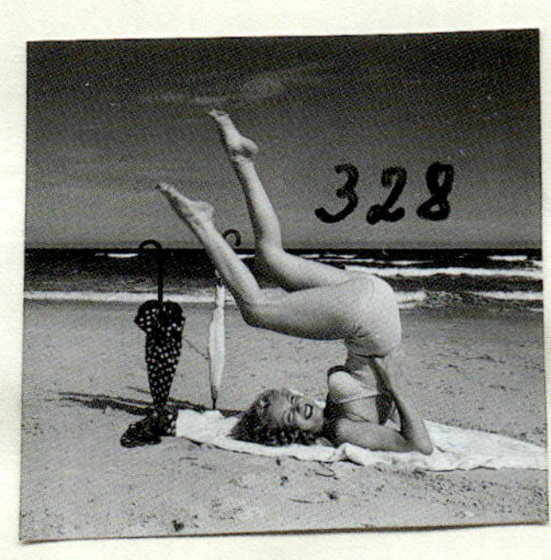

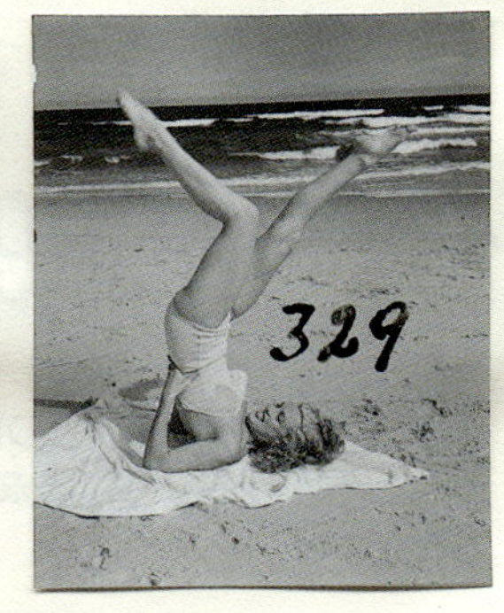

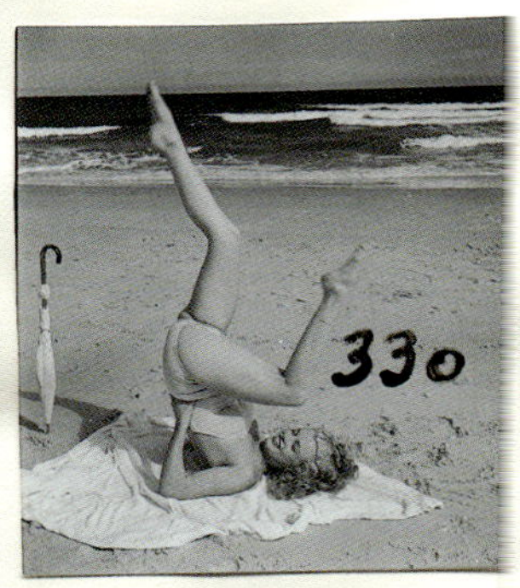

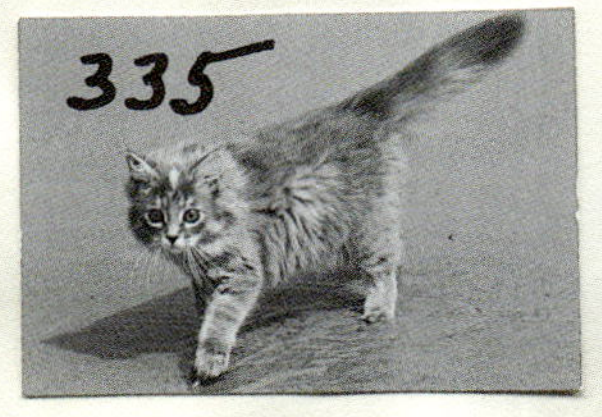

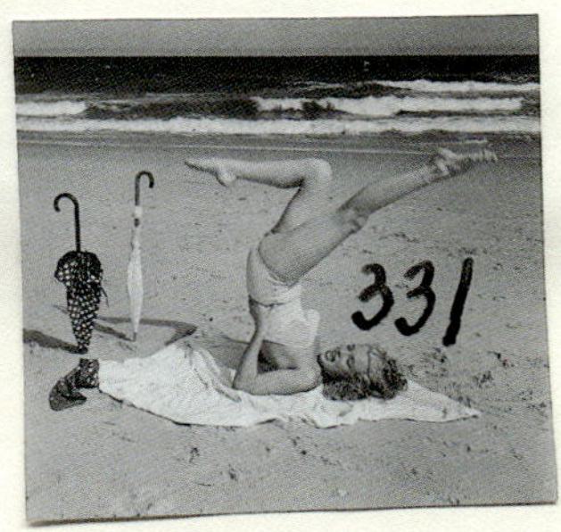

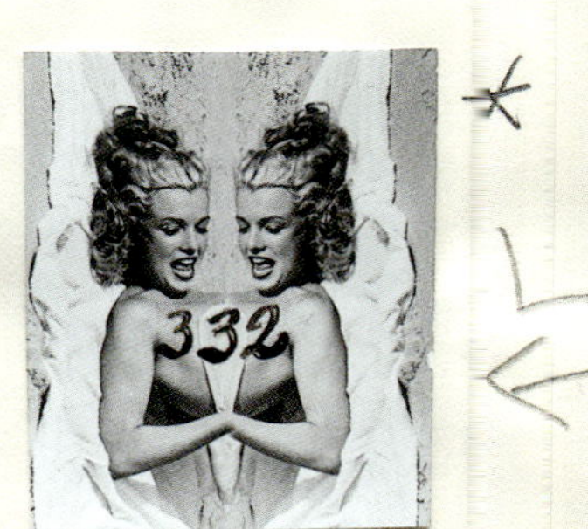

WE TOOK MY LITTLE CAT TO THE BEACH. MARILYN WAS DANCING, THE CAT WAS WATCHING US.

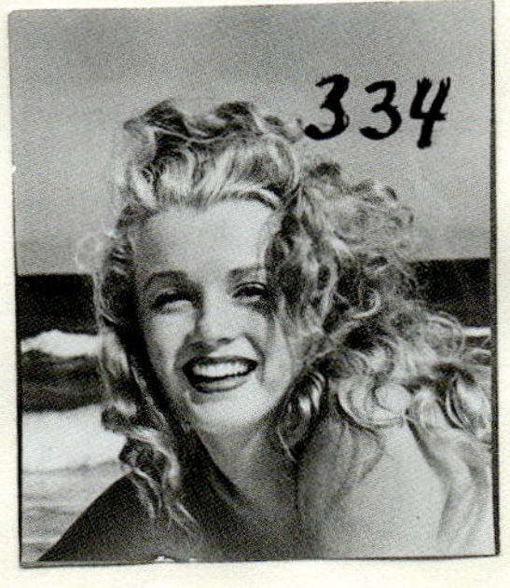

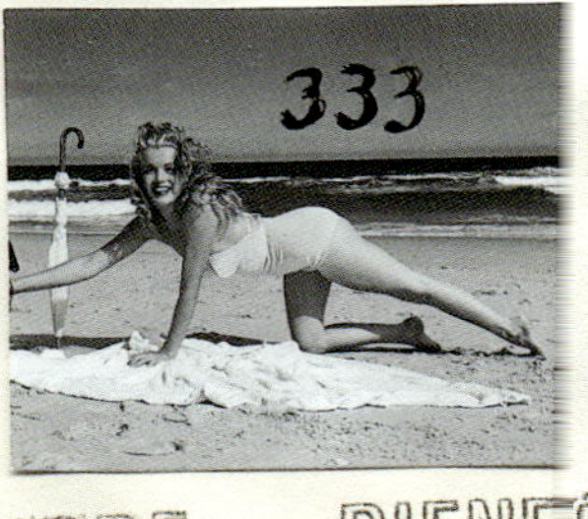

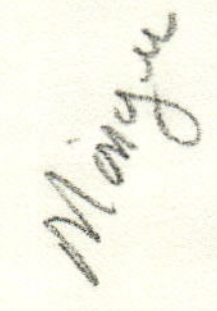

ANDRE DE DIENES
1401 SUNSET PLAZA DRIVE
HOLLYWOOD, CALIF. 900[illegible]9

1949

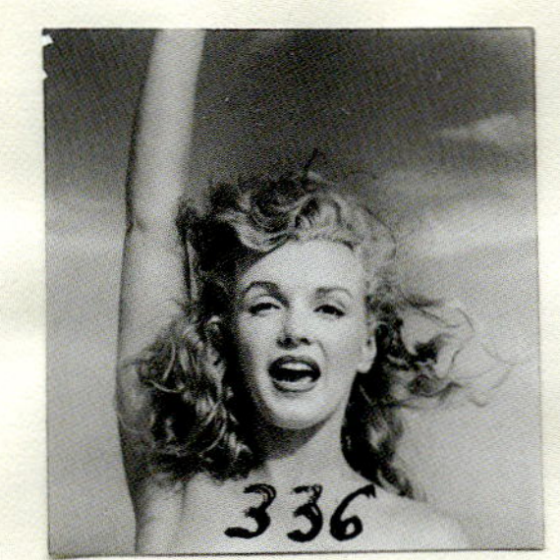

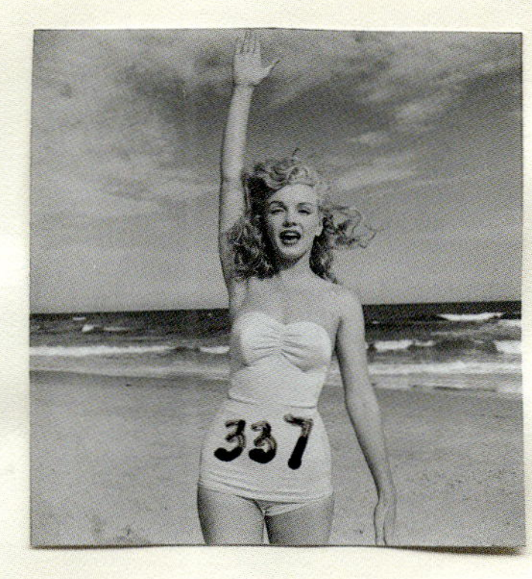

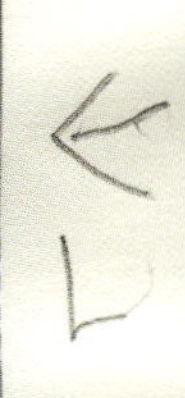

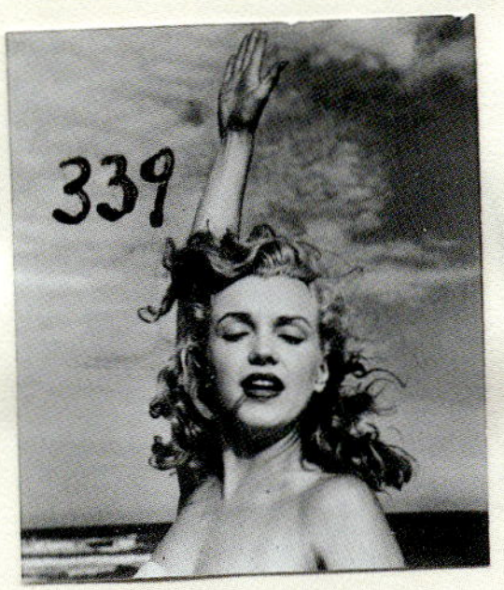

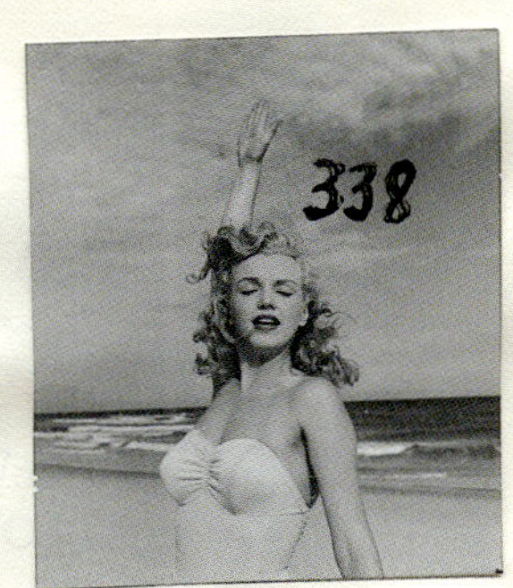

"EXALTATION"

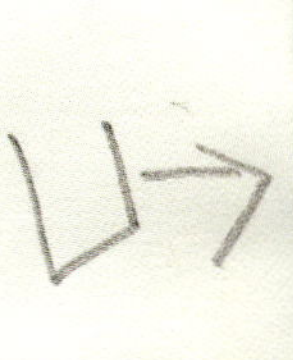

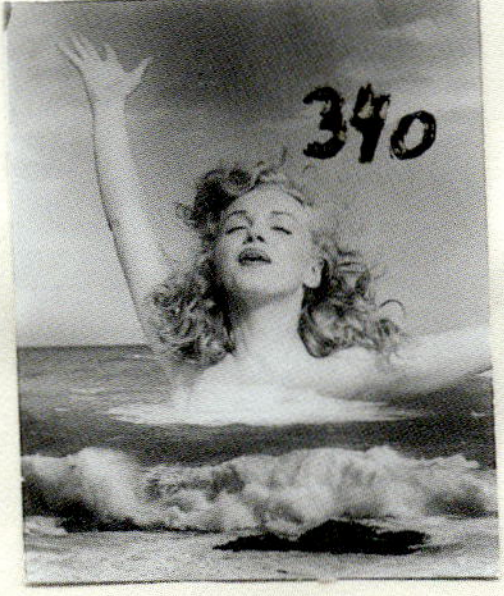

340

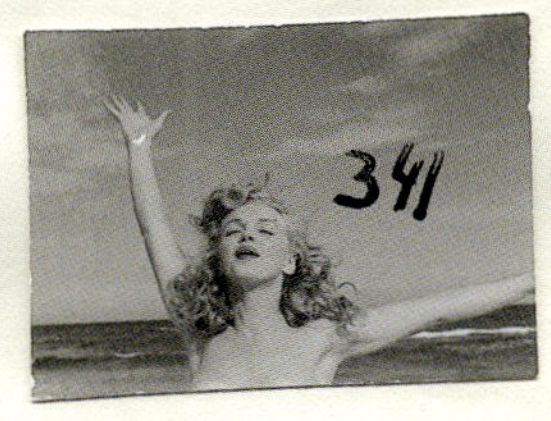

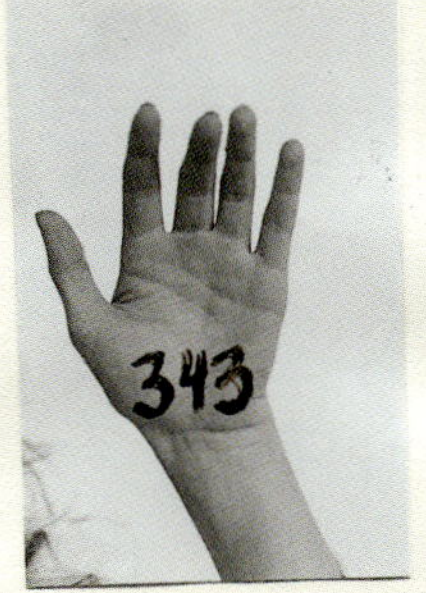

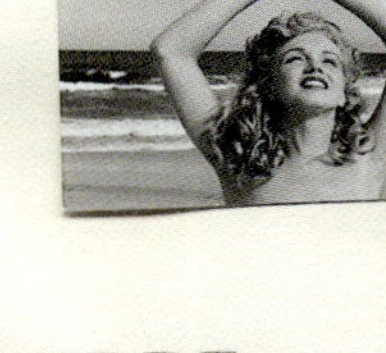

HER PALM

ANDRE de DIENES
1401 SUNSET PLAZA DRIVE
HOLLYWOOD, CALIF. 90069

1949

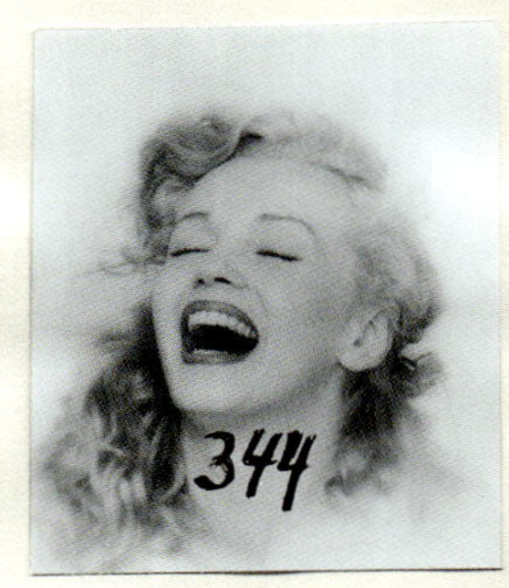

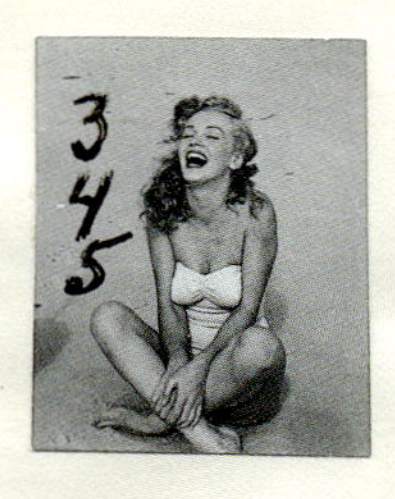

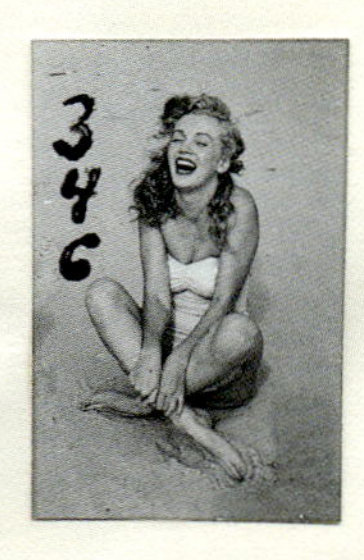

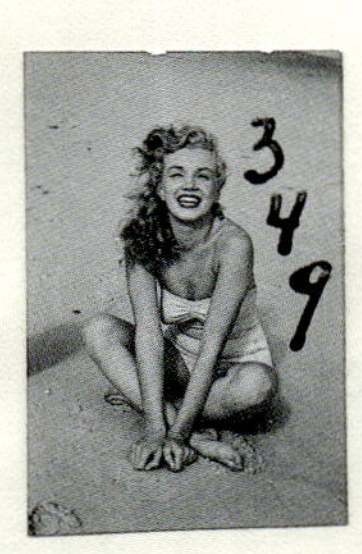

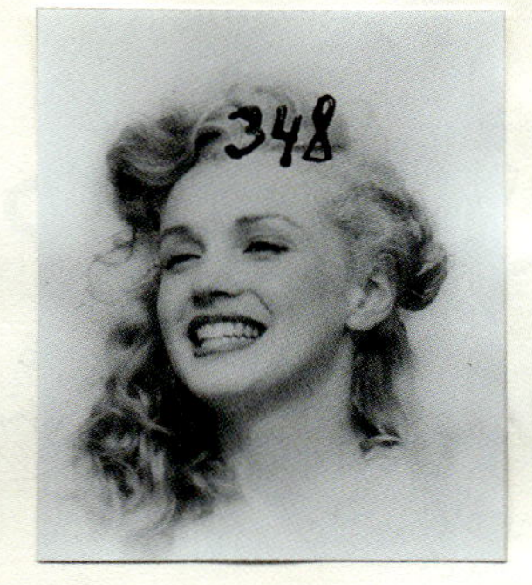

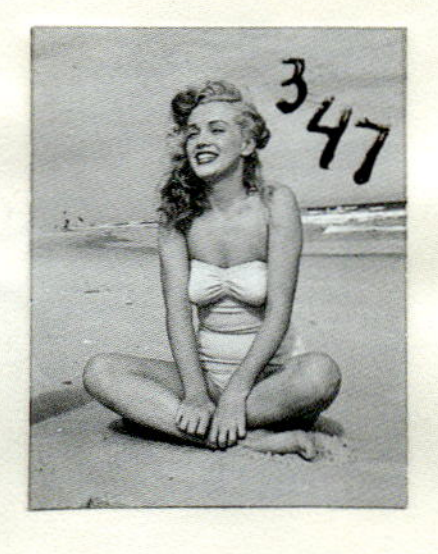

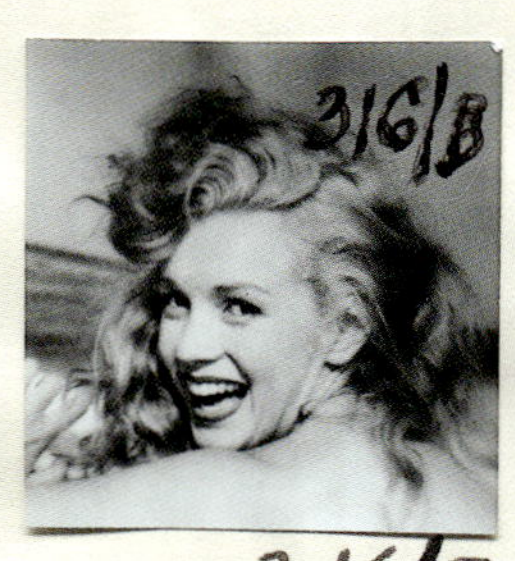

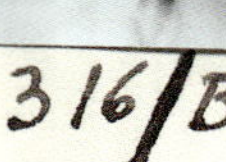

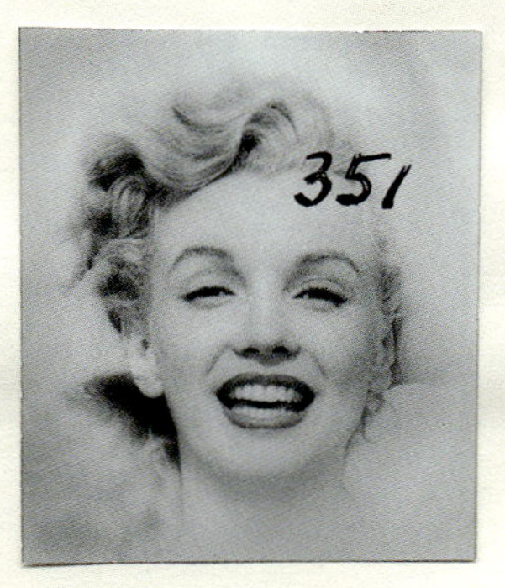

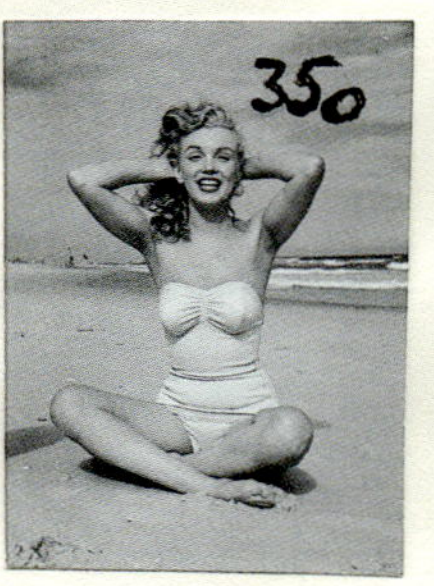

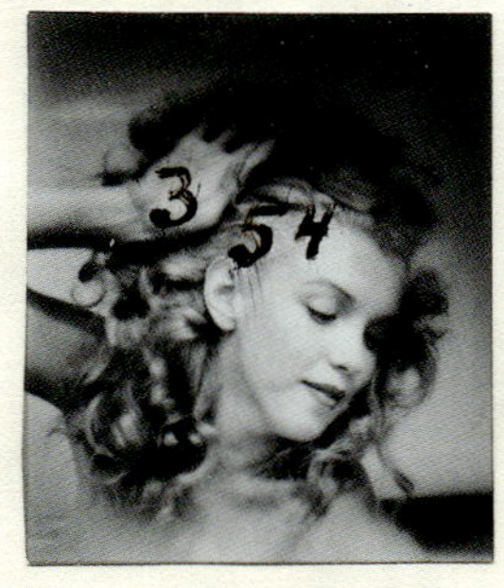

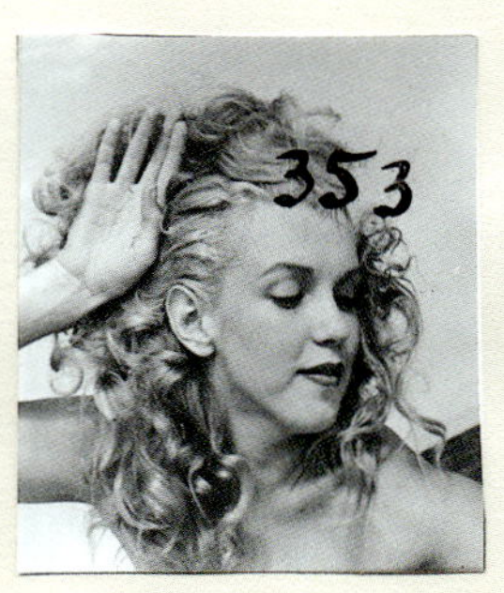

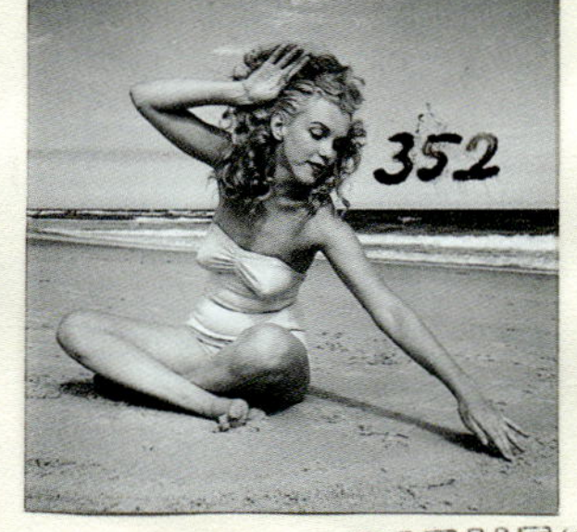

50

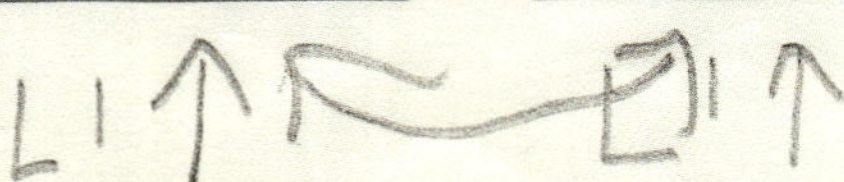

ANDRE DE DIENES
1401 SUNSET PLAZA DRIVE
HOLLYWOOD, CALIF. 90069

50

1949

L-1

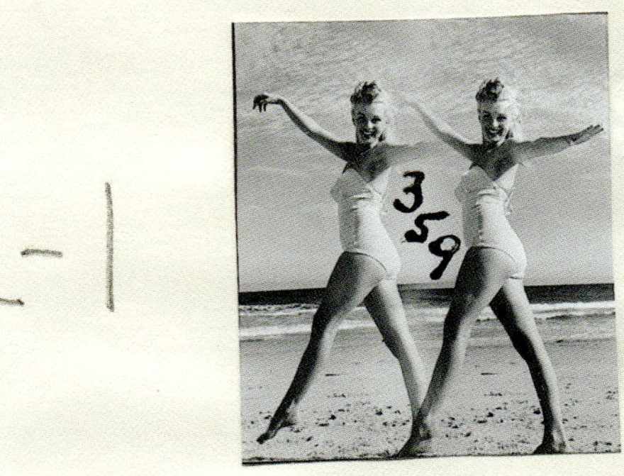

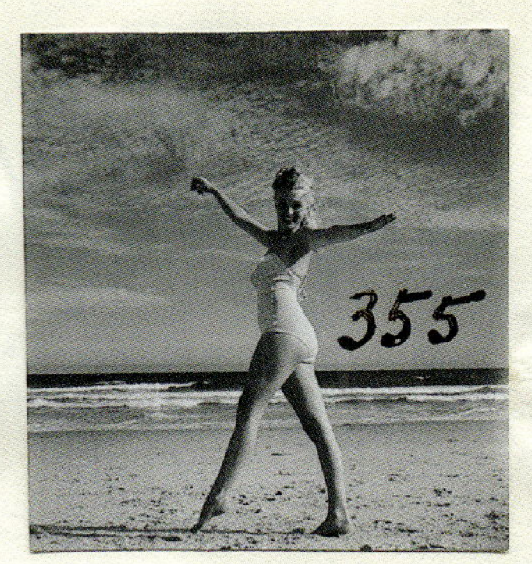

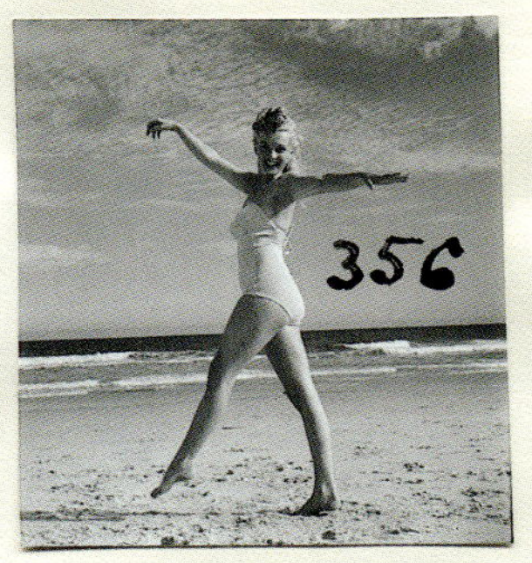

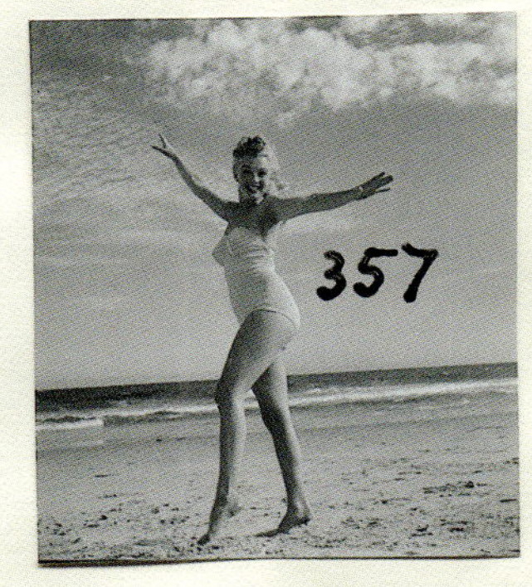

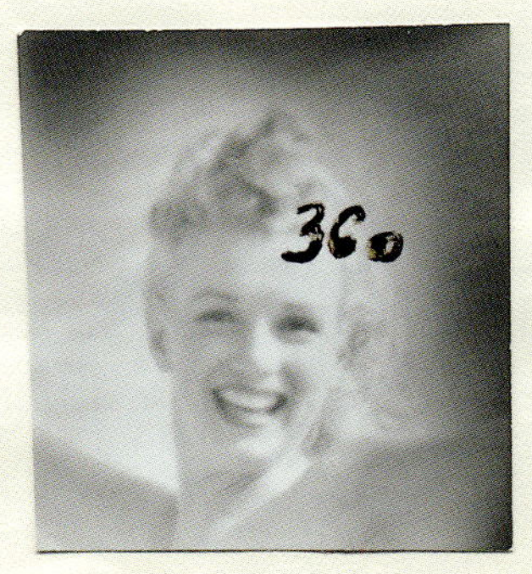

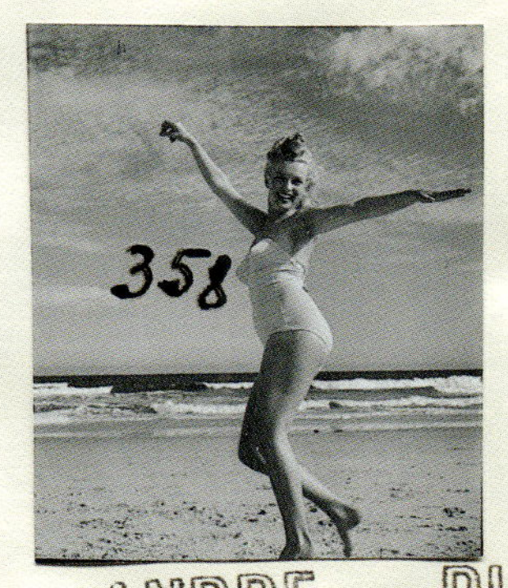

51

1949

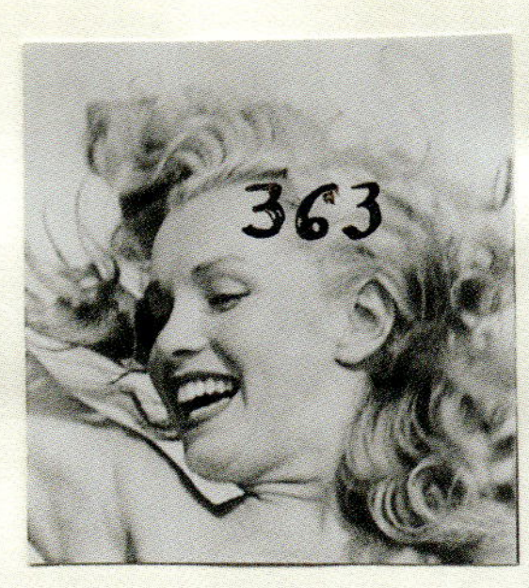

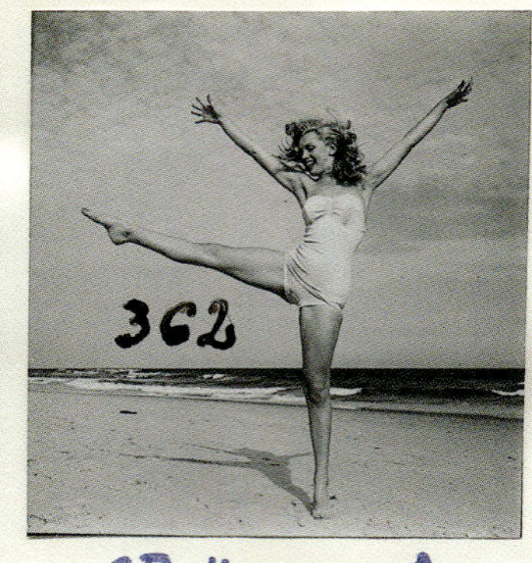

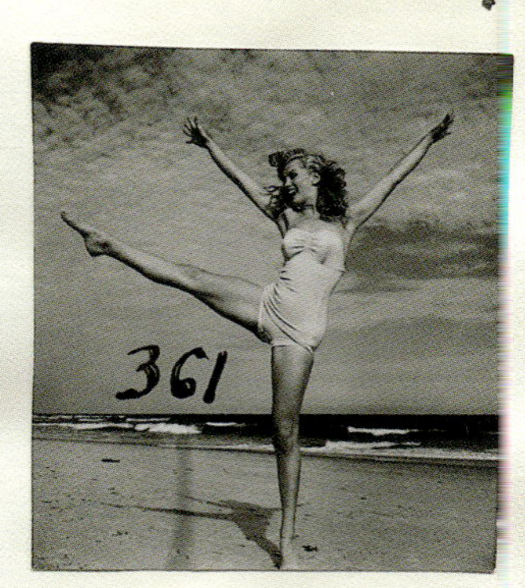

GR.H.

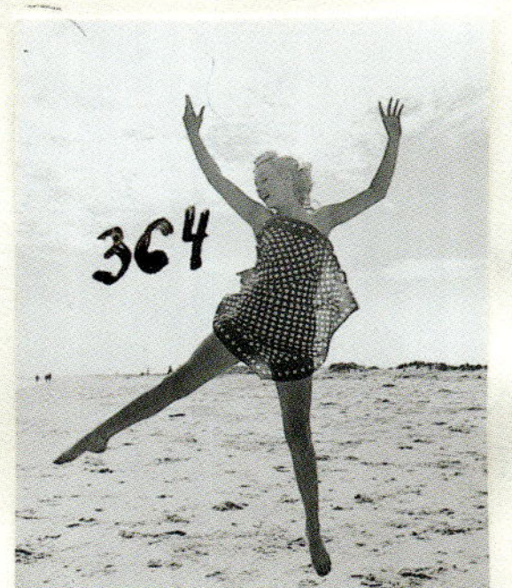

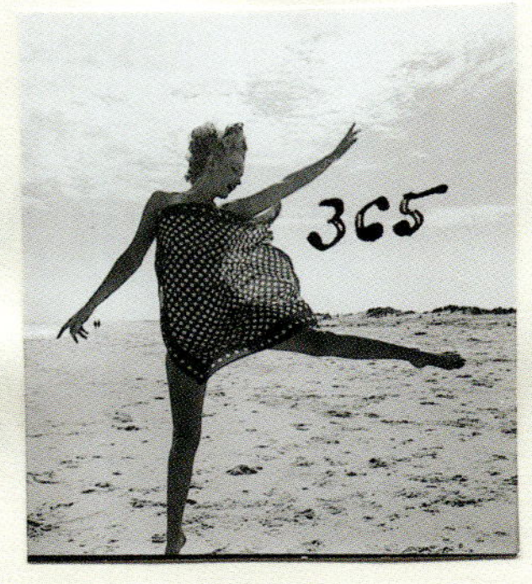

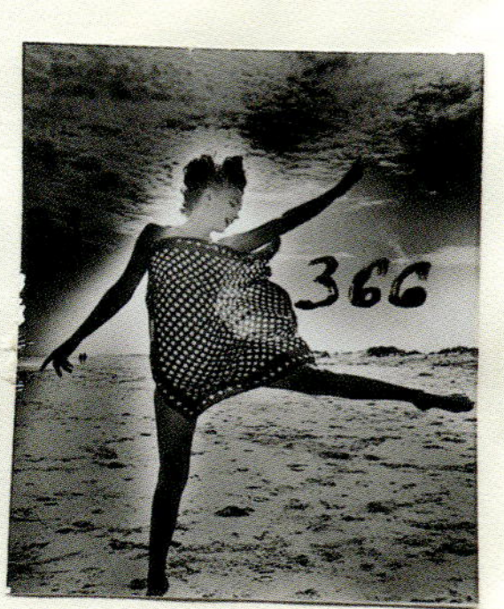

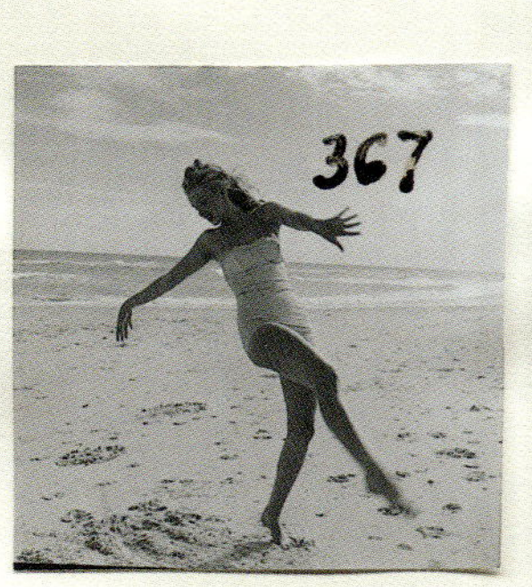

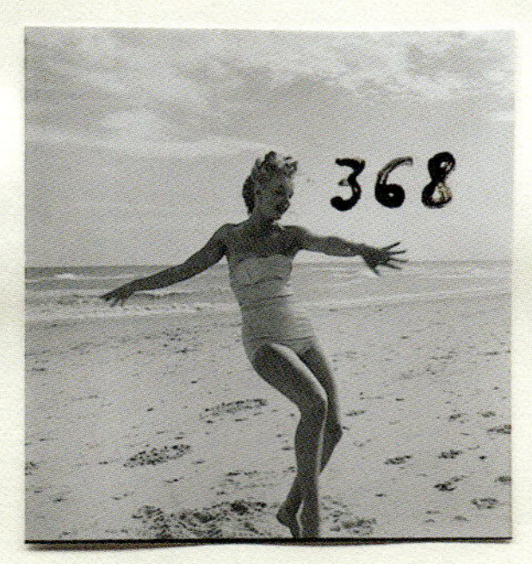

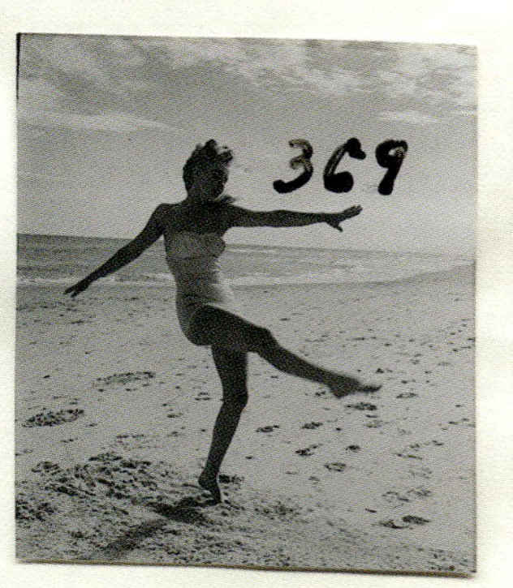

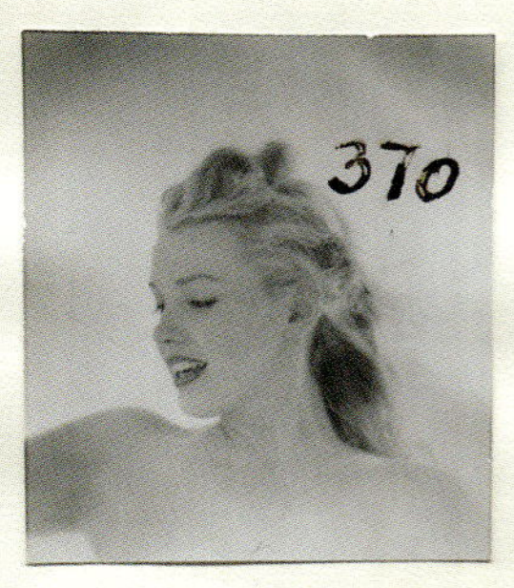

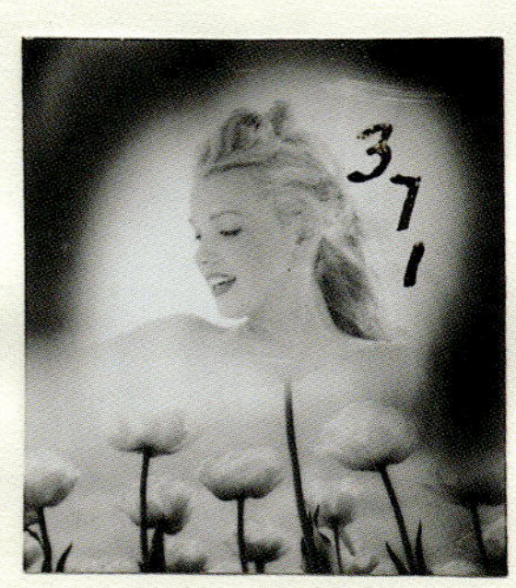

52

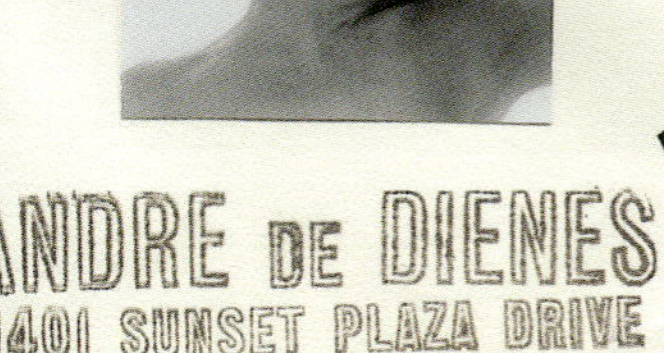

52

1949

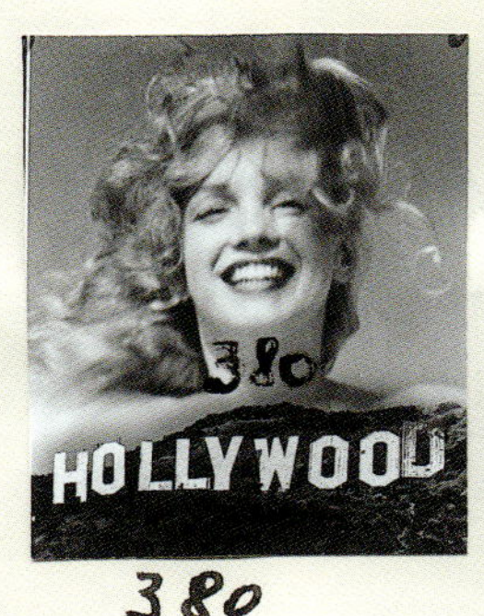

380

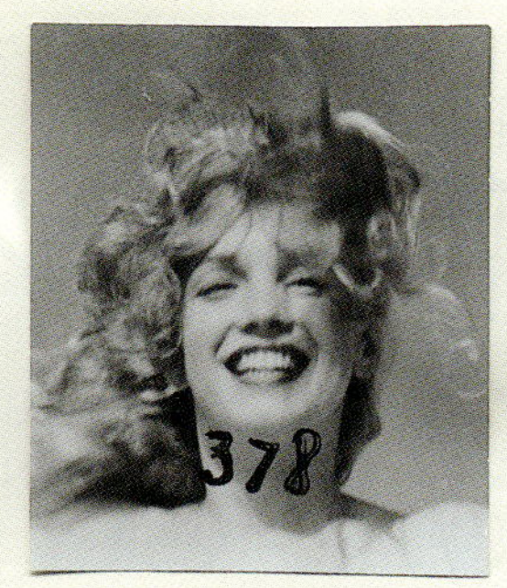

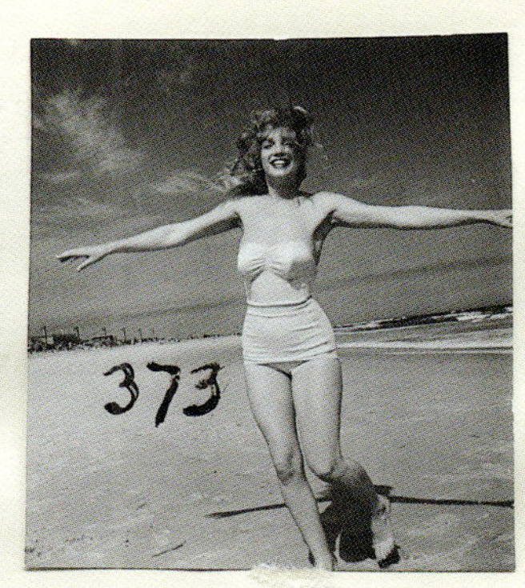

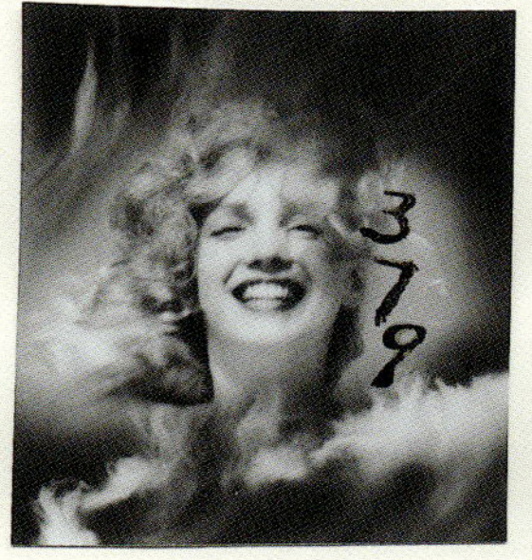

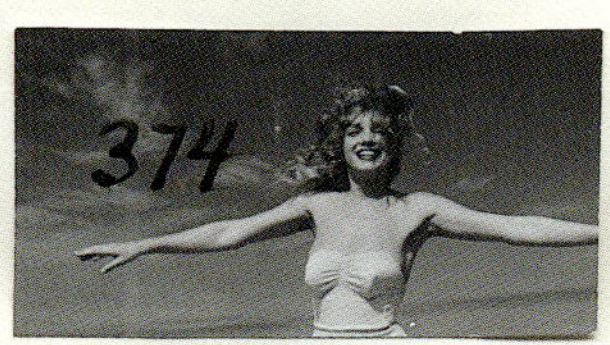

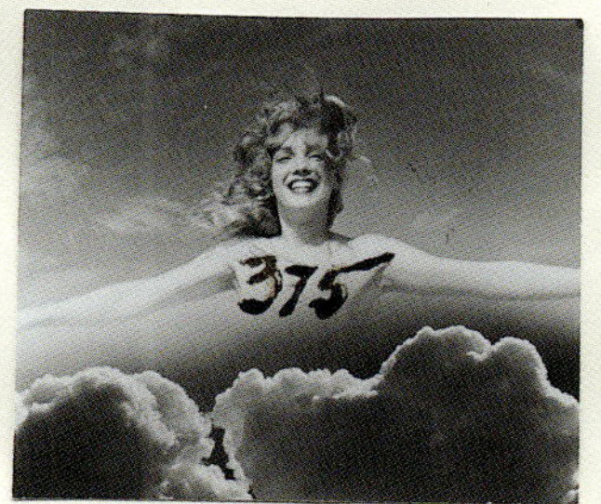

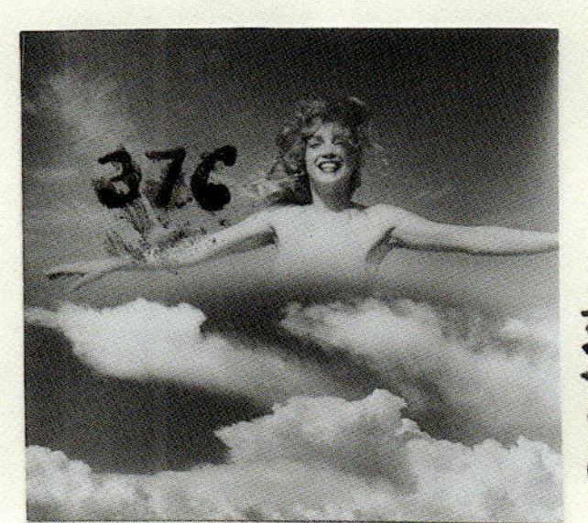

376

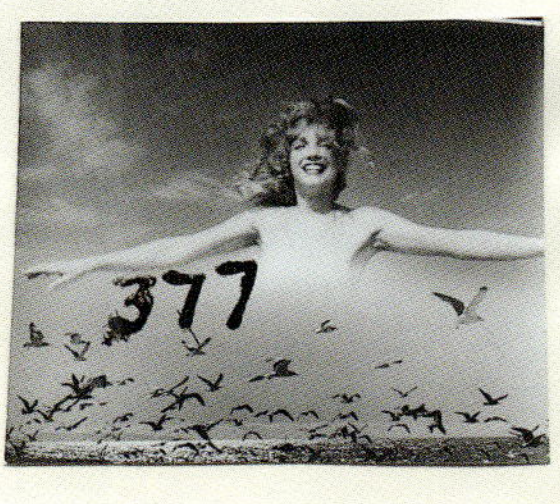

53

ANDRE de DIENES

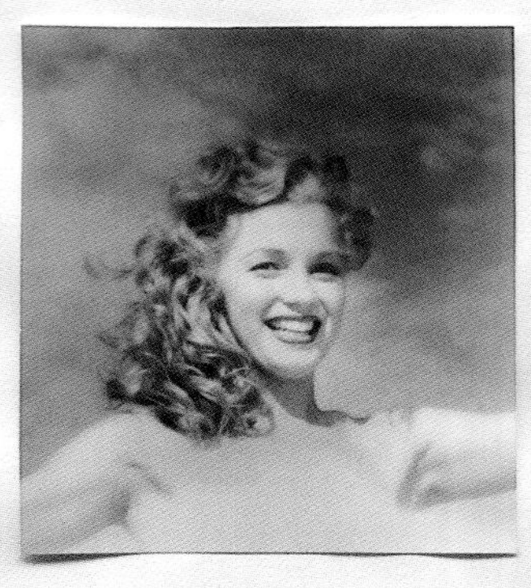
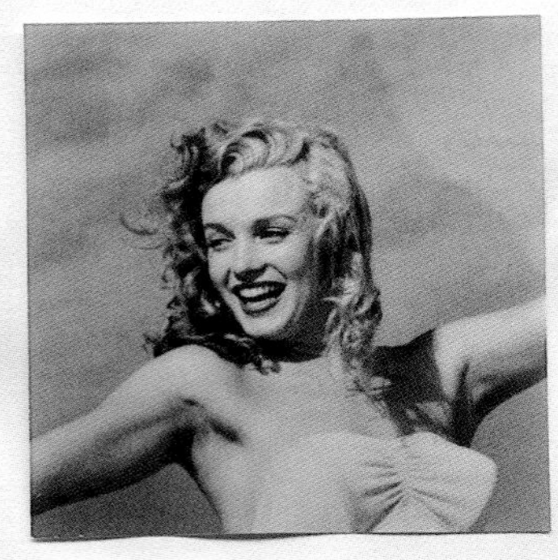
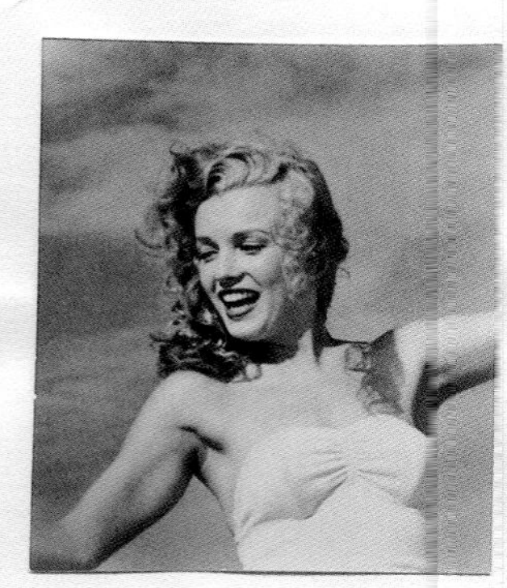
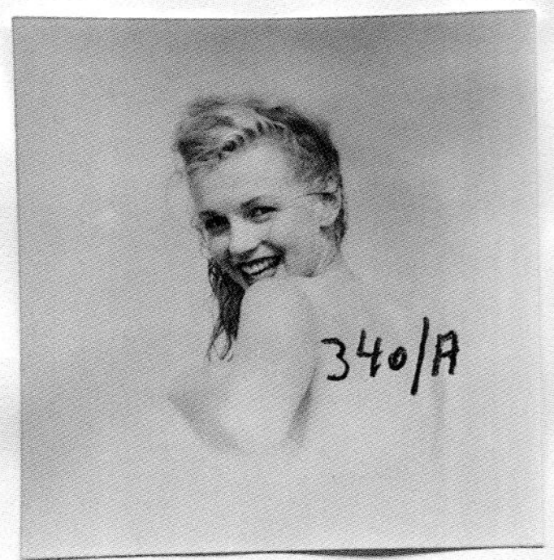

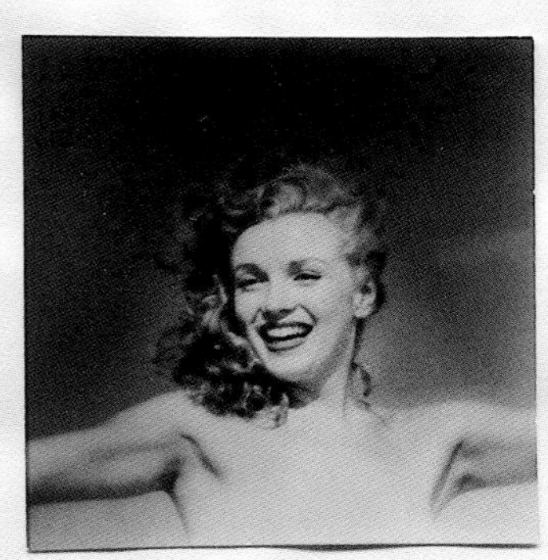
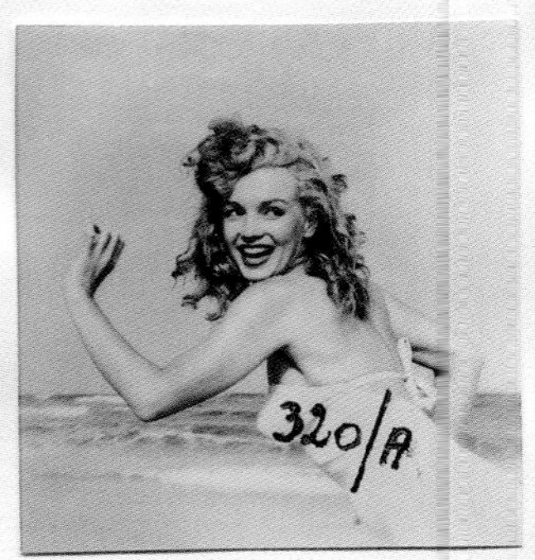

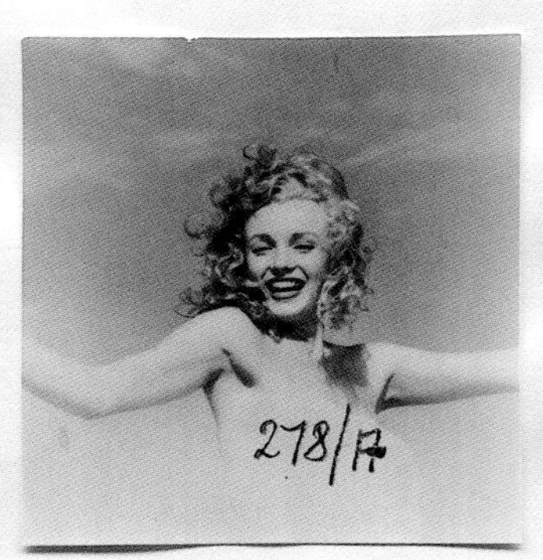

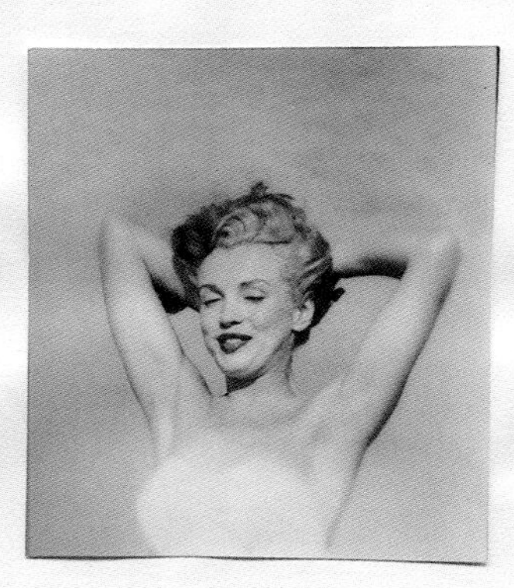
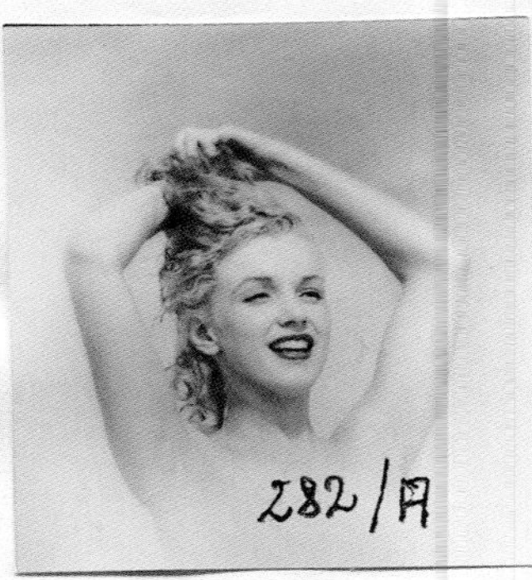

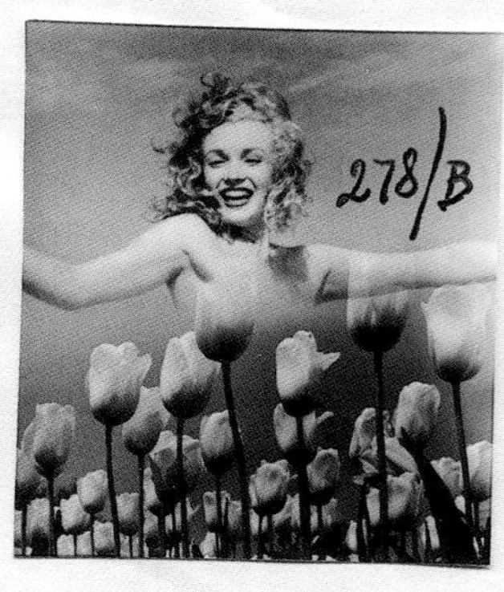

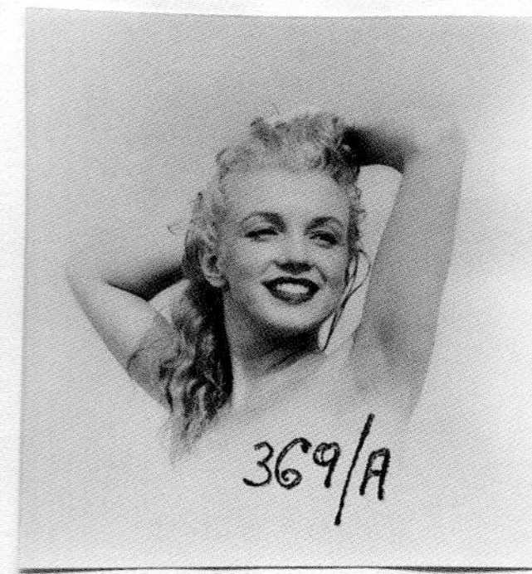

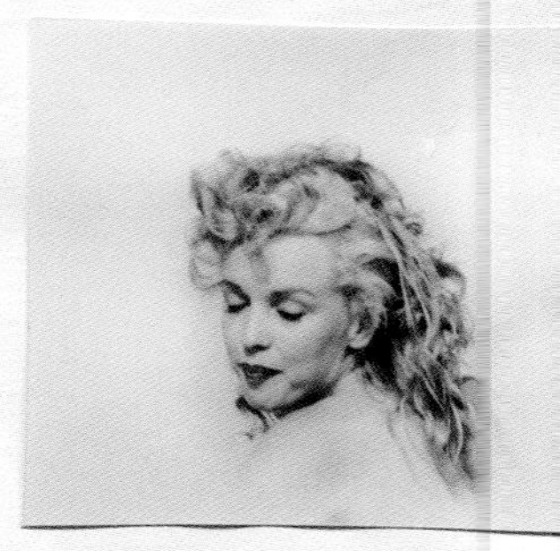

PAGE 53/A

ANDRE DE DIENES
1401 SUNSET PLAZA DRIVE
HOLLYWOOD, CALIF. 90069

1949

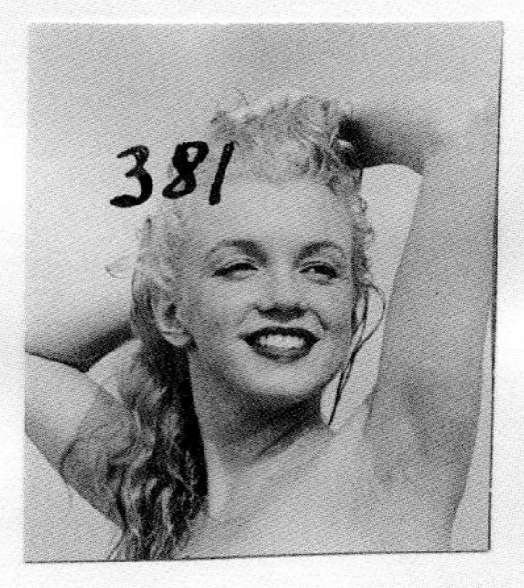

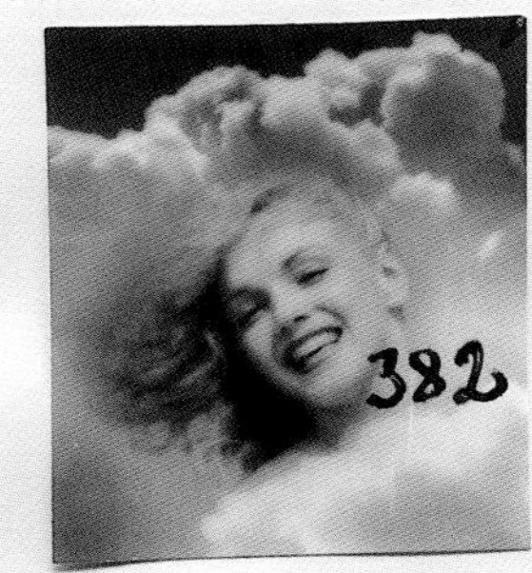

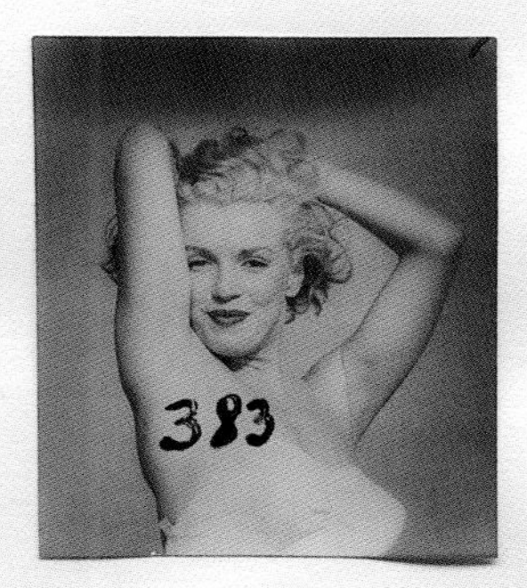

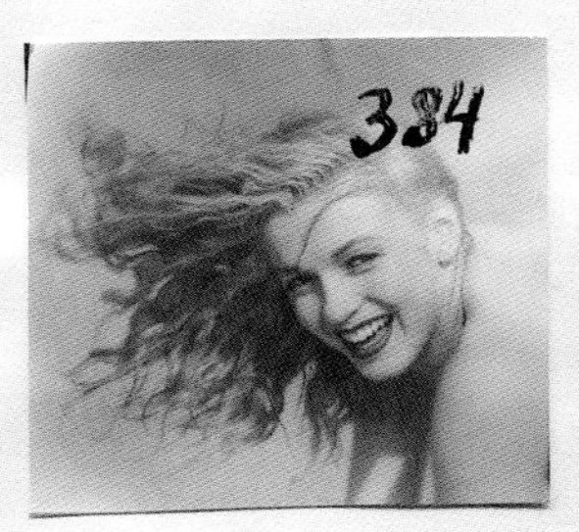

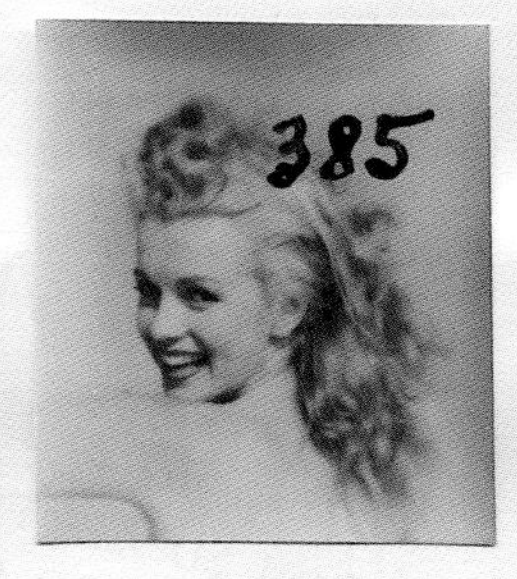

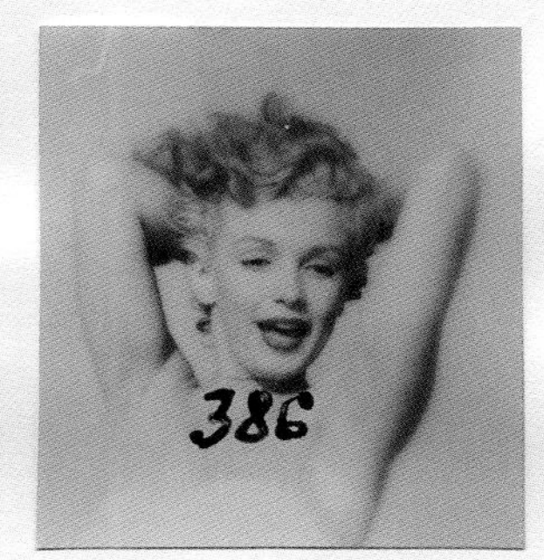

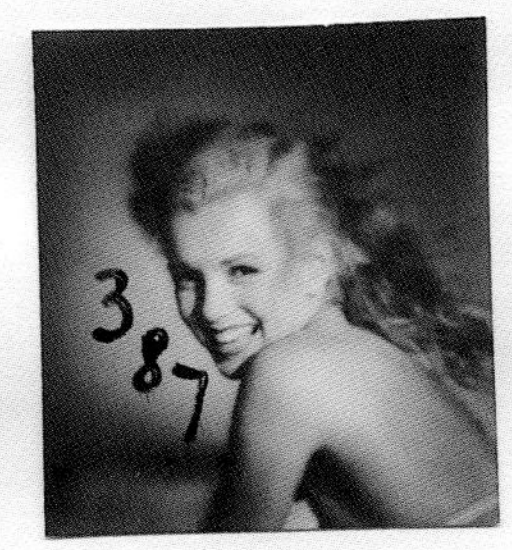

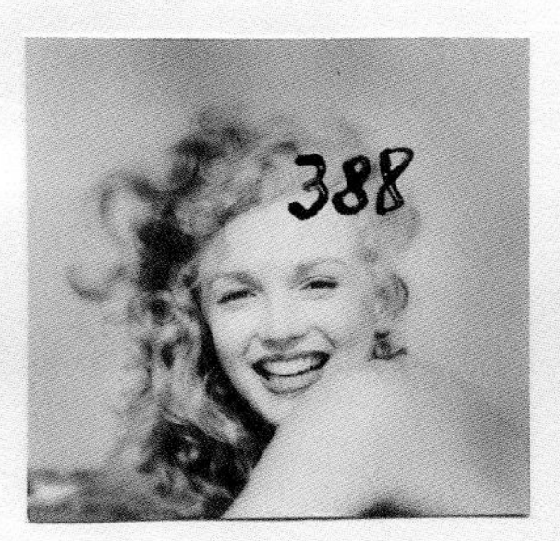

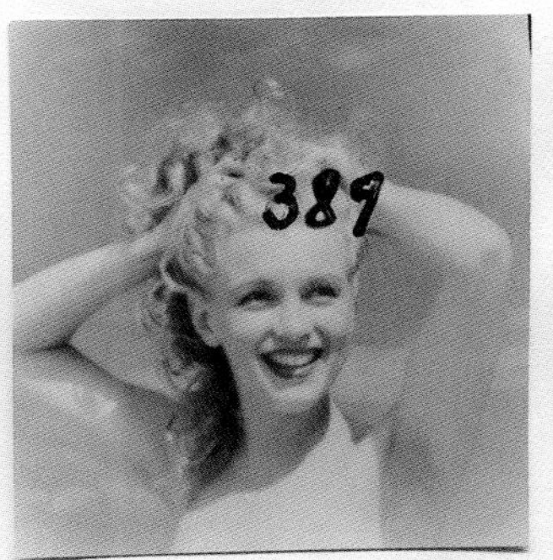

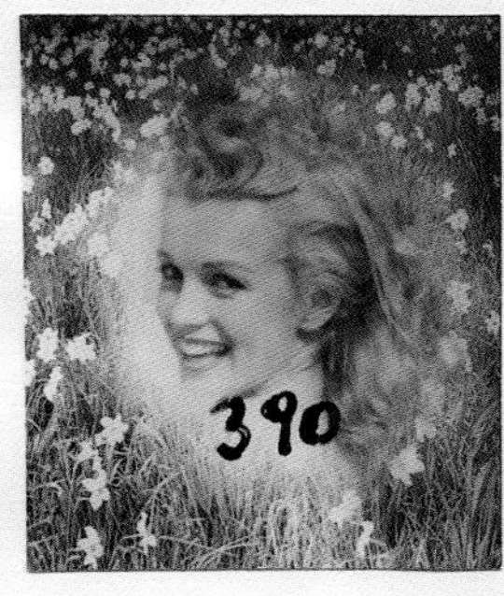

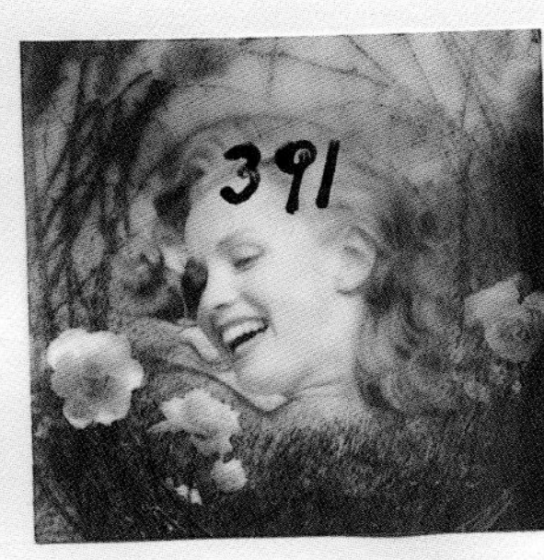

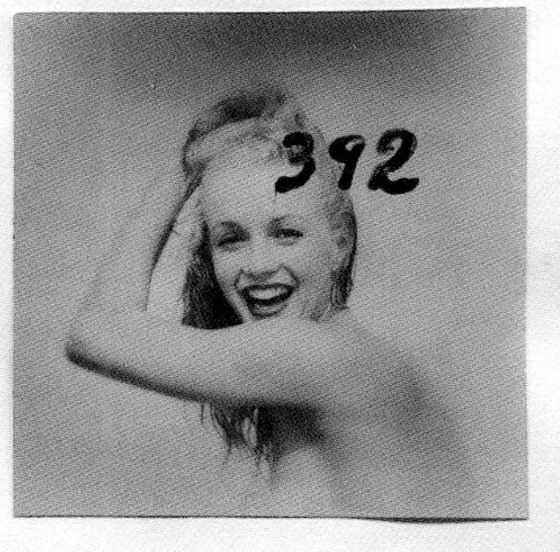

54

ANDRE DE DIENES
1401 SUNSET PLAZA DRIVE

L ↓ 1949

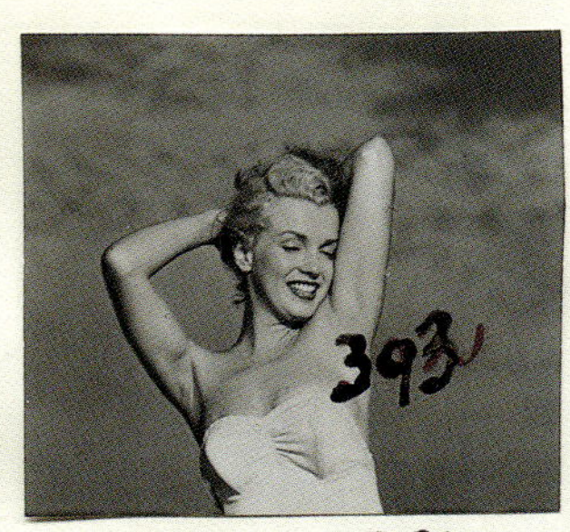

393

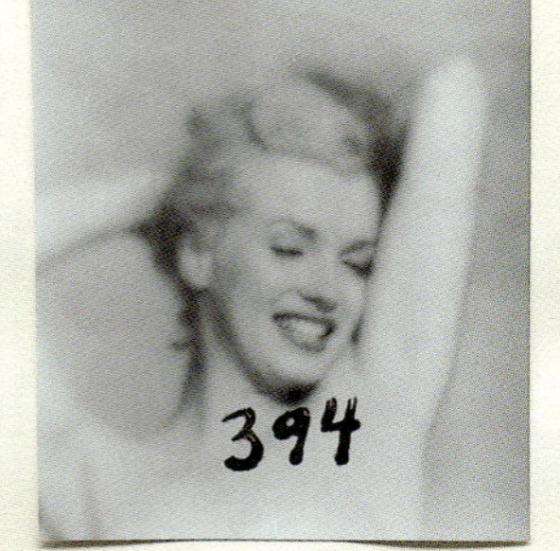

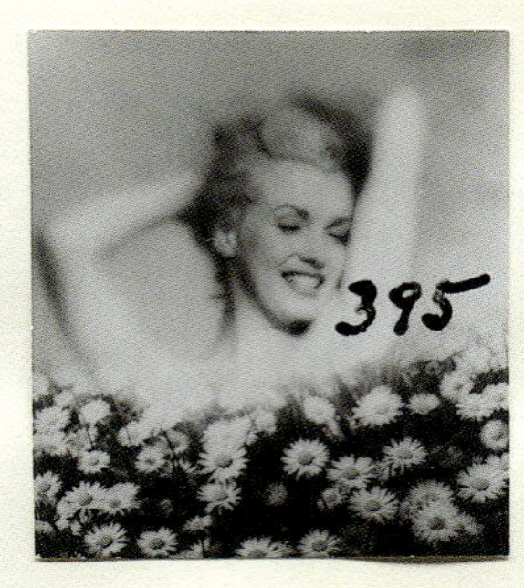

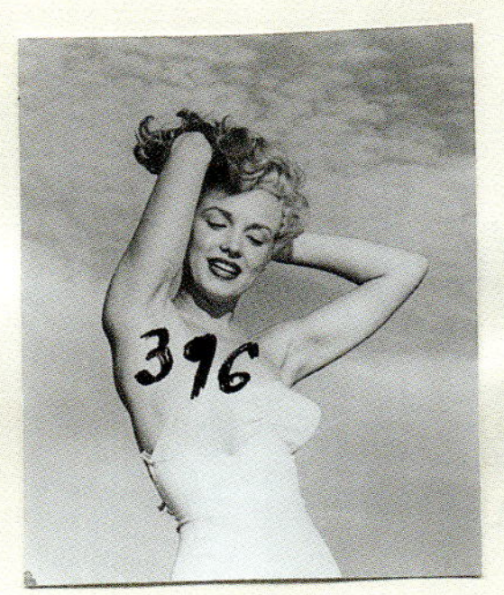

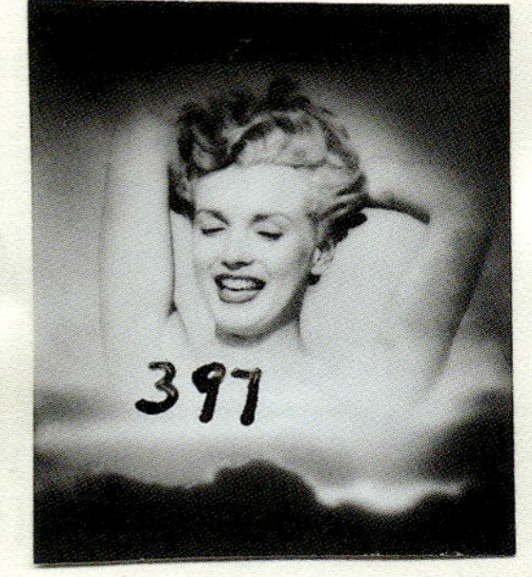

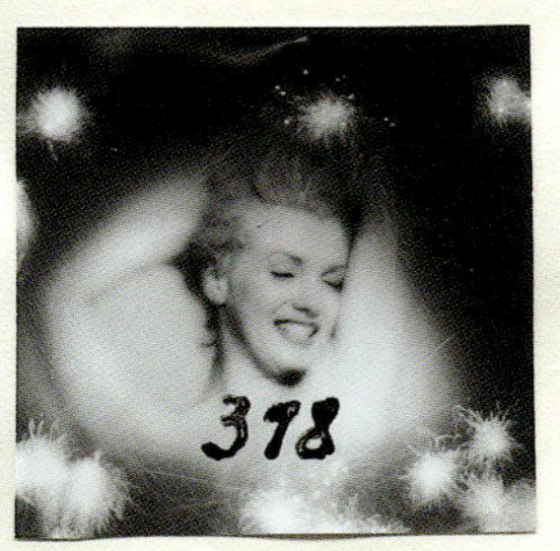

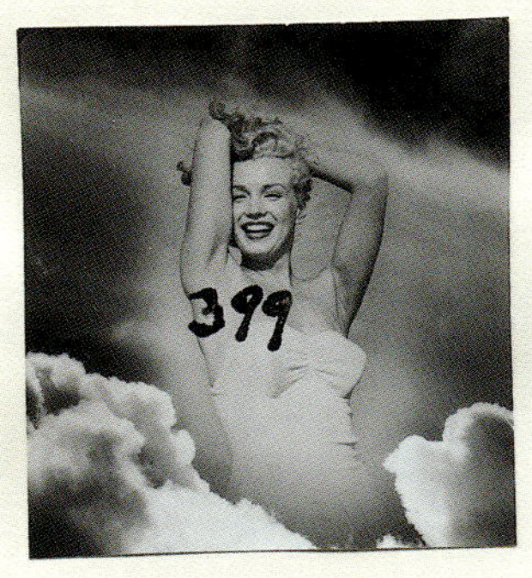

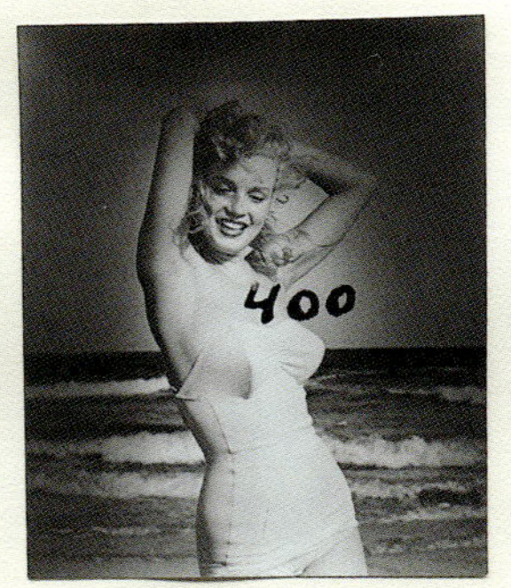

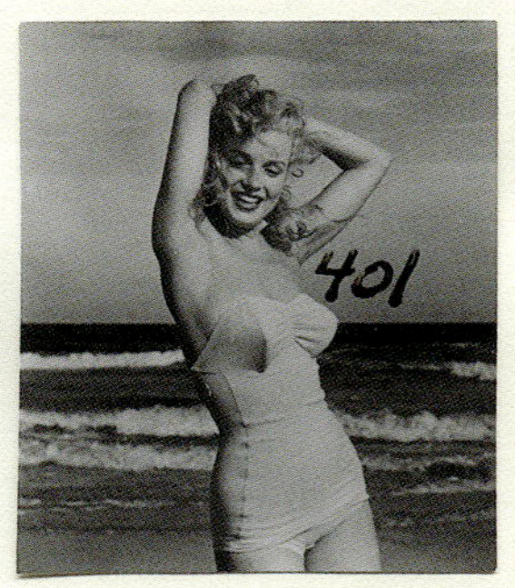

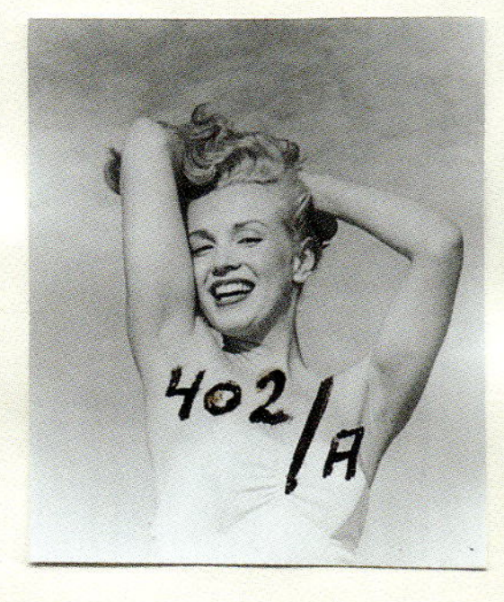

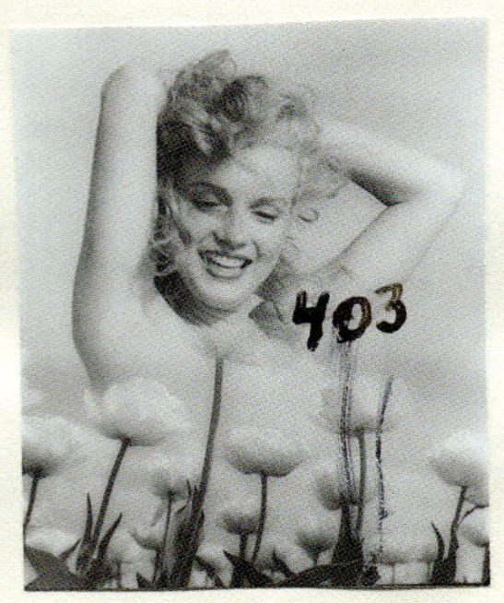

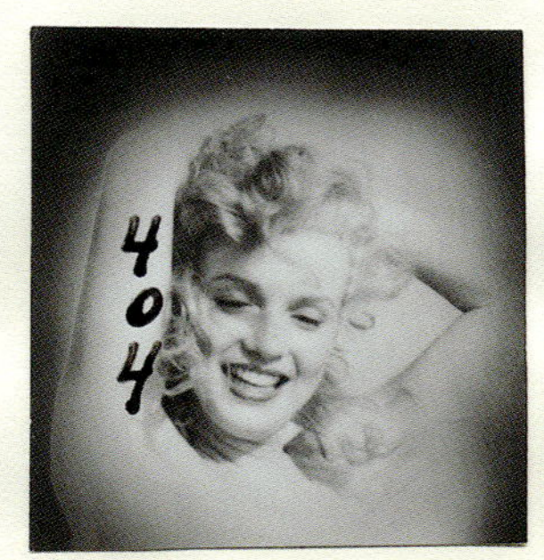

55

ANDRE de DIENES
1401 SUNSET PLAZA DRIVE
HOLLYWOOD, CALIF. 90069

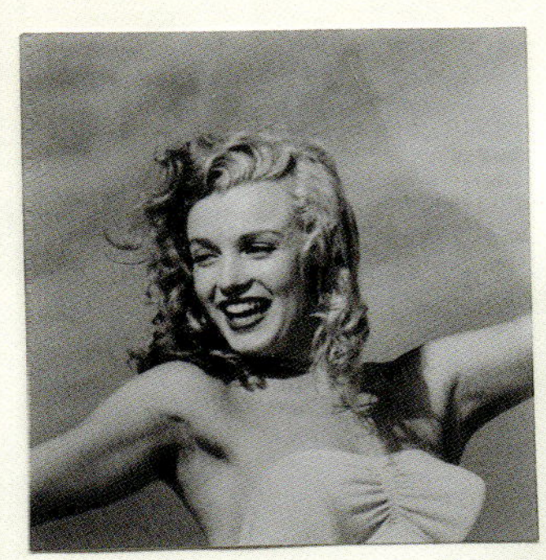

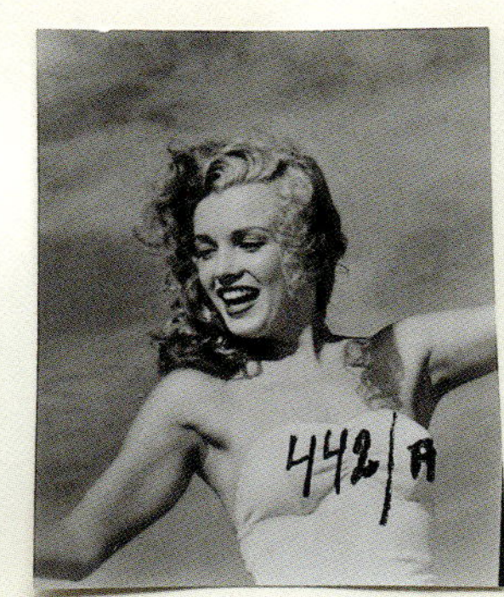

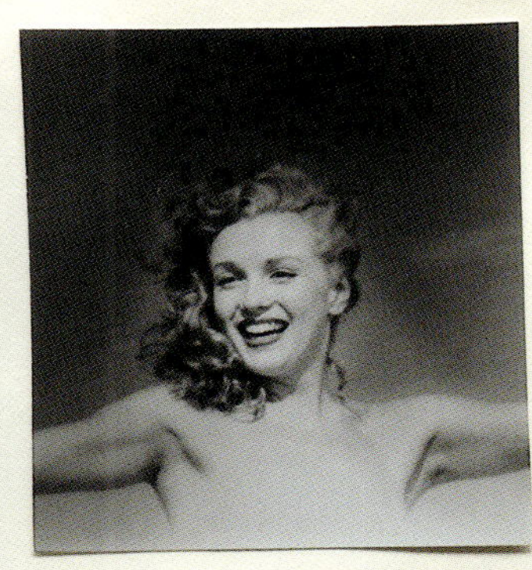

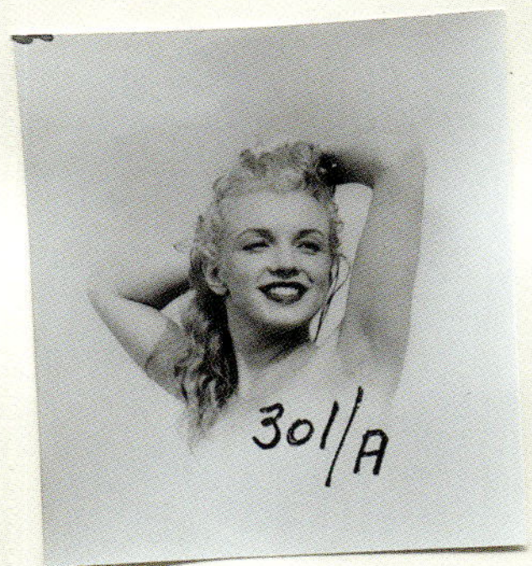

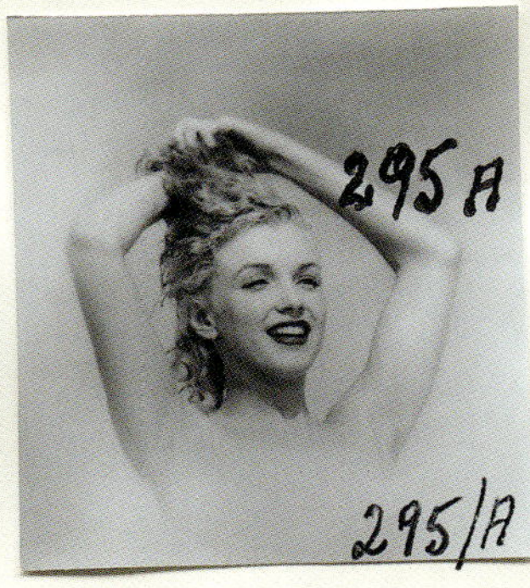

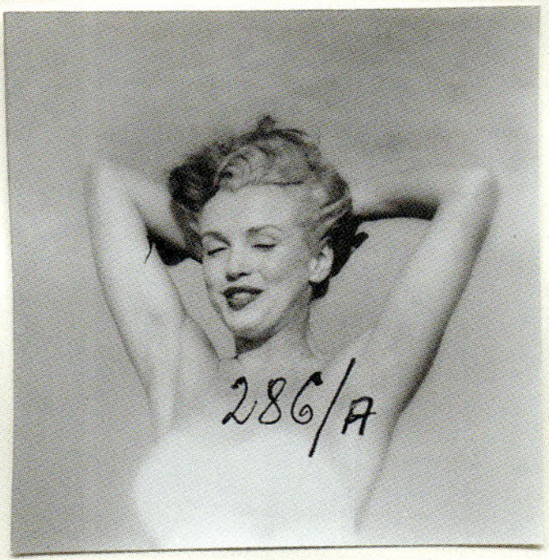

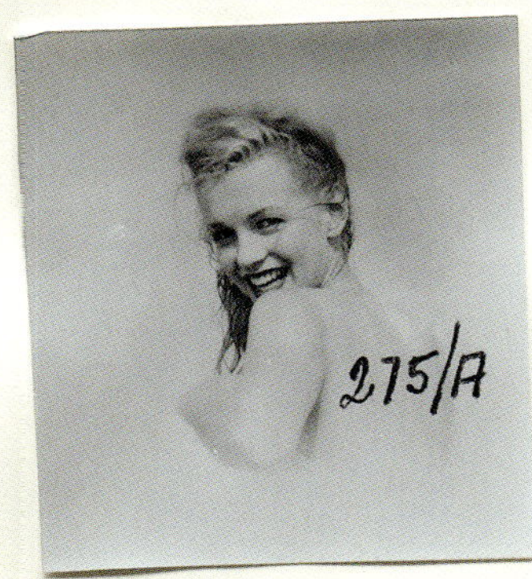

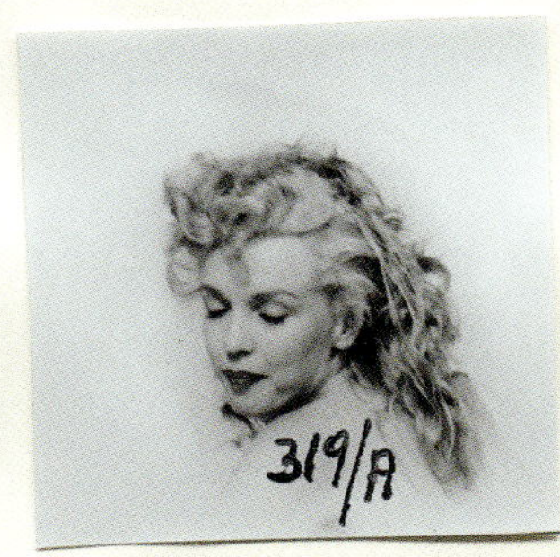

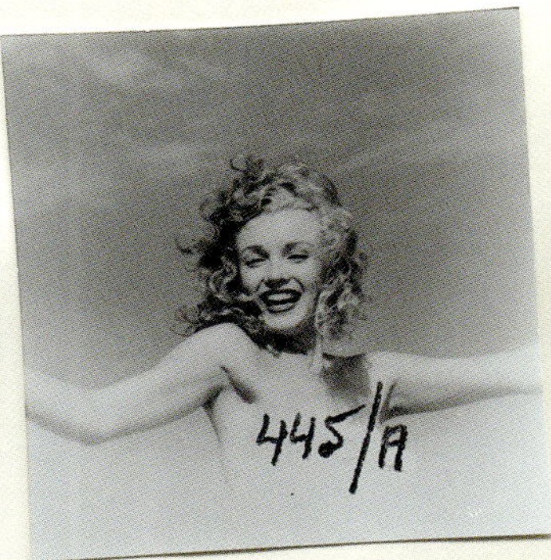

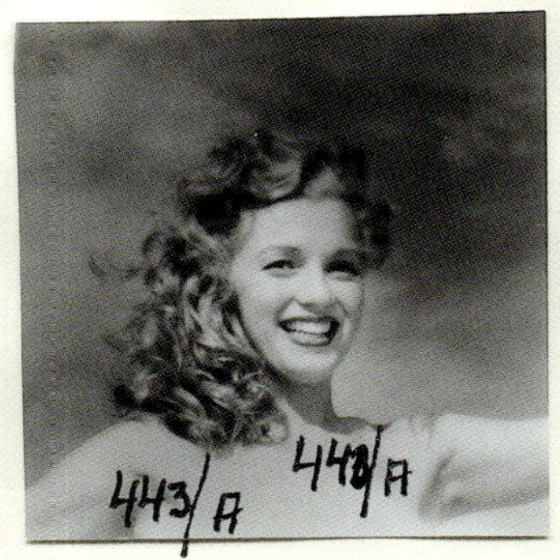

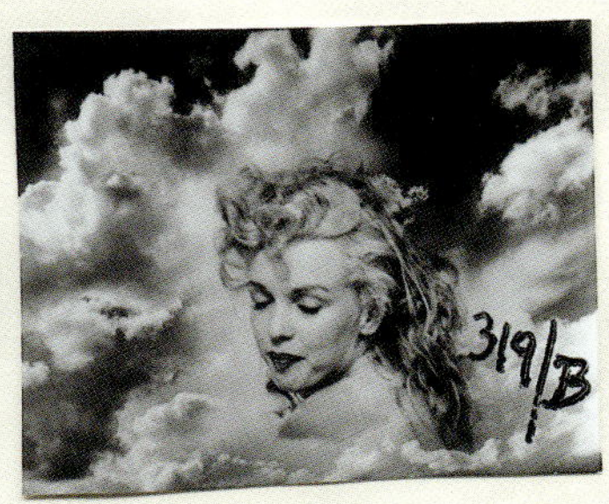

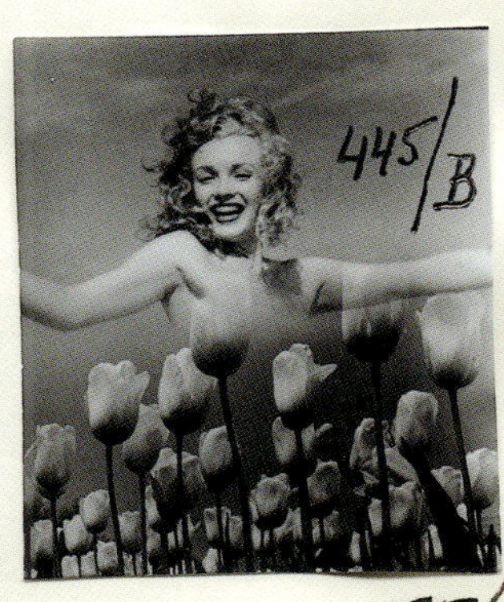

ANDRE de DIENES
1401 SUNSET PLAZA DRIVE
HOLLYWOOD, CALIF. 90069

Page 55/A

1949

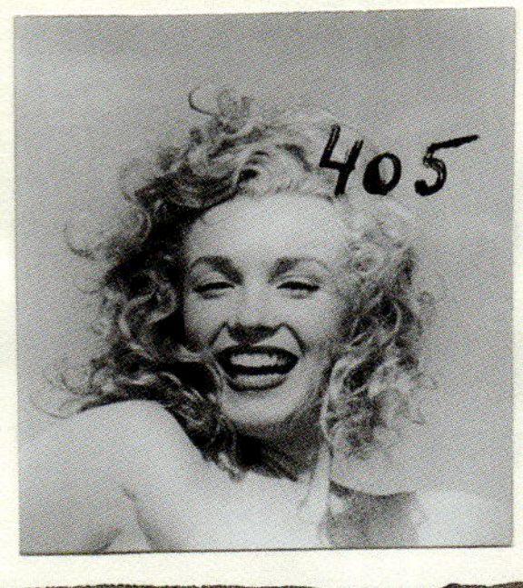

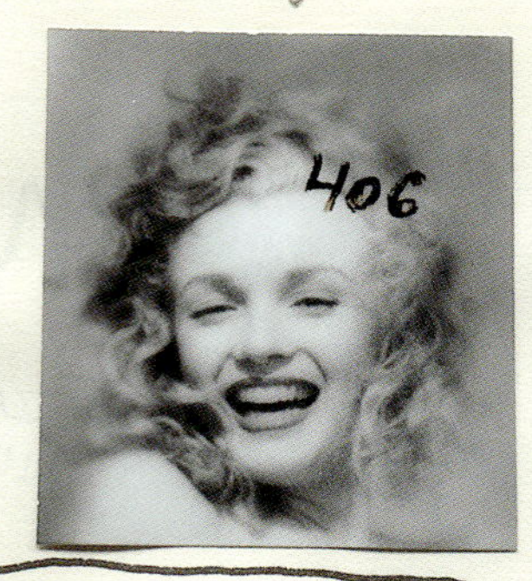

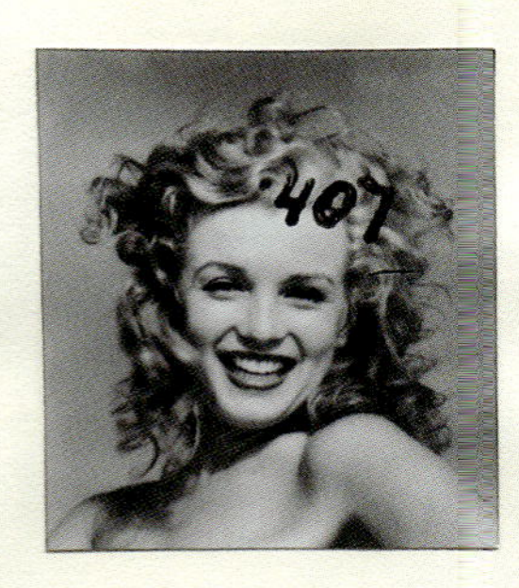

"GEMINI" (HER ZODIAC)

QUICK THINKER, STIMULATING, GENIAL, ETC.

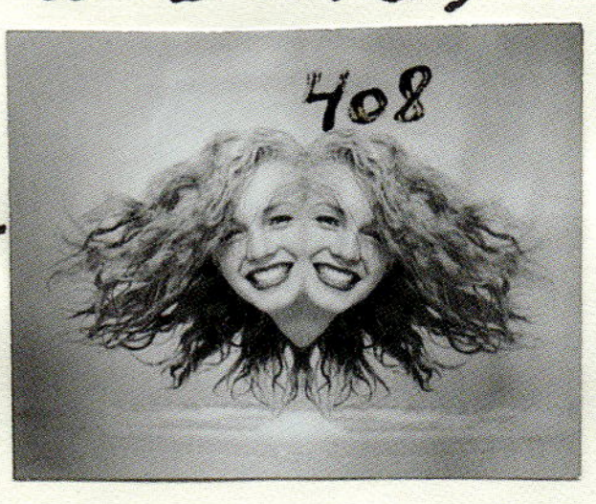

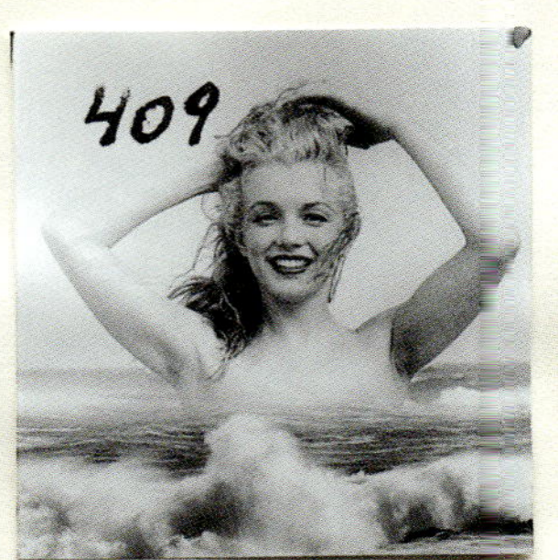

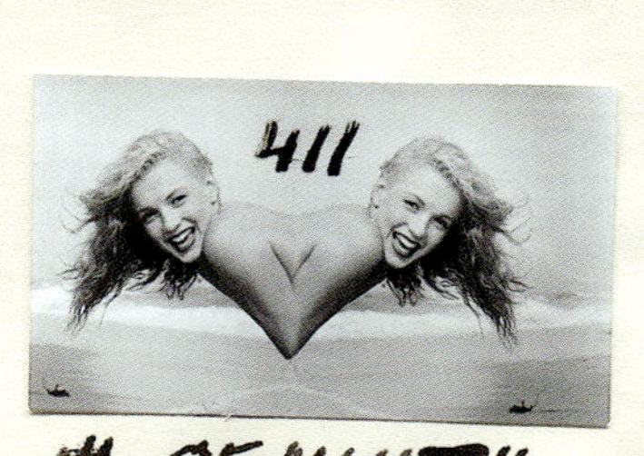

"GEMINI"

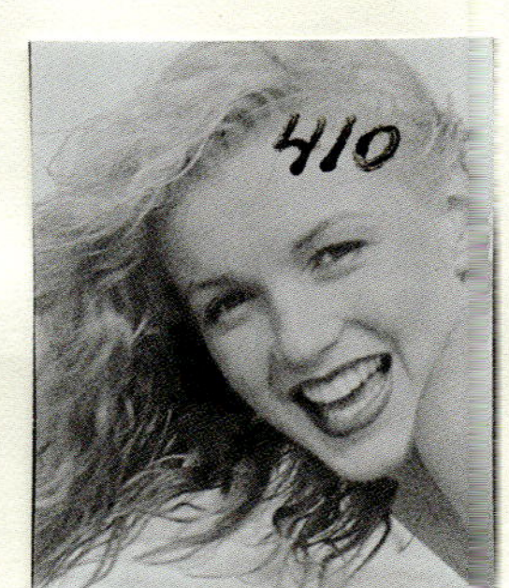

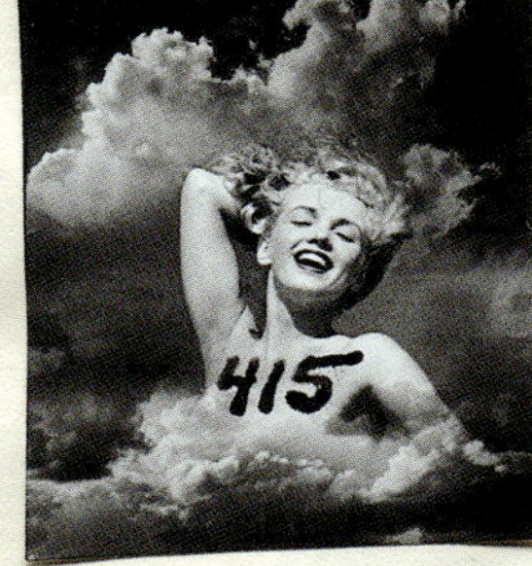

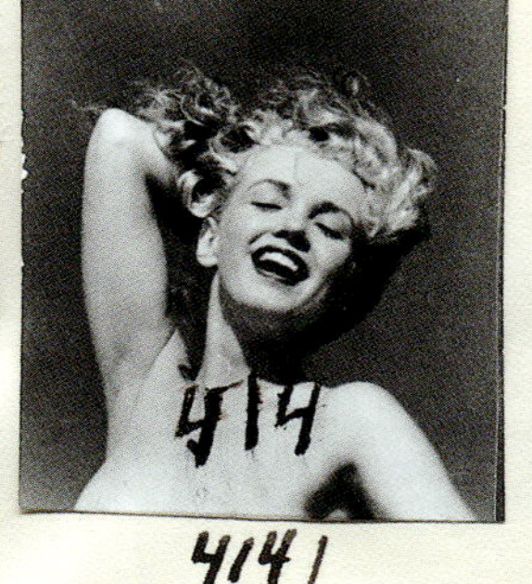

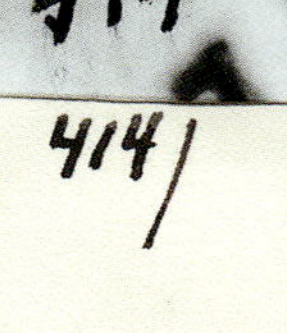

414

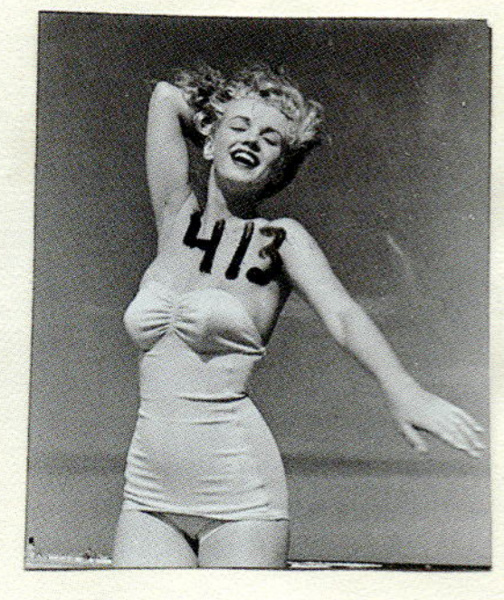

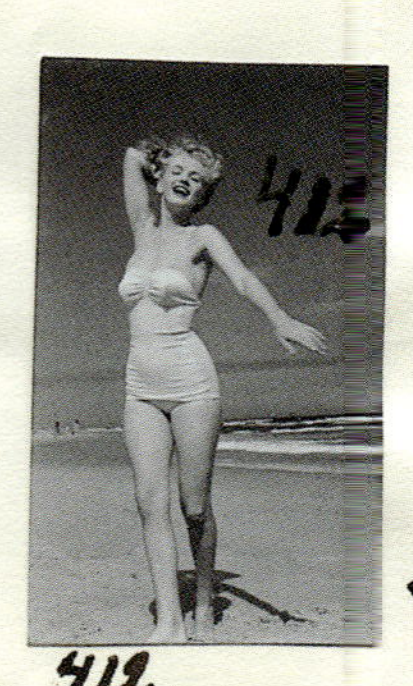

412

402/B

1949

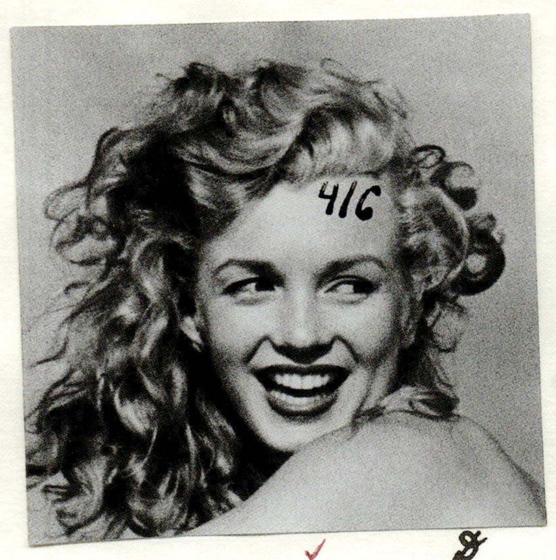

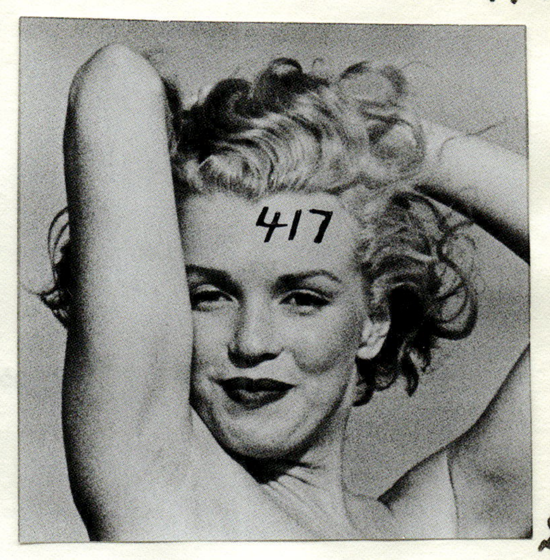

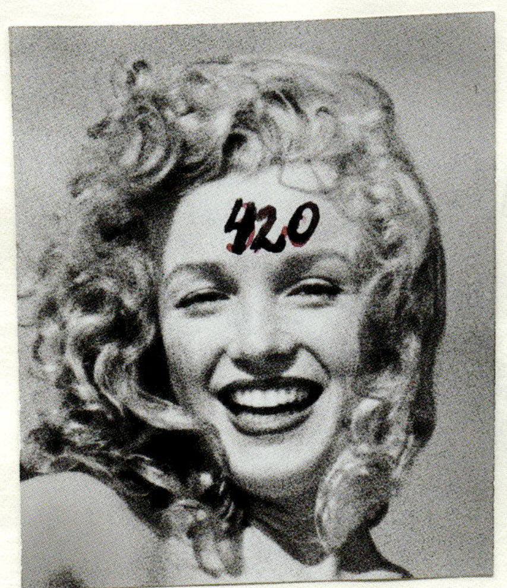

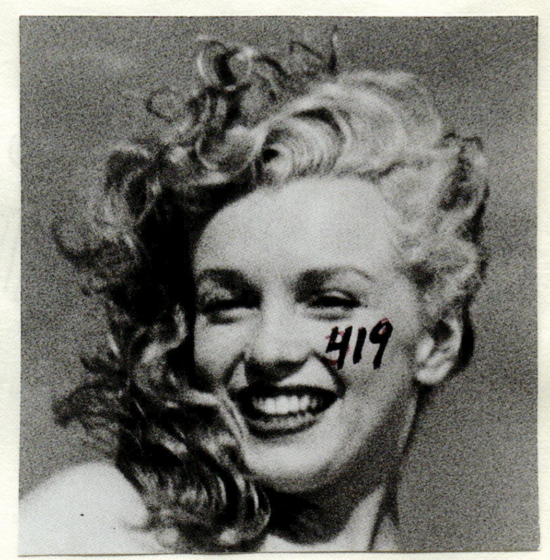

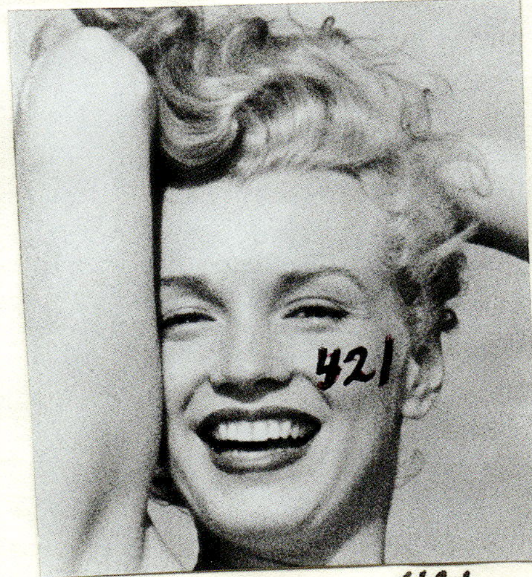

421

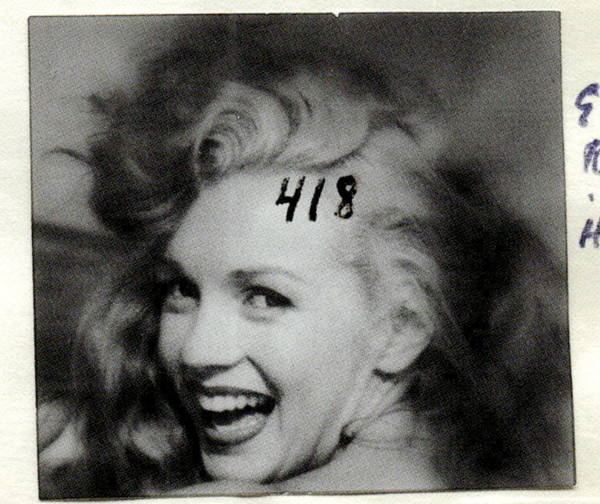

G. R. H.

ANDRE DE DIENES

57

194

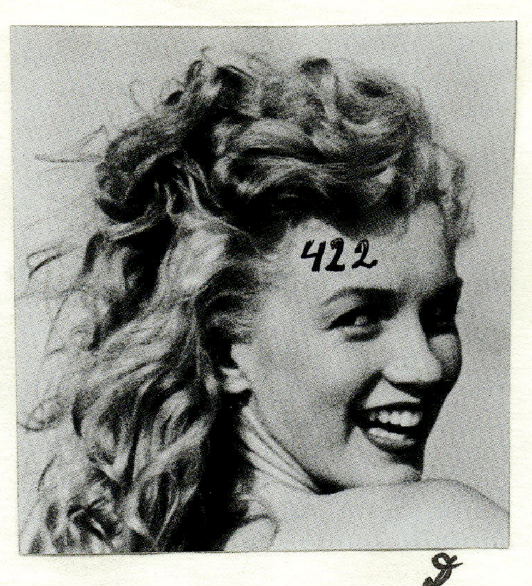

D

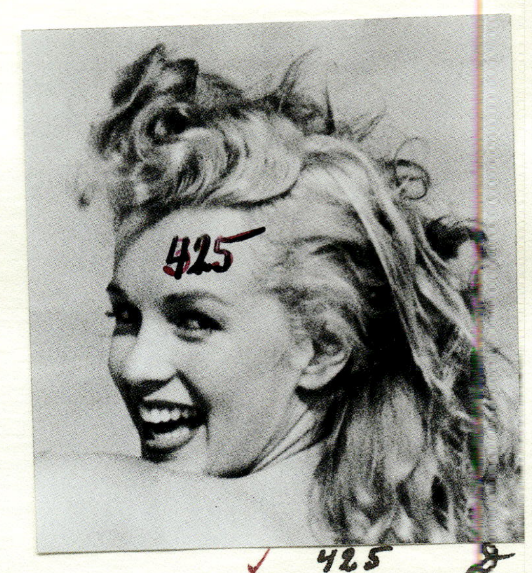

✓ 425 D

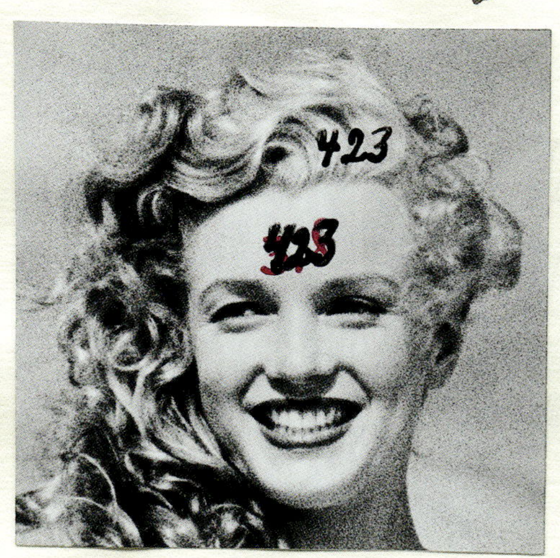

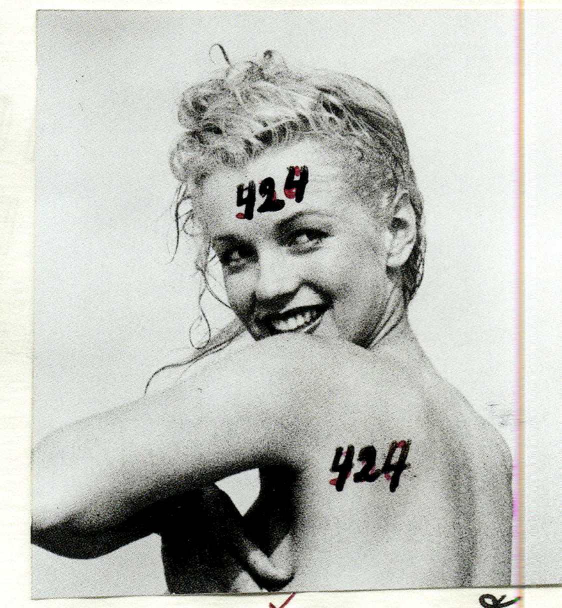

✓ D

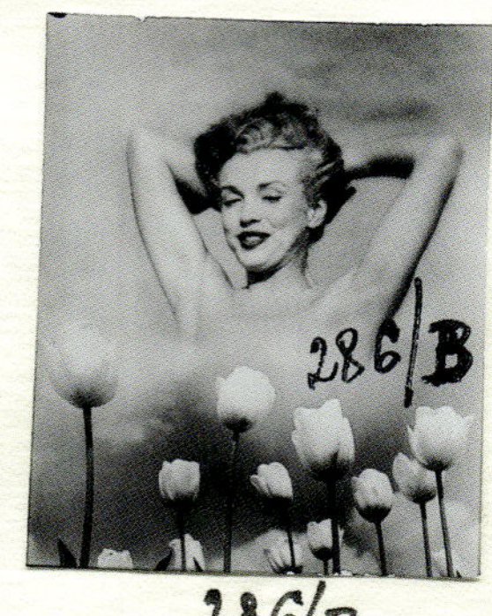

286/B

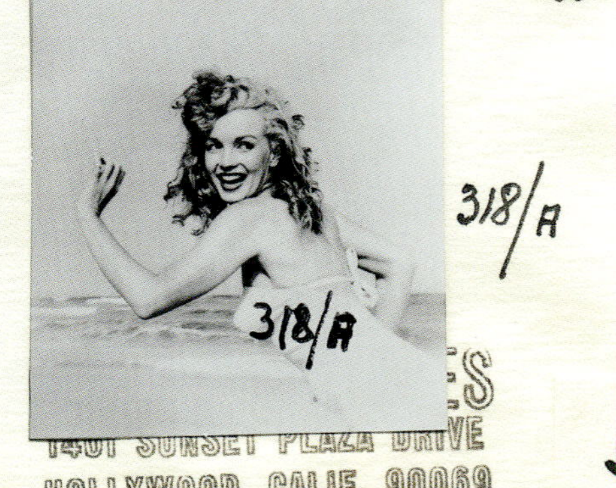

318/A

1401 SUNSET PLAZA DRIVE
HOLLYWOOD, CALIF. 90069

1949

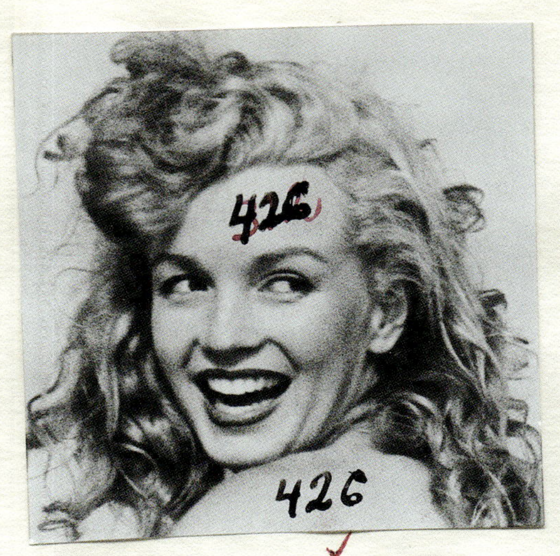

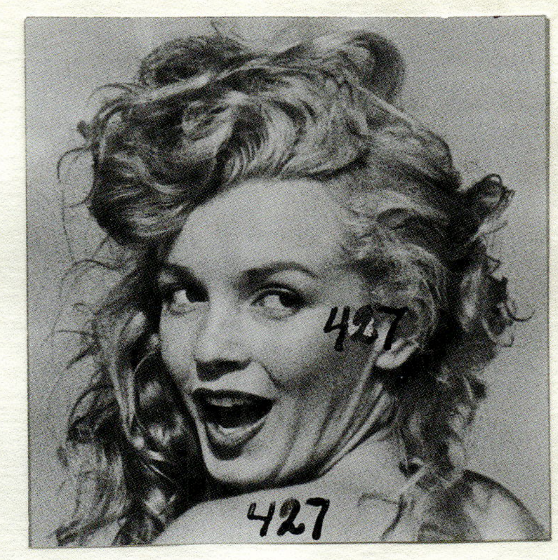

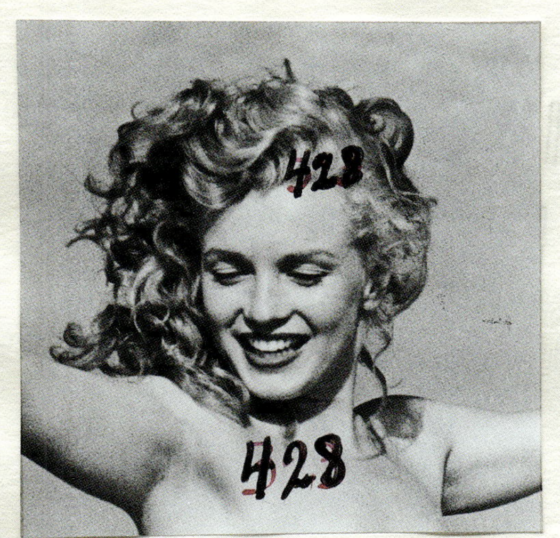

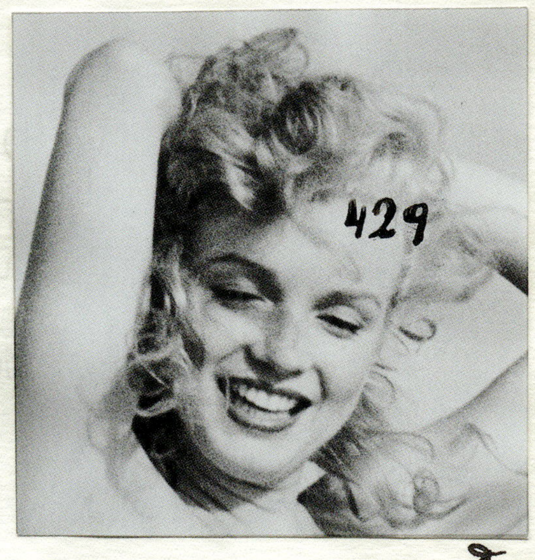

ANDRE DE DIENES
1401 SUNSET PLAZA DRIVE
HOLLYWOOD, CALIF. 90069

59

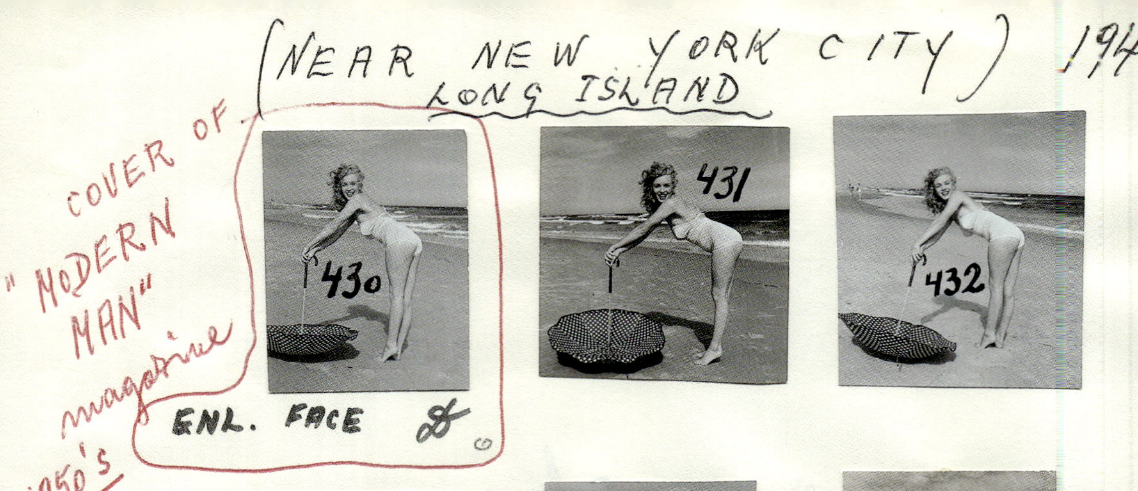

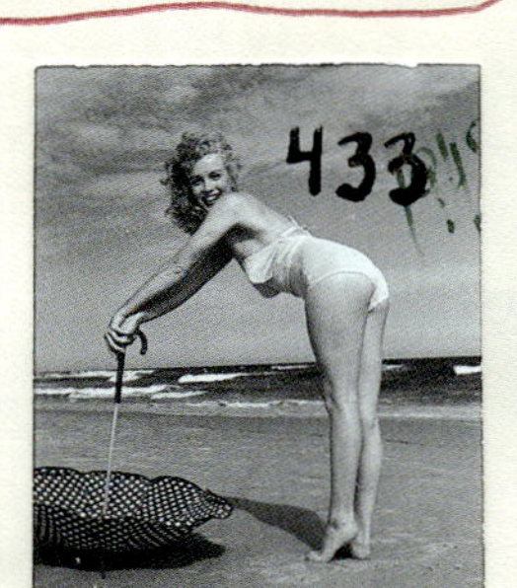

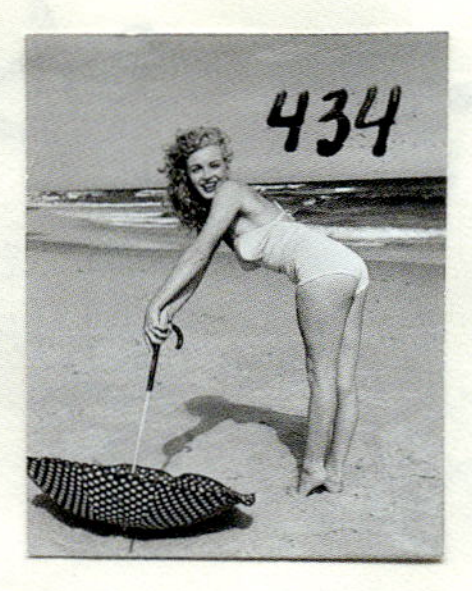

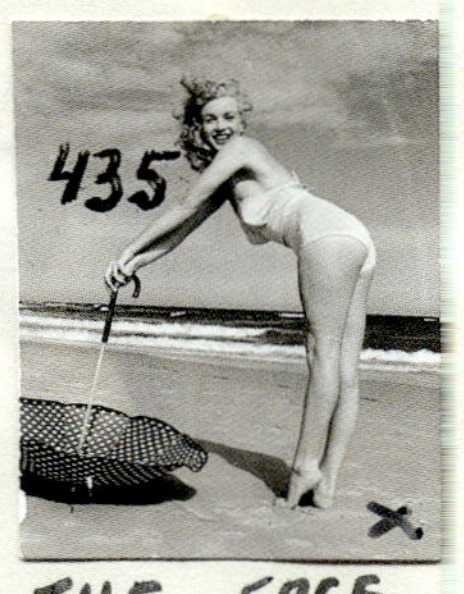

THE FACE

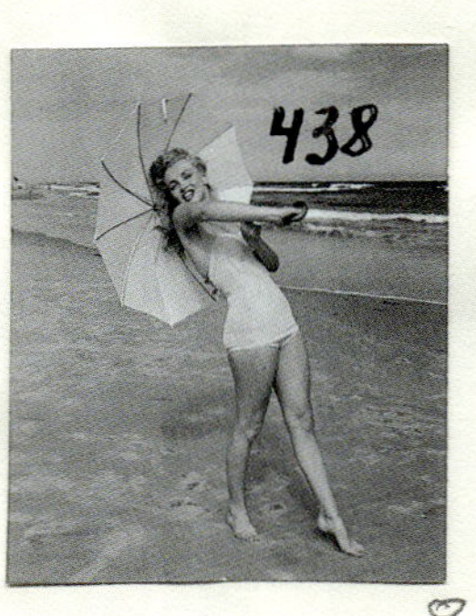

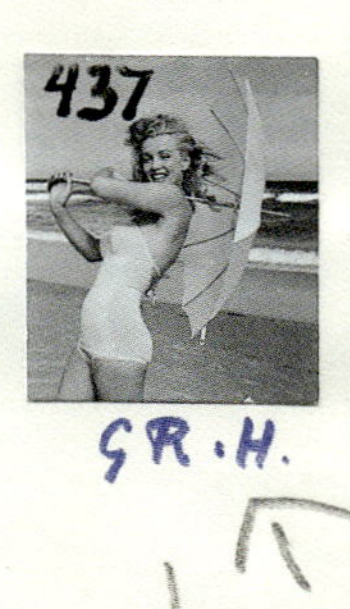

GR.H.

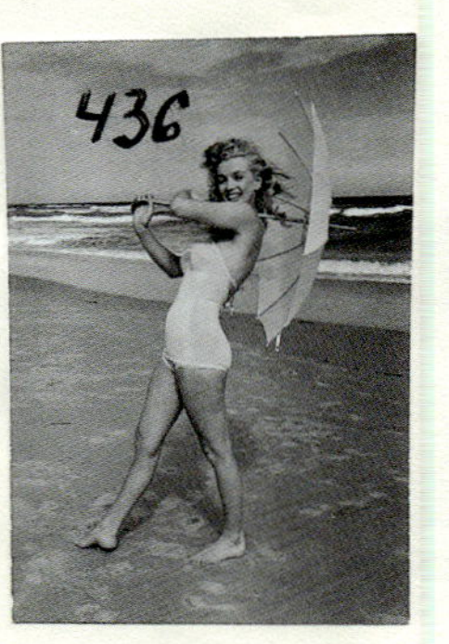

I BOUGHT 2 PARASOLS, ONE RED, THE OTHER WITE; A PINK BATHING SUIT, AND VARIOUS SILK SCARFS. THIS WAS JUST WHEN MARILYN WAS RISING TO FAME. (SHE WAS ON A PUBLICITY TOU ACCROSS THE U.S.A.)

ANDRE DE DIENES
1401 SUNSET PLAZA DRIVE
HOLLYWOOD, CALIF. 90069

6

1949

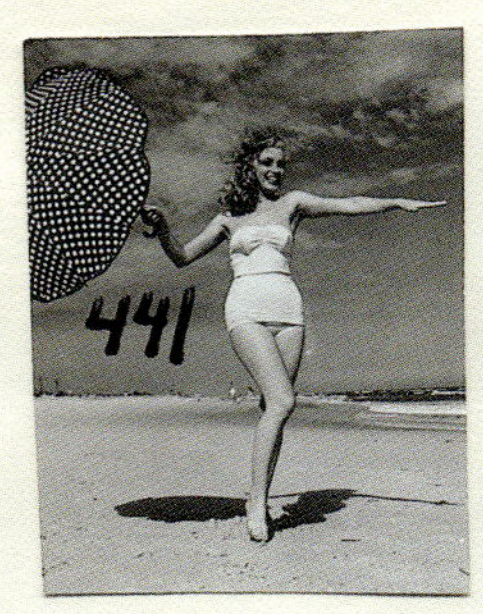

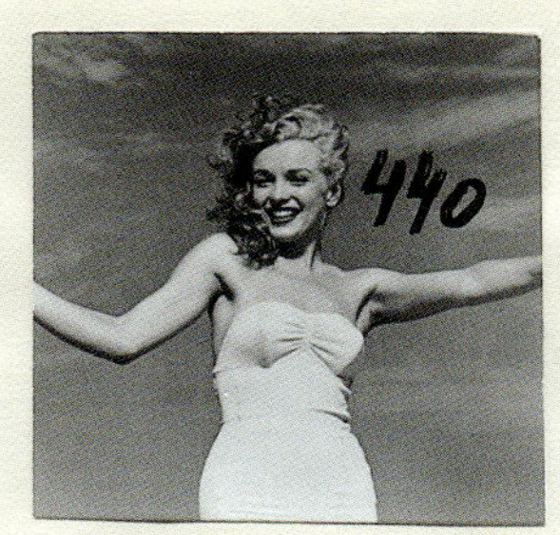

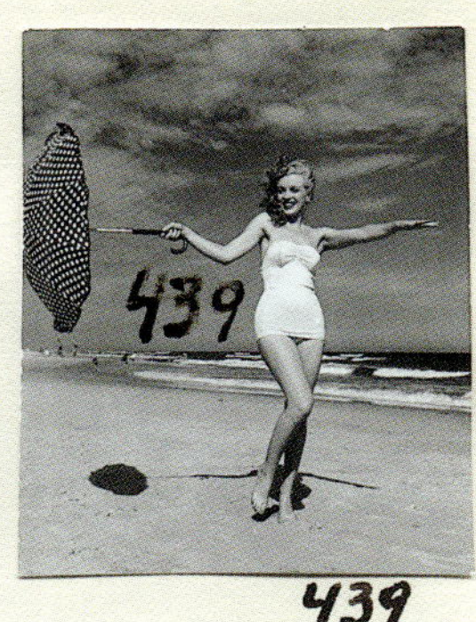

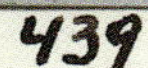

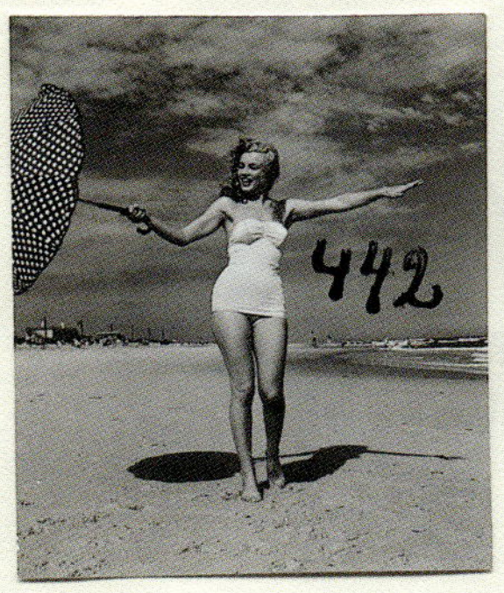

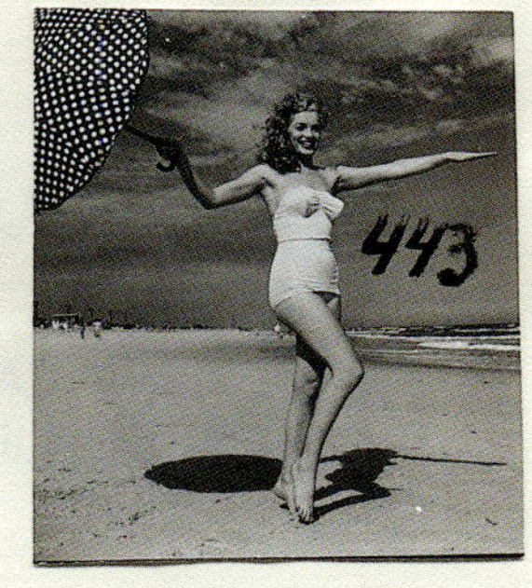

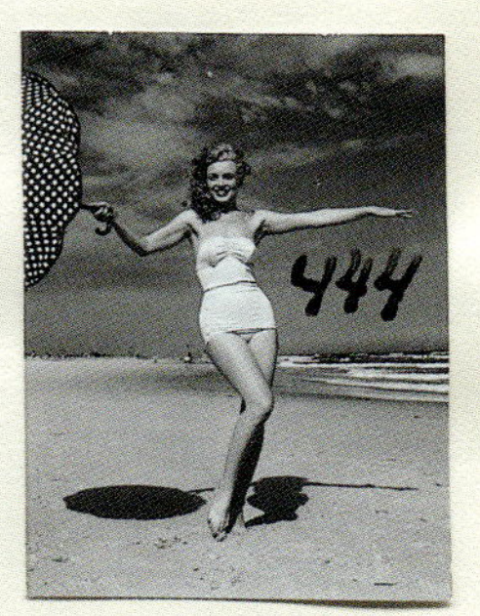

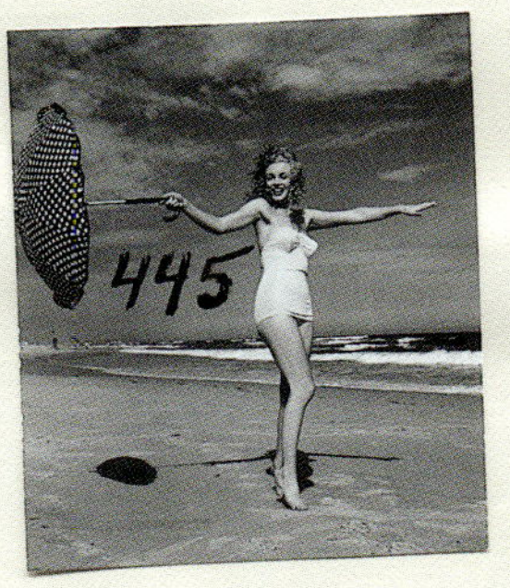

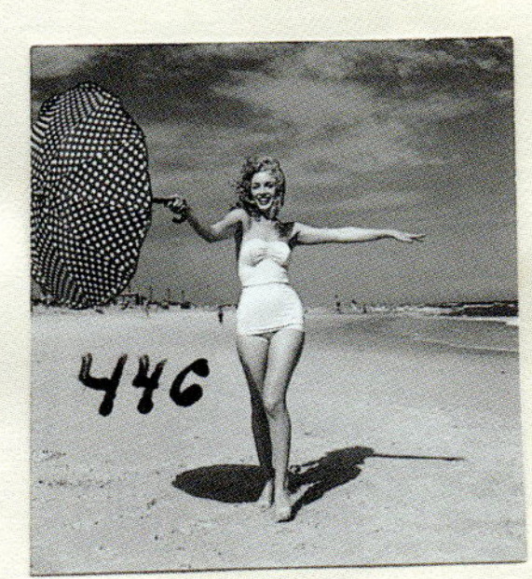

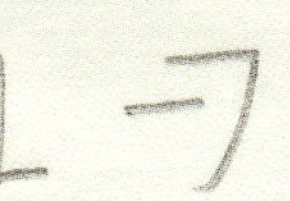

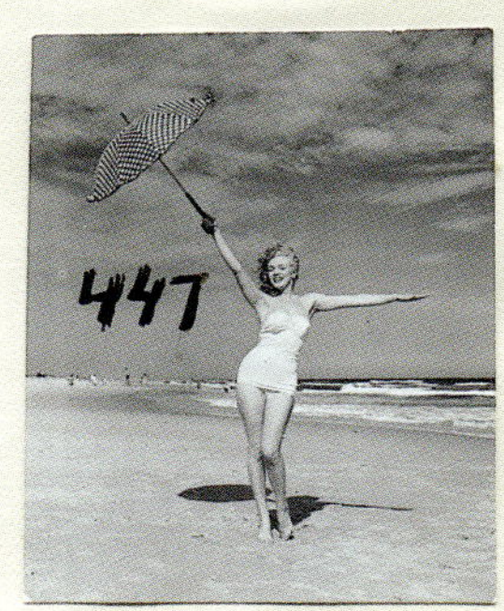

61

ANDRE DE DIENES
1401 SUNSET PLAZA DRIVE
HOLLYWOOD, CALIF. 90069

1947

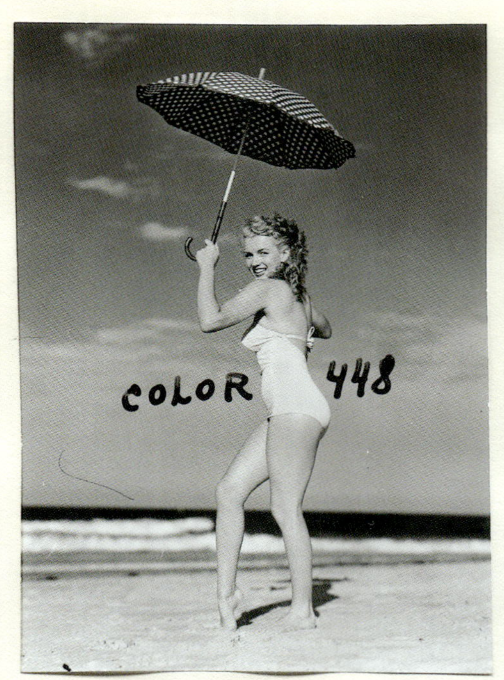

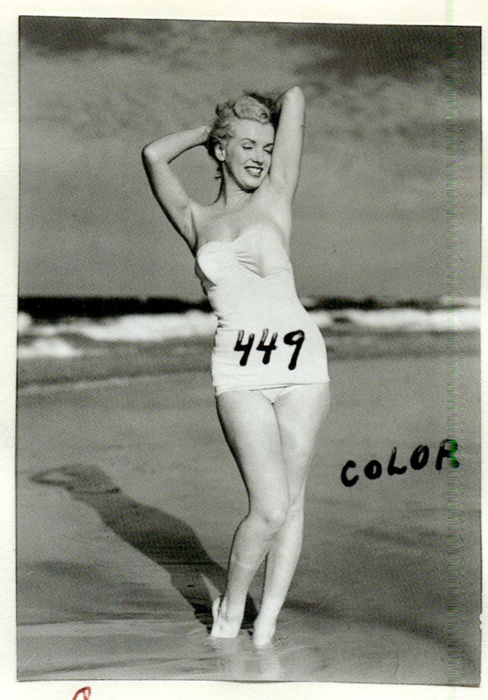

g.

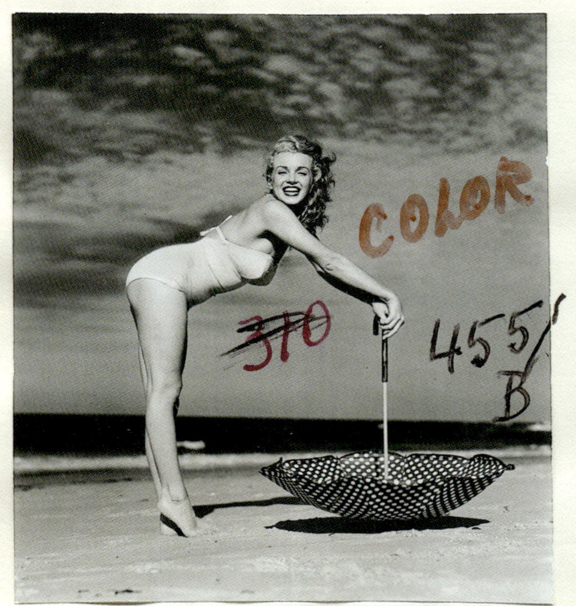

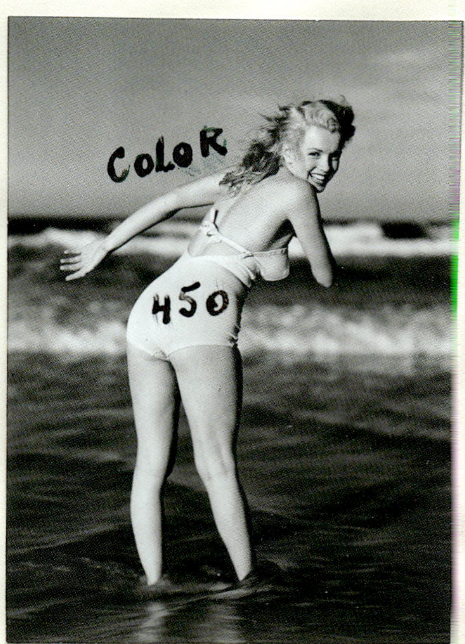

455/B
"GALA" Magazine
cover.....1950
COLOR

g

ANDRE DE DIENES
1401 SUNSET PLAZA DRIVE
HOLLYWOOD, CALIF. 90069

62

1949

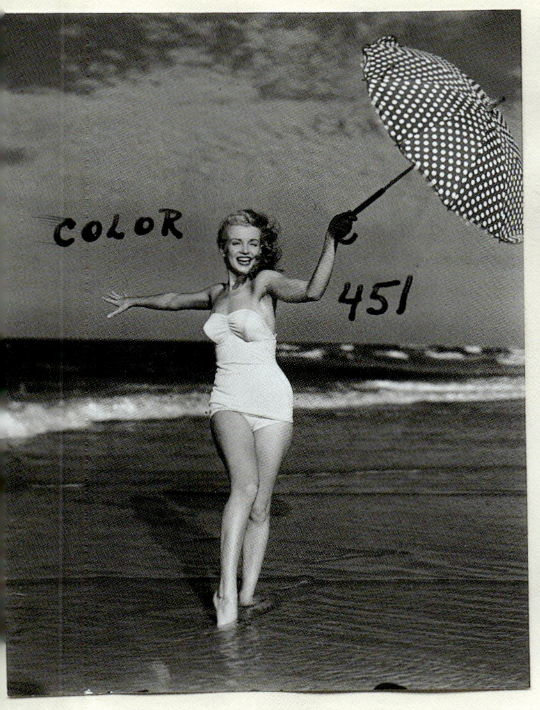

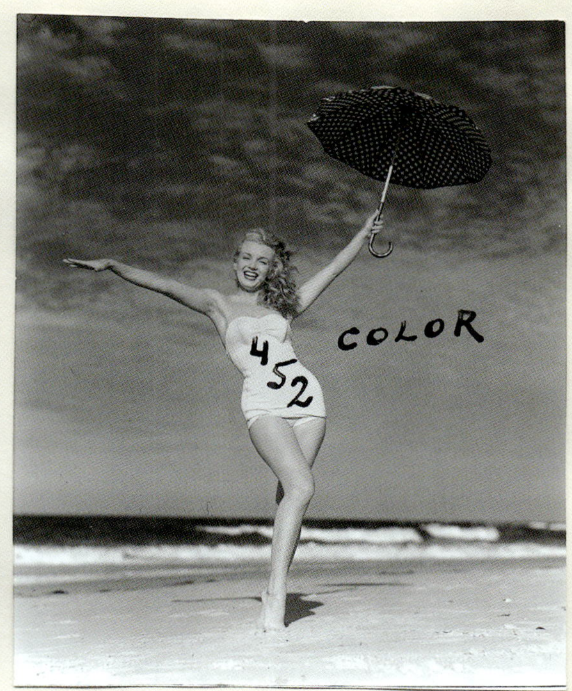

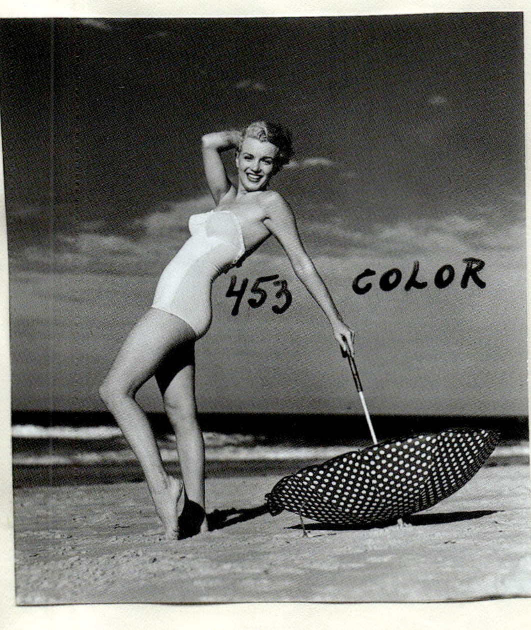

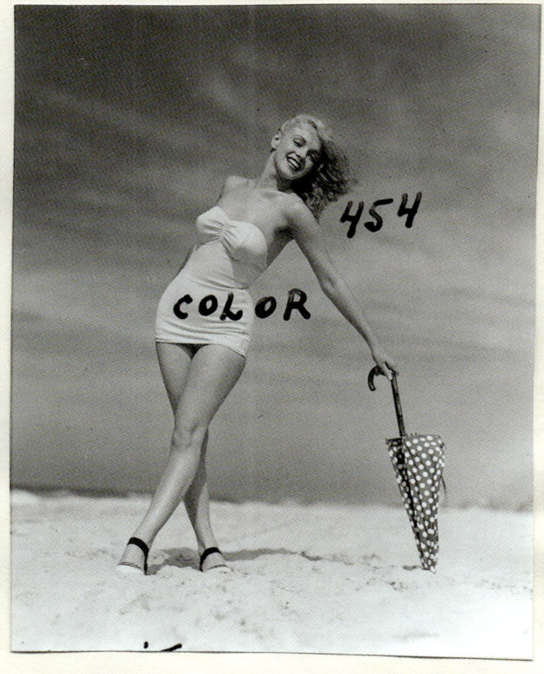

ANDRE DE DIENES
1401 SUNSET PLAZA DRIVE
HOLLYWOOD, CALIF. 90069

63

194?

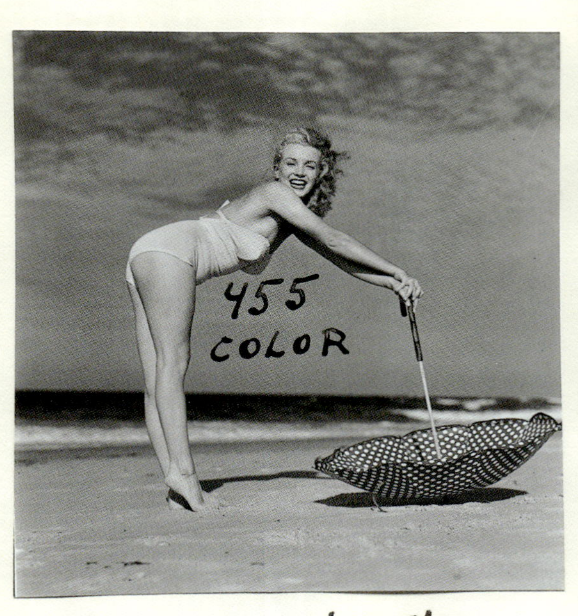

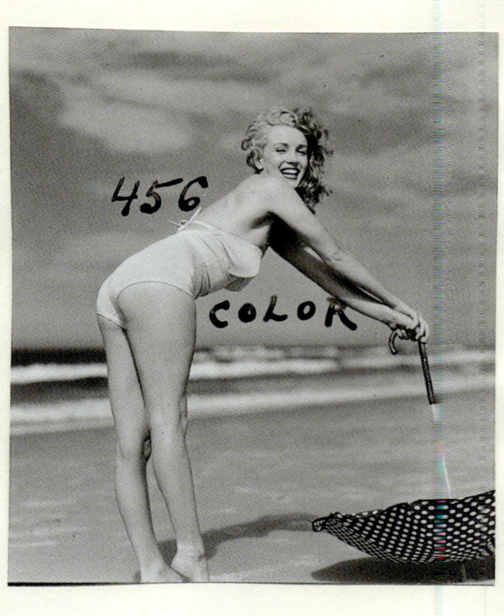

455/A

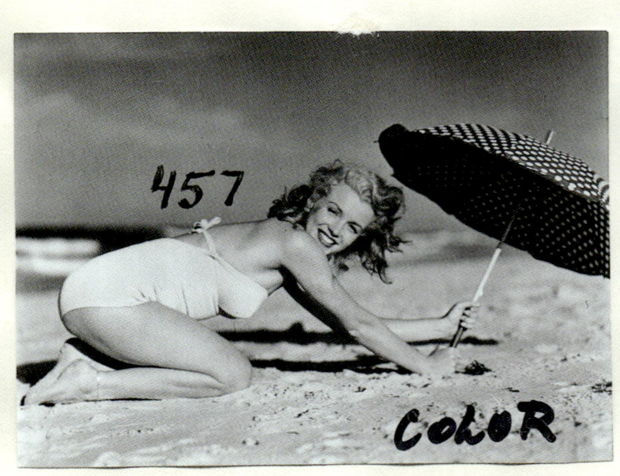

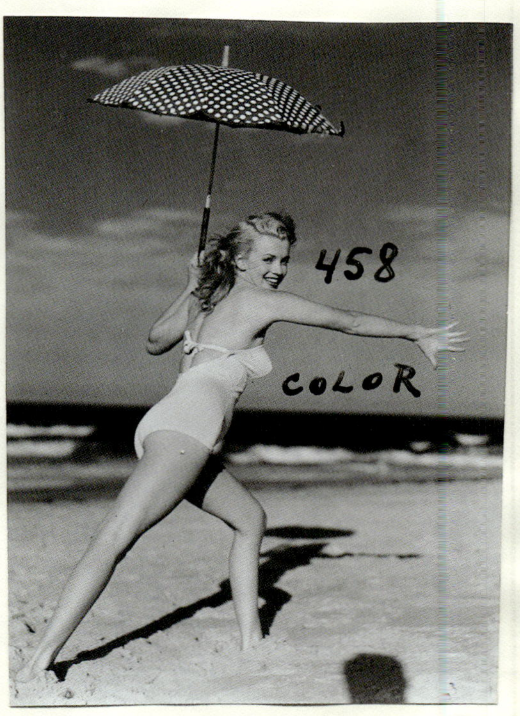

ANDRE DE DIENES
1401 SUNSET PLAZA DRIVE
HOLLYWOOD, CALIF. 90069

64

1949

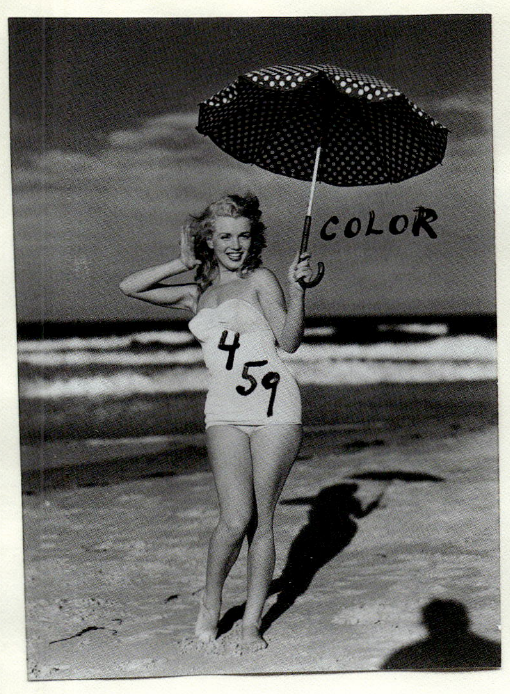

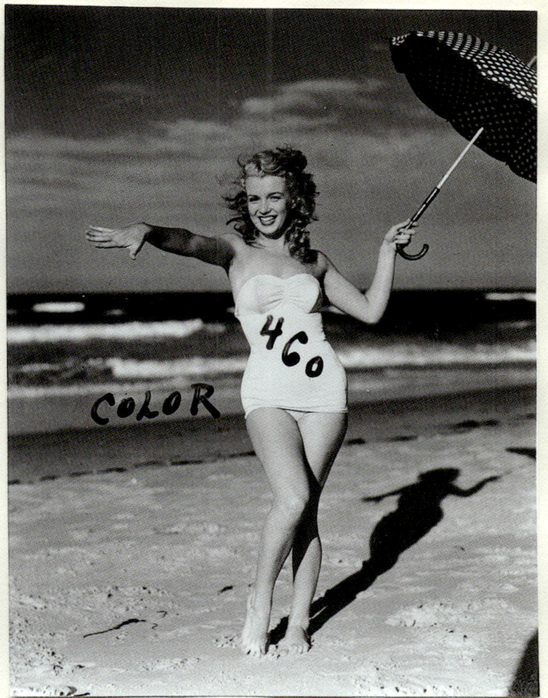

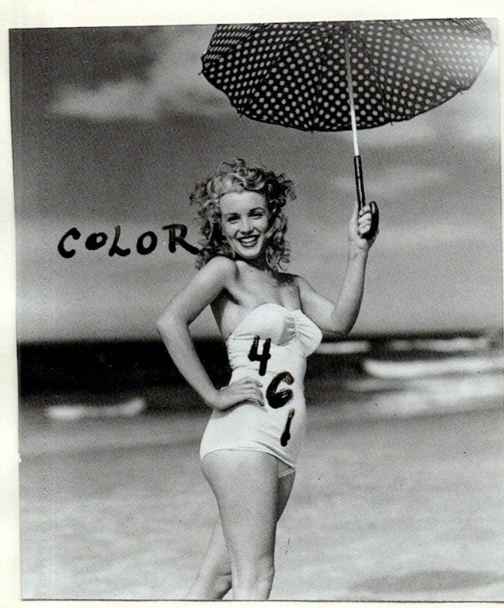

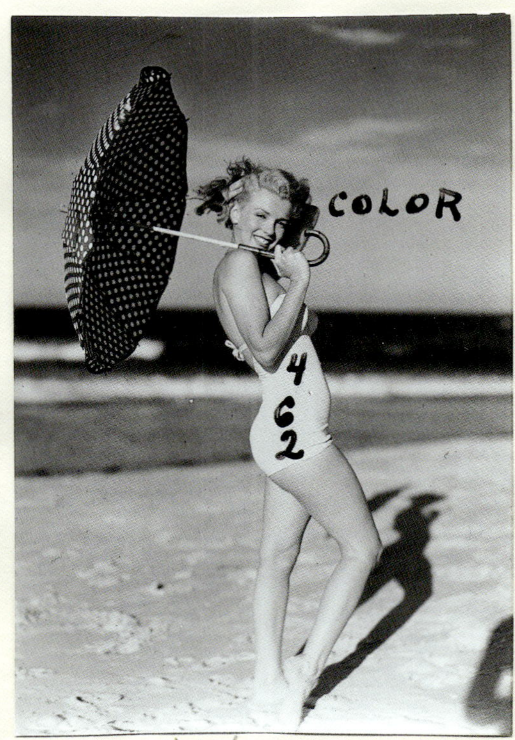

Reverse it!

ANDRE DE DIENES
1401 SUNSET PLAZA DRIVE

65

1949

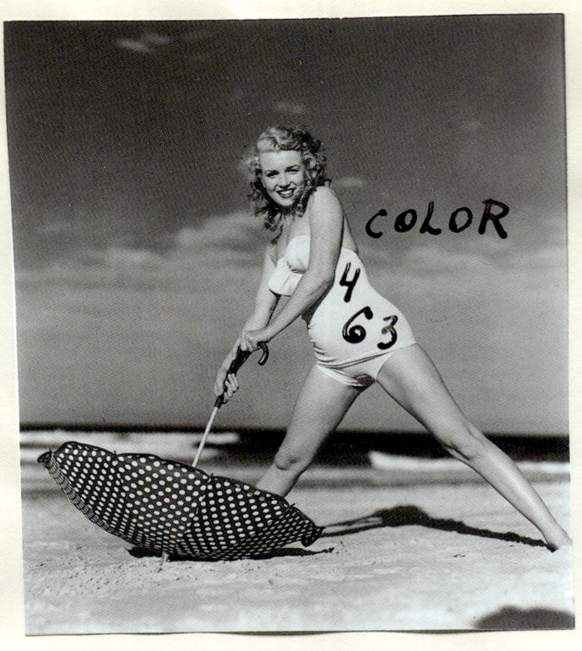

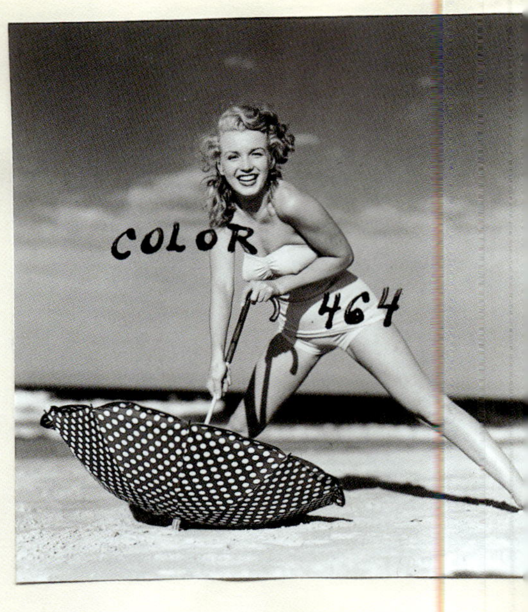

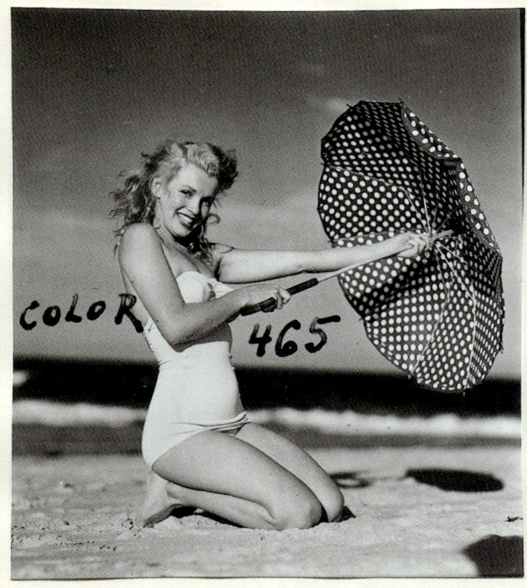

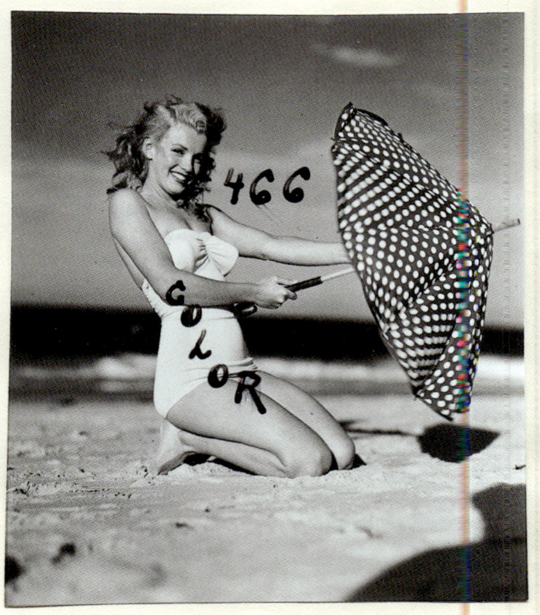

ANDRE DE DIENES
1401 SUNSET PLAZA DRIVE
HOLLYWOOD, CALIF. 90069

6

1949

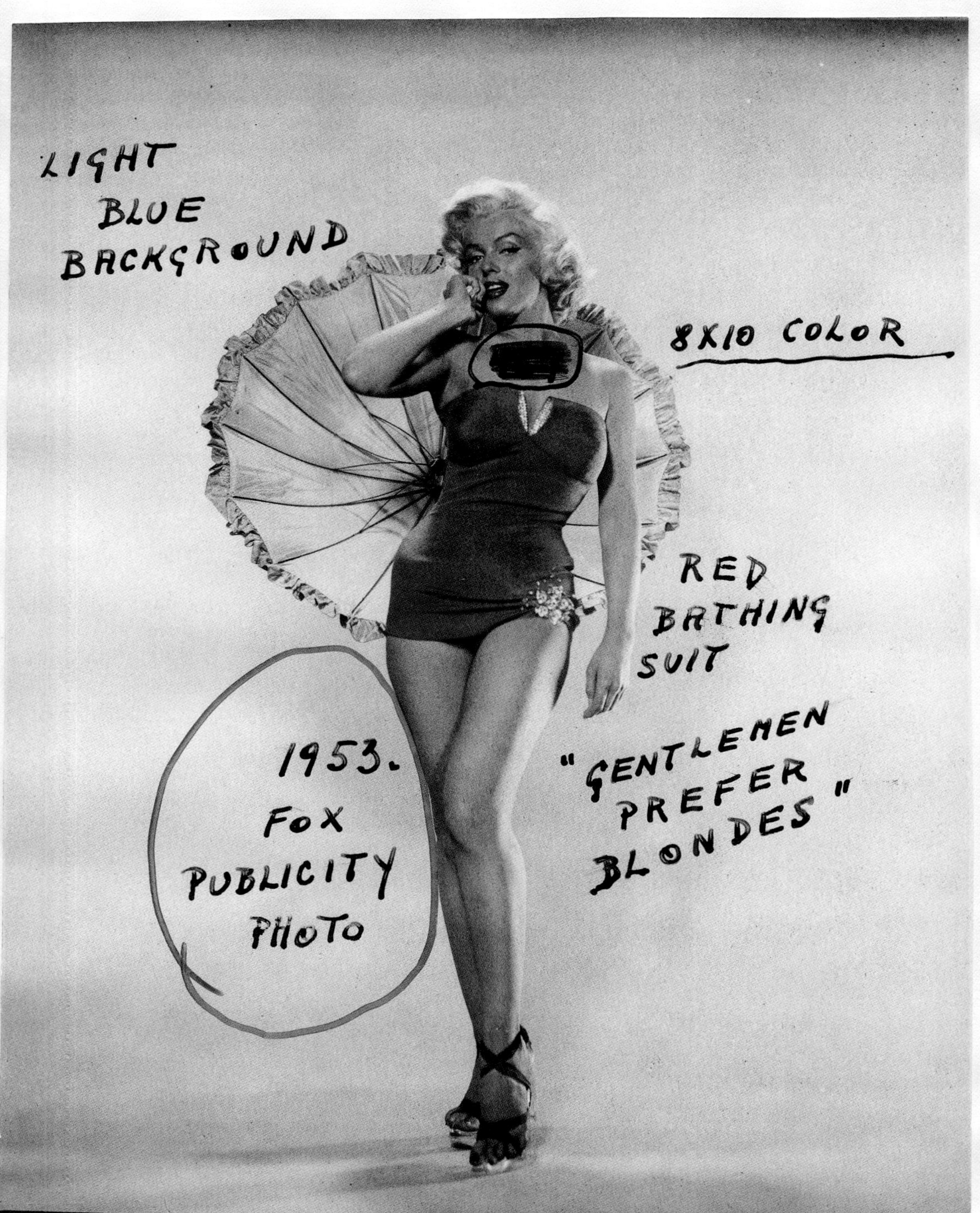

MARILYN TOOK ALL MY IDEAS.
HERE, 4 YEARS LATER, SHE
S POSING AGAIN WITH A PARASOL.

ANDRE DE DIENES
1401 SUNSET PLAZA DRIVE
HOLLYWOOD, CALIF. 90069

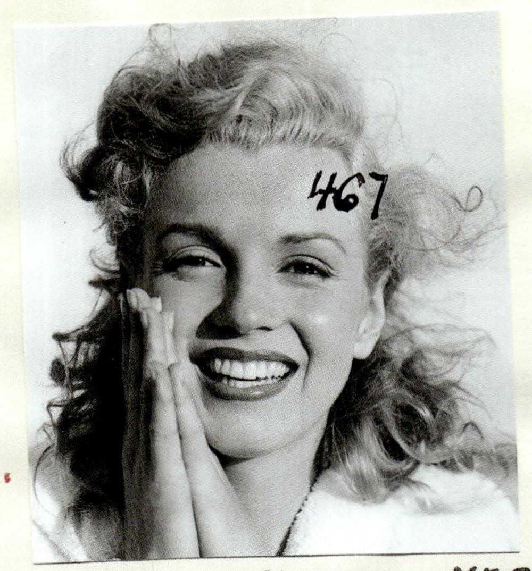

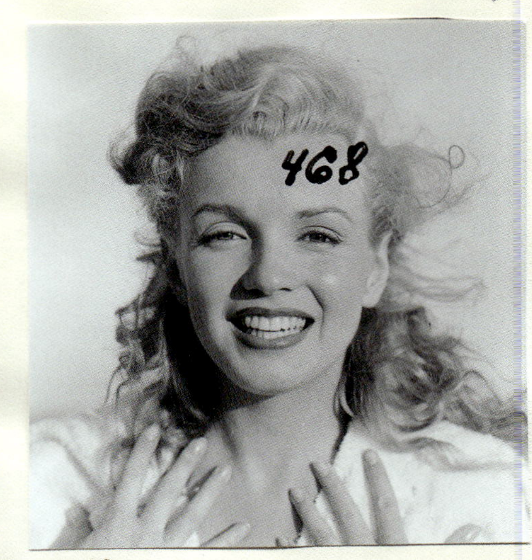

A VERY HAPPY MARILYN

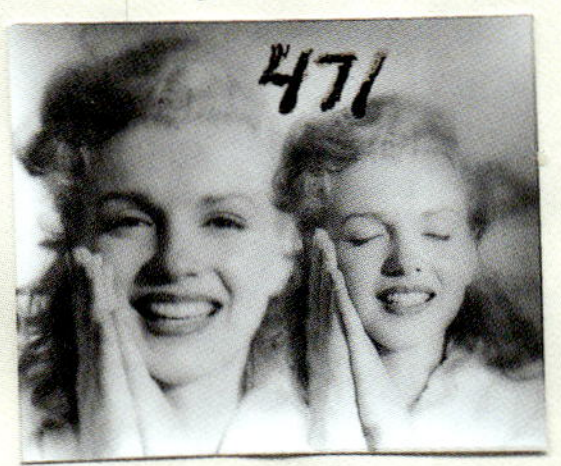

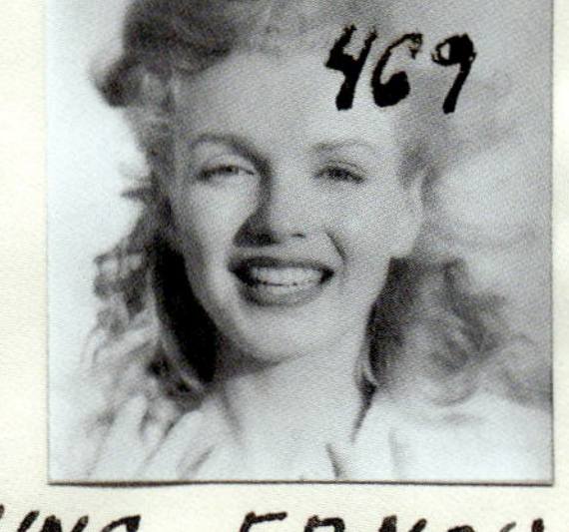

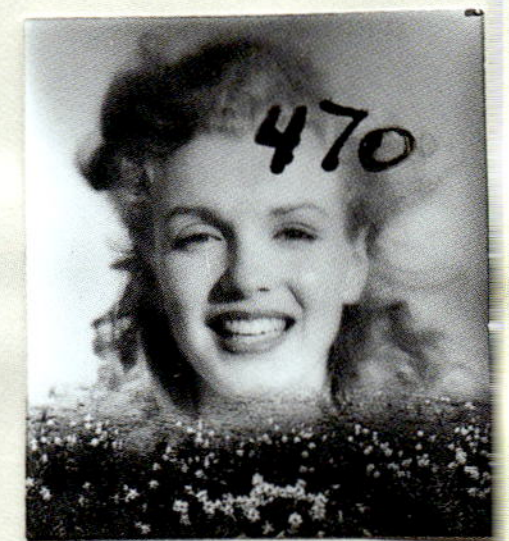

SHE IS BECOMING FAMOUS!

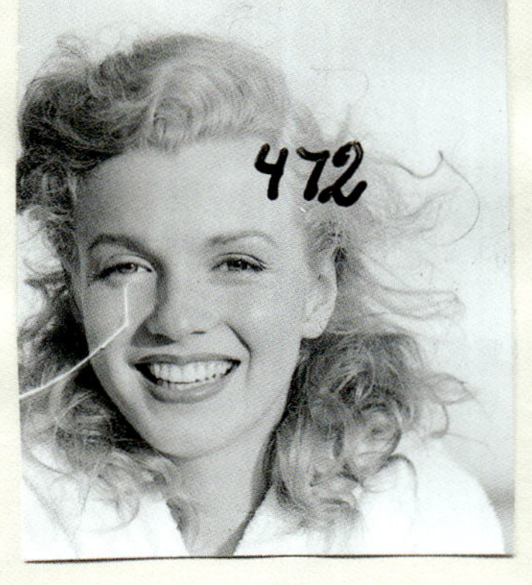

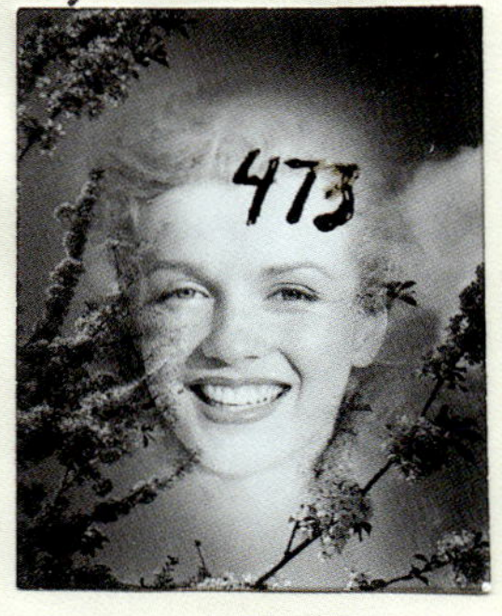

ANDRE DE DIENES
1401 SUNSET PLAZA DRIVE
HOLLYWOOD, CALIF. 90069

1949

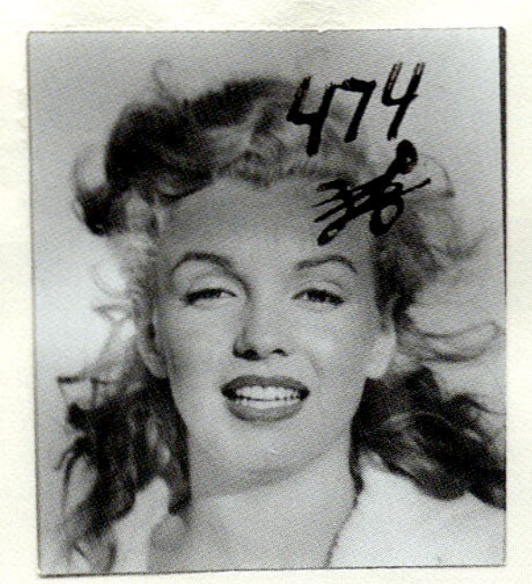

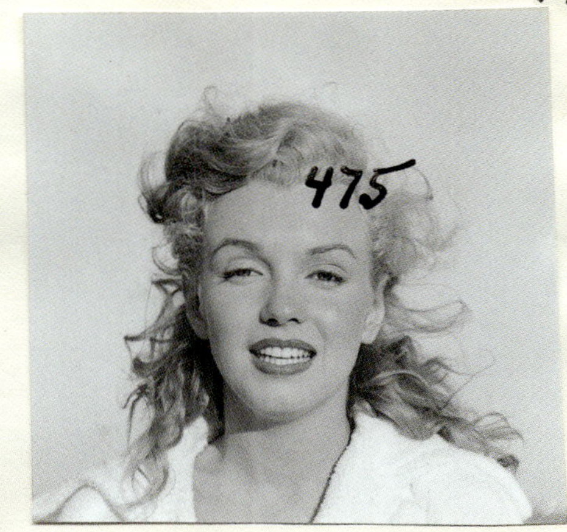

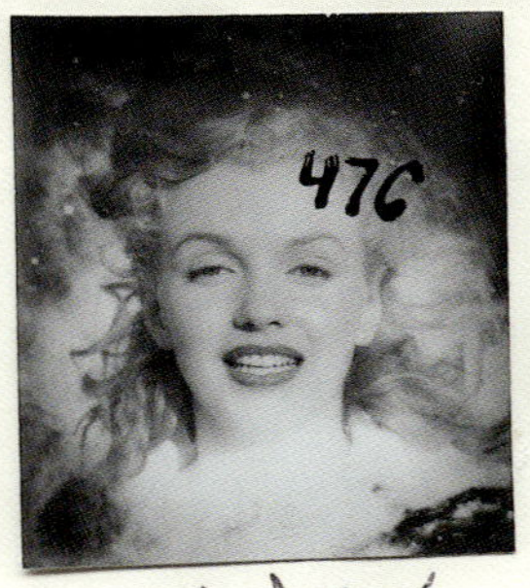

Beautiful!

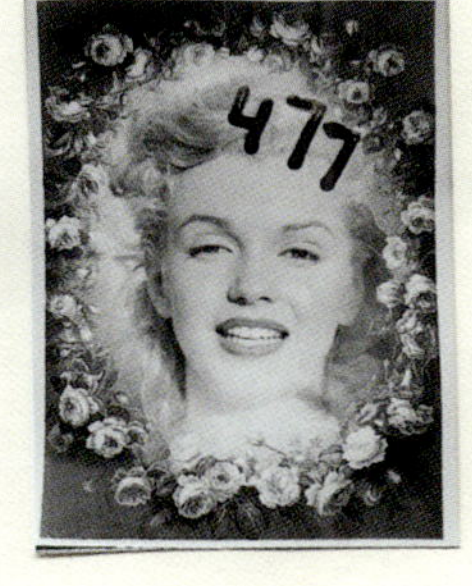

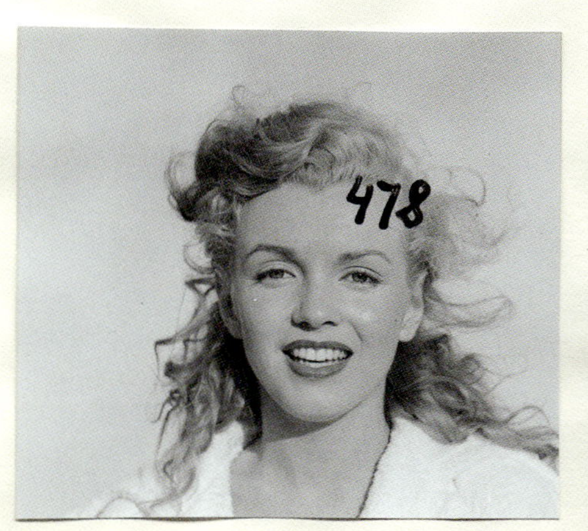

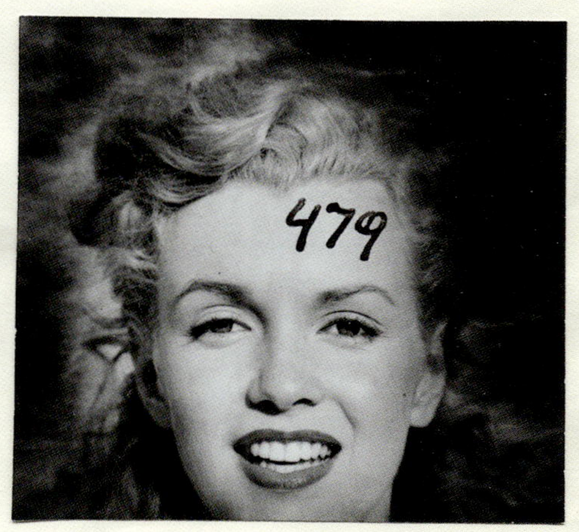

ANDRE de DIENES
1401 SUNSET PLAZA DRIVE
HOLLYWOOD, CALIF. 90069

1949

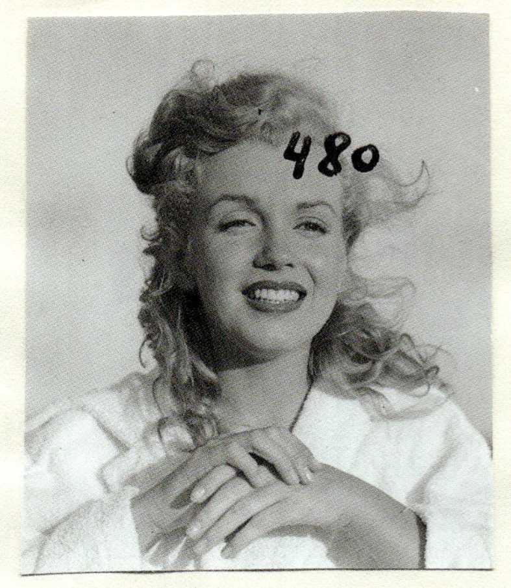

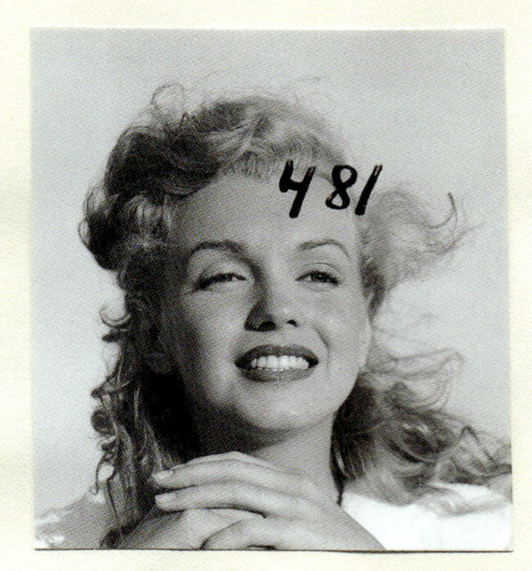

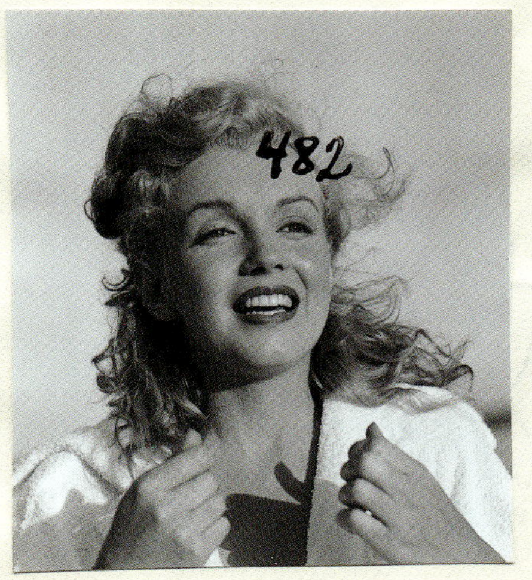

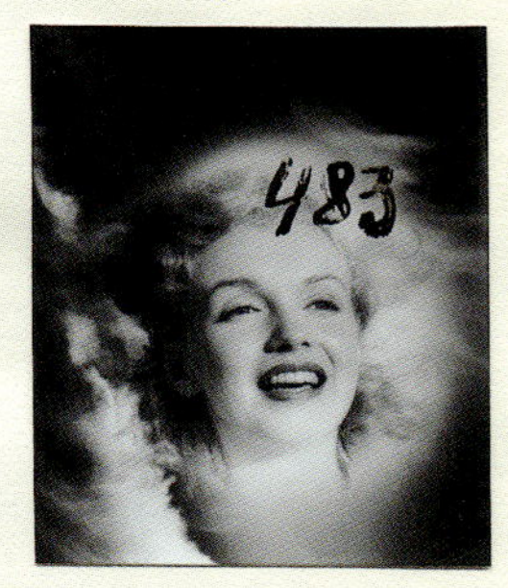

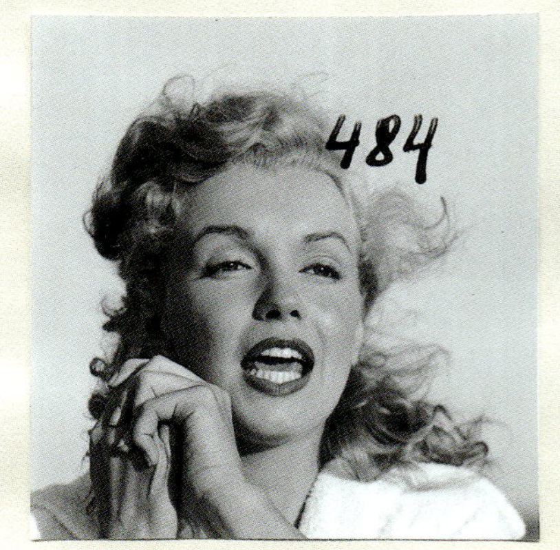

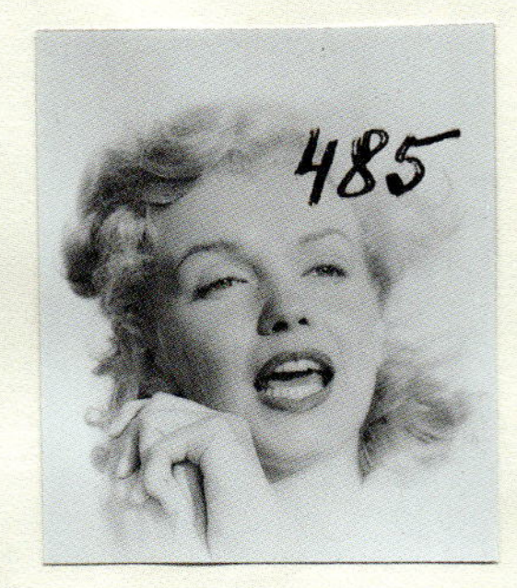

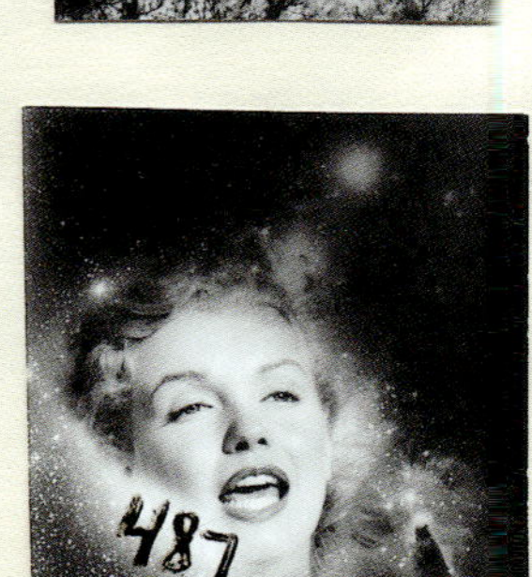

ANDRE DE DIENES
1401 SUNSET PLAZA DRIVE
HOLLYWOOD, CALIF. 90069

1949

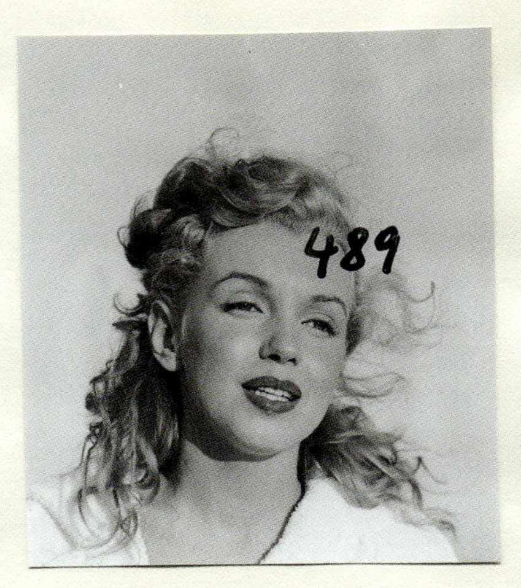

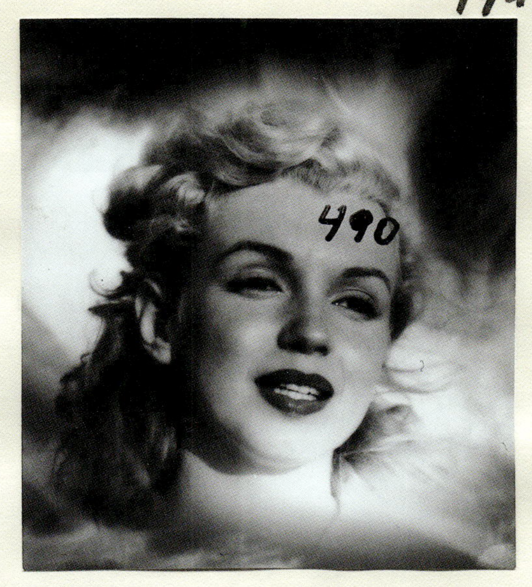

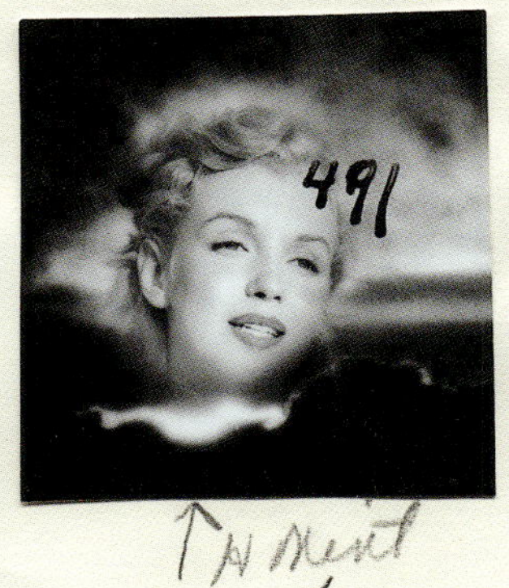

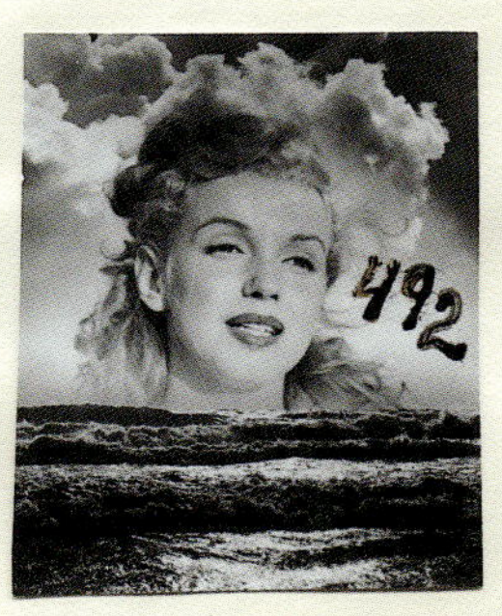

↑A Merit
7

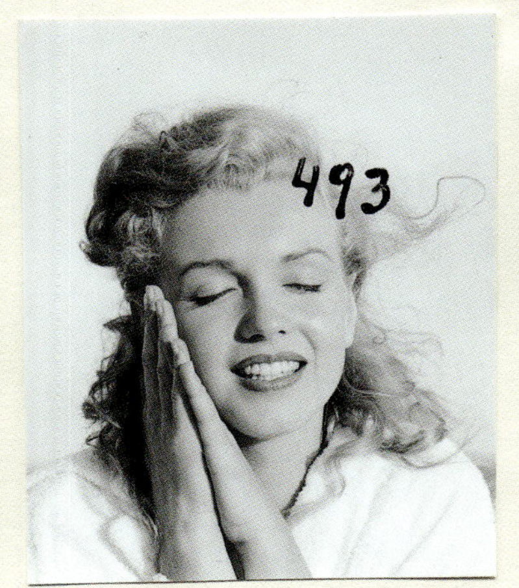

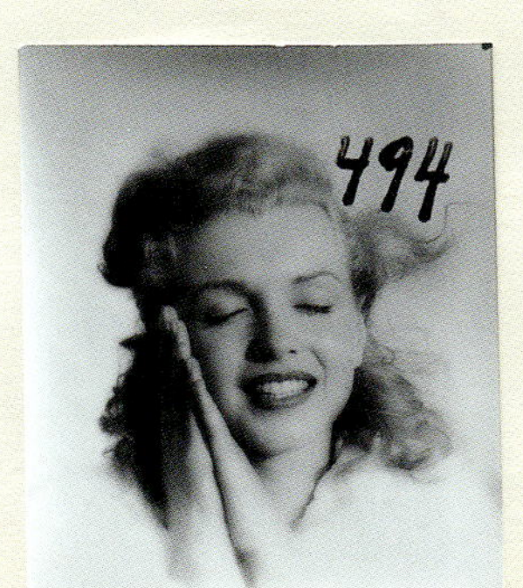

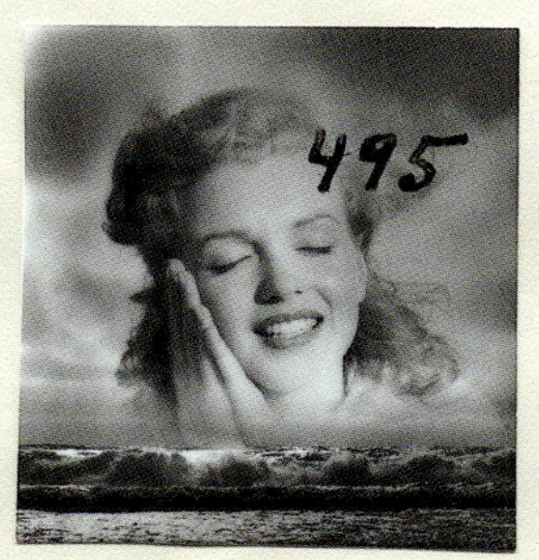

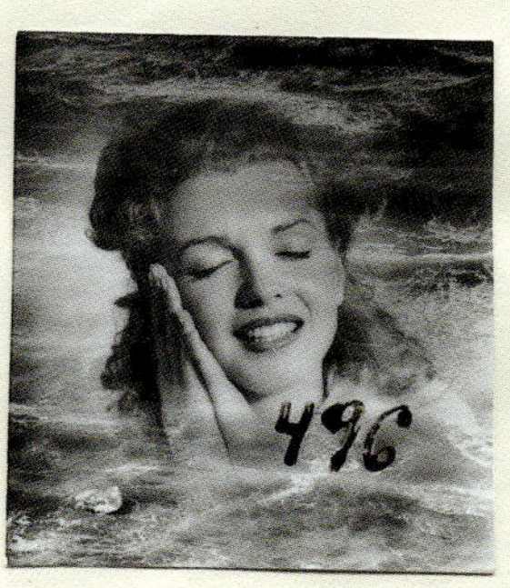

ANDRE DE DIENES 71
1401 SUNSET PLAZA DRIVE
HOLLYWOOD, CALIF. 90069

BK II

194

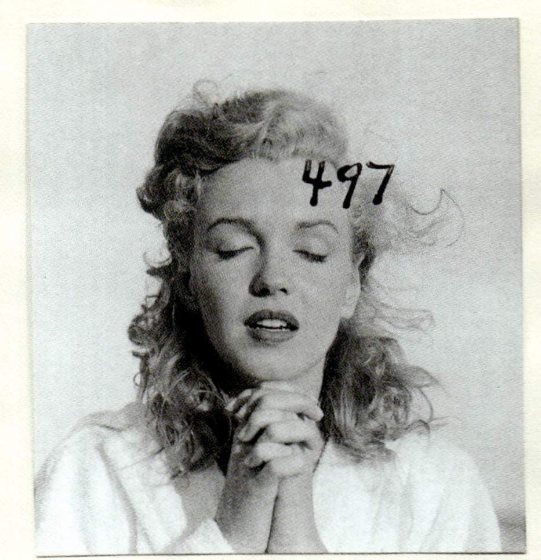

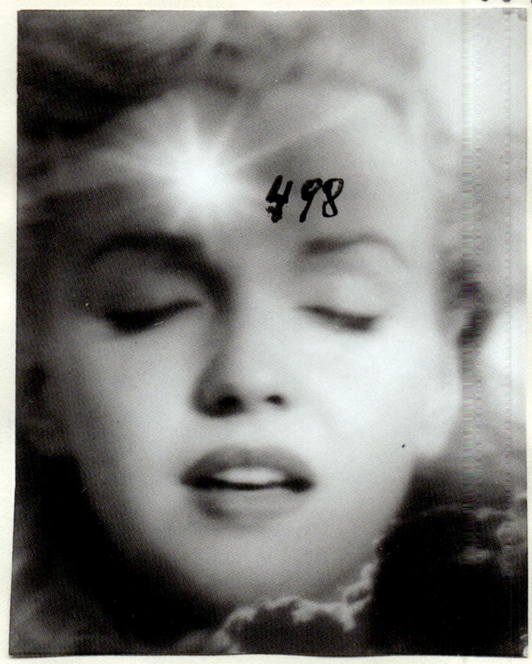

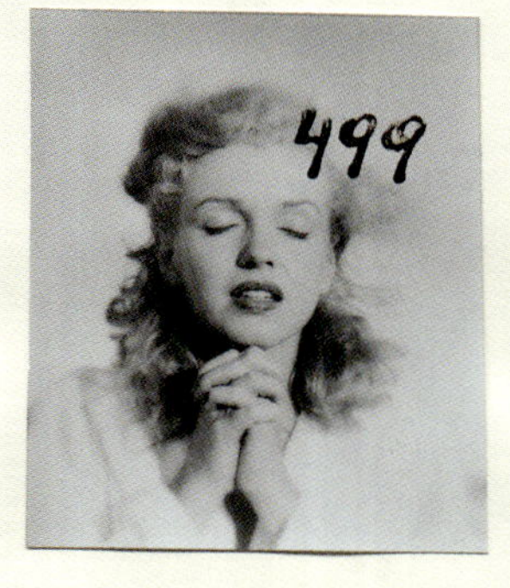

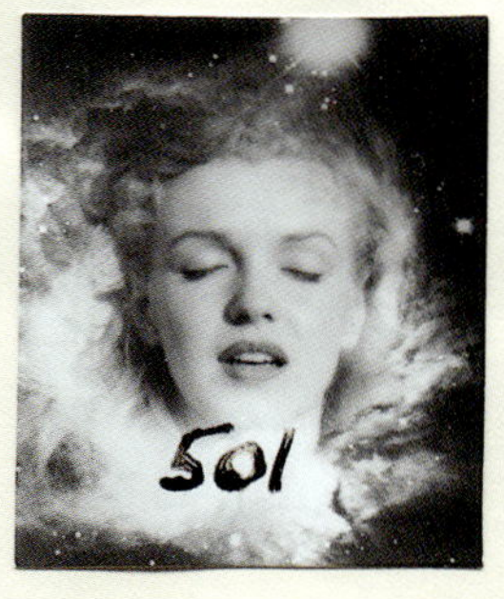

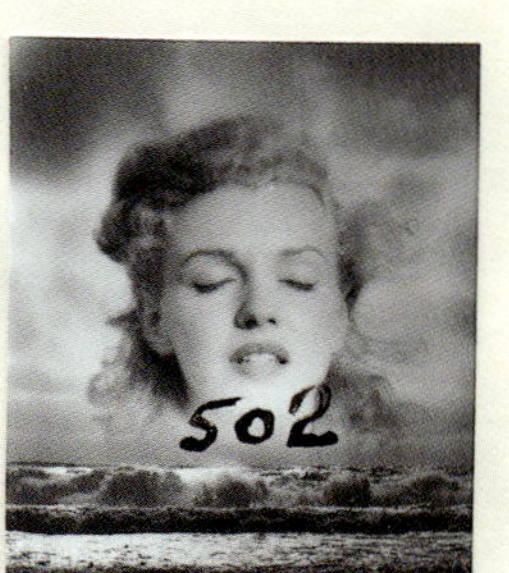

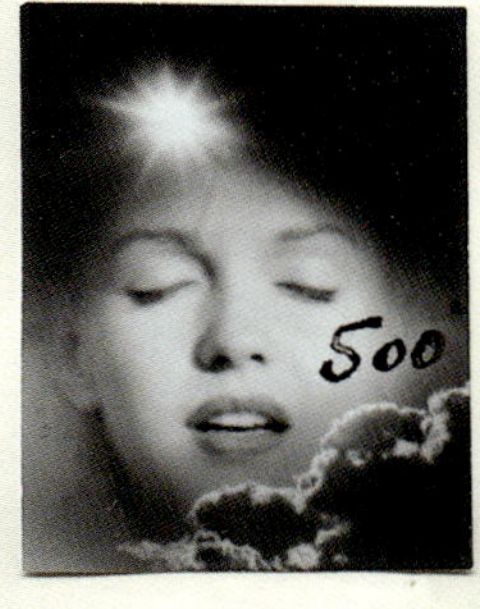

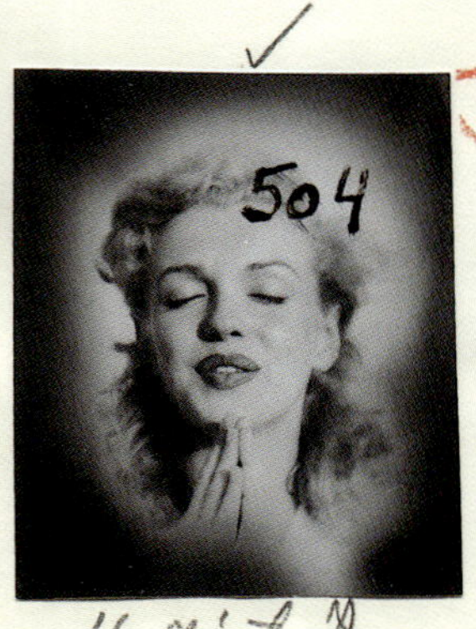

H. Miel

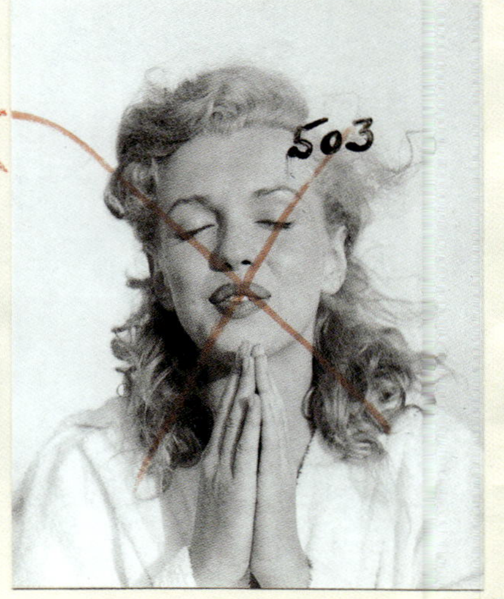

ANDRE DE DIENES

72

1949

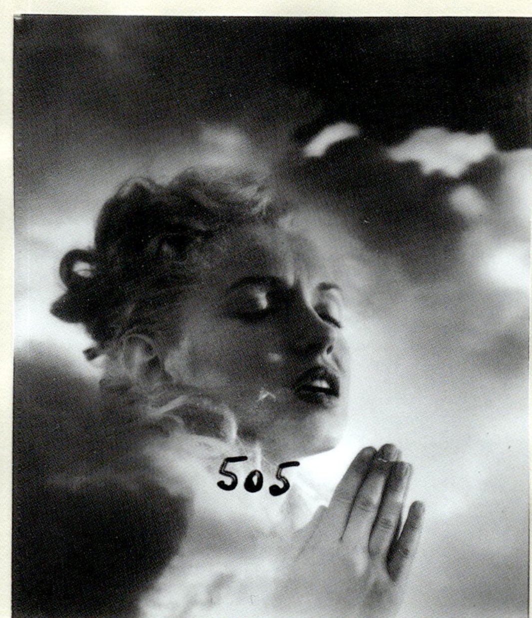

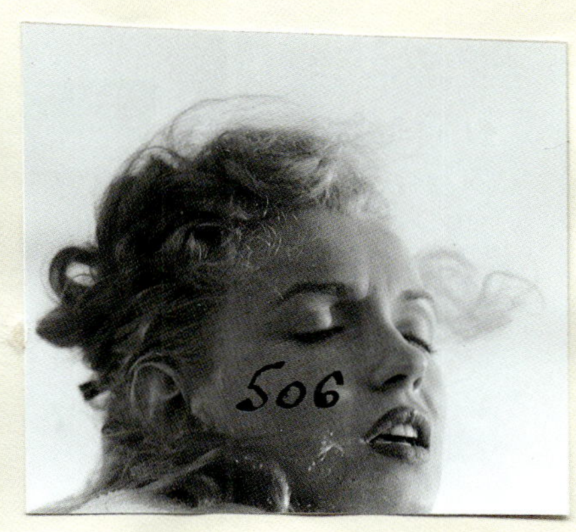

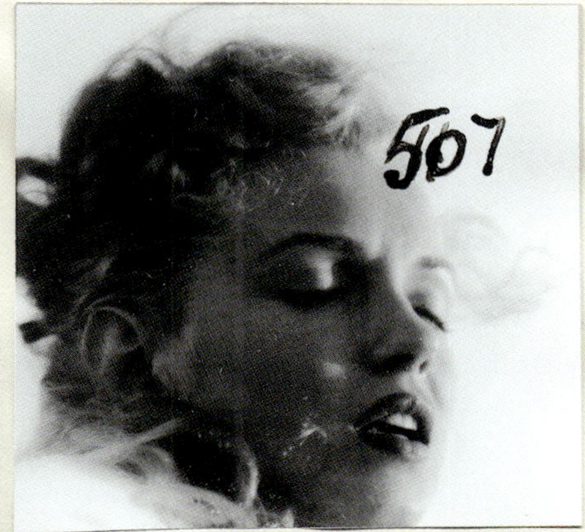

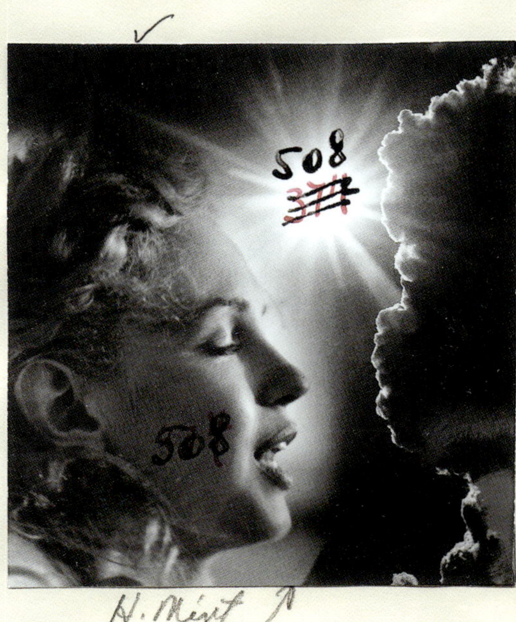

H. Mért

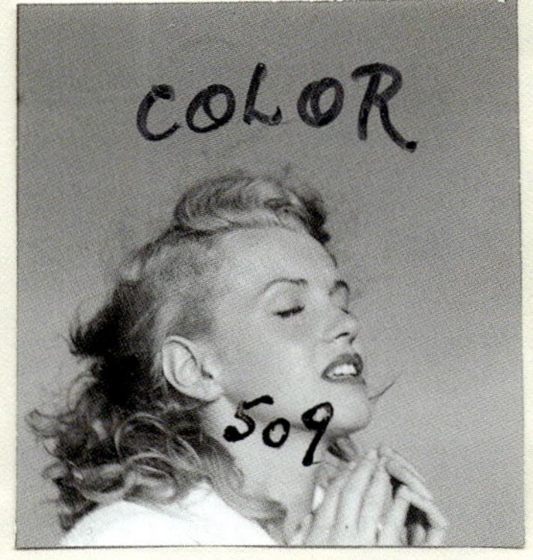

1949

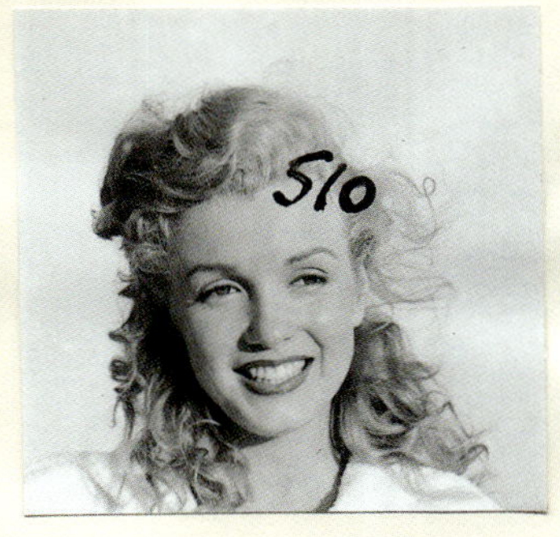

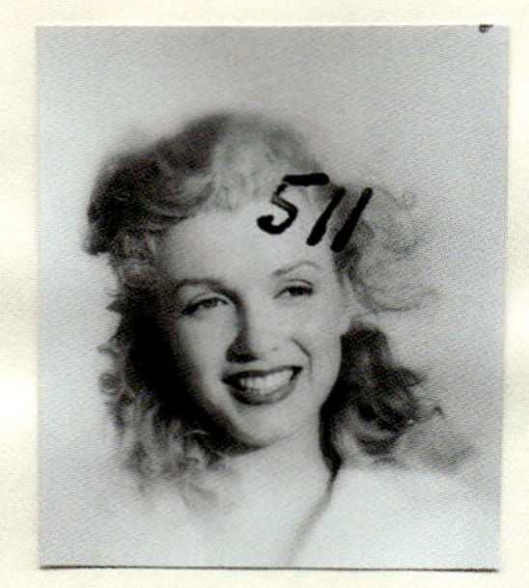

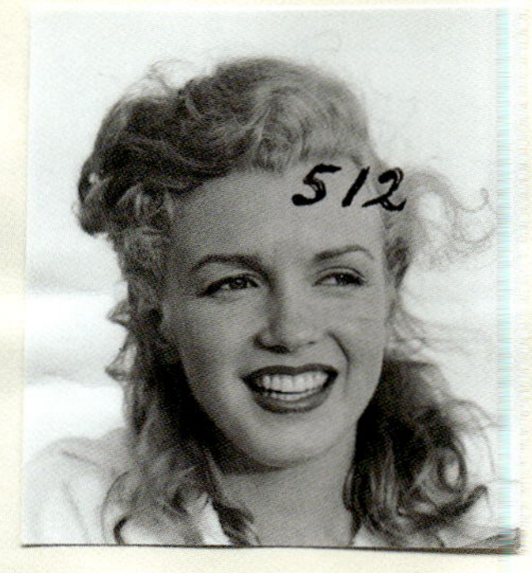

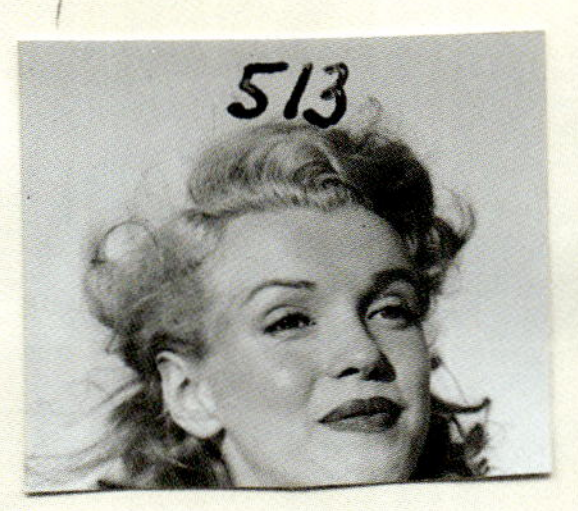

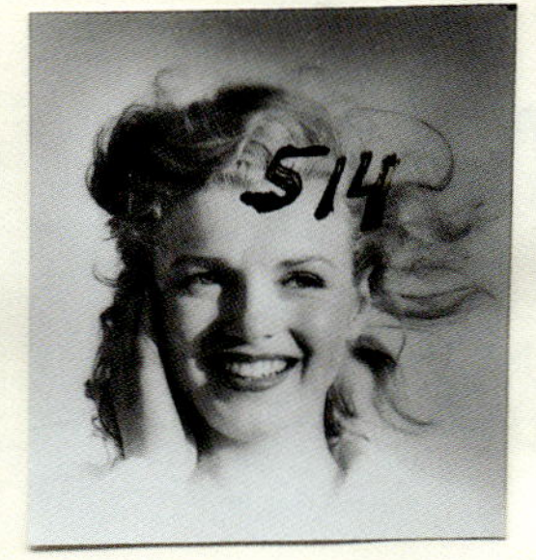

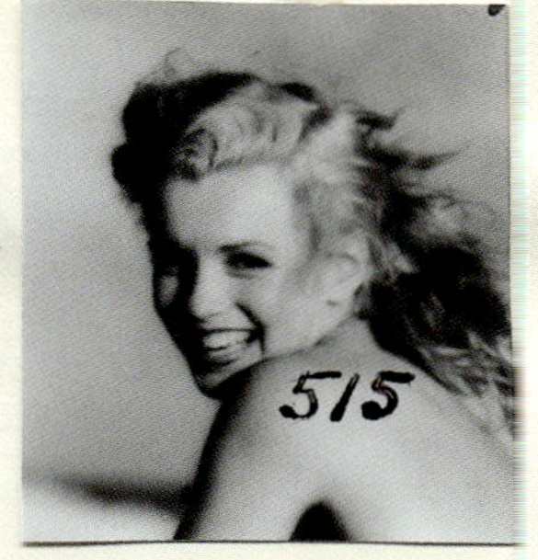

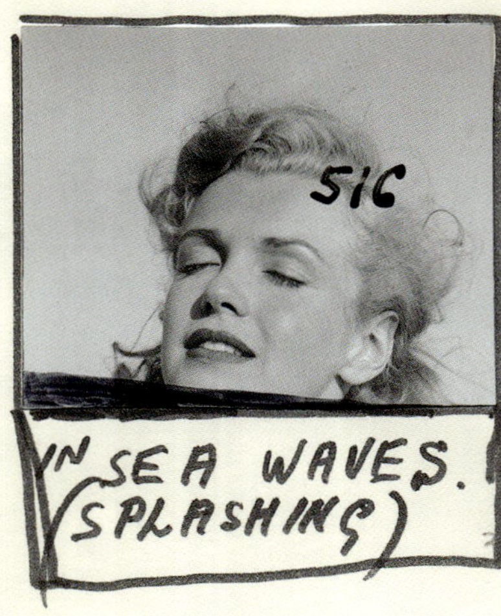

IN SEA WAVES.
(SPLASHING)

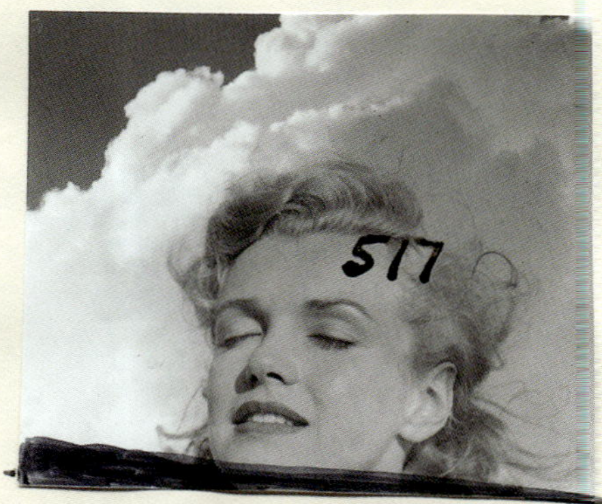

307/B

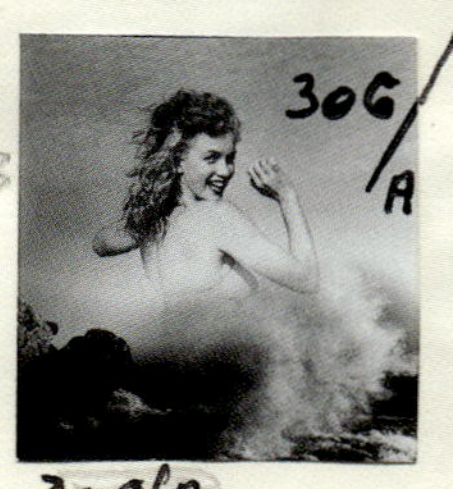

306/A

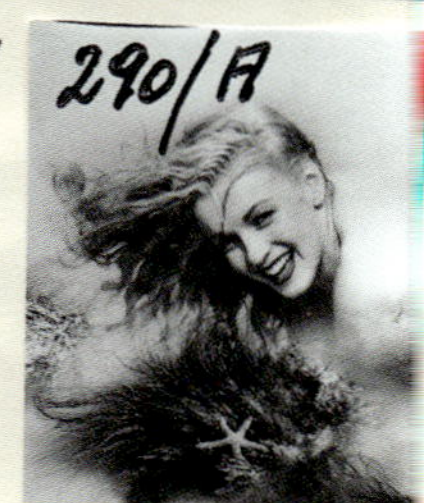

ANDRE DE DIENES
1401 SUNSET PLAZA DRIVE
HOLLYWOOD, CALIF. 90069

1949

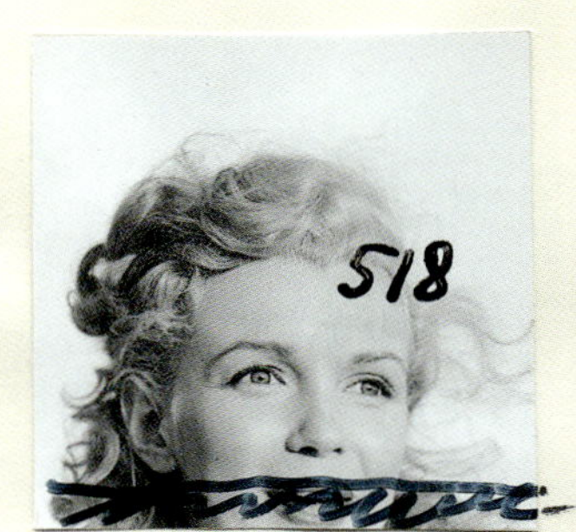

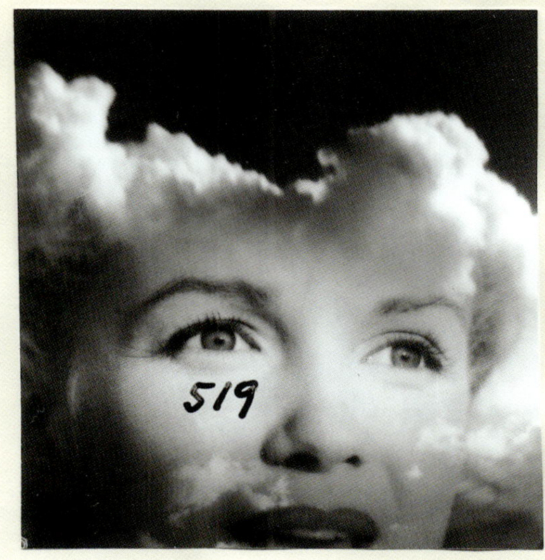

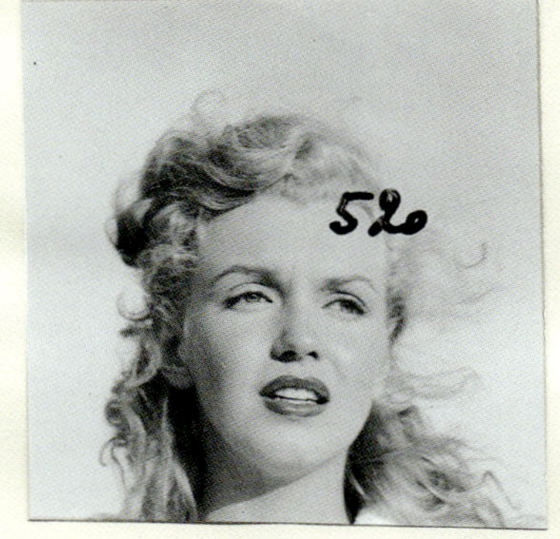

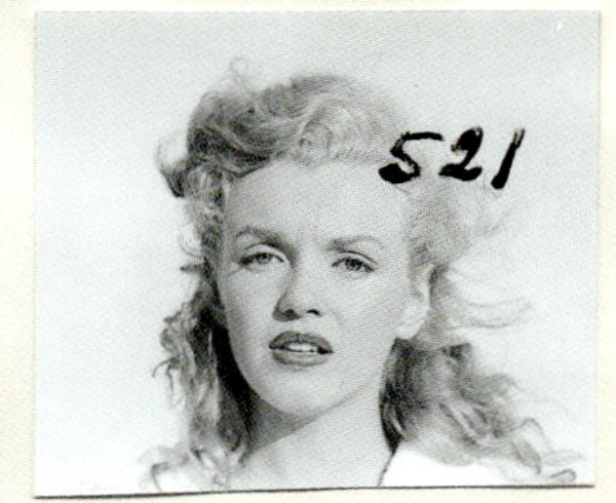

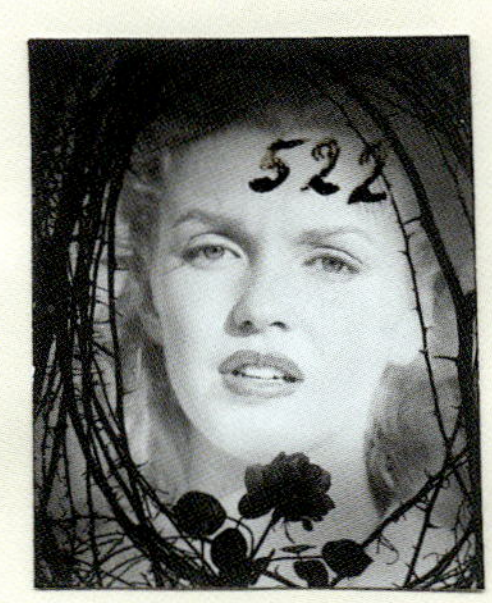

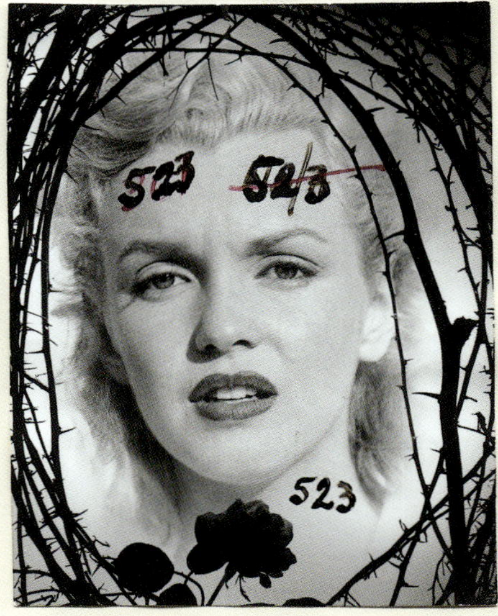

ANDRE DE DIENES 75
1401 SUNSET PLAZA DRIVE

1949

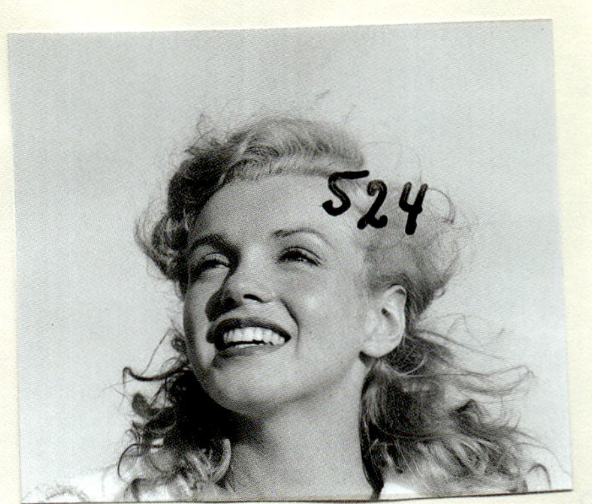

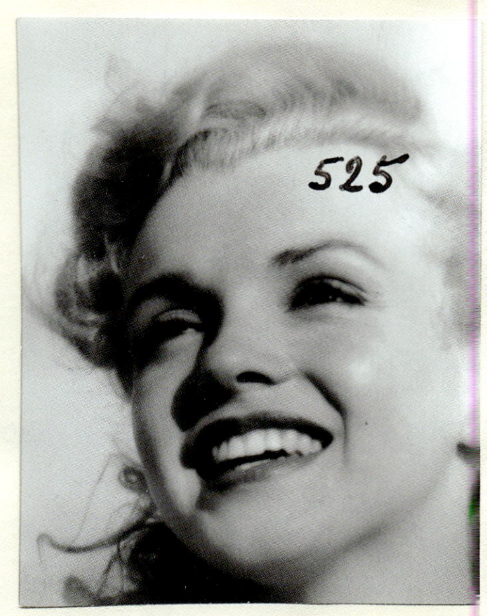

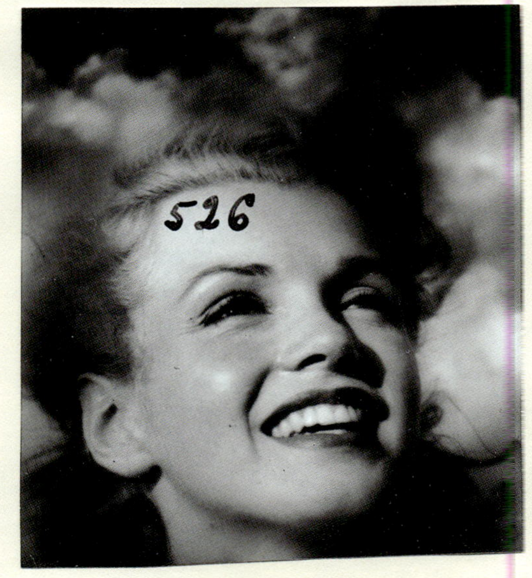

ANDRE DE DIENES
1401 SUNSET PLAZA DRIVE
HOLLYWOOD, CALIF. 90069

76

1949 ~~1950~~

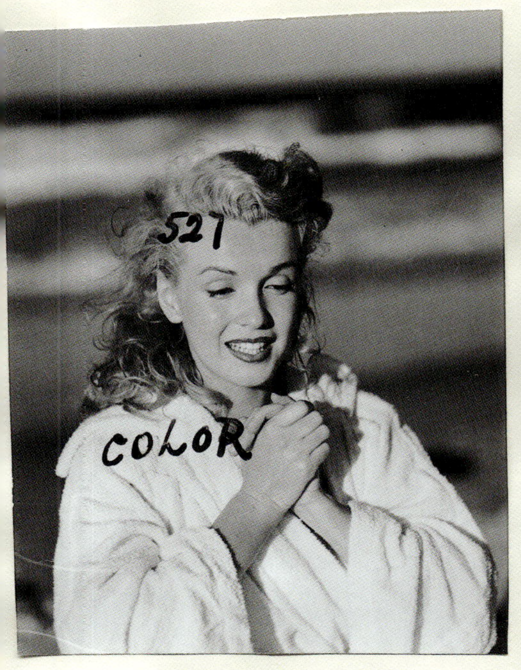

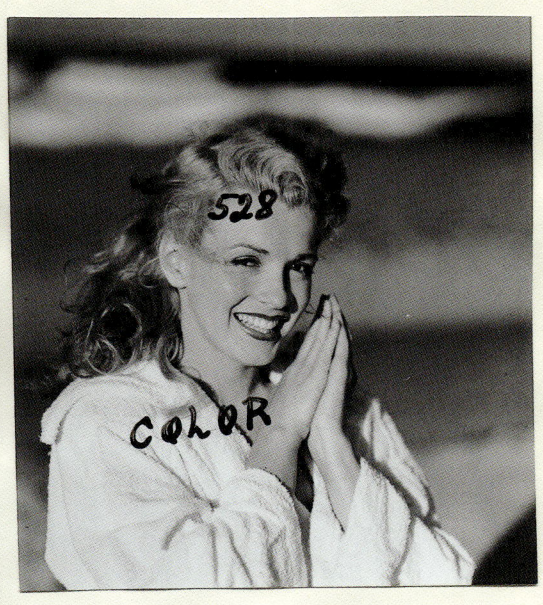

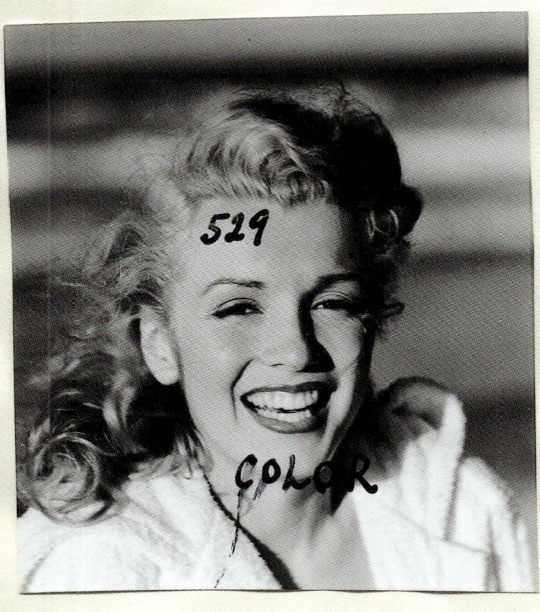

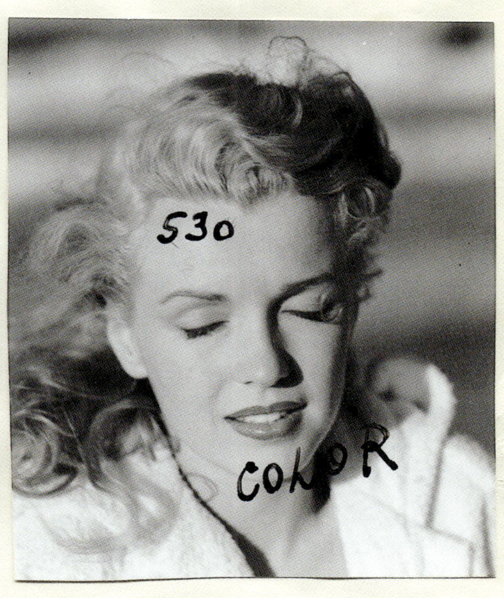

ANDRÉ DE DIENES
1401 SUNSET PLAZA DRIVE
HOLLYWOOD CALIF 90069

77

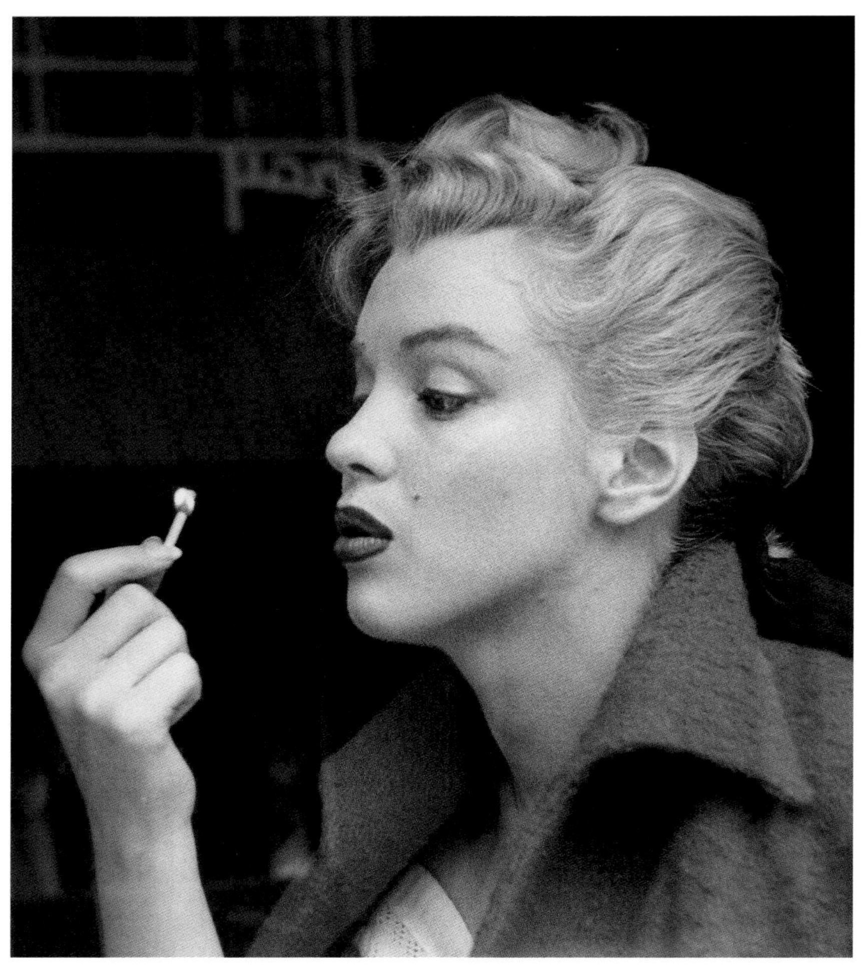

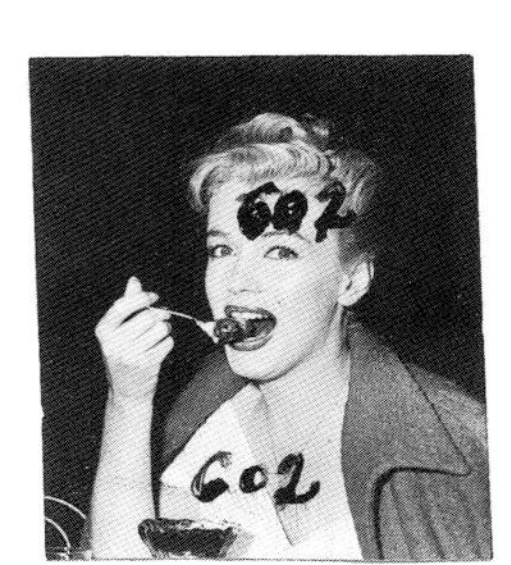

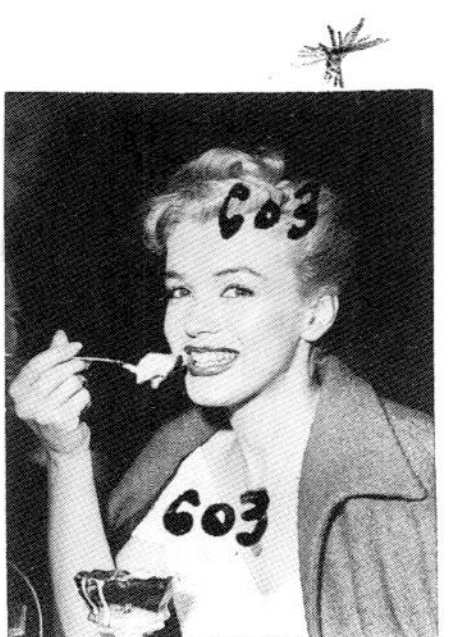

AT THE ICE CREAM PARLOR

<u>Unexpected Visitor</u> During the latter part of 1950, I decided to give up living in New York for good. The paintings, art and antiques that had taken me years to accumulate brought me a few thousand dollars at auction, and with a new Cadillac, my cameras, books, and my gray Persian cat, I left New York. After I got to Los Angeles, I went to see a real estate agent and explained frankly that I had eight thousand dollars to put down on a small house, somewhere on the hillside, not too far from Sunset Strip. I was shown only three houses and for a very peculiar reason I decided on one immediately. My choice was swift and final. The house was new, not even finished, a small modern ranch-type house with a long carport. I could see the city below from the small yard in front of the house. I told the agent that as soon as I gave him the down payment, he should let me move in right away, before the deal even went through escrow.

It sounds glamorous that I bought a house in Hollywood with Marilyn living not too far from me, but I hastily inform the reader that much of the adjacent hills were undeveloped land, covered with tall brush, which provided refuge to all kinds of rodents, lizards, spiders, scorpions, and snakes of several varieties. Every night small foxes and coyotes came to my yard looking for food. I lived only a few hundred feet from Sunset Boulevard, where famous movie stars gathered every night, but the hillside around me was dark and undeveloped!

I got busy photographing nudes, because I had an immediate market for them. Meanwhile, Marilyn was busy with her career. Occasionally,

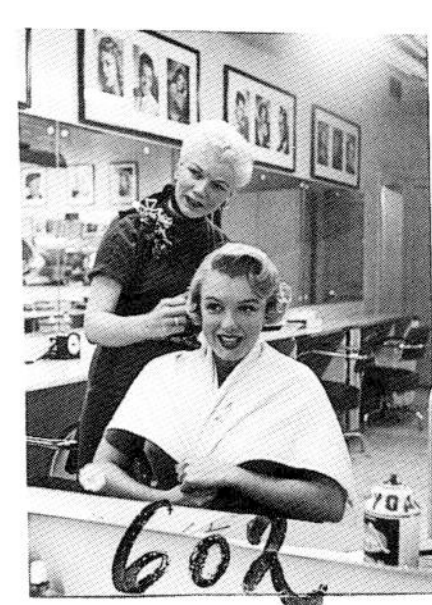

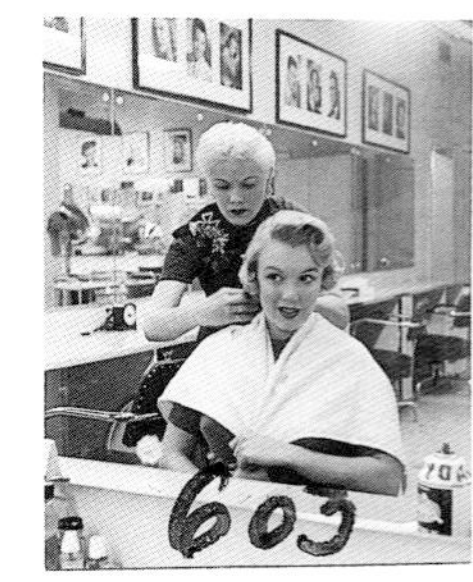

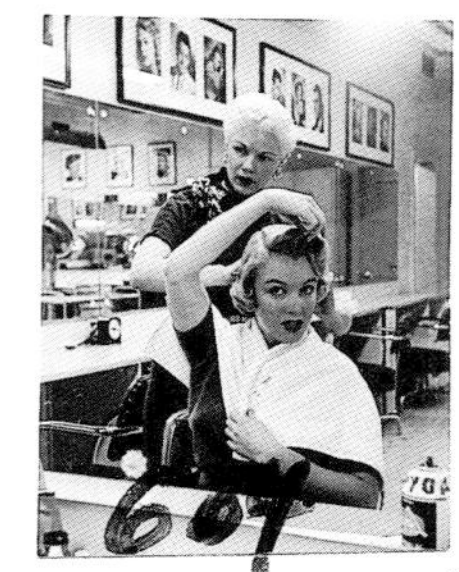

AT FOX STUDIO'S MAKEUP DEPT. 604
WITH "GLORIA" THE HAIRDRESSER

she visited me unexpectedly. I respected and treasured the joyful, occasional visits Marilyn paid me during her stardom. Usually, when she felt unhappy, very low in morale, unexpectedly she rang at my door. She came by taxi and left by taxi.

She came to complain and to discuss some of her problems and even to ask my advice about trifles. Then, she cooked a meal and washed the dishes. Each of her sporadic visits was like a little present to me. Usually, as soon as she arrived, I opened a bottle of French Beaujolais wine and I drank, purposely, because I did not want to continue cerebral conversations for too long, or to engage in any of my jealous outbursts. I became exhilarated, intoxicated, because I wanted her to listen to my favorite operatic arias from the stacks of records I had of Puccini – Tosca, La Bohème, Madame Butterfly, Manon Lescaut – and many others. I shed tears of joy and sadness, and one time I poured red wine on her feet and kissed them passionately, aroused by the gloriously happy music from the first part of Verdi's La Traviata. And later, when in the last act Violetta was dying, I was crying and kept pouring red wine on her feet and messed up the rug with the wine. She laughed and said I was completely mad! But she was happy, pleased, contented, satisfied! Nobody in the world knew where she was during those few hours. But only rarely could she escape her reality. Here, with me, it was as if she were on a desert island, in complete isolation from the outside.

Only once did the phone ring while she was with me, and an angry female voice I immediately recognized was asking for her. It was

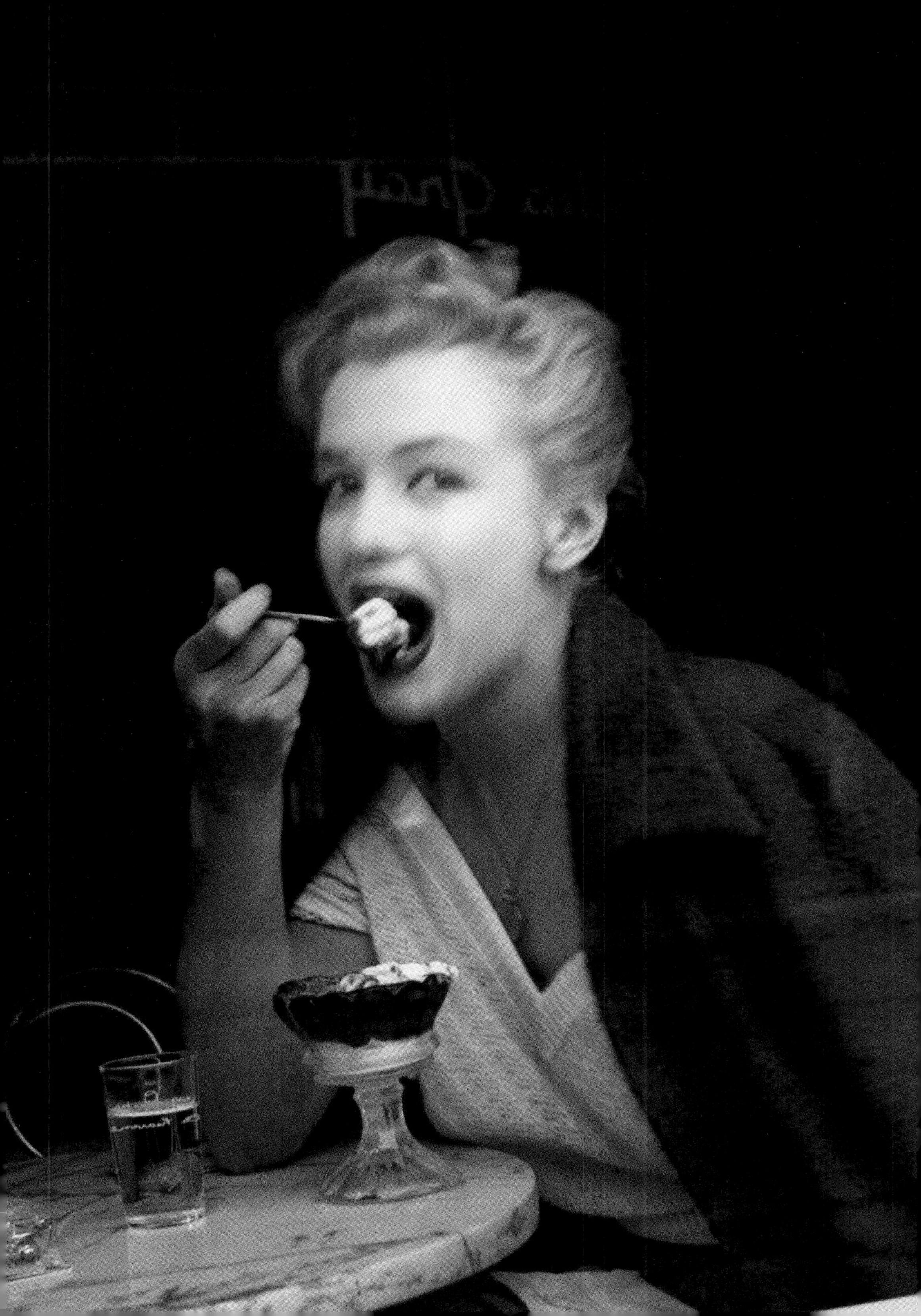

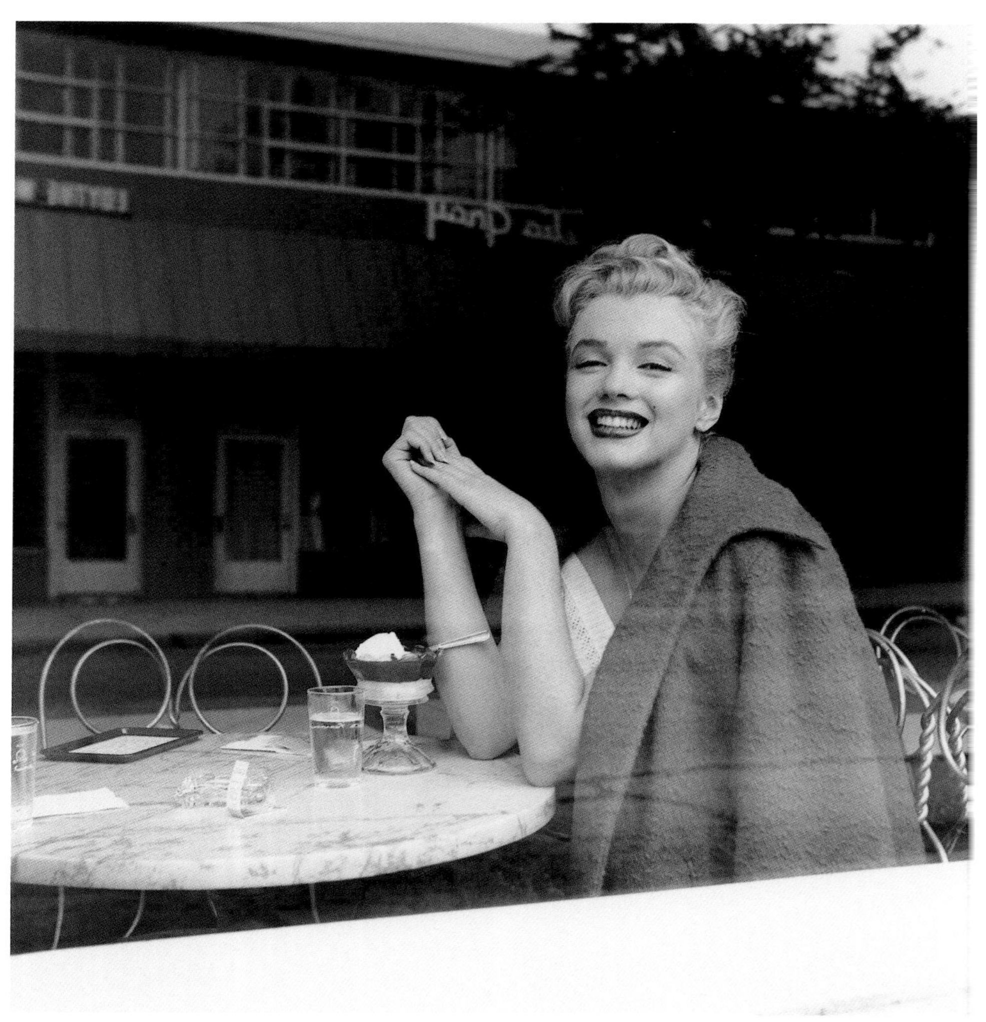

Marilyn's acting coach, Natasha Lytess, who dominated Marilyn's career in those years. I said Marilyn wasn't with me, but she shouted at me not to lie! She said she knew she was in my house! I can never forget that occasion. Marilyn and I were lying side by side on the living room rug, both of us transfixed, spellbound by the beautiful soprano voice singing Mimi's aria, "Si, mi chiamano Mimi" from the first act of La Bohème. And I was telling Marilyn in my wonderfully delirious state of mind that not in a thousand years, in fact, never again will there be another composer like Puccini. Marilyn herself was in tears, moved by the music, when the ringing of the phone and the harsh voice of Natasha interrupted us. I screamed at Marilyn for having been so stupid as to let the woman know where she was that afternoon. Marilyn left me in haste, greatly worried.

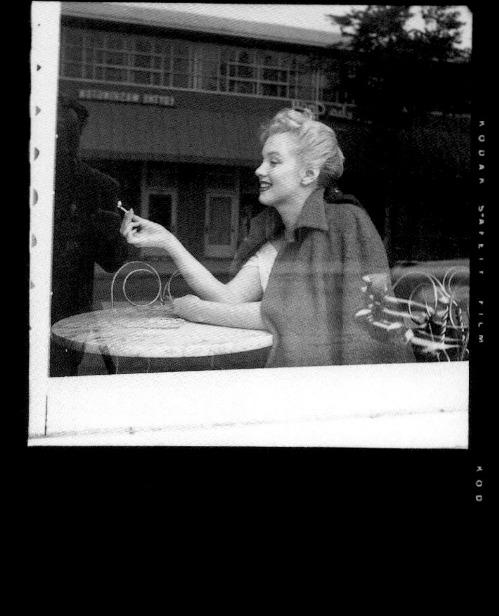
KODAK SAFETY FILM

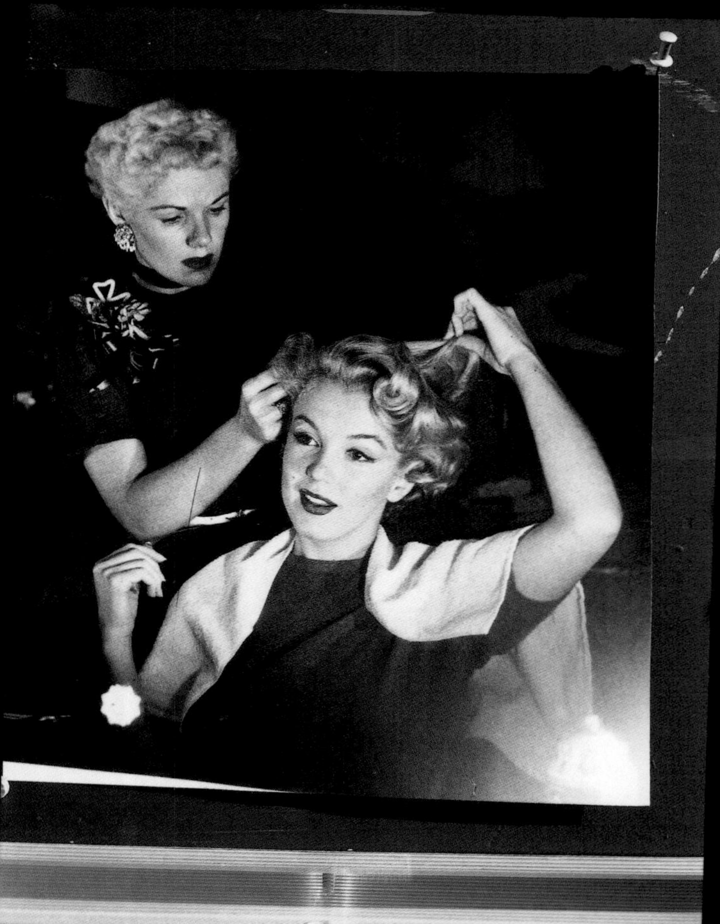

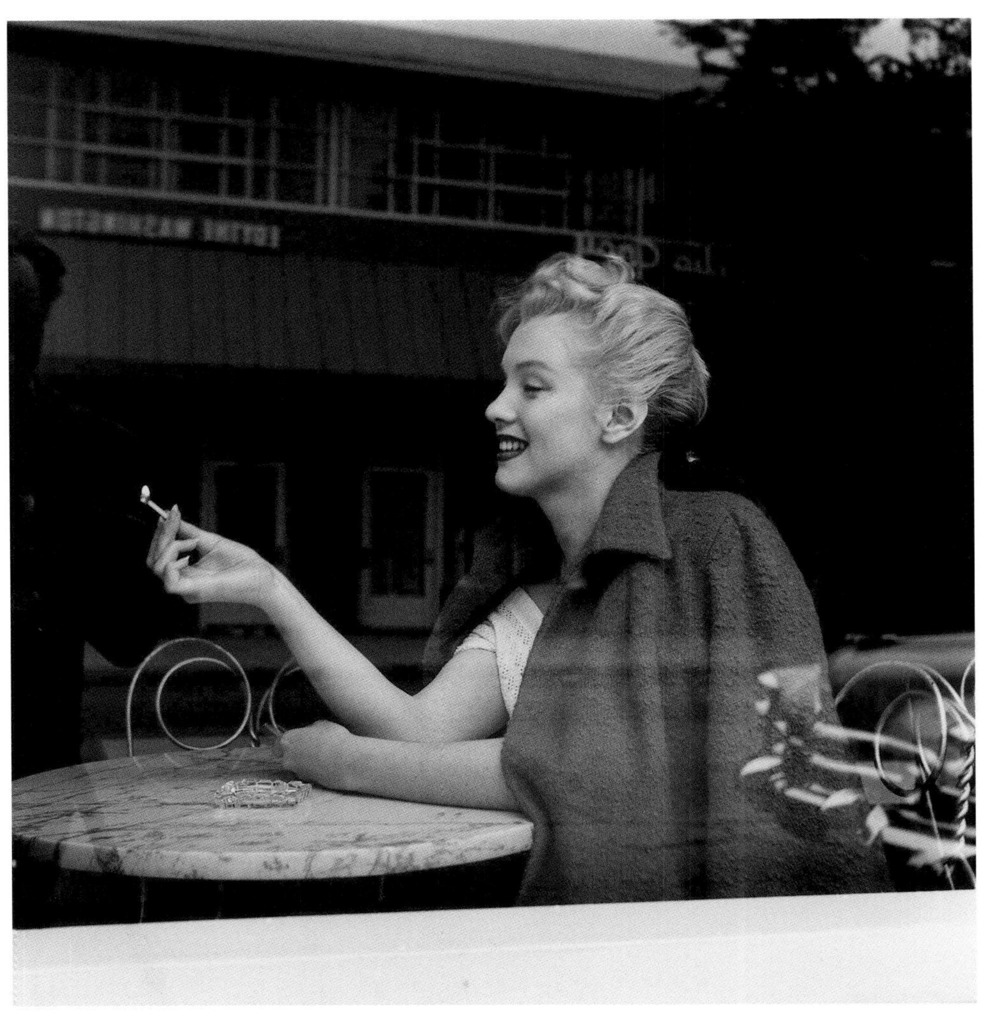

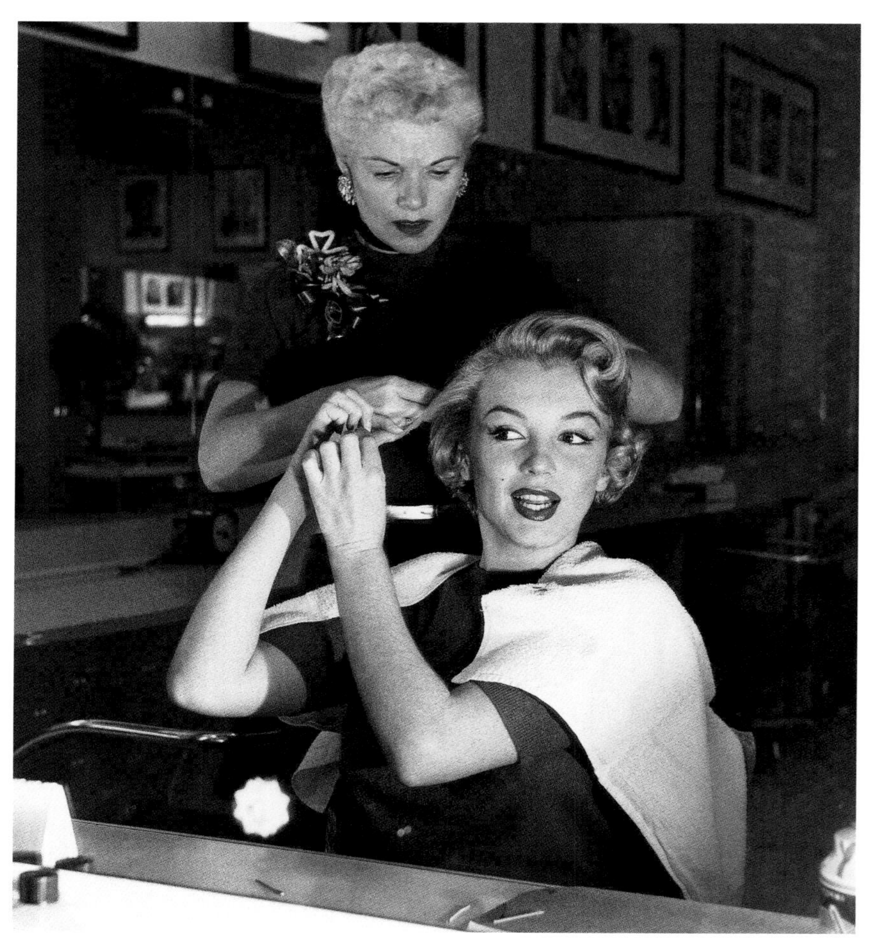

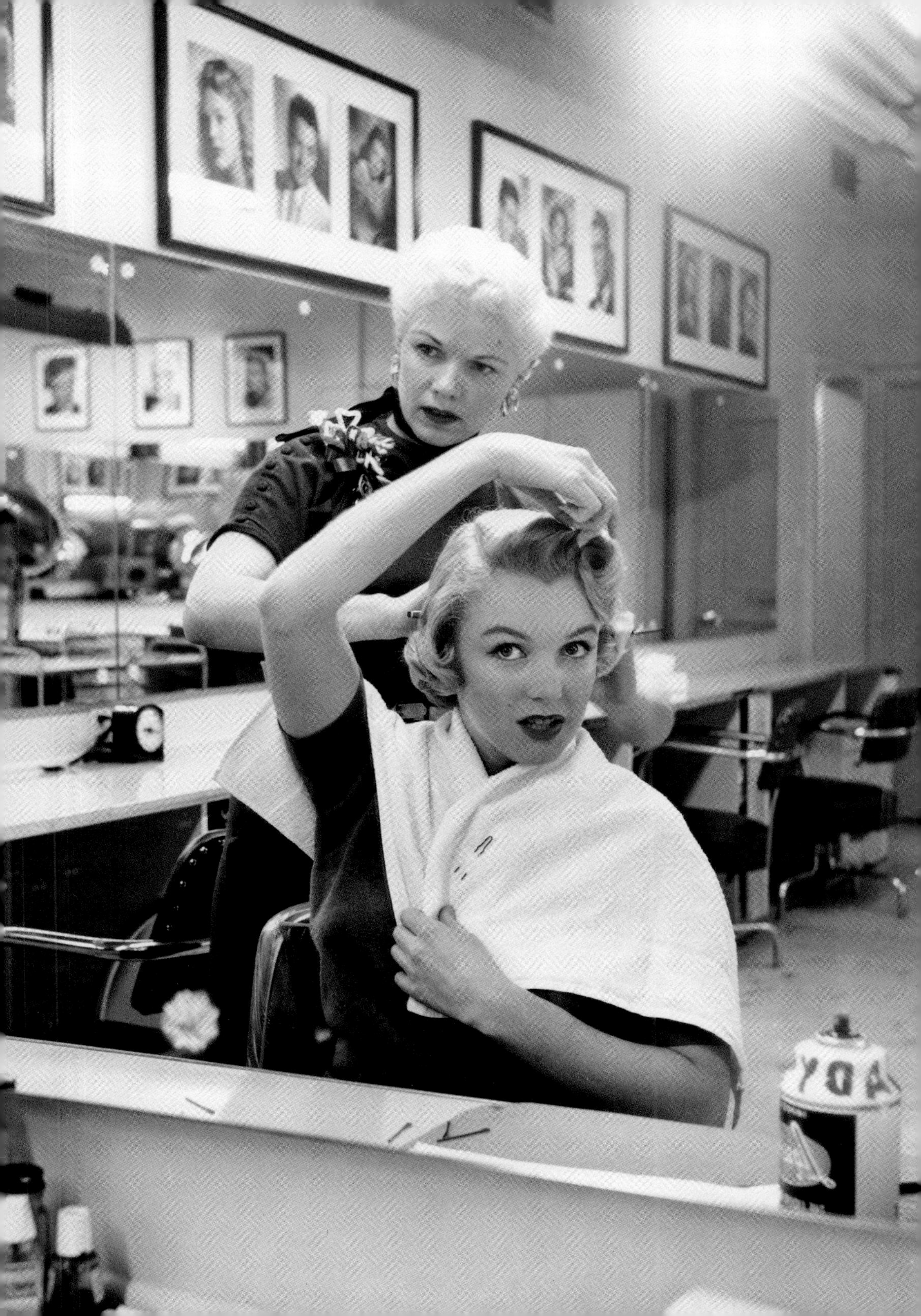

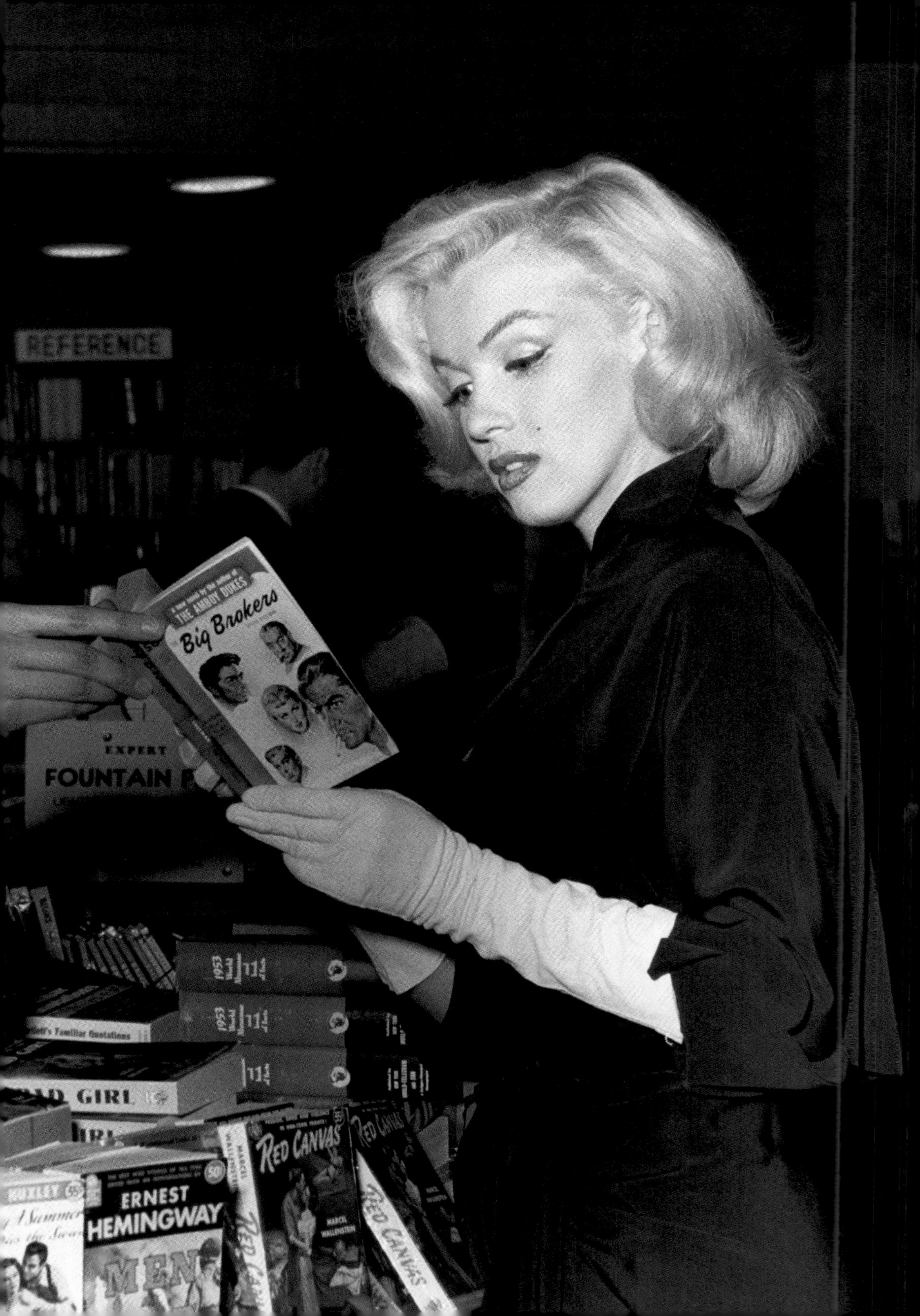

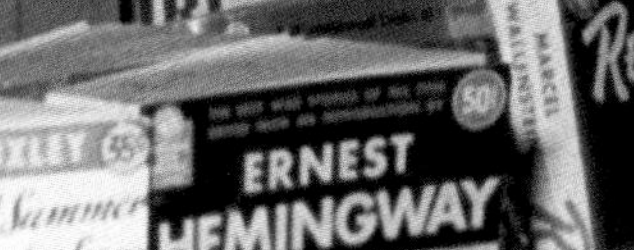
REFERENCE
THE AMBOY DUKES
Big Brokers
EXPERT
Familiar Quotations
RED CANVAS
MARCEL WALLENSTEIN
HUXLEY
ERNEST
HEMINGWAY

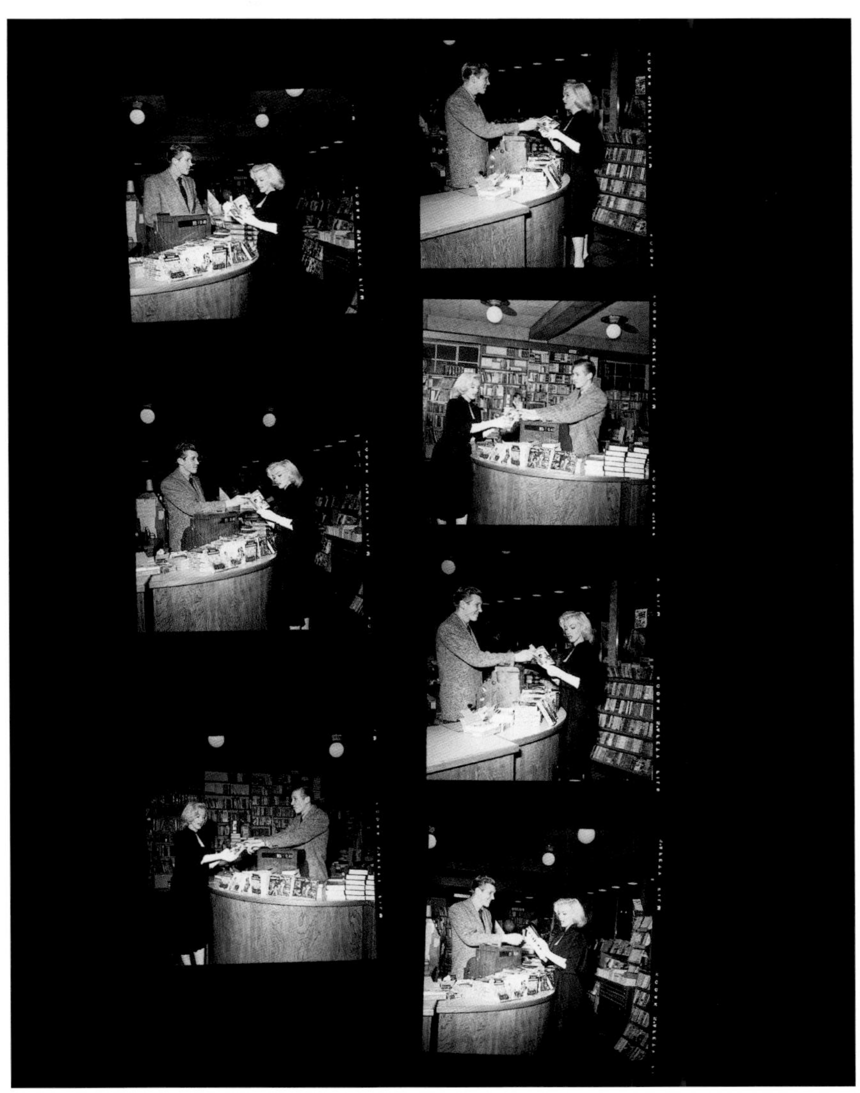

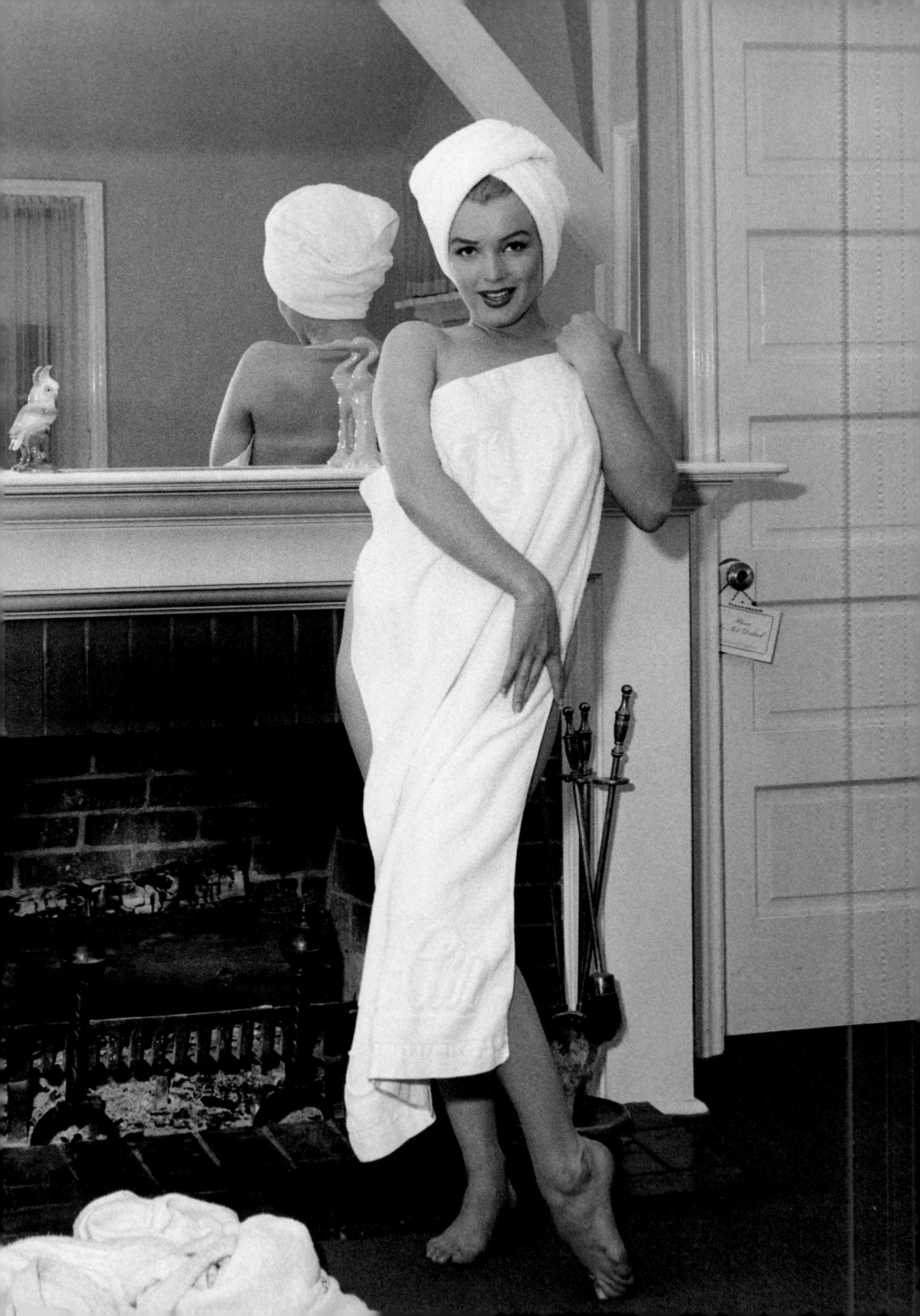

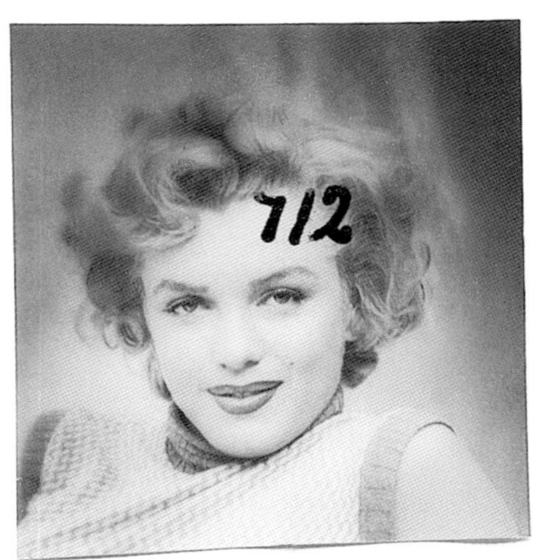

Bel Air Hotel   In 1949, Marilyn had posed nude for photographer Tom Kelley, because she needed the fifty dollars he paid for it. She never told me about it, but the truth came out three years later, in 1952. Ironically, I was with her when the story appeared in the newspapers that Marilyn had posed in the nude. Here I shall reminisce about it:

By late 1952, Marilyn had become an extremely successful actress. She was making one picture after another. I got a phone call from my agent in New York that *Pageant* magazine wanted a photo layout of the "Blonde Heat," as they called her. Roy Craft, the clever publicity man who had done a great deal to make Marilyn's fame an immense phenomenon, arranged for the sitting. Marilyn told him she and I were bosom friends and we wanted to be alone the day I would photograph her, that we didn't want any hairdressers, wardrobe ladies, or make-up men around us while we photographed. Marilyn's wish was a command — we had our privacy. I went to her bungalow at the Bel Air Hotel in Stone Canyon, an exclusive, beautiful place in a secluded canyon west of Beverly Hills. We started photographing about ten in the morning. Marilyn looked extremely lovely. She was in the happiest mood I had ever seen her. Then the phone rang.

I rushed to it and asked Marilyn not to touch it. We were going to take photographs all day and didn't want to be disturbed by anybody. I took many photos of her all morning and the phone kept ringing but she did not answer. She was extremely cooperative and greatly stimulated.

I had a delightful time photographing her and it was a rather unusual experience for me and for her, too, I guess, because she knew she was a great movie star and no longer my little Norma Jeane, not a girl whom I almost married! Yet we felt excessively comfortable with each other. She knew I respected and admired her and she had complete faith in my photography. No matter how I wished to pose her, she obeyed and all the pictures we took were delightful. There was absolutely no nervousness for any reason whatsoever. Only the phone's ringing bugged me, but I ordered her not to touch it!

I took pictures of her inside the bungalow and out on the patio, and by late afternoon she was taking a bubble bath. Afterward I began photographing her with a towel at the fireplace. She was in a bewitching mood! She had nothing on under the white towel, and mischievously she was opening and closing the towel, letting me see her nude for a split second, as if signaling to me that this was the occasion for me to photograph her nude – if I wanted to. These photos at the fireplace were to be the last photos of the day and we were planning to go out afterward to the most fancy restaurant, the most expensive place in Hollywood – Chasen's. Marilyn began insisting that she pay for dinner and for once I should let her be the boss! I told her we'd flip a coin. The phone rang again and rang and rang, and finally Marilyn picked it up. She kept listening and listening and gradually her expression turned frightened, practically horrified. She said something like, "Yes, I will, I will," and hung up the receiver. The change in her mood was

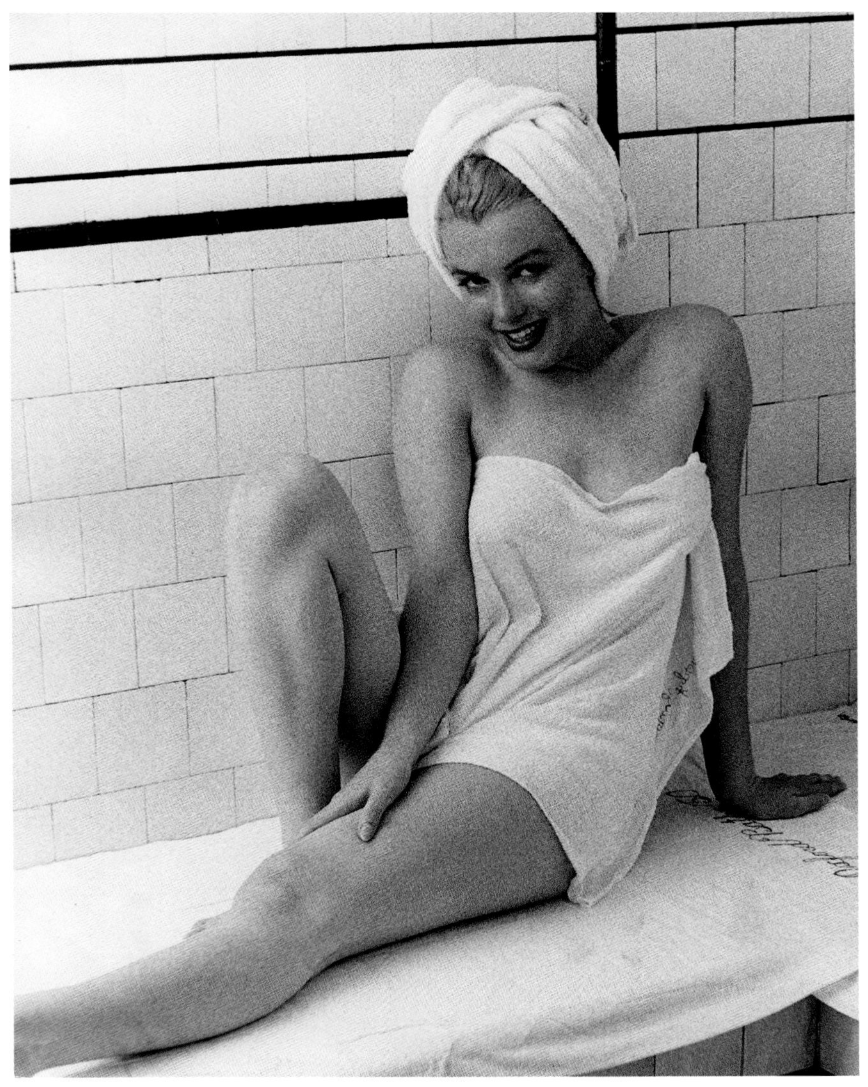

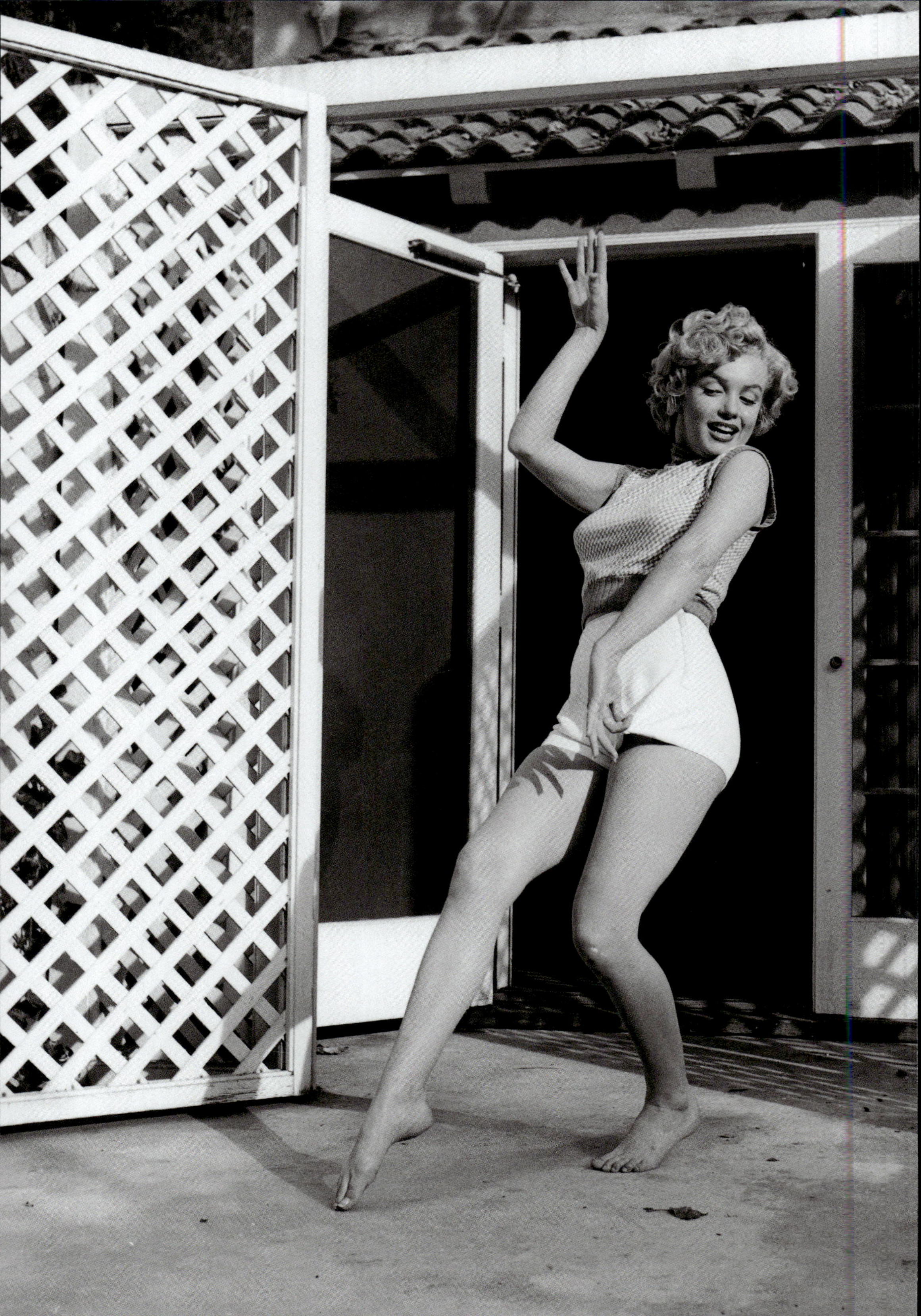

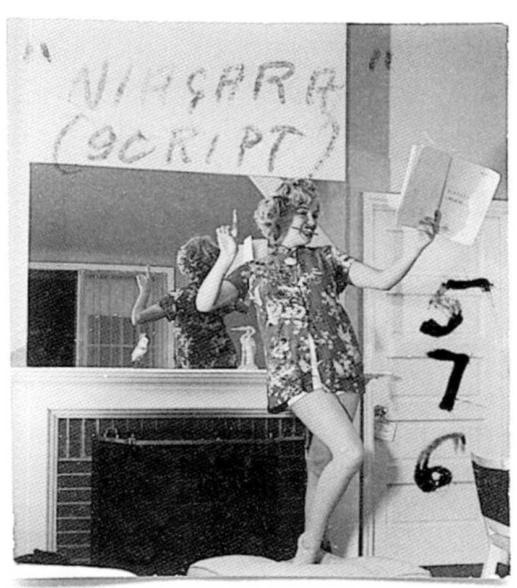

incredible. She was staggering away from the phone like someone who is ill, dizzy, ready to faint. I asked her what was wrong and she said she couldn't tell me. She said I had to leave her alone as she had to go to the studio at once to explain something. Even in those moments of distress she was so nice to me, she said I ought to order drinks for myself, and dinner, and charge it to her. I felt sad for her, and confused. I packed my equipment and left.

Days later, I found out what was the cause of her great distress. It was her studio that had called all afternoon; it was one of the executives at Fox who wanted her to come in at once, to explain the nude calendar which she had posed for. The story had just come out in the newspapers and the executives at Fox were worried her career might be totally ruined! A few evenings later, she came over to my house to look over the photos and I showed her all the lovely shots I had taken that day. She loved all the photos, she crossed out only one, and to reassure her I took the scissors and cut that negative to bits.

The nude calendar did not ruin her career. To the contrary! The write-ups about it in the newspapers coast-to-coast gave her even more publicity! And the public sympathized with her, thus her future fame was even more assured. In fact, I always suspected that all the brouhaha about the nude photo was a clever publicity stunt; Marilyn's publicity was always a stunning thing.

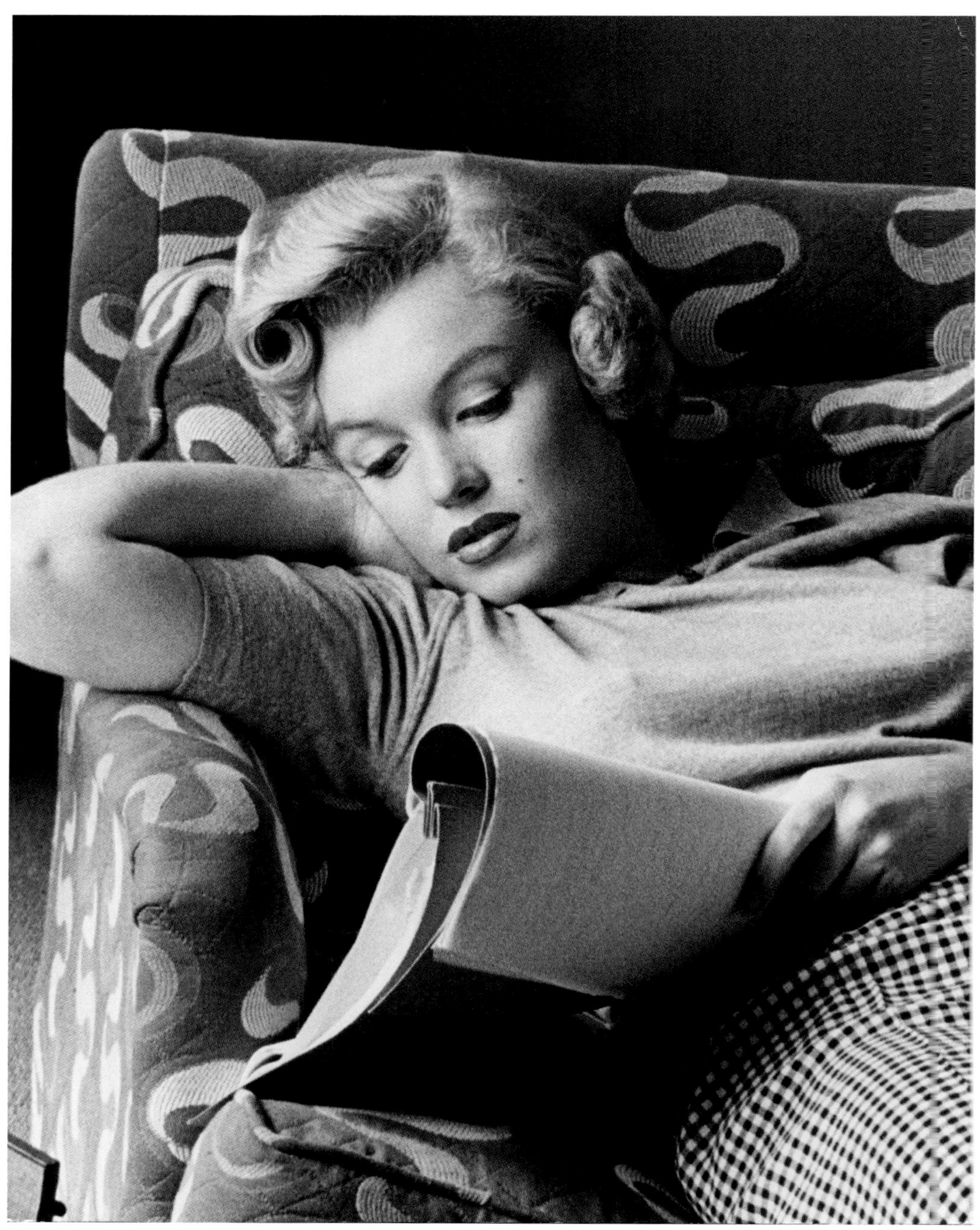

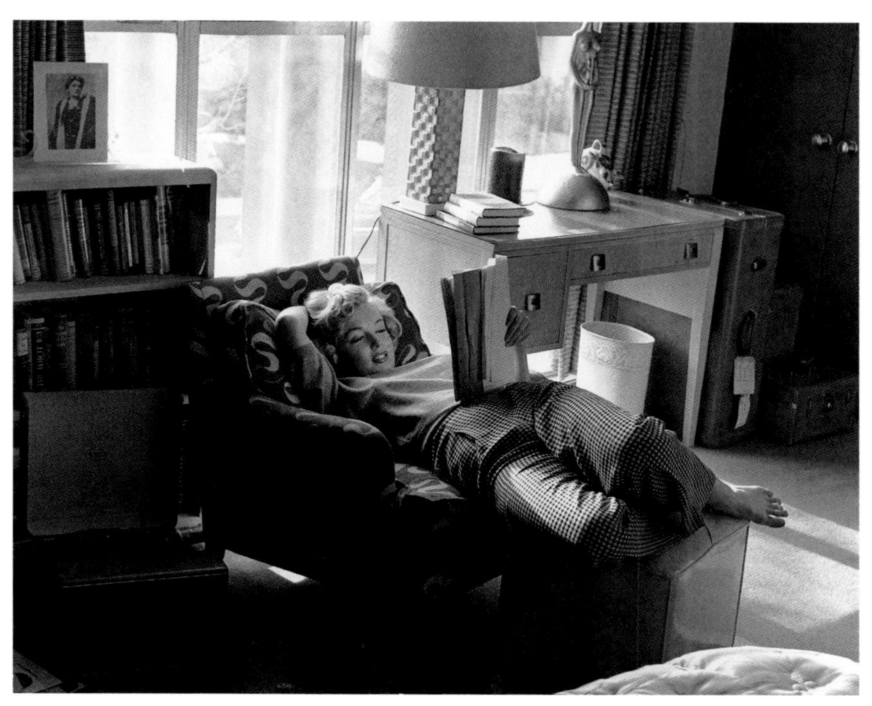

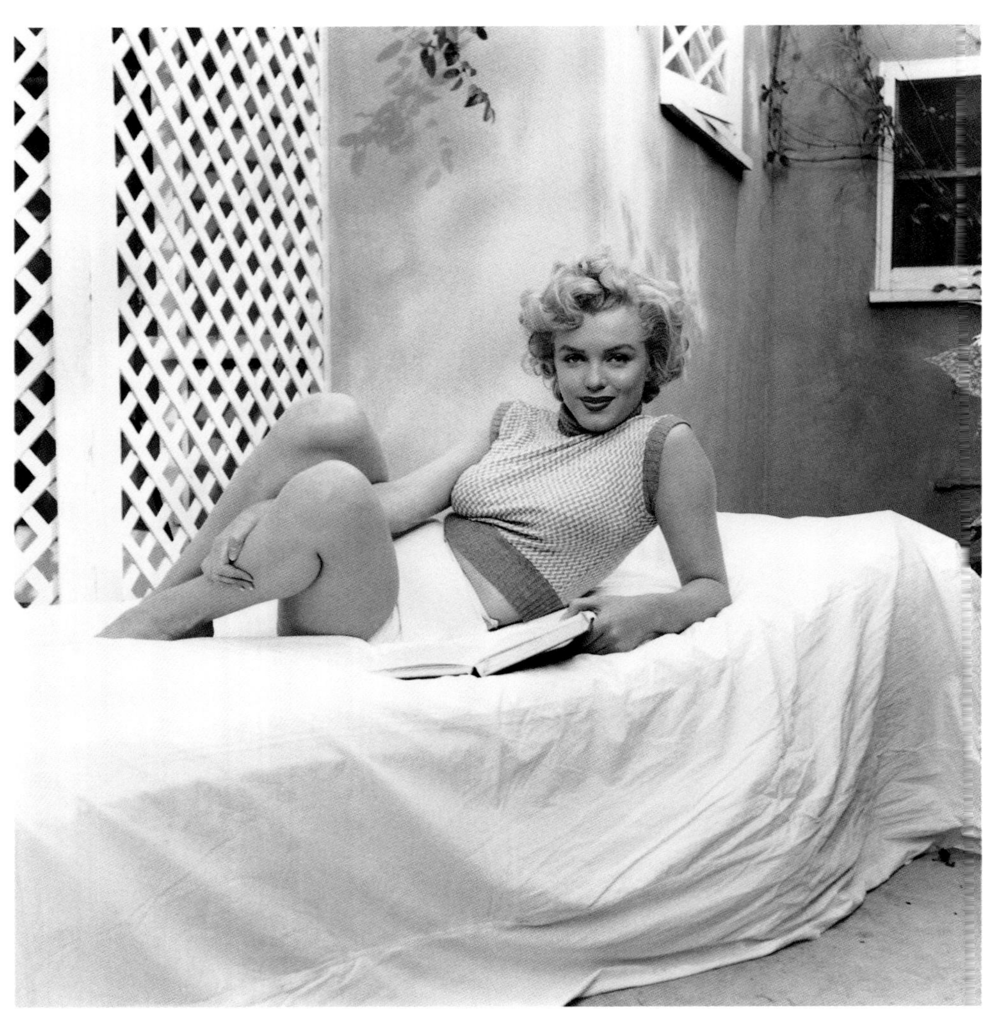

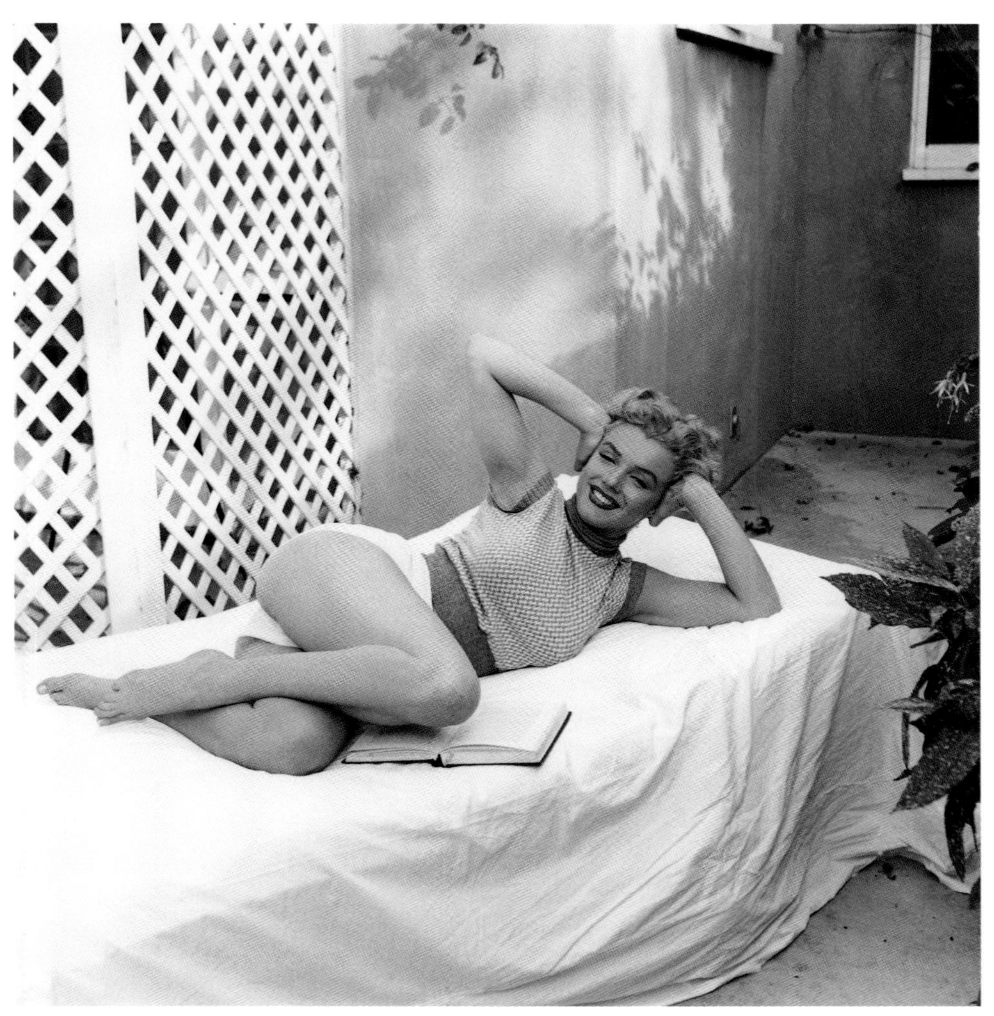

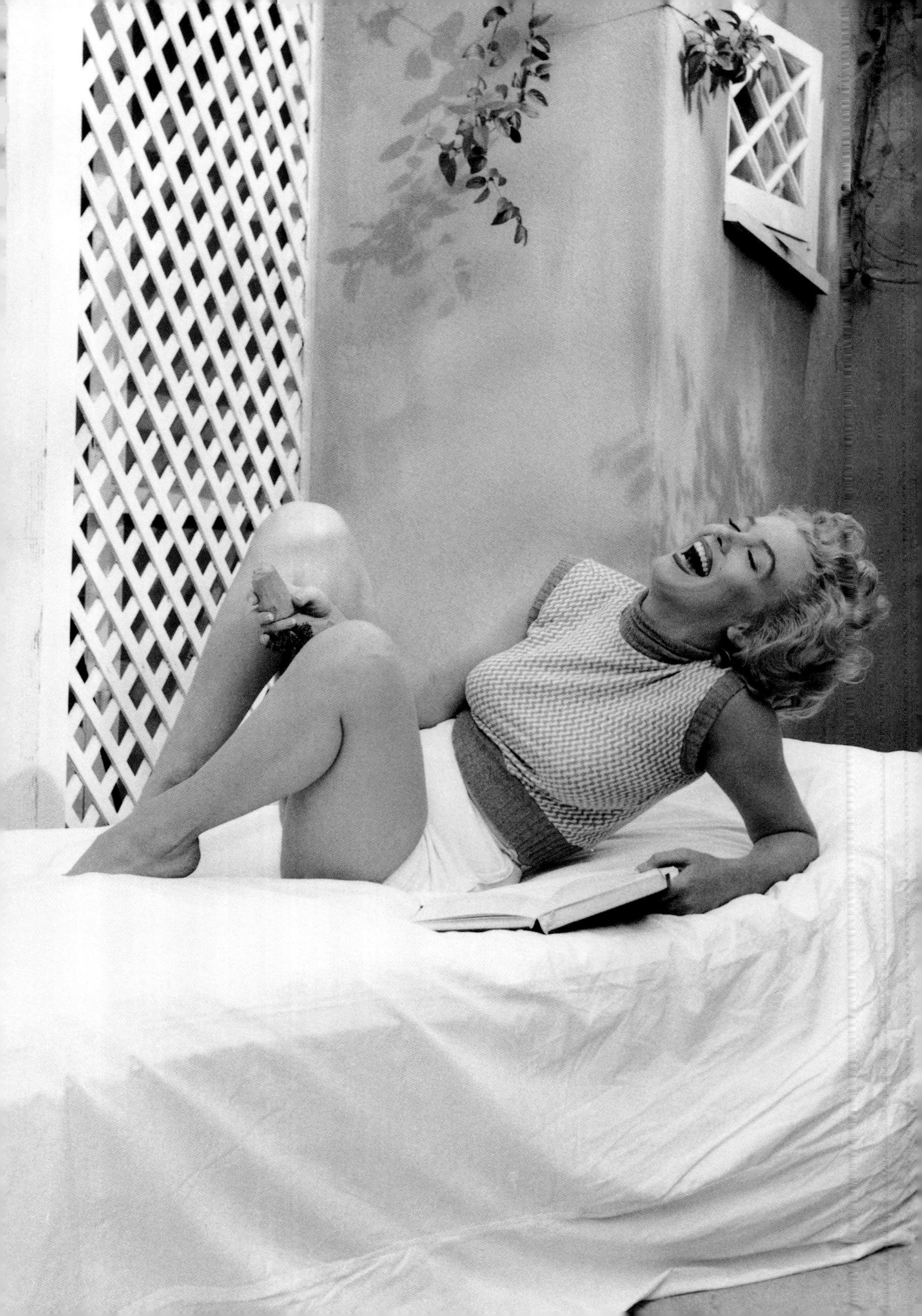

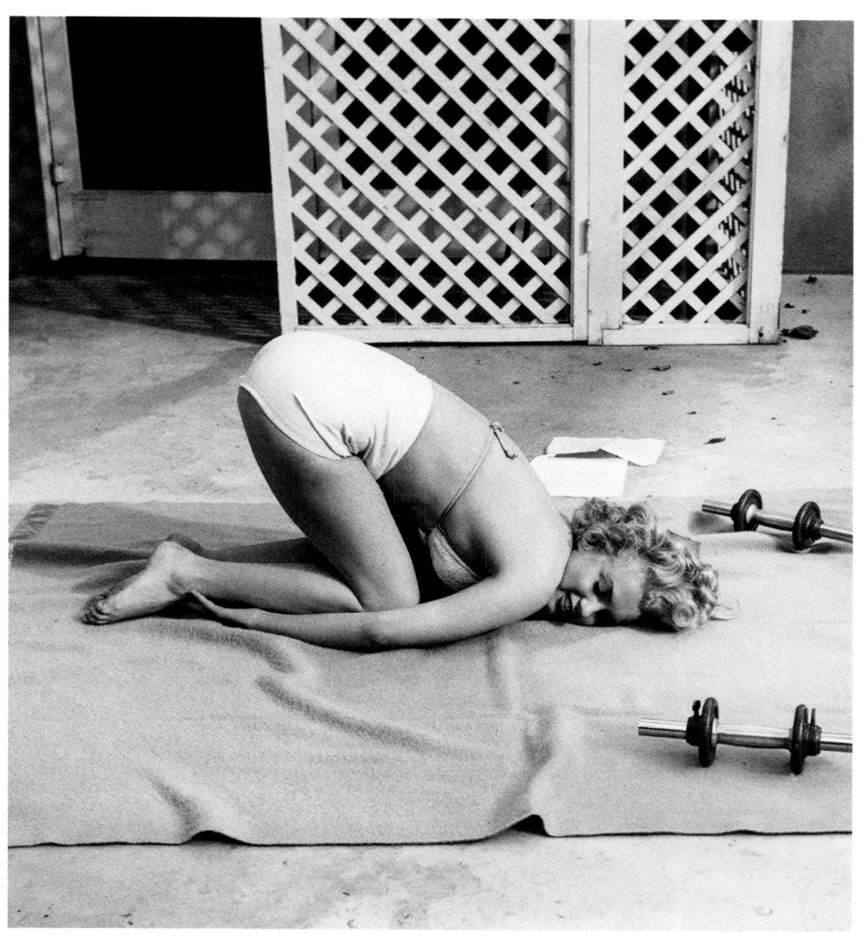

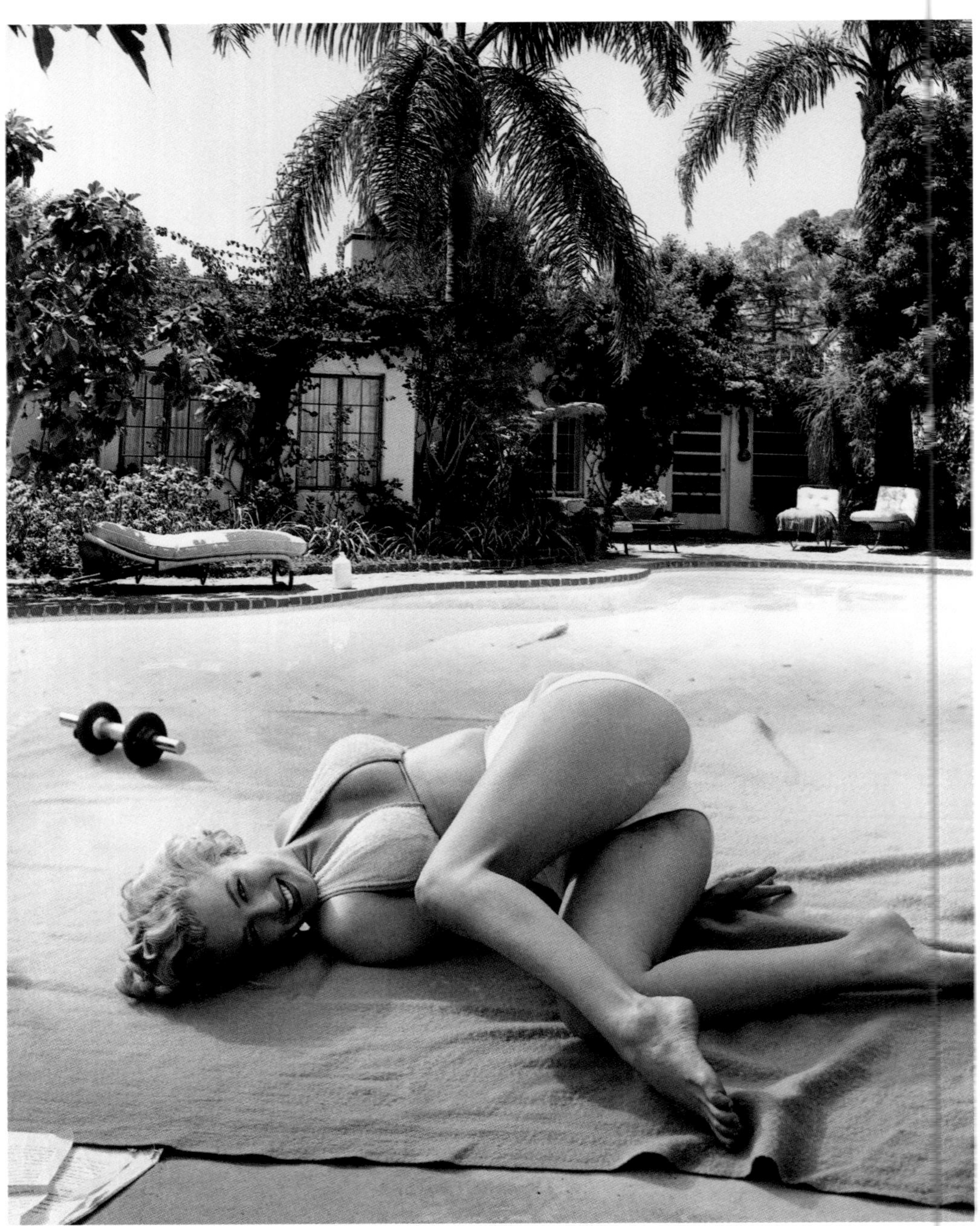

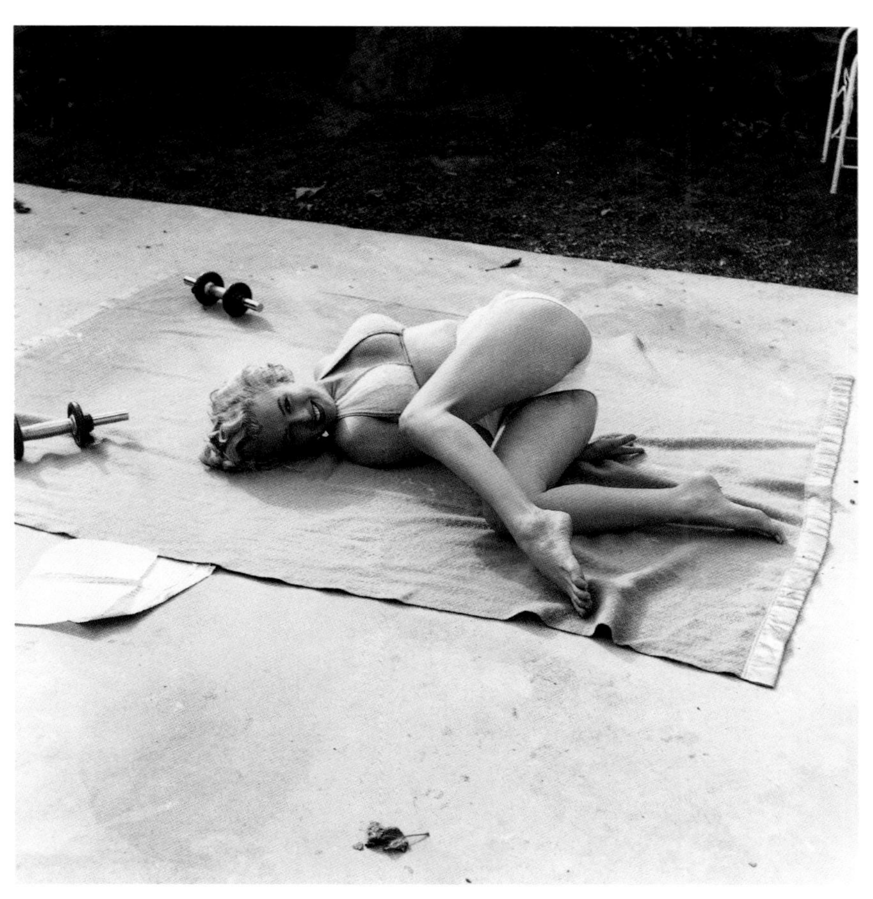

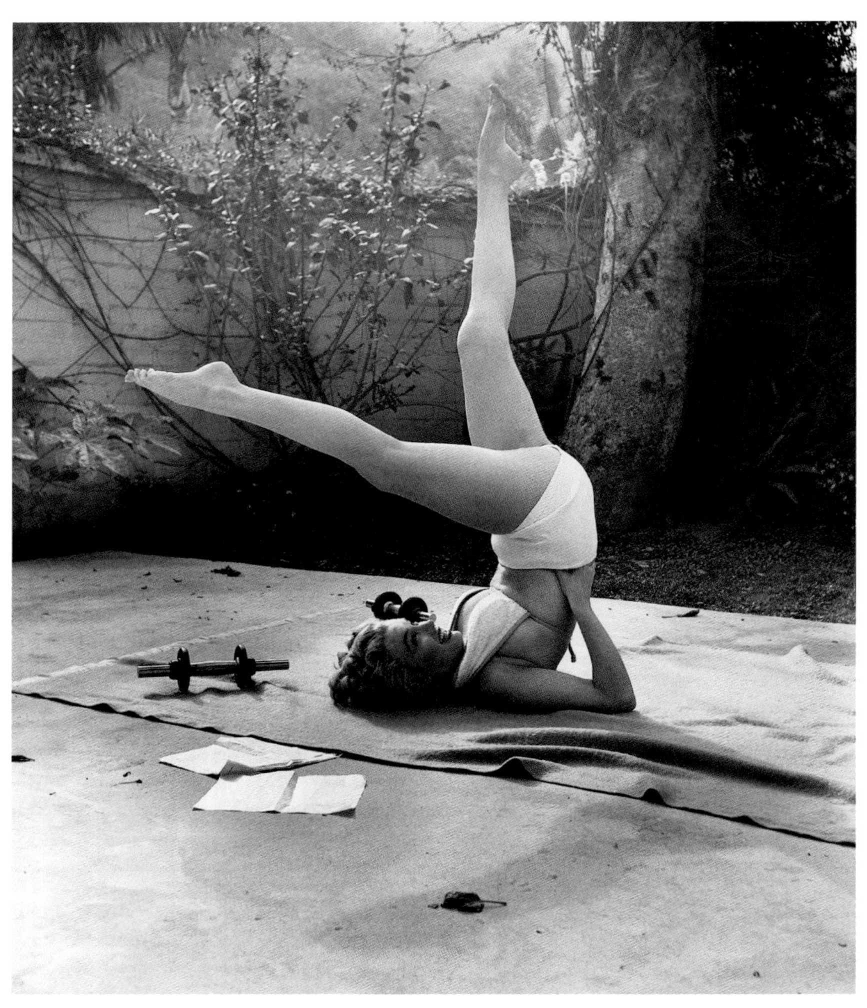

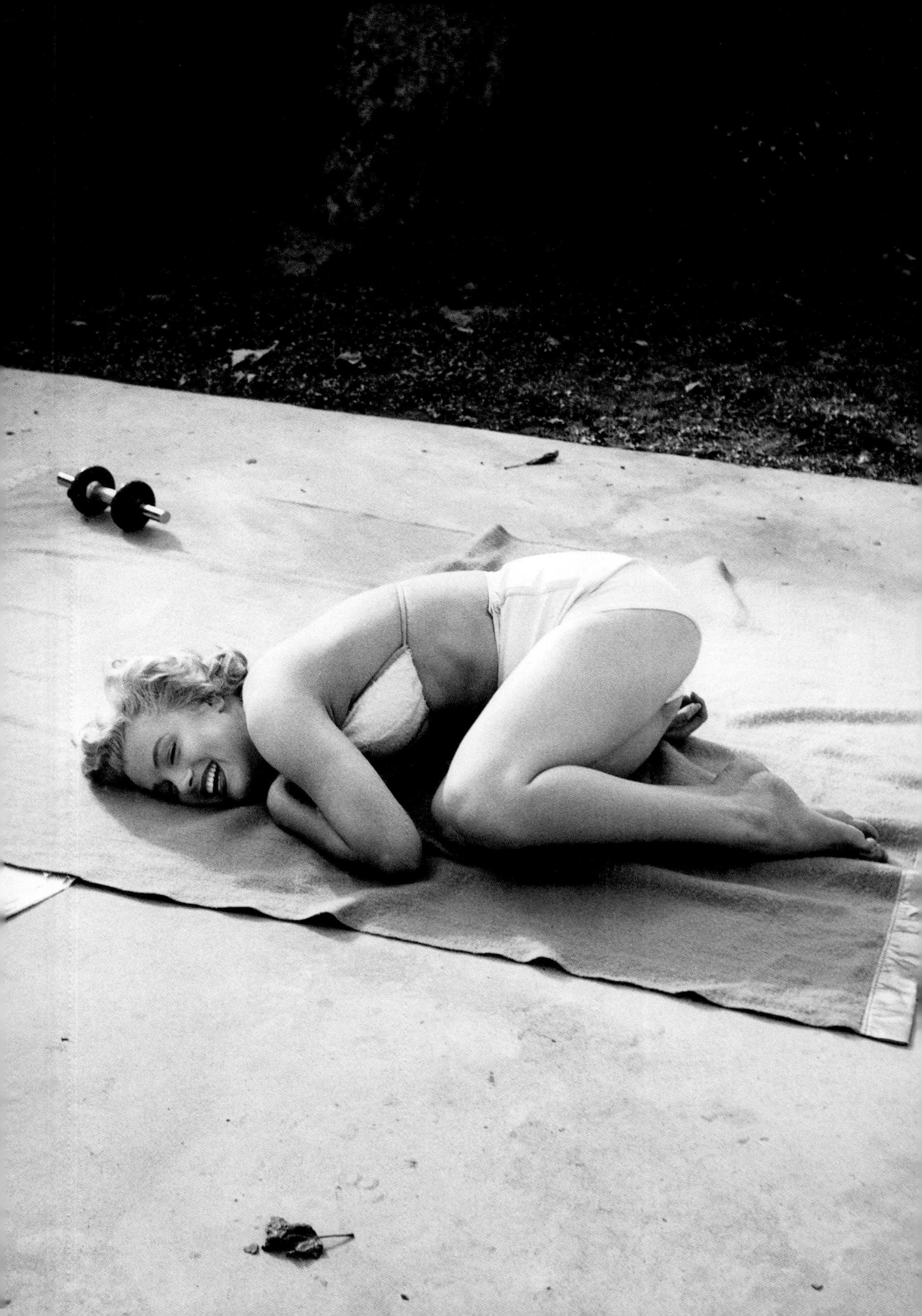

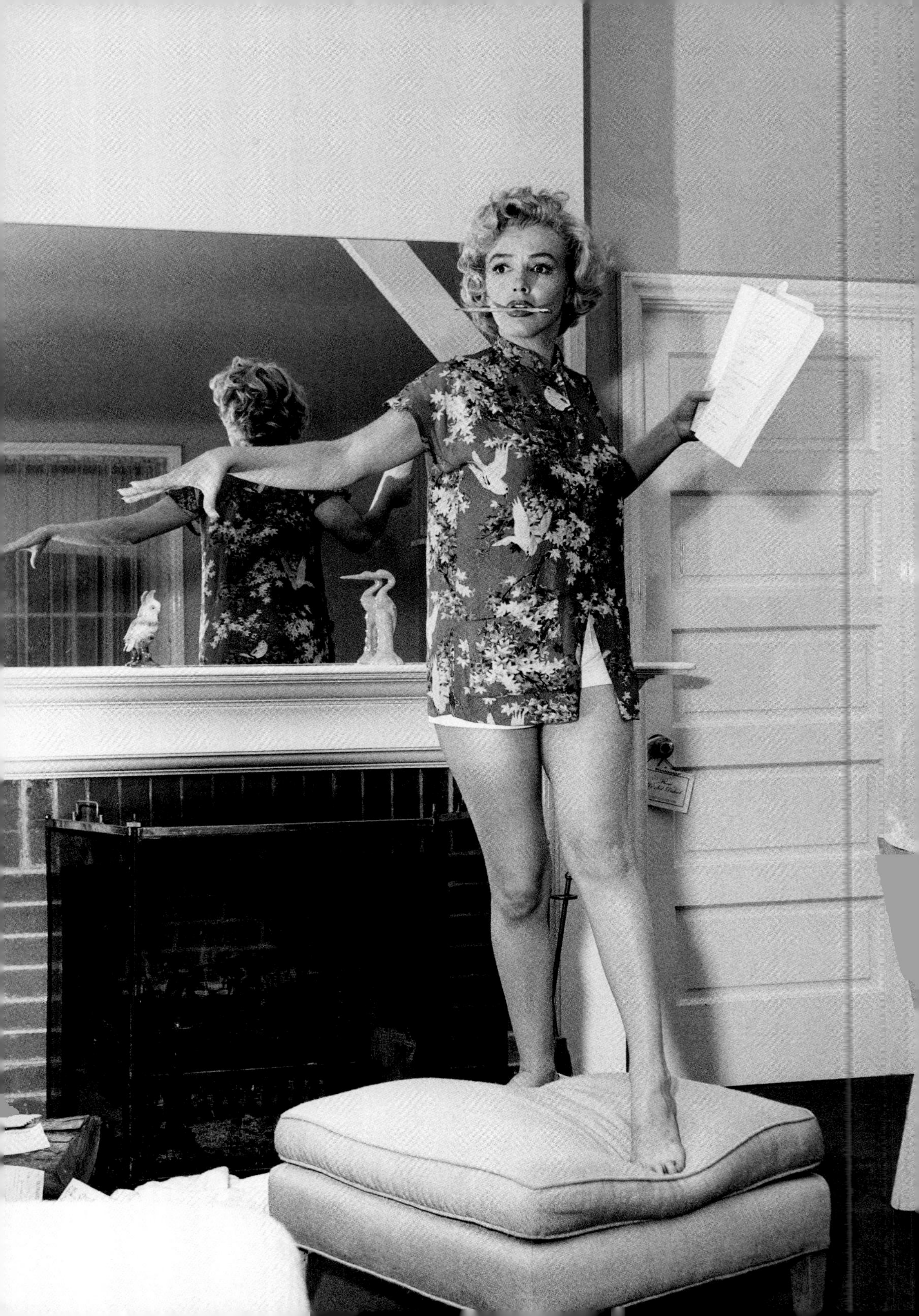

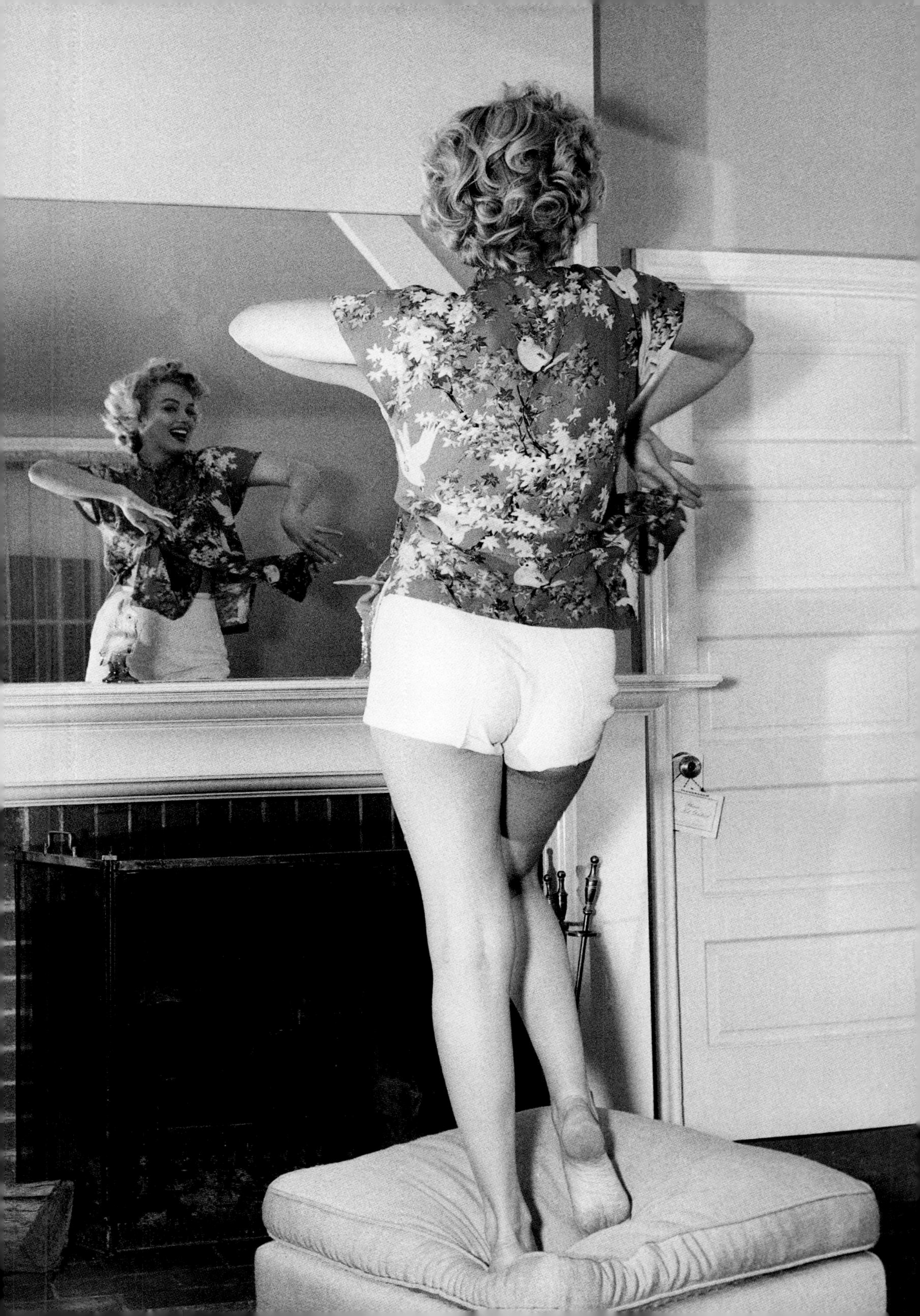

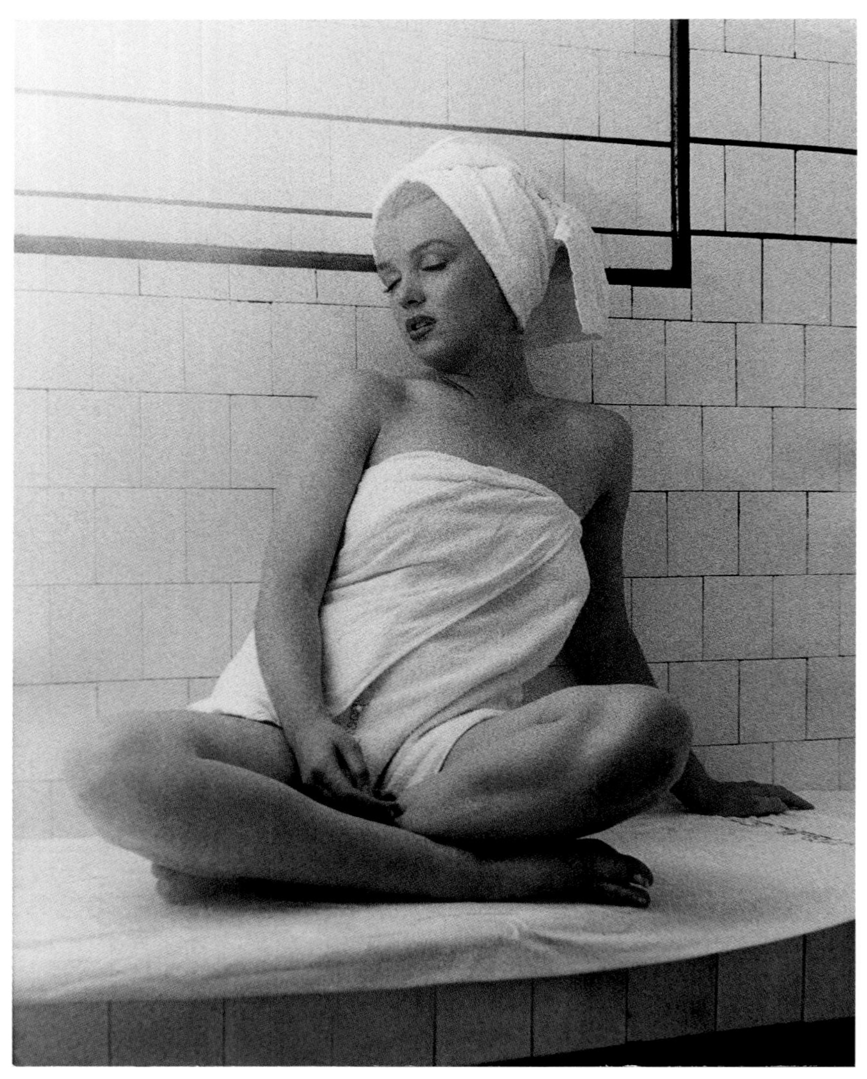

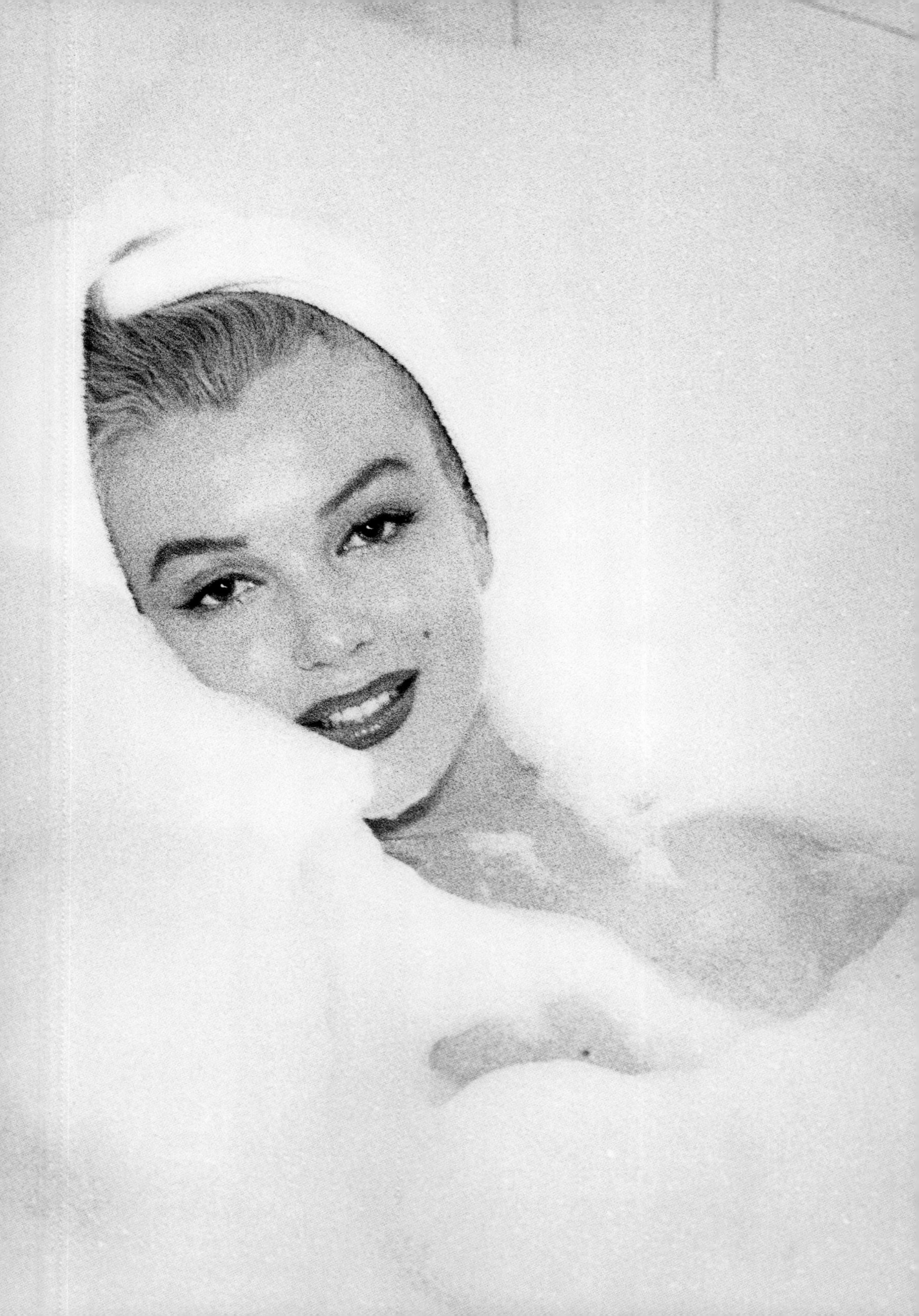

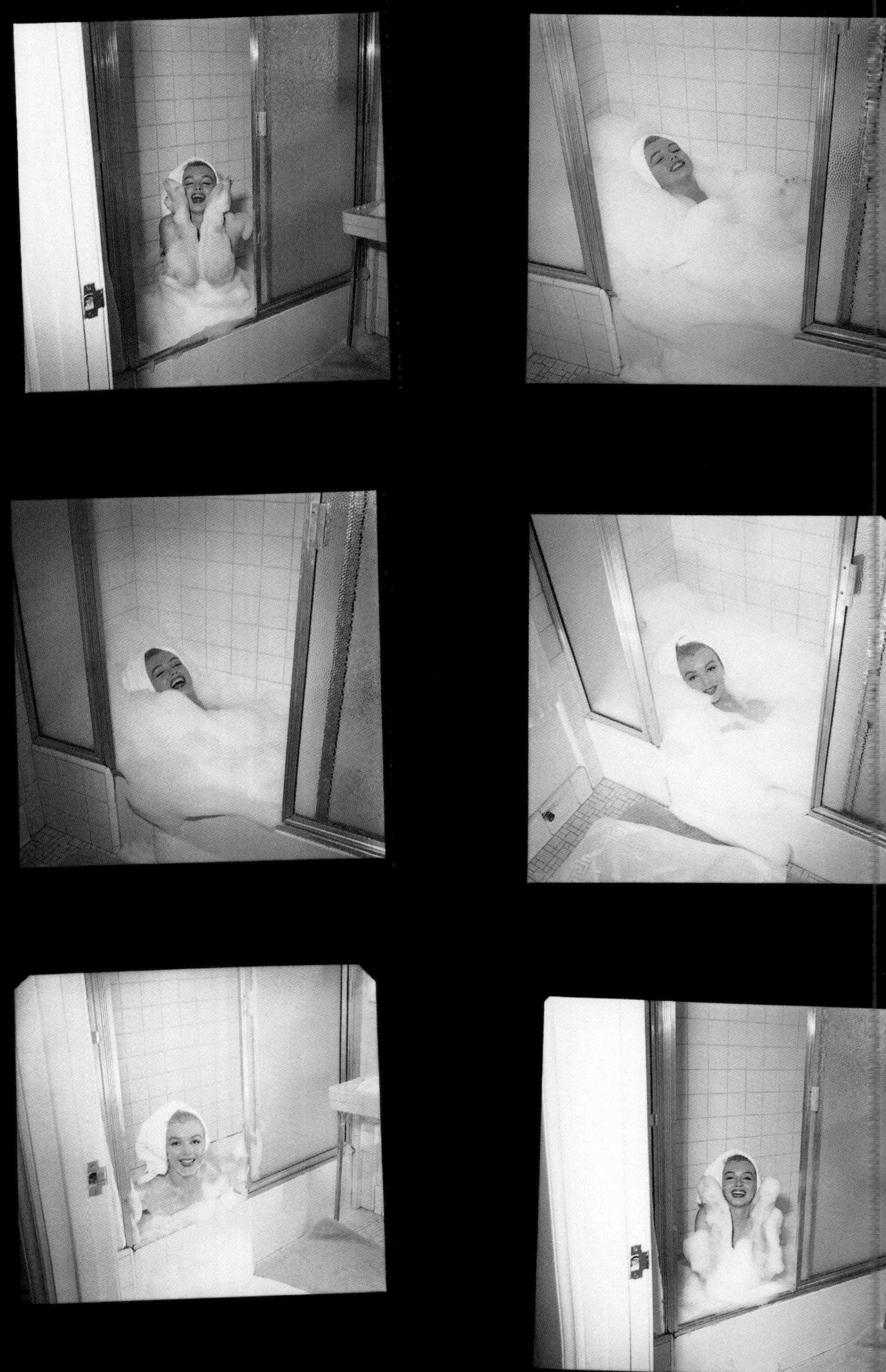

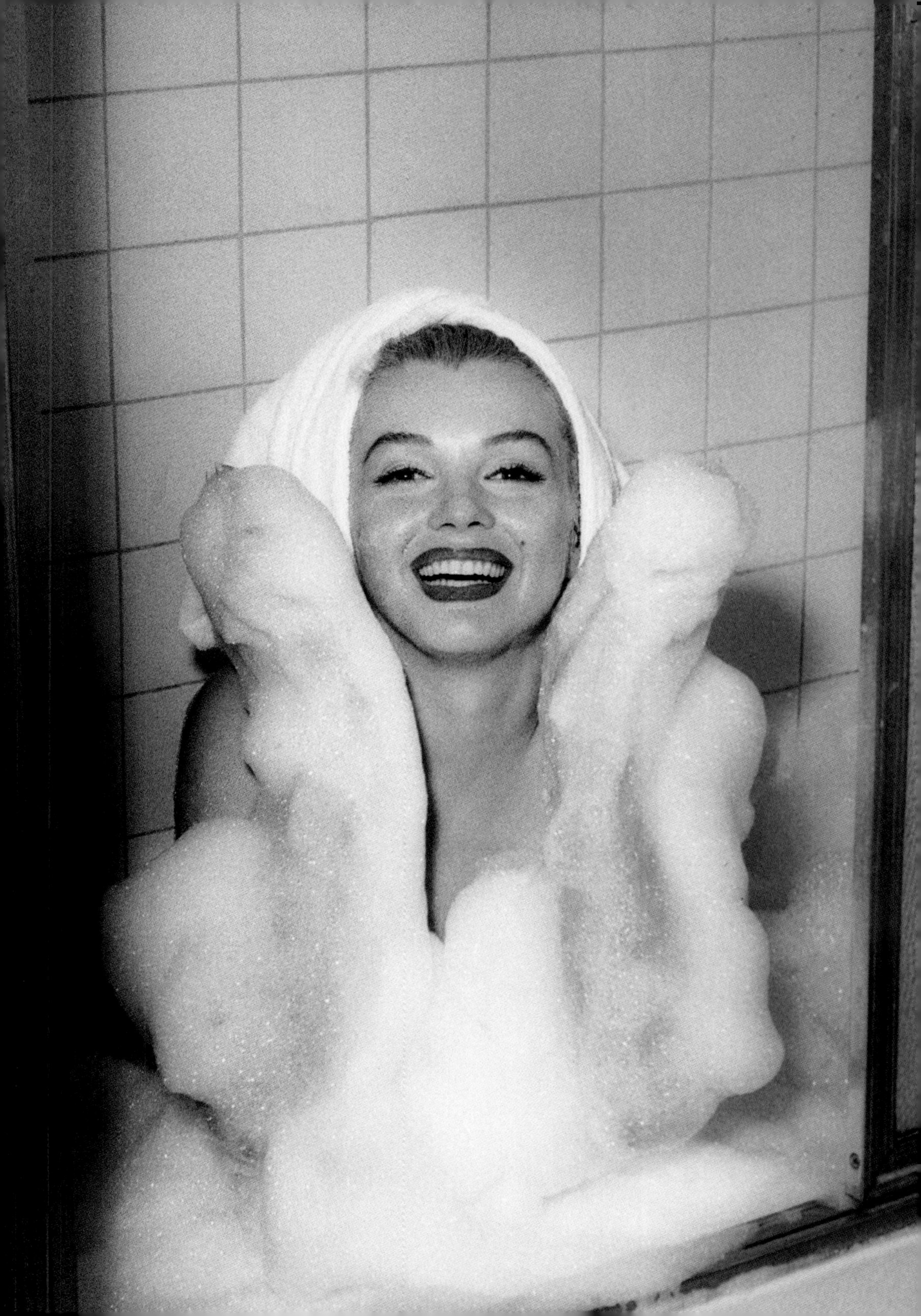

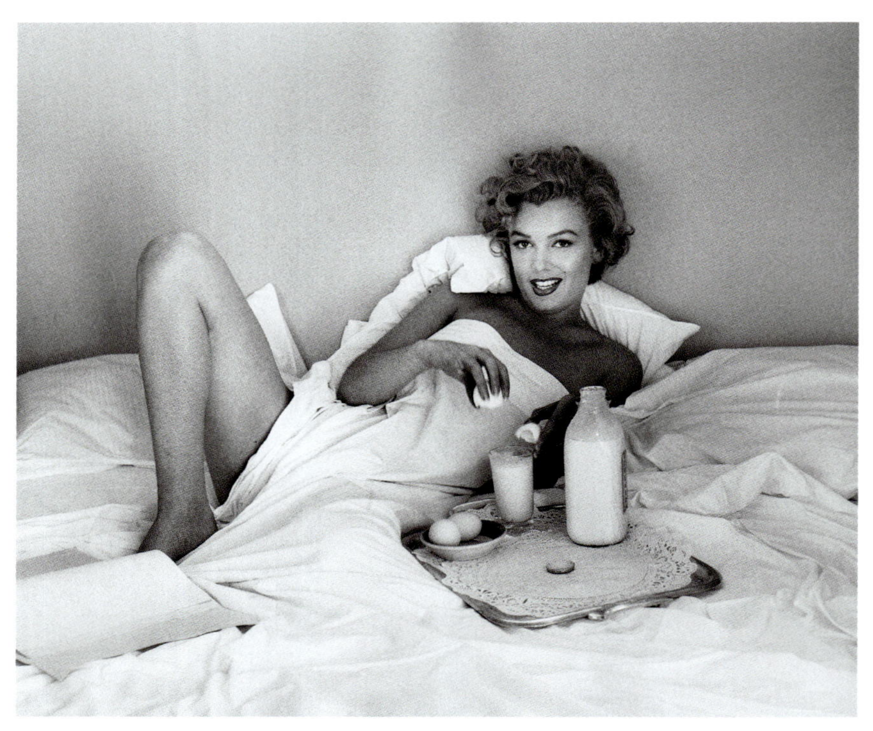

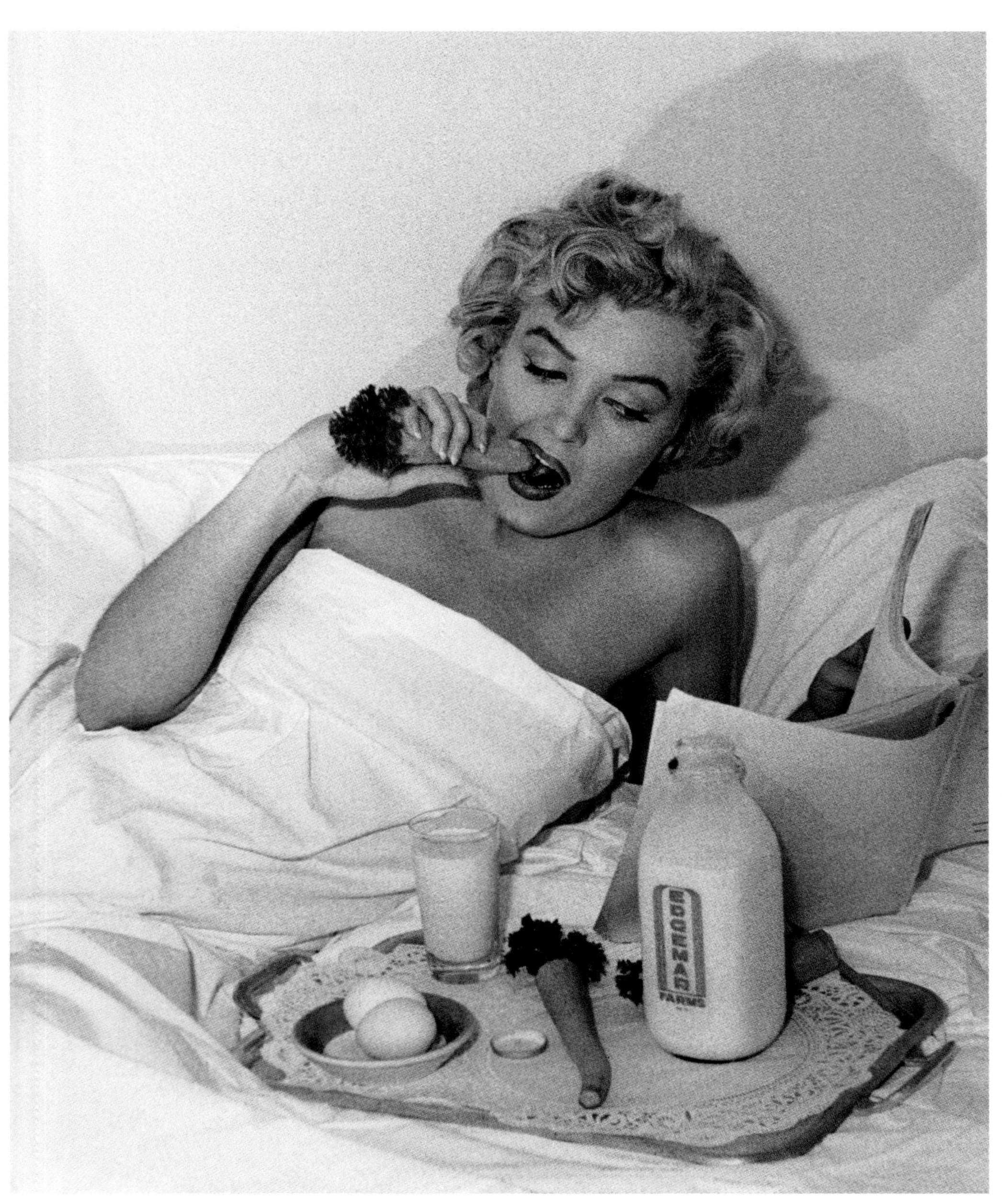
EDGEMAR
FARMS

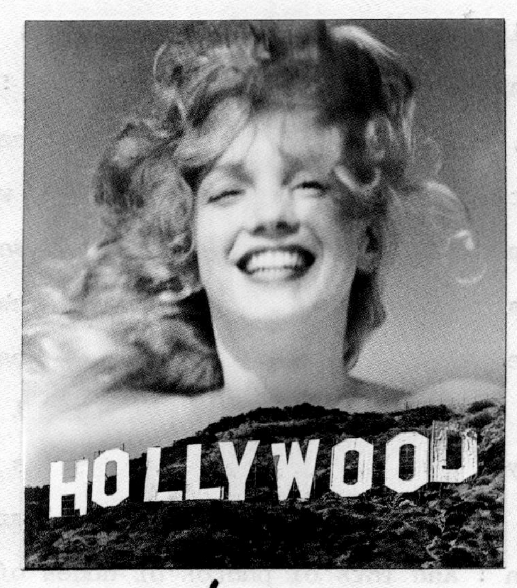

LONG AGO, THIS WAS "HOLLYWOODLAND" to advertise real estate land in the vicinity of Griffith Park. (in Los Angeles)

(Marilyn's face is a fragment from a photo where she is running joyfully, with outstretched arms)

ANDRE DE DIENES
1401 SUNSET PLAZA DRIVE
HOLLYWOOD, CALIF. 90069

After I got to Los Angeles during the first few weeks I was criscrossing the immensely large territory of the city, and adjoining Beverly Hills, and all the places along the ocean on the Pacific coast, north and south of Los Angeles. It's not an easy thing to decide immediately where to live permanently! I almost bought a house on a mountain top above Malibu, the movie colony for the elites of the film business, and acting business. The view from the house was fantastic, but except a narrow dirtroad leading to the house, accross almost unpenetrable brushland, there was no open field around the house. Fortunately, common sense told me not to fall for that incredibly wonderful privacy. The following year a devastating brushfire burnt the house to the ground, and burnt many many other homes also. I finally decided to live not too far from where Marilyn lived at that time, near the Sunset Strip, and where I too always stayed before, whenever I was in Hollywood. I always considered the "Sunset Strip" as the heart of California, and the heart of the movie business! And where the most beautiful girls live!

I went to see a Real Estate agent, explained frankly, that I had eight thousand dollars to put down on a small house, to be somewhere on the hillside not too far from the Strip. I was shown only three houses, and for a very peculiar reason I have decided on one immediately. My choice was swift and final. The reason I decided on it so fast, was an amazing, "deja-vu" experience to my mind. It was as if I lived there before, and walked up on the driveway many times before. The house was new, not even quite finished. A small, modernistic, ranch type house, with long carport. I could see the city below, from the small yard in front of the house. The place offered a certain ~~amount of~~ privacy. I told the agent that as soon as I give him the downpayment, he should let me move in right away, before the deal would even go through escrow. Yet gas and electirciy was not yet connected, so only cold water was available. And it was January! (1951) (chilly in California!)

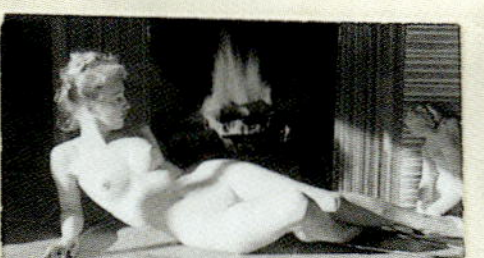
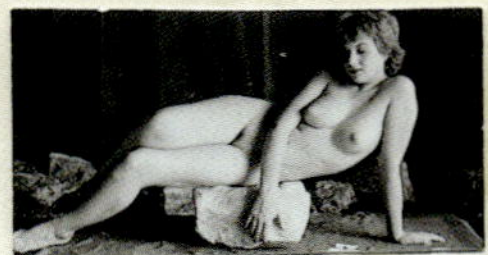
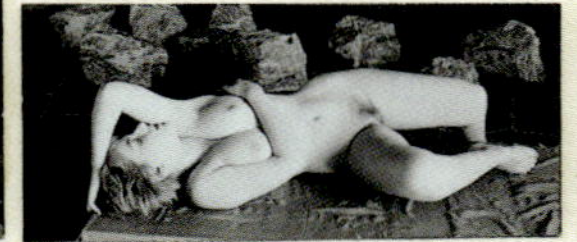
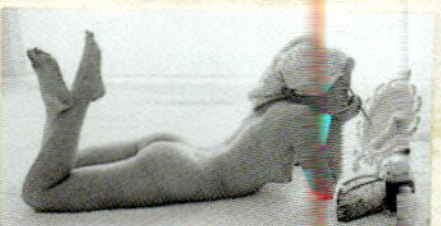

I bought a king-size mattress, sheets, pillows, blankets, a table, a chair, and brought up various sized empty crates I found in alleys, to fill the living room, where I intended to start photographing nudes as soon as possible. And I bought a few large, excellant oil paintings from an artist friend of mine which I hanged in the living room to create a necessary artistic atmosphere around me. And brought up a large quantity of empty liquor bottles from garbage cans, to create colors against the windows, and brought beautiful, heavy rocks from the seashore, as heavy as I could possibly lift, what I disperced throughout the house, and out in the yard. Either at dawn, or late afternoon, I drove to the ocean to bring home, each time, about a half a ton of rocks, which I loaded carefully into my beautiful Fleetwood Cadillac ! The rocks were essential for my mental equilibrium; messing the car up was a secondary matter. I had to have rocks inside my house to keep me company ! Strange isn't it !

At night, I had candles, or walked around with flashlight. As for water, to wash, I put four 50 feet long black garden hoses together, placed it on the flat roof of the house, and a shower head dangling at the side of the house, (outside) and even though it was January, and February, and March, I took rather nice, warm showers, when the sun was shining. On cloudy, foggy days, I suffered with the cold water, until finally, all the plumbing and electricity and the gas got connected in the house. Thus, I got started.

I took Marilyn to a friend, from whom I bought the oil paintings. He fell for her beauty right away! He wanted to start a painting of her right than! Marilyn was very please, but while the artist was setting up his canvas, and getting his colors ready, and brushes cleaned, the artist's wife took a look at Marilyn, made a lousy face, and started a complaining sort of conversation, about something unimportant. The artist got very angry at his wife! Great shoutings arose; they nearly got into hitting each other, while we looked at them, and treied to calm them down. Than, the wife nearly succeeded in getting into a fight with sweet Marilyn. Like a mad wasp, she wanted to take out her anger on HER! But I grabbed Marilyn's arm, and we got out from the house in great haste. From than on, Marilyn did not have any desire to accompany me on visits to artists, or to fool around with Art! Her mind was strictly on her own career! Too bad, though, that it turned out so badly with the artist. He was great ! Very talented! I was going to pay for that painting to the artist, and keep the painting ! As far as I know, there are hardly any paintings, good oil paintings in existance of Marilyn Monroe.

So, I have reminisced about my first few months, after I moved out to California, from New York, and into my house, January 1951. I am still living in the same house. Marilyn's memory fills it, and I have photographs of her, all over the rooms. I think, some of my photos of her are as beautiful as paintings ! I paint with my camera !

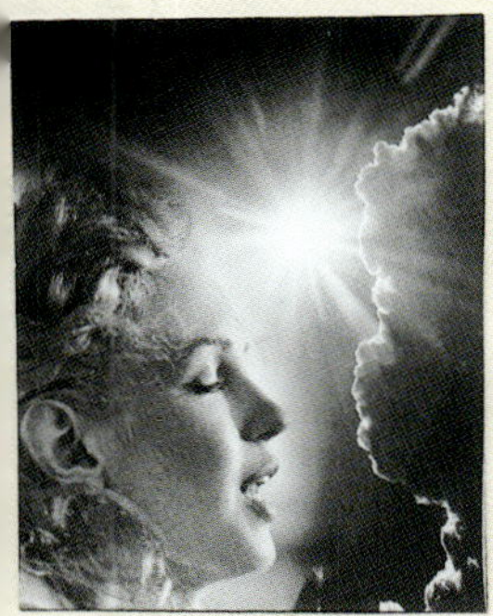
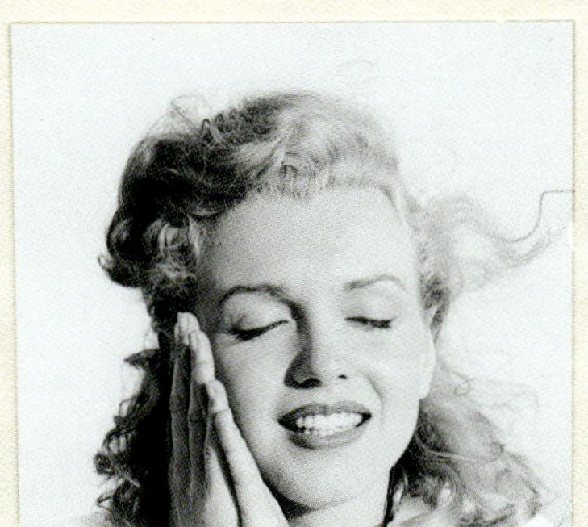
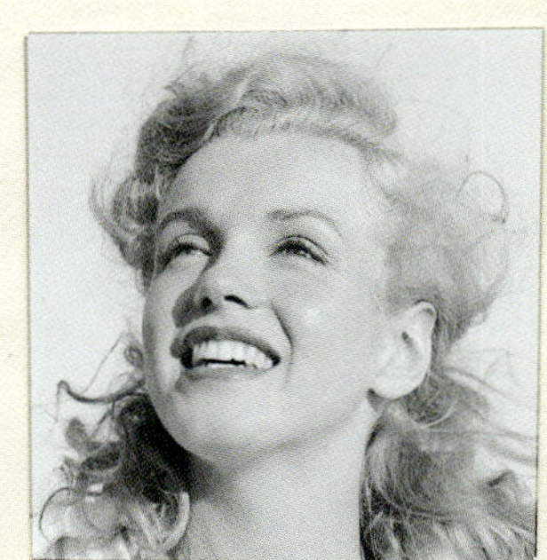
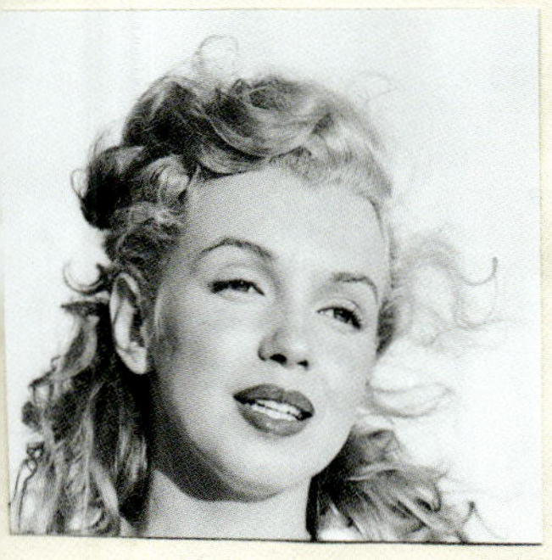
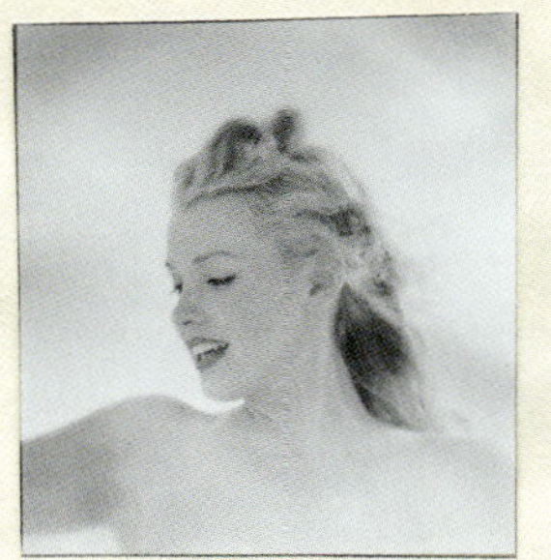
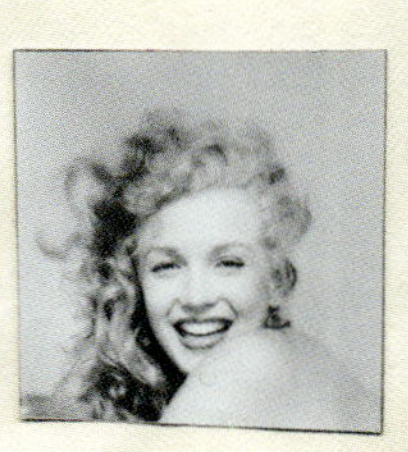
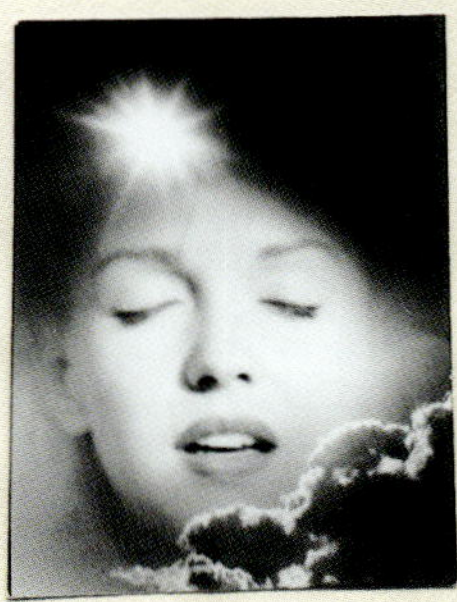

"BLONDE HEAT" (PAGEANT 1950)

By late 1952 Marilyn was a very successful actress. She was making one picture after another. I got a phone call from my agent in New York, Pageant magazine wanted a photo layout of the"Blonde heat " as they called her. I told my agent to arrange the assignment with the Publicity Department of Twentieth Century Fox Studios. Roy Craft, the clever publicity man who have done a great deal to make Marilyn' s fame an immense phenomena -- arreanged for me the sitting. Marilyn told him she and I were bosom friends, we want to be alone the day I would photograph her, we do not want any hairdresser, wardrobe ladies, make-up man, and any kind of people around us while we photograph. We want privacy ! Her wish was a command. We had our privacy. I went to her bungalow at the Bel Air Hotel,(In Stone Canyon) an excusive, beau-tiful place in a secluded Canyon west of Beverly Hills, and we started

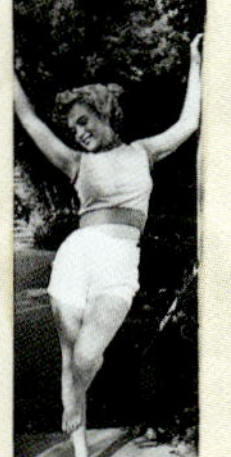

photographing about ten in the morning. Marilyn looked extremely lovely. She was in the happiest mood I have ever seen her. Than the phone reng, I rushed to it, and asked Marilyn not to tuch it. Because, that was a rare day for me, and for her,too, we are going to take photographs all day, and we do not wish to be disturbed by anybody. I took many photos of her all morning; The phone kept ringing but she did not answer. She was extremely cooperative, and greatly stimulated. I had a delightful time

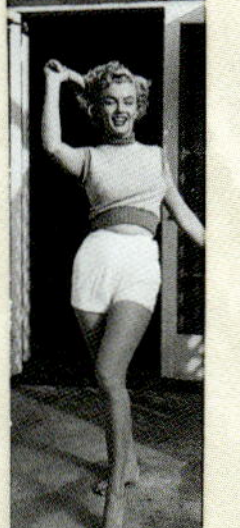

photographing her, and it was a rather unusual experience for me. For her,too, I guess, because SHE KNEW she was a great movie star, HELL, NO, not my little Norma Jeane! Not a girl whom I almost married! But an IMPORTANT, great movie star. Yet, we felt excessively comfortable with each other. She knew I was respecting her, admiring her, and she had complete faith in my photography. No matter how I wished to pose her, she obeyed and all the pictures we took were delightful. There was absolu-tely no cause for nervousness for any reason whatsover. Only the phone's constant ringing

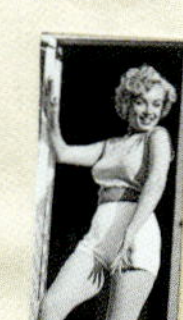

bugged me! I ordered her not to tuch the phone! We needed peace and privacy !

I took pictures of her inside her bungalow, and out in the patio, and by late afternoon she was taking a bobble bath. Afterward, I began photographing her with a towel at the fireplace. She was in a bewitching mood ! She had nothing on under the the white towel, and misciviously, she was opening and closing the towel, letting me see her nude, for a split second, as if signaling me that, that was the occasion for me to photograph her nude -- if I wanted. Those photos at the fireplace were to be the last photos for the day, and we were planning to go out afterward to the fanciest restaurant, most expensive place in Hollwywood , to Chasens. Marilyn began insisting she will pay for the dinner, AND for once, I must let her to be the the boss! I told her we will flipp a coin about it. I Was taking Her photos with electronic flashlight, I was going to install a bounce lighting-effect, to create a softer light for the subsequent MAYBE NUDES, but while I was fumbling with a long electric cord, the phone reng again, reng, and reng, and finally, Marilyn picked it up. She kept listening, and listening and gradually her expression turned frightened, practically horrified, and she said something " Yes I will, Yes, I will " and hanged up the receiver. The change of her mood was incredible. She was staggering away from the phone like someone who is ill, dizzy, ready to faint ! She set into an armchair, She looked sick; She could hardly talk. I asked her what was wrong. She said she can't tell it to me, she said I must leave her, she must be alone, and than she must go to the Studio at once, to explain something. Even in those moments of distress she ws so nice to me, she said I ought to order drinks for myself, and dinner, and charge it to her. I felt sad for her, BUT confused. I packed my equipment, and left.

DAYS LATER I found out what was the cause of her great distress, why HAD her morale collapsed so suddenly while listening on the phone,

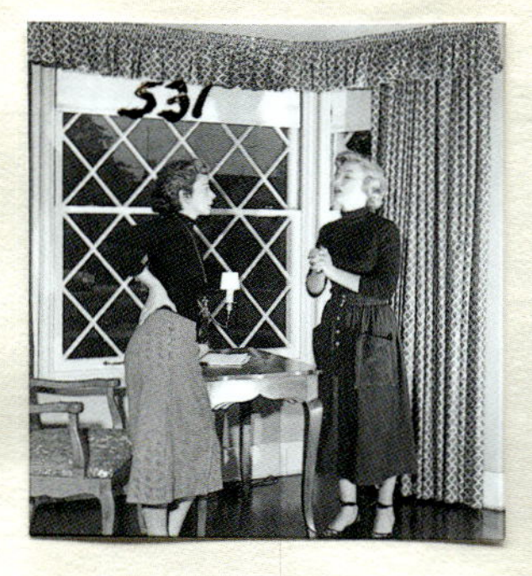

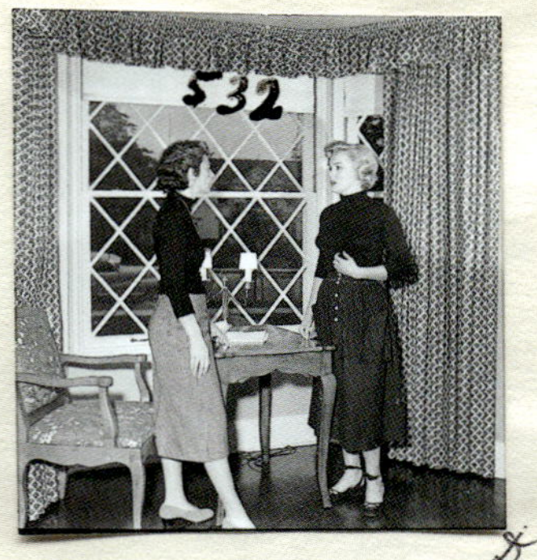

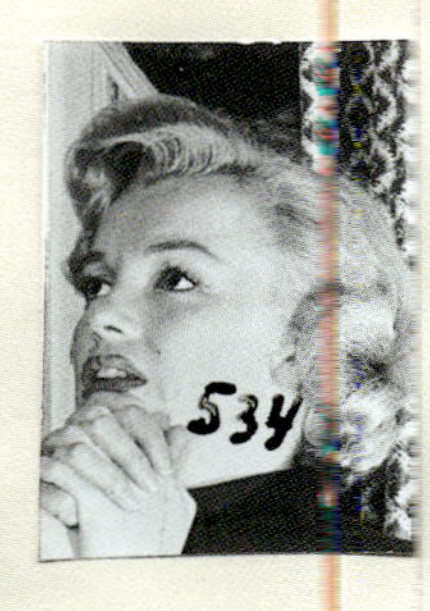

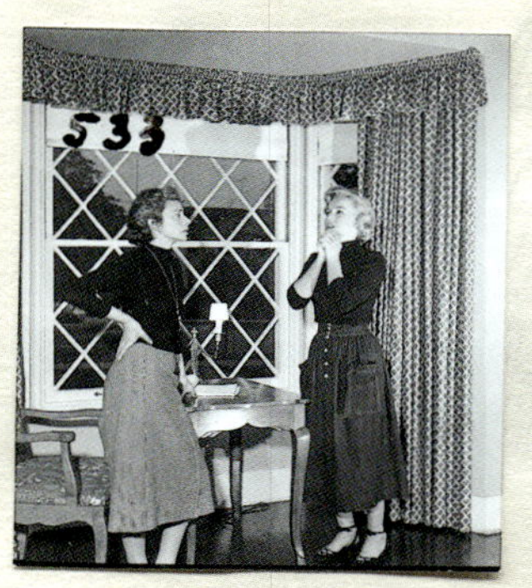

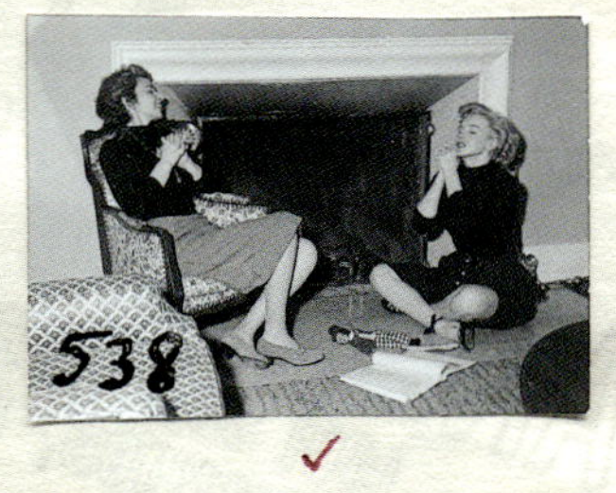

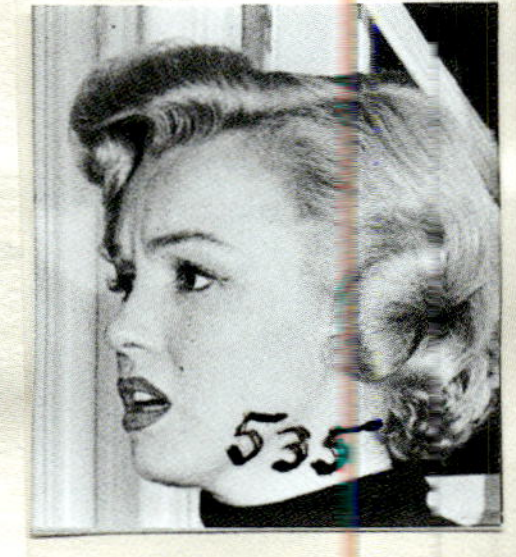

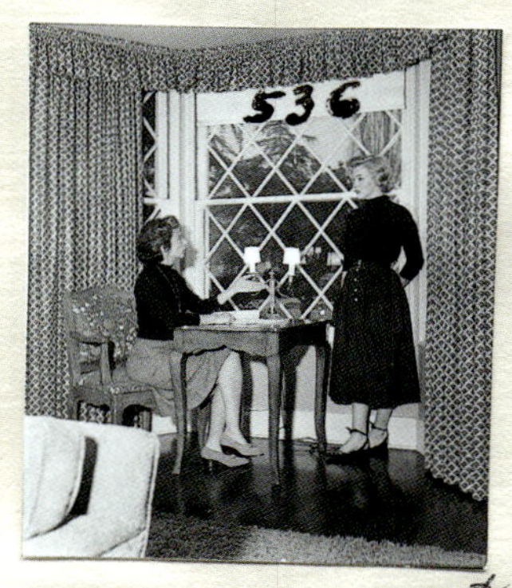

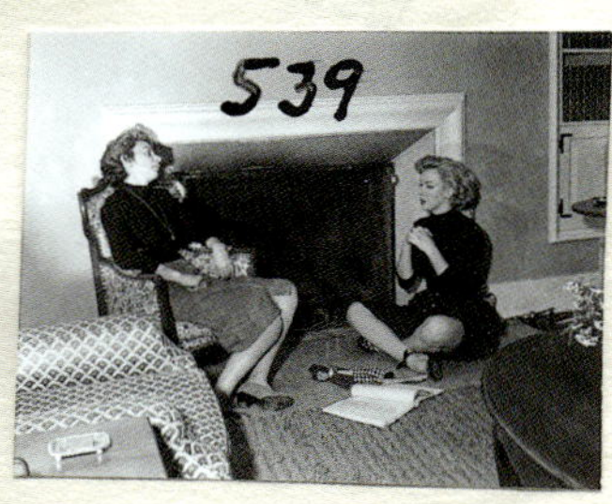

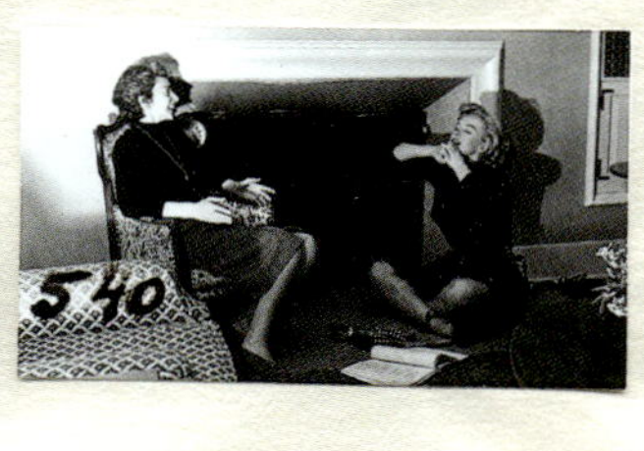

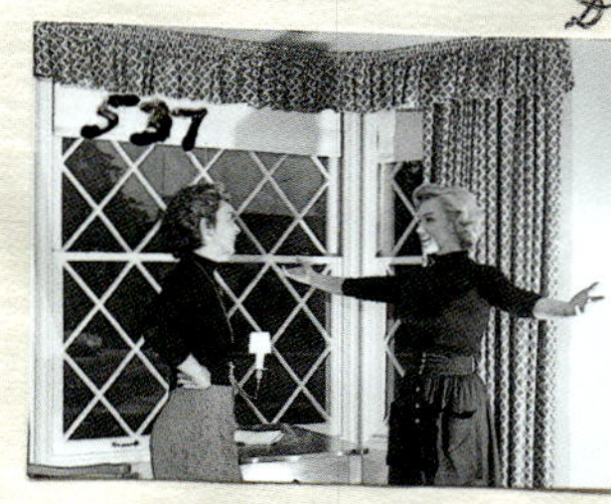

1952 WITH DRAMA COACH — NATASHA LEYTESS

1952

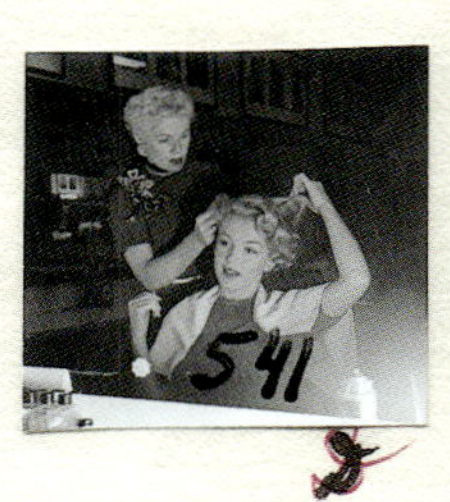

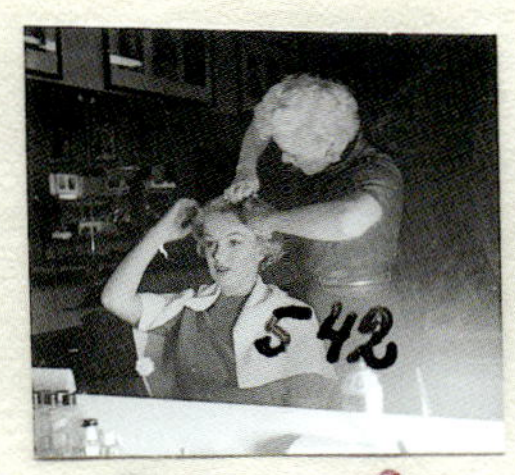

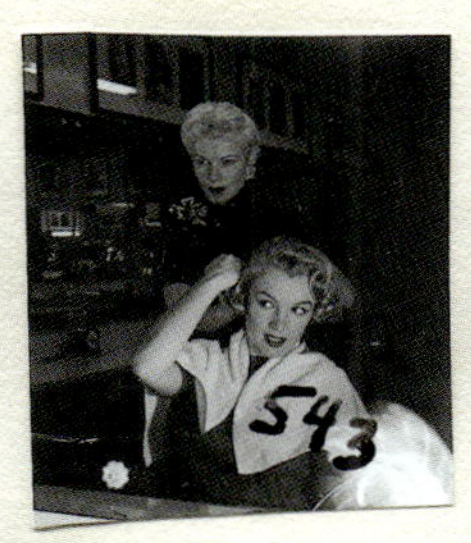

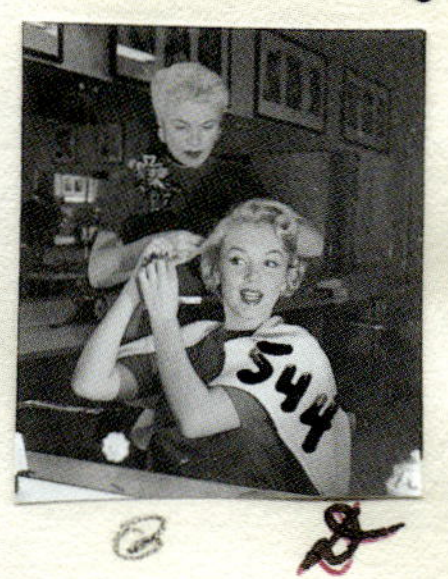

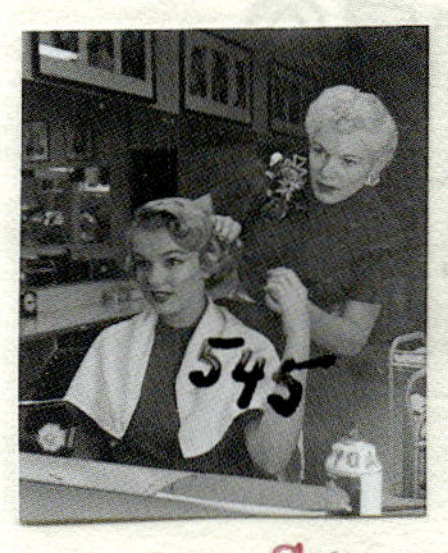

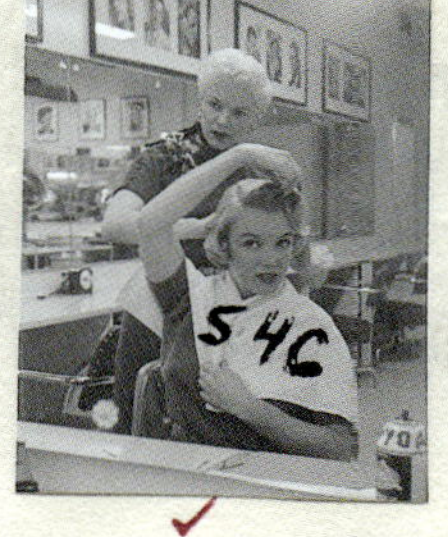

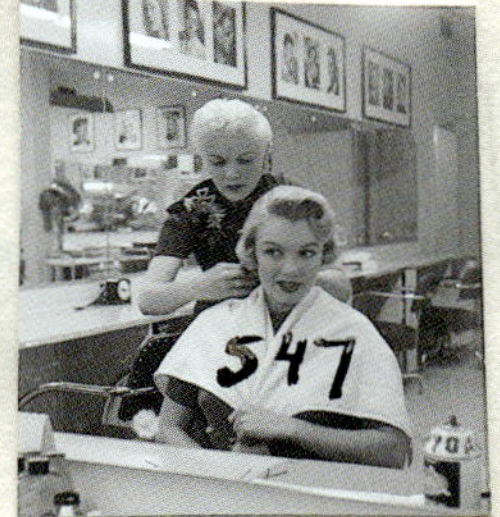

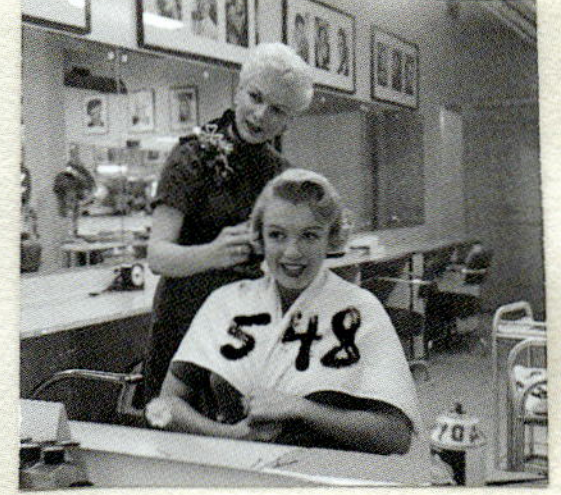

AT "FOX" STUDIO ↗

1953

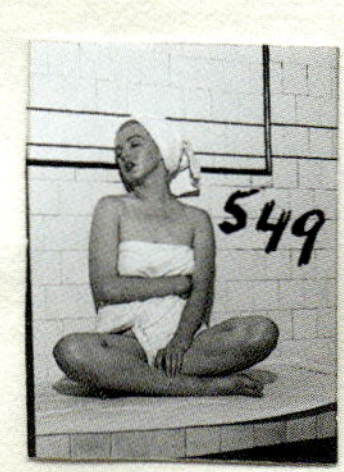

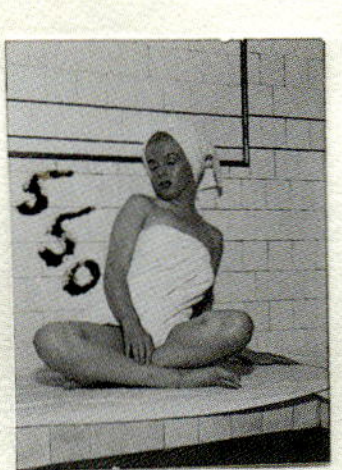

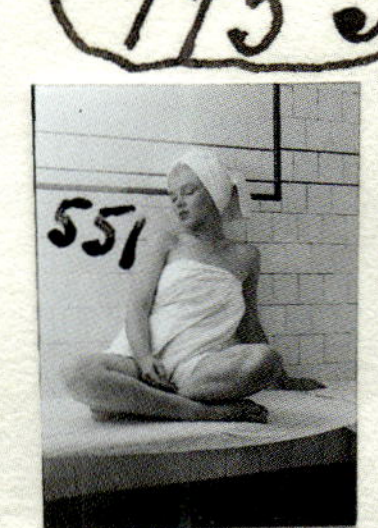

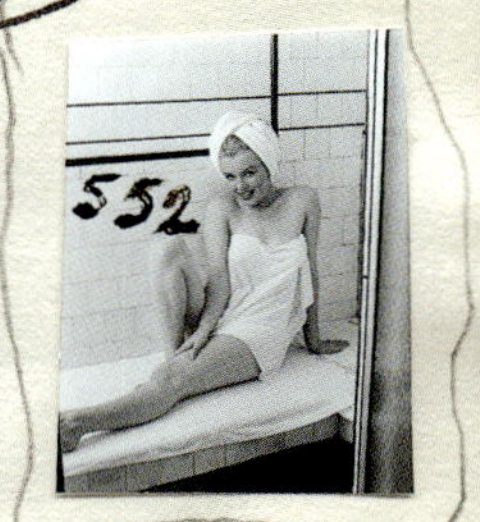

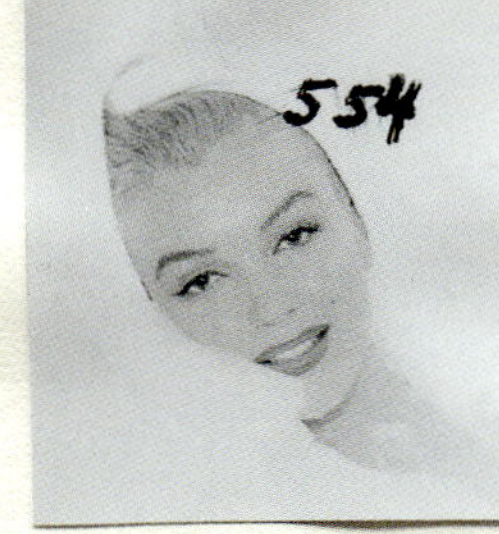

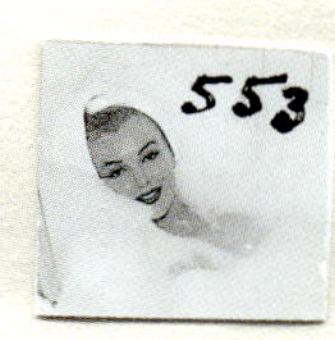

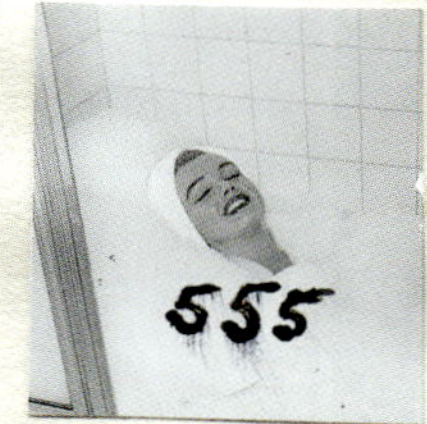

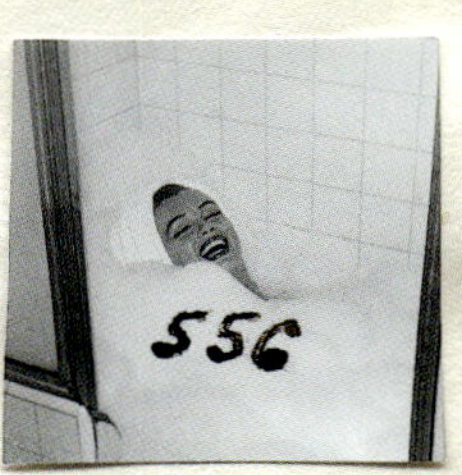

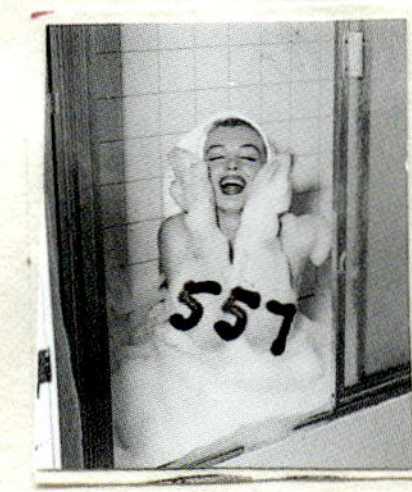

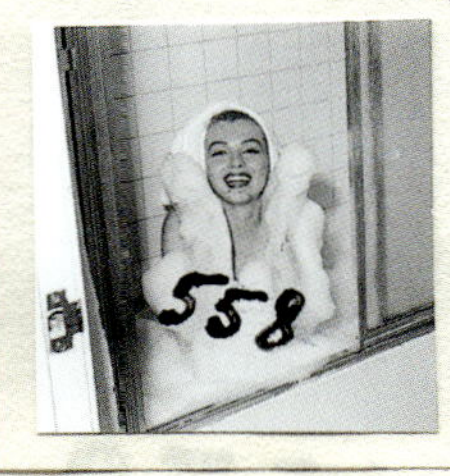

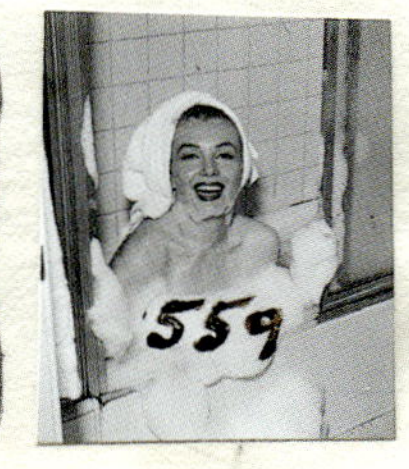

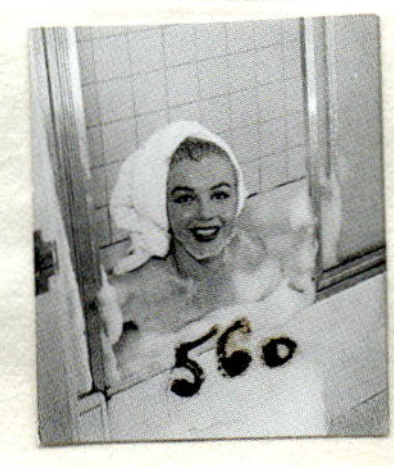

ANDRE DE DIENES 79

1952 — 1953 in BEVERLY HILLS, + BEL AIR

BK II

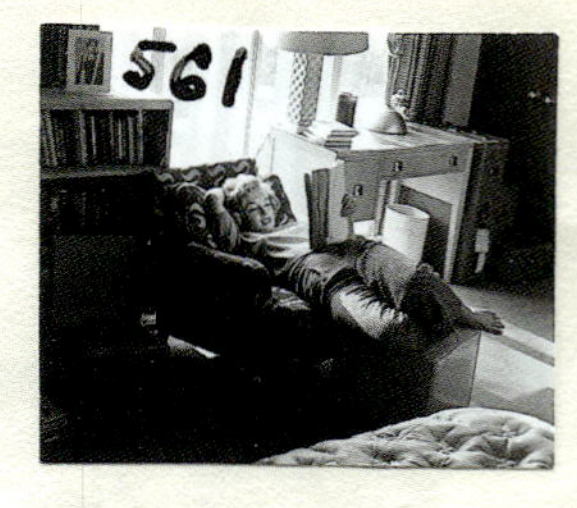

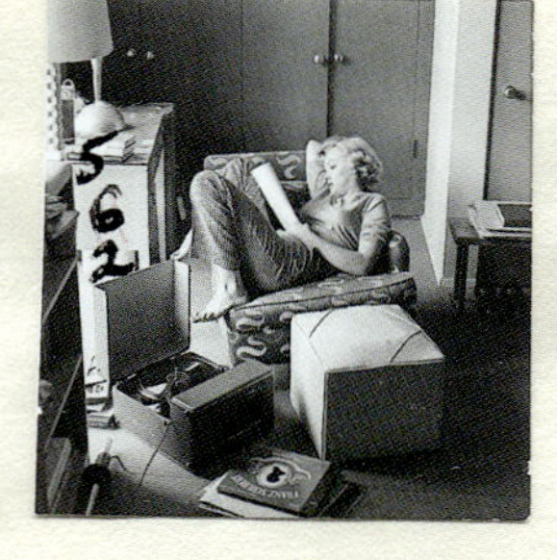

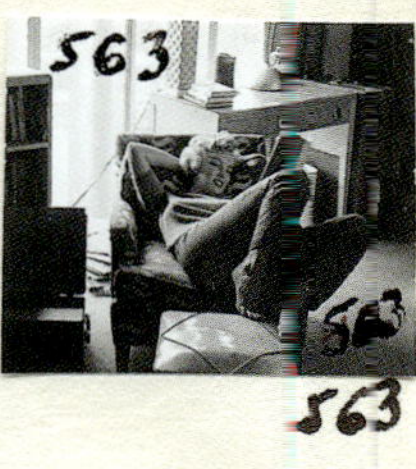

563

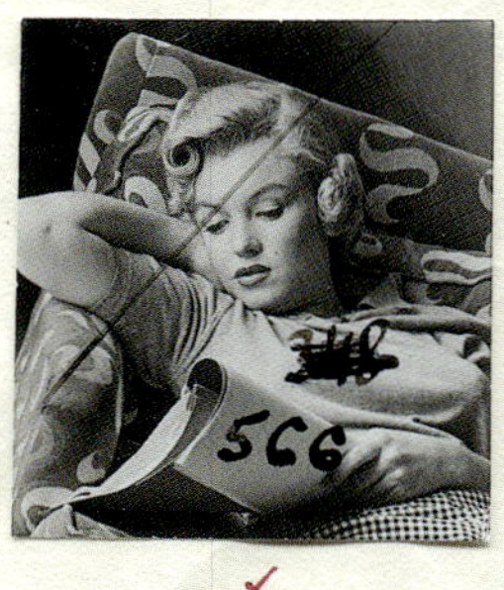

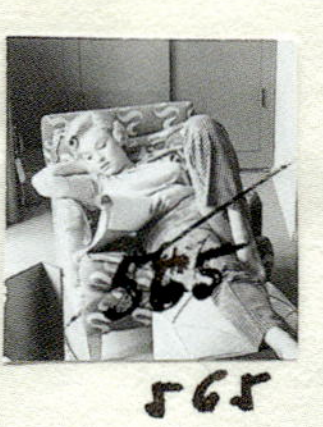

565

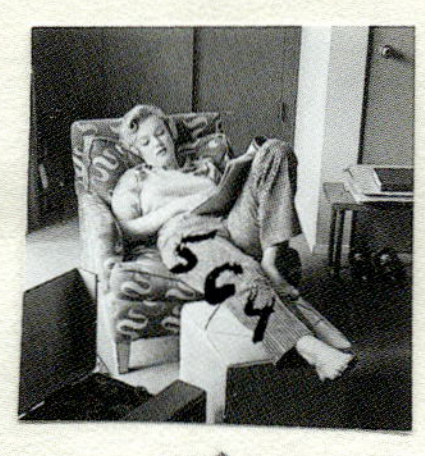

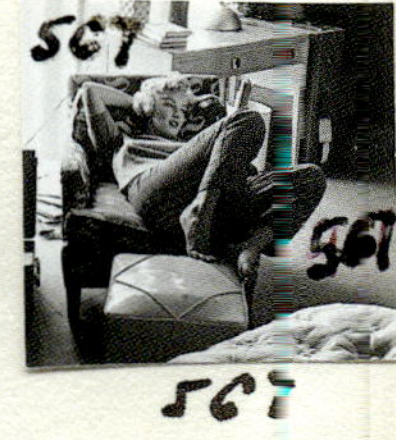

567

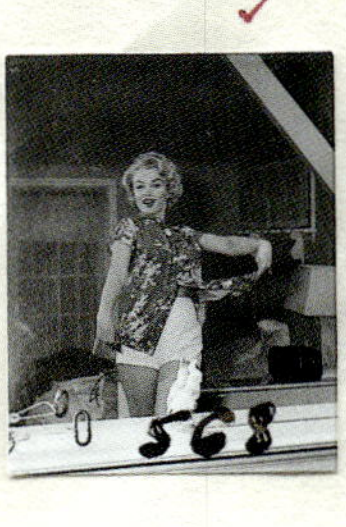

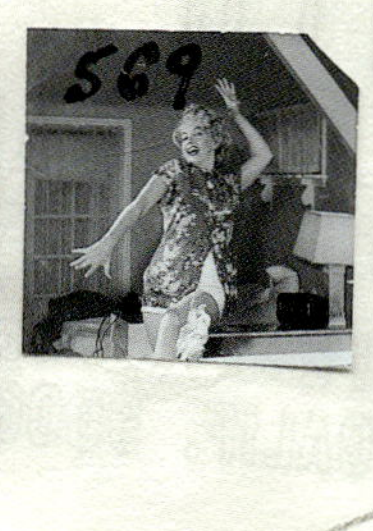

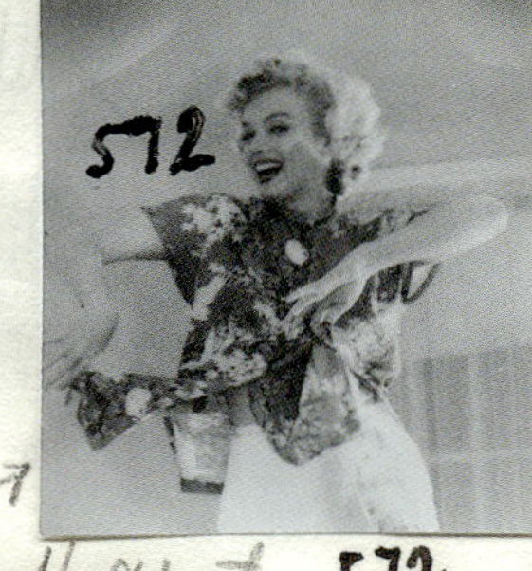

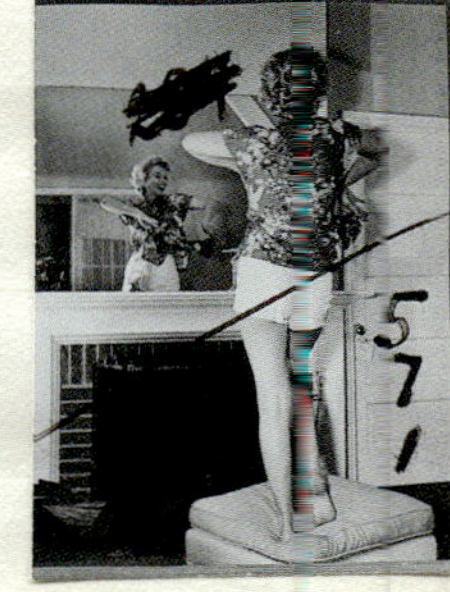

1st B H. Mint. 572

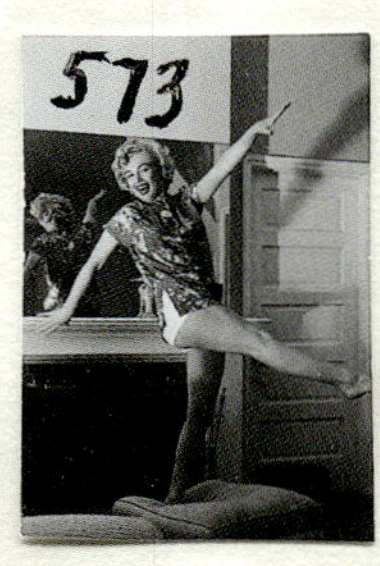

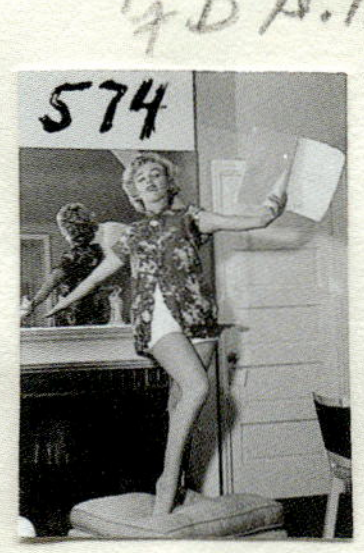

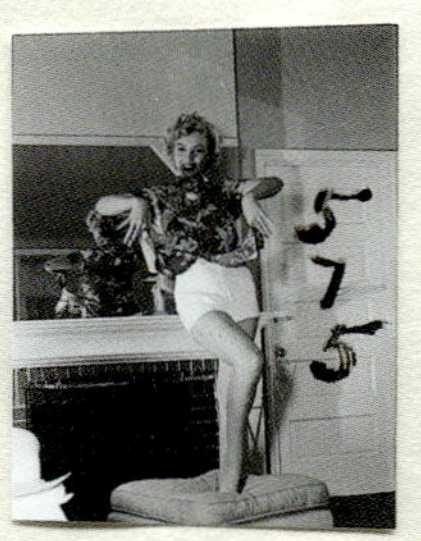

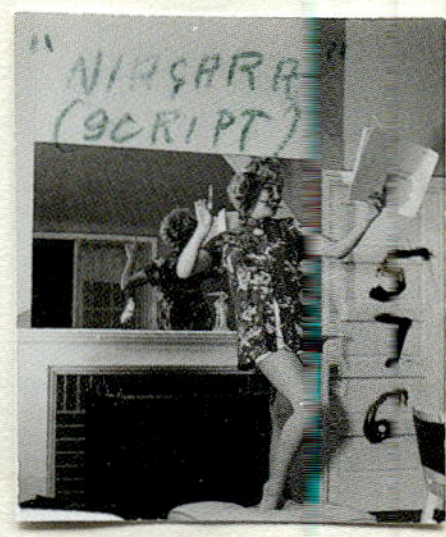

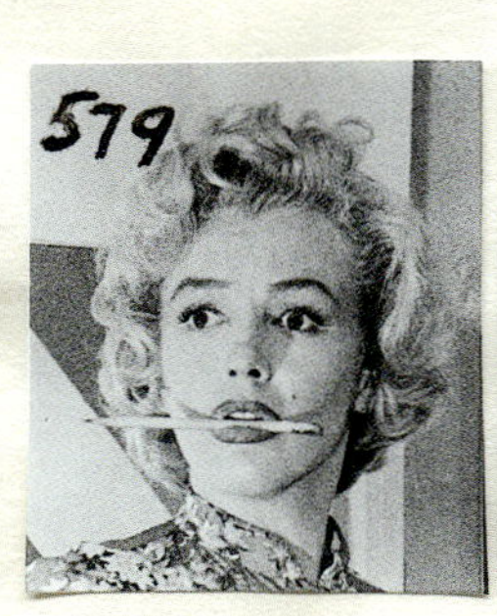

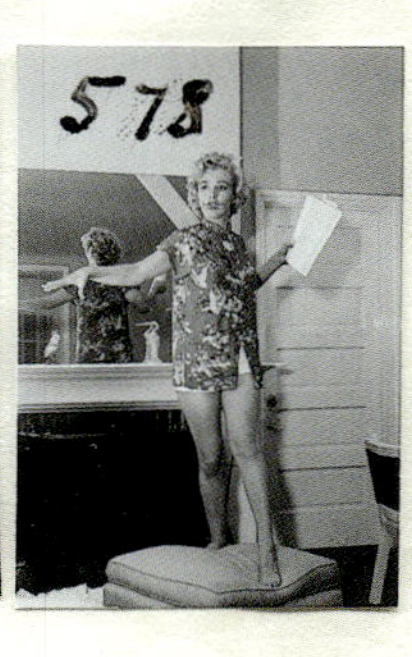

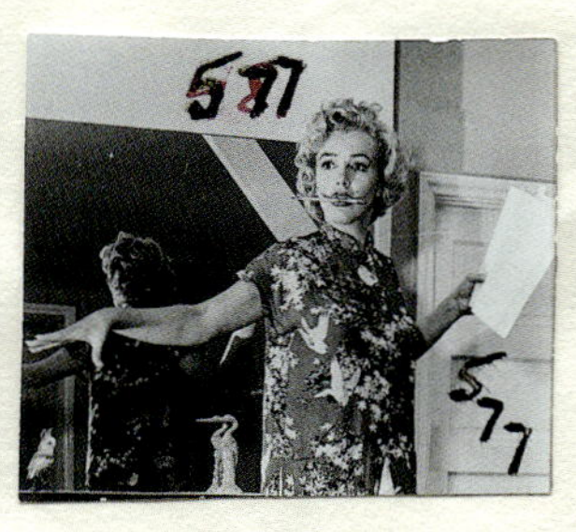

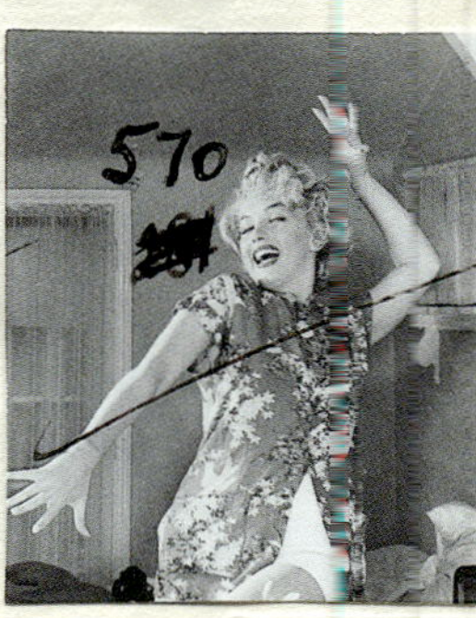

ANDRE DE DIENES

1953

GR. H.

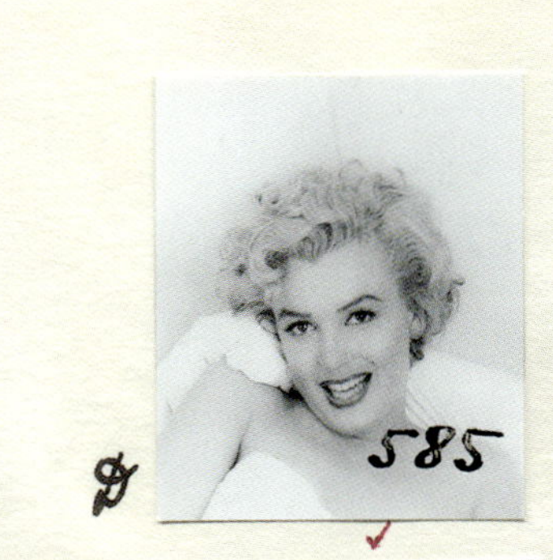

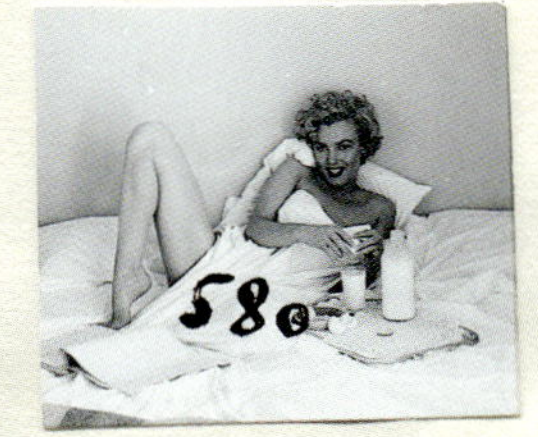

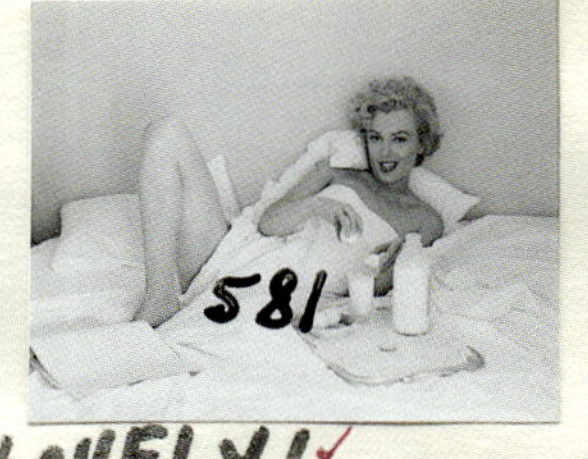

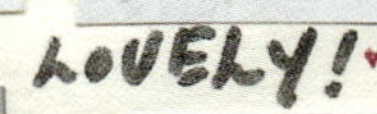

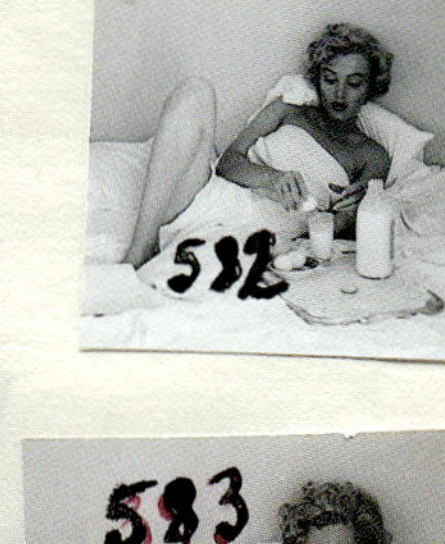

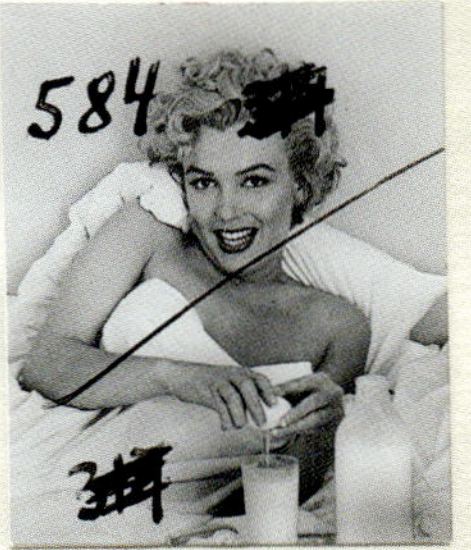

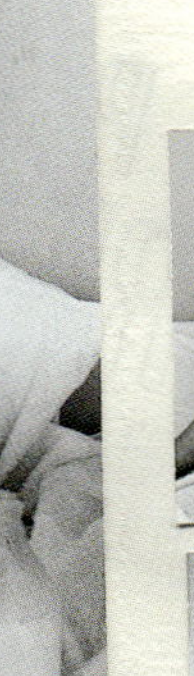

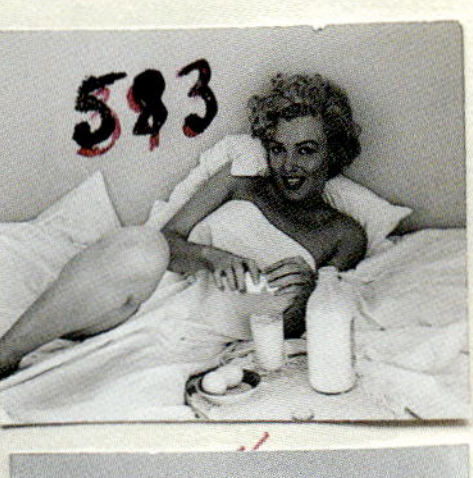

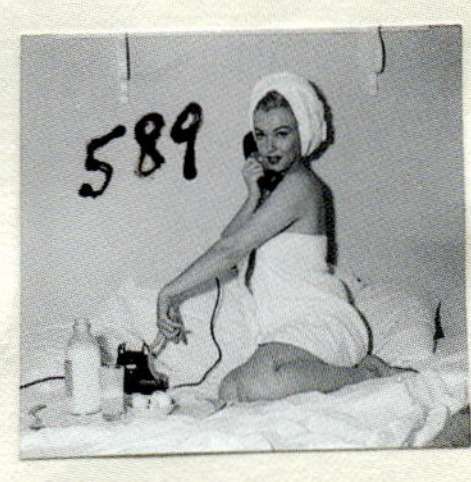

586

588

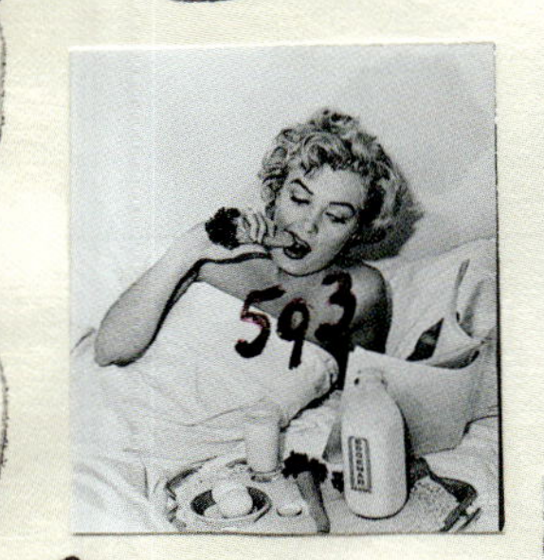

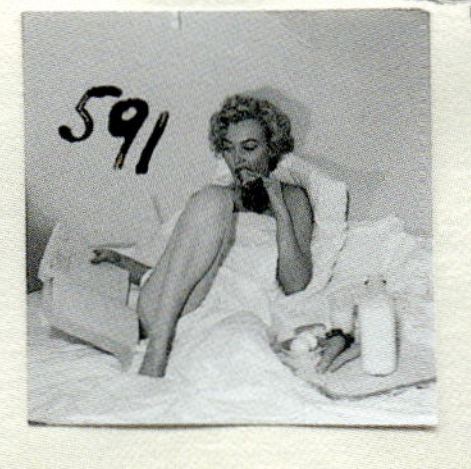

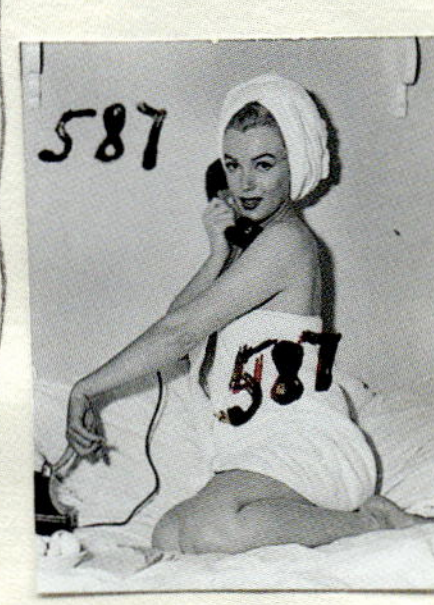

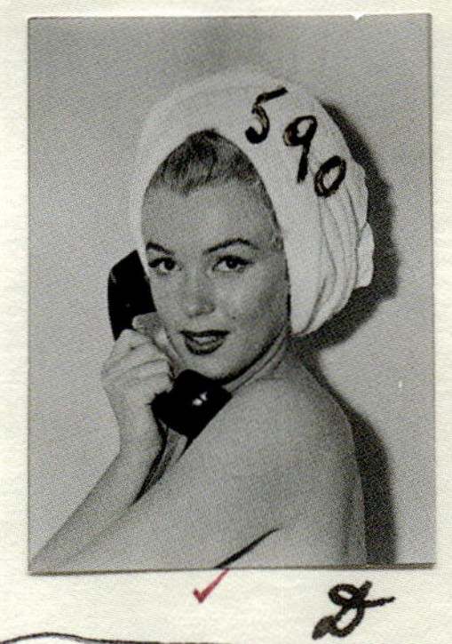

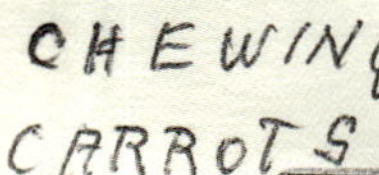

SHE WAS CHEWING CARROTS

592

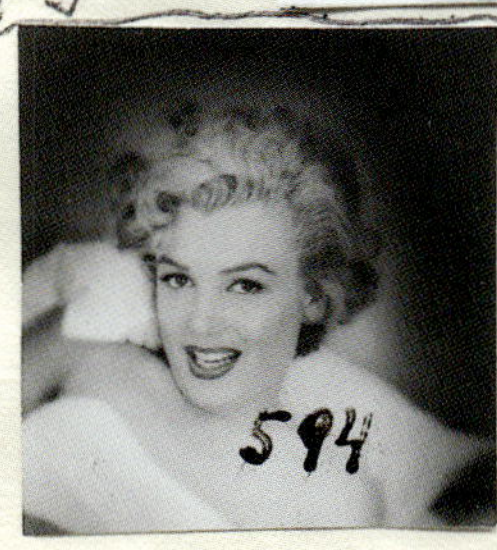

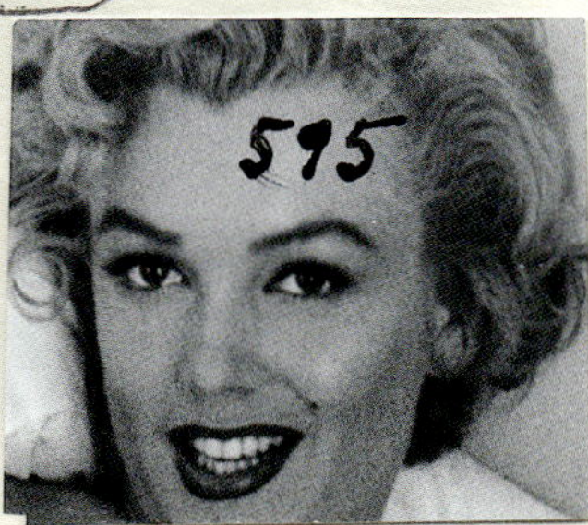

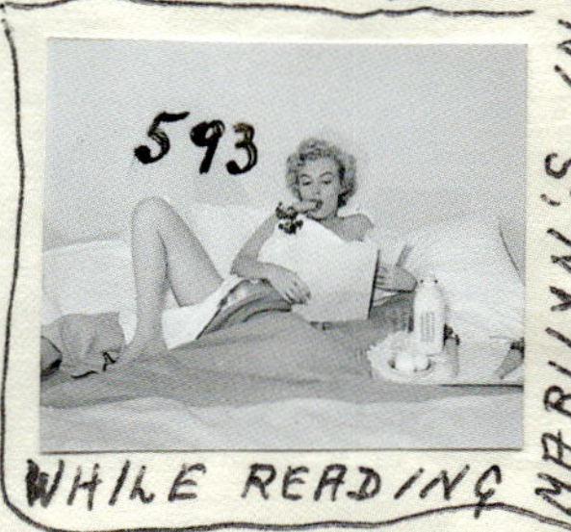

WHILE READING A SCRIPTT

MARILYN'S INNOCENT SEXUALITY HAD NO LIMIT!

ANDRE DE DIENES

BK II

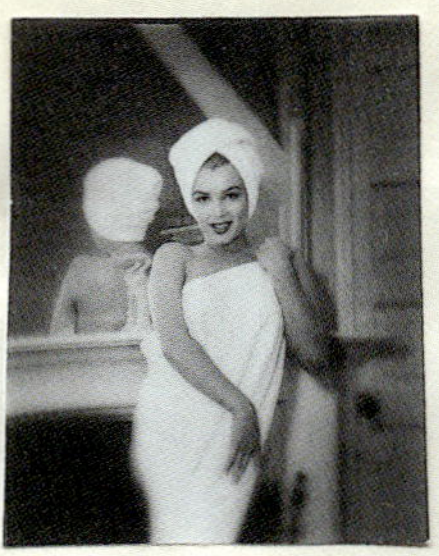

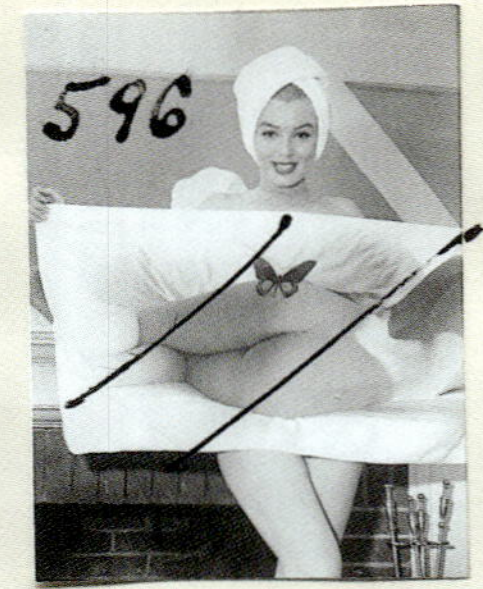

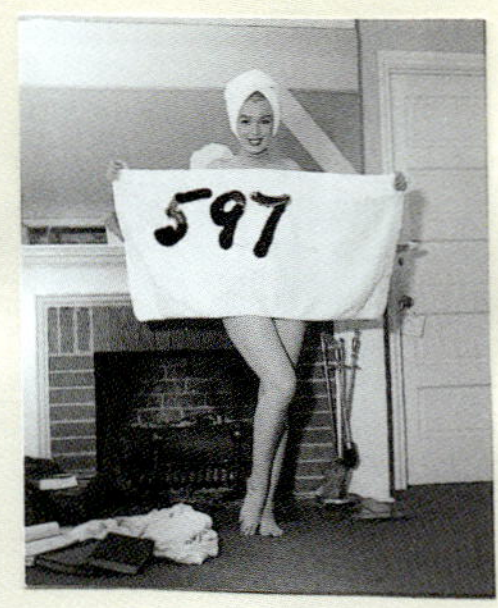

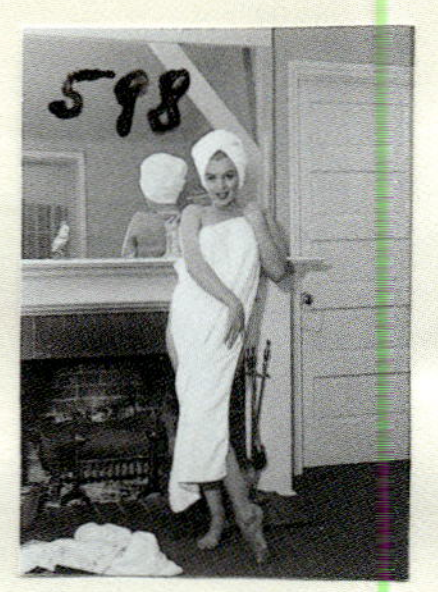

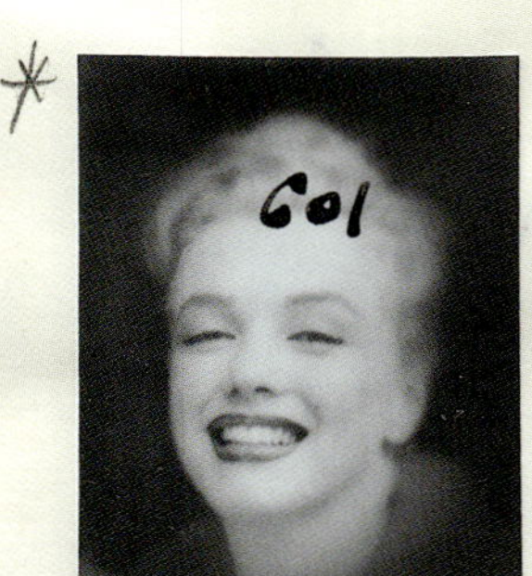

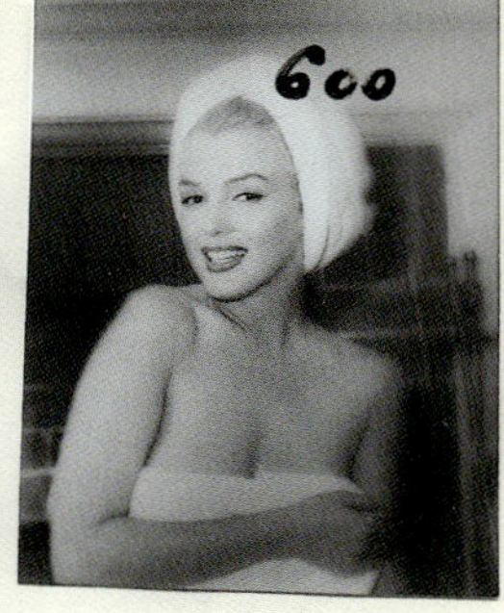

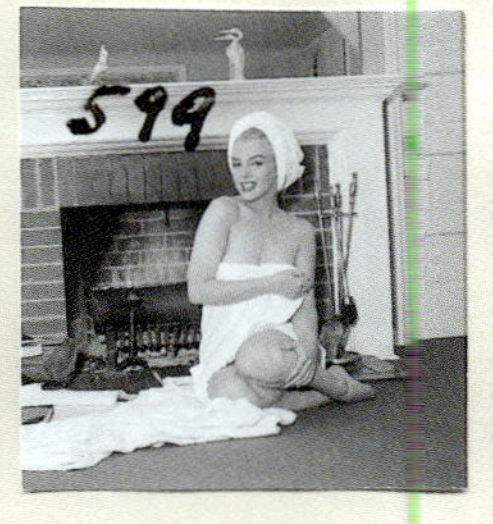

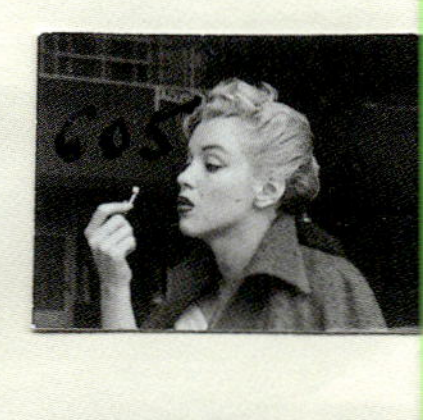

605

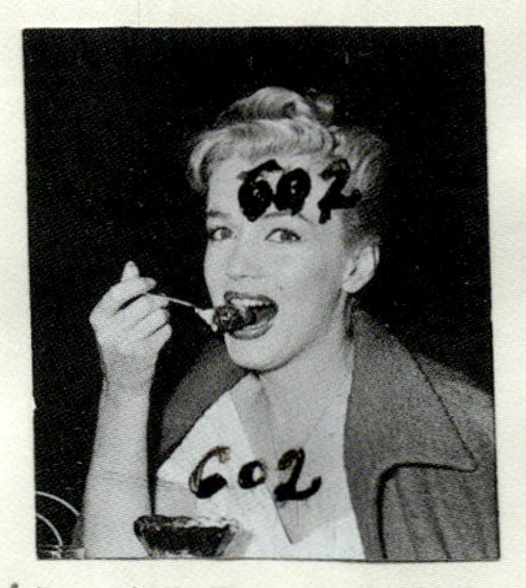

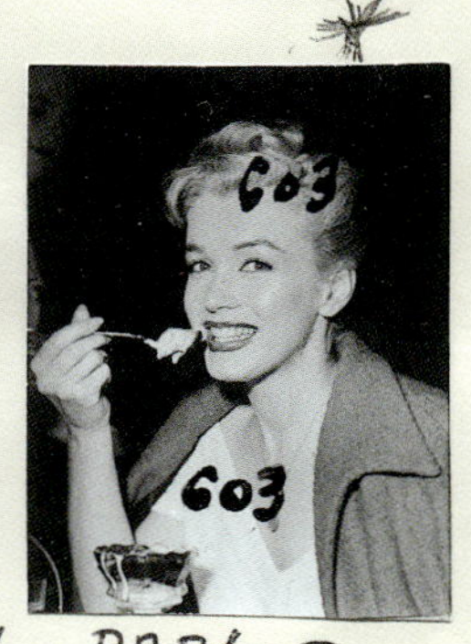

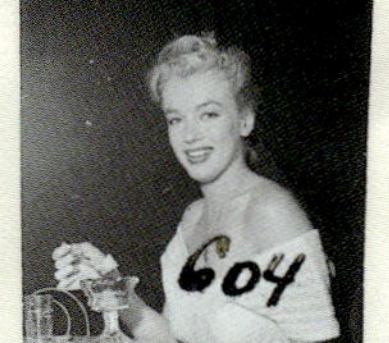

AT THE ICE CREAM PARLOR

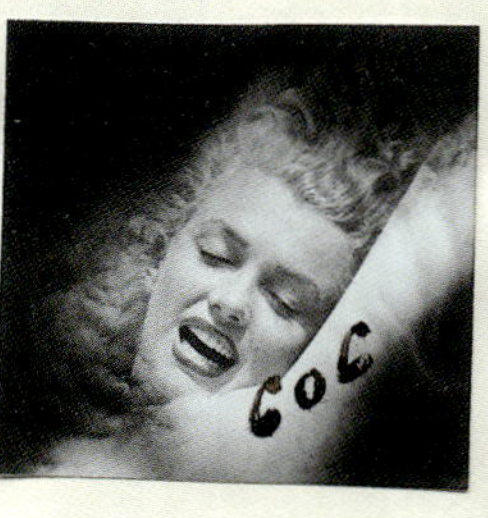

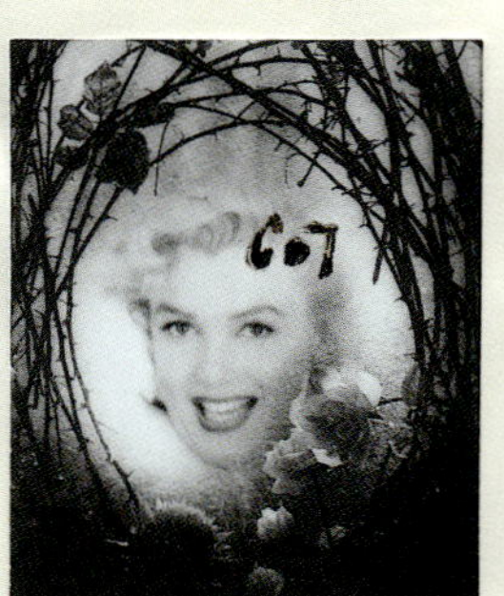

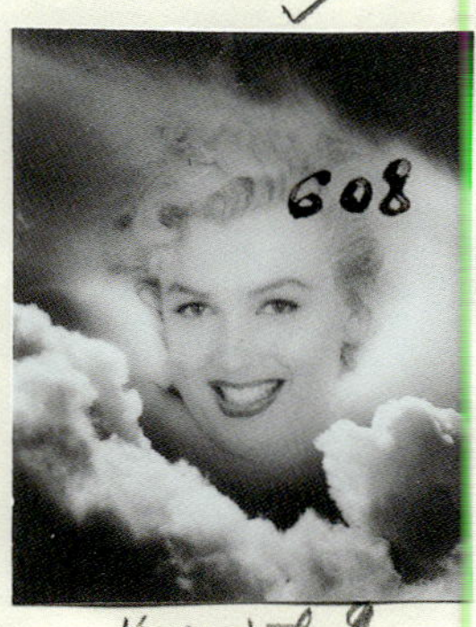

ANDRE DE DIENES

K II "MORNING" "GOOD MORNING, WORLD! 1953

H. Mint ↓7B

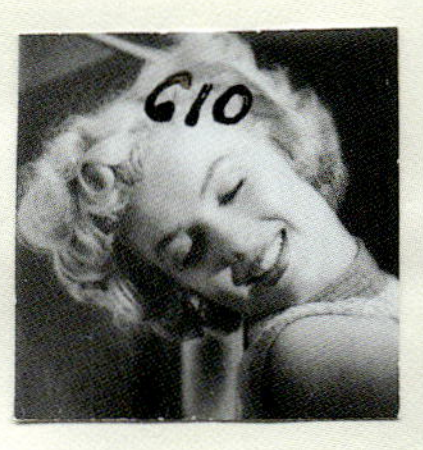

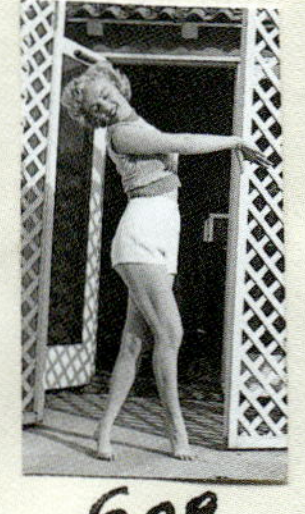

609

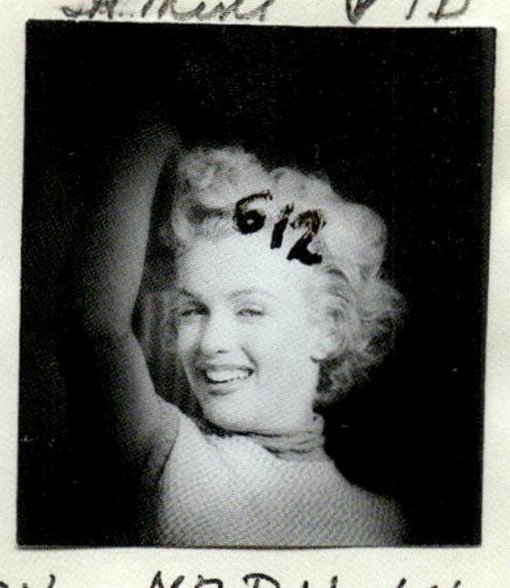

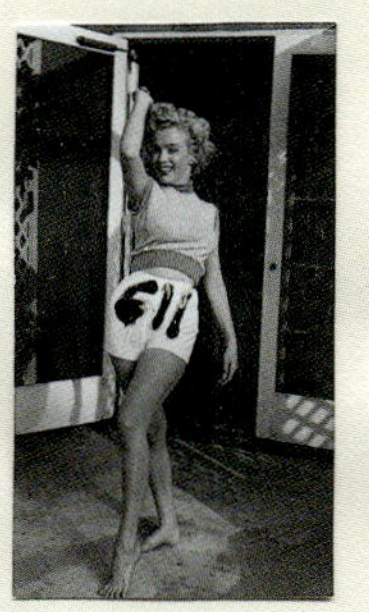

HERE, A VERY HAPPY MARILYN MONROE;

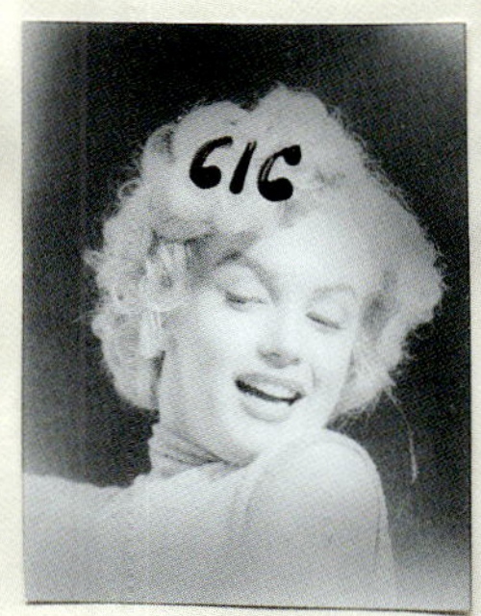

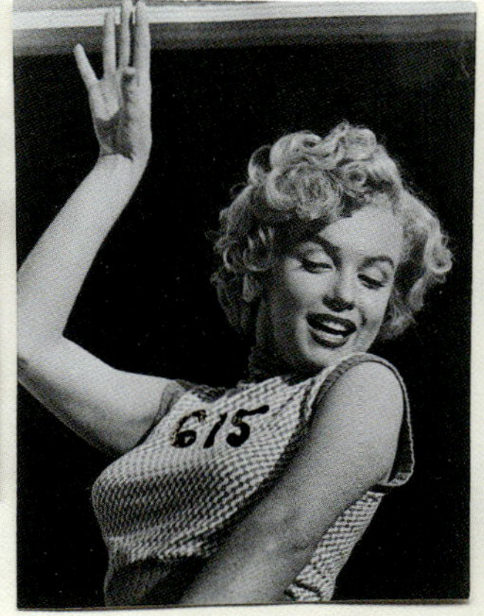

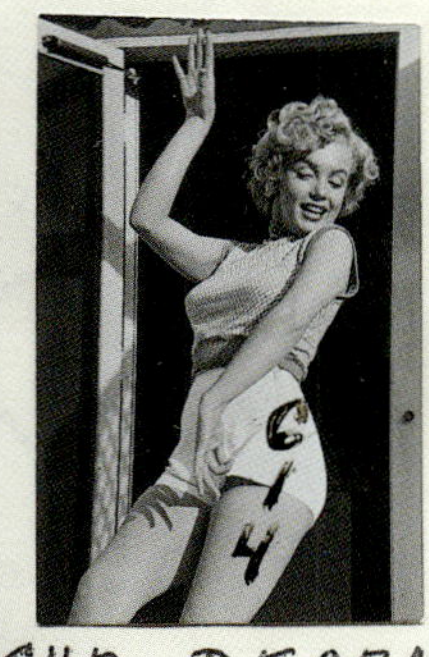

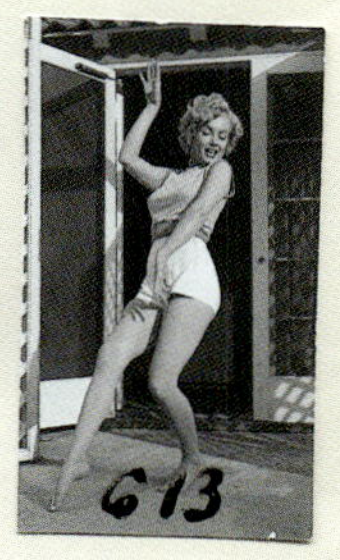

SHE BECAME WORLD FAMOUS! (1953)

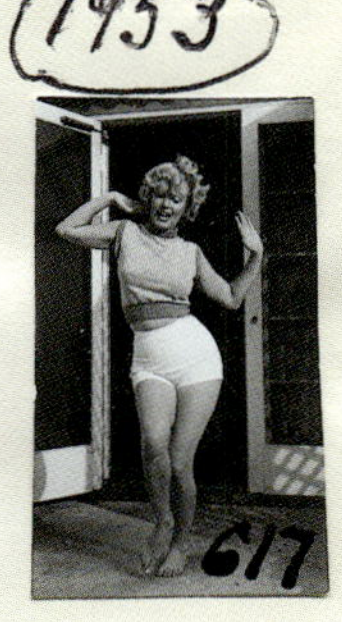

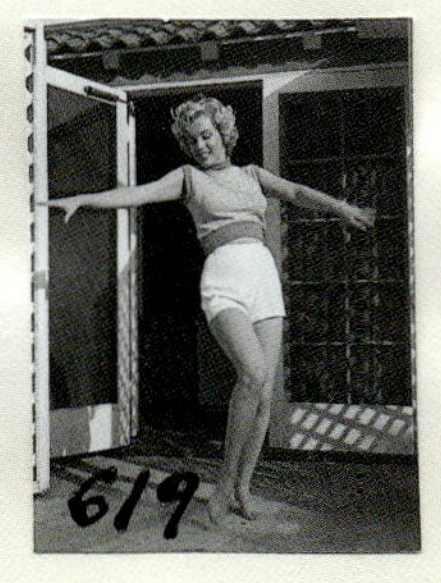

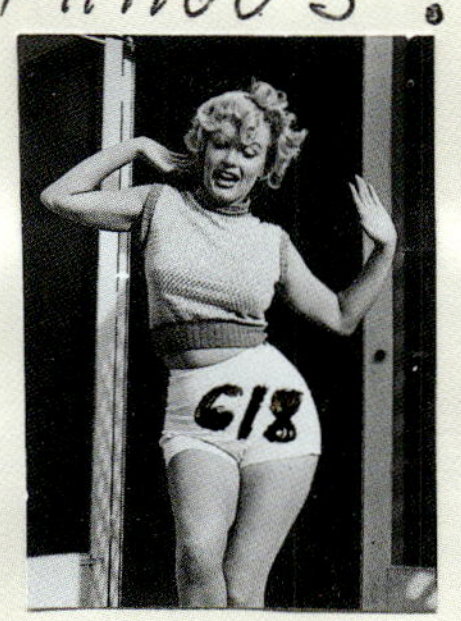

620

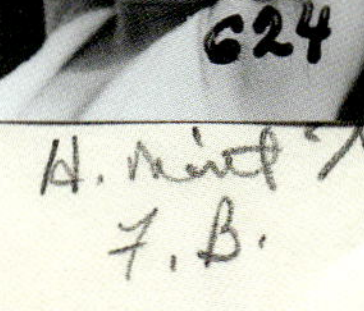

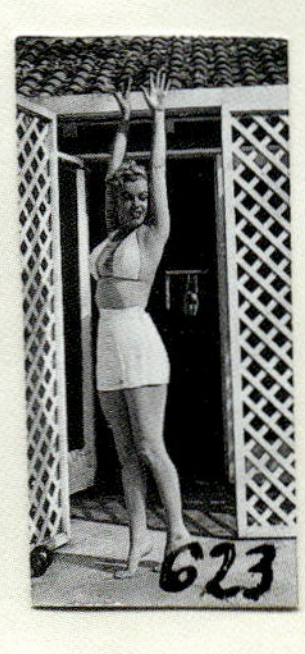

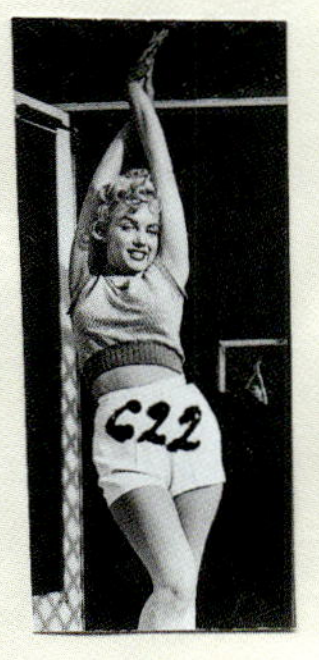

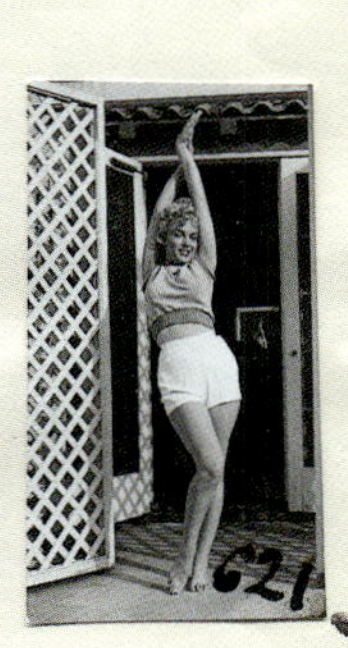

H. Mint 7.B.

ANDRE DE DIENES
1401 SUNSET PLAZA DRIVE

"GOOD MORNING WORLD!"

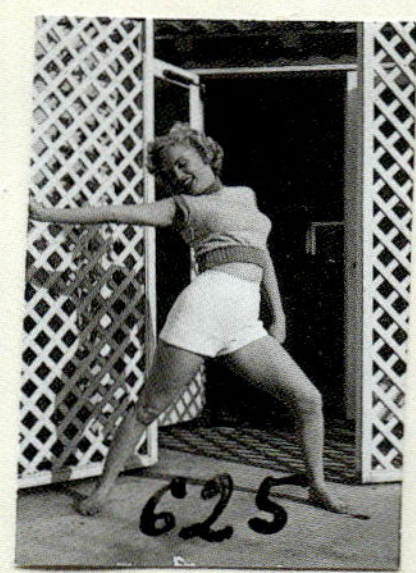

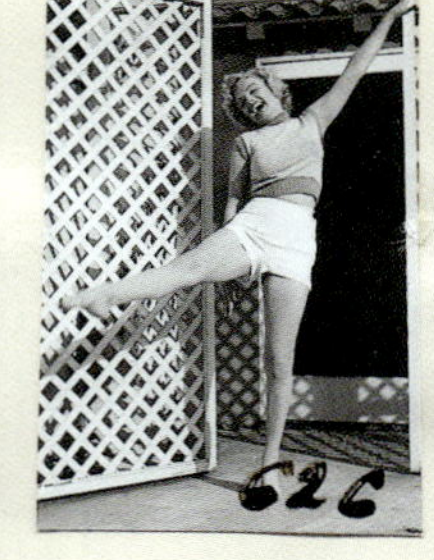

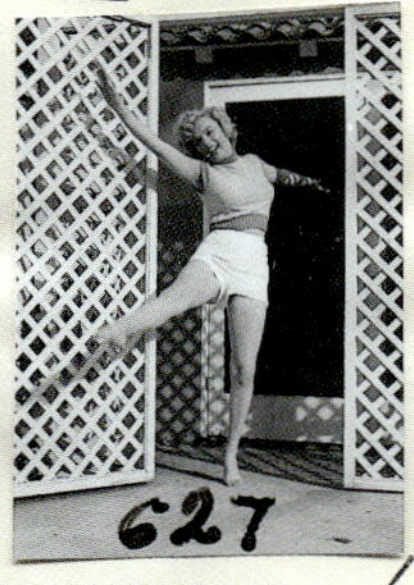

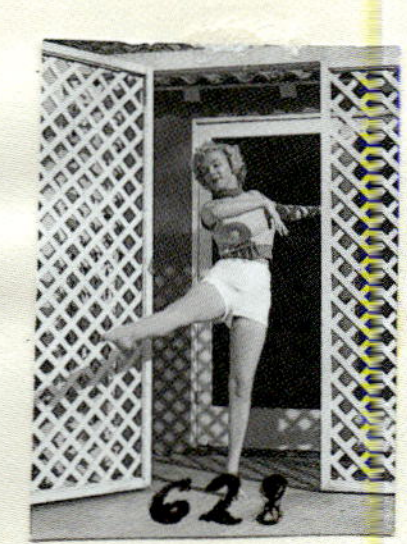

SEXY, TALENTED, HAPPY!

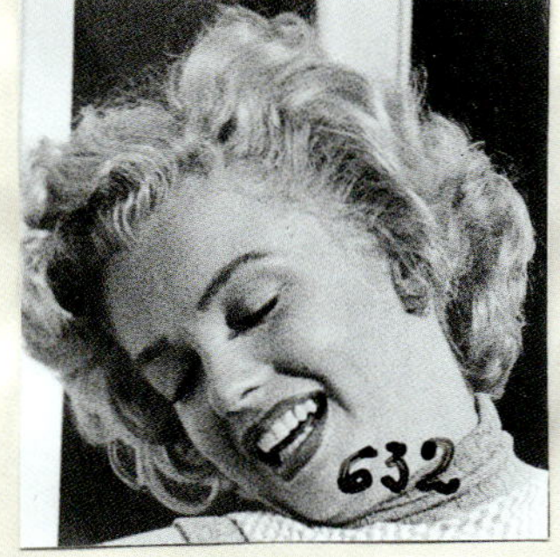

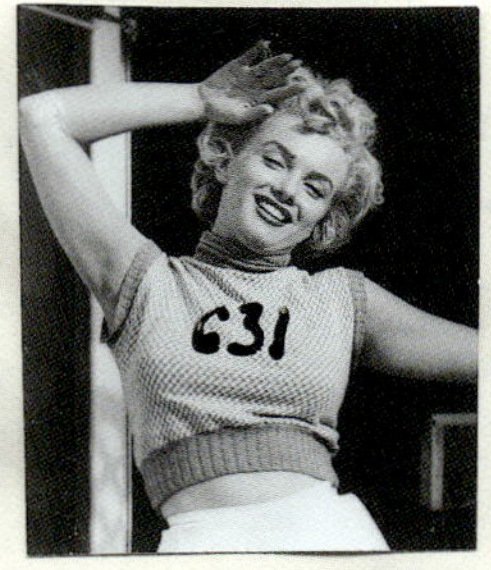

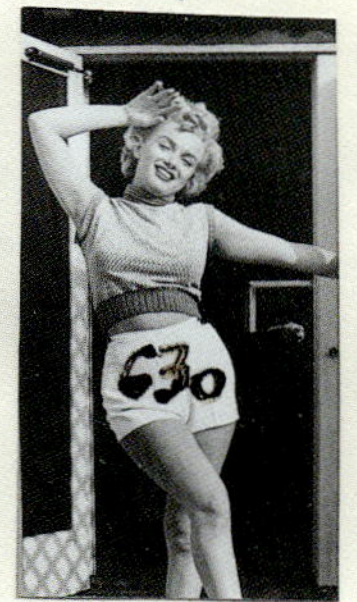

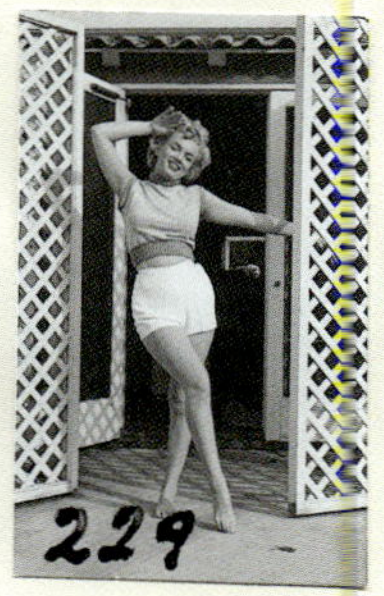

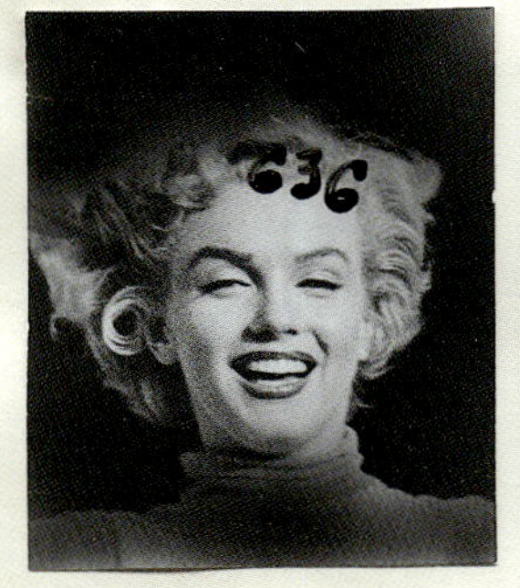

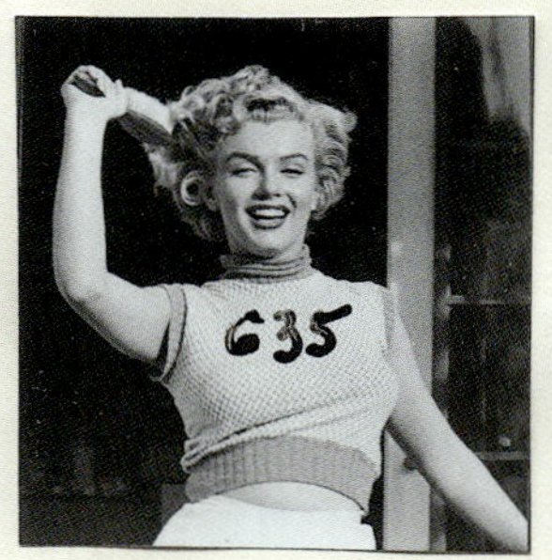

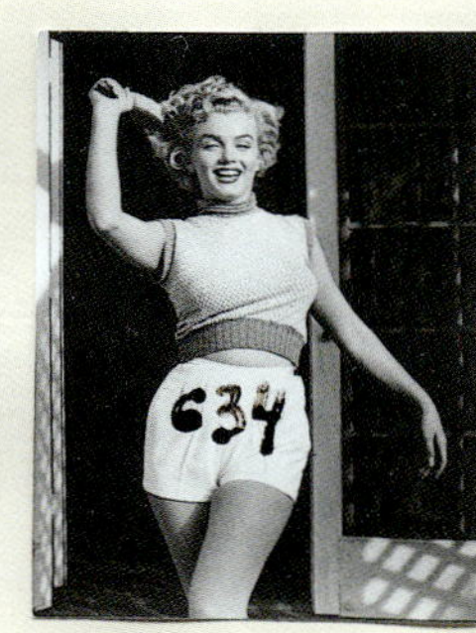

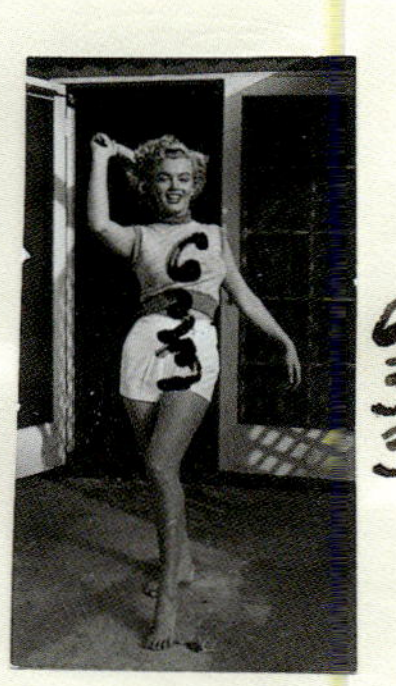

633

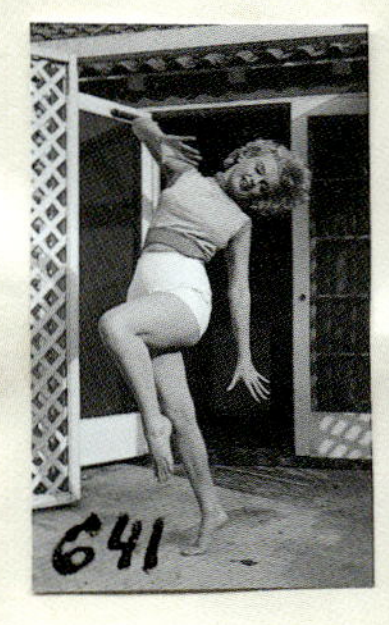

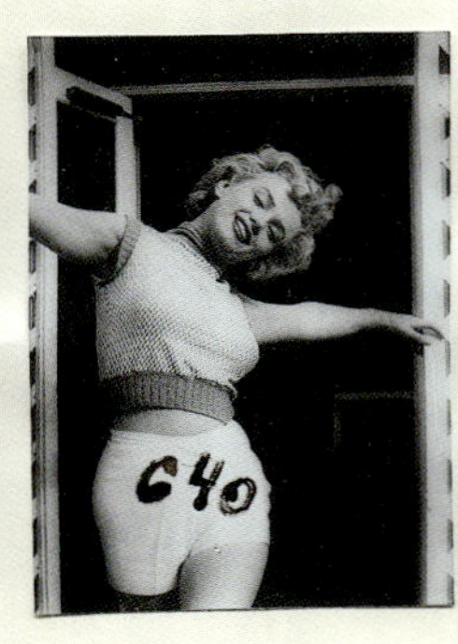

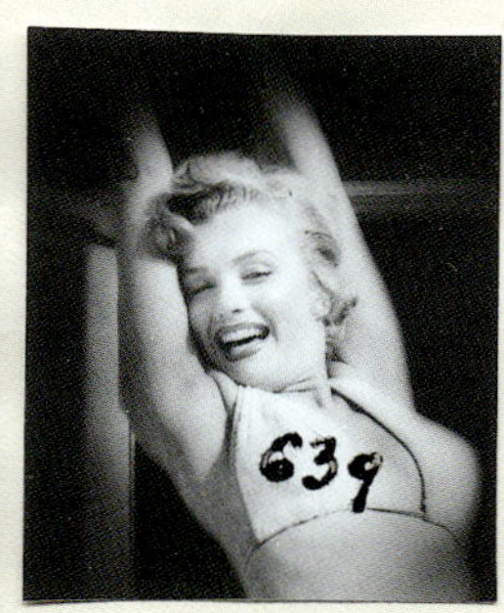

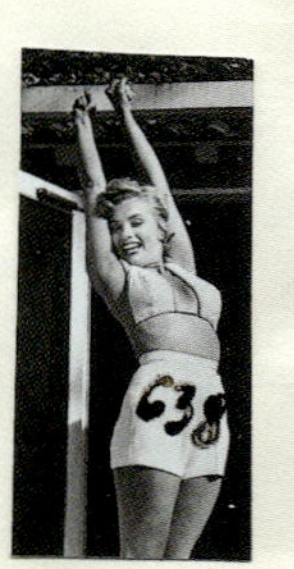

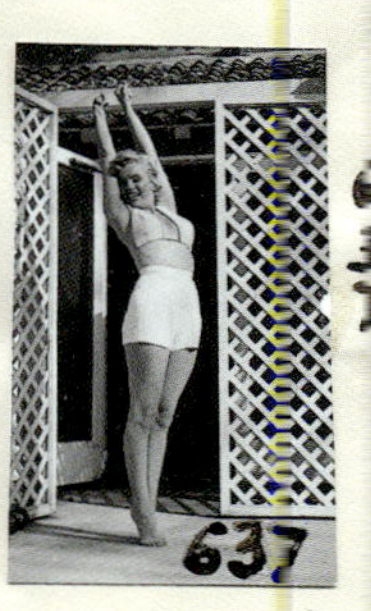

637

BK II "GOOD MORINING!"

Joy"! the whole Universe. Beautiful!

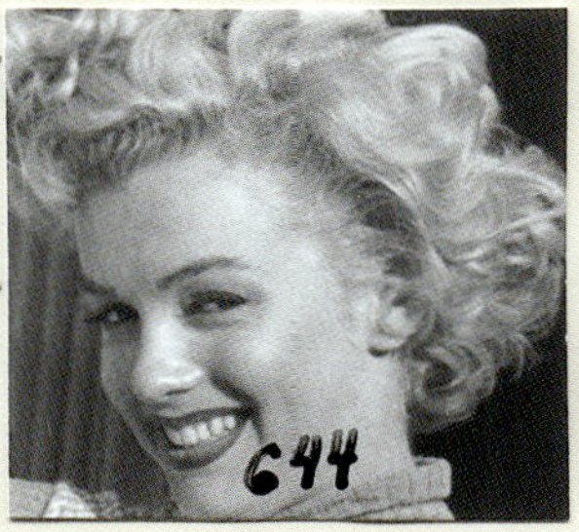

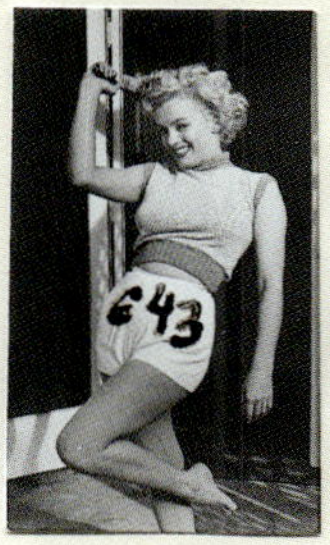

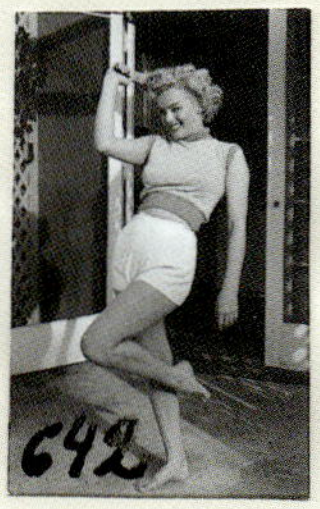

make a montage!

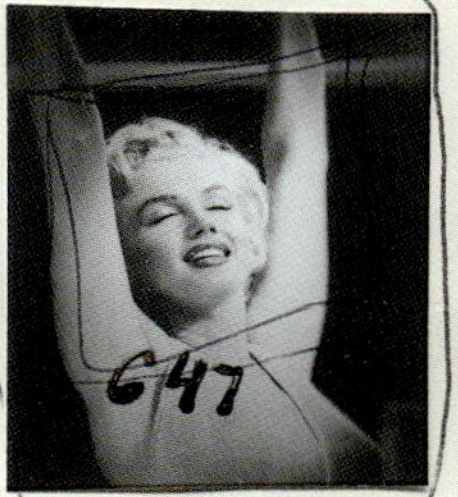

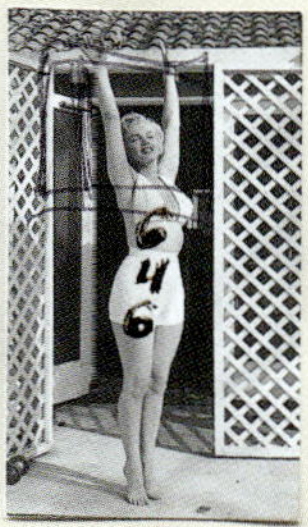

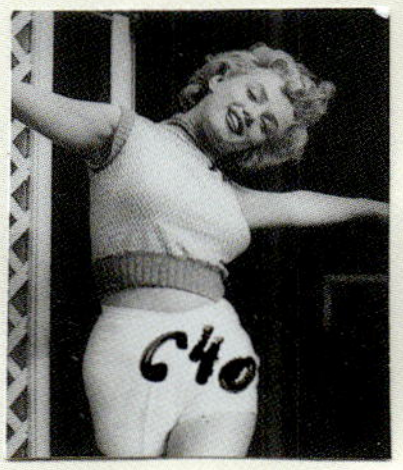

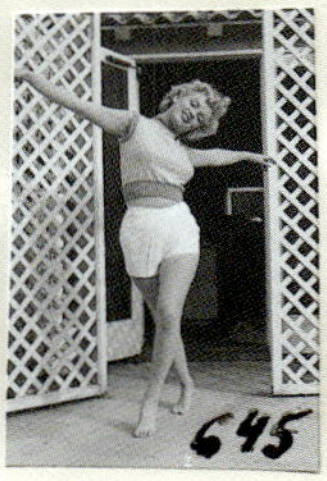

Joy!

644 643 642

647 646 640 645

651 650 649 648

636/A 654 653 652

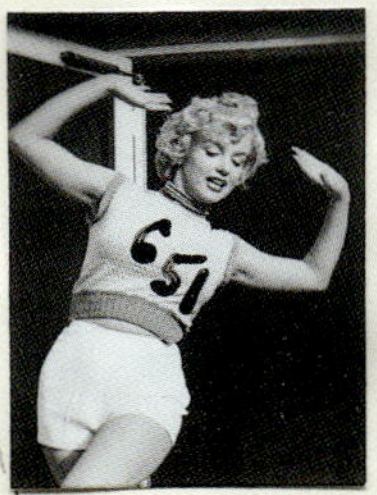

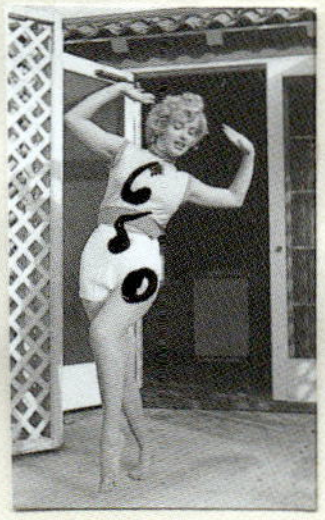

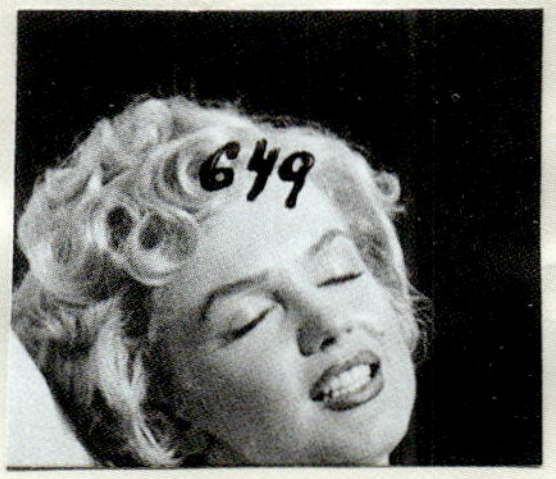

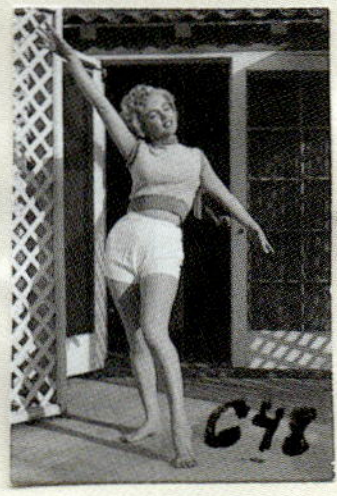

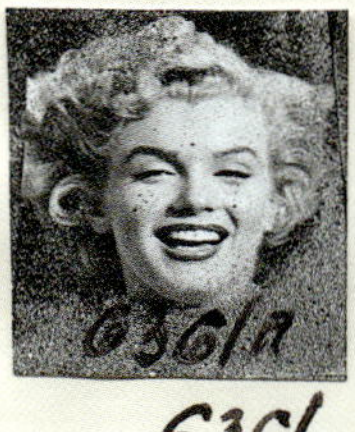

636/A

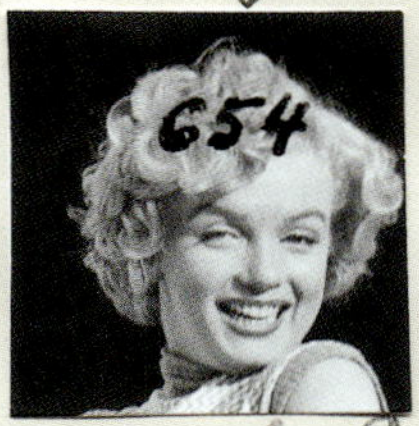

H. Mint-7
Full Body

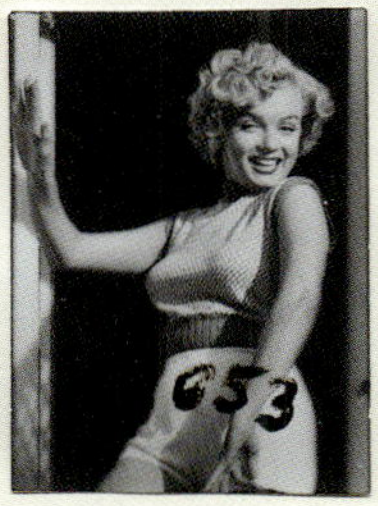

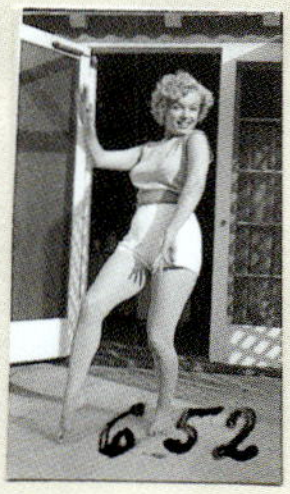

ANDRE DE DIENES
1401 SUNSET PLAZA DRIVE
HOLLYWOOD, CALIF. 90069

85

"GOOD MORNING"

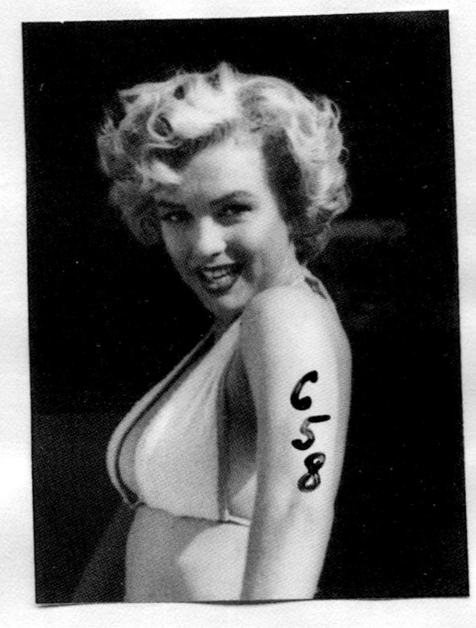

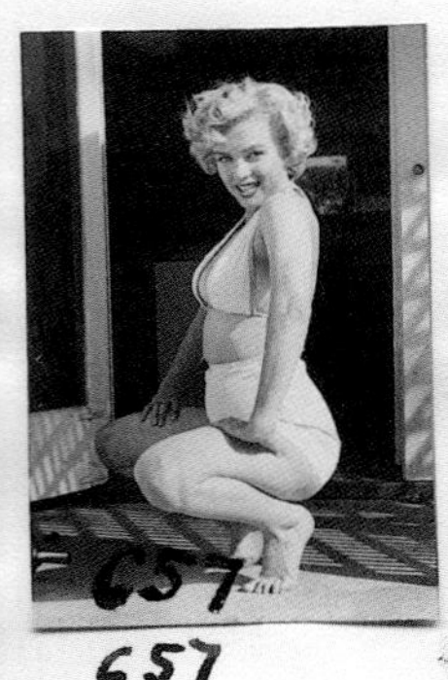

657

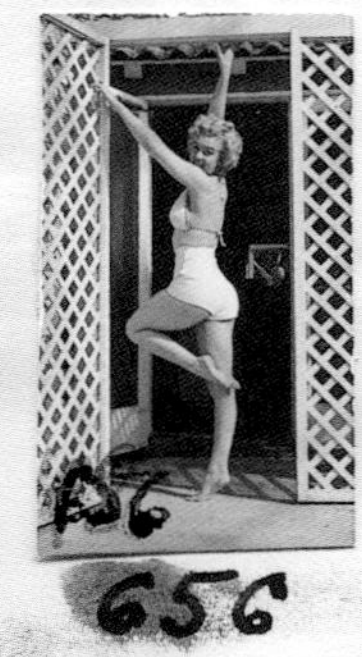
656

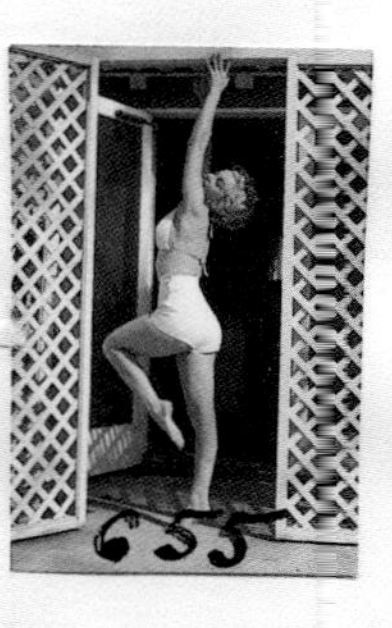

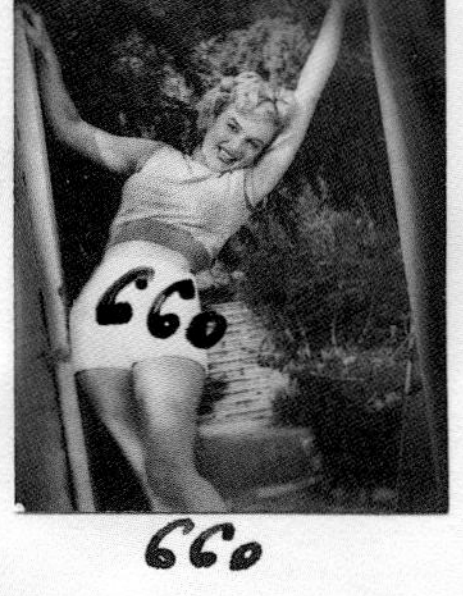

660

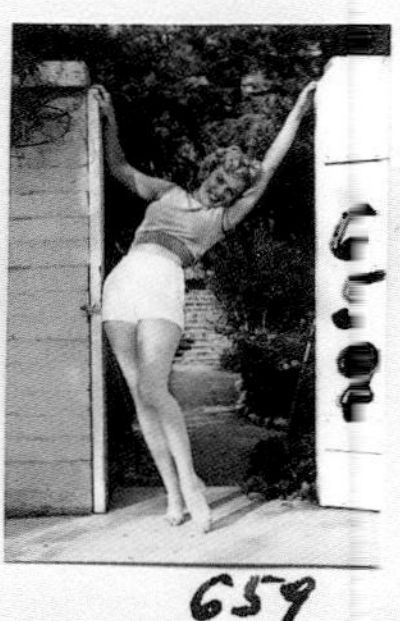
659

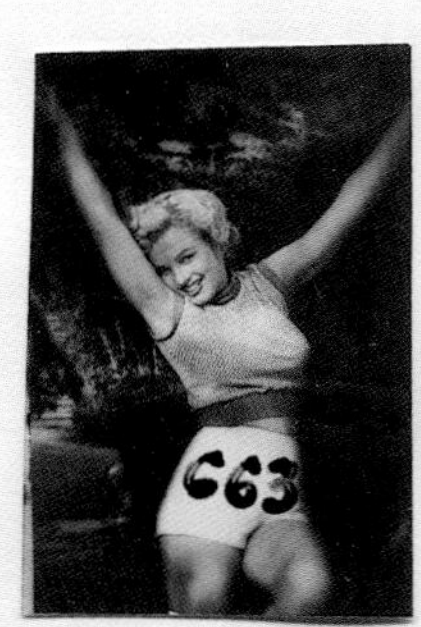

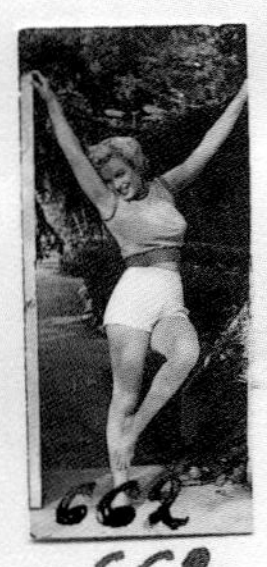

662

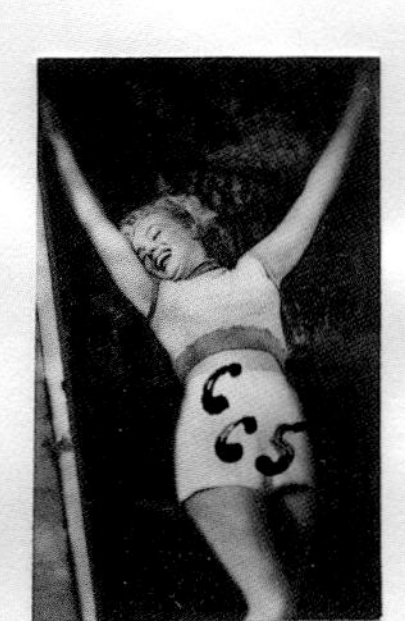

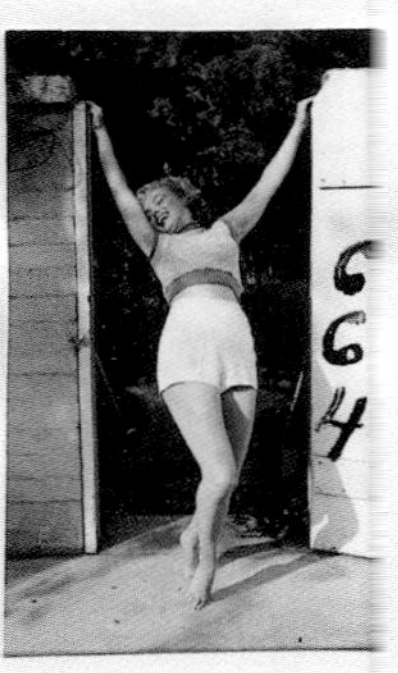

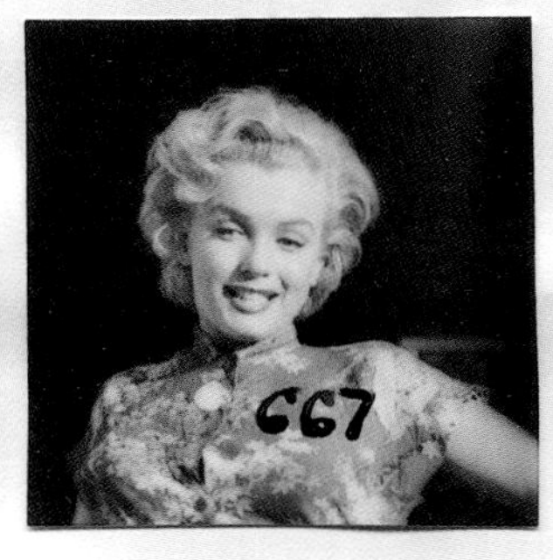

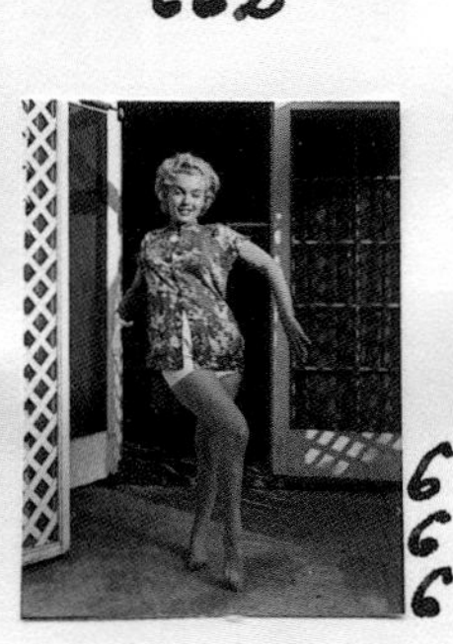
666

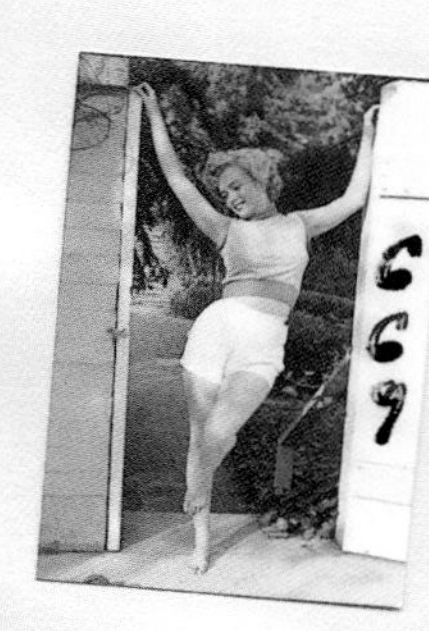

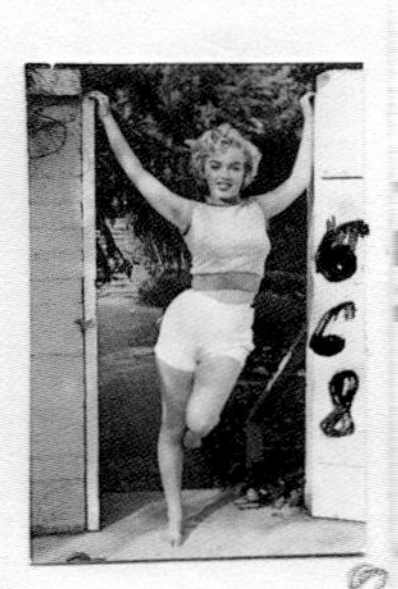

668

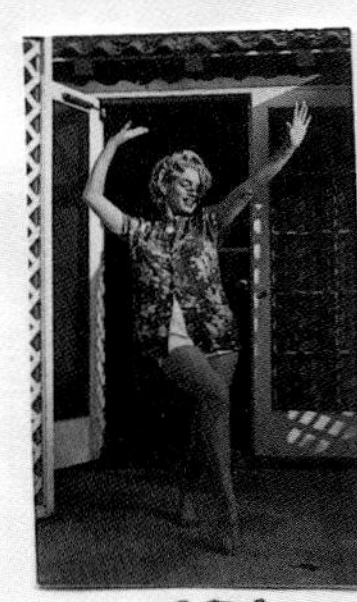
671

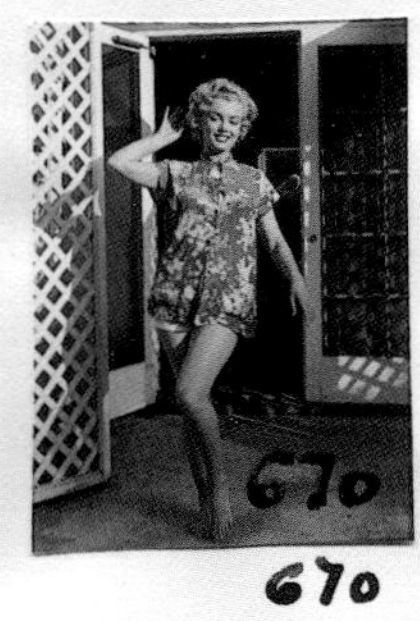

670

86

ANDRE de DIENES
1401 SUNSET PLAZA DRIVE
HOLLYWOOD, CALIF. 90069

Honest Face

674

"SHE DIED IN BEAUTY"

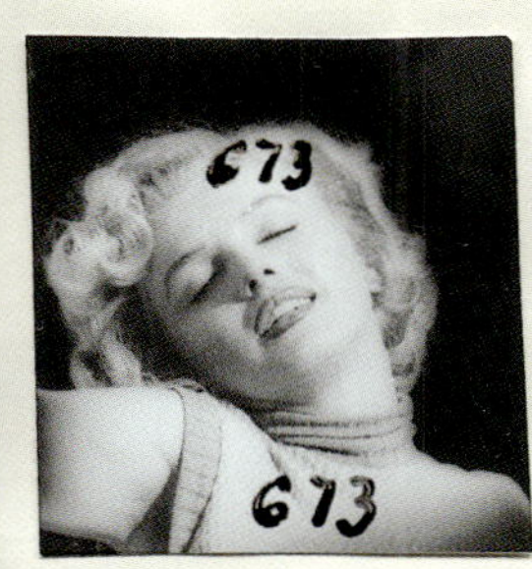

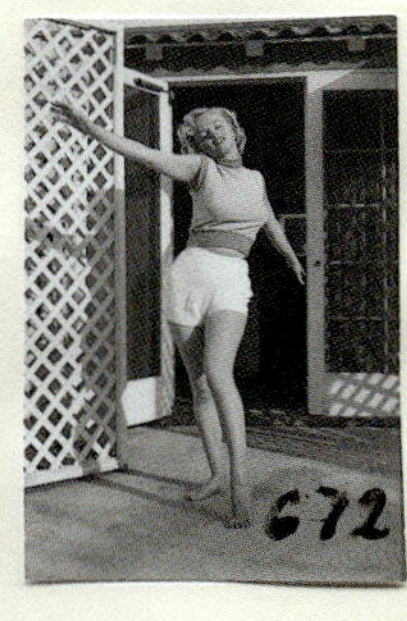

TO ILLUSTRATE A POEM I LIKE) "SHE DIED IN BEAUTY"

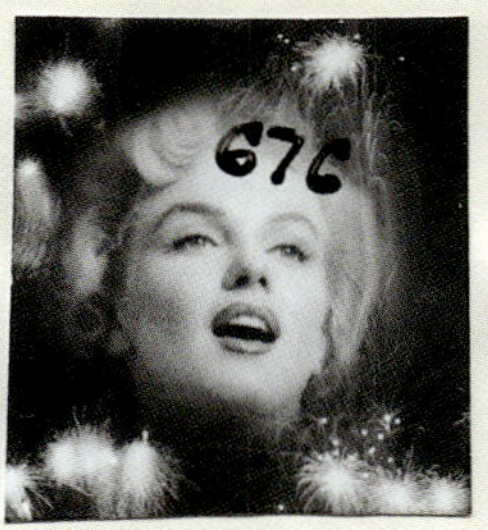

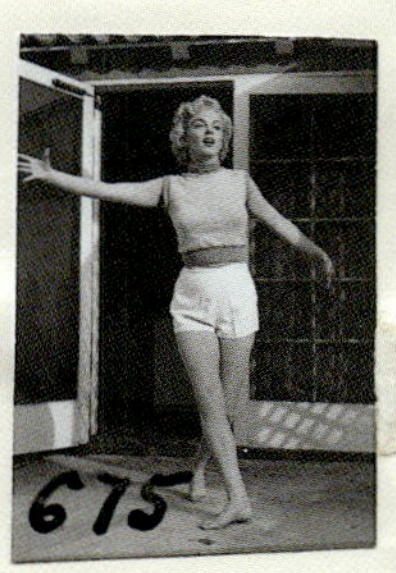

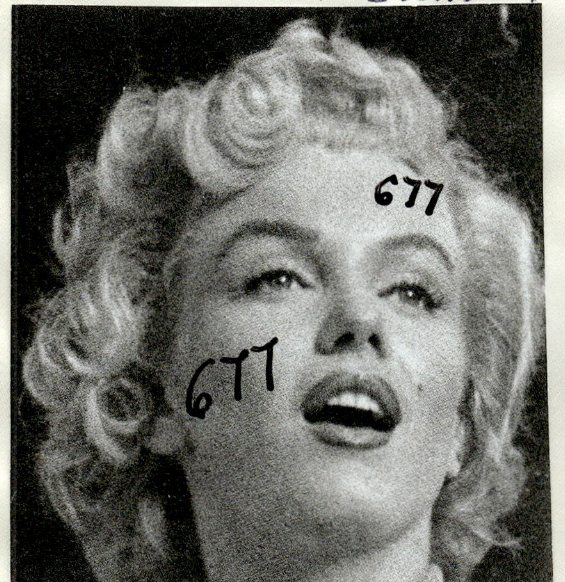

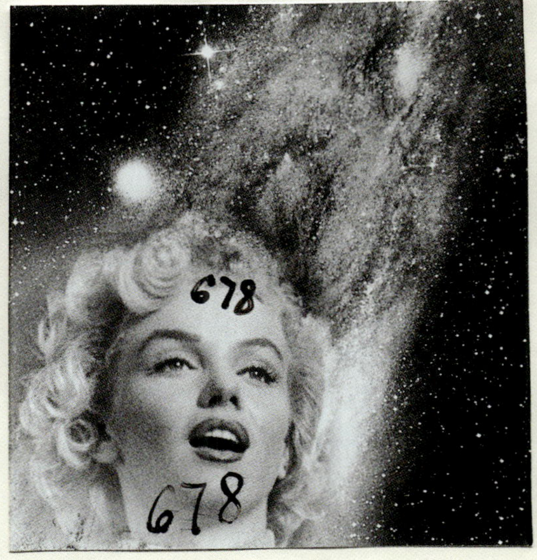

ANDRE DE DIENES
1401 SUNSET PLAZA DRIVE
HOLLYWOOD, CALIF. 90069

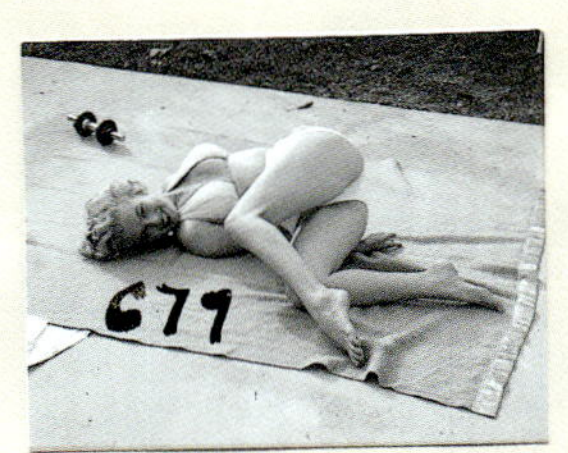

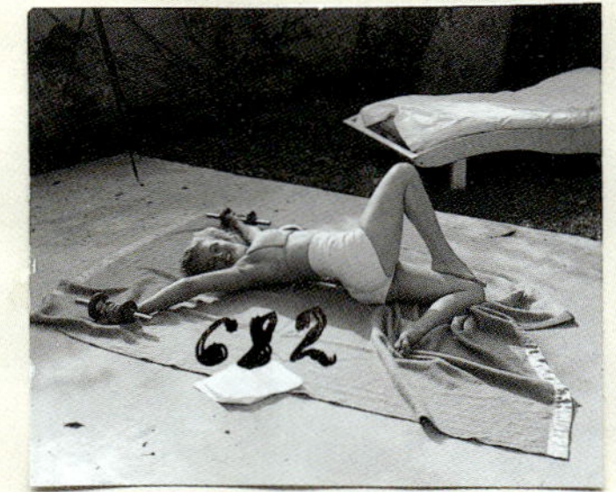

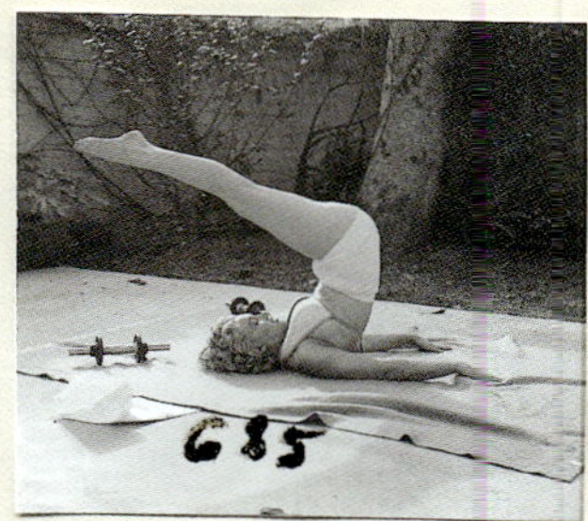

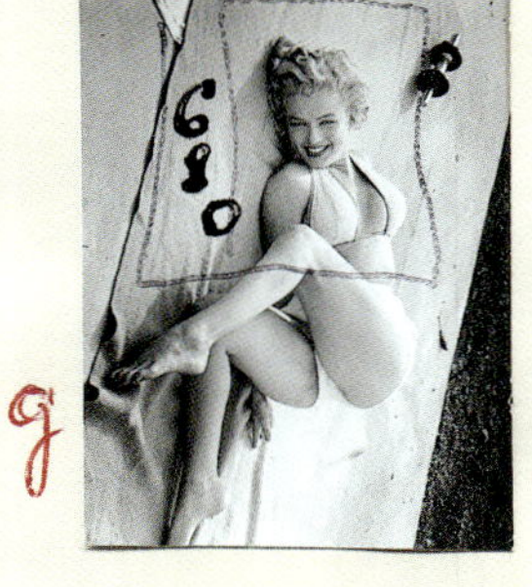

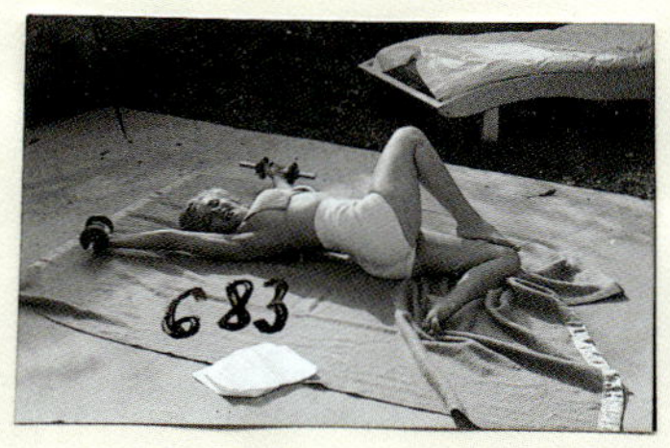

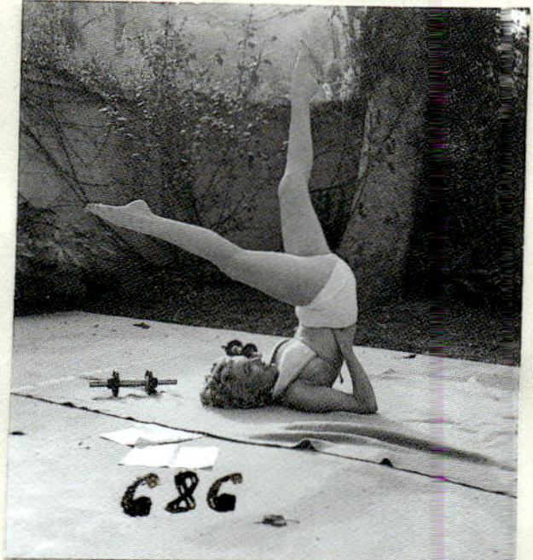

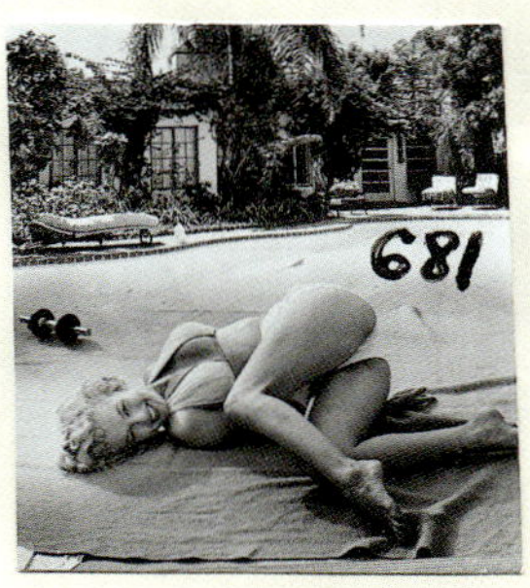

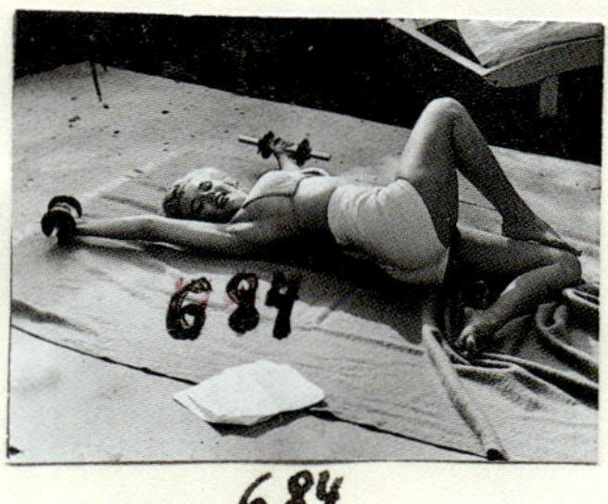

684

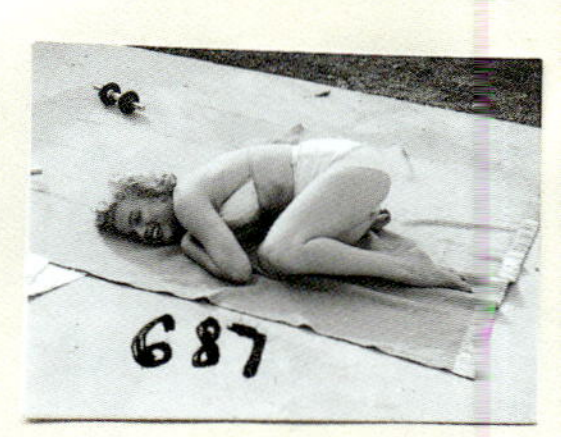

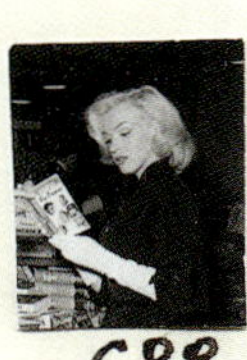

689

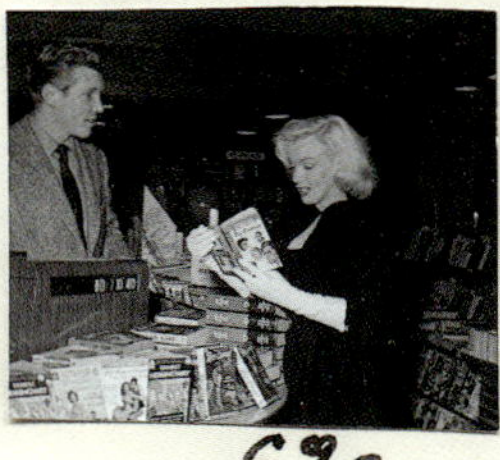

690

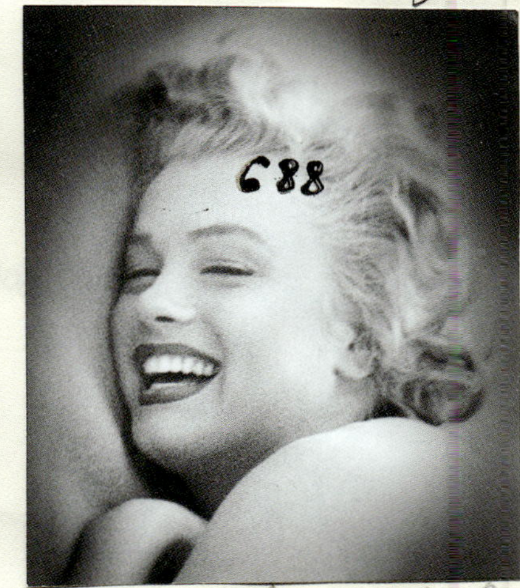

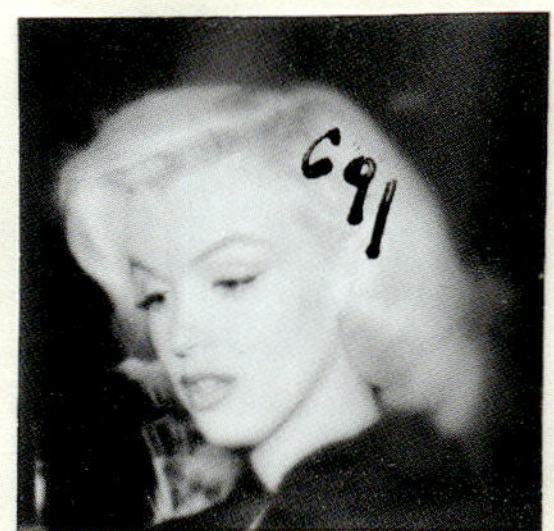

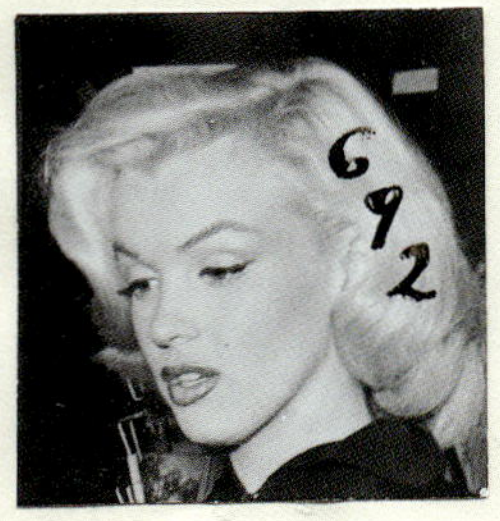

ANDRE de DIENES
1401 SUNSET PLAZA DRIVE

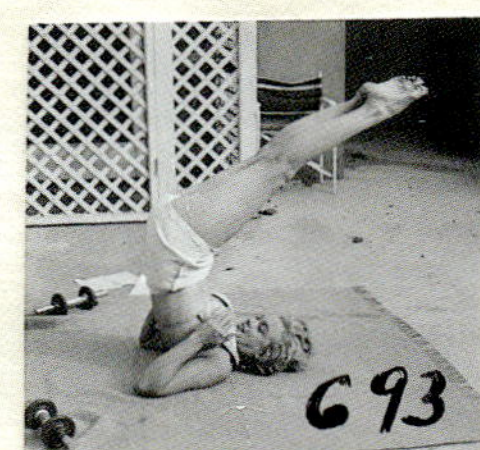

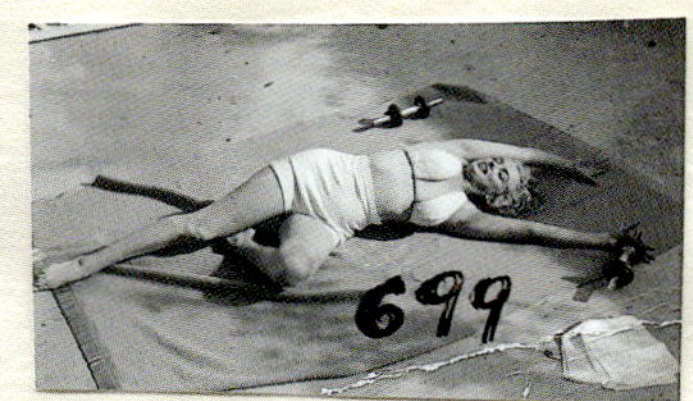

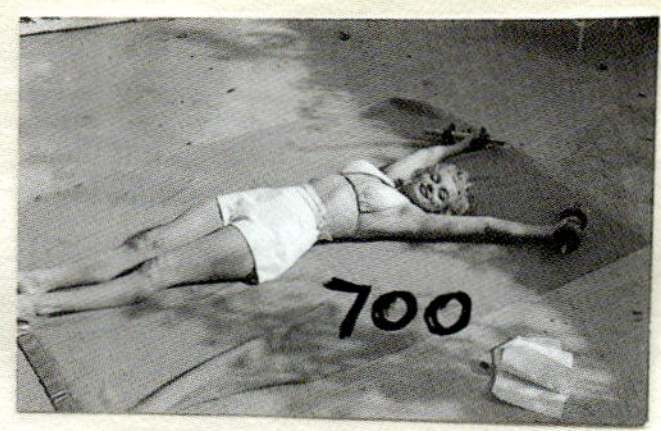

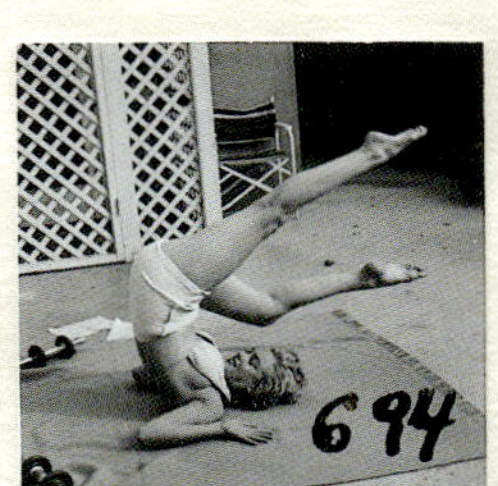

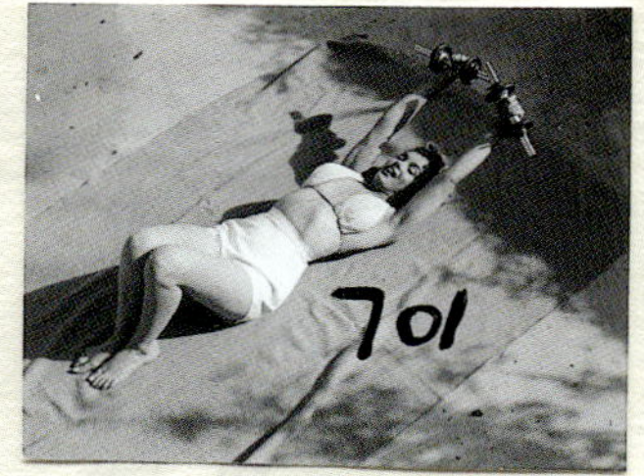

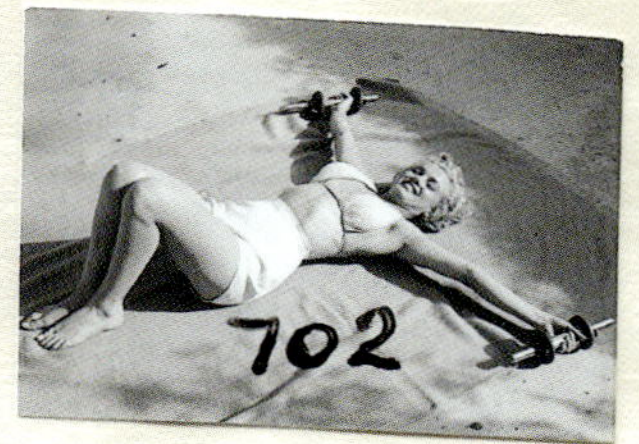

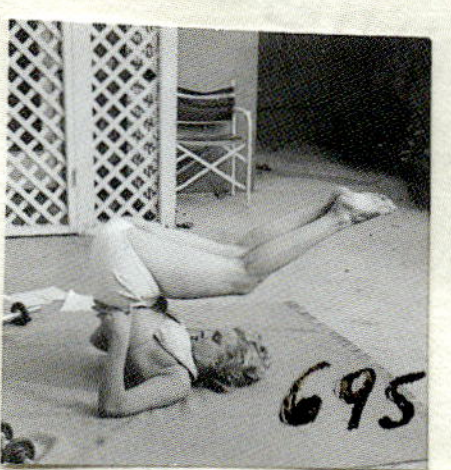

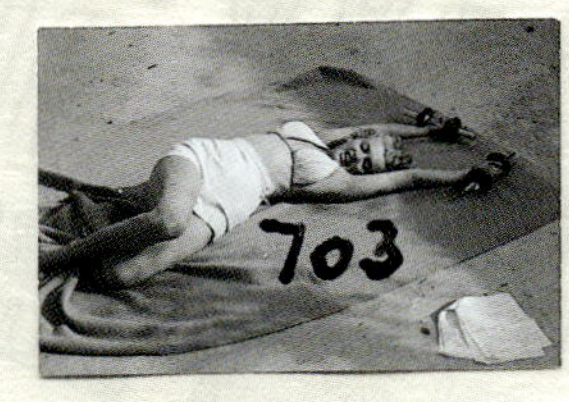

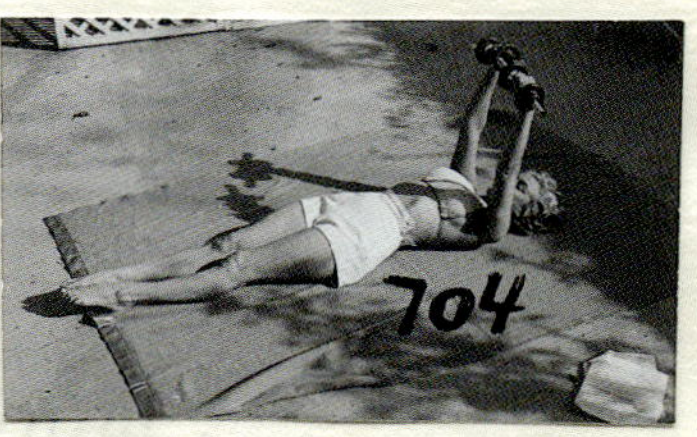

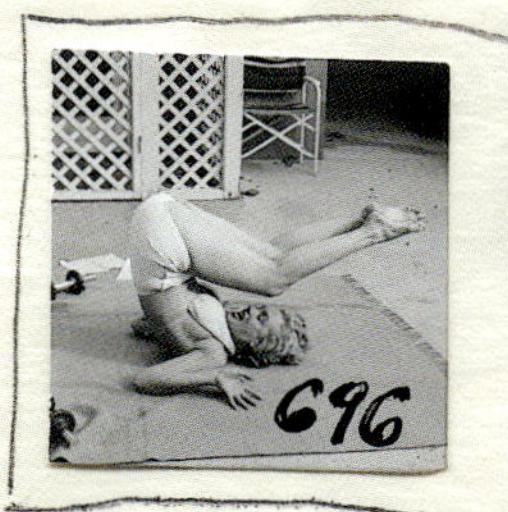

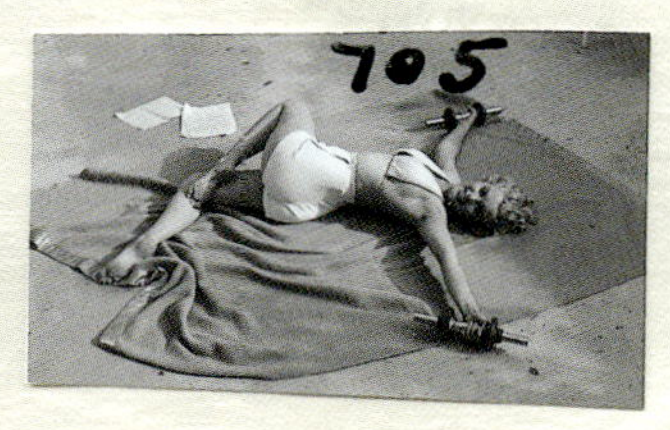

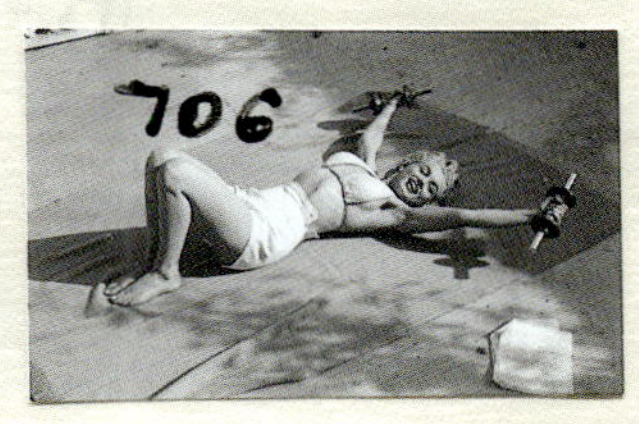

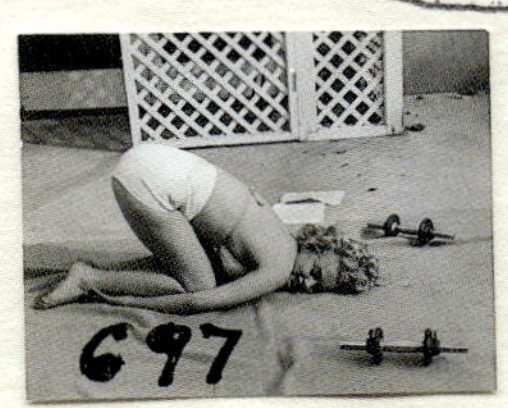

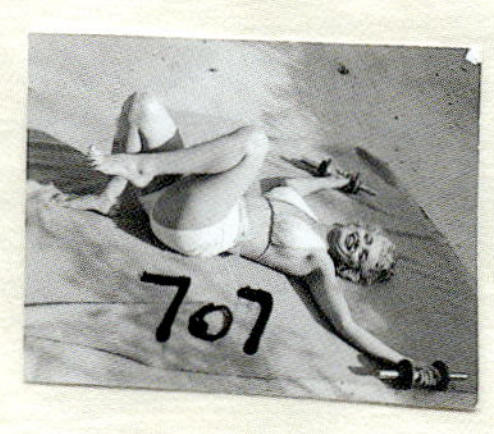

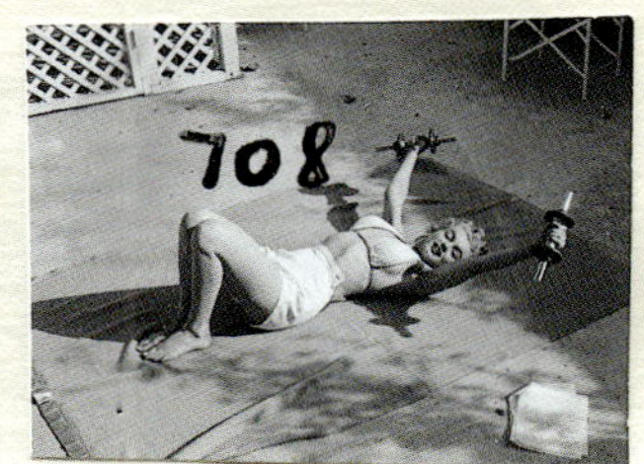

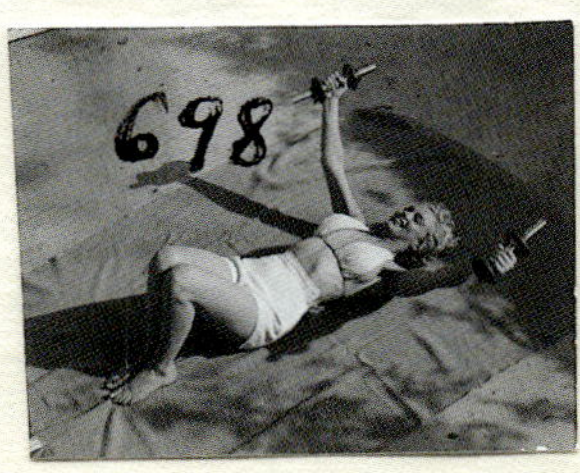

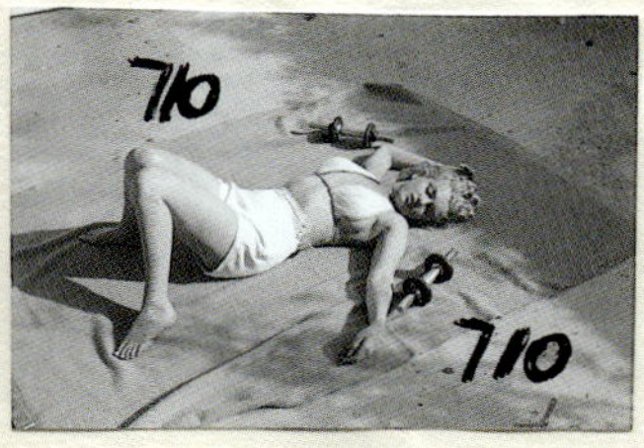

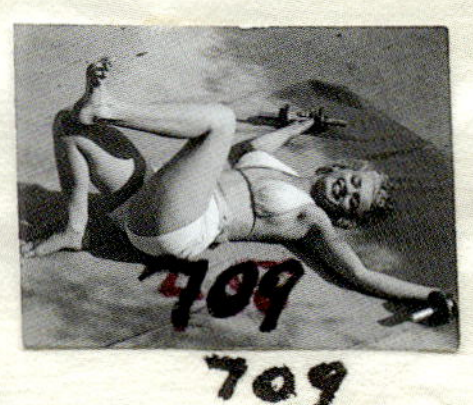

709

ANDRE DE DIENES
1401 SUNSET PLAZA DRIVE
HOLLYWOOD, CALIF. 90069

89

BK II

W ①

H Mint 7 + 7B

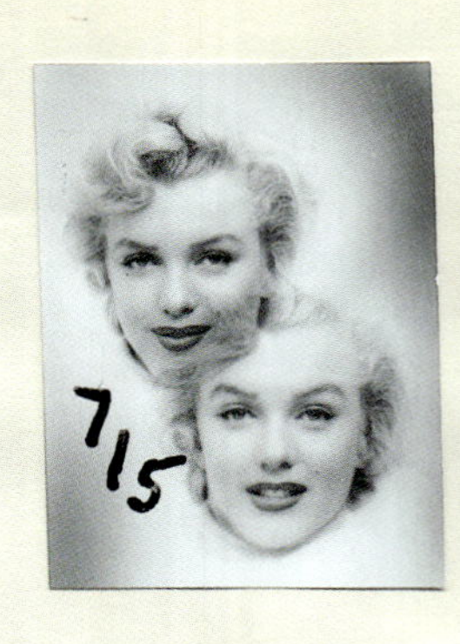

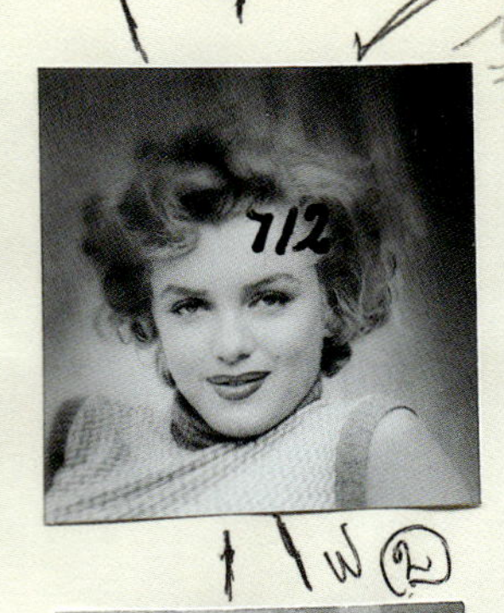

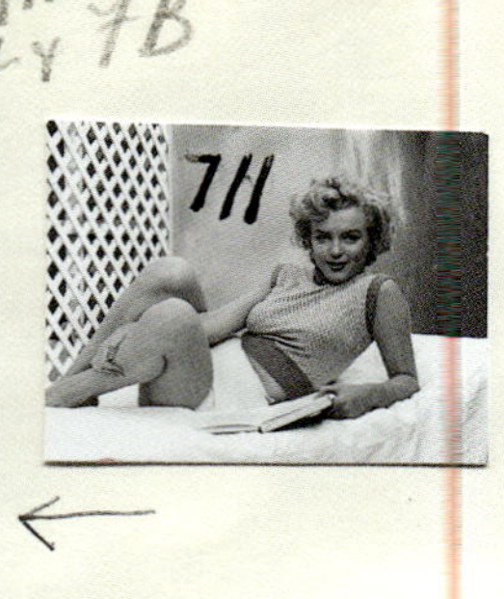

W ②

7B H Mint

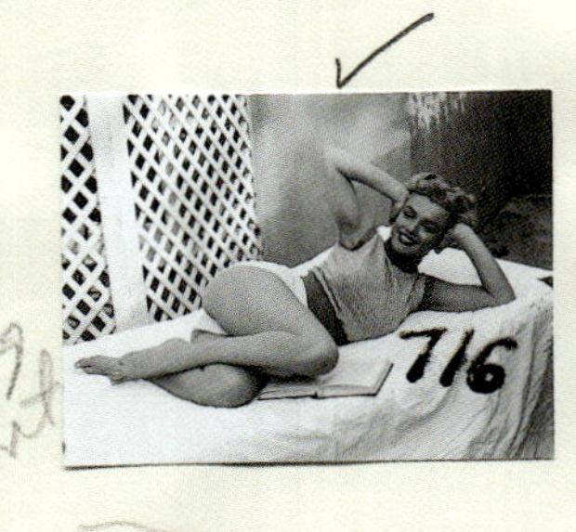

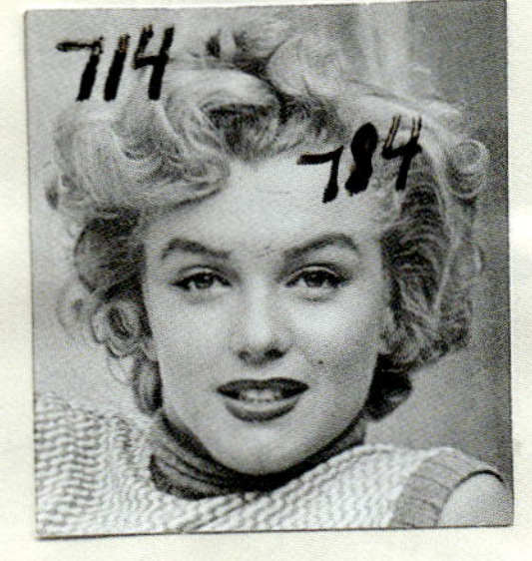

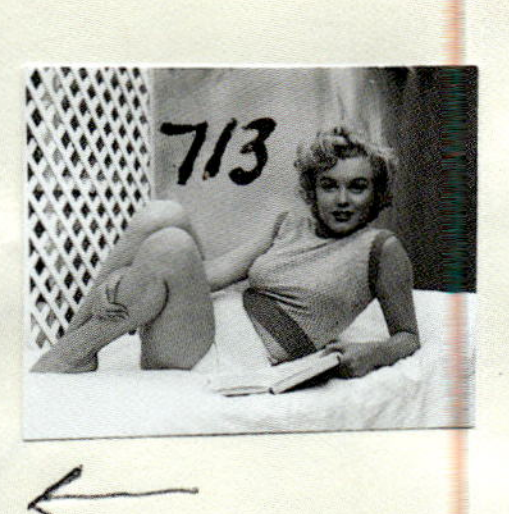

add a background

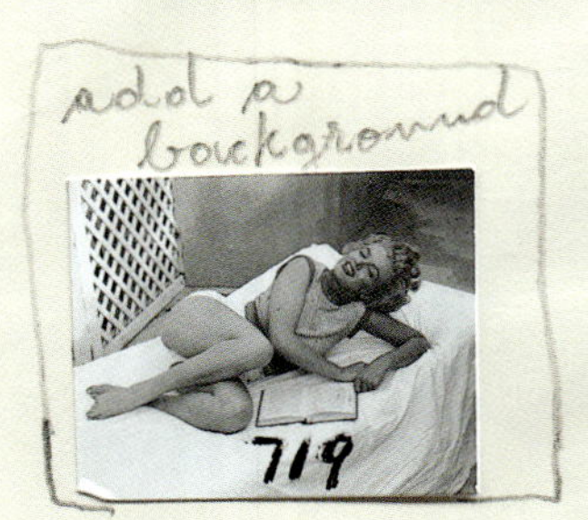

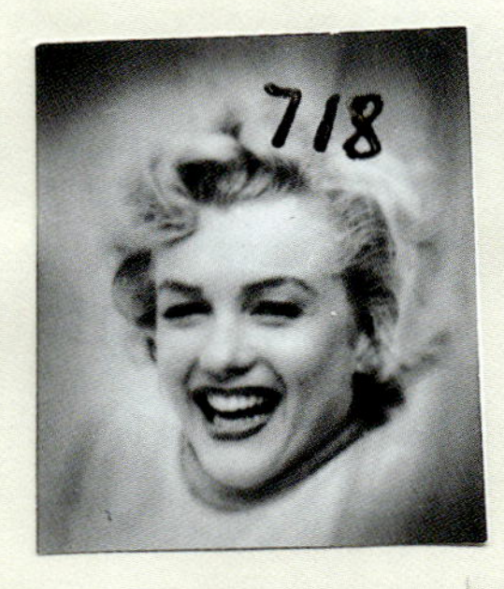

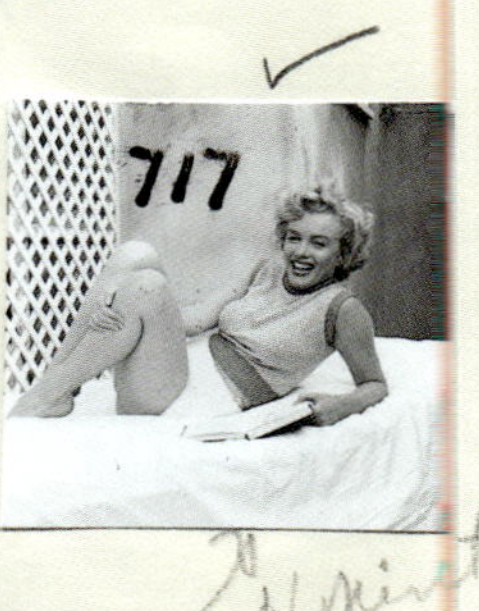

H Mint 7B

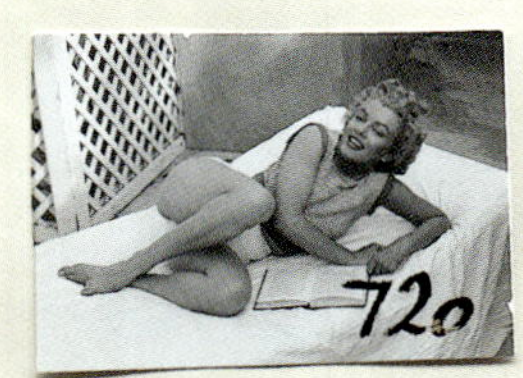

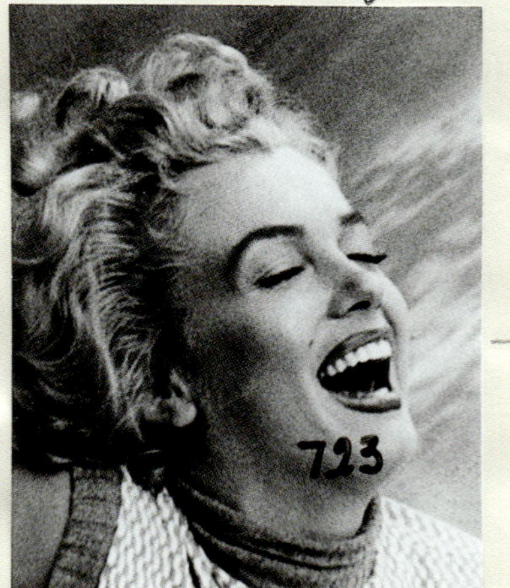

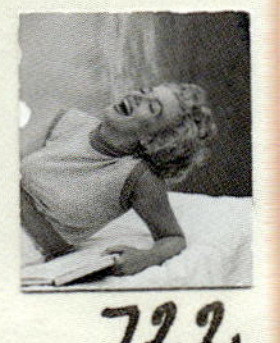

722

721

— H. Mint 7 + 7B

ANDRE DE DIENES
1401 SUNSET PLAZA DRIVE

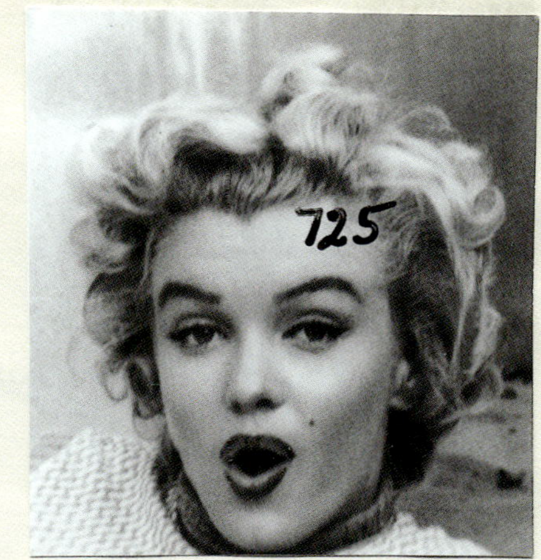

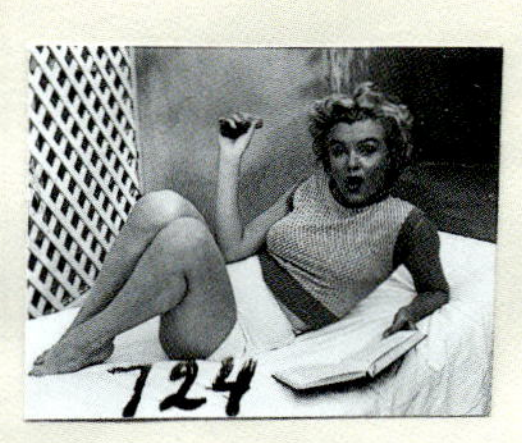

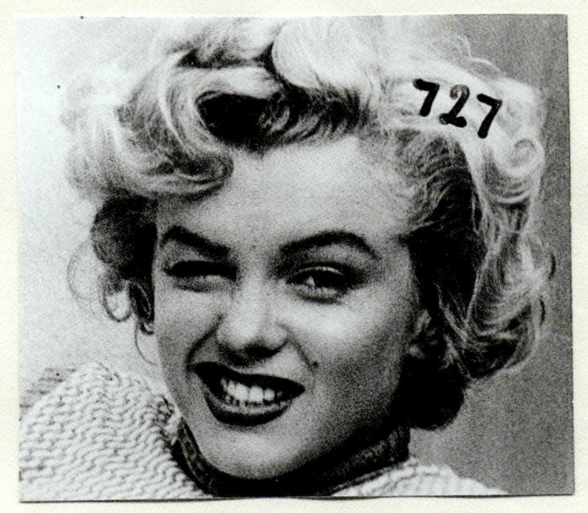

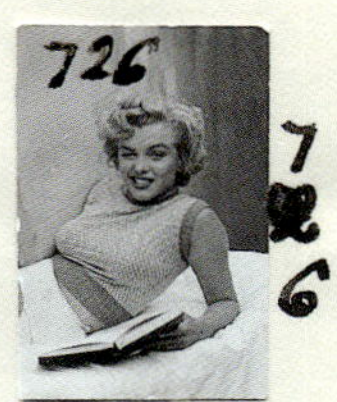

726

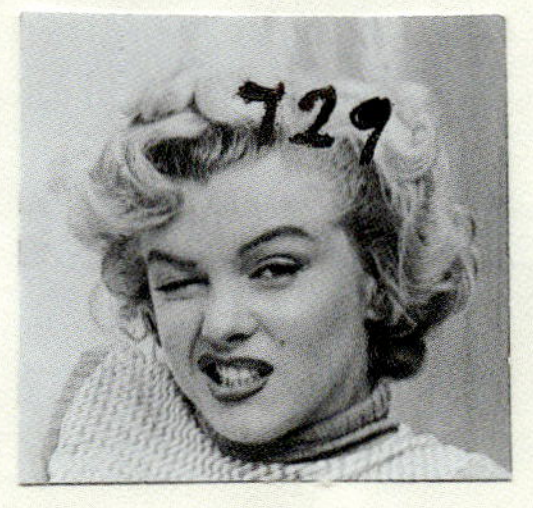

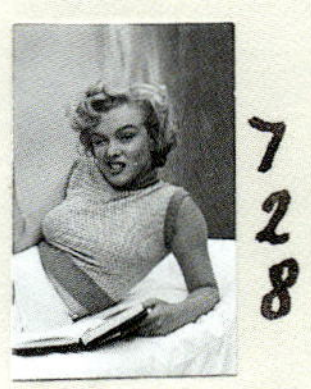

728

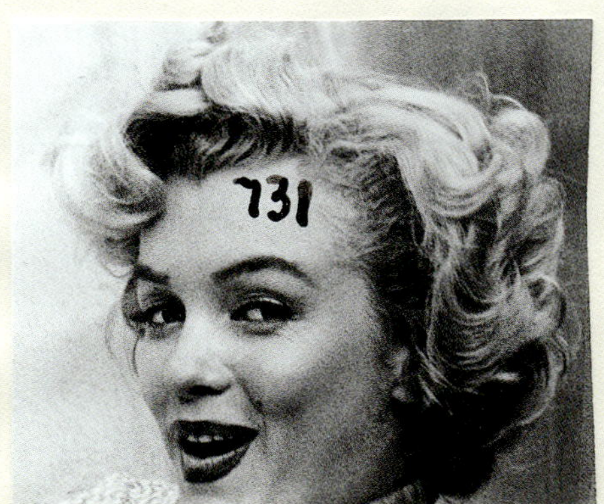

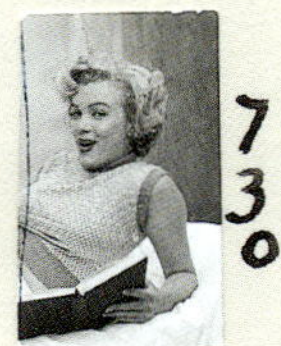

730

91

ANDRE de DIENES
1401 SUNSET PLAZA DRIVE
HOLLYWOOD, CALIF. 90069

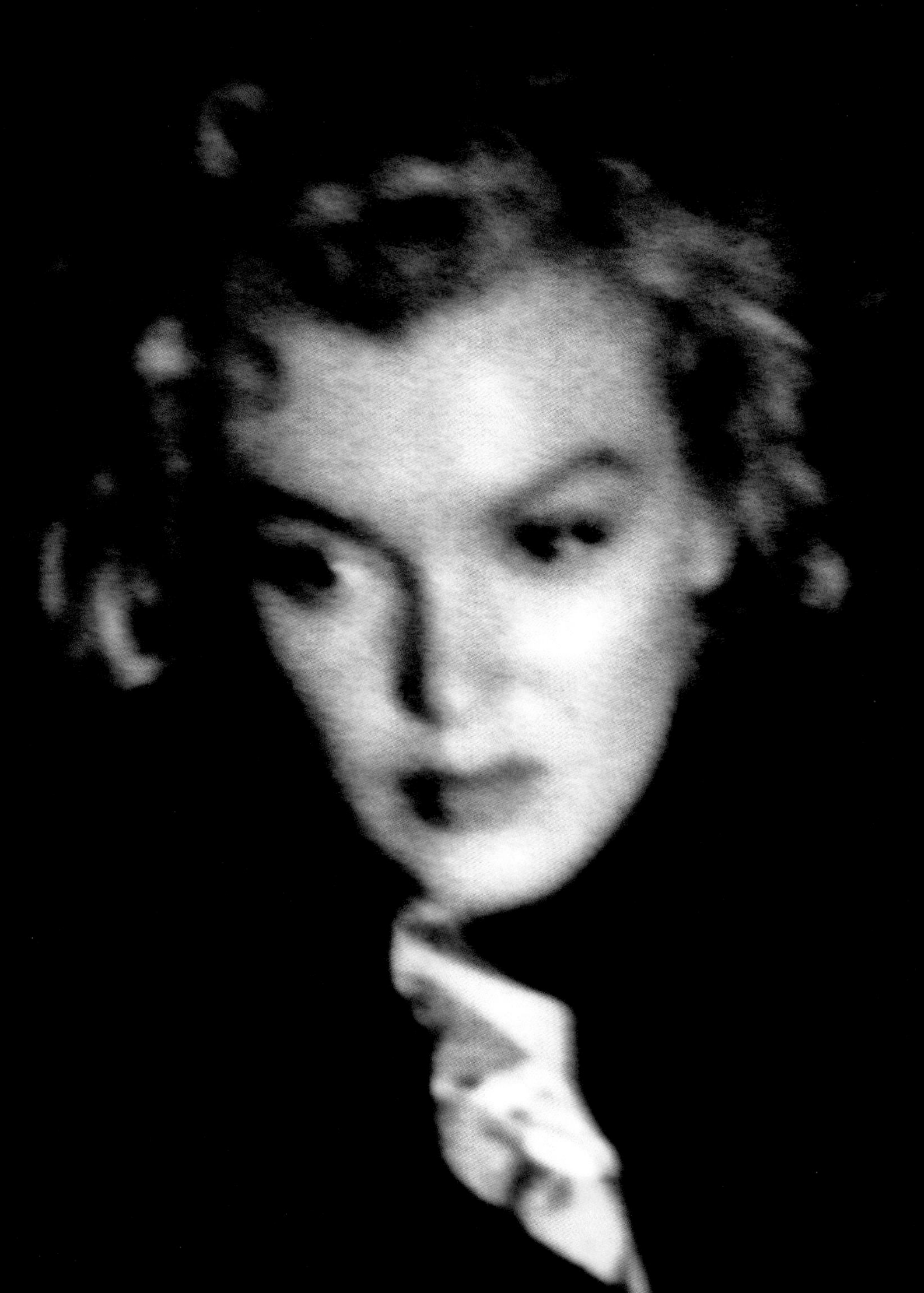

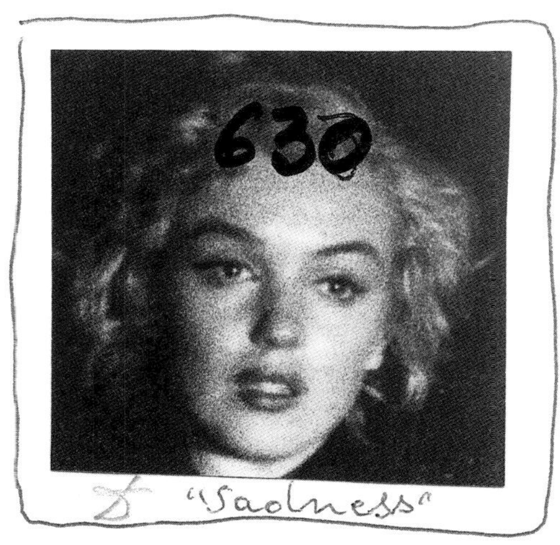

<u>Beverly Hills at Night</u> One late night, Marilyn phoned me and said she couldn't sleep. She proposed that we go take pictures of her somewhere in a dark alley in Beverly Hills. She would pose sad and lonely! I hopped out of bed, gathered my equipment, and we went to take pictures all night long. I had no flashlight, but as they say, necessity is the mother of invention; I lit Marilyn with the headlights of my car! Was she just playing a melodrama in those pictures, or was she conscious that something was wrong in her life, or that something tragic would happen to her?

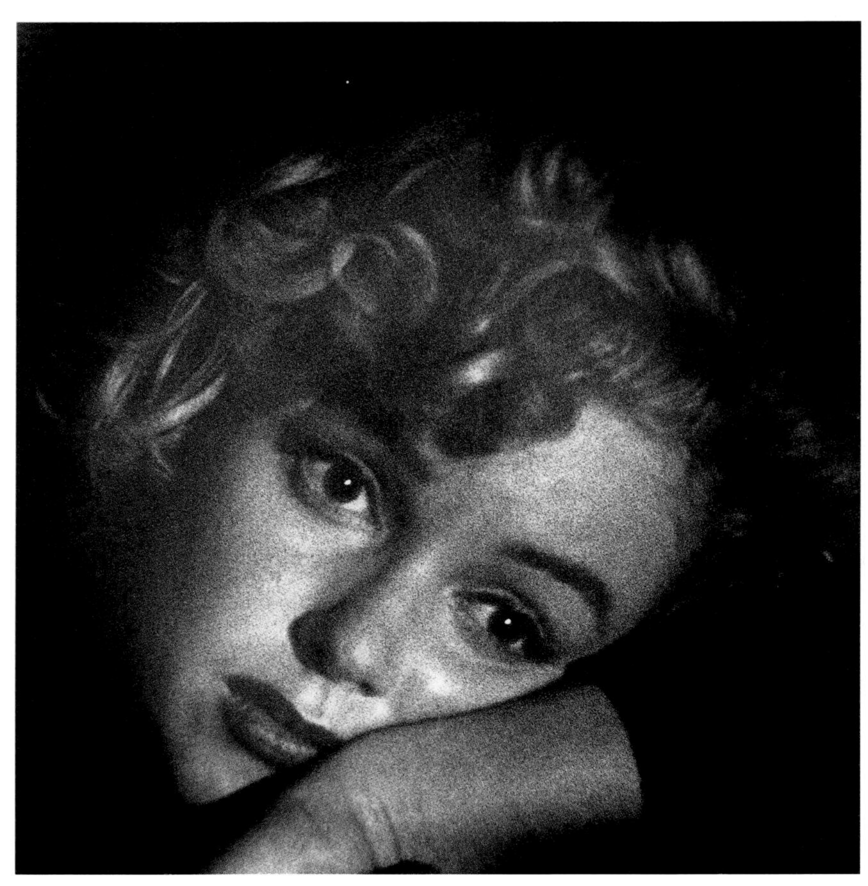

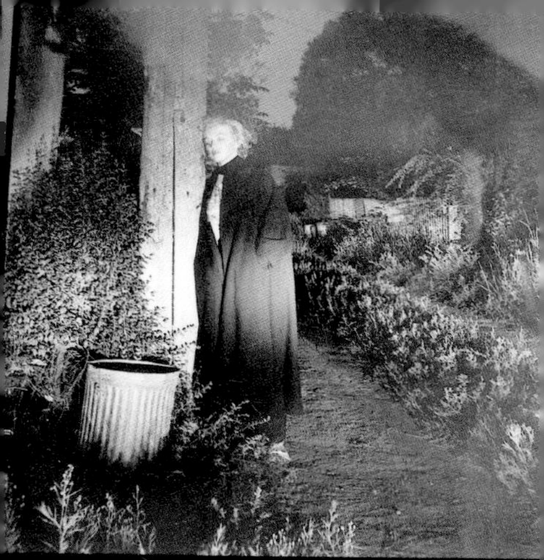

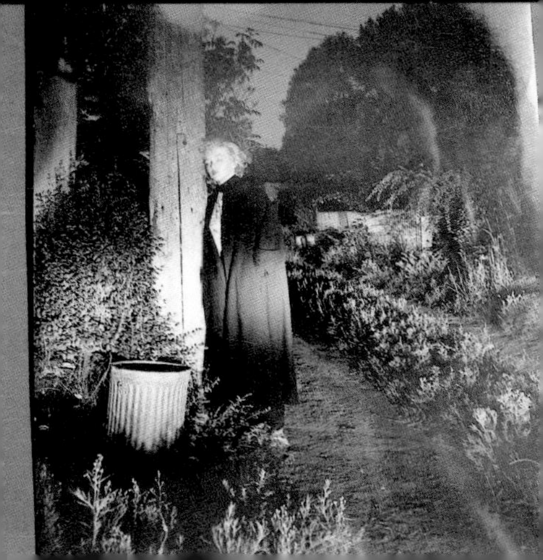

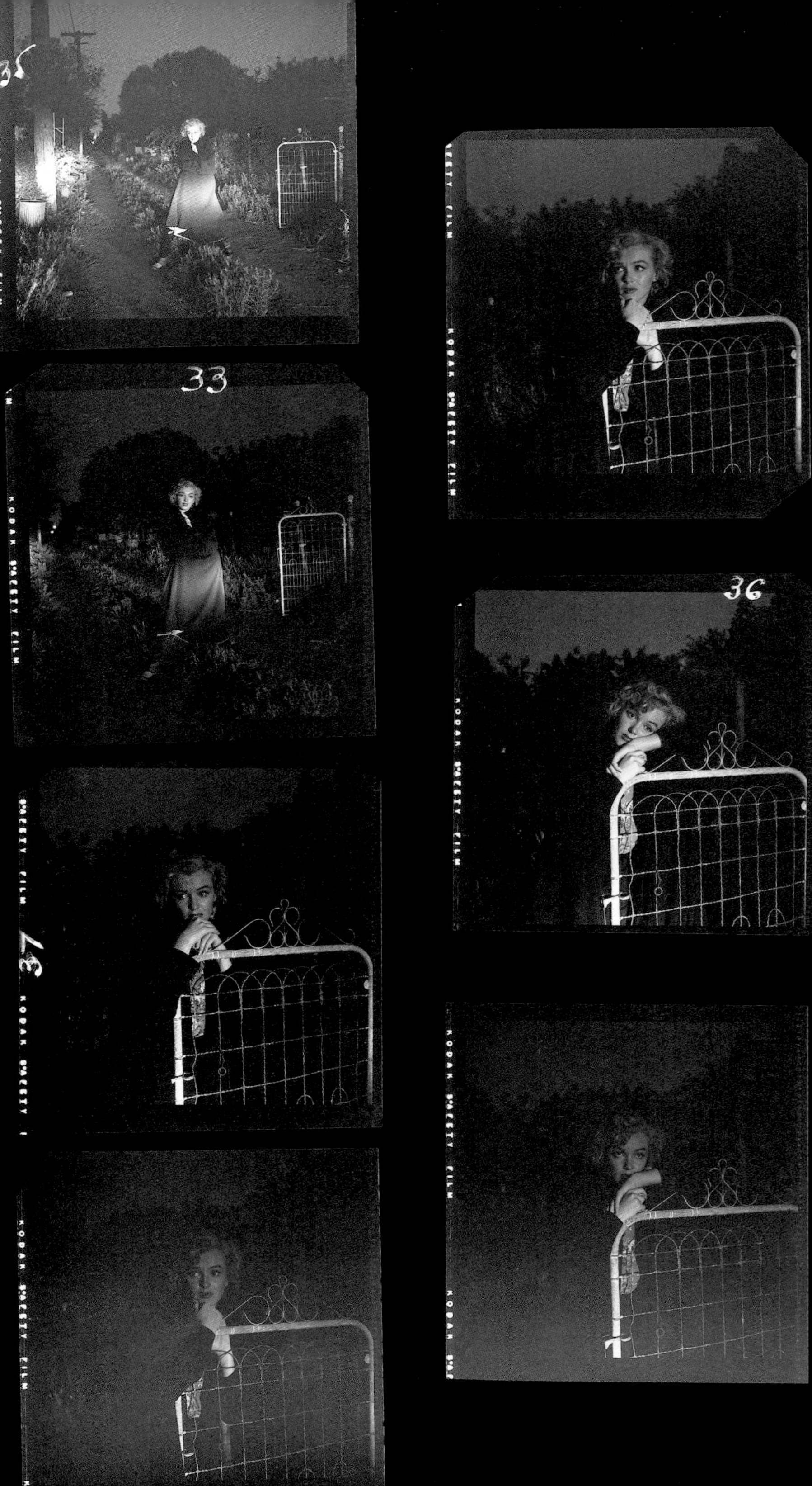

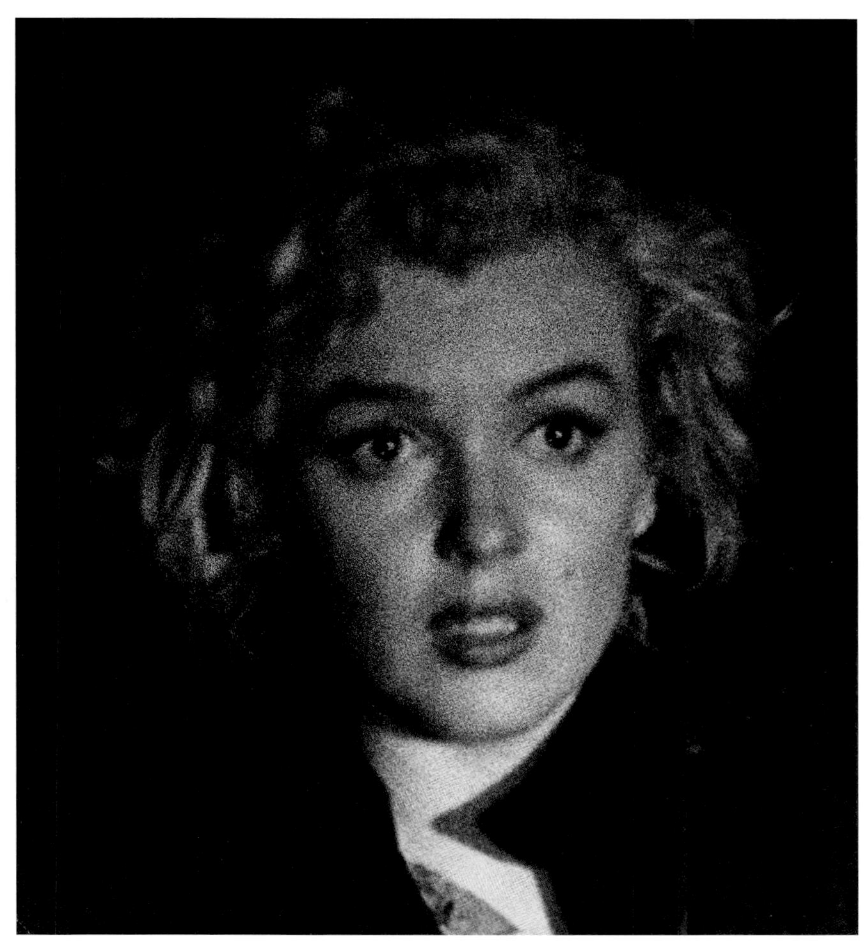

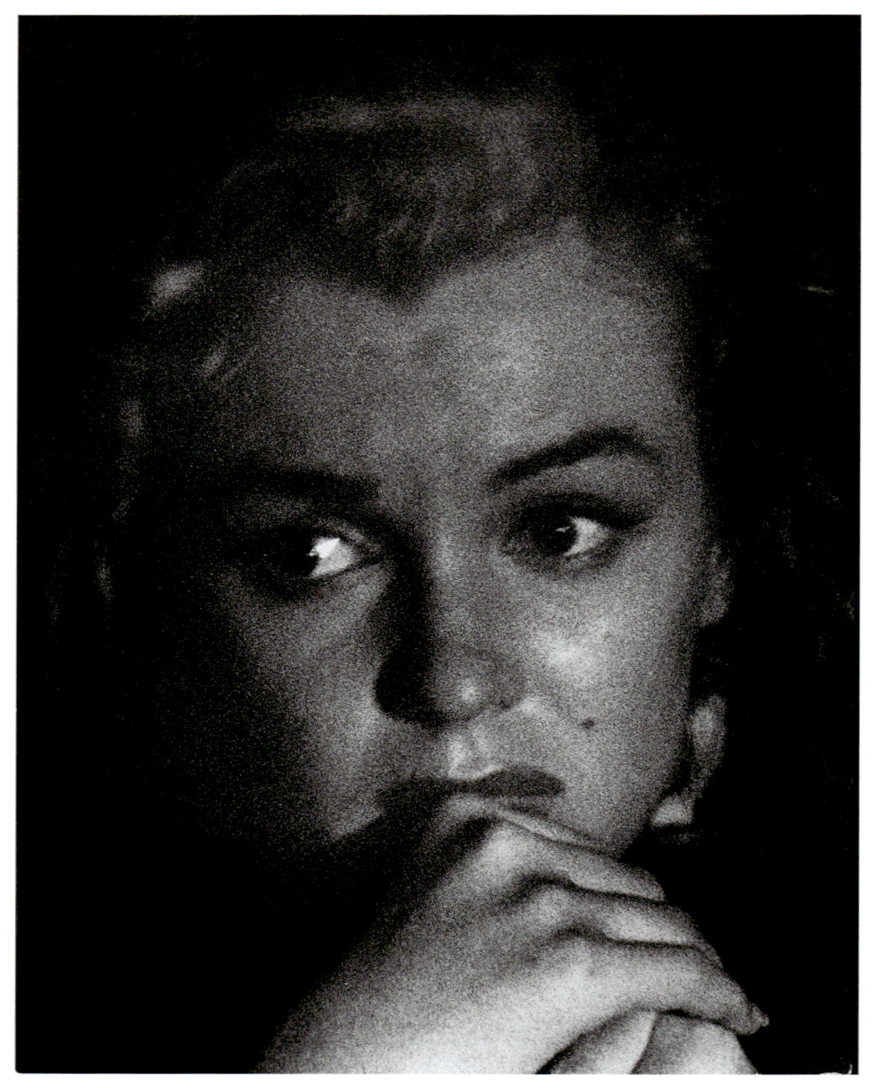

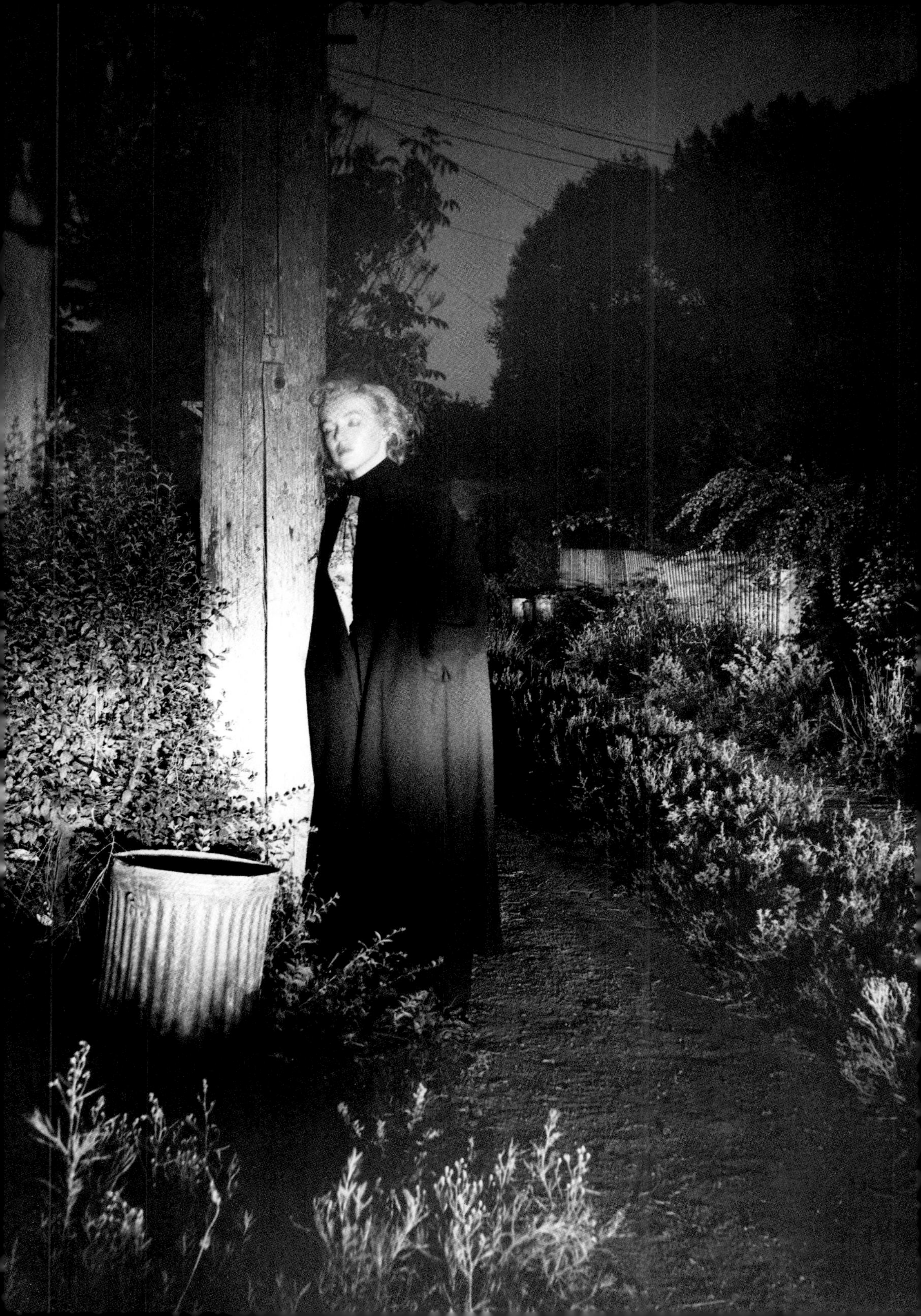

It was her studio who called all afternoon, AND WHEN she finally picked up the phone. One of the executives AT FOX wanted her to come in at once, to explain the nude Calendar which she posed for. The story just came out in the newspapers that she had posed nude. The executive at FOX were worried her career might be totally ruined by that sudden event ! The title for her nude photo on the calendar " Miss Golden Dreams nearly ruined her "dreams" -- she thought, everybody thought. A few evenings later, she came over to my house to look over the photos she posed for me. I showed her all the lovely shots I took that day, (with the Rolleiflex, my favorite camera) There were no nudes among the photos at the firepalce. She loved all the photos, she crossed over only one, and to reassure her, RIGHT AWAY I took the scissor and cut that negative to bits. The calendar " Miss Golden Dreams " DID NOT ruin her career. To the contrary ! The write ups about it, in the newspapers, coast-to-coast of course, gave her even more publicity! And the public symphatized with her, THUS her future fame was even more assured ! In fact, to tell the truth, I always suspected, that all that brouhaha, about a nude photo of her on a calendar, was simply a clever publicity stunt! Marilyn's publicity was always a stunning thing ! The publicity she got was fantastic ! Well done ! One of the greatest examples ever of American ingenuity ! Business ! The basis for a legendery fame is publicity !

(DIRECTED BY HARRY BRAND ! PUBLICITY DIRECTOR AT FOX.)

You can be very talented, yet remain nothing or nobody, if you don't get publicity! Enormous amount of publicity ! And Marilyn knew that well ! She had learnt it ! Good makeup, lots of sex-appeal, and good publicity men! And lots of good photography OF HER all over, in the papers, and in magazines !

(A good lesson to all newcomers in the future, FOR whoever wish to become very famous !)

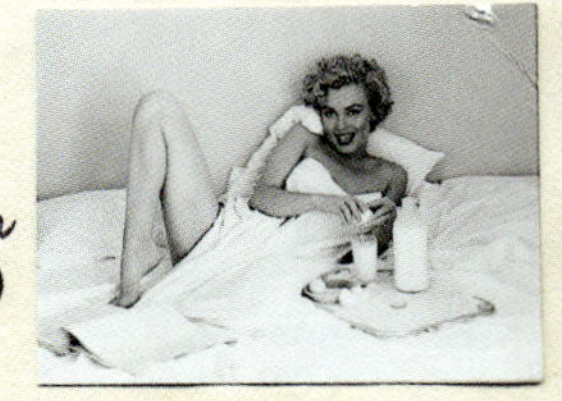

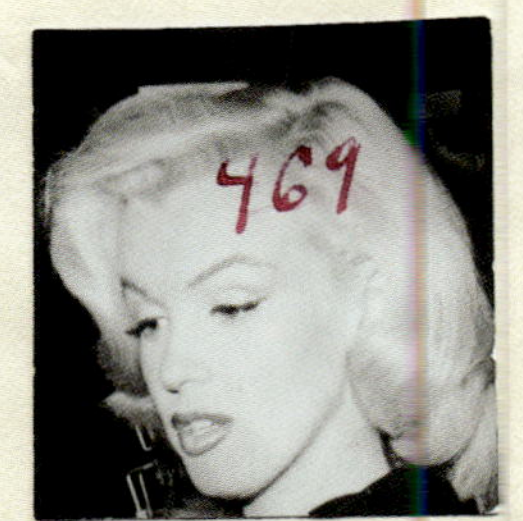
469

One late night, Marilyn phoned me, she said she can't sleep ! She proposed we should go to take pictures of her, somewhere in a dark alley, in Beverly Hills. She will pose sad and lonely ! I hopped out of bed, gathered my equipment, and we went to take pictures all night long. I had no flashlight, but as they say, necessity is the mother of invention; I lit Marilyn with the head-lights of my car !

Was she just playing a melodrama in these pictures, or was she conscious that something was wrong in her life.... something tragic will happen to her !

For Pg 307/A

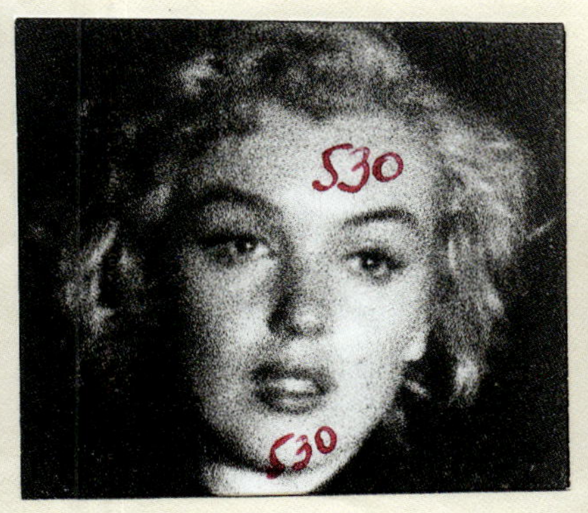

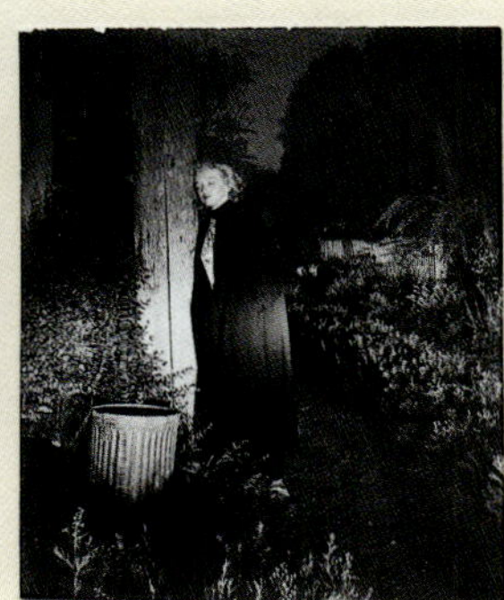

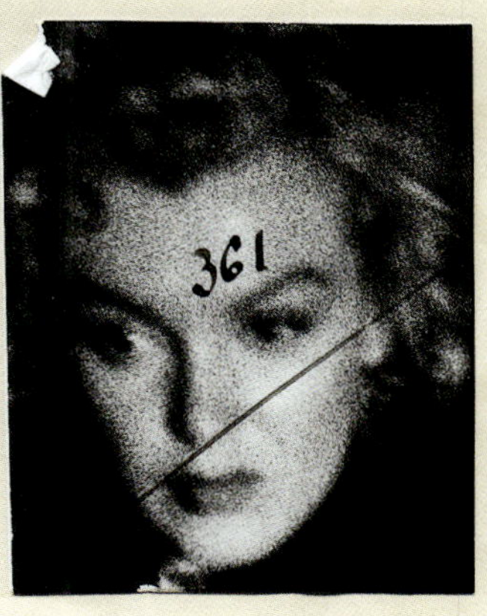

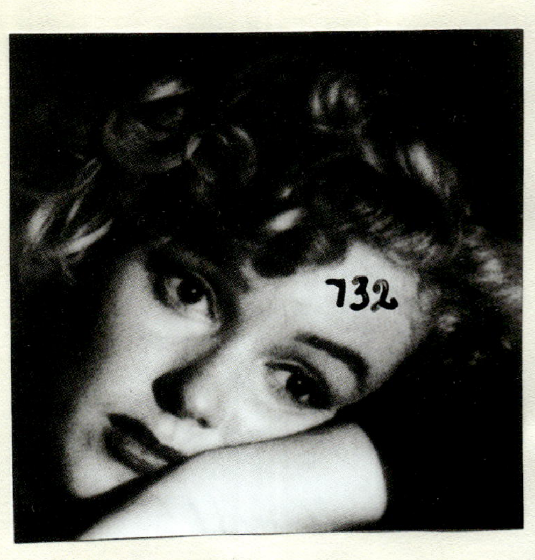

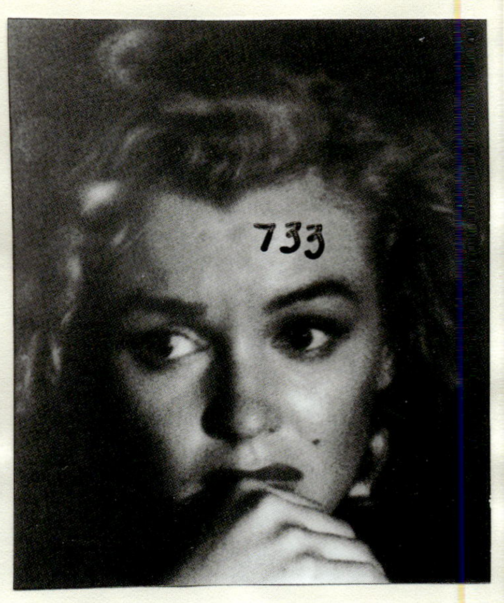

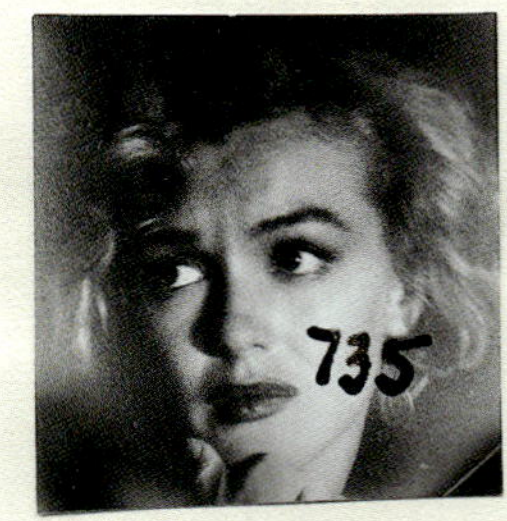

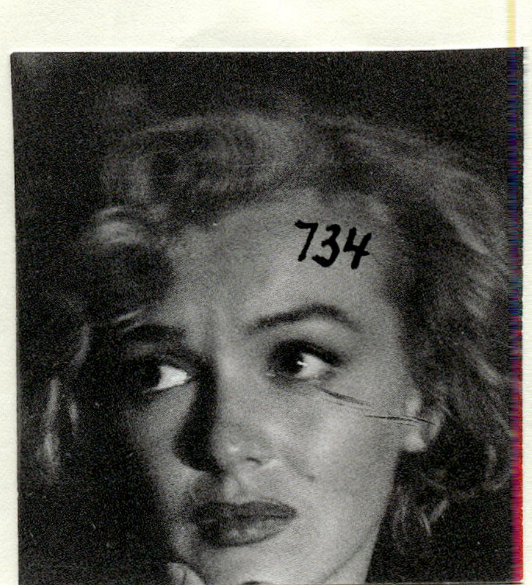

(STUDY IN SADNESS)

THE "SUNSHINE AND SHADOW" MARILYN. SHE COULD BE EFFERVESCENT, BUBBLING WITH JOY, OR ACT SAD AND TORMENTED, LONELY! SHE WAS ALL THAT, GENUINELY!

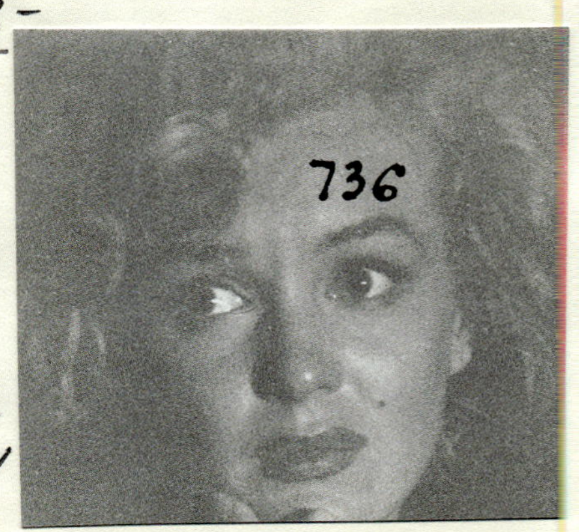

ANDRE DE DIENES

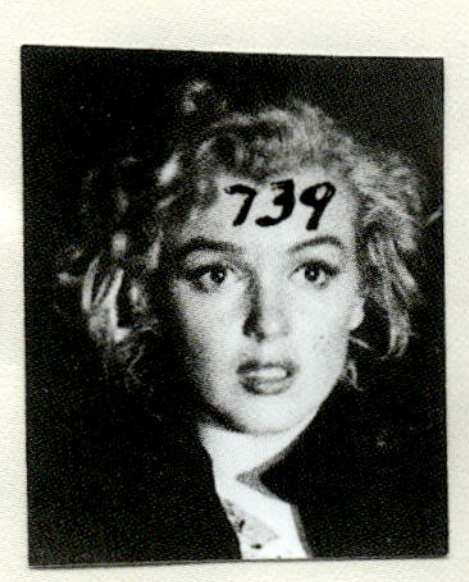

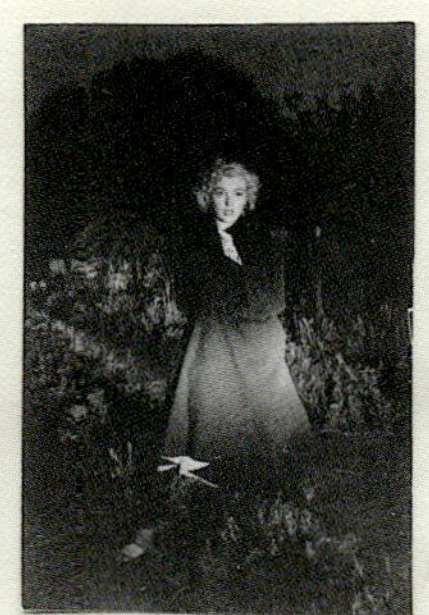

738

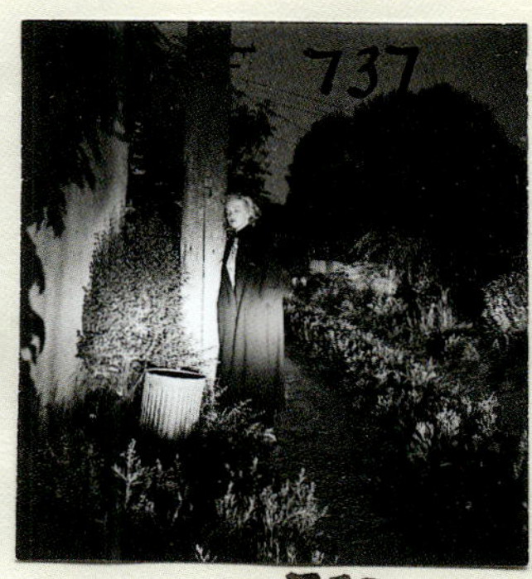

737

(A NOSTALGIC M.M) IN AN ALLEY IN BEVERLY HILLS

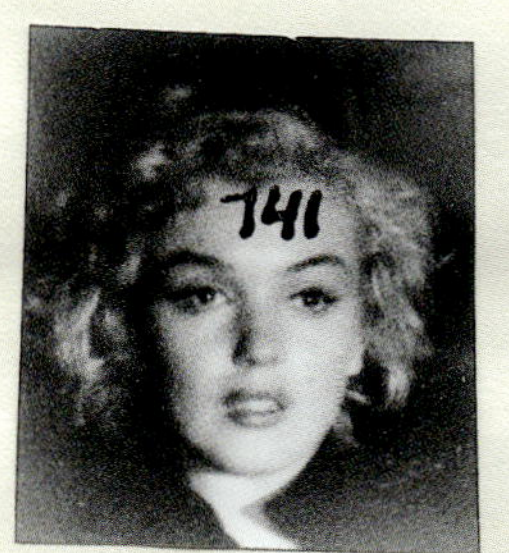

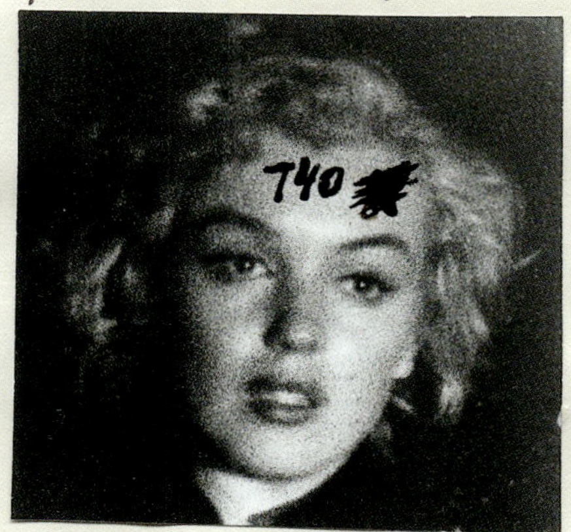

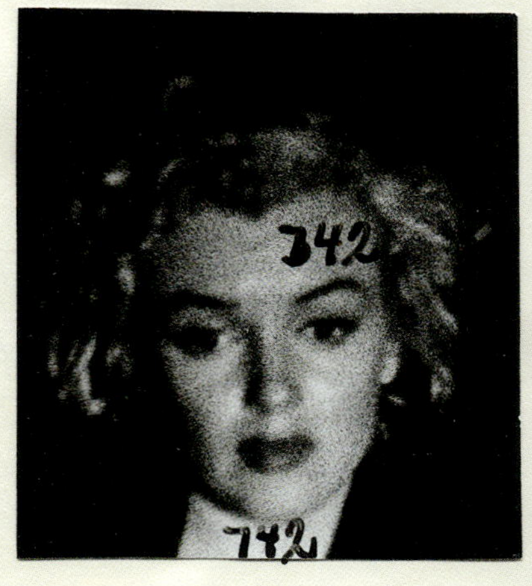

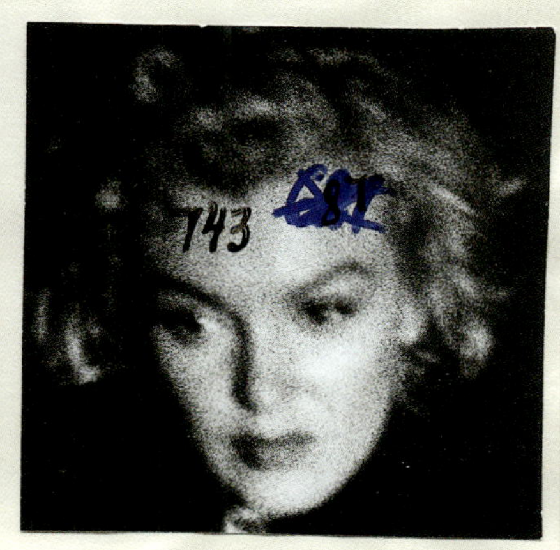

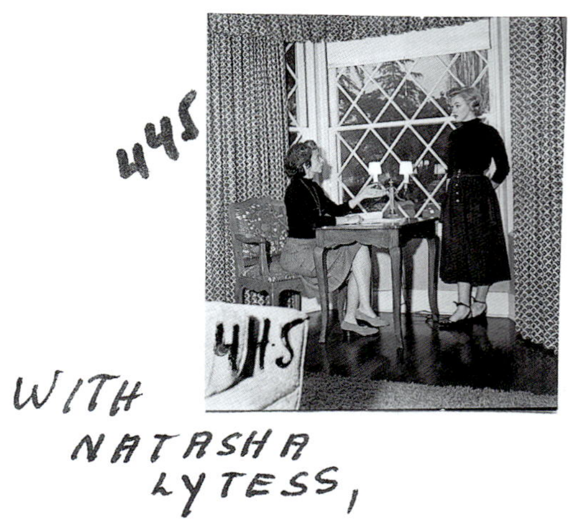

WITH NATASHA LYTESS,

LIFE Magazine Assignment I would be lying if I gave the impression to the reader that my involvement with Marilyn was just a lovey-dovey affair. Far from it – I had quite a few clashes with her. What comes to me most readily goes back to the early 50s while she was rising to great fame. I had an acting assignment from LIFE magazine to photograph Marilyn with her drama coach, Natasha Lytess. The scene was to be an acting lesson in Marilyn's house in the heart of Beverly Hills. No sooner had I started taking pictures when everything went wrong.

First, Natasha had a good fight with Marilyn about something I did not know of. Then the bad mood they had created influenced me and I started complaining that I simply hated the ensemble Marilyn was wearing. That blouse, which covered her completely, and that long, unattractive skirt which went almost down to her ankles – Marilyn was all covered up! And I even hated her formal hairdo. I wanted to photograph her sexy, very glamorous, provocative, very desirable to the minds of men who love women with sex appeal. I wasn't shy at all about my opinions, and suggested that Marilyn take off all her clothes and stand there, facing Natasha, wearing only her short black slip, with her hair messed up. There should be action going on for my pictures! Marilyn should make real dramatic movements! But Natasha had other thoughts. She was a cultured and very serious European woman and a domineering sort of person. She wanted to impose all her ego on Marilyn, and Marilyn was also, deep in her instincts, a very serious person, so she responded to Natasha's wishes and suggestions.

Marilyn would have been willing to take off her clothes and pose in her slip, but Natasha did not like my ideas. She was shouting that Marilyn should become a dramatic actress and not a sex-bobble! And I yelled back, reminding her that Marilyn was becoming famous because of her sex appeal! For once, I became a raging mad photographer. I packed my equipment and left, screaming that I did not want to associate with hypocrites and that I would never see any of them ever again! Of course, I was wrong; I should have continued photographing and I could have taken any kind of photos I wanted of Marilyn later that day. Instead, I got Marilyn angry at me!

That was just the beginning of other incidents between Marilyn and me of a very personal nature. Once, during a discussion, I shouted at her that she had ruined my life, that I could have continued to be a very successful commercial photographer had it not been that I fell in love with her so stupidly! And Marilyn shouted back something like, "Who asked you to fall in love with me? I wanted to become an actress, not your maid, not your whore!" And the whole thing became a terrible fight. She got dressed and left my house by foot, but by the time I went down by car to pick her up and take her home, she had vanished.

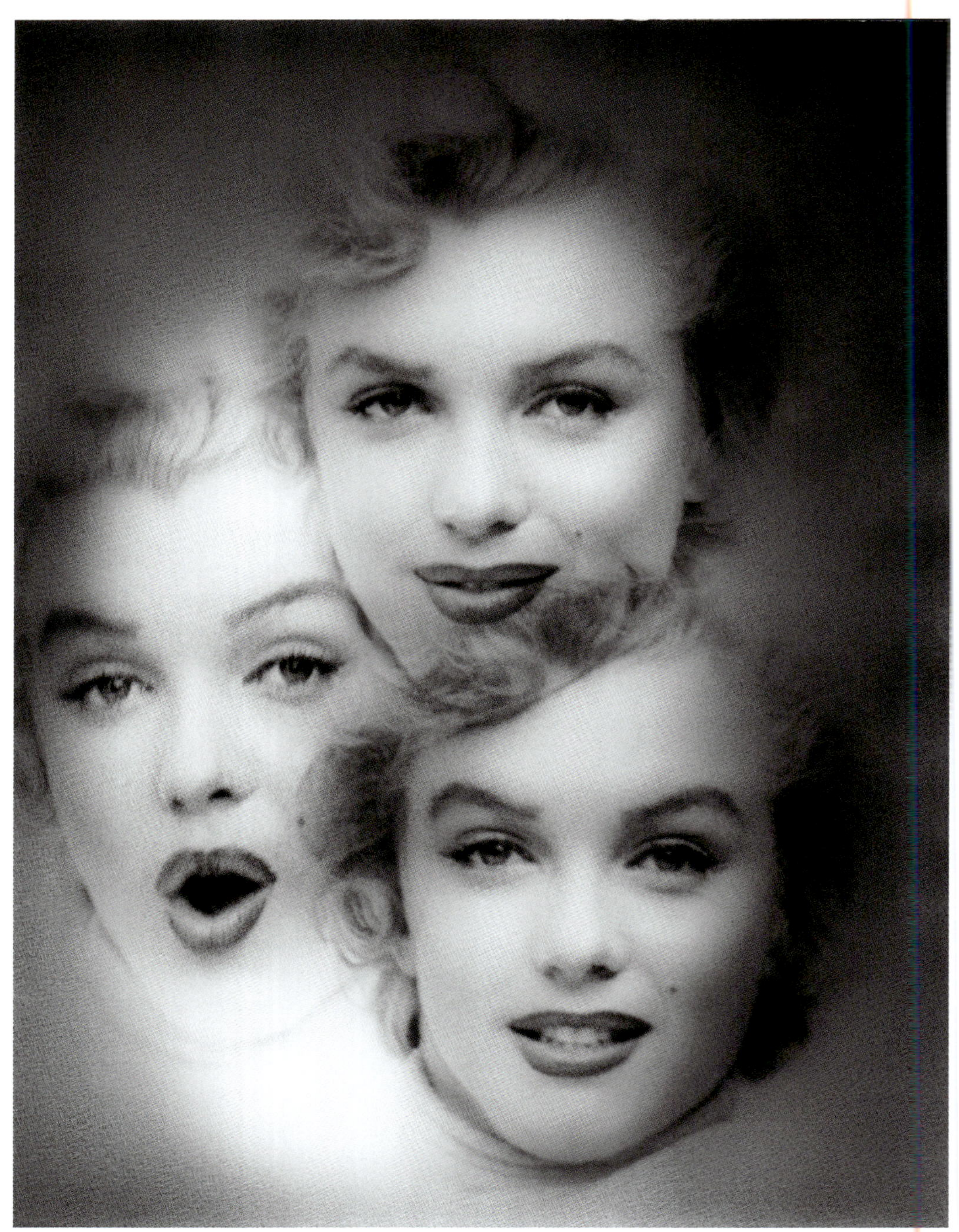

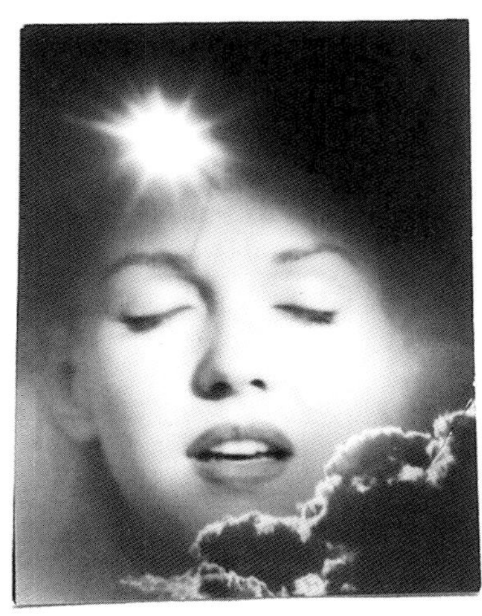

Later Years From 1953 on, my encounters with Marilyn became sparser and sparser. She became extremely famous, extremely busy, and in January 1954 she married Joe DiMaggio. But by October of that year, she had filed for divorce. In 1956 she married Arthur Miller and four years later she divorced him. While she was reaping success and glory, I photographed a couple hundred young, beautiful women – dressed and undressed. During the mid- and late-fifties I remember only a few things concerning Marilyn and me.

Once, when she was in the Cedars of Lebanon Hospital here in Hollywood, I sent her flowers. A few weeks after she came out of the hospital, she phoned me to thank me for the flowers and she said she thought of me when she entered the hospital, because they had asked the question "Who is your nearest relative?" and for a few moments she did not know what to answer, whose name to give, because she had nobody. She was divorced; she had a thousand friends, ten thousand acquaintances, and yet she felt all alone. She paid me a compliment by saying that she even thought to give my name as a reference at the hospital. Why? Because my case was like hers. I, too, was all alone in the world! Strange, how a person can be world-famous and still feel absolutely and completely alone.

The second incident was something humorous yet tragic. She phoned, I don't remember for what reason, and complained about a number of her problems. I was just in a very high-spirited, cocky mood, and I told her if she came over, I had a "cure for all ills" for her. I said she

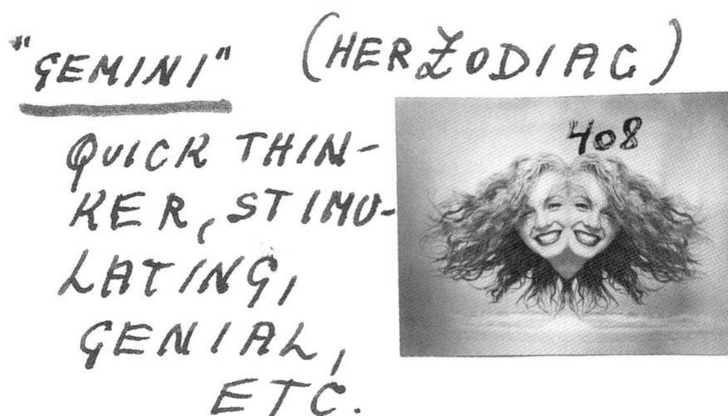

could leave all her cares behind and come to hear about my cure. But she did not come that day. A few weeks later a mysteriously dressed lady got out from a taxicab at the bottom of my driveway. Marilyn was so bundled up in things I did not recognize her until she walked up the driveway to my garage, where I was working on something. Her head was covered with a scarf, she wore dark eyeglasses, jeans, sandals, and a coat, looking completely unrecognizable.

I never forgot those first moments after she took off her eyeglasses and I recognized her from ten feet away. I was thinking, "What on earth happened to my lovely, happy, laughing-all-the-time Norma Jeane? How can she look so unglamorous, so unhappy?" She said she had come to find out what my "cure for all ills" was. The conversation that followed went something like this:

Me: What's bothering you?
Her: I didn't sleep all night!
Me: Did you drink much coffee yesterday?
Her: No.
Me: Are you broke?
Her: No.
Me: Are you worried about many things?
Her: Yes, quite a few things! I am being swindled!

And I snapped at her, "Well, that's cause number one for sleeplessness! You are angry, because you feel used!" Then I asked her whether she was physically tired when she went to bed. She said no. I told her that was cause number two for sleeplessness. Then I asked her: "Are you lonesome? Tell me the truth, Marilyn, the absolute truth! Are you lonesome?" And she said yes, she was! So that was the third cause for sleeplessness. The next questions (quite frank and straight to the point, as I usually am): "When did you last make love? When did you have your last orgasm?" She answered that it had been weeks and weeks! And I asserted that that was one of the most important reasons why she couldn't sleep all night.

I was going to remind her that when she used to travel with me in the car in 1945 and 1946, she used to need a great deal of sleep! After we would have transplanted a tree, I would have fixed her a drink or given her the red wine I loved (very healthy, in moderation!). She was about to respond, agreeing with me, when unfortunately our conversation got interrupted by an unexpected visitor, just like her, coming out of the blue.... A young beautiful model came to see me, sent by the model agent. In great contrast to Marilyn's disguise that did not show any of her sex appeal, the model wore a pink skin-tight silk dress to emphasize her sexy contour and dainty high-heeled shoes, her long hair flowing down on her shoulders splendidly. The young lady put on her best smile and all her charms as she entered my house, and as she was walking through the long corridor, I could see she was imitating

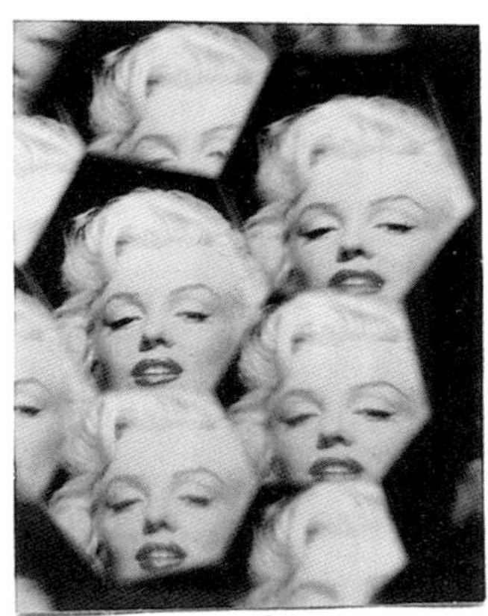

749

the famous Marilyn Monroe walk! For a few seconds the entire event became like an incredibly ironical confrontation with fate's trickery! The model who was willing to pose nude for fifty dollars was sexier than Marilyn!

She exposed all her sex appeal, but Marilyn, in great contrast to the girl, looked worn out, worried, and sad. She turned her head away to avoid being recognized by the young lady and while I was chatting with the girl, Marilyn disappeared to call a taxi. She locked herself in the bathroom until the cab arrived, then she asked me not to let the model see her on her way out of the house. Fortunately she was cheered up; her pride must have pepped her up! As she was entering the taxi she remembered to ask me what the "cure for all ills" was. But I was too embarrassed to talk about it in the presence of the taxi driver. I asked her to wait a few seconds, and dashed into my office to grab a copy of a little trifle I had copied from that old album from Scotland, the one I had so unexpectedly found in a bookshop a few years before. I handed the copy to her, then the cab left. That was the last time I saw her for quite a long time.

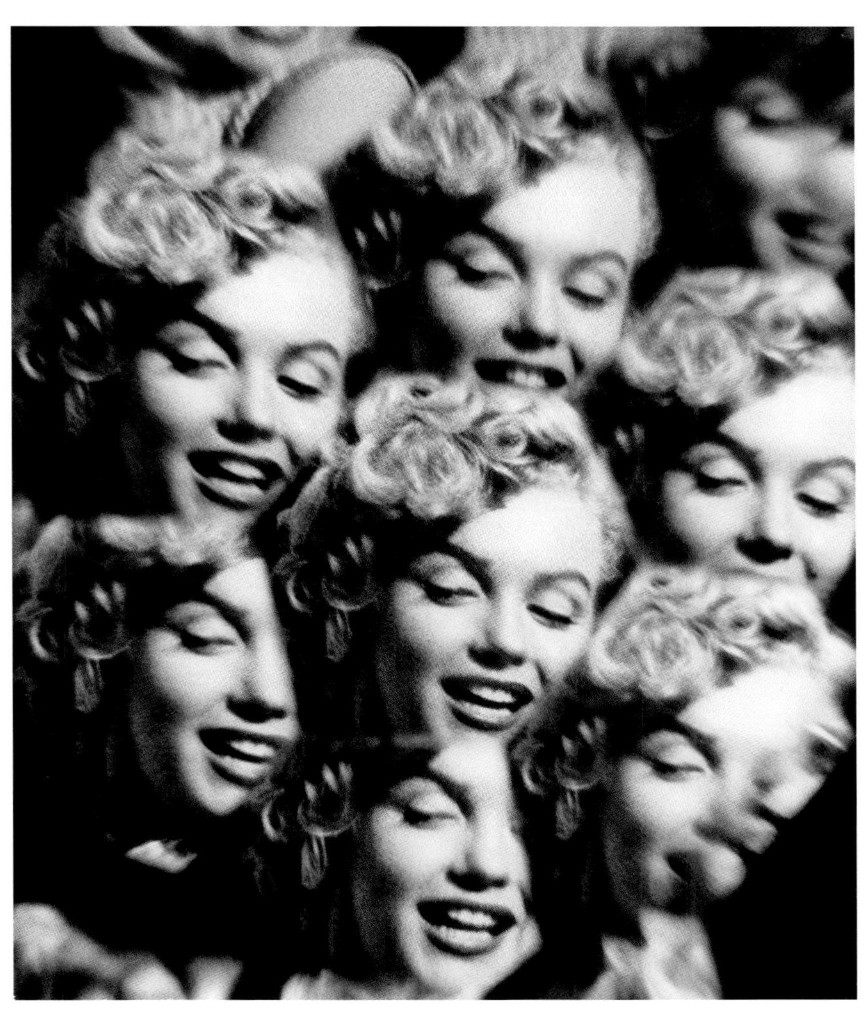

MEMO:

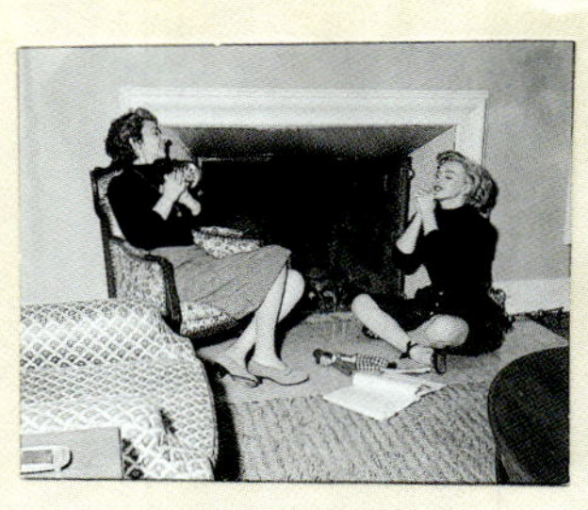

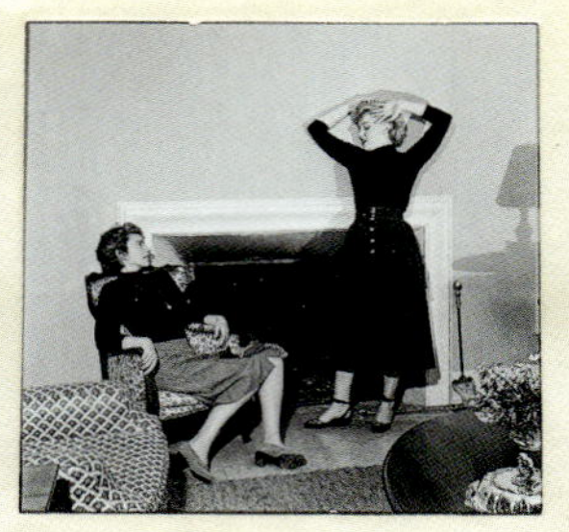

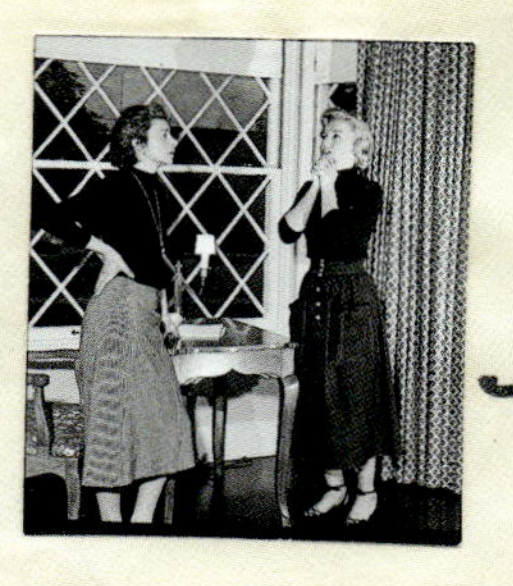

315/F.

Taking photographs, like the above ones, of Natasha Lytess, and Marilyn, simply to satisfy a magazine-editor, who assigned me the job -- simply bored me ! I always wanted to create photos of my own liking; I wanted to be be in charge of everything; I felt very relaxed, very contented when I took pictures what my instinct dicated me to take ! I had the complete control of everything ! Here, Marilyn is in bed, sexy, not vulgar, not naked, yet very provocative ! Both of us were very satisfied that we have not trespassed the normal, natural code of decency -- so important for those times,in th eraly 1950's !

But when I finished taking the photos, I ripped off the sheet from Marilyn's leggs, and I simply kept staring, and staring at her nakedness! And both of us said nothing. Nothing at all.....for a while, but we kept staring at each other for short while.....until I said to Marilyn, that, we shoud change the pose, and take other kinds of photos ! Time was too short for anything else ! I was extremely eager to photograph her! To photograph her for the magazine-layout I was assigned to do ! It was a fantastic after-effect of what have happend between us, years before, in 1945 ! When we became lovers ! In moments, in seconds, we have adapted ourselfs to new demands, new conditions, new of everything ! Marilyn was a big movie star now, not Norma Jean, the once sweet little girl...... of 1945.

LEGARTO 1953. BEL AIR HOTEL

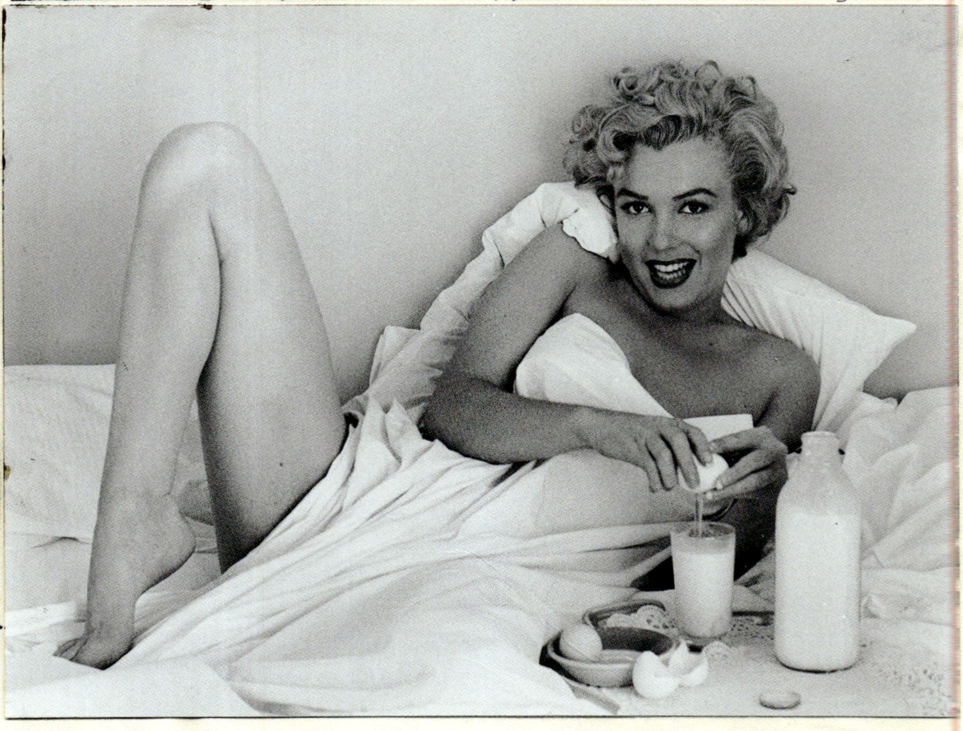

Fortunately, for me, it was always an easy thing to get rid of my frustrations because of Marilyn, or anybody or anything else. Marilyn was always cought up in her problems about her career, her fame, her involvments with such and such person -- with whom she never really found true love. For those love affaires, and marriages of hers, were always connected to getting FOR HERSELF even more fame, or to have her stories in the papers; but I could totally disconnect myself from thinking of Marilyn, or any problems; I could hire models for nudes, and we drove to faraway locations in the desert, in the mountains, up to Big Sur, on the northern California coast, and I took beautiful photographs of my liking. And absolutely nobody could tell me what to photograph, or what not to photograph, and I had nobody to exasperate me with anything, Except some models -- sometimes, either out on location, while photographing, or (for days sometimes) after I moved girls into my house -- in the hope that she might be the right person for me to marry, and to take care of my home ! What crazy stories I could tell about my escapades with the girls who posed for me, for nude photos ! But there is no place for those stories in this book.

I could do many other things to forget Marilyn. Every year, I spent several months building, (or, rather) rebuilding my house, what the storm destroyed in 1952. I became so fond of working with the hammer, and with the electric saw, cutting wood, and working with many different kinds of tools, that, for weeks, I was far happier building, constructing, mixing cement or doing anything of that kind of labor, than exasperating myself with glamorous girls and movie stars of Hollywood ! When you build, or construct something -- like a home, or a wall, (or, whatever) -- around your house--you see an immediate result. The wall you build, or whatever, will become an immediate utilitarian something, and it will stay there for decades to come, if you built it well. It is SOMETHING useful every day! It protects you, give you a home to live in for the rest of your life! But what benifit can you reap from arguing with women; or wasting yourself away on the love !

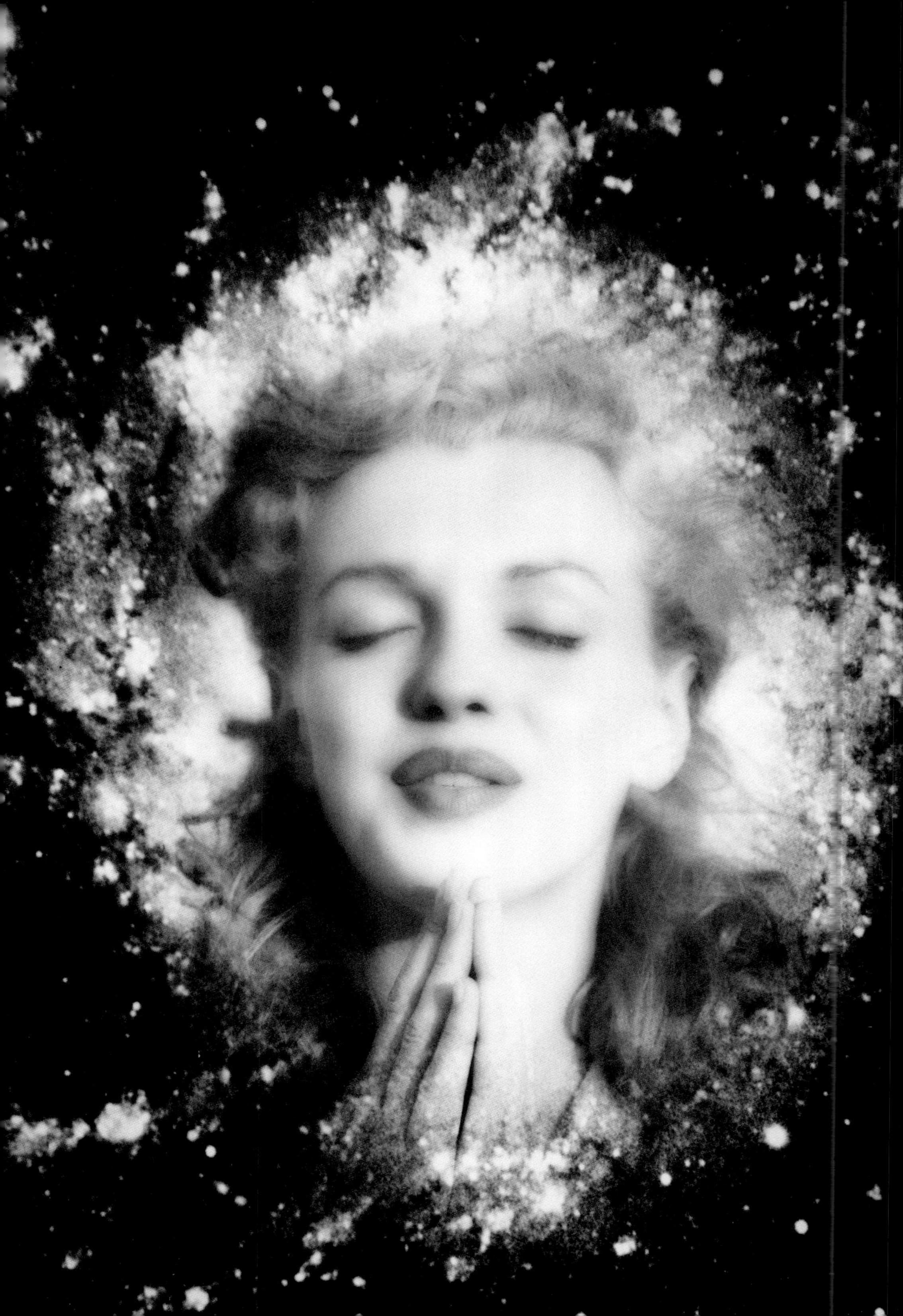

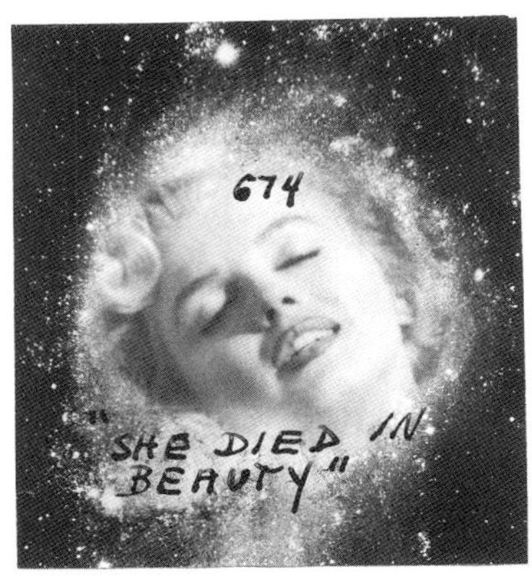

(TO ILLUSTRATE A POEM I LIKE) "SHE DIED IN BEAUTY"

Incredible Paradox In the latter part of 1960, on a Friday afternoon, Marilyn came to my house unexpectedly. She was dressed in a black suit, modest but elegant; she looked very beautiful. I noticed she was no more the youngish type I used to know, she had entered into womanhood (at age 34). She was calm, even sad. We were hardly over the first moments of greetings and hugs when she came right out saying, "André, take pictures of me again! Tonight, and tomorrow, too…. I'll stay with you."

I had just spent a long day working, selecting photos for a book I was putting together with glamour photos. My mind was tired when Marilyn arrived; the weekend was coming – time for fun, romance, lovemaking, anything except for taking pictures. Marilyn's request gave a good jolt to my mind – here we go again, I have to work! No matter how beautiful a woman is, photography is always hard work. I pointed to the hundreds of photos on my long worktable, and almost angrily I said to Marilyn that I was constantly oversaturated with "glamour" and I didn't care how beautiful or famous she was, I didn't care to take pictures of her at all! I went into a neurotic outburst stemming from sheer frustration. I needed to make love more than anything else in the world, not to work on capturing her beauty.

What I said must have hurt her feelings because soon after she decided to go back to her apartment at the Chateau Marmont, on Sunset Boulevard, just a few blocks away from my house. While I walked her

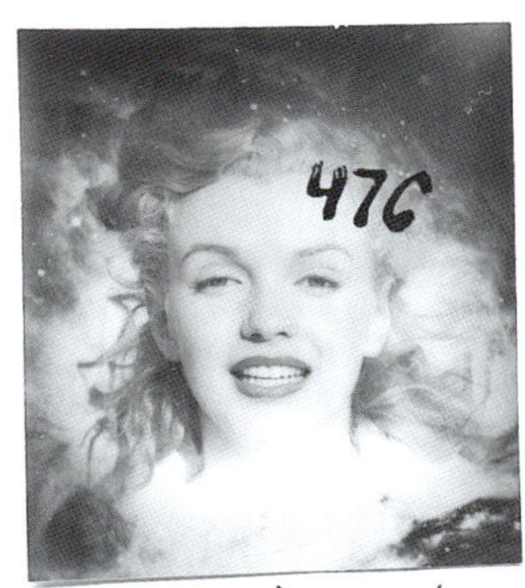

Beautiful!

home, she said she had just finished filming "The Misfits" and her marriage with Arthur Miller was over with.

At her two-room apartment, there were a good number of suitcases and two large wardrobe trunks, so I asked her whether she was leaving or had just arrived. She answered that she was going back to New York… maybe. But she wasn't sure whether she wanted to go, or where else to go, or, for that matter, where her home was. She was undecided, and perplexed as to where she belonged!

She put down her purse on a wardrobe trunk and sat down on one of the suitcases, and the scene seemed to me the most incomprehensible sight in the world, the most incredible paradox. I was looking at the world's most publicized, most glamorous, most adulated beauty, in that musty-smelling old lousy apartment; she was alone and had no place to go. What an incredible, sad sight!

I asked her about the farm she had bought in Connecticut, where she lived with Arthur Miller, wasn't that her home? Marilyn calmly answered that she had given the farm to Arthur. I blew up! I shouted, "Are you crazy? You gave away the only home you ever owned! Having a home is the most important thing in life, and you let yourself be out in nowhere, due to your stupidity, to your damned kind heart! Oh, Norma Jeane, what are you doing to yourself?" She only looked at me, vaguely smiling… saying nothing. I began to feel guilty for not accepting her offer to come to stay at my house and to take pictures of her. How absurd I had acted! How stupid I had been!

While she was occupying herself in the kitchenette to pour me a drink from the half-empty champagne bottle, I was asking myself what could have been the real purpose of her coming to my house that afternoon. What did she want from me that she could not get elsewhere, from somebody else? Why ask me to take pictures of her when she had just finished a film and had her pictures in magazines and newspapers all over the world? My ego began fantasizing.... Perhaps she came over to tell me, "André, I've had it, I quit! Take me away! Now you can have me!"

For a couple of minutes there was silence. I had the chance to sit in a big, old, comfortable armchair, wondering what famous movie star might have once sat there, maybe as unhappy as Marilyn Monroe.... She felt just as alone in the world as I felt, as I was.... While thinking that, suddenly it occurred to me that I was a damned fool! Perhaps Marilyn came to see me because she wanted to make love! Taking pictures was just an excuse to come to my house! Women are more shy than men in expressing their desires. She did not dare to come out with it so frankly, and I was a stupid fool not to realize it right away.

I emptied the second glass Marilyn handed me, and on an empty stomach, on a tired mind; the alcohol became like a magic sorcerer. I became exuberant, completely revived. Just off the cuff, I started a completely unmeditated scenario, saying, "Marilyn, let's quit everything! Let's elope! Let's go to live in North Africa or on Bora Bora in the South Pacific or in the Andes mountains in Peru! Or let's live in the forests of my native Transylvania and I shall rebuild a crumbling medieval castle just for you!" By then, Marilyn began to smile and she was chuckling when I was telling her the headlines in the newspapers the world over: "MARILYN MONROE DISAPPEARS…."

Suddenly, the telephone was ringing, and it rang and rang until she finally picked up the receiver. She kept listening, and talked back in a low, monotonous voice and her expression turned sad, sordid; after talking for a while she was wiping her tears while still listening on the phone.

I was never the snoopy kind of person who listens to other people's phone conversations, so I went into the bathroom. When I returned I heard Marilyn's last few words: "Yes, I am coming! I will be there tomorrow." Then she hung up the receiver and turned to me, saying, "André, please go home, I have to go back to New York tomorrow." She looked very strange; the mascara from her eyes was running down on her cheeks.

While I was walking home, a few blocks away, suddenly, I thought what a fool I was. I could have photographed Marilyn all night long at my house and made love to her afterwards! What an enormous blunder! I stopped and kept slapping my face with both hands, as hard as I could, to punish myself. It's a good thing it was dark and nobody saw me doing it! Quite suddenly, I turned around and rushed back to her apartment to tell her how stupid and sorry I was….

I did not even ring the doorbell or knock, I just charged in. She was still on the sofa, talking on the phone, crying. She wasn't at

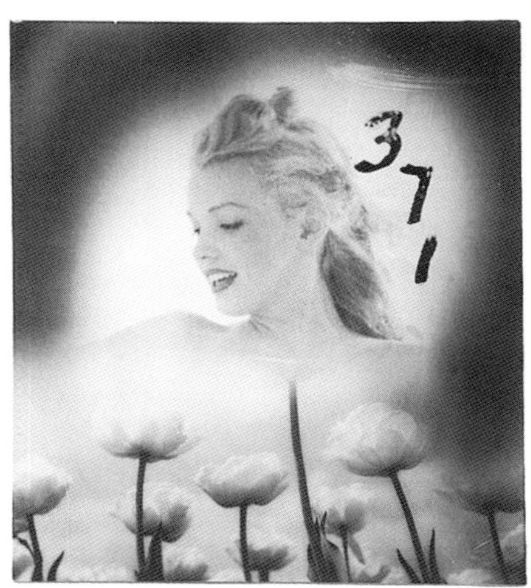

all surprised to see me again. She hung up the receiver; I knelt down and kissed her hands, asking her to come back to my house. I said, "Norma Jeane, we will take fantastic photos! I will fill the bathtub with flowers, and you will take a bubble bath among them. Please, Norma Jeane, don't go to New York yet! Come with me, let's go to my house!"

But my pleading was useless. She said I must go home and that people were waiting for her. That's how that Friday evening ended. The next morning when I phoned, the switchboard operator told me Marilyn had checked out. I felt sick from remorse and regret. And I shall regret it for the rest of my life, because sentiments can vanish like smoke, talk is cheap, but photographs remain.

In the latter part of 1960, on a Friday afternoon, Marilyn came to my house unexpectedly. Whether by taxi, or some one drove her here, I did not ask. She was dressed in a black suit, modest but elegant. She looked very beautiful ! I noticed she was no more the youngish type I used to know; she enetered into young womanhood [age 34]...She was calm, even sad. We were hardly over the first moments of greetings and huggings when she came right out saying " Andre, Take pictures of me again! Tonight, and tomorrow, too.... I stay with you...... "

I had just spent a long day, working, selecting photos for a book I was putting together with glamour photos, and beautiful photos of nudes for a publisher, in England. My mind was tired when Marilyn arrived; the weekend was coming; time for fun, romance, lovemaking, anything except to take pictures ! Marilyn's request gave a good jolt to my mind ! Here we go again; I have to work! Work hard to create pictures to glamorise her ! No matter how beautiful a woman is, photography always is a hard work! To direct the person, to observe the light on the face, to observe the background, to focus the camera, to compose the picture, to figure the exposure, and most importantly, to intently concentrate on catching the right expression at the right moment, all that is an extremely mind-wearing work, and that Friday afternoon I just wasn't in the mood for working at all..... I pointed at the hundreds of photos on my long worktable, and almost angrily I said to Marilyn, that I am constantly oversaturated with " glamour " , and I don't care how beautiful she is, how famous she is, I don't care to take pictures of her at all ! I went into a neurotic outburst .... stemming from shear frustration. I needed to make love more than anything else in the world; BUT not work on capturing her beauty ! To feed the world with more photos of her !

What I said must have hurt her feelings, because soon after that she decided to go back to her apartment, at the CHATEAU MARMONT, on Sunset Boulevard, (a famous, old, residential building in Hollywood) just a few blocks away from my house. While I walked HER HOME, she said she just finished filming THE MISFITS, and her marriage with Arthur Millar was over with.....

At her two room apartment, there were a good number of suitcases, and two large wardrobe trunks, groupped together, and I asked her whether she was leaving, or just arrived. She answered she was going back to New York....maybe, but she wasn't sure whether she wanted to go, or NOT, OR where else to go. Or for that matter--where her home was ? She was undecided, and perplexed as to where to go, where she belonged !

She put down her purse on a wardrobe trunk, and set down on one of the suitcases, and the scene seemed to me as the most incomprehensible sight in the world ! A most incredible paradox ! I was looking at the world's most publicized, most glamorous, most adulated beauty ; and I was thinking: dear, sweet Norma Jean, Marilyn.... in THIS rather musty-smelling ,old -looking, lousy apartment ; she is alone, and have no place to go ! How incredible ! What a sad sight !

I asked her ....what about the Farm she bought in Coonecticut, where she lived with her husband, Arthur Miller, wasn't that her home ? Couldn't she go there to rest up, read, relax for a while ? Hadn't she had enough of of all that hassle she went through in Nevada, during the filming of the MISFITS ? Marilyn calmly answered, that she gave the farm to Arthur ! I blew up! I shouted: " Are you crazy ! You gave away the only home you ever OWNED ! I struggled, worked hard to rebuild my house for 10 years, because, to me, having a home is the most important thing in life, and you let yourself be out in the nowhere — due to your stupidity, your damned kind heart ! Oh, Norma Jean, what are you doing to yourself ! " She only looked at me, vaguely smiling....

saying nothing.

I began to feel guilty for not accepting her offer to come to stay at my house, and to take pictures of her. How absurd I acted, How stupid I was !

While she was occupying herself in the kitchenett to pour me a drink from the half-empty champagne bottle, I was asking myself: what could have been the real purpose, the real truth in her mind for having come to my house that afternoon? What did she want from me, what she could not get elsewhere, from somebody else ? Why to ask me to take pictures of her, when she just finished a film, and she had been photographed by great deal by countless photographers, and her pictures were in all the magazines, and all the newspapers all over the world ! ? Why to take more pictures ? Why that hurry to work s more ? Why she chose me, to see that afternoon ?......

My eg[...] ame over to tell me: " Andre, I[...] Now you can have me Take me an[...] do what you wanted t do, in 19[...] re in the West; I wil be your si[...] the gardening, I sh plant tree[...] .....

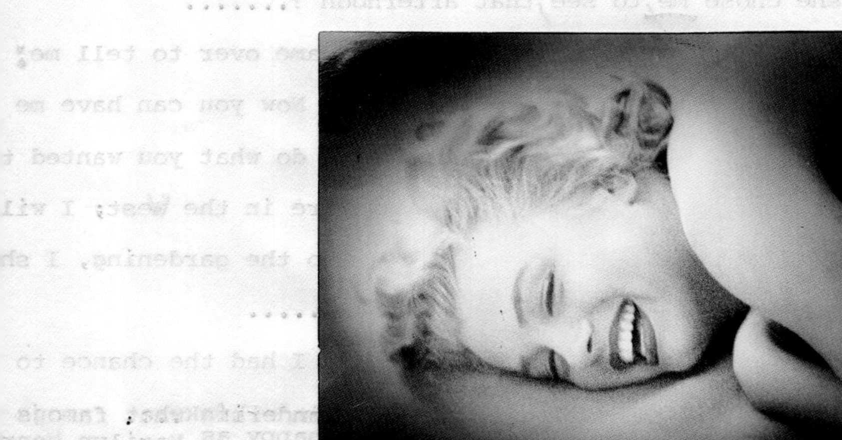

For a [...] I had the chance to just sit [...] nderinkwhat famous star migh[...] happy as Marilyn Monr How an[...] he amount of publicit Marilyn received, what success she achieved, how many millions of peopl would love to be with her -- even if for just a few minutes, but th we were, face to face, she had nobody, no home, I had nobody....ine that we knew so many people....She felt just as alone in the world as I felt, as I was... How many girls I could have married, but I didn't---because, she, Norma Jean, disillusioned me, forsaken me for her career ! How wrong I was, falling in love with a model !....

All those girls I met, as photographer, they just wanted pictures to further their career, to become "Marilyn". They were just using me..... hoping they would become famous with the photos I would take of them.....
And I was thinking how many people might have used HER, also !
I had my little sucesses, she had her big triumphal career, she was a glory in people's mind....yet the stark bitter truth was that loneliness was devouring our souls ! But we were too prudent, too proud to admit it ! Sometimes it is so difficult to tell the truth....How lonely we are ! What tragic lives many,many people live, inspite all that apparent successes they achieved ! How sad a Friday evening can be sometimes, when all of a sudden you realize that you have nobody to open your heart to, no one to embrace, kiss, love, make love with, sleep with.... How delightful a feeling it is to be alone sometimes, but how deadly, how heavy a feeling it is for the soul to bear that feeling of aloneness in certain times, certain days. Words can not express that feeling ! So we just remain silent about it.....

While thinking like that, suddenly it occured to me that I was a damn fool ! Perhaps,Marilyn came to see me because she wanted to make love ! Taking pictures of her was just an excuse to come by to my house ! What she wanted was to make love ! Just plain, ordinary, physical lovemaking ! But women are more shy than man to express their desires. Even married people can have those problems ! And sometimes women are tricky, devious, self-conscious, false, and God only knows what else. They do not dare to tell the truth ! If only she would have said as soon as she came to my house, " Andre, open a bottle of wine ! I feel horny ! Love me ! Do what you want ! Pour wine on my feet, kiss them, like you used to do ! Put on music ! I want to forget my problems !" Andre, go wild ! Love me ! I need it !

My Last Visit with Norma Jeane It was on June 1, 1961, on her birthday, that I last saw Norma Jeane alive. On that day, I was working in my garden and in the afternoon suddenly it came to my mind that this day was Marilyn's birthday. It was a most amazing telepathic experience, because without the slightest knowledge of where Marilyn was, I went inside my house, picked up the telephone and asked Information to give me the number of the Beverly Hills Hotel. Yet I did not know she would be staying there! I knew at least ten different places where she lived or stayed during those sixteen years I had known her, but why I suddenly chose the Beverly Hills Hotel is absolutely baffling to me! Then the hotel operator answered my call. Just like that, I asked for Miss Marilyn Monroe and got connected with her immediately! It was an extraordinary experience. I started by singing "Happy birthday" to Marilyn. She recognized my voice, and jubilantly asked me to come over right away. She said she was alone in bungalow ten. I was thinking, "Hurray, the weekend is coming and maybe I can persuade her to stay with me for a few days!"

Marilyn was very cheerful when I arrived. She took out a small jar of caviar and two bottles of champagne from the small refrigerator at the side of the bungalow living room and she kept refilling my glass. The same, sweet, considerate, good-hearted Norma Jeane! The same soul like years before….

We had a long discussion about many things, but the conversation became somber. She began complaining about her problems with her

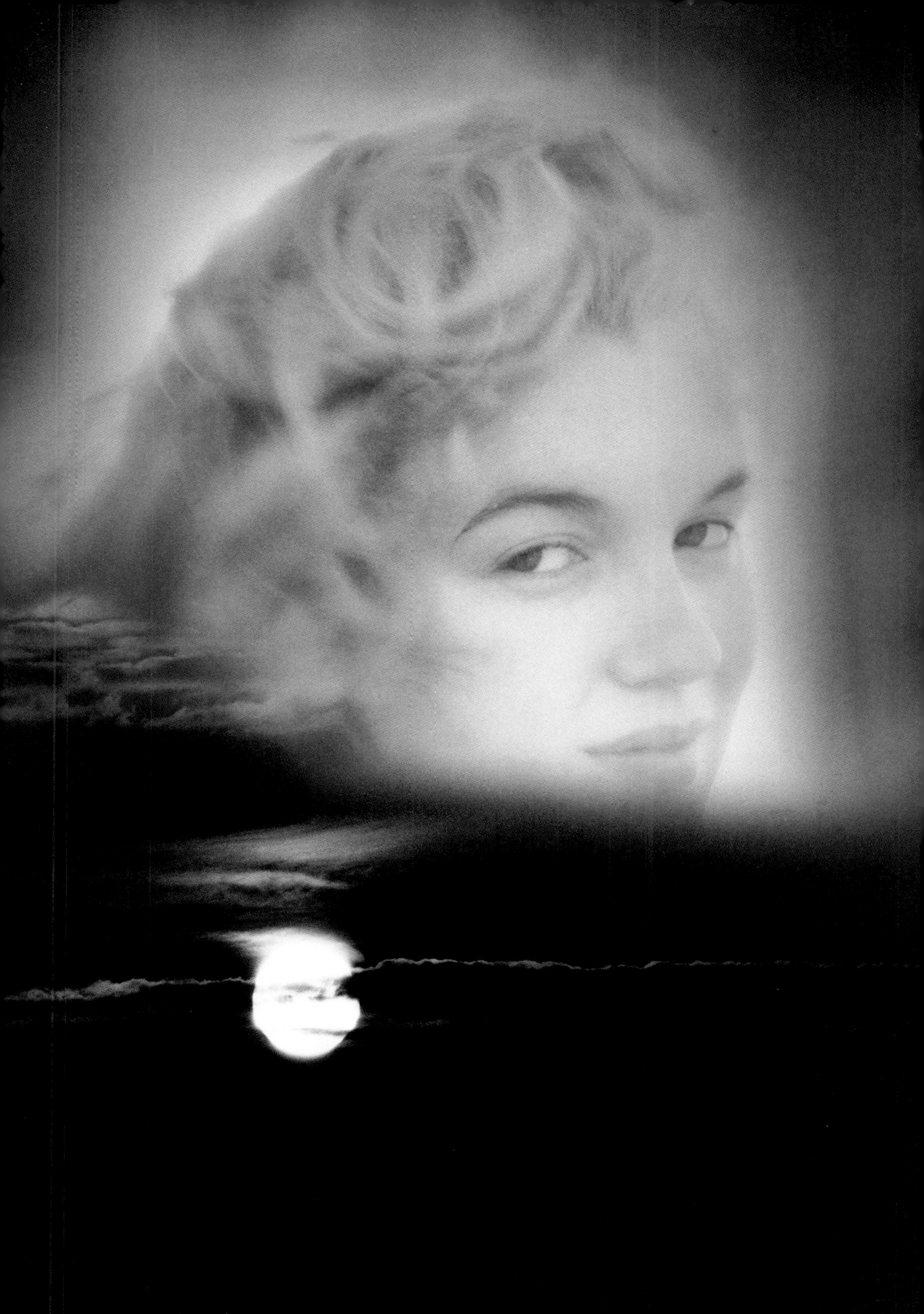

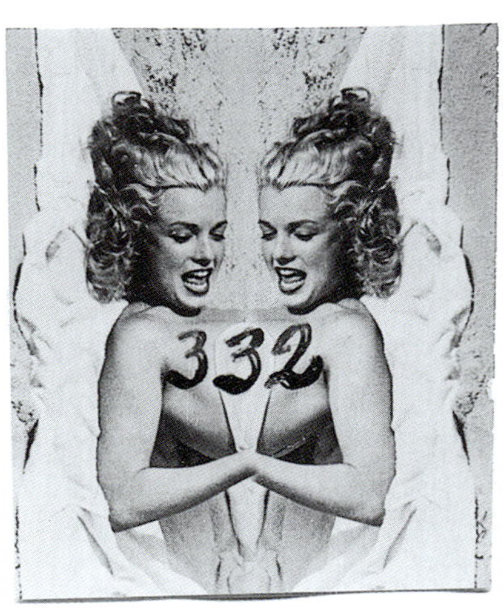

studio, 20th Century Fox. They had given her a birthday party that day at the studio, but she was tired and left early; she wanted to be alone. She felt unhappy and exploited by them. And she was glad to go back to New York.

Then, I asked her about her highly publicized habit of being last on the set when she was filming: “Why did you let, so often, a big crew of hundreds of people wait for you to appear on the set? Didn’t you realize that every hour of delay was costing the studio thousands of dollars? When we were traveling together in 1945, you were always up early in the morning, at daybreak, putting on your make-up, doing your hair… so why the hell did you let an entire crew wait and wait for you to appear on the set day after day? What the hell got into you, acting difficult when you were never like that before with me? What kind of snob have you become?”

And then Marilyn, Norma Jeane, answered me in a sort of pleading, painful way: “André, many times I could not help it! I was too tired, too exhausted to get up so early in the day. You remember how I used to get carsick during those long rides, when we were touring the West? You were driving endlessly, all day and night, and I just slumped over and went to sleep because I felt so tired…. So during all the filming at Fox, I was feeling the same way, just tired and needing rest! Sometimes I was drinking a little, with men I liked, and the nights were far too short, far too delightful, to go to work so early in the morning. Isn’t that all very human? I was simply too exhausted and it

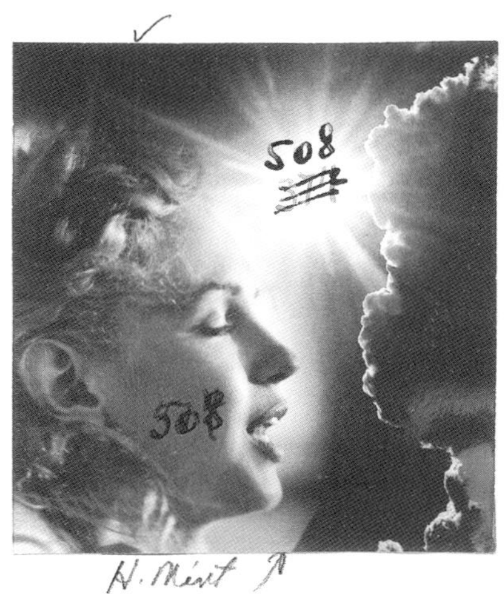

became almost impossible to cope with all that hard work. And now the studio is mocking me, saying openly that I am going insane!"

That struck me as strange, because with me, Marilyn was always rational, or almost always; she made good sense and she was correct, normal, never erratic or going into hysterics. But I observed that while she was talking, she became more and more downcast, bitter, and sad. She let herself go, telling me the bad things life had dealt her. She said people were swindling her and treated her rotten.

She looked so lovely, but so sad also, as she stood near the usual large pile of suitcases, everything all packed for her return to New York. This was just another of the many trips she made through the years between Hollywood and New York. I was thinking, what an amazing contrast, this meeting with her compared to when we had first met a little over fifteen years before. Now my darling little Norma Jeane's soul was very worn out. During the short hours we were conversing, she smiled very little and kept complaining about her problems with various people. She tried hard to conceal everything that was perturbing her, but she could not withhold her tears as she spoke. What a contrast her sad mood was to the flippant, flirtatious mood she was in when she first showed herself to me in her bathing suit in the center of my living room at the Garden of Allah in 1945! What a price we all pay sometimes for what we get in life.

I tried to cheer her up, to reassure her that she was now lovelier and more beautiful than ever. An intelligent, experienced, mature woman with the whole world at her feet, and that the best was just beginning for her. The talk helped her a little, we toasted to that. I could not help it, I was in a happy, jovial mood, so happy to see her again. My previous meeting with her at the Chateau Marmont had haunted me for months and now here I was again with the girl I used to love so much! I got quite intoxicated with champagne. I saw the bed in the adjoining room, uncovered, so I began hugging her, kissing her, like old times in years before, and I suggested we should make love because it would make her feel better. I had the right to suggest it – after all, we had nearly been married! But she said I should behave myself, and that she'd had an operation recently. She exclaimed, "You want to kill me! I need rest, André, please forgive me!" These were almost the last words I heard from Norma Jeane's lips, that June evening, a year before she died. Then, she handed me my jacket, walked me to the door of her bungalow, and bid me good night.

After she closed the door, I walked away a hundred feet, then removed my shoes and tiptoed back to her veranda, about twenty feet away from her bedroom window, and sat for a long while in the balmy, deliciously cool dark of the evening. I wanted to see what would happen later. Would she get up and leave, or would someone come to visit her? Instead, she turned out the lights in the bedroom. Through the open windows, the nylon curtains were blowing in the breeze, looking, in the darkness, like some kind of ghosts…. After that apparition, I left the scene.

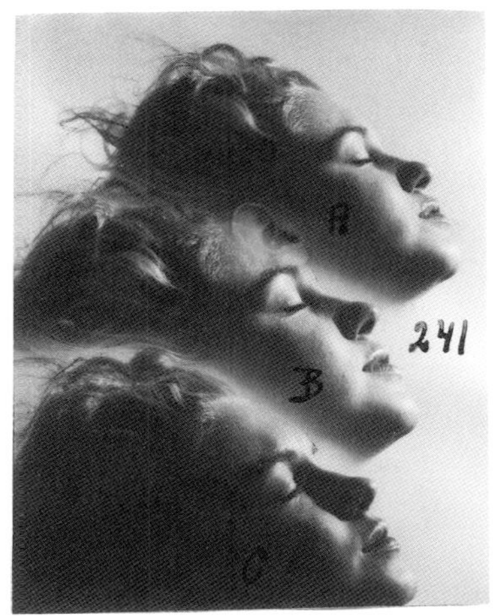

The next day, I rushed to Beverly Hills and bought a beautiful Italian ceramic fruit bowl. I filled it with oranges and bought flowers and wrote a letter to her to apologize for having been so "fresh" and wanting to make love with her. At the hotel, I gave a generous tip to the bellboy and instructed him to be sure to hand the things to Marilyn personally.

I know she received it, because a day later, I found one of the flowers at the front door of my house, and she had slipped an envelope full of studio stills of herself under my door. She must have passed by before going to the airport.

I never saw or talked with her again… only in my dreams.

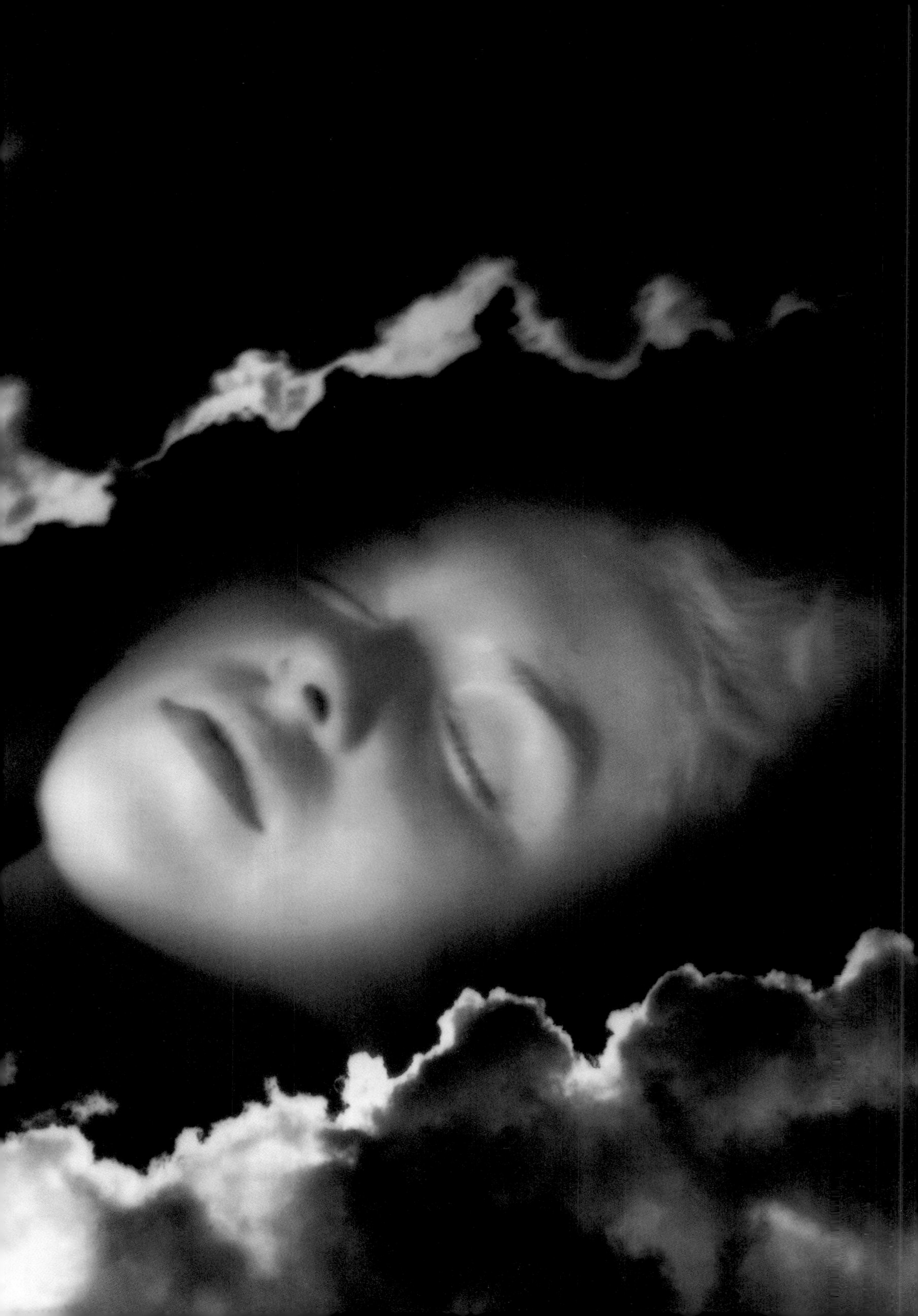

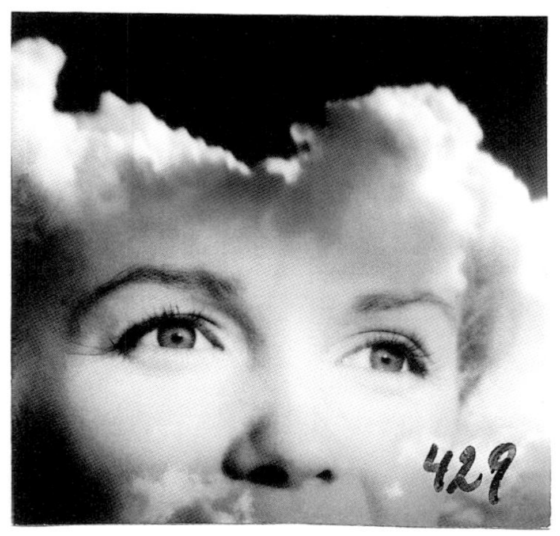

<u>Premonitions</u> Intuition and precognition can become an amazing and baffling experience. Marilyn's death was foretold to me in the most peculiar way; a very strange thing happened to me in June 1962, about two months before Marilyn's sudden death.

In 1952, when a big storm very badly damaged my house, my photo laboratory, and a large quantity of photos, letters, and negatives that were stored in cardboard boxes, instead of sorting anything, I dug a huge hole in the yard and threw everything in it, covering the hole with earth. It was somewhat like a burial. Ten years later, in June 1962, I was preparing a set of never-seen photos of Marilyn, showing her without makeup, that I had taken in 1946. I was going to propose that set of photos to *LIFE* magazine with the title "Who is she?" because I thought no one would recognize her. All of a sudden, a strong urge dictated to me to take a shovel and dig up my yard, hoping that perhaps I might find new negatives of Marilyn. While digging the hole, I had morbid thoughts; it felt as if I were digging a grave.

All the things made of paper had completely disintegrated, but the negatives protected each other and to my surprise, I found a few of Marilyn in a rather undamaged state – two negatives in particular. One was of Marilyn looking down at the ground, with a very sordid expression on her face. When I took that picture, Marilyn gave it a title. She said, "André, I am looking at my grave." This one is called "The End of Everything." The other negative I found was of her lying on the ground, eyes shut, pretending that she was dead. What was most particular about my preparing this unusual set of photos, and especially that I found these two negatives dealing with death, was that I didn't have the faintest idea that Marilyn was going through the most distressful period in her life that June. I was so involved with my work that I did not read any newspapers and did not know what was going on with Marilyn.

Early in July, while working with Marilyn's strange photos, I was having a mixture of very peculiar, disturbing nightmares. I saw my mother's coffin underneath my bed, and Marilyn, too, was intermingled in these nightmares. Right after I woke up one morning from one of these bizarre dreams, I had the strong urge to go to the nearest Western Union telegraph office, on Sunset Boulevard, to send a telegram to Marilyn. I addressed it to her studio where she was filming her last picture. The telegram said: TURKEY FOOT, I HAD VERY BAD DREAMS ABOUT YOU LAST NIGHT. PLEASE CALL ME. LOVE W.W.

I am sure the reader wonders what "Turkey Foot" and "W.W." are all about so I will explain briefly: in 1945, when I photographed Norma Jeane in the mountains, her hands often turned purple from the cold, and that color reminded me of the dark purplish color of turkey feet, hence I nicknamed her "Turkey Foot." And "W.W." stood for "Worry Wart." Norma Jeane had nicknamed me that because she thought I was always too cautious, too worried about things, especially about the state of my car, during that trip we took together. She laughed gaily whenever she called me W.W. instead of André. Those two names were our

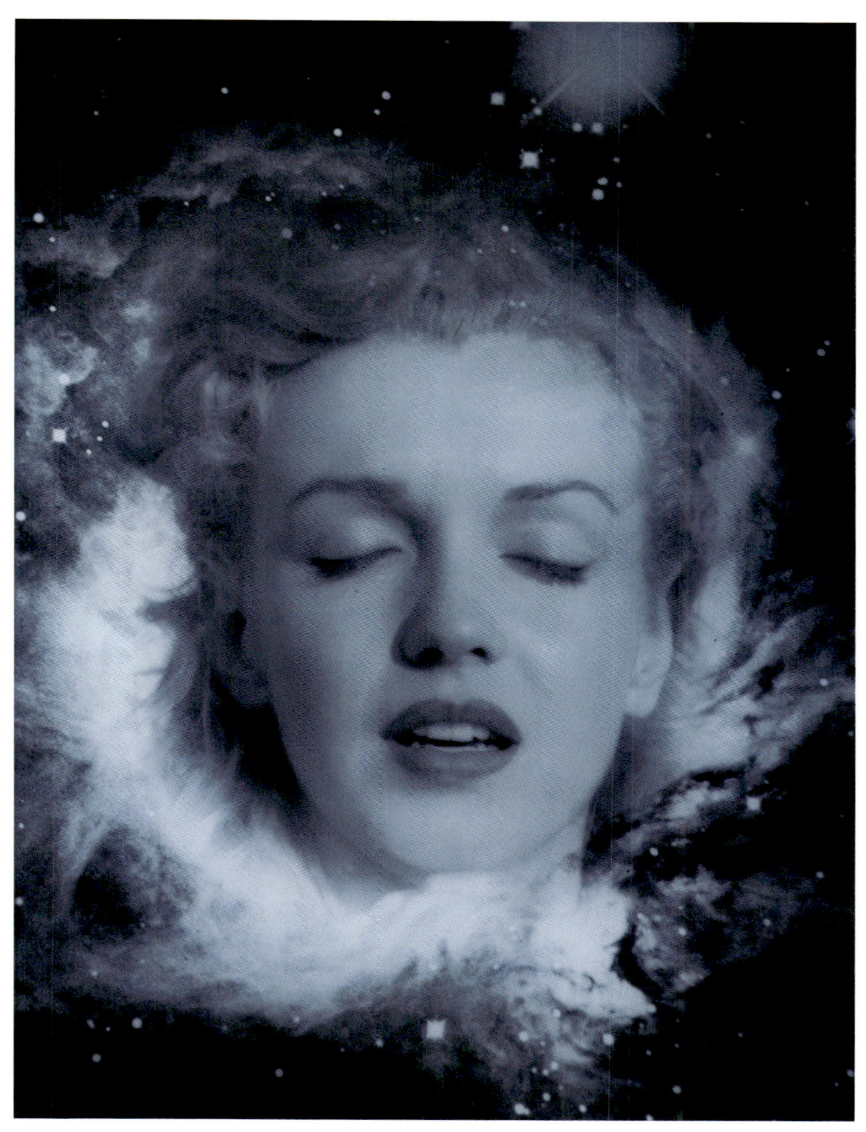

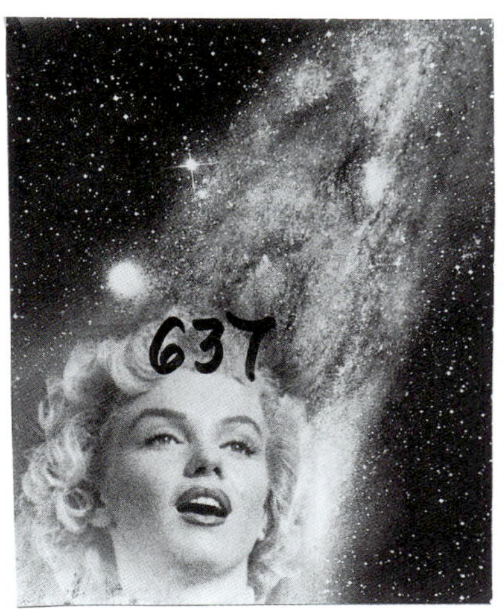

secrets. On some occasions, I used to send her notes or letters and nobody could have made any sense out of my funny messages except her…

I didn't receive a phone call or any response to that telegram. On August 4, Saturday evening, the night of her death, I went to the movies. When I came home, at the entrance door, I heard the phone ring and ring, while I was trying to find the key. After I rushed in and grabbed the receiver, the caller had just hung up. It was wishful thinking, but I thought perhaps she was the one who had called. One does not know whom one might call in moments of intoxication. Under the influence of alcohol or drugs, the mind goes berserk….

Nobody knows how many telephone calls she might have made during that fatal night, nor to whom. Several people who knew her closely thought, like me, that it might have been them she was calling. Much has been written about how she spent her last day alive, and why and how she might have died. Was she murdered? Did she commit suicide? Nobody knows for sure and perhaps it will remain a mystery forever. Accidental suicide is probably the best logical explanation.

I was shaving when I heard on the radio that Marilyn had died during the night. Of course, I was astounded, shocked, during the first few minutes, but after a while, while looking at her photos all laid out on my long worktable, I took it quite calmly. My mind was prepared. I looked at the first photo of Norma Jeane smiling, then at the next photos in which she looked more serious, and then at the last series of photos where she was… dead. I had worked for several weeks preparing those photos! It was a clear case of precognition!

Only some people can comprehend what Marilyn went through during her busy career, or the pressures she had to endure from the time when she gave her first important interview in 1949 until her last day, August 4, 1962. Probably, she didn't have a peaceful day during those thirteen years – and that's probably what killed her.

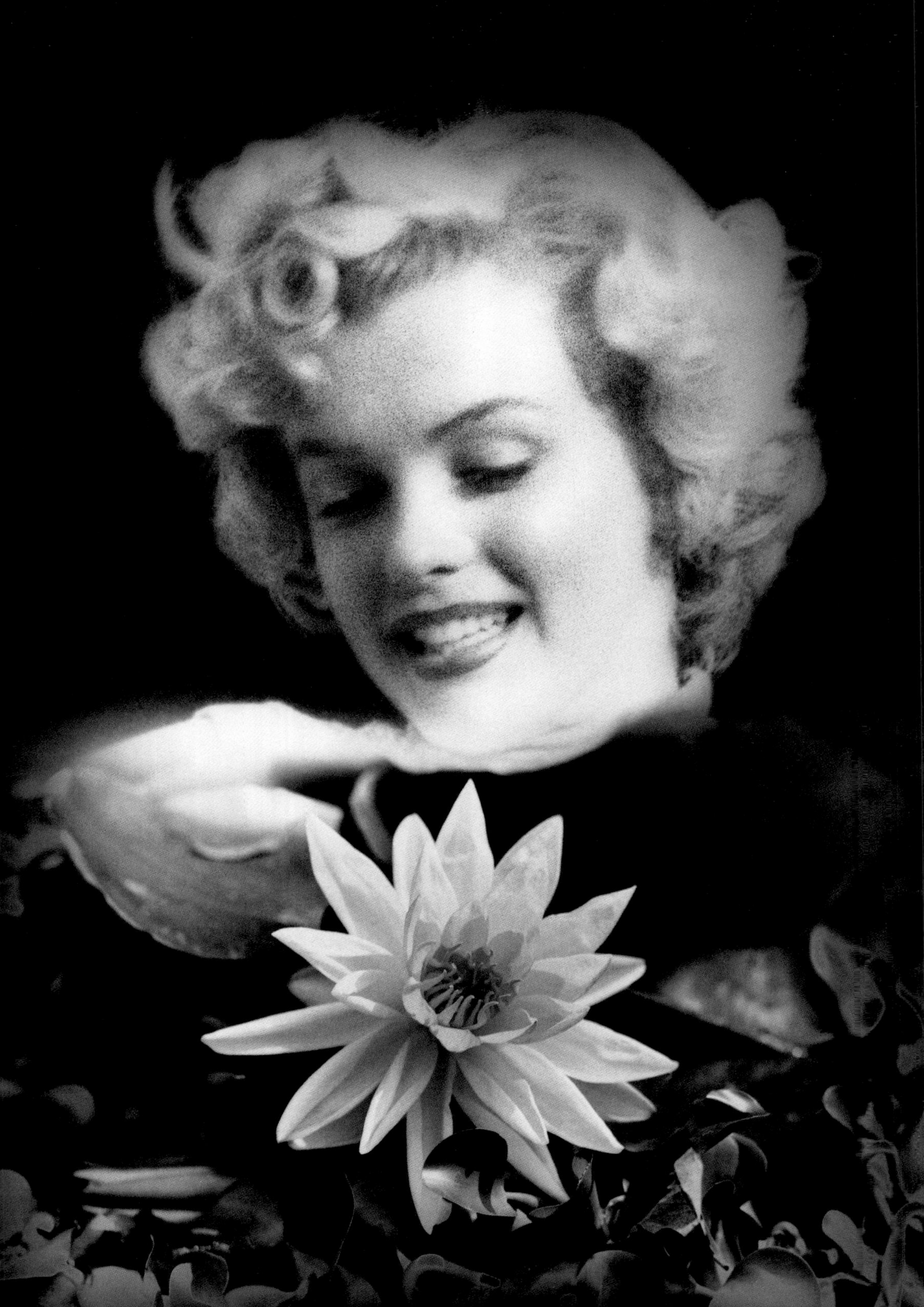

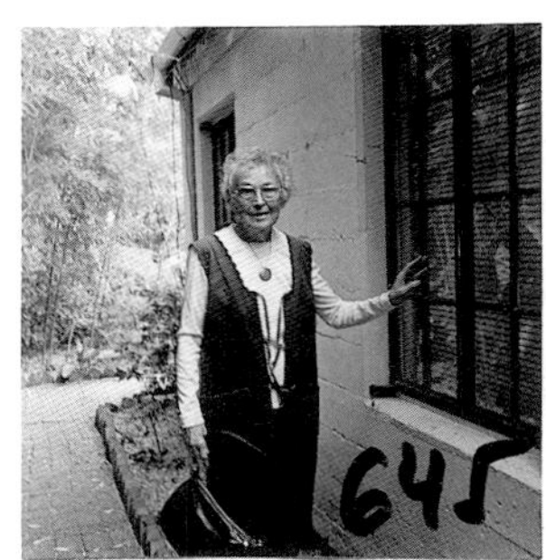

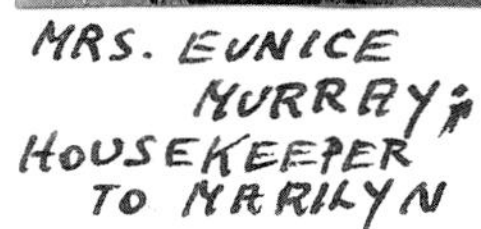
MRS. EUNICE MURRAY, HOUSEKEEPER TO MARILYN

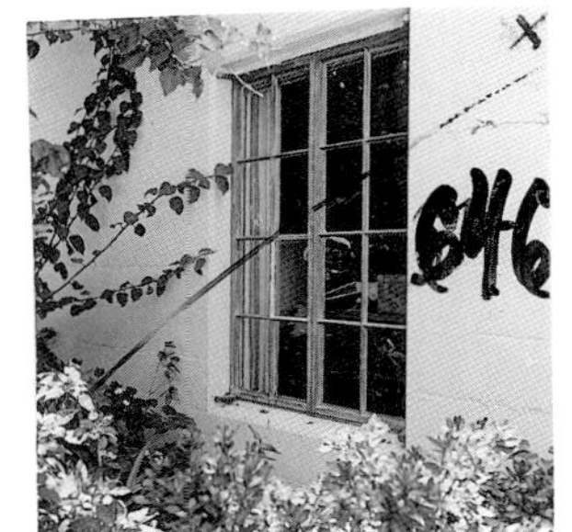

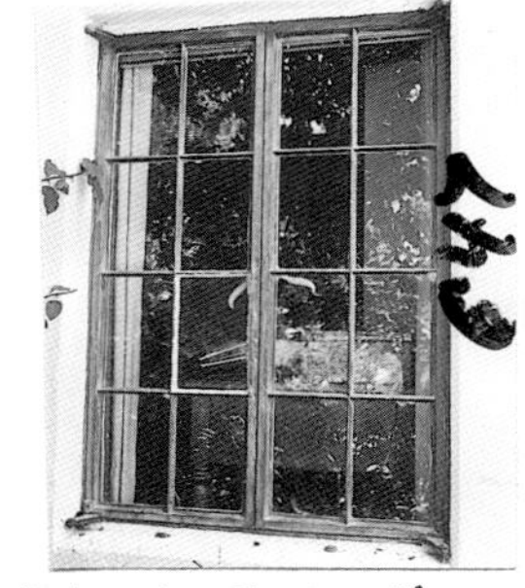

BEDROOM WINDOW, WHERE MARILYN DIED. AUG. 5. 1962

Remembrance   The day she died, August 5, 1962, a reporter named Jack Smith from the *Los Angeles Times* came over to my house to interview me. The long article appeared in the paper three days later with the headline: "'I LOVED MARILYN, STARTED CAREER,' MOURNS HOLLYWOOD PHOTOGRAPHER." From the day that newspaper article appeared, my telephone started ringing and I received call after call from all over the USA for days afterward. Journalists wanted to interview me, magazine editors were inquiring as to whether I had nude photos of Marilyn, and people wanted to tape interviews which would be made into phonographic records. Also, quite a few women called, saying they were as pretty as Marilyn, or even more so, and wished I would take pictures of them.

I gave only three interviews, to a reporter from France, another from Germany, and the third from New York, but after those interviews I felt completely exhausted and I had the guilty feeling that I had said the wrong thing<s, that I might have said things not too complimentary about Marilyn. During those hours of being interviewed, I was so nervous, I could hardly remember what I had said to the previous reporter. I phoned later to one of the reporters and asked him to please not print anything I had said. I know I did not say anything untrue, but I was angry at myself for saying things that were far too personal. I got so fed up that I refused any further interviews. I could well imagine what Marilyn endured year after year!

Marilyn is entombed in an outdoor mausoleum crypt, behind a marble slab, well protected by a shield of thick concrete to ensure that no

WESTWOOD MEMORIAL CEMETERY

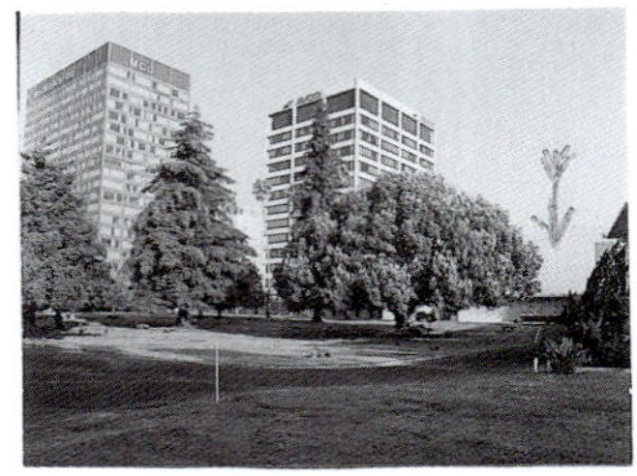

649

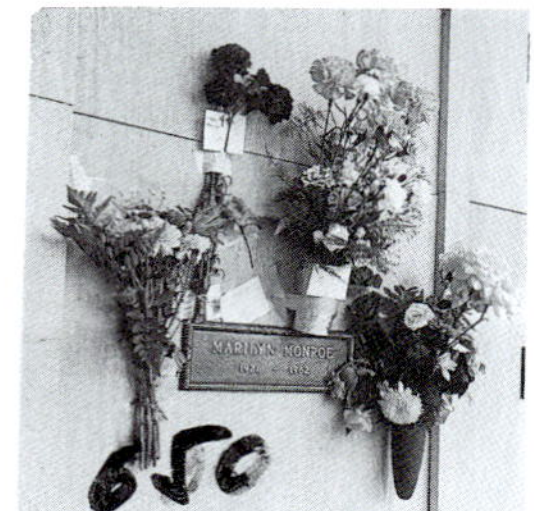

650

one will steal her remains. The cemetery is on Wilshire Boulevard in the heart of Westwood. It's like a small park, just a square block. It's all green in there, with flowers everywhere and a few beautiful trees. I never fail to drive in, park the car, and say hello to her whenever I am in that neighborhood; and I always visit her on June 1, her birthday, and August 5, the anniversary of her death. Usually, there are only a few people in there, while outside there are tall office and apartment buildings, and the neighborhood is jammed with traffic and often there is a long line of people waiting to get into the movie theater, which is near where Marilyn is resting. It always strikes me as strange that the people are in there, watching a film, but perhaps only a few know that Marilyn Monroe's coffin is right behind the movie screen, only fifty feet away!

I always meet visitors who, like me, come to see her, and I am amazed by the variety of people who come from the world over… from Europe, the Orient, Australia, and from all over the U.S. They bring flowers; they leave her letters and sentimental notes and poems. Her mother, too, an old lady in her eighties, is still alive and sends her flowers and brief messages, delivered by a florist.

Darryl Francis Zanuck (1902–1979), President of 20th Century Fox, is also buried there, just 200 feet away from Marilyn. How fantastic this life of ours is! Marilyn had so much trouble and unhappiness during her career because of her various problems with Fox studios… yet now, both of them are there, resting in peace forever.

Once, while I was photographing Marilyn, we went into a discussion about reincarnation. We were outdoors and it was a beautiful sunny day with lots of clouds in the sky. Marilyn was happy and laughing; she said in her next life she wanted to be a butterfly. I looked at the clouds and said to her, "Look, Norma Jeane, of course, there is a certain kind of reincarnation – most of the weight of our bodies is water, and when we die, that water evaporates and becomes clouds! Clouds create rain, rain fertilizes the soil, and from the soil grow things for animals and humans to eat. So the process of life keeps repeating itself!" Marilyn said to me, "You want me to become a cloud? Take pictures of it!" With her arms outstretched, she ran towards me with her head upward, her hair blowing out in the wind….

André de Dienes, November 1983

LINES ON THE DEATH OF MARILYN......

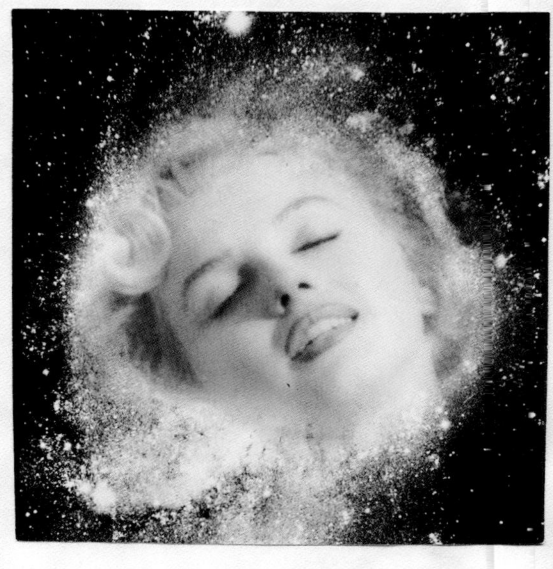

SHE DIED IN BEAUTY LIKE A ROSE
TORN FROM ITS PARENT STEM
SHE DIED IN BEAUTY LIKE A PEARL
DROPT FROM A DIADEM
SHE DIED IN BEAUTY LIKE A LAY
ALONG A MOONLIGHT LAKE
SHE DIED IN BEAUTY LIKE A SONG
OF BIRDS AMONG THE BRAKE

SHE DIED IN BEAUTY LIKE THE SNOW
ON FLOWERS DISSOLVED AWAY
SHE DIED IN BEAUTY LIKE A STAR
LOST ON THE BROW OF DAY
SHE LIVES IN GLORY LIKE NIGHT'S GEMS
SET AROUND THE SILVER MOON
SHE LIVES IN GLORY LIKE THE SUN
LOST AMID THE BLAZE OF NOON

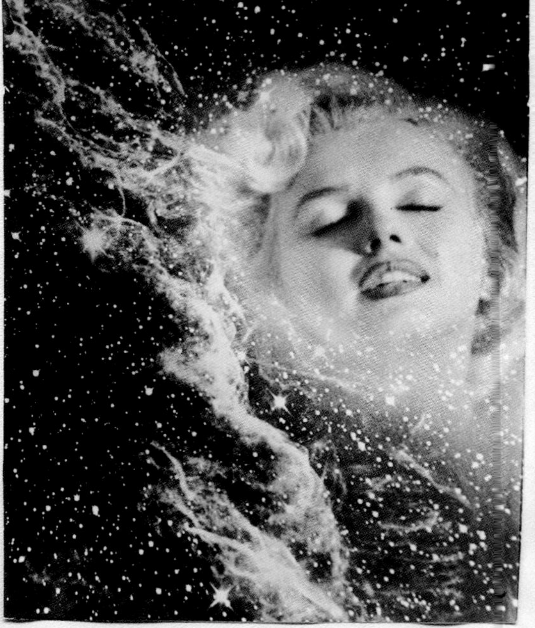

MARILYN MONROE
1926 - 1962

They bring flowers, they leave for her letters, sentimental notes, and poems....which I read.... They all express how much they admire her, how much they love her ! Reading those love-letters bring tears to my eyes....and I even cry a little...... Her mother, too, an old, lady in her eighties, still lives, and sends her flowers and brief messeges, delivered by a florist.

It's so nice to meet people there! They become talkative, sincere, direct, frank, The intercommunication is a delight for me ! The masks are down, people speak in honest terms, We are conscious that life does not last too long, and that we must die sooner or later.....

I don't particularly like the fact that Marilyn is resting in a concrete block wall. I have old-fashioned ideas; I prefer the ground; the earth.... to rot and assimilate with the elements.... But I don't think she had any say about that...... though she had made a very detailed will before she died, even had it altered a few times !

Natalie Wood is burried in the ground, 150 feet from Marilyn. Her grave is surrounded with LOTS OF flower pots. A bronze plaque reads:

NATALIE WOOD
Wagner
1938 - 1981

Her death, too, is a tragic, mysterious story... Exactly how she died; what went on during those last few hours of her life, just like in Marilyn's.. shall be never known !

I interupted writing the ending of this long chronicle of mine; I went to take pictures there....

Marilyn's cemetery is just"a drop in the bucket" what the visitors in South. California can see and enjoy visiting; but whoever comes here, please, please, do not miss it !

There are many other famous people burried there in that small cemetery: Darryl Francis Zanuck,[1902-1979] Co-Founder, President and Producer of 20th Century Fox Studio -- is also there; just 200 feet away from Marilyn ! That gives me things to think about ! How fantastic this life of ours is ! Marilyn had so much trouble, so many problems, so much heartackes, so much unhappiness during her career, because of the various problems she encoutered with ~~Mr. Zanuck~~ THE STUDIO....and how unhappy Marilyn was,because she did not make as much money as she should......
But now, both of them are there, dead; neighbors; resting in peace for ever !

* ***** ** ***

The cemetery was created at the turn of the century. At that time, the entire surrounding area was just farmlands,and orchards. The oldest grave dates to 1905. ALICE L. BROWN lays there; she was only 25 when she died. When I look at that stone slab, I am thinking....What difference does ~~it~~ that makes to the world,.... Nobody knows who she was, how she lived, why she died -- at such young age ! And I say to myself:there are so many aspiring writers,who are asking themselves what to write about....what new to find to write about ? Well, what about doing some research who that young lady was ! One never knows what amazing story one can stumble onto,by giving one-self to reseach!.... The winning people are always those who give efforts to something ! There are unlimited things to write about ! The mind has to be awakened by ideas ! And, there are different ways to be creative ! One can even break all the rules ! Doing things differently ! Just get started on something..... and keep going ! Our attitudes create our lives ! Always,be an optimist!

André de Dienes
Nov. 1983

Once, while I was photographing Marilyn, we went into discussion about reincarnation. We were outdoors, it was a bueautiful, sunny day, with lot's of clouds in the sky. Marilyn was loughing, HAPPY ! She said the next time she WANTS TO be a butterfly ! I looked at the clouds, and said to her: "Look, Norma Jean; Of course -- there is a certain kind of reincarnation ! Most of the weight of our body is water; when we die, that water evaporates .... It becomes clouds ! Clouds create rains, rain water fertilizes the soil; AND from the soil things grow what animals, and we human eat.... So the process of life keeps repeating itself! We are a compoundings of molecules that were part of something, or somebody else before us ! Sudenly, Marilyn said to me : "You want me to be a cloud ? Take pictures of it ! " With arms outstretched, she was running toward me, with her head upward, her hair blowing in the wind....

EPILOG

IT RAINED LAST night, but the sun was shining already when I went to the cemetery; (early this morning). Everything looked so clean, so green, so beautiful ! The roses, and all the other flowers were full of raindrops; the sunshine created many, many sparkling diamonds for Marilyn... And the birds were singing.... I could not help thinking, repeating to myself, how beautiful life is ! Than, a butterfly flew over, right to Marilyn. I took pictures of Marilyn's initials M M, reflecting the golden sunlight; AND WHEN I left the cemetery, instead of gloomy thoughts about death , I started to amuse myself thinking up words which began with two M-s. Even silly words...any words... like ..... MONROE MISHMASH, MAKING MONEY, MERRY MAKING, MANY MOODS, MYSTICAL MEMORIES, MONROE MEMORABLIA, MAGIC MOMENTS, MARVELOUS MOMENTS,... MASOCHISTIC MISFITS....... and I was thinking that, while I shall develop my films, and make prints, I shall listen to MARVELOUS MUSIC ! MAGICAL MINDS !.....

I felt so good ! Los Angeles is a Marvelous, Magic place to live in ! It's endless what one can do, and see here....each day !

MARILYN'S LAST HOME. 1962.

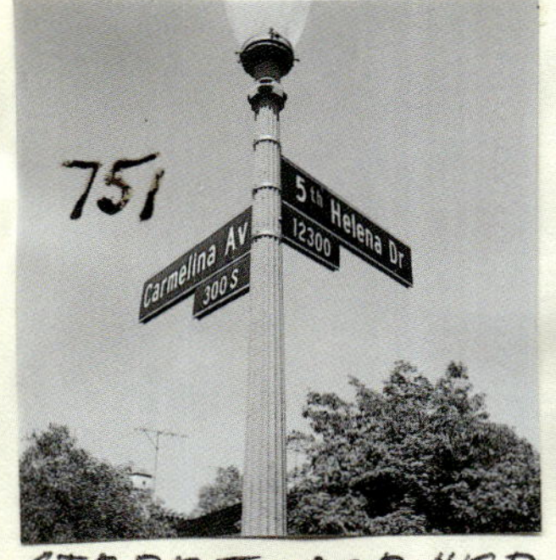

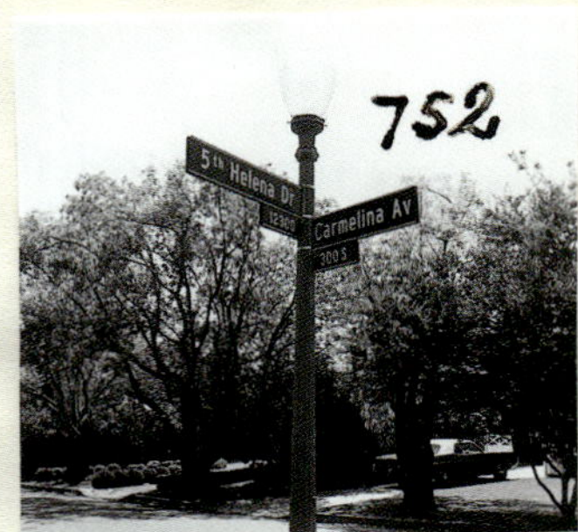

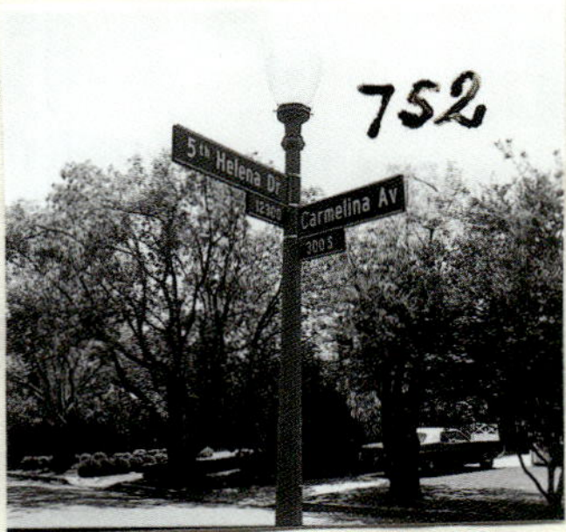

753

STREET CORNER. THE ENTRANCE GATE

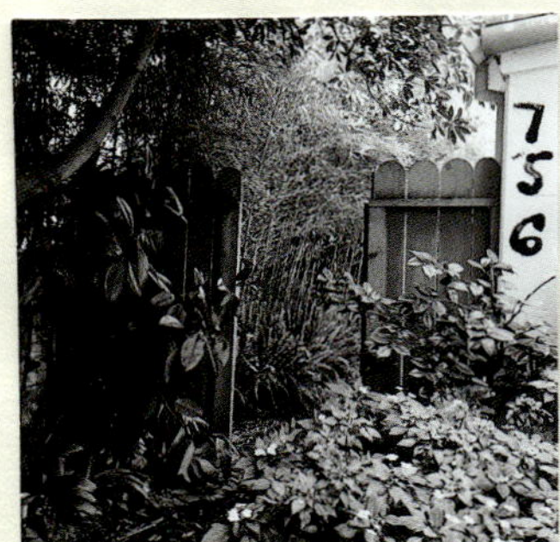

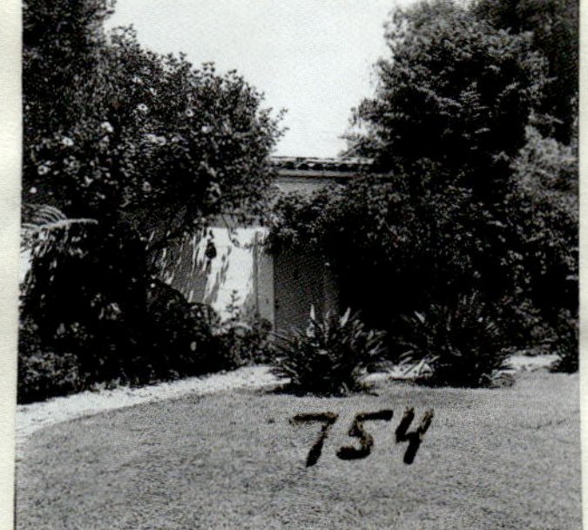

755

MAIN ENTRENCE

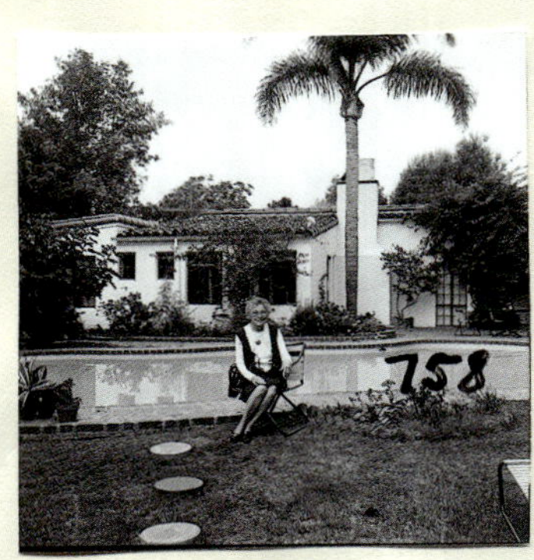

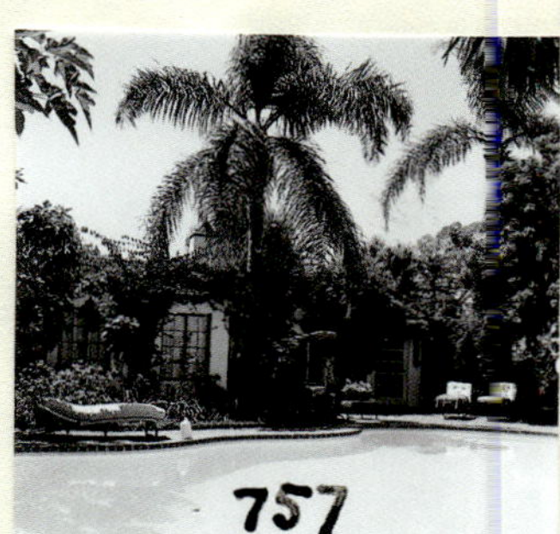

MRS. E. MURRAY

THE HOUSE-KEEPER WHO HAS SEEN MARILYN LAST. 8/4/1962 SHE IS POINTING AT MARILYN'S BEDROOM WINDOW WHERE MARILYN DIED. 8/5/1962

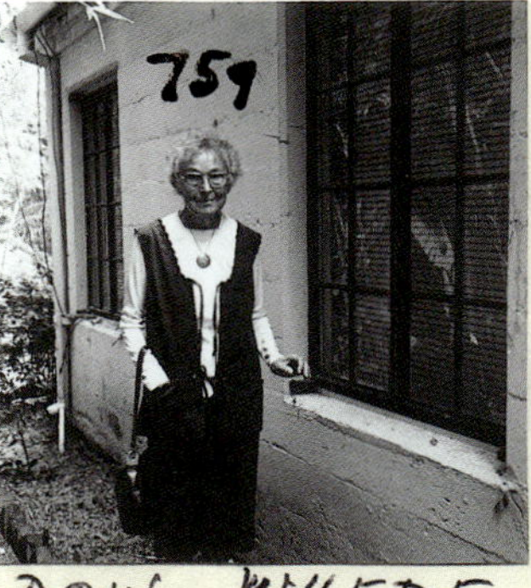

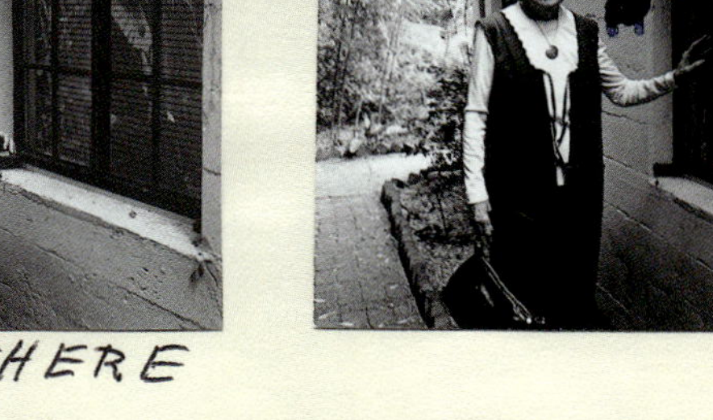

ANDRE DE DIENES

BK II

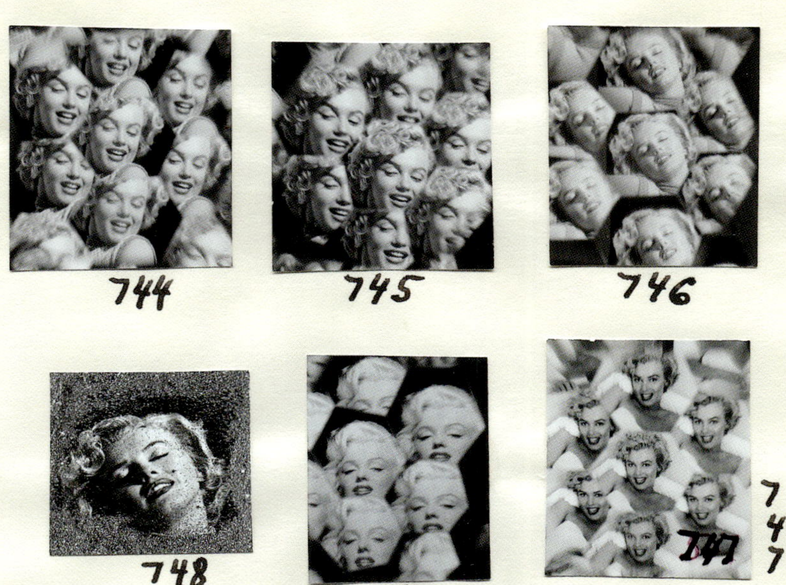

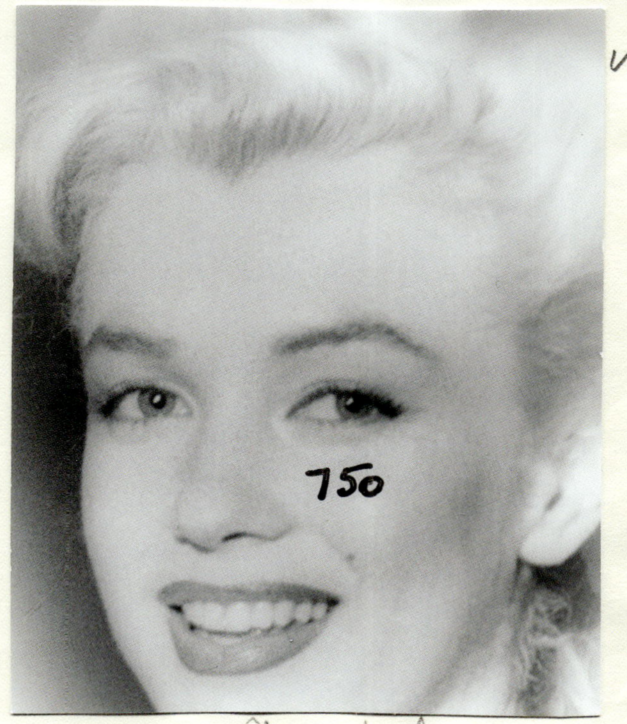

7 & 7B

95

ANDRE DE DIENES
1401 SUNSET PLAZA DRIVE
HOLLYWOOD, CALIF. 90069

SMALL CEMETERY, (1 BLOCK SQUARE)

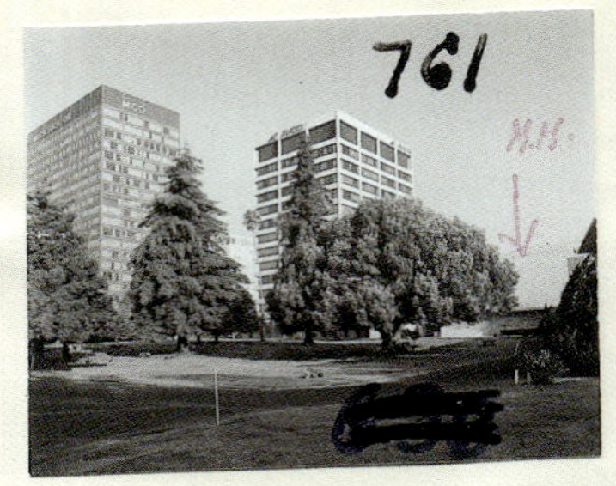

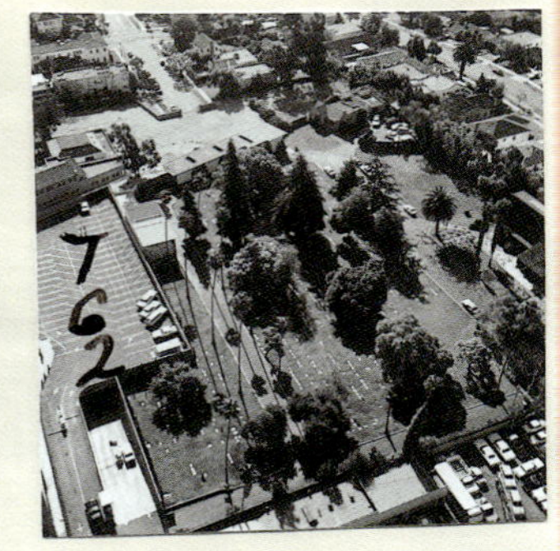

766

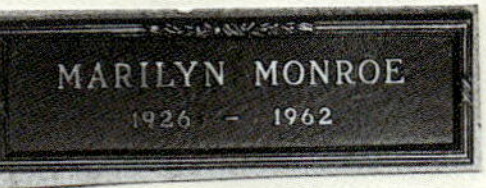

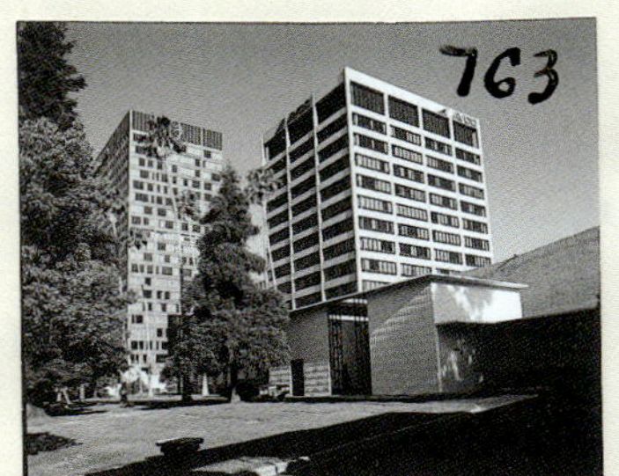

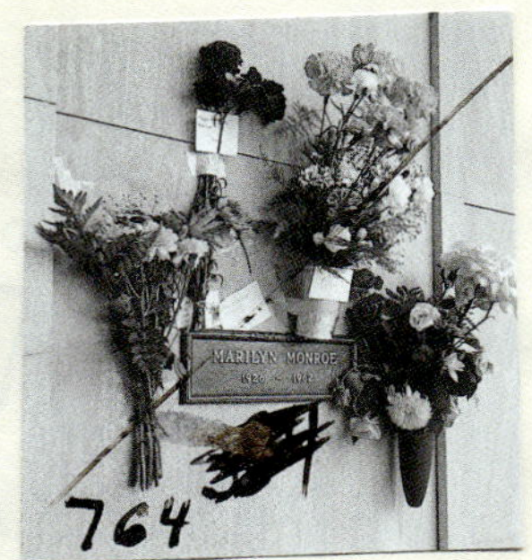

WESTWOOD,
WEST LOS ANGELES.

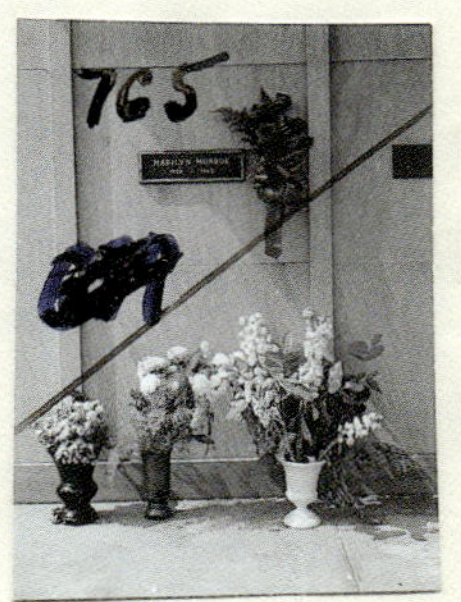

HOLLYWOOD BOULEVARD ..

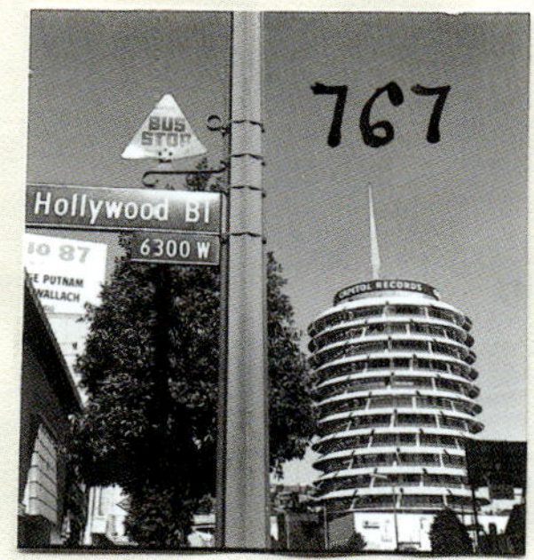

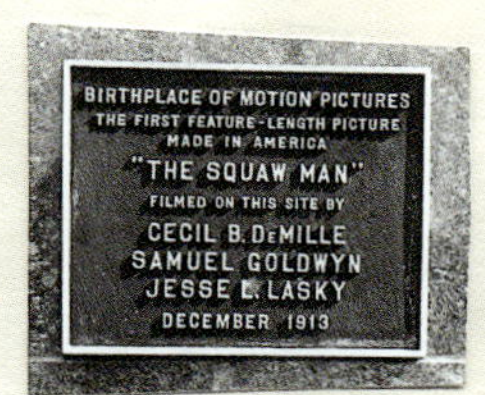

768

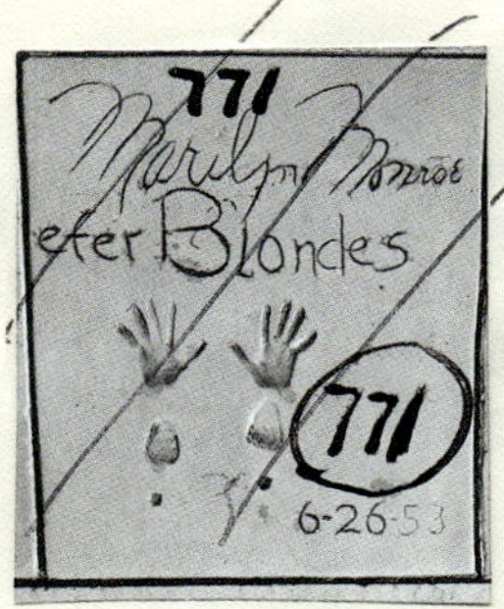

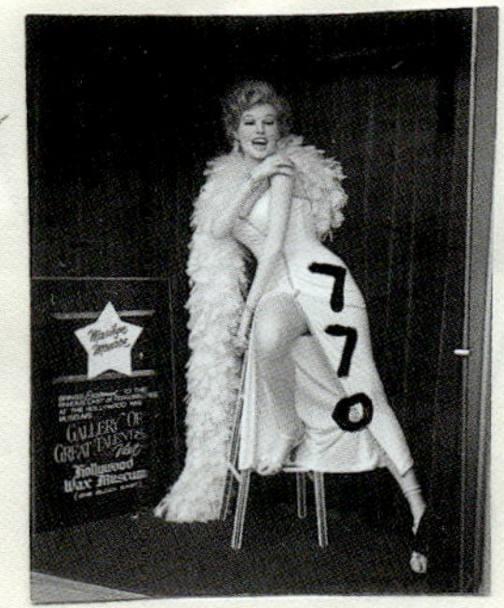

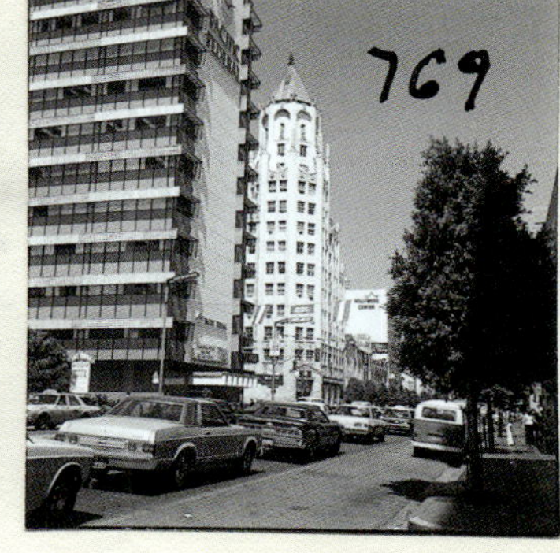

WAX MUSEUM
BEING ADVERTISED
BY MARILYN M.

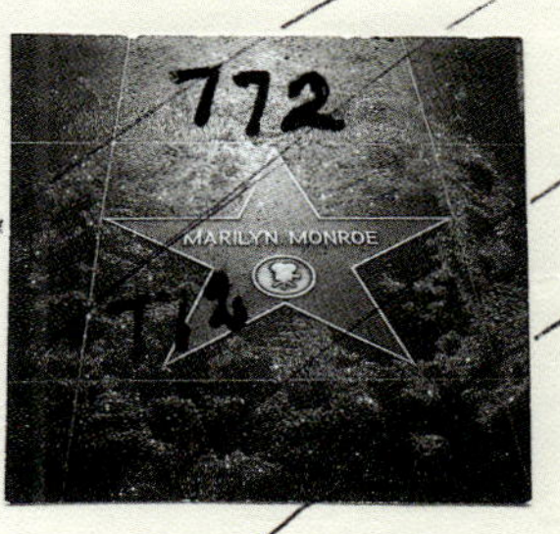

97

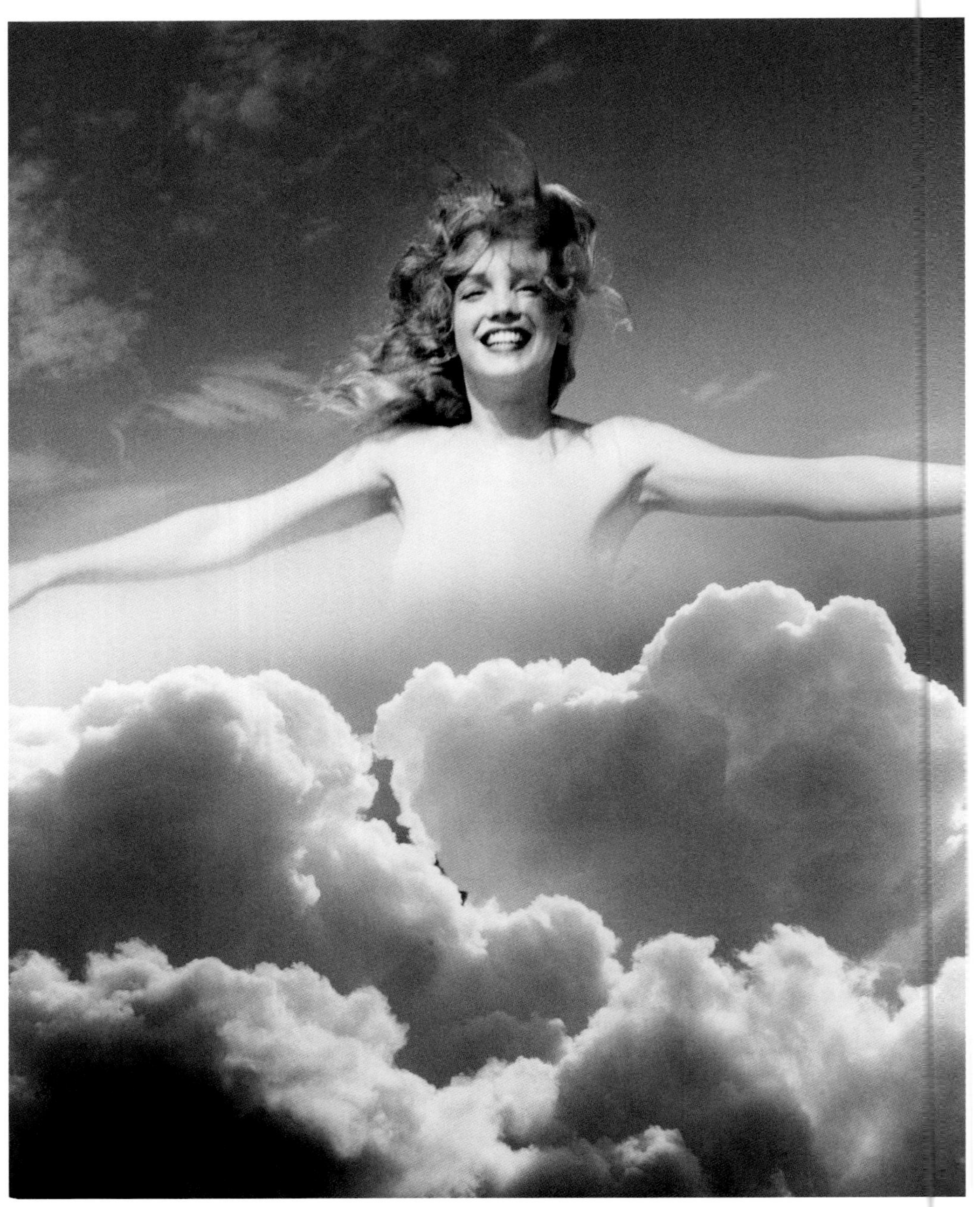

Epilogue It rained last night, but the sun was shining already when I went to the cemetery early this morning. Everything looked so clean, and green, and beautiful. The roses and all the other flowers were full of raindrops, and the sunshine created many sparkling diamonds for Marilyn. The birds were singing, and I could not help thinking how beautiful life is. Then, a butterfly flew over, right to Marilyn. I took pictures of Marilyn's initials reflecting in the golden sunlight. When I left the cemetery, instead of having gloomy thoughts about death, I started to amuse myself thinking up words which begin with two Ms, even silly words, like: Merry Making, Many Moods, Mystical Memories, Monroe Memorabilia, Masochistic Misfits, Magic Moments… and I was thinking that while I developed my film and made prints I would listen to Marvelous Music! I felt so good! Los Angeles is a Marvelous, Magic place to live in. It's endless what one can see and do here each day!

Acknowledgements Late in 1999, I had the opportunity to see the documentary film "Let's Get Lost" by photographer Bruce Weber. Somewhere in the film, Bruce showed a book of nude photographs to the musician Chet Baker, remarking how beautiful the unnamed artist's work was. Intrigued, I slowed down the videotape many times until I caught a brief glimpse of the photos and the name André de Dienes on the spine. Who was this unknown photographer? Why had his work slipped past me? I began to search. What had become of this photographer and his pictures? Perhaps I could purchase a print or an old book for my collection.

Eventually, with patience and a lot of luck, I tracked down André's widow less than a few hours away from my home. She reluctantly agreed to meet me, and we had our first encounter at a roadside diner in the middle of the California desert. She wore dark glasses and asked to see my driver's license to verify my identity. Satisfied, she produced a small box of André's photographs from underneath the table. Instead of the nudes I expected, she told a tale of Marilyn Monroe… lost images… and unpublished diaries. Right then, I knew I had stumbled upon a treasure and there was much more to this story than I ever imagined.

The weeks and months that followed were a blur of unboxing photographs, reading scribbled notes, and unfolding the actual umbrellas that a young Marilyn had held on the beach all those years before. In one box lay André's camera, with the letters MM inscribed on the case. Carefully tucked away in a bedroom closet were André's original diaries. I began to read, and the story started to come together…

Unknown to me at the time was the fact that Benedikt Taschen had been seeking out André's work in hopes of publishing it. Our mutual friend, the noted photographer William Claxton, had just introduced us around the time I was tracking down André – just another of the many coincidences in this project. I suppose now that all of this was simply fate unfolding before our eyes. Clearly, the resurrection of these photographs and diaries has been a series of strange coincidences and connections. Collecting, archiving, and piecing together this long overdue book has been a wonderful experience – equal parts photography, history, and mystery. Finally, the whole story can now be told as I know André would have wanted. It may well be the last untold story in the life of Marilyn Monroe, published exactly forty years after her death.

Thank you to the many people who have contributed to the creation of this book: Shirley de Dienes and family, Benedikt and Angelika Taschen and all at TASCHEN, William Claxton, Peggy Moffitt, Stephen Cohen and the staff of Stephen Cohen Gallery, Eric Ruffing at 13th Floor, Peter Shurkin, Monika Reynolds, Don Weinstein and the staff of Photo Impact Hollywood, Anita Teckemeyer, Horst Neuzner, Kim Goodwin, and Clark Kidder.

Most importantly, much love and gratitude to Gloria, Miles, and Lola.

Steve Crist

This book would never have come into being had I not had the good fortune to meet with Mr. Benedikt Taschen. To him, I owe my first debt of gratitude.

My greatest appreciation and love to my late husband, André de Dienes. Without his love and trust in me this beautiful material may well have never been preserved for you, the reader, to share. His genius in photography is unsurpassed. I love you, André, and thank you for your belief in me.

My deepest admiration and respect to Norma Jeane/Marilyn Monroe, whose beauty in body and soul touched our lives forever. Love is patient, love is kind, and love trusts always, hopes and has faith. The greatest of these you followed eagerly and made an indelible mark on history forever. Thank you Norma Jeane for leaving us with this beautiful gift.

No book can be published without the editor. My heartfelt appreciation and special thanks to Mr. Steve Crist, whose devotion and hard work made it possible for this project to succeed. Thank you Steve and your beautiful wife Gloria, who had to put up with both of us!

To the millions of fans all over the world, I salute and love you all, for without you, our Marilyn would not be alive today.

I thank my companion and my friend, Dennis E. Twohy, for sharing my journey of many trials and tribulations for the past fourteen years.

Most of all, for putting up with all the highs and lows which I have encountered in trying to honor André's memory, his work, and in fighting to keep his archive intact. I love you, Den Den. Thank you!

I thank my mother and father for their loving efforts to raise a family of five children. I thank my sisters, Irene Ellis Lynn and Mary Ellis Flory, for their love, support and understanding. I thank my deceased brother William (Billy), whose spirit has always guided me through many tough times.

Last, but most importantly, I'd like to express a very special thanks to my beloved sister, Charlotte, who was and remains my mentor, my teacher and my friend! Sweet sister Charl, you are my role model and without your endless understanding, faith and love where would I be? I love you and shall be eternally grateful for the special friendship we shared.

To all who made this beautiful book come together, I shall be forever indebted to you. Thank you!

Ms. Shirley T. Ellis de Dienes

ANDRE DE Dienes
1401 SUNSET PLAZA DRIVE
HOLLYWOOD, CALIFORNIA, 90069

<u>COVER SHOTS</u>

A selection of De Dienes's
magazine cover portraits

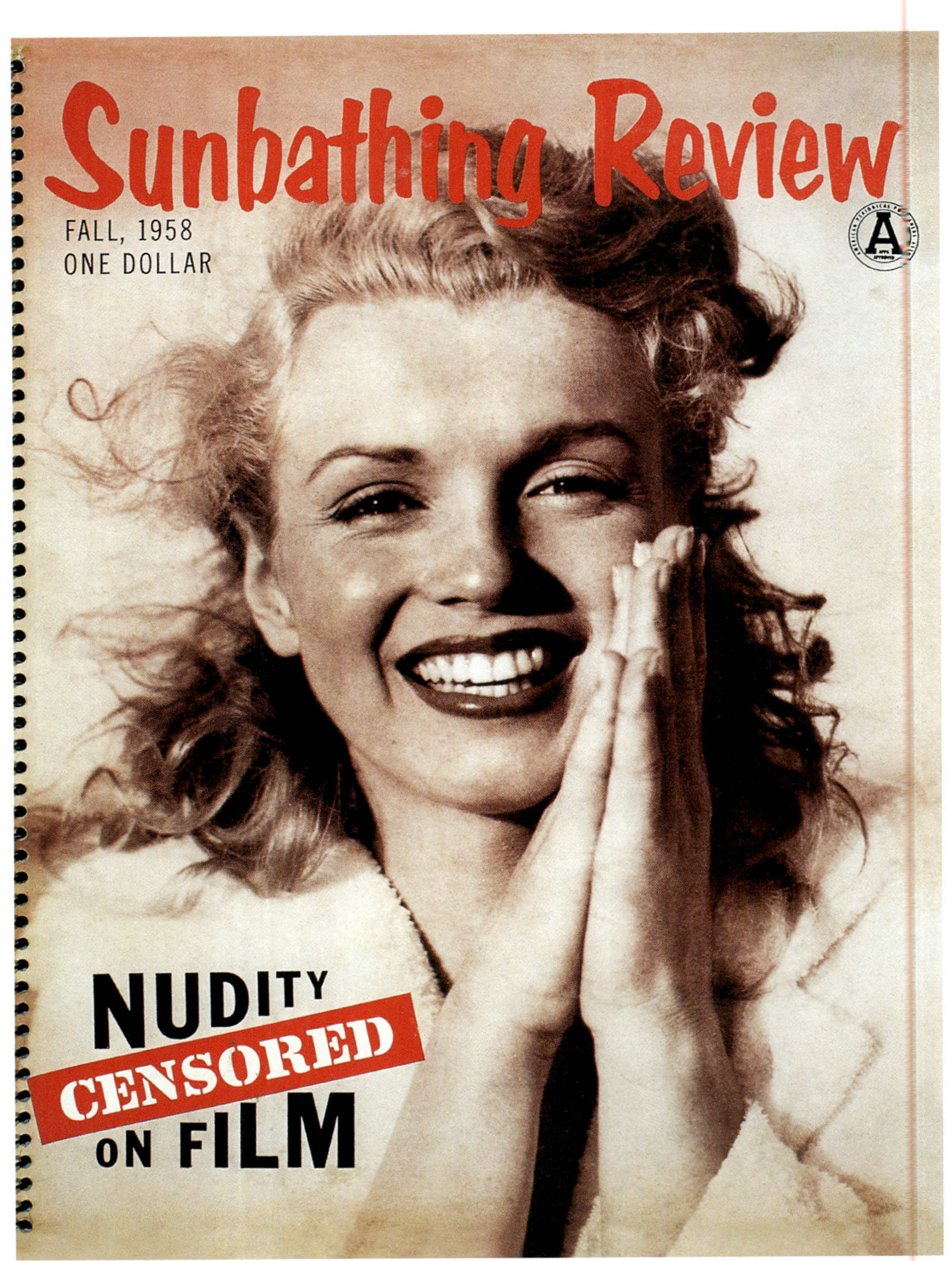
Sunbathing Review
FALL, 1958
ONE DOLLAR
A
NUDITY
CENSORED
ON FILM

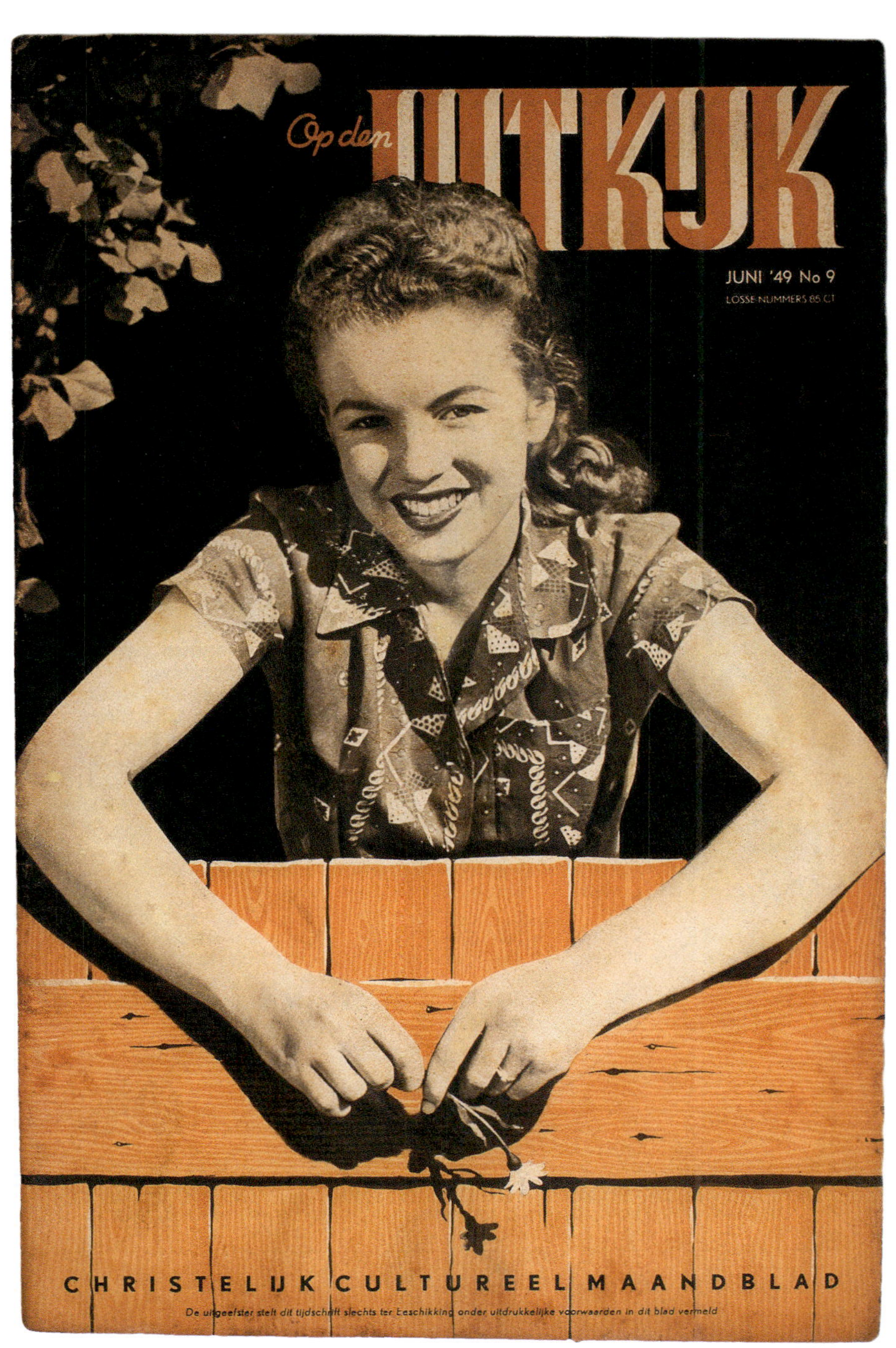
Op den UITKIJK
JUNI '49 No 9
LOSSE NUMMERS 85 CT
CHRISTELIJK CULTUREEL MAANDBLAD
De uitgeefster stelt dit tijdschrift slechts ter beschikking onder uitdrukkelijke voorwaarden in dit blad vermeld

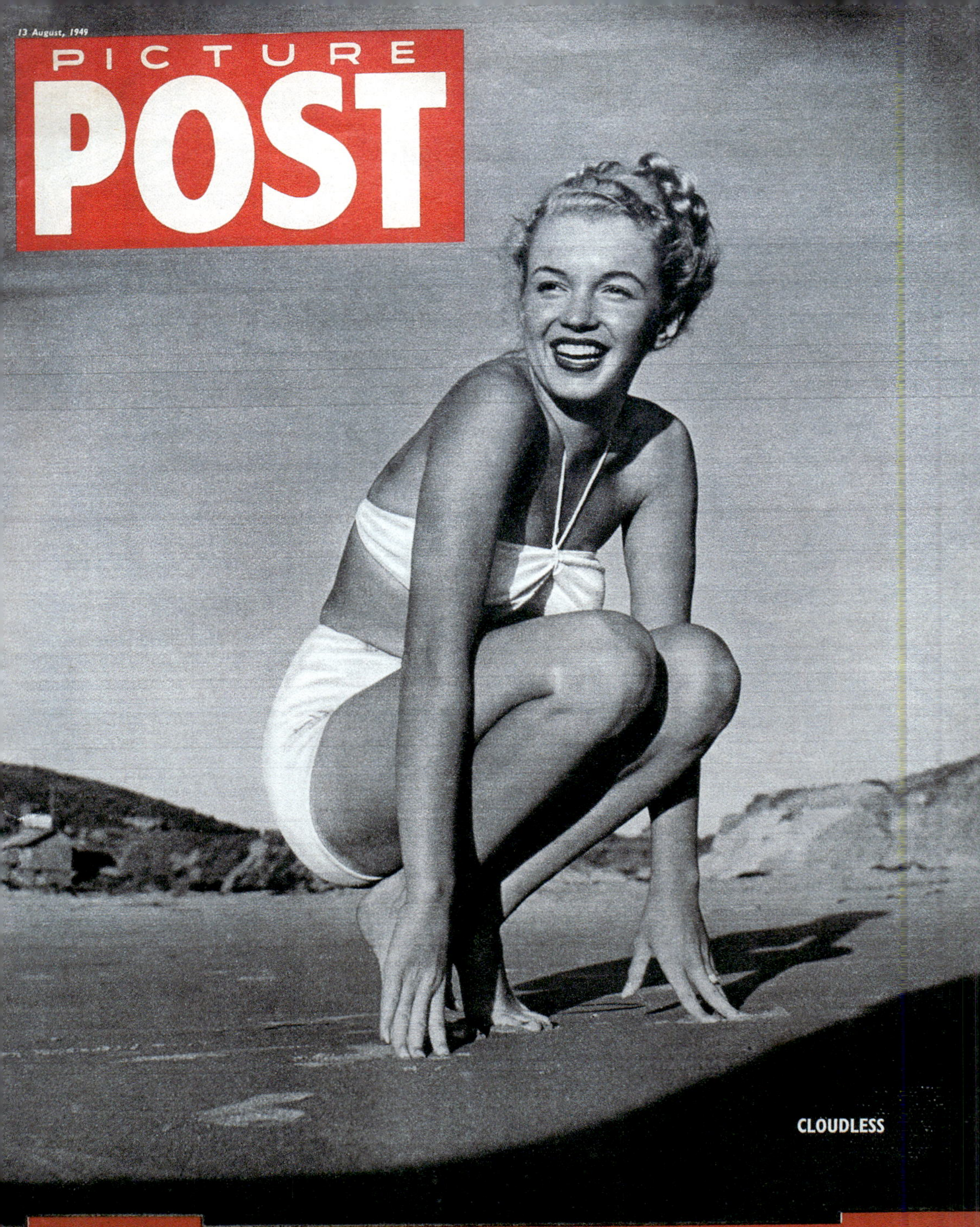

CLOUDLESS

HULTON'S NATIONAL WEEKLY

GERMANY TODAY

A Solemn Warning

13 AUGUST, 1949

Vol. 44 No. 7

4D

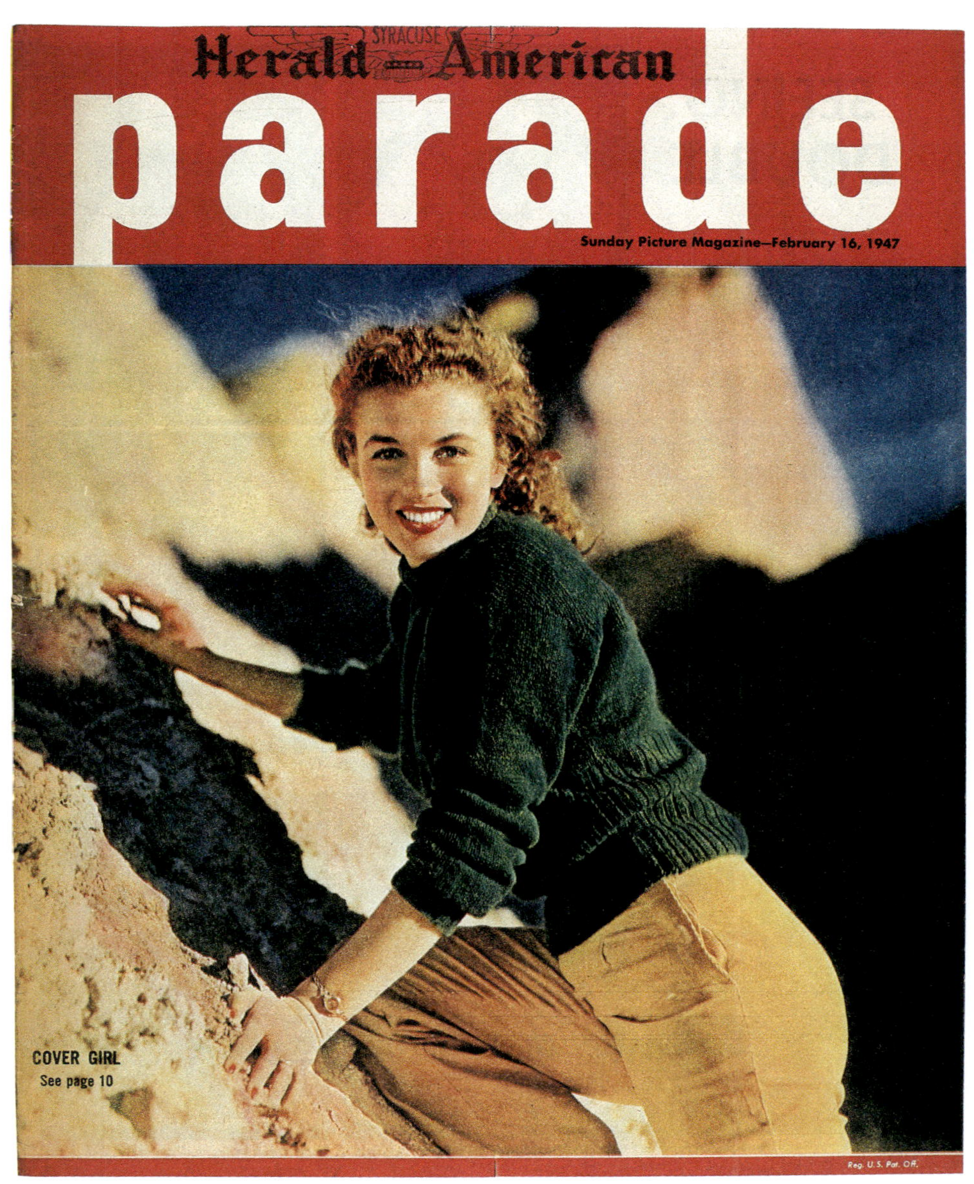

SYRACUSE
Herald-American
parade
Sunday Picture Magazine—February 16, 1947
COVER GIRL
See page 10
Reg. U.S. Pat. Off.

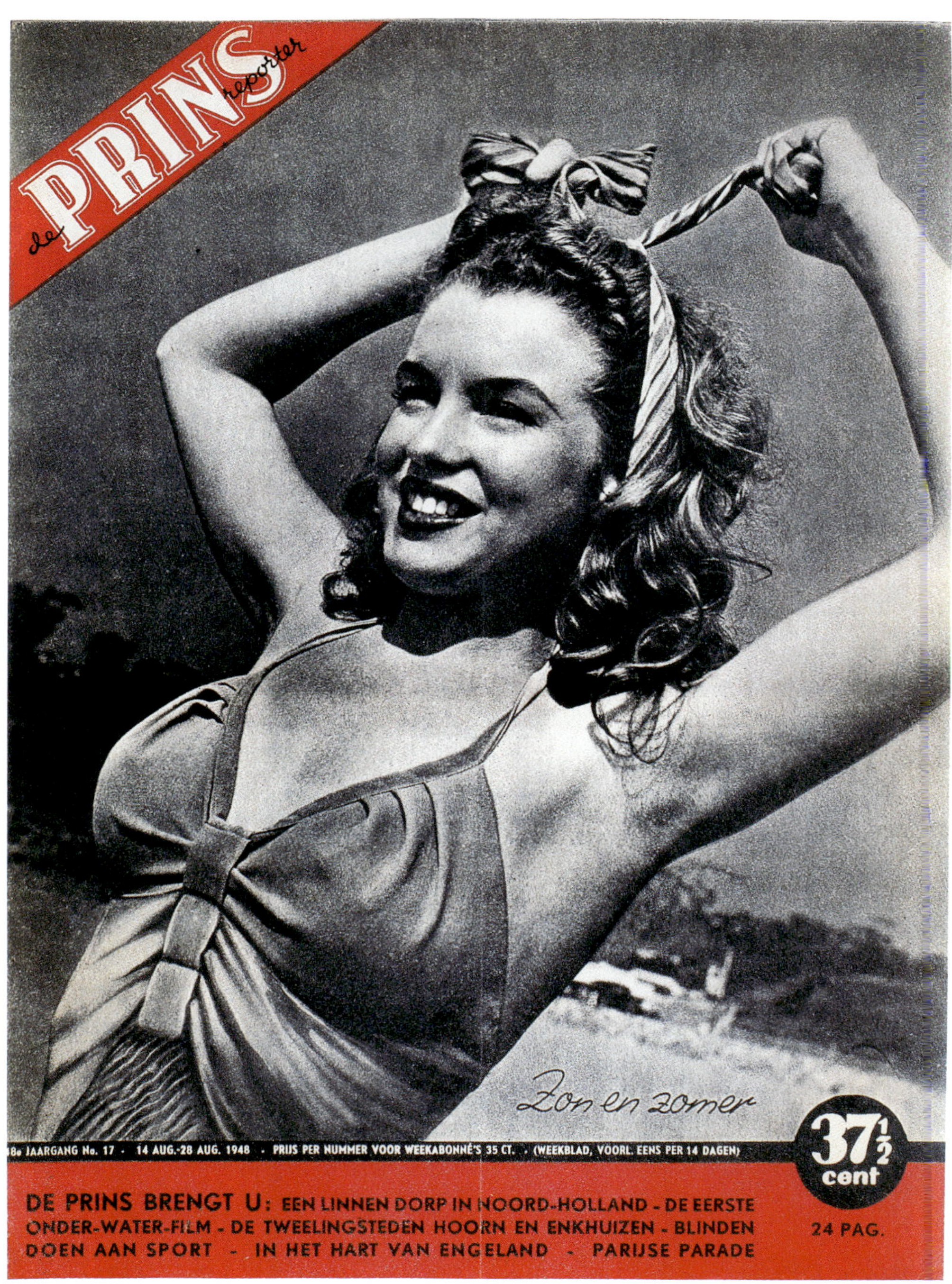
de PRINS reporter
Zon en zomer
18e JAARGANG No. 17 · 14 AUG.-28 AUG. 1948 · PRIJS PER NUMMER VOOR WEEKABONNÉ'S 35 CT. · (WEEKBLAD, VOORL. EENS PER 14 DAGEN)
37½ cent
DE PRINS BRENGT U: EEN LINNEN DORP IN NOORD-HOLLAND - DE EERSTE ONDER-WATER-FILM - DE TWEELINGSTEDEN HOORN EN ENKHUIZEN - BLINDEN DOEN AAN SPORT - IN HET HART VAN ENGELAND - PARIJSE PARADE
24 PAG.

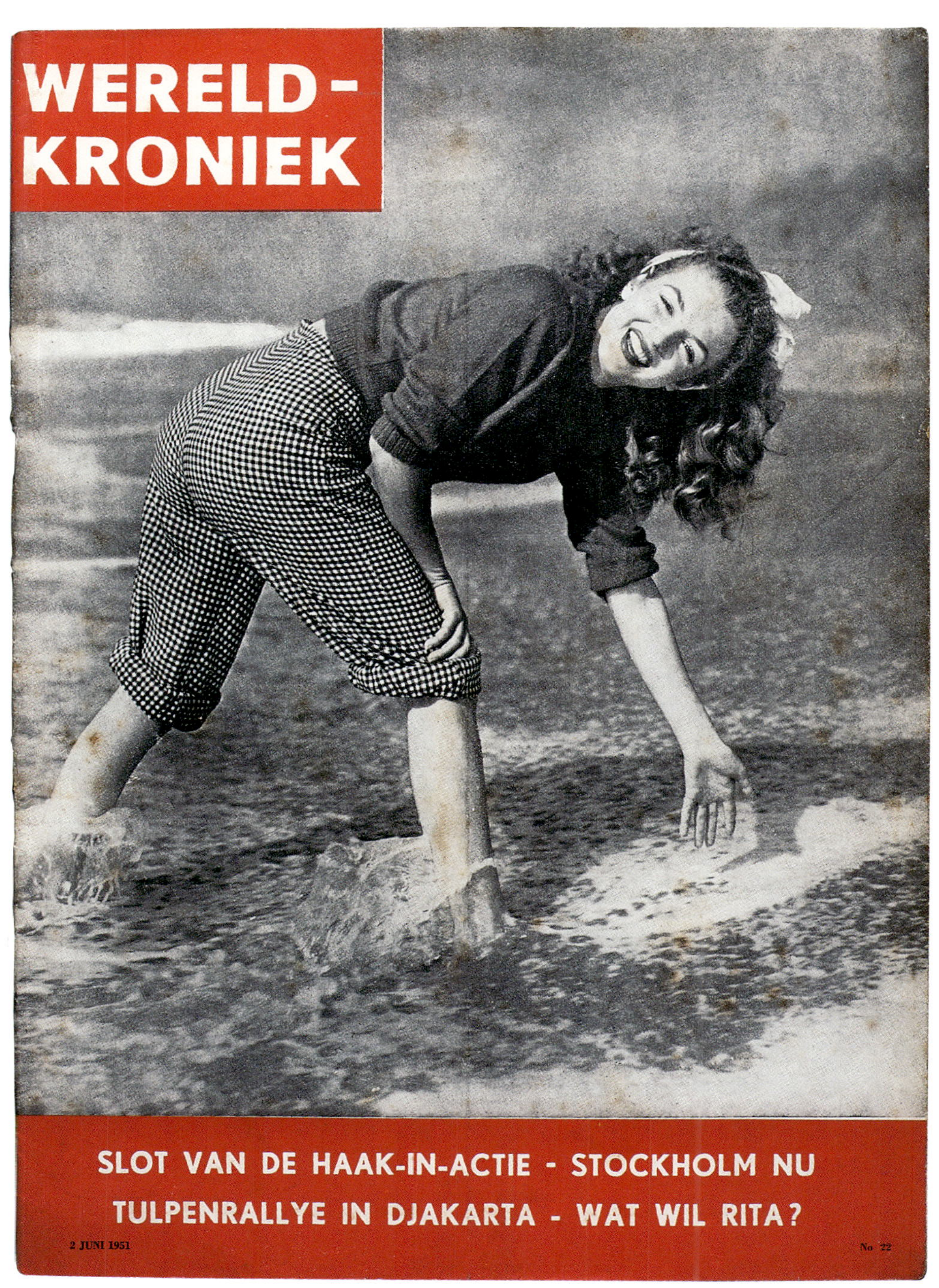
WERELD-
KRONIEK
SLOT VAN DE HAAK-IN-ACTIE - STOCKHOLM NU
TULPENRALLYE IN DJAKARTA - WAT WIL RITA?
2 JUNI 1951
No 22

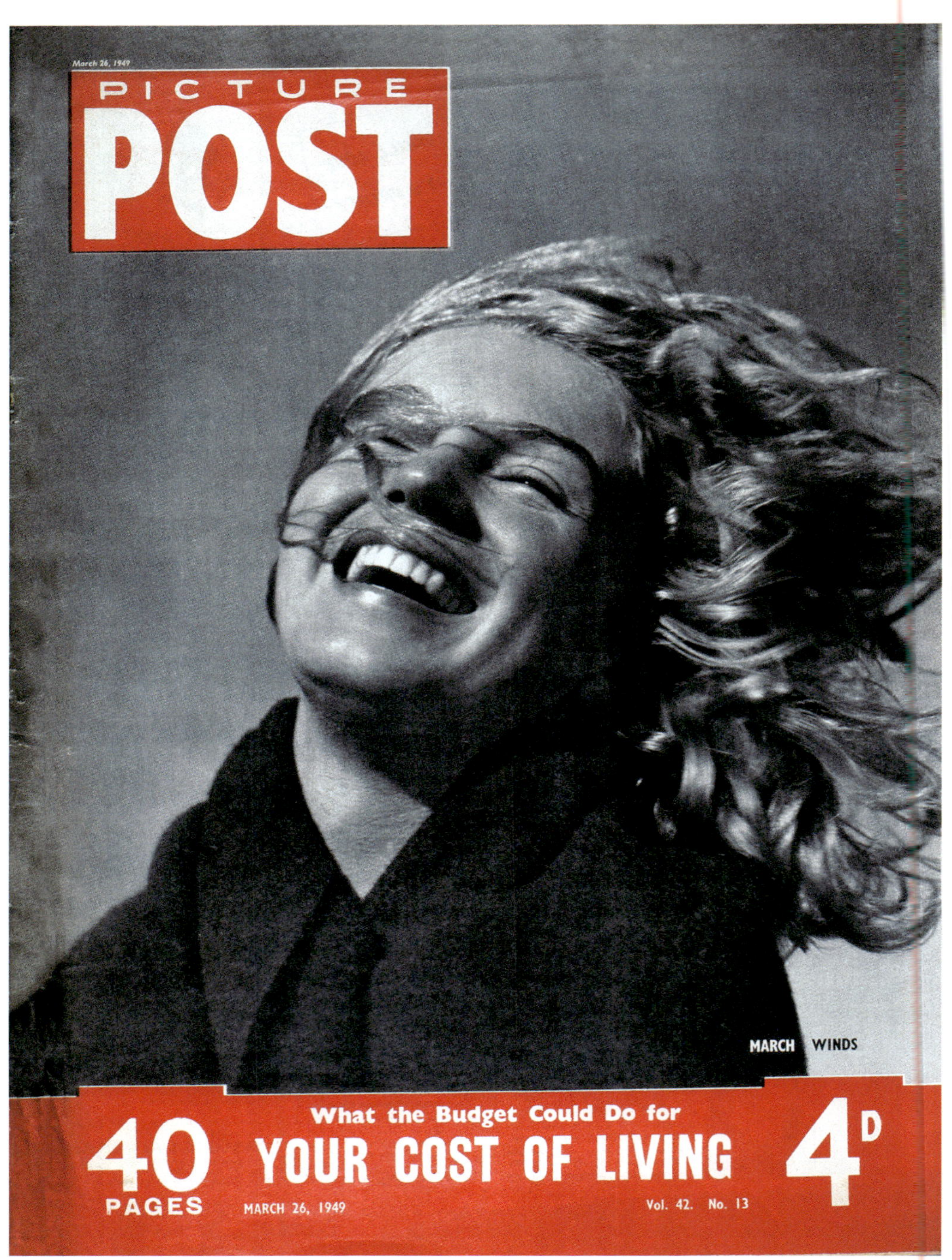

March 26, 1949
PICTURE
POST
MARCH WINDS
40
PAGES
What the Budget Could Do for
YOUR COST OF LIVING
MARCH 26, 1949
Vol. 42. No. 13
4D

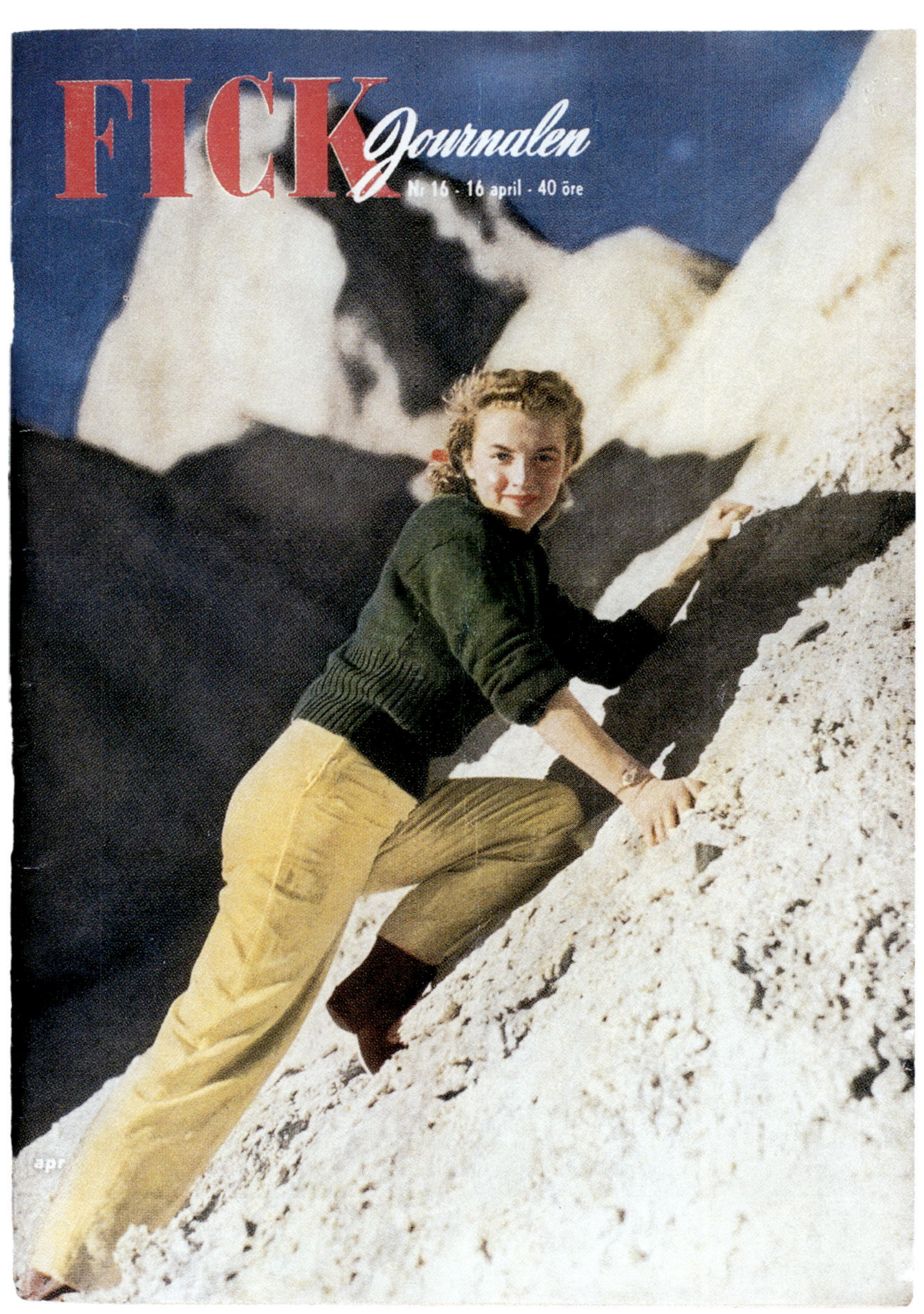
FICK Journalen
Nr 16 · 16 april · 40 öre

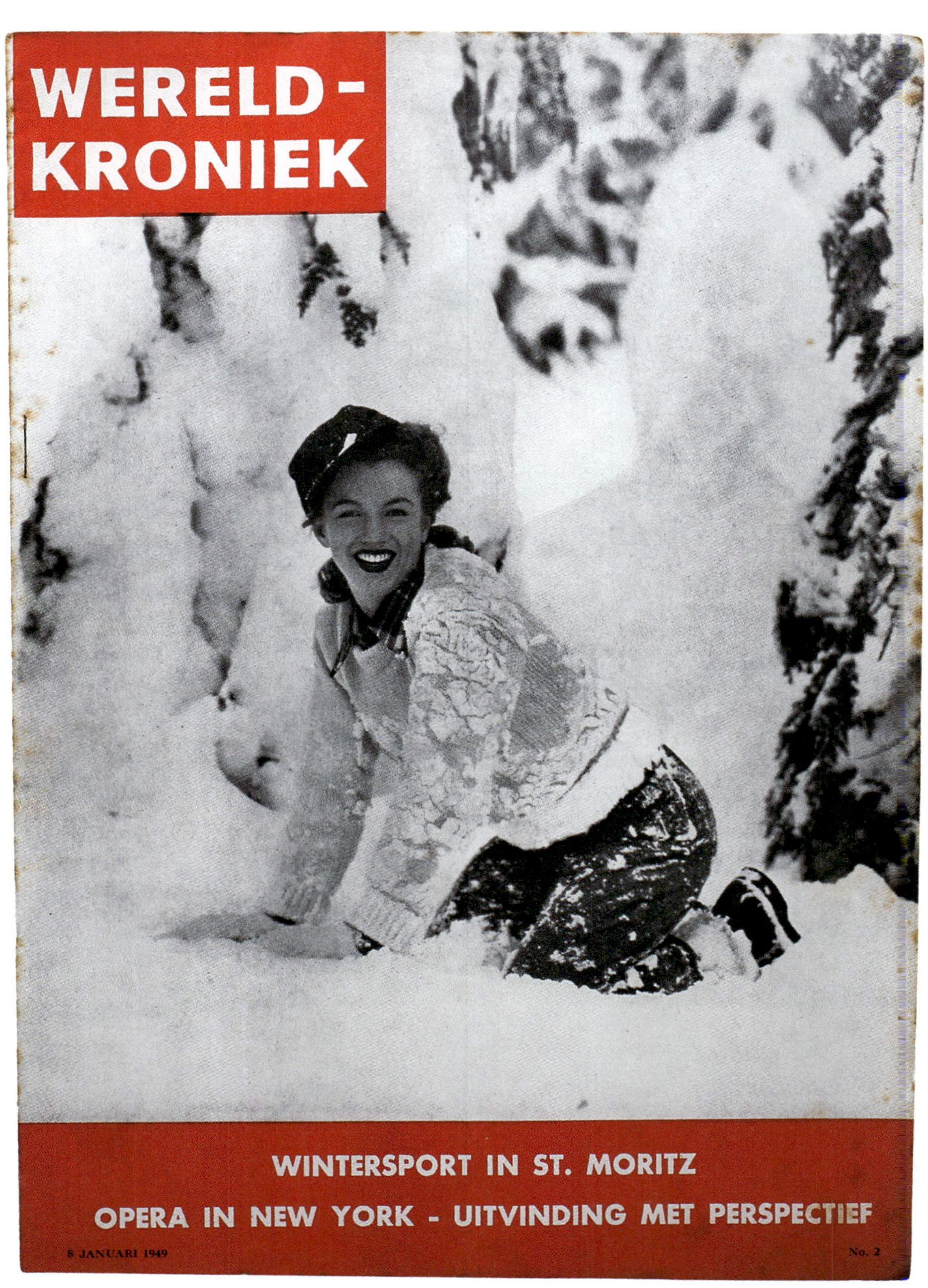
WERELD-
KRONIEK
WINTERSPORT IN ST. MORITZ
OPERA IN NEW YORK - UITVINDING MET PERSPECTIEF
8 JANUARI 1949
No. 2

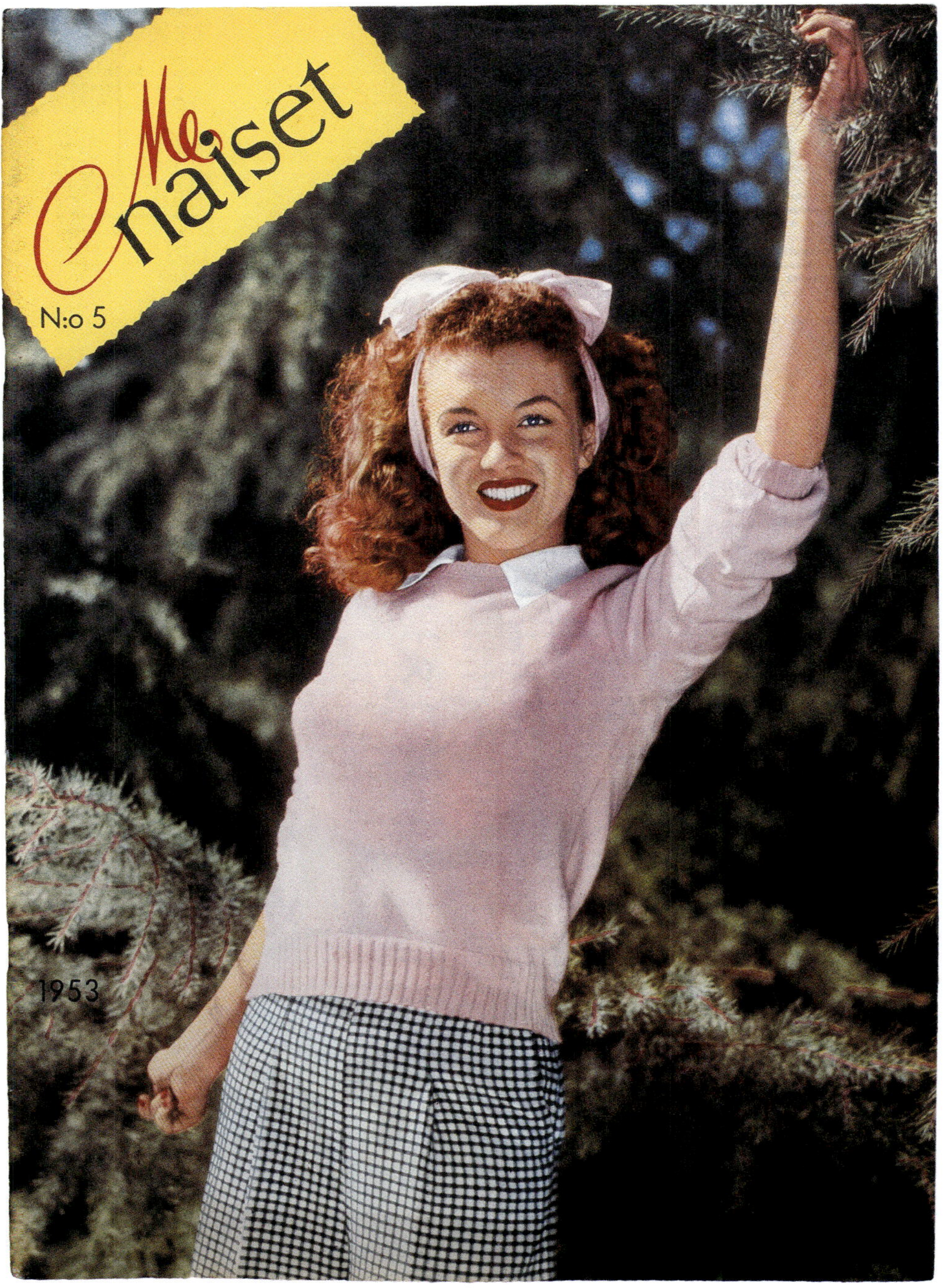
Me naiset
N:o 5
1953

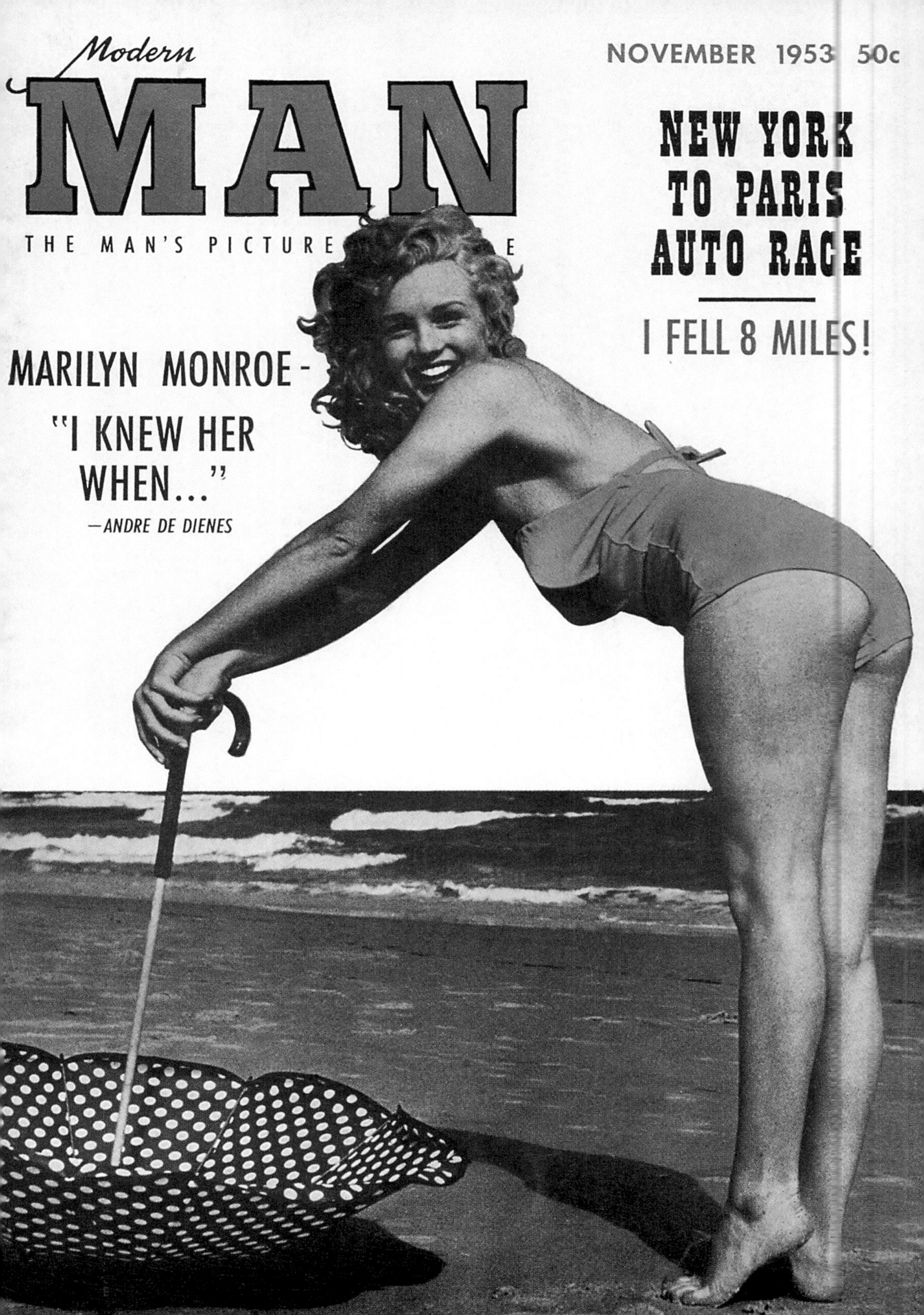

Modern
MAN
THE MAN'S PICTURE E
NOVEMBER 1953 50c
NEW YORK
TO PARIS
AUTO RACE
I FELL 8 MILES!
MARILYN MONROE-
"I KNEW HER
WHEN..."
—ANDRE DE DIENES

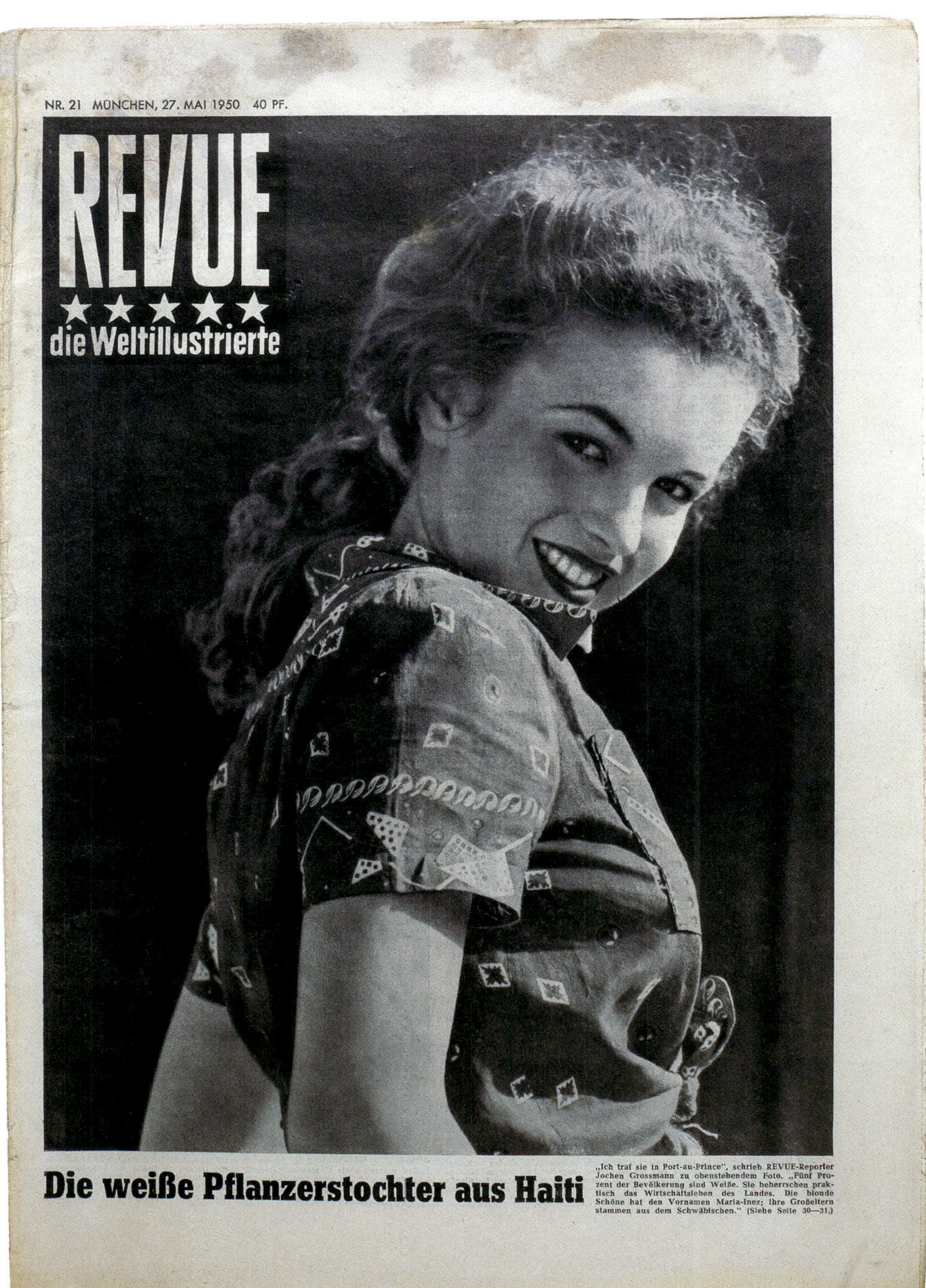

NR. 21 MÜNCHEN, 27. MAI 1950 40 PF.

REVUE

die Weltillustrierte

Die weiße Pflanzerstochter aus Haiti

„Ich traf sie in Port-au-Prince", schrieb REVUE-Reporter Jochen Grossmann zu obenstehendem Foto. „Fünf Prozent der Bevölkerung sind Weiße. Sie beherrschen praktisch das Wirtschaftsleben des Landes. Die blonde Schöne hat den Vornamen Maria-Inez; ihre Großeltern stammen aus dem Schwäbischen." (Siehe Seite 30—31.)

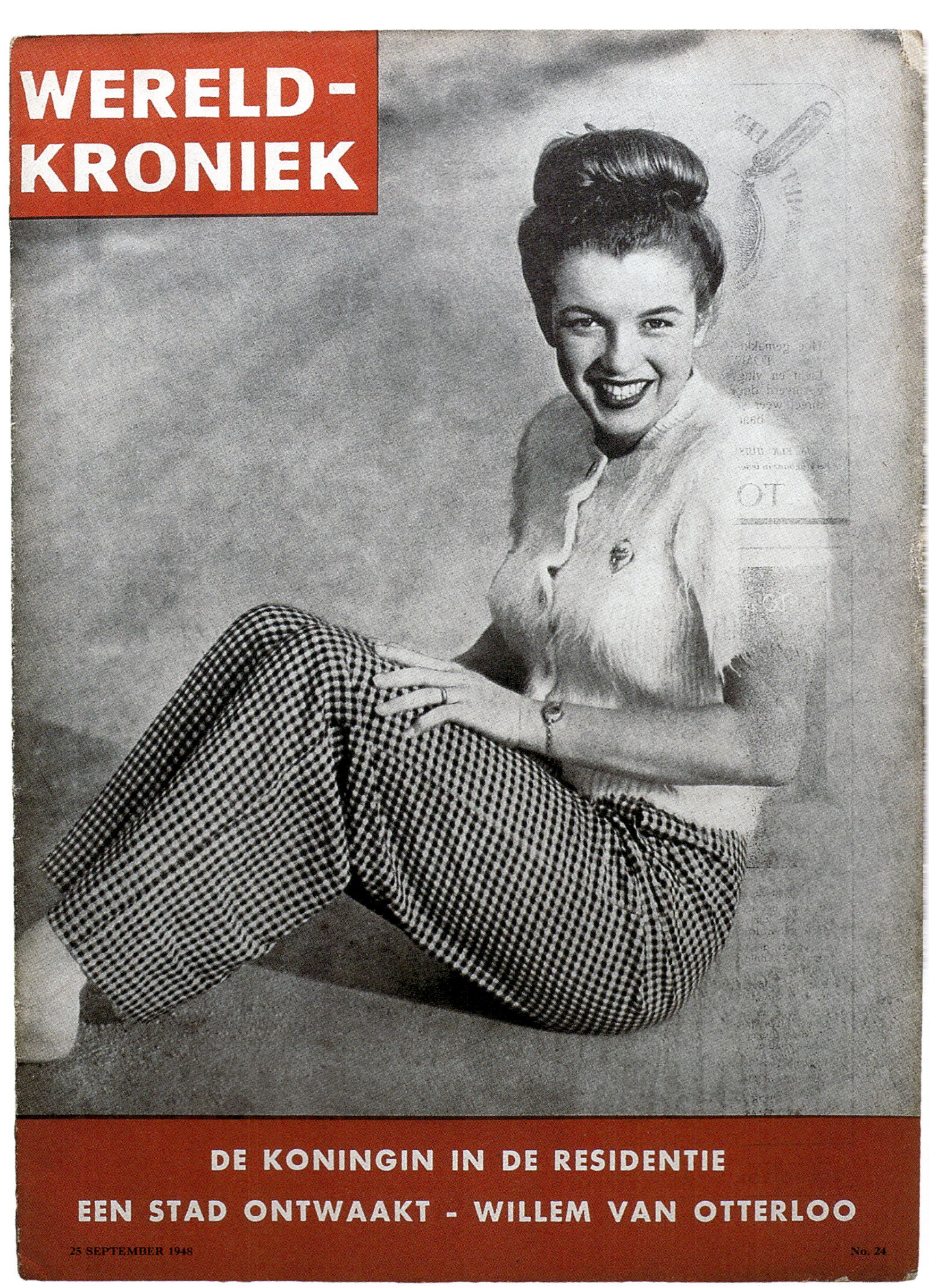
WERELD-
KRONIEK
DE KONINGIN IN DE RESIDENTIE
EEN STAD ONTWAAKT - WILLEM VAN OTTERLOO
25 SEPTEMBER 1948
No. 24

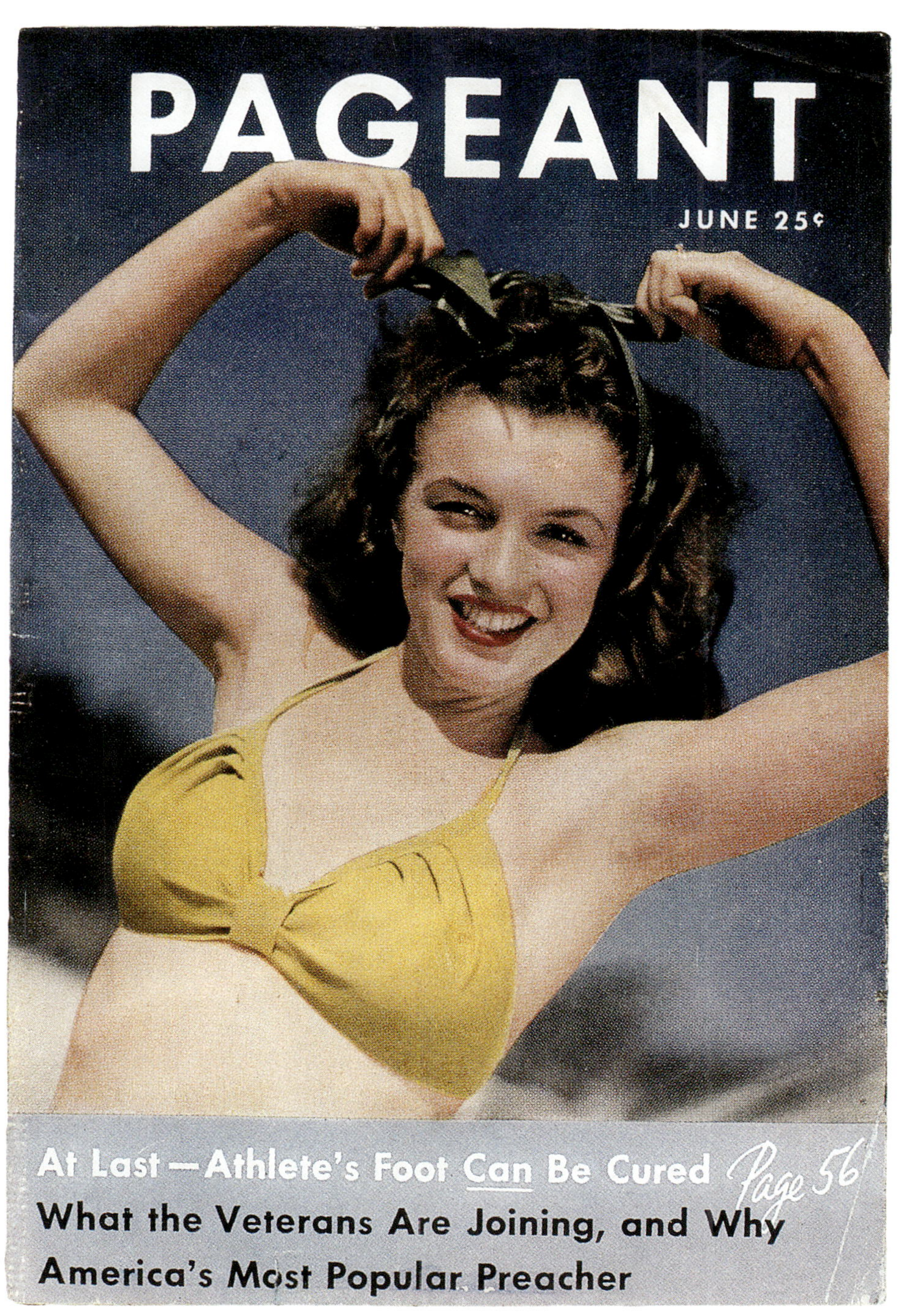
PAGEANT
JUNE 25¢
At Last—Athlete's Foot Can Be Cured
Page 56
What the Veterans Are Joining, and Why
America's Most Popular Preacher

VECKO REVYN

Nr 3 1950
20 JAN.
PRIS 35 ÖRE
I Danmark 60 øre.
I Norge 60 øre.

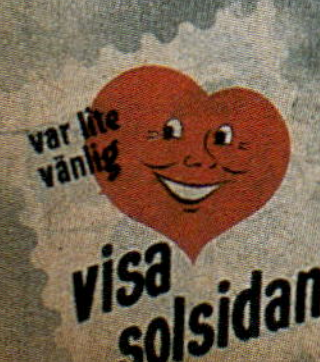

Vinter

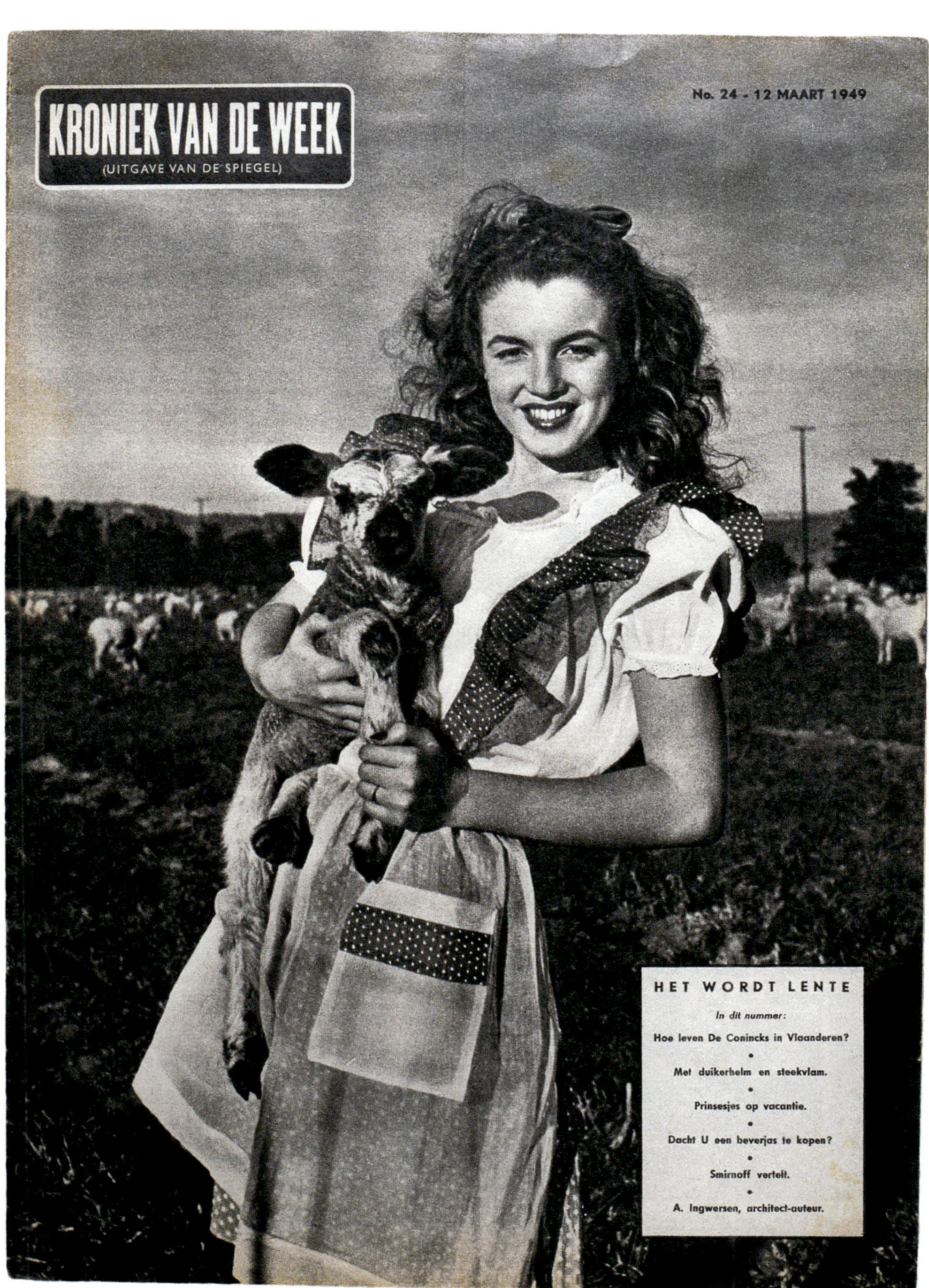
KRONIEK VAN DE WEEK
(UITGAVE VAN DE SPIEGEL)
No. 24 - 12 MAART 1949
HET WORDT LENTE
In dit nummer:
Hoe leven De Conincks in Vlaanderen?
Met duikerhelm en steekvlam.
Prinsesjes op vacantie.
Dacht U een beverjas te kopen?
Smirnoff vertelt.
A. Ingwersen, architect-auteur.

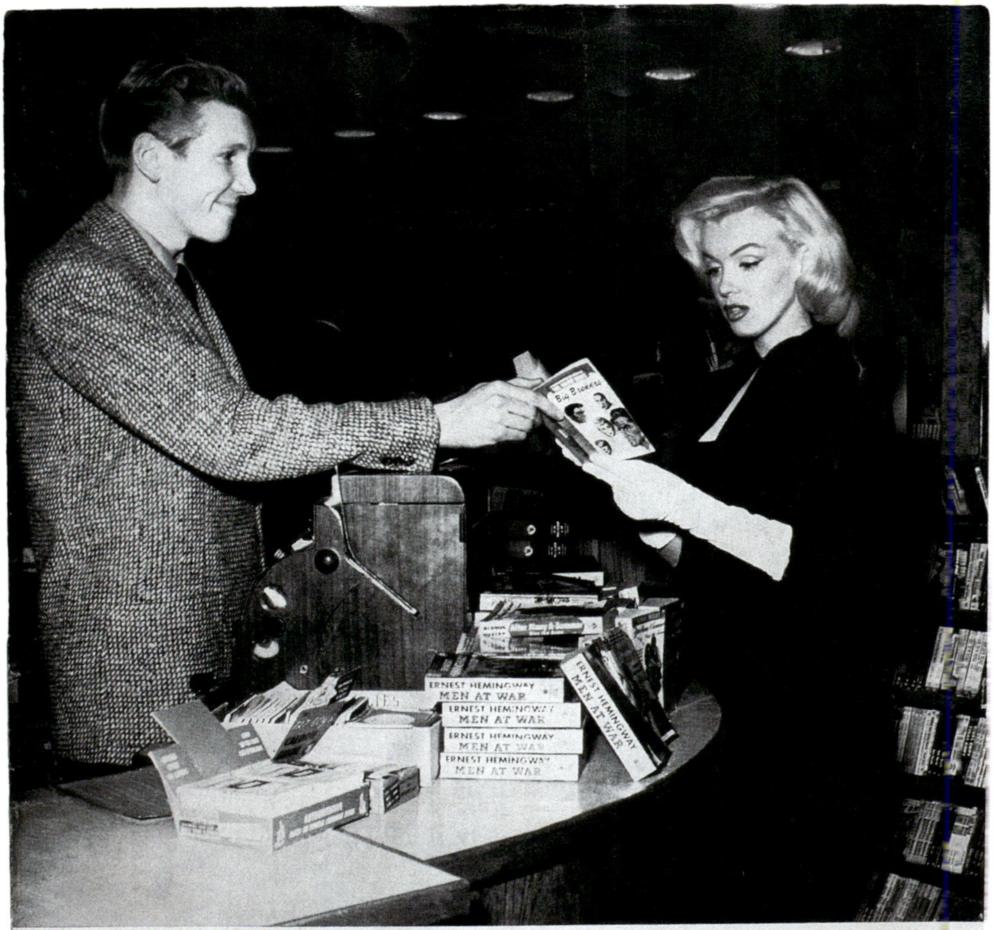

Vol. 35 No. 4

MARILYN MONROE SUCCUMBS TO WALTER MARTINDALE'S SALESMANSHIP

May 1953

THE AMERICAN NEWS

Trade Journal

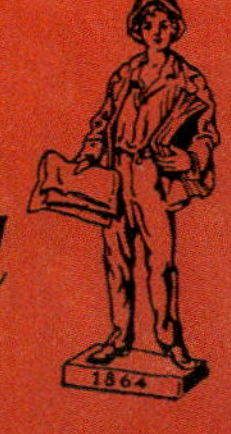

PUBLISHED BY THE AMERICAN NEWS COMPANY AS A SERVICE TO NEWSDEALERS

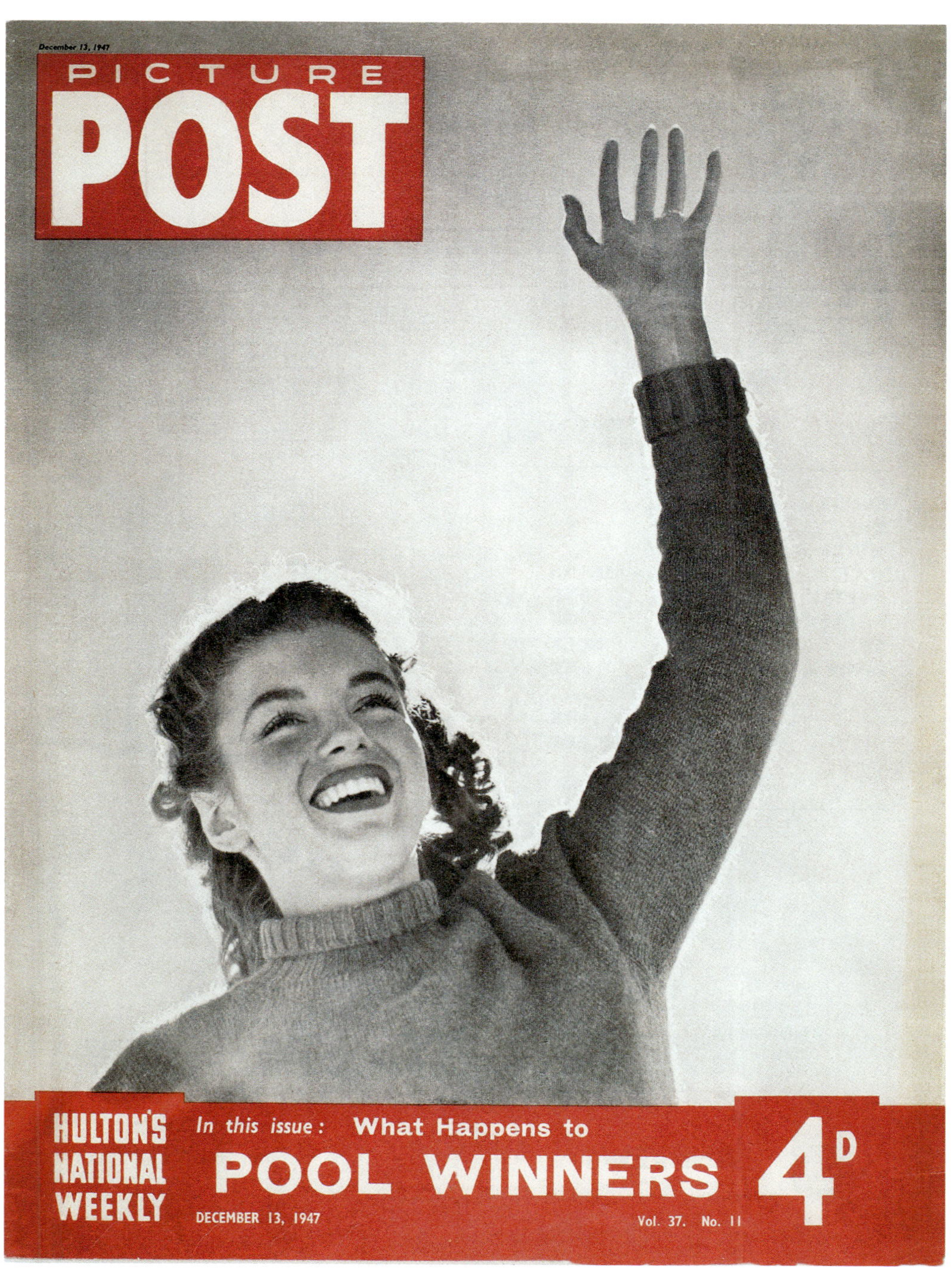
December 13, 1947
PICTURE
POST
HULTON'S
NATIONAL
WEEKLY
In this issue : What Happens to
POOL WINNERS
4D
DECEMBER 13, 1947
Vol. 37. No. 11

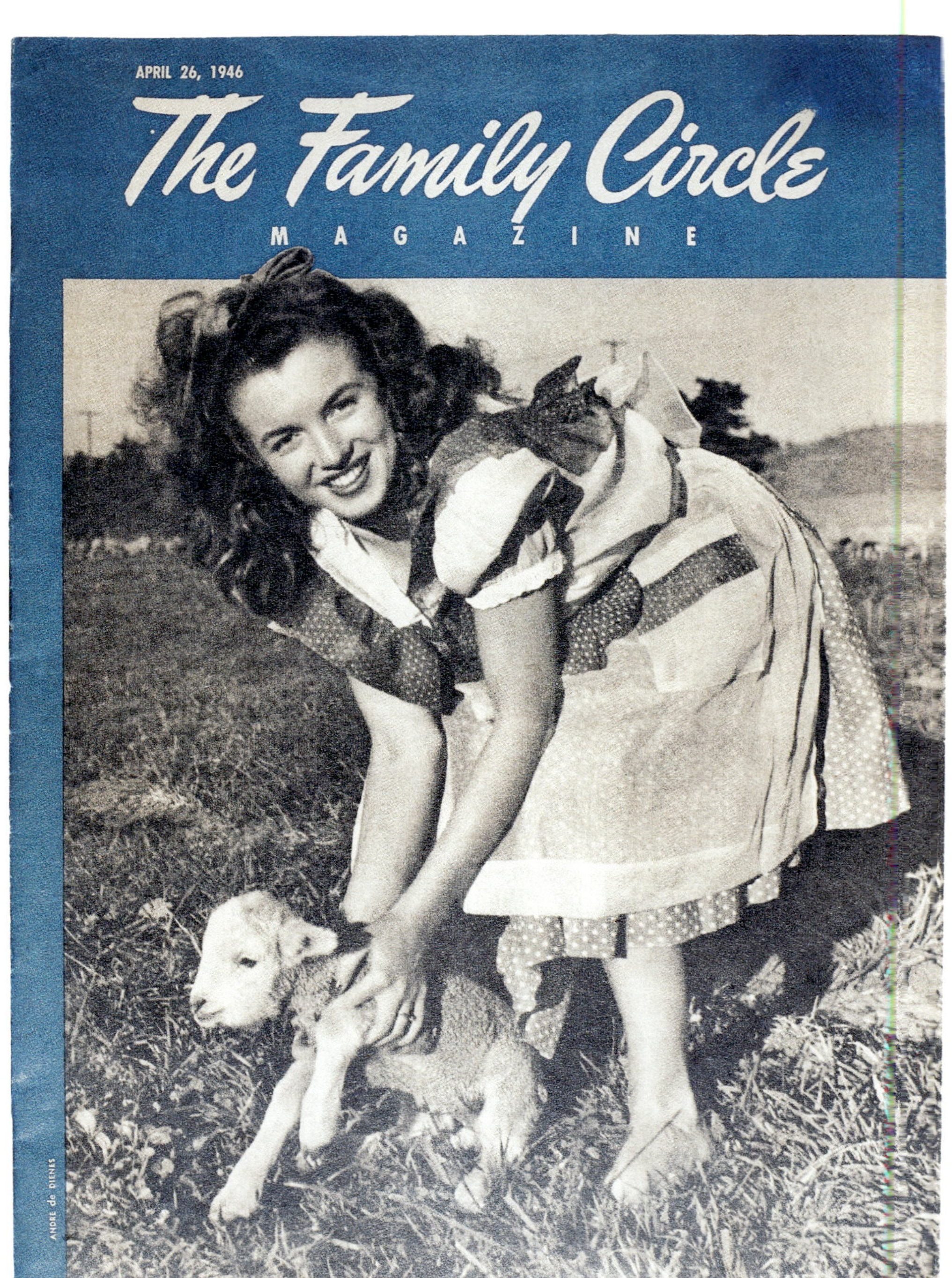
APRIL 26, 1946
The Family Circle
MAGAZINE
ANDRE de DIENES

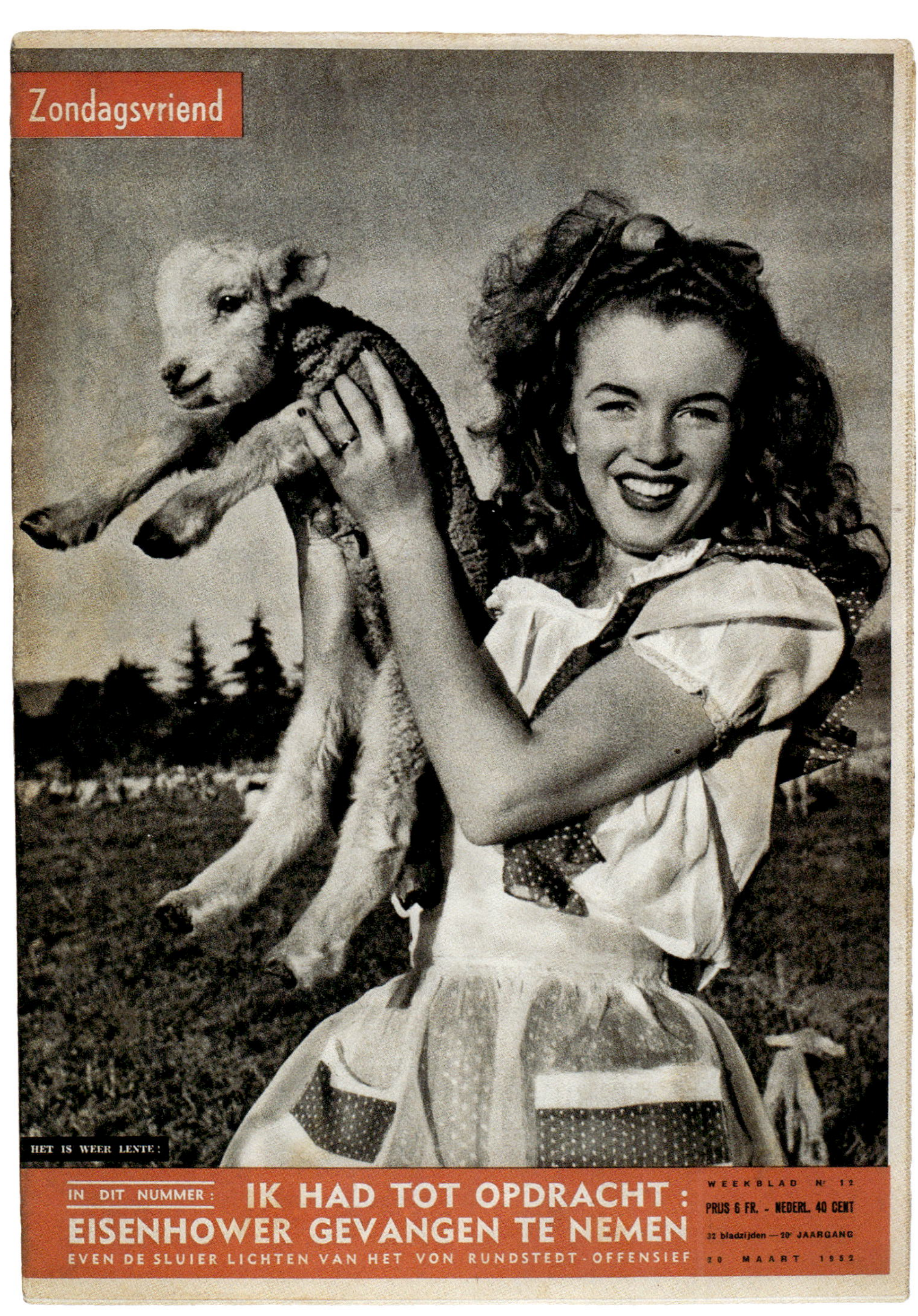
Zondagsvriend
HET IS WEER LENTE :
IN DIT NUMMER :
IK HAD TOT OPDRACHT :
EISENHOWER GEVANGEN TE NEMEN
EVEN DE SLUIER LICHTEN VAN HET VON RUNDSTEDT-OFFENSIEF
WEEKBLAD Nr 12
PRIJS 6 FR. - NEDERL. 40 CENT
32 bladzijden — 20e JAARGANG
20 MAART 1952

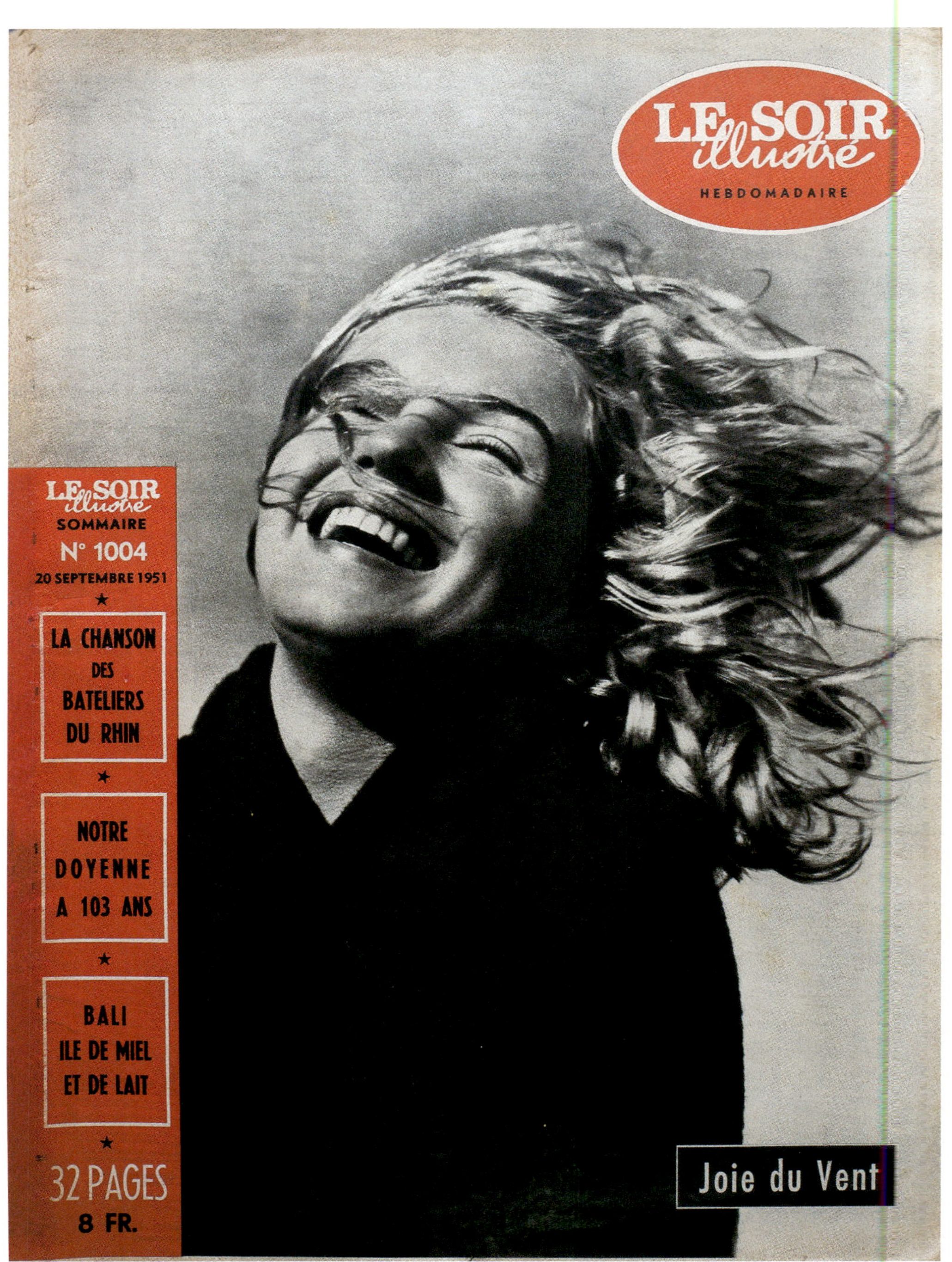
LE SOIR illustré
HEBDOMADAIRE
LE SOIR illustré
SOMMAIRE
N° 1004
20 SEPTEMBRE 1951
LA CHANSON DES BATELIERS DU RHIN
NOTRE DOYENNE A 103 ANS
BALI ILE DE MIEL ET DE LAIT
32 PAGES
8 FR.
Joie du Vent

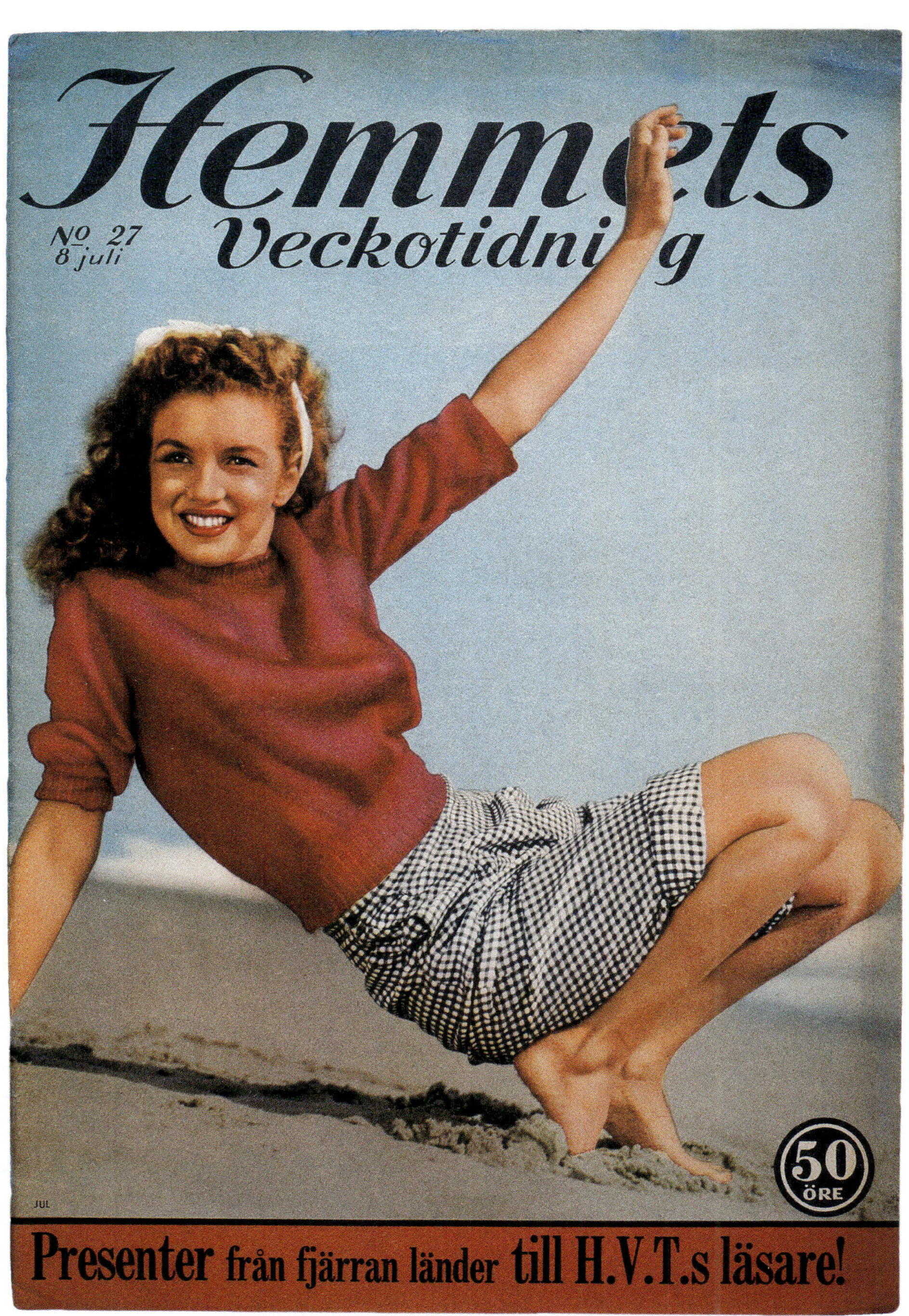
Hemmets
No 27
8 juli
Veckotidning
50
ÖRE
Presenter från fjärran länder till H.V.T.s läsare!

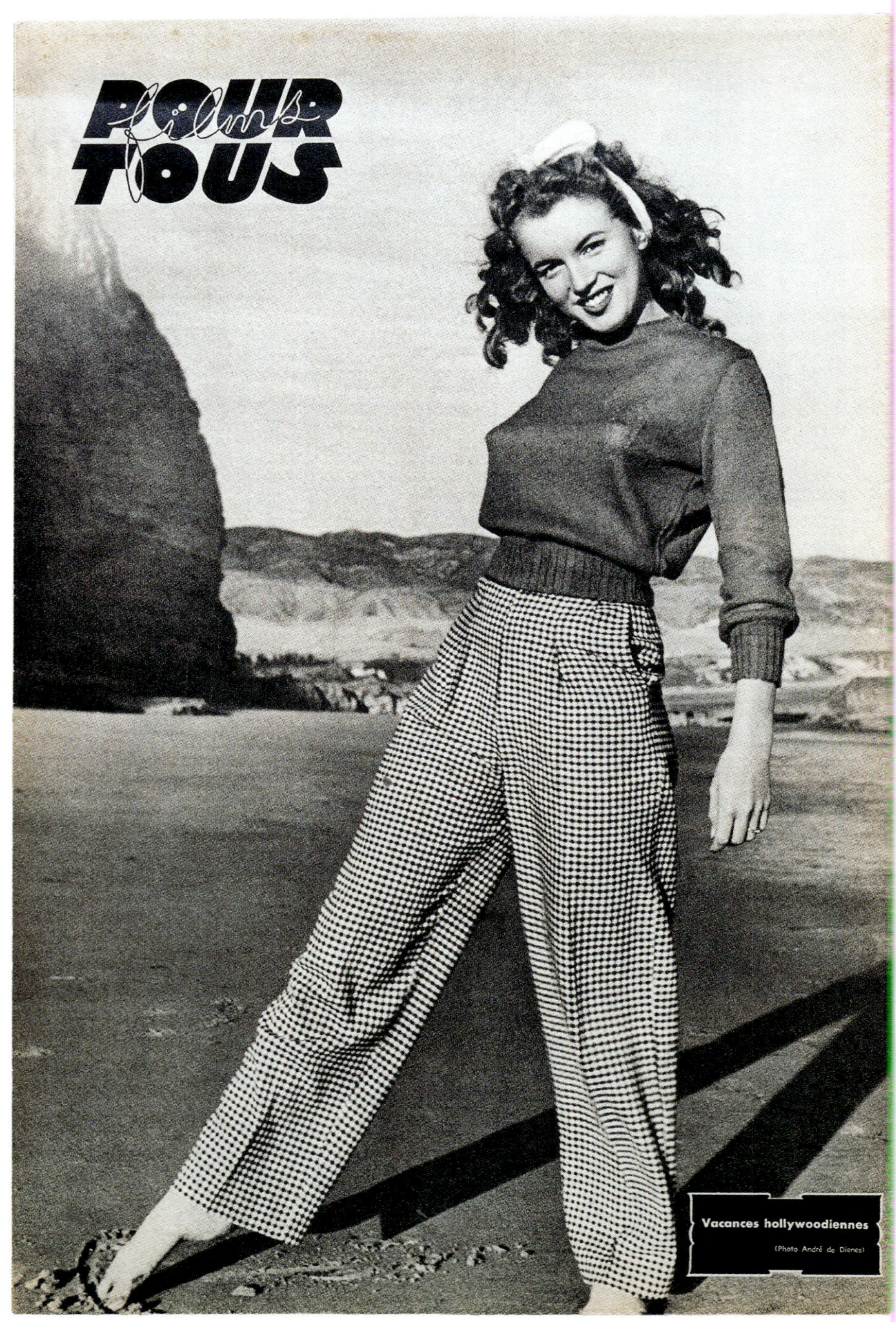

Vacances hollywoodiennes

(Photo André de Dienes)